For Christopher… now, as always.

—Don

For Beth, who makes all my dreams come true.

—Jeffery

Did you know that this book comes with free online
support directly from the authors?

Did you know that this book's sample scripts, along with late-breaking
updates, are accessible online for free?

Just visit www.ScriptingAnswers.com for support or
www.SAPIENPress.com for downloads!

You can also check out the SAPIEN Technologies blog at http://blog.sapien.com,
where you'll find the latest scripting news, PowerShell tips,
and much more. Drop by and subscribe today!

Contents at a Glance

Foreword

We are incredibly proud of this third edition of our PowerShell book, focused squarely on Windows PowerShell 2.0. This book is more than one-quarter larger than the original edition (in content, not just physical size), and contains probably more than 60% new material—and even the remaining 40% has been thoroughly re-visited and revised where necessary. It's also a testament to the popularity of Windows PowerShell itself, since it's that popularity that has led so many administrators into the intermediate and advanced topics that we're covering in this edition for the first time.

We've been fortunate to receive a lot of feedback—both constructive and sometimes not-so-constructive—from the first edition, and we've taken it all to heart. In addition to the new material we've created for this edition, we've also rewritten major sections of this book to provide clearer explanations of core concepts, and we've vastly expanded our explanations of other areas of Windows PowerShell that we didn't originally realize would be so interesting to Windows administrators. We've made a tremendous effort to make sure this book includes everything you might need, now and well into your PowerShell future.

Writing any book of this size is a labor of love. In the case of Windows PowerShell, it has to be, because so little in the way of formal documentation is available anywhere. Many things—such as PowerShell's custom formatting and type extensions—are either poorly documented, or completely undocumented by Microsoft (at least at the time we wrote this). So, we had to reverse-engineer a lot of these things in order to explain how they work and provide some practical examples for you. But we were happy to do it, because we know there are folks out there who will really utilize those features, using our examples as a jumping-off point for their own experimentation.

We're delighted that you've chosen our book for your Windows PowerShell learning needs. We hope you'll take advantage of the discussion forums, at http://www.ScriptingAnswers.com, for any follow-up questions, comments, or suggestions you may have. You'll find a lot of good information as well on the SAPIEN blog, http://blog.sapien.com as well as our own online ventures, http://www.concentratedtech.com and http://jdhitsolutions.com/blog. Finally, we also invite you to one of the many conferences we speak at, most of which we mention in our blogs from time to time. Most important, we don't want to be faceless entities, floating out in space somewhere writing books and magazine articles; we want to work with you to find answers to questions, and to find ways to put Windows PowerShell to practical uses in every Windows-based environment. Let this book be the beginning of your PowerShell career, but don't let it be the end. Drop by and say "hi."

Don Jones

Jeffery Hicks

About the Authors

Don Jones has been in the Information Technology industry for more than a decade, and has written more than thirty published books on IT topics. Today, he's a Windows PowerShell MVP Award recipient and an in-demand speaker at international conferences. Don is a columnist for *Microsoft TechNet Magazine* and in the past has written for *Windows IT Pro and REDMOND* magazines, among other publications. He founded ScriptingAnswers.com and continues to be one of the industry's leading advocates and experts for Windows administrative scripting and automation. Don co-founded Concentrated Technology, where he and Greg Shields deliver concentrated technology education to Windows professionals around the world.

Jeffery Hicks is an independent author, trainer, consultant, IT veteran and a Windows PowerShell MVP Award recipient. He is the author or co-author of several books including *Managing Active Directory with Windows PowerShell: TFM* (SAPIEN Press 2008), *WSH and VBScript Core: TFM* (SAPIEN Press 2007) and *Windows PowerShell: TFM* (SAPIEN Press 2007). He is currently a columnist and contributing editor for *REDMOND Magazine*, where he writes the popular "Mr. Roboto" column and the Prof. PowerShell column for MCPMag.com. Jeff is a frequent contributor to several online IT community web sites as well as an invited speaker at computer conferences and seminars. Jeff has been an IT professional for almost 18 years, much of it spent as a professional consultant. Throughout his entire career, Jeff has leveraged the available tools and techniques for automating Windows administration. His experience with a wide range of organizations and technologies provides a wealth of knowledge he is eager to share through speaking, teaching, writing, community participation, and mentoring.

Acknowledgements

We'd like to express our sincere gratitude to everyone who purchased the first and second editions of this book and took the time to send us their questions, comments, suggestions, and even the odd correction. Whether you contacted us via e-mail at errata@sapien.com (an address you're still welcome to use) or in the forums on ScriptingAnswers.com, we appreciate it, and we want you to know that everything you brought to our attention has in some way been incorporated into this new edition.

We'd also like to specifically thank the team at SAPIEN Technologies who have supported the SAPIEN Press brand and this revised edition of the brand's first book: CEO Ferdinand Rios and CTO Alex Riedel, along with Christopher Gannon, Margaret Pratt, Stephen Poon, and Maricela Soria.

We'd also like to thank the folks who provided such useful feedback during our Table of Contents review, including Marco Shaw, Michel Klomp, Bruno Guerpillon, Adam Ball, Hector Hernandez, Mark Ingalls, and especially Matthew Grogan, Greg Milner, and Jamie Bradford, who provided very detailed feedback that directly resulted in many of the things you'll find in this book.

The following folks also deserve thanks for their help in reviewing the draft chapters (but they deserve no blame for any mistakes you may find—those belong to use): Marco Shaw, Andy Bidlen, Michel Klomp, Colin Halford, Jamie Bradford, Shane Dovers, Alan Finn, and Adam Ball.

Finally, we'd like to thank our families and co-workers for their patience and understanding as we worked long hours on this project.

Contents

Windows PowerShell™ 2.0: TFM®

Don Jones

Jeffery Hicks

SAPIEN
PRESS

841 Latour Ct Ste D
Napa, CA 94558
www.SAPIENPress.com

The publisher offers discounts on this book when ordered in quantity for bulk purchases and special sales. For more information, please contact:

> SAPIEN Press
> 1-866-PRIMALS
> +1 707-252-8700
> sales@sapien.com

Visit SAPIEN Press on the Web: www.sapienpress.com.

Library of Congress Cataloging-in-Publication Data
Jones, Don; Hicks, Jeffery
> Microsoft PowerShell: TFM 3rd Edition/ Don Jones and Jeffery Hicks
>> p. cm.
> ISBN 0-9776597-6-3 (pbk. : alk. Paper)
1. Microsoft Windows (computer file)   2. Operating systems (Computers)
3. Windows PowerShell (Computer program language)   I. Title

3nd Edition / 1st Printing

Ground Zero

Windows PowerShell v2.0 Seven-step Speed Start

You've picked up a new book on Windows PowerShell and you're ready to get started! You want to see PowerShell in action! You want to see what it can do! You want to see if the authors will end every sentence with an exclamation point! That's what this chapter is all about: Putting PowerShell through its paces. We won't be explaining a lot as we go, since the goal here is just to show off some of PowerShell's capabilities. In fact, if you've already been tinkering with PowerShell, you might want to just skim this chapter and move right on to the next one, which is where the meaty stuff starts. Oh, and no, we won't use very many exclamation points from here on out.

1. Installing PowerShell

The first thing you need to do is install PowerShell. Exactly how you do that depends a bit on the operating system you're running, and as a caution: While this information was accurate at the time of writing, it may change a bit, since Microsoft may add PowerShell to the base Windows operating system in more versions of Windows.

You need to be running Windows XP (Service Pack 3 or later), Windows Server 2003 (Service Pack 2 or later), Windows Vista (Service Pack 1 or later), Windows Server 2008, or a later version of Windows in order to install PowerShell. You will find 32-bit and 64-bit flavors of PowerShell available. It *will not* install on Windows 2000 or anything older. Also, make sure you don't have any previous versions of PowerShell installed; if you do, uninstall them first. PowerShell v2.0 cannot co-exist with PowerShell v1.0.

Note that PowerShell v2.0 is preinstalled on Windows Server 2008 R2 (and later) and on Windows 7 (and later). If you're using those operating systems, you're good to go. Windows Server 2008 *comes with* PowerShell v1.0; you'll want to remove that feature using Server Manager, and then download and install PowerShell v2.0 for Windows Server 2008. You'll usually find the download links on www. Microsoft.com/powershell, or on Microsoft's main Downloads Web page.

Framework First

First, you need to make sure you have the latest (at least v3.5) version of the .NET Framework installed (you can get by with v2.0 of the Framework if you don't plan to use the graphical PowerShell tool or the **Out-GridView** cmdlet, and certain other features may be restricted or unavailable). Some versions of Windows, like Windows Vista and Windows Server 2008, may already have the latest Framework version installed. Look in your Windows folder (usually C:\Windows), and then under the Microsoft.NET folder. Under there, you'll either see a folder named Framework, or something similar—it has a different name on 32- and 64-bit systems. Under *there*, you're looking for the v3.5.xxxx folder. If it exists, you're good to go. If not, go to http://www.Microsoft.com/download and download the .NET Framework runtime for v3.5. You'll probably need to be a local administrator on your computer in order to do this. You might also be able to use the Windows Update or Microsoft Update feature of Windows to install the Framework; it'll be listed under Optional Components.

WinRM

Windows PowerShell v2.0 requires the Windows Remote Management service. The PowerShell installer will automatically prompt you to download and install this if it isn't already installed on your computer, and it will provide you with the URL where you can download WinRM.

Download and Install the Shell

With the Framework installed, see if PowerShell is already installed—usually, you'll find it right on your Start menu if it is. If not, you can also look for its installation folder: On 32-bit systems, it's in Windows\System32\
WindowsPowerShell. On 64-bit systems, it's usually the same path.

If you don't have PowerShell installed, go to http://www.Microsoft.com/PowerShell. From there, you'll find links to download it. *Be sure to download the right build!* A different build is available for *each* different version of Windows, and there's a different build for 32- or 64-bit editions, also.

....

Don't See a Download for Your Version of Windows?
If you go to the download page and don't see a build for your operating system, then either (a) your operating system isn't supported (that's the case for Windows 2000 and earlier), or (b) your operating system comes with PowerShell as a feature (as is the case for Windows Server 2008 R2 and Windows 7). In the latter situation, you'll need to install Windows PowerShell by using Windows Setup, Add/Remove Windows Components, Server Manager, or whatever other functionality is provided by the operating system itself.

Once you've downloaded the installer, just double-click it. As with the Framework, you'll probably need to be an administrator in order to complete the installation properly. The installer will install not only PowerShell itself, but also the documentation provided by Microsoft. It'll create Start Menu items for the shell and for the documentation. It's useful to pin the PowerShell icon to the Start Menu so it's easier to find.

2. Customizing the Shell

By default, the shell uses a blue background and white text. By clicking the control box (in the upper-left corner of the window), you can select Properties to modify the font, the colors, and even the window size. For the window size, you can control the physical size—that is, how many lines tall and how many columns wide the window is. You can also control the *buffer*, which is how many lines and columns actually exist. For example, if you configure the shell to use a 100-column window with a 200-column buffer, you'll see a horizontal scroll bar. Take a moment to tweak the shell to meet your liking—the wider the window, the better!

3. Performing Some Familiar Tasks in the New Shell

PowerShell works a lot like the shell you may have used before: the Windows Cmd.exe shell. For example, try these quick tasks:

- Enter **Cd ** to change to the root folder of your drive.

- Enter **Cd /Windows** to change into the Windows folder. Notice that you can use forward or backward slashes in paths!

- Enter **Cd ..** to go back up one folder level. Notice that in PowerShell v1.0, you did need a space between "Cd" and ".."—that's a difference from the old Cmd.exe shell. PowerShell isn't case-sensitive, so "CD," "Cd," and "cd" work equally well. In PowerShell v2.0, "cd.."—without the space—works fine.

- Enter **Dir** to see a directory listing.

- Press Up Arrow or Down Arrow to cycle through previously entered commands from your command buffer.

Many of the other commands you're familiar with will work, too: **Ren**, **Copy**, **Del**, **MkDir**, **RmDir**, and so forth. Commands like **Type** and **More** also work fine.

You can run the external command-line utilities you're accustomed to. For example, **Ping** and **TraceRt** work perfectly, as does **Net**, **Nbtstat**, **Netsh**, and many others. Try a few now to convince yourself. You'll even have access to some advanced commands, like **ps** for a process list or **kill** to terminate a process.

If you've used UNIX before, and prefer to use commands like **ls** or **man**, you'll find that those work, too.

4. Working with More Drives than C:

Now try this:

```
PS C:\> cd hkcu:
```

Then type:

```
PS C:\> cd software
PS C:\> dir
```

Cool, huh? PowerShell exposes your registry, your certificate store, and other forms of storage as if they were disks. You can use all the familiar disk commands to change keys, delete keys, and so forth. You can see a list of all available "drives" by entering **Get-PSDrive**. And yes, you can map a network drive in PowerShell, too: Use **New-PSDrive**.

5. Finding Help at Your Fingertips

PowerShell has a built-in Help facility. Just run **Help** *command* (or, as mentioned, **Man** *command*) to get Help on any command. For example:

```
PS C:\> Help dir
```

Displays Help on using the **Dir** command. You'll notice that it's a bit different from the old Cmd.exe version of Dir. For example, you can't use **/s** to include subdirectories. Instead, you'd run **Dir -recurse**. When asking for Help, the default screen is pretty concise. You can get more extensive Help by running something like this:

```
PS C:\> Help dir –detailed
```

Or, for even more Help:

```
PS C:\> Help dir -full
```

You can even ask for some examples of the command in use:

```
PS C:\> Help dir -example
```

The cool part about the **Help** command is that it'll show you what Help is available. For example, to see a list of everything it knows about:

```
PS C:\> Help *
```

Or, if you'd like to see what Help is available for working with Windows services, run this:

```
PS C:\> Help *service*
```

Wildcards like ***** can be used with many PowerShell commands, and in this case they're a great way to discover what PowerShell has to offer.

6. Performing Real Administrative Tasks Without Scripting

Try these quick tasks, which go far beyond what Cmd.exe could do:

- **Get-Service** will show a list of running services. **Stop-Service** and **Start-Service** provide control over those services.

- **Get-Process** and **Stop-Process** provide functionality similar to the Resource Kit tools Plist.exe and Kill.exe.

- **Get-ACL C:\Windows** will show you who has permissions to the Windows folder (note that if you're running on Windows Vista with User Account Control enabled, this may not work—try right-clicking the PowerShell shortcut to run it as Administrator, and then try again, or try a different folder).

- **Get-EventLog System** will get your System event log. Yes, it will probably take a few minutes to finish running! Try **Get-EventLog System -newest 10** to just see the first ten entries.

- Type **Notepad** to open a new instance of Notepad. Then run **Kill -name Notepad** to kill the process.

....

Leverage What You've Learned
Don't be afraid to try something new. Not sure what Get-EventLog does? Use Help to find out. Wondering what other things you can do with event logs? Try Help *event* and see if anything comes up. Running a script and want to stop? You just read about Ctrl+C, which will stop a script as well as a command like Get-EventLog. You can use many of the things in this book elsewhere in PowerShell—don't be afraid to try using things that you've learned in different combinations.

PowerShell has a lot of built-in commands that perform useful tasks. For example, try running **Help *service*** to see what commands are available for working with services—you may be pleasantly surprised! Always remember to use **Help** to discover more about what PowerShell can do, and to learn how a particular command works.

7. Taking a Peek at the Pipeline

PowerShell's commands—they're technically called *cmdlets* (pronounced, "command-lets")—don't actually produce text lists, although so far it seems like they do. Instead, they work with rich, fully functional *objects*. PowerShell's *pipeline* lets you pass (or "pipe") objects from one cmdlet to another. For example, try this to get a list of all running services:

```
PS C:\> Get-Service | Where-Object { $_.Status -eq "Running" } | Format-Wide
```

....

Hey, I Still Get a List!
At the end of every pipeline, PowerShell automatically takes whatever's left in the pipeline and makes a text list or table out of it. In this case, the syntax specifically tells PowerShell to make a wide list, so that's what it did.

PowerShell returned a collection of all the services by using **Get-Service**, and then piped those to **Where-Object**. The **Where-Object** cmdlet passed along all those with a status of Running, and dropped everything else. Finally, **Format-Wide** reformatted the results into a wide list of just the service names.

Do you want to see which processes on your computer have the largest memory working set?

```
PS C:\> ps | sort workingset -desc | select name,workingset | format-table -auto
```

The **ps** command returned a bunch of processes, and **Sort** ordered them by their working set in descending order (so the biggest users would be at the top of the list). The command then asked **Select** to grab just the name and working set information, and then used **Format-Table** to format the information into an automatically sized set of columns—a table, in other words.

This book will spend lots of time on the pipeline later—but for right now you can see that it enables some pretty powerful tasks, and it doesn't require you to use a bit of scripting.

Ready for More?

There's so much to learn in PowerShell! Hopefully, these few pages have given you a peek at what you can do with this new shell, and the entire rest of this book will be devoted to expanding upon and explaining those capabilities.

Let's get started!

Chapter 1
What's New in Windows PowerShell v2.0?

Windows PowerShell v2.0 offers a number of exciting new features. If you've never used any version of PowerShell, you might just want to skip this chapter—the authors will introduce you to all of the new features as you go. However, if you've been using v1.0 for a while, this chapter will give you a quick overview of major changes, and a pointer to where to find more detail in this book.

Note that this book is not covering new features related to software development, such as hosting the shell; instead it is focused on the new features that you'll find as you *use* PowerShell v2.0.

Remote Management and Background Jobs

PowerShell now has the ability to perform remote management, and it's a bit unlike any remote management you've ever seen before—in a good way! The shell now supports *fan-in remoting*, which is basically you sitting at your workstation and connecting to an instance of PowerShell running on a remote computer, such as a server. This is essentially the same as remote shell technologies like SSH or RSH, which have been around for years. *Fan-out remoting* is more flexible: It allows you to push a single command out from your workstation to *multiple* remote instances of PowerShell. Your command runs locally on all those remote machines, and then the results, in the form of serialized objects, come back to your workstation so that you can examine or manipulate them. Essentially, this gives you the ability to run a single command on multiple remote machines in parallel—it's a pretty impressive trick. The technology uses Windows Remote Management (WinRM), a new background service. WinRM is Microsoft's implementation of the WS-Management protocol, which is much more firewall-friendly than RPC. Any remote system you wish to manage will require an installation of Powershell v2.0 and WinRM.

Conceptually related is a new notion of background jobs, which allow PowerShell commands and scripts to run in the background, while you continue to use the shell for other tasks. You can start jobs, query them for results, and remove them, all using a series of new ***-Job** cmdlets.

```
PS C:\> get-command -noun job

CommandType     Name              Definition
-----------     ----              ----------
Cmdlet          Get-Job           Get-Job [[-Id] <Int32[]>] [-Verbose] [-Debug] [
Cmdlet          Receive-Job       Receive-Job [-Job] <Job[]> [[-Location] <String
Cmdlet          Remove-Job        Remove-Job [-Id] <Int32[]> [-Force] [-Verbose]
Cmdlet          Start-Job         Start-Job [-ScriptBlock] <ScriptBlock> [-Name <
Cmdlet          Stop-Job          Stop-Job [-Id] <Int32[]> [-PassThru] [-Verbose]
Cmdlet          Wait-Job          Wait-Job [-Id] <Int32[]> [-Any] [-Timeout <Int3
```

Making Cmdlets in a Script

In PowerShell v1.0, you needed to be a .NET developer to create new cmdlets. In v2.0, you can create the equivalent of a compiled cmdlet using PowerShell's own scripting language. Microsoft introduced new language elements that allow you to create fully fledged cmdlets capable of working within the pipeline. These cmdlets are covered in the chapter, "Creating PowerShell Advanced Functions," near the end of the book.

Steppable Pipelines

This new feature lets you turn a script block into a steppable pipeline, and then control the sequence of activities by calling special **Begin()**, **Process()**, and **End()** blocks on the pipeline. These blocks are covered in the chapter, "Script Blocks, Functions, and Filters."

Data Language and Internationalization

This subset of the PowerShell script language allows you to share scripts more easily, and to maintain a better separation between data and the actual script code. Conceptually related to this are PowerShell's new internationalization features, which allow you to write scripts that can be more easily translated into other languages by separating string data (which must be translated) from code (which stays the same). Both of these new features are covered in the chapter, "Separating Data and Code."

Debugging

Script debugging gets easier with a new set of debugging features. You can now set breakpoints on specific lines of a script, on columns, on functions, on variables, and on commands, causing your script to "pause" whenever a breakpoint is "hit." You can even specify custom actions to run when a breakpoint is "hit," and you can step into, over, and out of functions. These new features are covered in the chapter, "The PowerShell Debugger and Debugging Techniques."

New Operators, Variables, and Cmdlets

PowerShell v2.0 includes three new operators: **@**, called the "splat" operator, and the **–Split** and **–Join** operators for string manipulation. These operators are covered in the chapter, "Operators." Microsoft also exposed several new built-in variables; you'll find coverage of key ones in Appendix A, "Automatic Variables in PowerShell." Finally, Microsoft introduced an array of new cmdlets to handle many of

PowerShell's new features. This book covers these cmdlets along with their features, including many of the new features listed above.

Runspace Security

A new feature called *constrained runspaces* allows developers to create new runspaces—essentially, instances of the shell—that have a set of constraints applied. These constraints can restrict the new runspaces' ability to execute commands, scripts, and language elements. This effectively lets the developer create "restricted" instances of the shell that only have certain capabilities—perfect for testing, working in secure environments, and so forth. This is something more suited for a developer; we don't mean to imply that an administrator can configure a restricted runspace because, really, you can't. A developer, however, can create a sort of custom shell instance that includes restrictions, and can even restrict individual cmdlets to add or remove specific parameters. It's very flexible.

Transactions

When running on Windows Vista, Windows Server 2008, and later, PowerShell provides support for operations conducted with the transactional file system and transactional registry that Windows provides. You essentially begin a transaction, and then perform operations—like creating new items, deleting items, and so forth—as a part of that transaction. When you're done, you can either roll back the transaction, undoing all of those transacted operations, or you can complete, or *commit*, the transaction, making all of the changes permanent. Transactions are a great way to make sure that several discrete operations either succeed or fail as a unit, so that certain processes complete either in their entirety, or not at all.

Modules

PowerShell v2.0 introduces a new way of bundling together snap-in DLLs, scripts, and other code in a single unit called a *module*. Modules provide a convenient way to add custom-written functions, cmdlets, and other extensions to the shell with a single **Import-Module** command. The old **Add-PSSnapin** cmdlet still exists and still works to add snap-in DLLs, but the new module functionality is easier and doesn't require that you register snap-ins in advance, which is nice.

Events

PowerShell now provides support for responding to asynchronous events. For example, you can create a **Timer** object that "ticks" every 60 seconds, and designate a function that runs each time a "tick" occurs. It also provides support for responding to WMI events, such as the creation of a new process or other trigger.

Error Handling

New, easier techniques for detecting and dealing with errors are now available in PowerShell. These make it vastly simpler to write scripts that anticipate, and respond to, errors that occur when the script executes. PowerShell v2.0 now supports **Try…Catch** in addition to the old Trap construct, and you can read more about it in the "Error Handling" chapter of this book.

Graphical PowerShell

PowerShell includes an entry-level graphical shell and script editor, which provides basic functionality such as syntax coloring, snippets, and so forth. Microsoft refers to this officially as Windows PowerShell ISE (Integrated Scripting Environment). In addition, a new cmdlet named **Out-GridView** produces a graphical, grid-based view for PowerShell output. While you can use it in the text-based console window, it's the perfect companion for the graphical shell now included with v2.0.

The new graphical shell provides a tabbed interface for working with multiple files simultaneously, and supports the creation of multiple shell instances in parallel. The graphical shell requires version 3.0 of the .NET Framework; apart from the graphical shell, PowerShell v2.0 can run on v2.0 of the .NET Framework.

Other Changes

A number of existing features have been improved in PowerShell v2.0:

- The **Select-String** cmdlet supports new parameters, including **–Context**, which allows you to see lines before and after the match line; **-AllMatches**, which allows you to see all matches in a line; **-NoMatch**, which is the same as running **grep –v** in Unix; and **–Encoding**, which allows you to specify a particular character encoding.

- PowerShell improved type adapters to include base members, which are now directly accessible on objects. This removes the need to use PSBASE to access base members.

- The **Get-Member** cmdlet now supports a **–View** and **–Force** parameter. **–View** accepts values such as "**Extended**," "**Adapted**," "**Base**," and "**All**;" the default is "**Extended,Adapted**." "**Get**" and "**Set**" methods are now hidden by default. Use **–view** "**All**" to list base members when using **Get-Member**.

- The [ADSI] type adapter now adapts base methods and properties, including **SetInfo()** and **SetPassword()**. PowerShell added the [ADSISearcher] type accelerator as a shortcut to the .NET Framework's System.DirectoryServices.DirectorySearcher class. PowerShell added two new code methods to the **DirectoryEntry** type to simplify data conversion: **ConvertDNBinaryToString** and **ConvertLargeIntegerToInt64**.

- The **Get-WMIObject** cmdlet now supports new parameters: **-Impersonation**, **-Authentication**, **-Locale**, **-EnableAllPrivileges**, **-Amended**, **-DirectRead**, and **–Authority**. These allow setting the **Authentication** and **Impersonation** properties, which are needed when working with remote computers.

- Bitwise operators now work with Int64 data types.

- **Get-WMIObject** has always supported the ability to retrieve objects from multiple computers; now, it supports an **–AsJob** parameter, which causes long-running operations to run as one of PowerShell's new background jobs. Use **Get-Job** to view the status and **Receive-Job** to retrieve the results.

- The new **ConvertTo-XML** cmdlet takes objects and converts them into an XML document object, which you can manipulate (the chapter on "Working with XML" shows you how).

More changes are doubtless forthcoming: Future revisions to this manuscript will reflect the latest CTP at the time. This version of the manuscript is based upon CTP 3.

Backward-compatibility and Breaking Changes

PowerShell v2.0 is basically compatible with v1.0—in other words, most things you did in v1.0 should still work in v2.0. However, v2.0 does add new keywords, such as **data**, which may cause problems for v1.0 scripts that use those as function or command names.

Here's a cool trick, though: You can tag your v2.0-specific scripts so that v1.0 won't try to run them. Just add this comment to the top of your script:

```
#REQUIRES -version 2.0
```

Version 1.0 will return an error if you try to use it to run that script. That way you can clearly "tag" any v2.0 scripts, so that you don't get errors or unexpected behaviors when running them in v1.0.

Obviously this chapter doesn't cover every new detail in PowerShell v2.0. But hopefully we've offered enough to get you excited and ready to go!

Chapter 2
Windows PowerShell Architecture and Overview

Windows PowerShell occupies a fairly unique place in the Microsoft world. Never before has Microsoft really created a command-line shell: The original MS-DOS of the 1980s wasn't a *shell*; it was the entire *operating system*. The original Windows was a *graphical* shell on top of MS-DOS, but when Windows NT came out the *operating system* was a graphical environment. The Cmd.exe "shell" that we're accustomed to is really just a Windows console application; it doesn't actually "wrap around" the operating system in the way that a UNIX shell does, like Bash. PowerShell, however, is a *true* shell that is uniquely designed for the complex Windows operating system and the various server products—such as Exchange Server and the System Center family—that we all use every day.

What Is PowerShell, and Why Should I Care?

Administrators of UNIX and Linux systems (collectively referred to as "*nix" throughout this book) have always had the luxury of administrative scripting. In fact, most *nix operating systems are built on a command-line interface (CLI). The graphical operating environment of *nix systems—often the "X Windows" environment—is itself a type of shell; the operating system is fully functional without this graphical interface. This presents a powerful combination: Because the operating system is typically built from the command line, there's nothing you can't do, from an administrative sense, *from the command line*. That's why *nix administrators are so fond of scripting languages like Python and Perl: They can accomplish real administration tasks with them.

Windows, however, has always been different. When a Microsoft product group sat down to develop a new feature—say, the Windows DNS Server software—they had certain tasks that were simply required. First and foremost, of course, was the actual product functionality—such as the DNS Server service, the bit of the software that actually performs as a DNS server. Some form of management interface was also required, and the Windows Common Engineering Criteria specified that the minimum management interface was a Microsoft Management Console (MMC) snap-in—that is, a *graphical* administrative interface. If they had extra time, the product team might create a Windows Management Instrumentation (WMI) provider, "connecting" their product to WMI, or they might develop a few command-line utilities or Component Object Model (COM) objects, allowing for some scriptable administrative capability. Rarely did the WMI or COM interfaces fully duplicate all the functionality available in the graphical console; this often meant that *some* administrative tasks could be accomplished via the command line or a language like VBScript, but you couldn't do *everything* that way. You'd always be back in the graphical console for something, at some point.

Not that graphical interfaces are *bad,* mind you. After all, they're how Microsoft has made billions from the Windows operating system. But clicking buttons and check boxes can only go so fast, and with commonly performed tasks like creating new users, manual button-clicking is not only tedious, it's prone to mistakes and inconsistencies. Administrators of *nix systems have spent the better part of a decade laughing at Windows' pitiable administrative automation, and third parties have done very well creating tools like AutoIt or KiXtart to help fill in the gaps for Windows' automation capabilities.

That's no longer the case, though. PowerShell is now a part of the Windows Common Engineering Criteria, and it occupies a similar position of importance with product groups outside the Windows operating system. Now, *administrative functionality is built in PowerShell first.* Any other form of administration, including graphical consoles, utilizes the PowerShell-based functionality. Essentially, graphical consoles are merely "script wizards" that run PowerShell commands in the background to accomplish whatever they're doing. Exchange Server 2007 is the first example of this: The graphical console simply runs PowerShell commands to do whatever corresponds to the buttons you click (the console even helpfully displays the commands it's running, so you can use those as examples to learn from). In fact, that graphical console only exposes roughly 80% of the product's total functionality: For everything else, you have to use the PowerShell command line. PowerShell is now the single source for administrative functionality; as it is a command-line interface, which means *every piece of functionality* can potentially be scripted or automated!

Of course, only *new* Microsoft products conform to this vision. Even Windows Server 2008 originally didn't, since its development—under the code-name "Longhorn"—began prior to PowerShell's availability. But the next version of Windows will have to be built on PowerShell. It's a huge step, and it's a major change for the way administrators work with Windows. A change that is definitely for the better.

How Do I Use PowerShell?

When you open a new PowerShell window, you're actually running a program called PowerShell.exe. It's a small application—just about 300 kilobytes, in fact. Its job is to fire up the *real* PowerShell, what we call the "PowerShell engine," an application written in C# and housed in a DLL file. PowerShell.exe—called a *hosting application*—is what provides you with the command-line interface to issue instructions to the PowerShell engine, and provides you with a means of reviewing the results that the engine generates.

You operate PowerShell primarily by running *cmdlets* (pronounced, "command-lets"). These are special mini-applications written in a .NET language, such as C# or Visual Basic. They're designed to run exclusively within PowerShell, and they form the basis of PowerShell's functionality. Cmdlets are named according to a consistent, documented standard created by Microsoft. All cmdlet names are constructed of a verb, such as *get* or *set,* and a noun, such as *service* or *process.* Nouns are always singular; even though **Get-Process** returns all running processes, the noun is still the singular *process.*

PowerShell comes with about 410 cmdlets built-in, including ones that work with services, permissions, processes, WMI, and more. More cmdlets can be "snapped in" to PowerShell. Exchange Server 2007, for example, snaps in about 300 or so additional cmdlets, which handle Exchange administration tasks. Most cmdlets provide instant gratification: Open PowerShell, type **Get-Service**, and press Enter, and you'll see a list of services installed on your computer. But that's really just scratching the surface: These cmdlets can, as you'll learn, do much more.

Parameters

Like the command-line utilities you may have used in the past, PowerShell cmdlets often support a number of parameters. However, unlike the old command-line utilities, PowerShell's cmdlet parameters use a consistent naming pattern, which makes the parameters easier to learn. For example, both the **Get-Content** and **Set-Content** cmdlets allow you to specify a path—such as a file path—and so both use the same parameter name, **-path**, for that parameter.

PowerShell uses spaces as parameter delimiters. For example:

```
PS C:\> Get-Content -path C:\Content.txt
```

If a parameter value contains spaces, then you must enclose the value in either single or double quotation marks:

```
PS C:\> Get-Content -path "C:\Test Files\content.txt"
```

Typically, the most commonly used parameter for any given cmdlet is *positional,* meaning you don't even have to specify the parameter name. Therefore, the following is also valid:

```
PS C:\> Get-Content C:\Content.txt
```

What's more, when you *do* need to type a parameter name, you need to type only as much of the name as necessary to distinguish the parameter from others. For example, here's a command that will retrieve operating system information from a remote computer, passing along a previously created set of alternate credentials:

```
PS C:\> Get-Wmiobject win32_operatingsystem -computer Server02 -credential $cred
```

The following, however, would also be valid, because you can abbreviate the parameter **-credential** to just a couple of letters and no other parameter begins with *cr.* You can also abbreviate the computer parameter:

```
PS C:\> Get-Wmiobject win32_operatingsystem -co Server02 -cr $cred
```

Parameters allow you to customize the way cmdlets behave. For example, when retrieving a list of files from a folder, you can specify a parameter that causes the cmdlet to recurse subfolders.

Aliases

Aliases are basically just nicknames for cmdlets, either to make it easier to type the cmdlet name, or to associate the cmdlet with a familiar command from the older Cmd.exe shell. After all, it's certainly easier to type **Dir** than to type **Get-ChildItem** all the time, and **Dir** corresponds with a Cmd.exe command that performs basically the same function as **Get-ChildItem**. PowerShell comes with a number of predefined aliases that can make typing faster. For a complete list, simply run **Get-Alias**, and you'll see a list of all aliases, as well as the cmdlets they point to.

You can make your own aliases, too. For example, it's useful to occasionally pop up Windows Notepad to jot down a few notes as you're working in the shell, and simply typing **Notepad** over and over takes too long. Instead, it's easier to use a shorter alias, **Np**, which you can create by running this:

```
PS C:\>new-alias np notepad
```

Notice that you didn't even have to type the parameter names, since with this cmdlet both of the required parameters—alias name and command name—are positional, and don't need to be specifically named. Also notice that *you aliased an external command!* **Notepad** isn't a PowerShell cmdlet, but it is something you can run in PowerShell. Therefore, you can create an alias for it. Of course, your alias will "go away" the minute you close the shell session, so add it to your profile script. Now the alias will be added each time you run PowerShell. You'll learn more about PowerShell profiles later in the book.

Aliases have some downsides. For one, while they're certainly easier to type, they can be harder to read. Consider this:

```
ps | ? { $_.CPU -gt 50 } | % { $_.Name }
```

Yikes. Even punctuation marks like **?** and **%** get into the act with aliases! This is a lot easier to figure out when full cmdlet names are used:

```
Get-Process | '
 Where-Object { $_.CPU -gt 50 } | '
 ForEach-Object { $_.Name }
```

This command retrieves all currently running processes, selects those instances that have CPU utilization greater than 50, and then for each of those instances, just displays the process name. We haven't yet covered exactly how all of those cmdlets work, but you can probably see how the full cmdlet names make this easier to follow than the aliases.

Aliases are limited to providing a shorter, alternate name. You cannot create an alias for an expression that includes a parameter:

```
PS C:\ > new-alias -name os -value get-wmiobject win32_operatingsystem
New-Alias : A parameter cannot be found that matches parameter name 'win32_operatingsystem'.
At line:1 char:10
+ new-alias <<<< -name os -value get-wmiobject win32_operatingsystem
```

This is not to say you can't create a shortcut for something like the above expression. You'll have to create a function or use a script block rather than an alias, which will be covered later in the book. You can only create an alias for a cmdlet name:

```
PS C:\ > new-alias -name wmi -value get-wmiobject
```

Another downside to aliases is that, unless you stick to the aliases predefined in PowerShell itself, any scripts you write won't run on another computer unless you first take the time to define your custom aliases on that computer.

When it comes to writing scripts, you can work around both of these downsides by using a script editor. In fact, a very basic one comes with PowerShell v2.0, or you can invest in a full, commercial, visual development environment like SAPIEN PrimalScript (www.primalscript.com). Type all the aliases you want—after all, they *are* faster—and then go to PrimalScript's Edit menu. Open the Convert submenu, and then select Alias to Cmdlet to have PrimalScript expand all of your aliases into their full cmdlet names. You'll get instant readability and portability!

There are a couple of other cmdlets that you can use to work with aliases. **Export-Alias** exports your aliases into a special export file, allowing you to import those aliases on another system using **Import-Alias**. The **Set-Alias** cmdlet lets you change an existing alias. Remember, you can read more about using these cmdlets by asking PowerShell for Help—read on, and you'll learn how.

Backward-Compatible

PowerShell doesn't require you to give up all the external command-line utilities you've become accustomed to over the years. With few exceptions, utilities like Nslookup.exe, Ping.exe, Tracert.exe, Pathping.exe, and nearly any other will still run from within PowerShell—meaning you don't need to maintain two separate shells. PowerShell v2.0 uses these older command-line utilities in more or less the same way that they always have been used; however, you'll run into some situations where you need to enclose command-line parameters in quotes from within PowerShell, but that's about the only major difference. You'll also notice that most of your batch files and VBScript files should also run from within PowerShell. If you run into something that just won't run under PowerShell, you can always resort to calling CMD:

```
PS C:\ > cmd /c c:\scripts\myoldscript.bat
```

When either of us speaks at conferences we're often asked, "Can PowerShell also run graphical applications?" We're glad you asked, although, really, you should just try it and see! After all, what's the worst that could happen? In fact, if you open PowerShell and run **Calc** or **Notepad** or even **MSPaint**, you'll find that the graphical application pops right up, exactly as it would if you ran those applications from Cmd.exe or even the Windows "Run" dialog box. So, there aren't many reasons to keep Cmd.exe around. Consider deleting its shortcuts from your Start menu or wherever else and replacing those with shortcuts to PowerShell!

Navigation

Much like the Cmd.exe interface, PowerShell allows you to quickly and easily navigate the file system on your computer. Commands like **Dir, Cd, Del, Mkdir,** and others work "almost" flawlessly. "Almost" is in quotes because these are *not* PowerShell commands or cmdlets. Instead, they're *aliases,* or nicknames, to built-in PowerShell cmdlets. For example, **Dir** is an alias to the **Get-ChildItem** cmdlet, which retrieves a list of child items for a given object. Since a folder's "children" are its files and subfolders, **Get-ChildItem** has the same practical use as the old **Dir** command. However, when using **Dir** in Cmd. exe, you'd type something like **Dir /s** to see a list of files and folders and to recurse through subfolders. In PowerShell the same command line would be **Dir -recurse,** because **-recurse** is the equivalent parameter of **Get-ChildItem.**

Interestingly, cmdlets can have more than one alias. For example, **Get-ChildItem** is aliased to **Dir,** but also to **Ls,** the *nix equivalent to **Dir.** This lets folks with some *nix experience quickly jump in and start navigating. For the same reason, PowerShell will accept both backslashes and slashes in file paths, helping to bridge the gap between the MS-DOS world and the *nix world.

Scripting

PowerShell scripts are simple text files with a .PS1 filename extension. Inside each file is a list of PowerShell command lines *exactly as you might type them interactively in the command-line window*. There is *no difference* in functionality between using the shell interactively and running a script. Essentially, you can type commands interactively until they do what you want, and then paste them into a script for long-term use. PowerShell does have some scripting-specific language elements, which you'll learn about later in this book, but you can also use these elements interactively at the shell's command line—you don't have to "save" them for a PS1 file.

PowerShell scripts are also capable of being fully secured, much more so than prior Microsoft scripting languages like KiXtart, VBScript, or JScript.

Variables

Like any good scripting environment, PowerShell supports the use of variables. However, as mentioned above, there's no strict difference in functionality between using the shell interactively and writing a script. Therefore, you can use variables interactively! For example, the following will retrieve a list of services that are installed on the remote computer Server2:

```
PS C:\> Get-WmiObject Win32_Service -computerName Server2
```

The results will simply be listed on your screen. However, you *could* save those results into a variable:

```
PS C:\> $wmi = Get-WmiObject Win32_Service -computerName Server2
```

The variable **$wmi** is easy to spot: Variable names always begin with a dollar sign. Once the variable contains the results of the **Get-WmiObject** cmdlet, you can display those results simply by typing the variable name and pressing Enter:

```
PS C:\> $wmi
```

You can, of course, expect more than one service to be installed on that remote computer, and $wmi would contain them all. To view just the *first* service—something it's tougher to do by just using **Get-WmiObject** alone—you could do something like this:

```
PS C:\> $wmi[0]
```

Of course, we're getting a bit ahead of ourselves, but this does illustrate how powerful and flexible the shell is without ever needing to use a script.

Built-in Help

Microsoft ships PowerShell with extensive Help for all of the built-in cmdlets. To ask for Help, simply type the keyword **Help** (which is actually a special, built-in function that utilizes the **Get-Help** cmdlet), followed by whatever you want Help on:

```
PS C:\> Help Get-WmiObject
```

If all you know is an alias name, you can use that, too:

```
PS C:\> Help Dir
```

If you're not even sure what you need Help on, try using wildcards. For example, to see everything PowerShell can do with services, try this:

```
PS C:\> Help *service*
```

The default Help display is fairly concise, designed to fit on a single screen. Use parameters like **-full**, **-detailed**, or **-example** to get full Help, moderately detailed Help, or command examples, when available. To see **Get-ACL** in action, for example:

```
PS C:\> Help Get-ACL -example
```

This Help functionality makes PowerShell's capabilities easier to discover.

In addition to the cmdlet **Get-Help**, PowerShell includes a number of topic-oriented Help files. Want to know more about associative arrays? Run this:

```
PS C:\ > Help about_associative_array
```

You'll get a useful summary with examples. If you want to see a listing of all the available topics, run:

```
PS C:\ > Help about*
```

Of course, sometimes it can be a distraction to have to refer to Help while you're trying to work out a command line, and sometimes you don't want to have to page through the information the way the **Help** function does. If you'd prefer an on-screen, electronic cmdlet reference, there are several options available. The authors suggest that you go to www.primaltools.com/communitytools/ and download the free PowerShell Help tool. It provides a nicely formatted version of Help in a graphical window that you can have up and running alongside your PowerShell console, giving you access to the built-in Help without distracting you from the command you're trying to construct.

Object Oriented

Perhaps the most important part of PowerShell—and one of the toughest concepts to grasp—is that PowerShell is completely object oriented. If you're an old hand at *nix, this object orientation is a big conceptual leap; PowerShell looks and feels so much like a *nix shell (such as Bash, which provided a lot of PowerShell's inspiration), that it's easy to think of PowerShell as a text-based shell. But it isn't.

Almost all PowerShell cmdlets deal with *objects*. This is perhaps easiest to see with a cmdlet like **Get-Service**.

```
PS C:\> $services = Get-Service
PS C:\> $services[0]
PS C:\> $services[0].Name
PS C:\> $services[0].Pause()
```

The first line retrieves all installed services and stores the result in the variable **$services**. The "result," in this case, is a *collection* of service *objects*. That is, for each service installed on your computer, Windows produces a unique software component to represent the service. That component can do all the things a service can do, such as starting or stopping. The component also contains all the properties, or attributes, that service has, such as a name and description and start mode.

The second line displays the first service in the collection. Collections are zero-based, so the first item has an index of zero, the second an index of one, and so forth. Placing the index in square brackets just retrieves that particular item. The third line is still working with the first service, but now PowerShell will *just* display the contents of that service's Name property.

Finally, the last line grabs the first service and executes its **Pause()** *method*. A method is essentially a command, telling the object—in this case, a service—to do something, such as pause itself.

The thing to remember is that even when you're looking at a text list in PowerShell—such as the list you see when you run **Get-Service**—what really happened under the hood is that a cmdlet produced one or more objects. Having nothing else to do with those objects, PowerShell selected certain properties of those objects and used those properties to construct a text list. That doesn't mean the **Get-Process** cmdlet creates a list of processes. The cmdlet assembles a *collection* of process *objects*. It's PowerShell that selected key properties of those objects to create that text list. PowerShell will only create a text list when you haven't given it something else to do with those objects.

Objects are a software way of representing complex computer functionality. For example, the objects returned by **Get-Service** represent services and all the things a service can do; the objects returned by **Get-Process** are quite different, since processes have different attributes and capabilities than a service. Even strings of text are, to PowerShell's way of thinking, a kind of object:

```
PS C:\> "this is a string".ToUpper()
THIS IS A STRING
```

The string of characters, "this is a string," is enclosed in double quotation marks, identifying them to PowerShell as a single unit. That single unit is an *object* of the String type; that is, the object is a string of characters. PowerShell knows how to do certain things with strings, including displaying an all-uppercase version of them. That particular capability is accessed via the **ToUpper()** method of the String object, as shown in the example. The object itself is followed by a period, which indicates that you're ready to type a property or method name, and then the method name, **ToUpper()** (methods always have parentheses after their name).

This example illustrates that you can treat anything, even a literal string, as an object. If the string were in a variable, as with the earlier example on pausing a service, things would work exactly the same:

```
PS C:\> $var = "this is a string"
PS C:\> $var.ToUpper()
THIS IS A STRING
```

In this case, you put the string of characters into a variable, **$var**. At that point, **$var** represents that string of characters and has the same capabilities. In programmer-speak, then, **$var** is a String variable, with all the capabilities of any String, including the **ToUpper()** method.

Curious about the capabilities a particular object might have? PowerShell has a cmdlet, **Get-Member**, which displays the properties and methods of any object. To use **Get-Member**, simply *pipe* the object you're curious about to **Get-Member**:

```
PS C:\> $var = 5
PS C:\> $var | get-member


  TypeName: System.Int32
```

```
Name              MemberType      Definition
----              ----------      ----------
CompareTo         Method          System.Int3...
Equals            Method          System.Bool...
GetHashCode       Method          System.Int3...
GetType           Method          System.Type...
GetTypeCode       Method          System.Type...
ToString          Method          System.Stri...


PS C:\>
```

In this example, you put the number 5 into **$var** and piped it to **Get-Member**. The results, as you can see, indicate that **$var** represents an Int32 type of variable—that is, an integer—and that the Int32 type has six methods you could use. Try putting the results of **Get-Process** into a variable, and then piping that variable to **Get-Member**. What can you do with a process object, once you have one?

You'll spend a lot more time on objects, variables, and piping in upcoming chapters, so if this didn't make a lot of sense right now, don't worry. There are more elaborate examples later to help make things clearer.

Danger! Danger! Danger!

The question often comes up, "Is PowerShell dangerous?" To which the answer is always, "Of course it is!" After all, PowerShell is an administrative tool, capable of doing the same amount of damage as any such tool. Imagine, for example, what you could do in Active Directory Users & Computers with an injudicious mouse click and the Delete key on your keyboard!

But PowerShell does try and offer you some protection through two common parameters, **-whatIf** and **-confirm**. Supported by almost any cmdlet that has the potential to do something damaging or irreversible, these parameters give you an opportunity to see what the cmdlet *would do*, without actually doing it, and a chance for you to change your mind. To see how they work, consider this:

Caution: Please don't actually run this next bit until you've read this entire section. Seriously.

```
PS C:\> Get-Process | Stop-Process
```

The first cmdlet retrieves all running process, and then *pipes,* or sends, them to the second cmdlet, which will stop them all one at a time. The result is that your computer crashes. Whoops! Now consider this safer alternative:

```
PS C:\> Get-Process | Stop-Process -whatif
```

You can run the above safely because it won't *do* anything. Instead, **Stop-Process** simply shows you *what it would have done,* if you'd let it. This is an excellent way of testing a command line to see what would happen, without actually letting anything happen that might get you into trouble with the boss. As a next step, you might try this:

```
PS C:\> Get-Process | Stop-Process -confirm
```

Now, **Stop-Process** will stop before every process and ask you what you want to do. You'll have the option to stop each process, one at a time, or skip ones that you've changed your mind about. This is essentially the same as the "Are you sure?" dialog boxes you'd find in a graphical user interface, and it's a good way to help avoid potentially damaging situations. Remember, shells don't damage systems, *people* damage systems: By using **-whatif** and **-confirm** appropriately, you'll help yourself avoid any unintended damage to your computers.

Sometimes, PowerShell will automatically do the "Are you sure?" thing. That's because every cmdlet which changes something and supports the confirmation capability also specifies its *impact level*, which might be something like "high" or "low." A built-in PowerShell preference—which defaults to "high"— automatically confirms any operation with an impact level equal to or higher than the preference's setting. You can't modify a cmdlet's impact level, but you can modify the threshold for automatic confirmation by modifying the built-in **$ConfirmPreference** variable.

Bottom Line: Do I Need to Know All This?

Yes. Look, clearly graphical user interfaces are easier to use than esoteric command-line utilities. Hopefully, though, PowerShell's consistent naming and architecture make its utilities less esoteric and easier to use. But, in the end, it's all about the command line. A Windows administrator who operates from the command line can create a hundred new users in the time it takes to create just *one* in the graphical user interface. That's an efficiency savings managers just can't ignore. PowerShell lets you perform tasks *en masse* that can't be done at all with the GUI, like updating the password a particular service uses to log on across dozens of computers.

If you've been with Windows since the NT 4.0 days, you may remember a time when earning your Microsoft Certified Systems Engineer (MCSE) certification was not only a way to differentiate yourself from the rest of the administrators out there, it was also a ticket to a $20,000 or more pay raise. Those days, of course, are gone; today, management is looking at production-applicable skills to differentiate the highly paid administrators from the entry-level ones. And before long, PowerShell is going to be *the* skill management is after. As an industry, we know it, because we've seen it: Try finding an IT manager who'll pay top dollar for a *nix administrator who can't script in Perl, or Python, or some similar language. Before long, Windows managers will have figured it out, too: A PowerShell-savvy administrator can do more work, in less time and with fewer mistakes, than an administrator who doesn't know PowerShell. That's the type of bottom-line, dollars-and-cents criteria that any smart manager can understand. So, *yes*, you will need to know this stuff. Ideally, you started learning it with PowerShell v1.0, when there was a bit less to learn. If not, you'd sure better jump in now—because wait a few years and there will be *even more* to learn, and it'll become increasingly difficult for someone starting from scratch.

Is PowerShell a Good Investment of My Time?

Absolutely. That can be tough to believe, given all the scripting technologies Microsoft has inflicted on the world in the past and then quickly abandoned: KiXtart, VBScript, batch files, JScript, and more— the list goes on. But PowerShell's different. First of all, PowerShell is currently in version 2.0 (and that's the version this book covers, and it's a big improvement over 1.0, which itself was *great*). But there *will be* a v3.0, and a v4.0… so while today's PowerShell is far from perfect, it's pretty darn good, and in almost all ways it's already better than any similar technology we've had in the past.

But, as this book has already described, PowerShell is here to *stay*. Microsoft's not going to be able to walk away from PowerShell as easily as they did VBScript, primarily because so many products are being built *on top of* PowerShell. With PowerShell embedded in Exchange Server 2007, the System Center family, much of Windows Server 2008 R2, and in future versions of Windows, well, it's a safe bet that we're going to be working with PowerShell for a decade or more, at least. In computer time that's about a century, so it's definitely a good investment.

Help and Additional Resources

If you ever get stuck, please know that www.ScriptingAnswers.com is available to help. It's a free online community for Windows scripting and automation. They have a dedicated forum for PowerShell questions, and they encourage you to post any questions you run across. You can also check out PowerShellCommunity.org, which is where a lot of the Windows PowerShell MVP Award recipients hang out and answer questions, and you can also visit ConcentratedTech.com, where one of this book's authors (Don) answers questions and posts PowerShell tips.

If you're looking for additional training resources, visit www.ScriptingTraining.com, which offers a variety of instructor-led and self-paced training products related to PowerShell.

Finally, you should download a trial version of PrimalScript from www.PrimalScript.com. This all-in-one visual development environment supports PowerShell scripting, as well as cmdlet development, should you ever venture in that direction. It makes PowerShell scripting vastly easier and more intuitive, and provides a lot of little tricks to help you construct scripts more quickly and efficiently.

If you're interested in participating in the larger PowerShell community, start at http://blogs.msdn.com/powershell, which is the home of the Windows PowerShell Team Blog. There, you'll find many members of the PowerShell product team—that's right, real Microsoft employees—sharing tips and tricks about their product. Our own blogs, at blog.sapien.com, and concentratedtech.com are also chock-full of scripts, tips, techniques, news, and more, and we hope you'll take a moment to check it out.

So, that's our introduction! Now, let's dive in and see how this PowerShell thing ticks.

Chapter 3
PowerShell Drives

PowerShell introduces a unique concept called *PSDrives*, or PowerShell Drives. There's an interesting philosophy behind these: The team that created PowerShell knew that they'd have an uphill battle convincing administrators to drop their graphical tools and turn to the command line. They figured the switch would be easier if they could leverage the relatively small set of command-line skills that most Windows administrators already had. PowerShell's cmdlets, with their command-line parameters, are one example of that. Most admins are already familiar with command-line utilities and switches, and PowerShell simply expands on that familiarity, adding in better consistency for a shorter learning curve. The other main skill that the team wanted to leverage was the ability to navigate a complex hierarchical object store. Bet you didn't know you had that skill, but you do!

Navigating a Hierarchical Object Store

Suppose you were using an operating system, like Windows, that had the ability to store long strings of text in some sort of container. That container would have various properties, such as a name, its size, and information about when it was created and last accessed. You'd be able to view those properties at any time, modify some of them, like the name, and access the contents of the container. Now suppose that "container" was called a "text file" and you'll realize that you already know all about them! You probably even know how to manipulate them, to a degree, from the command line. You probably know how to use **Ren** to rename a file, **Type** to see its contents, and **Del** to remove it from the storage device. In fact, PowerShell supports all three of those commands by aliasing them to actual PowerShell cmdlets.

Now suppose your operating system had *tens of thousands* of files like these. You'd need some way to organize them, right? Something like the hierarchy of folders and subfolders that you've doubtless seen in Windows Explorer. And you probably know how to work with that hierarchy from the command line, too, using commands like **Cd** to change into a different folder, **Cd ..** to move up one level in the hierarchy, **Rmdir** to remove a folder, **Mkdir** to create a new folder, and **Dir** to see a list of the objects (files and subfolders) within a folder. And again, PowerShell supports these commands by aliasing them to the appropriate PowerShell cmdlets.

In other words, you can jump right into PowerShell and navigate a complex, hierarchical, object-based store, using the same commands and techniques that you've probably been using for years in something like Cmd.exe.

So, why can't *all* of Windows' hierarchical stores be navigated in the same fashion?

More Stores than Just the File System

Windows has several different hierarchical stores aside from the file system. The registry, for example, looks a lot like the file system, don't you think? It has folders (registry keys) and files (registry settings), and the files have contents (the values within settings). The Certificate Store in Windows is similar, too. So is Active Directory, for that matter.

PowerShell lets you leverage all of these hierarchical stores using the same techniques you use to work with the file system (well, not *all*—PowerShell v1.0 didn't ship with a way to make Active Directory look like a file system, although Windows Server 2008 R2 does include the functionality). Open a PowerShell console and run **Get-PSDrive**. You'll see a list of all the "drives" attached to your PowerShell console, and you'll see the *provider* that connects each drive. For example, you'll doubtless see drives C: and D:, and perhaps others, using the FileSystem provider—and these drives are the ones you're probably already familiar with. But you'll also see drives HKCU: and HKLM:, which use the registry provider. You'll see a CERT: drive for the Certificate Store, and an ENV: drive for environment variables. Other drives like Function: and Variable: connect to PowerShell's own internal storage mechanisms.

Try accessing the HKEY_LOCAL_MACHINE hive of the registry. How? The same way you'd access your D: drive:

```
PS C:\> cd hklm:
```

Simply change to the HKLM: drive and you're there. Need to see the keys that are available at list level? Ask for a list:

```
PS HKLM:\> dir
```

Want to change into the SOFTWARE key? You can probably guess how that's done:

```
PS HKLM:\> cd software
PS HKLM:\Software >
```

Note that PowerShell isn't even case sensitive! Want to delete a registry key (be careful)? The **Del** command will do it. There is much more that you can do, and this book will cover working with the registry in more detail in "Managing the Registry" . But it was important for you to see the flexibility of PSDrives.

Mapping Drives

You can create your own drives using whatever providers you have installed. For example, to map your

Z: drive to \\Server\Share, you'd run something like this:

```
PS C:\> new-psdrive Z -psprovider FileSystem -root \\server1\share
```

The -**Psprovider** parameter tells PowerShell exactly which provider you're using. You can even map to local folders:

```
PS C:\> new-psdrive Z -psprovider FileSystem -root C:\test
```

This maps the Z: drive to the local C:\Test folder. Unfortunately, PowerShell doesn't provide any means for using the other providers remotely. Mapping to a remote UNC is about your only option, and that only works with the FileSystem provider. You can't map to remote registries or certificate stores. That'd be a useful capability, but it doesn't exist in v1.0 or v2.0.

Any mappings you create in PowerShell are preserved only for the current session. Once you close PowerShell, they're gone. Also, your drive mappings don't show up in Windows Explorer; they only exist in PowerShell. If you need to re-create a particular mapping each time you open a PowerShell console, then add the appropriate **New-PSDrive** command to a PowerShell profile (more on that in "Scripting Overview").

You should pay special attention to the fact that PowerShell's drives *exist only within PowerShell itself.* For example, if you map the Z: drive to a UNC, and then try to launch Windows Notepad to open a file on the Z: drive, *it won't work.* That's because the path is passed to Notepad, which has to ask *Windows,* not PowerShell, to get the file. Since *Windows* doesn't "have" the Z: drive, the operation will fail.

More Providers!

You're not limited to the providers supplied by Microsoft. Go to www.codeplex.com and, in the search box near the top of the page, type **powershell** and hit Enter. You'll find a variety of projects that extend PowerShell's functionality. Some of these include providers for other hierarchical storage systems, allowing you to "attach" them as PSDrives:

- The PowerShell Community Extensions includes a provider for Active Directory.

- A SharePoint Provider connects SharePoint 2003 and 2007 as a PSDrive.

- A BizTalk provider connects BizTalk Server as a file system, including applications, orchestrations, and schemas.

The possibilities are endless. Microsoft also releases new providers, as appropriate, with server products, and Windows Server 2008 R2 includes an officially-supported PSDrive provider for Active Directory. Imagine being able to delete users using the **Del** command, or being able to navigate organizational units (OUs) using **Cd**!

PSDrives = Ease of Use

The beauty of the PSDrive model is that *any* hierarchical store supported by a PSDrive provider looks like a file system. If Microsoft releases yet another hierarchical storage product in the future, it can be "snapped" into PowerShell to look like a file system, meaning your investment in file system-management commands will last you for a good, long time. You also have to be creative in using PSDrives. For example, if you know how to write a batch file that copies a bunch of files from one place to another, then you also know how to write a PowerShell script that copies *registry keys* from one place to another! Every skill you already possess for managing files from the command line can now be re-purposed for many different types of storage—and that's a *real* benefit of using PowerShell.

Chapter 4
Key Cmdlets for Windows Administration

Now that you've had a quick overview of PowerShell and you know how to navigate your computer's various storage systems, it's time to put PowerShell to use. Understand that the rest of this book will build on these concepts, and in fact go into more depth on a lot of what we'll show you right now, but we want you to be able to do something *useful* with PowerShell as quickly as possible. Also, don't think that this chapter represents the sum total of PowerShell's capabilities—nothing could be further from the truth! Our plan is to just scratch the surface a little bit and introduce you to some key cmdlets that you'll use almost every day in Windows PowerShell. We want to show you how these cmdlets relate directly to production administration tasks. Ready to get started?

Cmdlets for Navigating Your System

We reviewed a bunch of these in "Windows PowerShell Architecture and Overview" and "PowerShell Drives," but we primarily focused on their aliases—such as **Dir, Cd, Ls, MkDir,** and so forth. Now, we'd like to focus on the actual underlying cmdlets. Hey, you're still welcome to type the aliases, if you prefer them, but knowing the names for these particular cmdlets gives you some valuable insight into how PowerShell thinks.

Listing Child Items

First up, remember that PowerShell thinks of *everything* as an object. A folder on your hard drive, for example, is an object. Of course, folders have subfolders and files, which PowerShell thinks of as *children* of the folder. That's not an uncommon term, for example many of us are accustomed to thinking of "parent folders" and so forth. So, if you're working with a particular folder, meaning that PowerShell is "inside" that folder, then the way you'd get a list of child items is simple: **Get-ChildItem**. Remember,

PowerShell cmdlets always use a singular noun, so it's not "Get-Children" or "Get-ChildItems," it's **Get-ChildItem**. Typed alone, the cmdlet—or one of its aliases, such as **Dir**, **Ls**, or **GCI**—will return a list of child items for the current object; that is, the folder the shell is currently "in." Like this:

```
PS C:\test> Get-ChildItem


    Directory: Microsoft.PowerShell.Core\FileSystem::C:\test


Mode                LastWriteTime     Length Name
----                -------------     ------ ----
d----        4/9/2007  11:10 AM              subfolder
-a---        3/20/2007 11:37 AM        435   demo1.ps1
-a---        3/20/2007 11:46 AM        481   demo2.ps1
-a---        3/20/2007  9:44 AM        354   demo3.ps1
-a---        3/20/2007  9:44 AM        349   demo4.ps1
-a---        3/20/2007 11:55 AM        676   scope.ps1
-a---        3/19/2007 11:15 AM       1825   webcast.zip
```

By default, this information is displayed in a table format. However, if you ask for help on **Get-ChildItem**, you'll see that it has a lot of additional options, which are exposed via parameters. For example, one useful parameter is --**recurse**, which forces the cmdlet to retrieve *all* child items, even those deeply nested within subfolders.

You can get the child items for a specific path, too:

```
PS C:\> gci -path c:\test
```

Notice that we've used the **GCI** alias, and specified the name of the --**path** parameter. The online help indicates that the actual parameter name is optional, in this case, because the first parameter is positional. Therefore, the following would achieve the same thing:

```
PS C:\> dir c:\test
```

Of course, we used a different alias, but it doesn't matter. The command works the same either way. Other parameters let you filter the results. For example, consider this:

```
PS C:\test> dir -exclude *.ps1


    Directory: Microsoft.PowerShell.Core\FileSystem::C:\test


Mode                LastWriteTime     Length Name
----                -------------     ------ ----
d----        4/9/2007  11:10 AM              subfolder
-a---        3/19/2007 11:15 AM       1825   webcast.zip
```

The -**exclude** parameter accepts wildcards, such as * and ?, and removes matching items from the result set. Similarly, the -**include** parameter filters out everything *except* those items that match your criteria. One important thing to remember about -**include** and -**exclude** is that they force the cmdlet to retrieve all of the child items *first,* and *then* filter out the items you didn't want. That can sometimes be slow, when a lot of items are involved. An alternate technique is to use the -**filter** parameter. Its use differs depending on the PSDrive provider you're working with, although with the file system it uses the familiar * and ? wildcards, like this:

```
PS C:\test> dir -filter *.ps1


    Directory: Microsoft.PowerShell.Core\FileSystem::C:\test


Mode                LastWriteTime     Length Name
----                -------------     ------ ----
-a---         3/20/2007 11:37 AM        435 demo1.ps1
-a---         3/20/2007 11:46 AM        481 demo2.ps1
-a---         3/20/2007  9:44 AM        354 demo3.ps1
-a---         3/20/2007  9:44 AM        349 demo4.ps1
-a---         3/20/2007 11:55 AM        676 scope.ps1
```

Only items matching your criteria are included in the output. If that output contains too much information, you can just have the cmdlet return the names of the child items:

```
PS C:\test> dir -filter *.ps1 -name
demo1.ps1
demo2.ps1
demo3.ps1
demo4.ps1
scope.ps1
```

Here, by combining the **-filter** and **-name** parameters, we've generated a very customized list: just the names of the PowerShell scripts in this folder.

Occasionally, PowerShell can annoy you by attempting to interpret characters in a path as a wildcard. For example, in the file system, the question mark character is used as a single character wild card:

```
PS C:\temp > dir t?st.txt


    Directory: Microsoft.PowerShell.Core\FileSystem::C:\temp


Mode                LastWriteTime     Length Name
----                -------------     ------ ----
-a---         8/23/2007  4:40 PM      44194 tast.txt
-a---         8/23/2007  4:40 PM      44194 test.txt
-a---         8/23/2007  4:40 PM      44194 tzst.txt
PS C:\temp >
```

However, within the Windows registry, the question mark character is a legitimate character. To see how this works temporarily, create some new keys in the registry:

```
PS HKCU:\software > mkdir Micr?soft
PS HKCU:\software > mkdir Micr?soft\test1\
```

Now try the following:

```
PS HKCU:\> dir Micr?soft -recurse
```

You might be expecting a listing of registry keys underneath the key "Micr?Soft," but PowerShell interprets the question mark as a wildcard, and will instead search for any key like "MicrzSoft," "Micr0soft," and so forth. If you run into this situation, just use a slightly different technique:

```
PS HKCU:\> dir -literalPath Micr?soft -recurse
```

Here, the **-literalPath** parameter tells PowerShell to take the path literally—that is, to not try and interpret any characters as wildcards. Now you should see only the specified key and its children.

Finally, remember that PowerShell is designed to work with a variety of different storage systems. When you're working with the CERT: drive—the "disk drive" that's connected to your local certificate store—**Get-ChildItem** supports a parameter named **-codeSigningCert**. It filters the display of child items to those that are code-signing certificates rather than other types; this makes it easier to retrieve a code-signing certificate when you want to digitally sign a PowerShell script file. For example:

```
PS CERT:\> get-childitem -codesign
```

Notice that we didn't specify the full name of **-codeSigningCert**; we didn't need to, because you only need a few characters to differentiate the parameter name from the other ones available (actually, we could have used fewer characters, but this way it's still relatively obvious what's going on when you read the command line).

Changing Location

Now that you know how to get a list of child items from a single location, you'll also need to know how to change locations. In MS-DOS and *nix, that's done with the **Cd** command, short for "Change Directory," and in many operating systems the longer **ChDir** command will also work. PowerShell aliases **Cd** to **Set-Location**.

Generally speaking, you just tell **Set-Location** where you want to go:

```
PS C:\> Set-Location -path CERT:
```

Or, using an alias and omitting the parameter name:

```
PS C:\> cd C:\Test\Subfolder
```

As with the **Get-ChildItem** cmdlet, you can also specify a literal path, if you don't want PowerShell interpreting wildcard characters:

```
PS C:\> cd -literal HKCU:\SOFTWARE\Manu?\Key
```

If you're curious, you *can* provide wildcards if you don't use the **-literalPath** parameter:

```
PS C:\> cd tes*
```

On the test system, the above changes into the C:\Test folder. You'll get an error if the path you specify resolves to more than one path; this is different than the Cmd.exe behavior of simply changing into the first matching path in the event of multiple matches.

By the way, you *will* notice some quirks in how **Set-Location** behaves compared to Cmd.exe. For example, the following will produce an error:

```
PS C:\test> cd..
```

In Cmd.exe, that would move up one directory level to C:\; in PowerShell it generates an error because PowerShell needs a space between the command and any parameters:

```
PS C:\test> cd ..
```

That's just a little thing you'll have to get used to as you work with PowerShell. Before long, you'll be dropping your old Cmd.exe habits and picking up new PowerShell habits!

Cmdlets for Working with Items

Remember, PowerShell uses the word *item* to generically refer to the "stuff located in a PSDrive." That means an *item* could be a file, a folder, a registry value, a registry key, a certificate, an environment variable, and so forth. For example, try this:

```
PS C:\> cd env:
PS Env:\> type systemroot
C:\Windows
PS Env:\>
```

This uses **Set-Location** (or its alias, **Cd**) to change to the ENV: drive—the "disk drive" that contains all the environment variables on your computer. It then uses the **Type** alias—that's the **Get-Content** cmdlet, by the way—to retrieve the contents of the item named "systemroot." In this case, that "item" is an environment variable and **Get-Content** displays its contents: "C:\Windows." So, you've just learned a new cmdlet: **Get-Content**! That cmdlet has a *lot* of parameters that customize its behavior, allowing you to filter the content as it's being displayed, read only a specified number of characters, and so forth; we won't be covering the cmdlet in any more depth right now, but feel free to look it up in PowerShell's help if you like.

PowerShell has a variety of cmdlets for manipulating items:

- Copy-Item
- Clear-Item
- Get-Item
- Invoke-Item
- New-Item
- Move-Item
- Remove-Item
- Rename-Item
- Set-Item

Some of these will look familiar to you. For example, **Remove-Item** is an alias for s **Del**, and is used to delete items, whether they are files, folders, registry keys, or whatever. The old **Move**, **Ren**, and **Copy** commands are now aliases to **Move-Item**, **Rename-Item**, and **Copy-Item**. For example, here you can see a directory listing that includes a folder named Subfolder; you then use the **Copy-Item** cmdlet to create a copy of it named Newfolder:

```
PS C:\test> dir
```

```
Directory: Microsoft.PowerShell.Core\FileSystem::C:\test


Mode                LastWriteTime     Length Name
----                -------------     ------ ----
d----         4/9/2007  11:10 AM            subfolder
-a---        3/20/2007  11:37 AM        435 demo1.ps1
-a---        3/20/2007  11:46 AM        481 demo2.ps1
-a---        3/20/2007   9:44 AM        354 demo3.ps1
-a---        3/20/2007   9:44 AM        349 demo4.ps1
-a---        3/20/2007  11:55 AM        676 scope.ps1
-a---        3/19/2007  11:15 AM       1825 webcast.zip


PS C:\test> copy subfolder newfolder
PS C:\test> dir


    Directory: Microsoft.PowerShell.Core\FileSystem::C:\test


Mode                LastWriteTime     Length Name
----                -------------     ------ ----
d----         4/9/2007  11:37 AM            newfolder
d----         4/9/2007  11:10 AM            subfolder
-a---        3/20/2007  11:37 AM        435 demo1.ps1
-a---        3/20/2007  11:46 AM        481 demo2.ps1
-a---        3/20/2007   9:44 AM        354 demo3.ps1
-a---        3/20/2007   9:44 AM        349 demo4.ps1
-a---        3/20/2007  11:55 AM        676 scope.ps1
-a---        3/19/2007  11:15 AM       1825 webcast.zip
```

The **Copy-Item** cmdlet is incredibly powerful, though. It supports a **-recurse** parameter which lets it work with entire trees of objects, and supports the **-include** and -**exclude** filtering parameters, as well as -**filter.** For example, the following will copy all files with a .PS1 filename extension to a folder named Newfolder. However, it will not copy files matching the wildcard pattern Demo?.ps1:

```
PS C:\test> copy *.ps1 newfolder -exclude demo?.ps1
```

The cmdlet also supports the -**whatif** and -**confirm** parameters we introduced in "Windows PowerShell Architecture and Overview." The **Move-Item** cmdlet supports a similar set of functionality. Even **Rename-Item** supports the -**whatif** and -**confirm** parameters, so that you can test what it's doing before actually committing yourself.

Clear-Item works similarly to **Remove-Item**. However, it leaves the original item in place, and clears out its contents, making it a zero-length file. That might not seem useful with files and folders, but it's definitely useful with other PSDrive providers, such as the registry, where **Clear-Item** can eliminate the value from a setting but leave the setting itself intact. Similarly, **Set-Item** might not seem to have any use in the file system, but it's useful for changing the value of registry settings.

Last up is **New-Item**, which, as you might guess, creates an all-new item. Of course, you will need to tell PowerShell what *kind* of item you'd like created, and that type of item must match the drive where the item is being created. You can't, for example, create a new file within one of the registry "drives," because the registry can't store a file. For example, this will create a new file and place some text in it:

```
PS C:\> New-Item -path . -name example.txt -type "file" -value "hello!"
```

The **-path** parameter indicates where the system should create the item, and the remaining parameters specify its name, its type, and its initial contents. You might also specify "directory" to create a new directory—and, by the way, you've just found the cmdlet that's used instead of the old **MkDir** command! Unfortunately, PowerShell doesn't contain an alias for **MkDir**, because an alias can't specify parameters—and in order to create a new folder, you must specify the **-type directory** parameter.

....

Note
You don't have to include parameter values like "file" in quotation marks, unless the value contains a space. It doesn't hurt to enclose them in quotation marks, though, and it's not a bad habit to get into, because quotes will always work, even if the value contains spaces.

Use PowerShell's built-in help to explore some of the other options available to these cmdlets, and you'll soon be working with all types of items from the various PSDrives available to you.

Cmdlets for Working with Text Data

Although PowerShell itself always works with objects, as an administrator you're often forced to work with text, or strings of characters. For example, some administrators need to scan through Internet Information Server (IIS) log files, searching for HTTP application errors, so they can report the errors to the appropriate Web developers for resolution. This is a bit tricky: The HTTP error code you're after is 500, but you can't just search for the string "500," since it also occurs in page names, port numbers, byte counts, and so forth. Here's an example log file line with HTTP status code 500 logged:

```
2007-03-05 09:08:45 W3SVC122167217 DATAPIPE-OG0E5E 65.17.251.151 GET /forum/member_profile.asp
PF=|110|800a000d|Type_mismatch:_'CLng' 80 - 66.249.65.243 HTTP/1.1 Mozilla/5.0+(compatible;+Google
bot/2.1;++http://www.google.com/bot.html) - - www.sapien.com 500 0 0 641 248 93
```

The status code immediately follows the domain—in this case, "www.sapien.com 500" is the string we're after. The **Select-String** cmdlet can help quickly scan an entire log file looking for lines with this pattern of characters:

```
PS C:\> get-content c:\sample.log | select-string "www.sapien.com 500" -simple
```

The **-simple** parameter tells **Select-String** that we're not matching on a regular expression, but rather a simple string of characters. The output is every line of the input that has a match for the pattern. We could have stored those matches in a variable, if desired:

```
PS C:\> $matches = get-content c:\sample.log | select-string "www.sapien.com 500" -simple
```

We didn't even have to use **Get-Content** to retrieve the text file, as **Select-String** provides a **-path** argument, which loads the file automatically:

```
PS C:\> $matches = select-string "www.sapien.com 500" -simple -path c:\sample.log
```

Now, the **$matches** variable actually includes a collection of MatchInfo object, not just pure text. For example, by treating it as a collection, we can refer to specific matches:

```
PS C:\> $matches.filename
sample.log
PS C:\> $matches.line
2007-03-05 09:08:45 W3SVC122167217 DATAPIPE-OG0E5E 65.17.251.151 GET /forum/member_profil
e.asp PF=|110|800a000d|Type_mismatch:_'CLng' 80 - 66.249.65.243 HTTP/1.1 Mozilla/5.0+(com
patible;+Googlebot/2.1;++http://www.google.com/bot.html) - - www.sapien.com 500 0 0 641 2
48 93
PS C:\> $matches.linenumber
5416
PS C:\> $matches.path
C:\sample.log
PS C:\> $matches.pattern
www.sapien.com 500
PS C:\>
```

You can see that the Filename, Line, LineNumber, Path, and Pattern properties all return useful information. Now, in this example the **$matches** variable only contained one match (the $matches.Count property would verify this). But we can modify the search slightly:

```
PS C:\> $matches = select-string "500" -simple -path c:\sample.log
```

Now we're not just getting HTTP 500 errors, but also anything with "500," including byte counts and other data. This time the log generated 503 matches:

```
PS C:\> $matches.count
503
```

And we can reference individual matches by using their index number:

```
PS C:\> $matches[0].linenumber
93
```

This tells us that the first match was on line 93. The **Select-String** cmdlet also works with regular expressions; in fact, it's *primarily* designed to work with regular expressions, although we've been using it in a simpler fashion in the examples. We discuss regular expressions in their own chapter, later in this book.

The **Select-String** cmdlet has a lot of additional capability for working with text data—consider reading its online help to see its various options. If you're a *nix administrator accustomed to working with the Grep utility, then you'll find much of the same functionality within **Select-String**.

Cmdlets for Working with Windows

Even though current versions of Windows—Vista, XP, Server 2003, Server 2008, and even Server 2008 R2—aren't specifically built on PowerShell, you can still perform a lot of administrative automation in PowerShell. That's because PowerShell comes pre-packed with cmdlets designed for administering specific portions of Windows, and because PowerShell makes it easy to utilize Windows Management Instrumentation (WMI), a key management technology that's present in all modern versions of Windows. Windows Server 2008 R2 ships with several PowerShell modules that enable PowerShell-based administration of Active Directory, AD Rights Management, AppLocker, BITS, Group Policy, Server Manager, Troubleshooting, and much more.

Note

Keep in mind that files, folders, registries, and other aspects of Windows are also manageable through Windows PowerShell, using the various cmdlets and techniques discussed earlier in this chapter. There aren't specific cmdlets used to deal with files or folders, for example; you use the "generic" Item cmdlets to move, copy, rename, delete, and create these items.

The goal here is *not* an exhaustive exploration of these cmdlets. In fact, later chapters in this book focus on using these and other cmdlets to perform administrative tasks. The goal right now is just to make you aware of these cmdlets, since we'll be using them in a lot of examples and samples in upcoming chapters.

Perhaps the easiest cmdlet to start working with is **Get-Process**. By itself, it returns a collection of all the currently running processes on your computer. You can also give it a specific process name, or a numeric process ID, and it'll retrieve just the specified process. The following example retrieves a specific process and stores it in the **$psh** variable. Then, it displays the path of the executable that the process is running by using the Path property of the process object.

```
PS C:\test> $psh = get-process PowerShell
PS C:\test> $psh.path
C:\WINDOWS\system32\WindowsPowerShell\v1.0\powershell.exe
```

The other cmdlet used to work with processes is **Stop-Process**. It can also accept a process name or ID, or you can simply give it a process object. It supports the -**whatif** and -**confirm** parameters we described in "Windows PowerShell Architecture and Overview." The following example continues to use the **$psh** variable we created in the previous example. As you can see, we chose *not* to stop the process after all. But by using the -**confirm** parameter, we can see what the **Stop-Process** cmdlet was doing:

```
PS C:\test> stop-process -inputobject $psh -confirm

Confirm
Are you sure you want to perform this action?
Performing operation "Stop-Process" on Target "powershell (2008)".
[Y] Yes [A] Yes to All [N] No [L] No to All
[S] Suspend[?] Help (default is "Y"): n
PS C:\test>
```

See Also

We'll give you more examples of process management in the chapter, "Managing Processes."

Another straightforward cmdlet is **Get-Service**, which retrieves one or more Windows services. It supports the same -**include** and -**exclude** parameters that the various Item cmdlets did, allowing you to filter the results that the cmdlet provides. You can specify either the name of the service you want or its display name. If you don't specify any name, you get a collection of all installed services. The following example retrieves the LanManServer service and displays its status:

```
PS C:\> $svc = get-service lanmanserver
PS C:\> $svc.status
Running
PS C:\>
```

Other cmdlets used to work with services include **Stop-Service**, **Start-Service**, **Suspend-Service**,

Resume-Service, and **Set-Service**, which allows you to reconfigure a service. **New-Service** permits you to create new services. For example, the following would stop the LanManServer service (stored in the **$svc** variable)—that is, if we hadn't specified the **-whatif** parameter:

```
PS C:\> stop-service -inputobject $svc -whatif
What if: Performing operation "Stop-Service" on Target "Serv
er (LanmanServer)".
```

See Also

"Managing Services" provides examples of performing various service management tasks using these cmdlets.

The last set basic cmdlet we'll explore for now is for event log management. **Get-EventLog** retrieves an event log, such as the Application, System, or Security log. Not sure what logs are installed? Try this:

```
PS C:\> get-eventlog -list
```

Max(K)	Retain	OverflowAction	Entries	Name
512	7	OverwriteOlder	109	ACEEventLog
20,480	7	OverwriteOlder	1,296	Application
15,168	0	OverwriteAsNeeded	6	DFS Replic...
20,480	0	OverwriteAsNeeded	0	Hardware E...
512	7	OverwriteOlder	0	Internet E...
512	7	OverwriteOlder	0	Key Manage...
8,192	0	OverwriteAsNeeded	0	Media Center
16,384	0	OverwriteAsNeeded	0	Microsoft ...
16,384	0	OverwriteAsNeeded	117	Microsoft ...
20,480	7	OverwriteOlder	25	Security
20,480	7	OverwriteOlder	4,677	System
15,360	0	OverwriteAsNeeded	345	Windows Po...

Yes, that last one *is* "Windows PowerShell." Bet you didn't realize Windows PowerShell had a log all its own! When you retrieve a log, what you're really retrieving is a collection of the log's entries. For example, here's part of a Security log:

```
PS C:\> get-eventlog security
```

Index	Time		Type	Source	EventID	Message
25	Apr 04	03:05	Succ	Microsoft-Windows...	1108	T...
24	Apr 04	03:05	Succ	Microsoft-Windows...	1100	T...
23	Mar 30	14:46	Succ	Microsoft-Windows...	4616	T...
22	Mar 30	14:46	Succ	Microsoft-Windows...	4616	T...
21	Mar 23	14:48	Succ	Microsoft-Windows...	4616	T...
20	Mar 23	14:48	Succ	Microsoft-Windows...	4616	T...
19	Mar 23	08:09	Succ	Microsoft-Windows...	4616	T...
18	Mar 23	08:09	Succ	Microsoft-Windows...	1100	T...
17	Mar 19	17:45	Succ	Microsoft-Windows...	1108	T...
16	Mar 19	17:45	Succ	Microsoft-Windows...	1100	T...

Note

We're truncating our output throughout this book to save space and to prevent unnecessary line-wrapping. When you run this on a full-sized monitor, you'll see more comprehensive results.

Don't want the full list of events? No problem!

```
PS C:\> get-eventlog security -newest 10

Index Time               Type Source              EventID Message
----- ----               ---- ------              ------- -------
   25 Apr 04 03:05        Succ Microsoft-Windows...   1108 The description for E...
   24 Apr 04 03:05        Succ Microsoft-Windows...   1100 The description for E...
   23 Mar 30 14:46        Succ Microsoft-Windows...   4616 The description for E...
   22 Mar 30 14:46        Succ Microsoft-Windows...   4616 The description for E...
   21 Mar 23 14:48        Succ Microsoft-Windows...   4616 The description for E...
   20 Mar 23 14:48        Succ Microsoft-Windows...   4616 The description for E...
   19 Mar 23 08:09        Succ Microsoft-Windows...   4616 The description for E...
   18 Mar 23 08:09        Succ Microsoft-Windows...   1100 The description for E...
   17 Mar 19 17:45        Succ Microsoft-Windows...   1108 The description for E...
   16 Mar 19 17:45        Succ Microsoft-Windows...   1100 The description for E...
```

See Also

"Managing Event Logs" provides samples for production event log management in PowerShell.

Just this handful of cmdlets provides a lot of administrative functionality. Of course, we haven't even talked about WMI, yet, or about ways of managing Directory Services from PowerShell—those topics will come later. But right now you know enough cmdlets to start working with PowerShell in more depth.

Cmdlets for Working with PowerShell

Another category of cmdlets is used to manipulate PowerShell itself, working with the shell's variables, commands, and so forth (and, remember, we covered commands to work with aliases earlier).

Creating Output

PowerShell supports a number of different *output streams*. These can be kind of tough to visualize in the console, because in the end, everything appears as text within the console window. But, if you can imagine PowerShell being embedded inside another application—such as the Exchange Server 2007 graphical management console, where the PowerShell command line itself isn't visible—you can start to imagine how you can use these different "streams." PowerShell provides a cmdlet for writing to each of these streams:

- **Write-Debug** writes debugging information—primarily from a script. Whether PowerShell displays the information written to the debugging stream depends upon the contents of a special PowerShell variable named **$DebugPreference**. Its default value, "SilentlyContinue", suppresses anything written to the debugging stream. Any other valid value—"Stop", "Continue", and "Inquire"—will display the information written to the debugging stream. This cmdlet is useful within scripts, where you can use it to output status information as the script runs. By setting **$DebugPreference** to "SilentlyContinue", you can then suppress the debug output without having to remove the **Write-Debug** commands from the script.

- **Write-Error** writes information to the error stream. This cmdlet has a large number of parameters that permit you to customize its output. Generally speaking, you should use this only when a script needs to output an error message. By default, the console displays errors in red text, helping them stand out from other output.

- **Write-Host** writes information to the application that is hosting PowerShell. Remember, when you're using PowerShell.exe, *this* is the hosting application, and it's what provides you with the command-line interface you're accustomed to seeing. Other applications can host the PowerShell engine, though, and what *those* applications do with **Write-Host** output may differ. A best practice is to use **Write-Host** only when you *know* your scripts will only be run in the PowerShell.exe host and when you want to take advantage of the formatting options **Write-Host** offers, like alternate text colors.

- **Write-Output** sends output to the "success" output stream. This has a number of uses. Within the PowerShell.exe console host, the "success" output stream is usually just whatever output you want the user to see. Within a PowerShell function, the "success" output stream is where you send the information you want to return from the function when the function completes. From the command line, **Write-Output** may seem indistinguishable from **Write-Host** (except that **Write-Host** offers some formatting options for text), but under the hood these two cmdlets do serve different purposes. **Write-Host** always creates output to be displayed in a host window. **Write-Output** sends output to a specific output stream, which doesn't, in all cases, display as text to the user.

- **Write-Progress** creates a progress bar within the PowerShell window. Whether PowerShell displays the bar depends upon the special **$ProgressPreference** variable. When set to "SilentlyContinue", no progress bar is displayed; other values—"Continue", "Stop", and "Inquire"—will display the progress bar. Note that you can generally display a progress bar only within a script or some other construct; if you issue a single call to **Write-Progress** from the command line, the bar will appear and disappear too quickly to even see.

- **Write-Verbose** writes a string to the hosting application's "verbose" stream. The contents of the special **$VerbosePreference** variable determine whether PowerShell actually displays verbose output. A value of "SilentlyContinue" suppresses output, while other values—"Continue", "Stop", and "Inquire"—will display the output.

- **Write-Warning** writes a string to the hosting application's "warning" stream. The contents of the special **$WarningPreference** variable determine whether PowerShell actually displays verbose output. A value of "SilentlyContinue" suppresses output, while other values—"Continue", "Stop", and "Inquire"—will display the output. By default, warnings are displayed in reversed colors to help make them stand out from other output.

Now, here's where things may get confusing. In reality, none of the Write cmdlets *actually produce output.* As described above, these cmdlets simply write to various different streams (or pipelines—same thing). *Rendering* those streams—that is, turning the objects in the streams (which are technically called *pipelines*) into text output—is the job of the various Out cmdlets:

- **Out-Default** is a placeholder; that is, it doesn't really do anything except pass objects right along to the shell's default output cmdlet, **Out-Host**. The only reason **Out-Default** exists is in case a developer wanted to create a different default behavior.

- **Out-Host** turns objects into strings and displays them in the console host; that is, it creates command-line output. The cmdlet does not pass any objects down the pipeline.

- **Out-Printer** turns objects into strings and sends them to the specified Windows printer. The cmdlet does not pass any objects down the pipeline.

- **Out-File** turns objects into strings, and writes them to the specified file. You can use cmdlet parameters to append to an existing file rather than overwriting it, and so forth. The cmdlet does not pass any objects down the pipeline.

- **Out-Null** doesn't do anything with whatever it's given; it just discards it. The cmdlet does not pass any objects down the pipeline.

- **Out-String** turns objects into strings, and then passes them down the pipeline. This is the only Out cmdlet that passes things down the pipeline. **Out-String** is designed to render objects into strings so that they can be passed to older, external utilities that can work only with strings and not with objects.

For example, when you run this:

```
Write-Output "Hello"
```

You're really running a lot more than that: The cmdlet is writing the text "Hello" to the success pipeline; since there are no other cmdlets in the pipeline, PowerShell sends everything to **Out-Default**, which reroutes it right to the default output cmdlet, **Out-Host**. So, really, what you ran, even though you didn't realize it, is this:

```
Write-Output "Hello" | Out-Default | Out-Host
```

And that's what resulted in the word "Hello" being displayed on the command line. **Write-Host** does something similar, although it explicitly sends objects to **Out-Host**. So, this:

```
Write-Host Hello
```

Is actually running this:

```
Write-Host Hello | Out-Host
```

Generally speaking, the output cmdlets (those beginning with "Out") are designed to have things piped to them. They then take care of turning that output into strings of text and getting the text to whatever output device—file, screen, printer, and so forth—that you've specified.

Here's Another Way to Think About Writing and Output

All of the Write cmdlets, with the exception of Write-Host, are writing to a *stream*, or, more properly, a *pipeline*. For example, **Write-Output** writes to the success pipeline, which is the pipeline that cmdlets run on and is what we're generally referring to when we use the term *pipeline* generically. **Write-Debug** writes to the debug pipeline, **Write-Error** writes to the error pipeline, and so forth.

As we've already discussed, when PowerShell comes to the end of a pipeline, its default action is to render whatever's in the pipeline into text and display it. More specifically, all of the pipelines are connected to the **Out-Default** cmdlet. So, anything left at the end of a pipeline goes to **Out-Default**, which sends the objects along to **Out-Host**. **Out-Host** then renders the objects into text and displays the result.

You can suppress all of the pipelines except the success pipeline by using the various Preference variables described earlier in this section. Essentially, the Preference variables put a "plug" into the associated pipeline so that the content in that pipeline never reaches **Out-Default**, and, therefore, never displays.

The **Write-Host** cmdlet is an exception: It does *not* write to a pipeline. Instead, it implicitly pipes its output directly to **Out-Host**, displaying the output in the console window as text.

So, to summarize: The Write cmdlets (except **Write-Host**) put objects into a pipeline. Preference variables determine whether a given pipeline (except the success pipeline) is connected to **Out-Default**. The Out cmdlets are responsible for rendering pipeline objects into text and sending the text to the associated output device, such as a printer, file, or the console window.

Because **Out-File**, **Out-Printer**, and the other Out cmdlets aren't directly connected to a pipeline, the only way to use them is to explicitly send objects their way. *Technically,* when you pipe objects to a cmdlet such as **Out-File**, that pipeline is *still connected to **Out-Default***, because the main success pipeline *always* ends in **Out-Default** (which then sends whatever it received on to **Out-Host**). However, **Out-File**, **Out-Printer**, **Out-Host**, and **Out-Null** don't pass anything down the pipeline. So, even though **Out-Default** is always implicitly called after every **Out-Printer** (for example), **Out-Default** is given no objects to work with, and so it doesn't create any visible result.

Clearing the Console

PowerShell also has a cmdlet named **Clear-Host**, which simply clears the hosting application's window. Its alias, **Cls**, is one you may be familiar with from the Cmd.exe console or versions of MS-DOS. **Clear-Host** doesn't have any parameters, and most people just run the **Cls** alias instead.

Accepting Input

PowerShell offers one cmdlet for accepting text input from the command line: **Read-Host**. You can specify a text prompt, and PowerShell returns whatever the user types from the cmdlet and you can store it in a variable, if you like, as follows:

```
PS C:\> $username = Read-Host "Type your username"
```

You can add the **-asSecureString** parameter to have PowerShell encrypt whatever the user types as a secure string—this is useful when you're asking them to type a password or other sensitive information. Whatever they type will be obscured by * characters on the screen, as shown here:

```
PS C:\> $var = read-host "Password" -assecurestring
Password: *********
PS C:\>
```

Secure strings are a bit more difficult to work with than normal strings of text. For example, you can't simply output the contents of a secure string, as shown here. Instead, PowerShell simply informs you that the variable contains a secure string:

```
PS C:\> $var
System.Security.SecureString
```

The **ConvertFrom-SecureString** cmdlet can convert a secure string into an encrypted string, but all you wind up with is the encrypted version, not the original, clear text that was typed:

```
PS C:\> convertfrom-securestring $var
01000000d08c9ddf0115d1118c7a00c04fc297eb01000000c3fa04e02c086948b8384ff78af7b2a0000000000
200000000000003660000a800000001000000099bf997ab82c7d2ed347fbc67cab7ed20000000004800000a00000
0010000000a91c2fa70a5ed0080b523499a48bc4f718000000a89c92a8fd1d1596f07c70c5c799b3bab1befd7
722a0b19514000000a15e2a9e566a7bb748a542080fa89b0aec580e5f
```

The purpose of secure strings is just that: They're *secure*. They can be stored in files and retrieved for later use (and certain PowerShell cmdlets *accept* a secure string as input and know how to retrieve the clear text version of the string).

Working with Variables

You don't *need* to use cmdlets to work with variables. Creating a new variable is as easy as assigning a value to it (and there's currently no way to make PowerShell insist on advance variable declaration, as some programming languages can do). For example:

```
PS C:\> $var = 5
```

Retrieving a variable is just as easy: Type it, and hit Enter. The default **Out-Host** cmdlet will display the variable's contents:

```
PS C:\> $var
5
```

But PowerShell does provide cmdlets for working with variables. In fact, it also has a PSDrive, since PowerShell's variable storage is exposed as a "disk drive" within the shell:

```
PS C:\> cd variable:
PS Variable:\> dir


Name                      Value
----                      -----
Error                     {RuntimeException, RuntimeException, RuntimeException, ...
DebugPreference           SilentlyContinue
PROFILE                   C:\Users\Don\Documents\WindowsPowerShell\Microsoft.Powe...
HOME                      C:\Users\Don
Host                      System.Management.Automation.Internal.Host.InternalHost
MaximumHistoryCount       64
MaximumAliasCount         4096
foreach
input                     System.Array+SZArrayEnumerator
StackTrace                at System.Number.StringToNumber(String str, NumberSt...
names                     {computers.txt, computers.txt, computers.txt}
ReportErrorShowSource     1
ExecutionContext          System.Management.Automation.EngineIntrinsics
true                      True
VerbosePreference         SilentlyContinue
var                       5
ShellId                   Microsoft.PowerShell
name                      DON-PC
false                     False
```

The variable-manipulation cmdlets are:

- **Clear-Variable** removes a variable's value.

- **Get-Variable** retrieves the contents of a variable.

- **New-Variable** creates a new variable. Optionally, using parameters, you can assign a specific data type to the variable and assign an initial value.

- **Remove-Variable** deletes a variable.

- **Set-Variable** changes the value of a variable.

Again, however, it's unusual to see these cmdlets being used, since you can manipulate variables directly, just as with most programming languages.

Working with Commands

PowerShell provides a few cmdlets for working *with* cmdlets, or commands. They are:

- **Get-Command** retrieves basic information about a cmdlet. If you don't provide a cmdlet name, then it retrieves a list of all cmdlets. You can use the **-verb** or **-noun** parameters to just retrieve cmdlets related to a specific verb, such as "Get", or a specific noun, such as "Variable." You can also just retrieve the cmdlets contained within a particular snap-in by using the **-pSSnapIn** parameter.

- **Measure-Command** allows you to measure the time it takes to run script blocks or cmdlets. Simply give it the command or script block you want to run, and it'll output the execute time.

- **Trace-Command** traces the execution of a specific command. It has a wealth of parameters, which you can review in the built-in help. This is primarily useful in debugging short script blocks that contain a few cmdlets, so that you can trace the progress of the block's execution.

Working with Command-line History

As you may know, PowerShell maintains a history of everything you type into the command line. Normally, you access this history using the up and down arrow keys on your keyboard (we'll cover that and other tips in "Command History"). PowerShell also provides three cmdlets used to manipulate the shell's command-line history:

- **Add-History** adds a command to the command-line history. You can read a text file containing a command-line history, for example, and pipe that to **Add-History** to re-create the command-line history for a past PowerShell session.

- **Get-History** retrieves a list of what's in the command-line history buffer. You could pipe this list to one of the "Out" cmdlets to save the command-line history into a file, or, even better, use one of the "Export" cmdlets (which we cover in Chapter 5) to create a CSV or XML file.

- **Invoke-History** runs commands from the session history. You specify the desired command by using its history ID (viewable with **Get-History**). You can use the **-whatif** or **-confirm** parameters to review what would happen and get confirmation, if desired.

Working with PSDrives

Finally, PowerShell provides three cmdlets for working with PSDrives:

- **Get-PSDrive** retrieves information about a specific PSDrive or, if you don't specify one, lists all available drives.

- **New-PSDrive** creates a new drive using the specified provider. Use this, for example, to map network drives, as we showed you in the "PowerShell Drives" chapter.

- **Remove-PSDrive** removes an existing drive from the shell.

Chapter 5
The PowerShell Pipeline

Perhaps the most powerful concept in Windows PowerShell is its rich, object-oriented pipeline. You may already be familiar with pipelines from the Cmd.exe console, or from MS-DOS. For example, one common use was to pipe a long text file to the **More** utility, creating a paged display of text:

```
C:\> type myfile.txt | more
```

This technique evolved directly from *nix shells, which have used pipelines for years to pass, or *pipe*, text from one command to another. In PowerShell, this concept takes on whole new meaning as cmdlets work with rich *objects* rather than text, and pipe those objects to one another for great effect. For example, consider this cmdlet:

```
PS C:\> get-process
```

Run that, and you get a list of processes. It's easy to assume that what you're seeing is the actual output of the cmdlet; that is, it's easy to think that the cmdlet simply produces a text list. But it doesn't. The cmdlet produces a set of Process objects. Because there's nothing else in the pipeline waiting for those objects, PowerShell sends them to the default output cmdlet (**Out-Default**, as discussed in the previous chapter). That cmdlet calls one of PowerShell's formatting cmdlets, which examines various properties of the objects—in this case, the Process, Handles, Nonpaged Memory, Paged Memory, Working Set, Virtual Memory, CPU, ID, and ProcessName properties—and creates a table of information. So, the result that you *see* is certainly a text list, but you're not seeing the intermediate steps that created that text list from a collection of objects.

By the Way...
How does PowerShell decide what properties to use when it converts objects into a text-based listing? It's not arbitrary: For most object types, Microsoft has pre-defined the "interesting" properties that PowerShell uses. These pre-defined formats are in a file called DotNetTypes.format.ps1xml, located in the PowerShell installation folder. Other pre-defined types are defined in other files, such as FileSystem.format.ps1xml, Certificate.format.ps1xml, and so forth. These files are digitally signed by Microsoft, so you can't modify them unless you're prepared to re-sign them using your own code-signing certificate. However, you can build custom formats, a topic covered in the chapter "Creating Custom Formats."

Piping Objects from Cmdlet to Cmdlet

Once you have a collection of objects, however, you can do a lot more than let PowerShell create text lists. For example, take a look at the Help for the **Stop-Process** cmdlet:

```
PS C:\> help stop-process

NAME
    Stop-Process

SYNOPSIS
    Stops one or more running processes.


SYNTAX
    Stop-Process [-id] <Int32[]> [-passThru] [-whatIf] [-confirm] [<CommonParameters>]

    Stop-Process -name <string[]> [-passThru] [-whatIf] [-confirm] [<CommonParameters>]

    Stop-Process -inputObject <Process[]> [-passThru] [-whatIf] [-confirm] [<CommonParame
    ters>]


DETAILED DESCRIPTION
    The Stop-Process cmdlet stops one or more running processes. You can specify a proces
    s by process name or process ID (PID), or pass a process object to Stop-Process. For
    Get-Process, the default method is by process name. For Stop-Process, the default met
    hod is by process ID.


RELATED LINKS
    Get-Process, Start-Process

REMARKS
    For more information, type: "get-help Stop-Process -detailed".
    For technical information, type: "get-help Stop-Process -full".
```

Did you notice that there are *three* ways in which **Stop-Process** can be used? If the first parameter is an integer, the cmdlet assumes you've given it a process ID, and it tries to stop that process ID. If you give it a string, it tries to stop a process with that name. Or, if you give it a Process object, it will try to stop the process represented by that object. The Help indicates that the **-id** parameter name is optional, but that **-name** or **-inputObject**, should you use those, are required. In other words, you can do this:

```
PS C:\> stop-process 505
```

But you can't do this:

```
PS C:\> stop-process notepad
```

Instead, if you're providing a string, you need to provide the parameter name:

```
PS C:\> stop-process -name notepad
```

That's because only the **-id** parameter is *positional*; any other parameter, like **-name**, needs to be specified, which is easy enough to do from the command line. Where would you have learned that if you didn't have this book? By using the **Help** command, naturally! **Help Stop-Process –Full** would have explained. Let's take a look.

Finding Cmdlets that Accept Pipeline Input

That's all well and good from the command line, but from within the pipeline, things are somewhat different. Inside the pipeline, only certain parameters can accept input. To see this, you need to ask for full Help (using the **-full** parameter of the **Help** command). Here's an excerpt:

```
PARAMETERS
    -id <Int32[]>
        Specifies the process IDs of the processes to be stopped. To specify multiple IDs
        , use commas to separate the IDs. To find the PID of a process, type "get-process
        ". The parameter name ("-Id") is optional.

        Required?                true
        Position?                1
        Default value            Null
        Accept pipeline input?   true (ByPropertyName)
        Accept wildcard characters? false

    -inputObject <Process[]>
        Stops the processes represented by the specified process objects. Enter a variable
        that contains the objects or type a command or expression that gets the objects.

        Required?                true
        Position?                named
        Default value
        Accept pipeline input?   true (ByValue)
        Accept wildcard characters? False
```

Notice that the **-id** parameter can accept input from the pipeline, *as can the -inputObject parameter.* That means these parameters can accept pipeline input without specifying a parameter name. More importantly, **-inputObject** can accept pipeline input "ByValue", meaning it can accept entire Process objects. The **-id** parameter can only accept pipeline input if that input is actually a property *named* "ID"—that's what "ByPropertyName" means. In other words, if you can produce an object that has an ID property (other than a Process object), and that ID property's value corresponds to the ID of a process you want stopped, then you can pipe that object into **Stop-Process**. Sound confusing? It is.

The practical upshot of this is that, when you're reading the full Help, look for parameters that can accept pipeline input "ByValue". Those are the ones you want to work with. In this case, it tells you that you can pipe a bunch of Process objects to **Stop-Process**, and it'll stop those processes. But where do you get a collection of Process objects?

```
PS C:\> get-process
```

So, all you have to do is pipe those to **Stop-Process**:

> **Caution:** Don't run the following on your computer.

```
PS C:\> get-process | stop-process
```

And the computer will crash as its critical processes are stopped in their tracks. Oops! It's a good demonstration, though, right? The point is that you can continue piping objects down the pipeline to keep doing things with them. For example, most cmdlets that do something with an object also have a -**passthru** parameter, which tells the cmdlet to do whatever it's going to do, and then continue passing the objects down the pipeline. So, you could do this:

```
PS C:\> Get-service | stop-service -passthru | out-file c:\stopped.txt
```

This will retrieve a collection of Service objects, stop them, and then output a text list to a file named C:\Stopped.txt. Yes, it's unlikely you'd want to stop *all* of a server's services all at once—so how about just the ones start with the letter "A"?

```
PS C:\> Get-service -include a* | stop-service -passthru | out-file c:\stopped.txt
```

True, this technique would be more useful if you had a more powerful way of filtering the objects that **Get-Service** retrieves—and you'll learn more powerful ways in the very next chapter, in fact—but this example serves to illustrate what the pipeline can do for you. By stringing together cmdlets that successively refine a collection of objects, you can accomplish extremely powerful administrative tasks with a *single line*—what the PowerShell community has taken to calling *one-liners*. One-liners can literally replace hundreds of lines of VBScript code, or tens of hours of manual effort.

The Pipeline Enables Powerful One-Liners

Okay, we'll jump ahead of ourselves a bit and give you a *really* good example:

```
PS C:\ > get-wmiobject -query "Select Name,StartMode,State from win32_service
>> where startmode<>'disabled' AND state='Stopped'" | select Name | start-service
>>
```

This retrieves all services using **Get-Wmiobject** that have not been disabled and are not running. The **Select** cmdlet extracts the names of the services, and then passes the list of stopped services to **Start-Service**. Here's another one:

```
PS C:\>$svcname=Read-Host "Enter a service name" ; get-process | where {$_.id -eq (Get-WmiObject
win32_service | where {$_.name -eq $svcname}).ProcessID} | select -property StartTime
```

Yes, that's all one line of text. It asks you for a service name, and then gets a list of all processes. It filters out all the processes *except* the one that matches the service name you typed—it actually executes **Get-WmiObject** to get the process ID of the service you specified). Then it retrieves just the StartTime property—the practical upshot is that you can see exactly when the specified service started. Yes, it's pretty complicated, but you assemble these things one step at a time. For example, the first task is to get a service name:

```
PS C:\> $svcname=Read-Host "Enter a service name"
```

Easy enough. That stores the service name in the variable **$svcname**. Next, you want to start a new pipe-line: Notice in the original command where the semicolon occurs? That tells PowerShell to begin a new logical line, as if you'd hit Enter. So, *technically,* this is a two-liner. Given the service name in **$svcname,** though, the rest occurs on one line. So, you know you need to get a **Process** object in order to get a start time, so how do you get **Process** objects?

```
PS C:> get-process
```

Now, you only want the process that represents the specified service. So, you need to make a call to **Get-WmiObject** (this will be covered in an upcoming chapter—we said we were getting ahead of ourselves, here!) to retrieve the desired service:

```
PS C:\> Get-WmiObject win32_service
```

Well, okay, that gets *all* the services. Let's filter that down to get just the one you want:

```
PS C:\> Get-WmiObject win32_service | where { $_.name -eq $svcname }
```

That $_ variable, by the way, is a placeholder for "the current pipeline object." So, **Get-WmiObject** will retrieve all instances of the win32_service class, or services, and then **Where-Object** (or its alias, **Where**) will look at each one to see if its ID property matches the process ID of the service you retrieved from WMI. Don't worry if this a little confusing. You'll learn about the **Where** cmdlet in the next chapter.

The upshot is that the **Where** cmdlet gets rid of all services except the one you're looking for. Specifically, what you're interested in from the service is its process ID. So, the entire call to **Get-WmiObject** will result in only one object being returned. Therefore, you can bundle that whole call into parentheses to treat it as a standalone object, and then just refer to the process ID property:

```
PS C:\> (Get-WmiObject win32_service | where { $_.name -eq $svcname }).ProcessID
```

And now you combine that with the original call to **Get-Process** so that you can filter out the processes that don't have the process ID you're after.

```
PS C:\> get-process | where {$_.ID -eq (Get-WmiObject win32_service | where { $_.name -eq $svcname }).ProcessID}
```

Once you've gotten the process you're after, just select the StartTime property using **Select-Object,** or its alias, **Select:**

```
PS C:\> get-process | where {$_.ID -eq (Get-WmiObject win32_service | where { $_.name -eq $svcname }).ProcessID} | select -property StartTime
```

And that's it. Yes, it's a bit funny-looking, and it definitely takes some time to wrap your head around it. Not to mention the fact that you haven't really explored some of these cmdlets yet! But the point is that you construct complex one-liners one cmdlet at a time, which is a pretty easy way to work, since you can immediately see your results and decide what step will be next in order to get to your final goal.

The Pipeline Enables Simple Output Redirection

For now, don't worry about complex one-liners. They'll come to you naturally enough as you learn more of PowerShell's cmdlets. For now, remember that the pipeline can be a great way to create output. For example, the previous chapter mentioned that you could export a command-line history to a text file. Well, here's how:

```
PS C:\> Get-History | Out-File C:\History.txt
```

That retrieved the command history and *piped* it to the **Out-File** cmdlet. See, as you learn more cmdlets, you'll learn more techniques for making the pipeline useful! And the next chapter is all about some cmdlets designed to work almost entirely within the pipeline.

The End of the (Pipe)line

What you rarely see is the *end* of the pipeline. Invisibly connected to the end of the pipeline is the **Out-Default** cmdlet, which basically does nothing except transfer objects to **Out-Host**. The **Out-Host** cmdlet is both clever and stupid: It's stupid, in that the only thing it knows how to deal with are formatting directives which tell it what text to display; it's smart in that, if it doesn't *get* formatting directives, it'll send whatever it *does* get to a Format cmdlet first.

So, here's a set of basic rules to remember about the end of the pipeline:

- If you end a pipeline by using an **Out** cmdlet (like **Out-File**), then the **Out** cmdlet doesn't pass anything else down the pipeline (unless it's **Out-String**, which is definitely an exception). So, **Out-Default** is still there at the end, but it has nothing to work with and so nothing else happens.

- If you end a pipeline with a **Format** cmdlet, then the pipeline contains formatting directives. **Out-Default** passes them to **Out-Host**, which loves formatting directives—it does whatever the directives say, thus producing text.

- If you don't end the pipeline with either a **Format** cmdlet or an **Out** cmdlet, then whatever's in the pipeline goes to **Out-Default**, which turns right around and sends them to **Out-Host**. Because **Out-Host** doesn't see formatting directives, it gets scared and calls on PowerShell's formatting system to format the pipeline objects. **Out-Host** then gets the formatting directives it wants, and displays whatever they tell it to.

In other words, *all* pipelines end in **Out-Default** (which, practically speaking, means they end in **Out-Host**). The various **Out** cmdlets all work with formatting directives, so if they see "raw" objects, they'll ask PowerShell to format them first. That means even a simple cmdlet:

```
PS C:\> Get-Process
```

This is really running *four* cmdlets: First, **Get-Process**. Then, **Out-Default**. Then, **Out-Host**. Then, a formatting cmdlet—PowerShell would choose **Format-Table** in this case (you'll see in a bit why that's so).

Chapter 6
Cmdlets to Group, Sort, Format, Export, and More

Because Windows PowerShell's output is almost entirely text based, it's easy to mistake it for a text-based shell. However, what is really happening behind the scenes is that PowerShell is using .NET and cmdlets to carry out your commands and manipulate data as needed. Only when all processing is complete is the final data formatted for textual presentation. However, there are many things you can do to control how PowerShell ultimately presents the data.

Formatting

Just about every PowerShell cmdlet is designed to produce textual output. The cmdlet developer creates a default output format based on the information to be delivered. For example, the output of **Get-Process** is a horizontal table. However, if you need a different output format, PowerShell has a few choices that are discussed below.

Formatting Rules
PowerShell uses a fairly clever system of priorities to determine which formats it uses. Refer to "Formatting Rules" toward the end of the book for more information on these rules, if you're interested. You don't need to know these rules in order to use PowerShell's formatting capabilities.

Format-List

This cmdlet produces a columnar list. Here's a sample using **Get-Process**:

```
PS C:\> get-process | format-list
Id      : 720
Handles : 63
CPU     : 0.1301872
Name    : ApntEx

Id      : 584
Handles : 105
CPU     : 0.5107344
Name    : Apoint

Id      : 404
Handles : 130
CPU     : 0.4706768
Name    : avgamsvr

Id      : 444
Handles : 205
CPU     : 2.1130384
Name    : avgcc
...
```

Even though we've truncated the output, you get the idea. Instead of the regular horizontal table, PowerShell lists each process and its properties in a column. As we've pointed out when this cmdlet has been used in other examples, the **Format-List** doesn't use all the properties of an object; PowerShell instead follows its internal formatting rules, which may include using a *view*—essentially a set of pre-selected properties. Microsoft provides views for most of the common types of information you'll work with, and in many cases provides both table- and list-style views so that PowerShell doesn't just pick random properties for its output.

If you prefer more control over what information is displayed, you can use the **-property** cmdlet parameter to specify the properties:

```
PS C:\> get-process winword |format-list -property '
>> name,workingset,id,path
>>


Name       : WINWORD
WorkingSet : 32522240
Id         : 564
Path       : C:\Program Files\Microsoft Office\OFFICE11\WINWORD.EXE

PS C:\>
```

In this example we've called **Get-Process** seeking specific information on the WinWord process.

How Did You Know?

You might wonder how we knew what properties PowerShell can display when we use the -property cmdlet. To review, it is important to get to know the Get-Member cmdlet. This command lists all the available properties for the process object:

```
get-process | get-member
```

Different cmdlets and objects have different properties, especially in WMI.

Note that if you don't specify any properties, **Format-List** either uses a pre-defined view, or if none exists, **Format-List** looks in PowerShell's Types.ps1xml type definition file to see if any properties are marked as "defaults." If some properties are marked as defaults, then PowerShell uses those properties to construct the list. Otherwise, PowerShell uses all of the object's properties to construct the list. To force the cmdlet to list all of an object's properties, use * for the properties list:

```
PS C:\> get-process | format-list *
```

Format-Table

Just as there are some cmdlets that use a list format as the default, there are some that use a table format. Of course, sometimes you may prefer a table. The format of this **Get-WmiObject** expression produces a list by default:

....

Why a List?
Why does this cmdlet produce a list by default? There are two possibilities: Microsoft provided a pre-defined view which happens to be a list, or Microsoft provided no pre-defined view. In the latter case, PowerShell selected the list type because the object has more than five properties—if it had fewer, PowerShell would select a table under the same circumstances.

```
PS C:\> Get-WmiObject -class win32_logicaldisk


DeviceID     : C:
DriveType    : 3
ProviderName :
FreeSpace    : 2815565824
Size         : 15726702592
VolumeName   : Server2003

DeviceID     : D:
DriveType    : 5
ProviderName :
FreeSpace    :
Size         :
VolumeName   :

DeviceID     : E:
DriveType    : 3
ProviderName :
FreeSpace    : 2891620352
Size         : 24280993792
VolumeName   : XP
```

This is not too hard to read. However, here's the same cmdlet using the **Format-Table**:

```
PS C:\> Get-WmiObject -class win32_logicaldisk |format-table

DeviceID    DriveType    ProviderName    FreeSpace       Size VolumeName
--------    ---------    ------------    ---------       ---- ----------
C:                  3    2815565824      15726702592     Server2003
D:                  5
E:                  3    2891620352      24280993792     XP
```

```
PS C:\>
```

Since the ProviderName property is blank, we can clean-up this output even more by using **-property** as we did with **Format-List**:

```
PS C:\> Get-WmiObject -class win32_logicaldisk |format-table '
>> -property deviceID,freespace,size,volumename,drivetype
>>


deviceID        freespace      size       volumename   drivetype
--------        ---------      ----       ----------   ---------
C:              2815565824     15726702592 Server2003          3
D:                                                             5
E:              2891239424     24280993792 XP                  3


PS C:\>
```

Notice that the property headings are in the same order that we specified in the expression. They also use the same case. You *can* use * for the property list. However, doing so will often create unreadable output, because PowerShell tries to squeeze all the properties into a single screen-width table, and most objects simply have too many properties for that to work out well. For example, you can see here how PowerShell has made the column headers vertical in an attempt to fit as much as possible, dropped 20 columns, and still created essentially useless output. What you're seeing after the verticalized column headers is the first character of the value that would normally appear in each column—the columns, in other words, are only one character wide.

....

Have fun

Try this with PowerShell's colors set to a black background and a green text color. Looks a bit like a screen saver from "The Matrix."

```
PS C:\> get-process | ft *

WARNING: 20 columns do not fit into the display and were removed.

_ N H V W P N P C C F P D P I P H W P P V T B E H E H M M M M M M N N P P P P P P P P
_ a a M S M P a o P i r e r d r a o a r i o a x a x a a a a a a i o o o a a a e e e e e
N m n     M t m U l o s o   i n r g i r t s i s i n c i i i x n d n n g g g a a a a a a
o e d     h p e d c d o d k e v t a e t E t d h n n n W W u p p e e k k k k k k
u   l     a   V u r u   r l i d a u l P C x T l i W W M o o l a a d d d P P W W V V
n   e     n   e c i c   i e n M t a P r o i i e n i i o r r e g g M S S a a o o i i
N   s     y   r t p t   t C g e e l r i d t m   e n n d k k s e e e y y g g r r r r
a             s V t     y o S m M M o o e e e   N d d u i i   d d m s s e e k k t t
m             i e i     C u e o e e c r   d     a o o l n n   S S o t t d d i i u u
e             o r o     l n t r m m e i         m w w e g g   y y r e e M M n n a a
              n s n     a t   y o o s t         e H T   S S   s s y m m e e g g l l
              i         s     S r r s y         a i   e e     t t S M M m m S S M M
              o         s     i y y o           n t   t t     e e i e e o o e e e e
              n               z S S r           d l           m m z m m r r t t m m
                              e i i T           l e           M M e o o y y 6 o o
                              z z i             e             e e 6 r r S S   4 r r
                              e e m                            m m 4 y y i i     y y
                                  e                            o o   S S z z     S S
                                                              r r   i i e e     i i
```

```
                        y y  z z  6     z z
                        S S  e e  4     e e
                        i i     6        6
                        z z     4        4
                        e e
                          6
                          4
- - - - - - - - - - - - - - - - - - - - - - - - - - - - - - - - -
P A 5 0 4 0 2        4  5 4 0 0 0  8    . 0    2 2 0 6 6 4 4 4 4 4 4
P A 2 4 8 8 4        6  2 8 8 8 4  8    . 0    4 4 8 2 2 4 4 4 4 2 2
P A 6 6 6 0 8 C L 0 4 4 T T 4 N 6 6 0 0 6 0 8  F  1 . 0  S 1 2 { 8 8 0 6 6 8 8 6 6 0 0
P c 6 8 0 8 4        0  6 0 8 8 8  3    . 0    4 4 8 4 4 2 2 0 0 4 4
```

Format-Table lets you tweak the output by using **-autosize**, which automatically adjusts the table output based on the date:

```
PS C:\> Get-WmiObject -class win32_logicaldisk |format-table '
>> -property deviceID,freespace,size,volumename,drivetype -autosize
>>


deviceID   freespace    size         volumename drivetype
--------   ---------    ----         ---------- ---------
C:         2815565824   15726702592  Server2003         3
D:                                                      5
E:         2890489856   24280993792  XP                 3


PS C:\>
```

This is the same command as before, except it includes **-autosize**. Notice how much neater the output is. Using **-autosize** eliminates the need to calculate how long lines will be, add padding manually, or use any scripting voodoo.

Tables can also include custom, or calculated columns. These are great for adding columns that provide more detailed or better-formatted output. For example, consider the previous example, which displayed the size and free space of logical disks. Since those two properties store a number in bytes, that's what gets displayed. However, it might be more readable to display those values in megabytes, and you can do just that with a custom column.

A custom column is included in the list of properties passed to **Format-Table**. The column definition has a very specific format:

```
@{"Label"="column label";"Expression"={ expression }}
```

For example, we might want a column labeled FreeSpace(MB) that displays the free space property in megabytes. Within the *expression*, use the special $_ variable to refer to the object that is being displayed on the current line of the table. In other words, $_.FreeSpace represents the unmodified free space property of the current logical disk. Displaying that in megabytes would require an expression such as:

```
($_.FreeSpace / 1MB) -as [int]
```

We haven't discussed data types and the **–as** operator yet, but the basic gist of this is that we're taking the FreeSpace property and dividing it by one megabyte. The result will have a fractional (decimal) component; converting the result to an integer will round it off to the nearest whole number. Turning all that into an actual command looks like this:

```
PS C:\> gwmi win32_logicaldisk | format-table -property deviceID,@{"Label"="FreeSpace(MB)";"Expre
ssion
"={($_.FreeSpace / 1MB) -as [int]}},@{"Label"="Size(MB)";"Expression"={($_.Size /1MB) -as
[int]}},volu
mename,drivetype -autosize

deviceID FreeSpace(MB) Size(MB)   volumename     drivetype
-------- ------------- --------   ----------     ---------
A:                   0        0                          2
C:               13073    20466                          3
D:                   0        0                          5
I:              752775   953869   Storage                4
Y:                   0        0                          4
Z:              114785   476612   Shared Folders         4
```

As you can see, we've added calculated custom columns for both the FreeSpace and Size properties. The *expression* you use can be as complex as you want, and can even include complete blocks of scripts. That's a bit too complex for where we are in the book right now, but once you see some of PowerShell's scripting capabilities all sorts of possibilities will come to mind.

Format-Wide

Some cmdlets, like **Get-Service**, produce a long list of information that scrolls off the console screen. Wouldn't it be nice to get this information in multiple columns across the console screen? We can accomplish this with the **Format-Wide** cmdlet:

```
PS C:\> get-service |format-wide


Alerter                         ALG
AppMgmt                         aspnet_state
AudioSrv                        Avg7Alrt
Avg7UpdSvc                      AVGEMS
BAsfIpM                         BITS
Browser                         CiSvc
ClipSrv                         clr_optimization_v2.0.50727_32
COMSysApp                       CryptSvc
CVPND                           DcomLaunch
Dhcp                            dmadmin
dmserver                        Dnscache
ERSvc                           Eventlog
EventSystem                     FastUserSwitchingCompatibility
GrooveAuditService              GrooveInstallerService
GrooveRunOnceInstaller          helpsvc
HidServ                         HTTPFilter
...
```

If you prefer more than two columns, which is the default, use the -**column** parameter to specify the number of columns:

```
PS C:\> get-service |format-wide -column 3


Alerter              ALG                    AppMgmt
aspnet_state         AudioSrv               Avg7Alrt
Avg7UpdSvc           AVGEMS                 BAsfIpM
BITS                 Browser                CiSvc
ClipSrv              clr_optimization_v2.0.5. COMSysApp
```

```
CryptSvc              CVPND              DcomLaunch
Dhcp                  dmadmin            dmserver
Dnscache              ERSvc              Eventlog
...
```

However, don't get carried away. The more columns you specify, the more you'll find the output getting truncated.

The **Format-Wide** cmdlet also lets you specify which single property you would like to display:

```
PS C:\> get-service |format-wide displayname -column 3
```

```
Alerter                      Application Layer Gatew...   Application Man...
ASP.NET State Service        Windows Audio                AVG7 Alert Mana...
AVG7 Update Service          AVG E-mail Scanner           Broadcom ASF IP...
Background Intelligent       Computer Browser             Indexing Service
ClipBook                 .   NET Runtime Optimizati...    COM+ System App...
Cryptographic Services       Cisco Systems, Inc. VPN...   DCOM Server Pro...
DHCP Client                  Logical Disk Manager Ad...   Logical Disk Ma...
DNS Client                   Error Reporting Service      Event Log
COM+ Event System            Fast User Switching Com...   Groove Audit Serv
Groove Installer Service     GrooveRunOnceInstaller       Help and Support
...
```

Unlike **Format-Table** and **Format-List** that allow multiple properties, **Format-Wide** permits only a single property. In this example, we've specified the service's display name.

Format-Custom

PowerShell provides the ability for you to display data in a custom format; that is, in neither a list nor a table. Unfortunately it requires defining a new format in a custom XML file, and then using the **Update-FormatData** cmdlet to register it in PowerShell. Frankly, for most administrators, this cmdlet requires more effort than it's worth since it requires a certain degree of knowledge about .NET classes. We do cover custom format creation in the chapter "Creating Custom Formats," in case you're interested (you can also create custom list, wide, and table formats, if you like).

If you don't specify a specific custom view using the **-view** parameter, then **Format-Custom** will default to a *class* view of an object. In this view, you can see the exact structure of the object you're trying to display, including any child objects. The **-depth** parameter can limit how deeply into an object hierarchy **Format-Custom** will go; for example, displaying your hard drive's root folder would normally generate a very large and deep list, since your root folder contains every other file and folder on that drive. Here's an excerpt:

```
PS C:\> dir \ | format-custom -depth 1

class DirectoryInfo
{
 PSPath = Microsoft.PowerShell.Core\FileSystem::C:\DRIVERS
 PSParentPath = Microsoft.PowerShell.Core\FileSystem::C:\
 PSChildName = DRIVERS
 PSDrive =
   class PSDriveInfo
   {
     CurrentLocation =
     Name = C
     Provider = Microsoft.PowerShell.Core\FileSystem
```

```
    Root = C:\
    Description = Local
    Credential = System.Management.Automation.PSCredential
  }
PSProvider =
  class ProviderInfo
  {
    ImplementingType = Microsoft.PowerShell.Commands.FileSystemProvider
    HelpFile = System.Management.Automation.dll-Help.xml
    Name = FileSystem
    PSSnapIn = Microsoft.PowerShell.Core
    Description =
    Capabilities = Filter, ShouldProcess
    Home = C:\Users\Don
    Drives =
      [
        C
      ]

  }
PSIsContainer = True
Mode = d----
Name = DRIVERS
Parent =
  class DirectoryInfo
  {
    Mode = d--hs
    Name = C:\
    Parent =
    Exists = True
    Root = C:\
    FullName = C:\
    Extension =
    CreationTime = 11/2/2006 5:18:56 AM
    CreationTimeUtc = 11/2/2006 10:18:56 AM
    LastAccessTime = 4/19/2007 10:26:56 AM
    LastAccessTimeUtc = 4/19/2007 3:26:56 PM
    LastWriteTime = 4/19/2007 10:26:56 AM
    LastWriteTimeUtc = 4/19/2007 3:26:56 PM
    Attributes = Hidden, System, Directory
  }
Exists = True
```

As you can see, the output indents child objects slightly and provides a very "under the hood" look at the objects you're viewing. Normally, there's little use for this view; in some instances it can be useful for debugging or what we call "object spelunking," but, for the most part, you'll only use **Format-Custom** if you have a custom view definition that you want the cmdlet to use.

Formatting Rules Overview: When Does PowerShell Use a List or Table?

PowerShell will automatically format with one of the Format cmdlets, depending on a couple of things. First, if PowerShell has a custom output view for the first object in the pipeline, it'll use that view—and the view itself defines whether it's a table, list, custom, or wide view—and PowerShell comes with tons of custom views for many different types of objects.

If there is no custom view, however, PowerShell will use **Format-List** if the first object in the pipeline has five or more properties; otherwise, it'll send the output to **Format-Table**. If **Format-Table** is selected, then it'll use the properties *of the first object in the pipeline* to form the table columns. So, if the first object has three properties and every other object in the pipeline has ten properties, you'll get a three-column table.

Note that PowerShell's formatting files—or a custom formatting file you create—can contain *multiple* different possible views for a given type of data. We'll get into these files in more detail in "Creating Custom Formats," which starts on page 502. For now, though, you need to know that PowerShell's formatting files—or custom formatting files you create—can contain more than one "view" for a given data type. Normally, when you explicitly use **Format-Table**, **Format-List**, **Format-Wide**, or **Format-Custom**, PowerShell will select the first registered view that matches that layout option. That is, if you send data to **Format-Table**, PowerShell will find the first table-style view and use it.

All of the formatting cmdlets, however, support a **-view** parameter, which lets you specify an alternate view. For example, normally **Get-Process** returns a view like this:

```
PS C:\> get-process

Handles NPM(K)    PM(K)     WS(K) VM(M)   CPU(s)     Id  ProcessName
------- ------    -----     ----- -----   ------     --  -----------
    135      5     2680      4296    56               584 AcPrfMgrSvc
    260      7     5856      6064    74              2476 AcSvc
     86      6    10140      4972    73     0.16     3044 ACTray
     82      6    10236      4836    72     0.16     3048 ACWLIcon
    109      3    11300      9136    43              1236 audiodg
    106      5     8700      4500    70     0.09     2892 AwaySch
```

That's a table view. Yes, it has more than five properties, but it's a view specifically registered for Process objects, and PowerShell will always use a registered, type-specific view if one is available. However, you could specify an alternate view:

```
PS C:\> get-process | ft -view priority

ProcessName          Id  HandleCount  WorkingSet
-----------          --  -----------  ----------
AcPrfMgrSvc         584          135     4399104
AcSvc              2476          260     6205440




PriorityClass: Normal

ProcessName          Id  HandleCount  WorkingSet
-----------          --  -----------  ----------
ACTray             3044           86     5091328
ACWLIcon           3048           82     4952064
audiodg            1236          109     9355264
```

Notice that this particular view is grouping Process objects on their PriorityClass property, and it has defined a different list of columns. We had to explicitly use **Format-Table** (or rather its alias, **Ft**) because we needed to specify the view's name, Priority. If we'd used another formatting cmdlet, this wouldn't have worked, because the Priority view is defined as a table—it can't be selected by anything but **Format-Table**.

Unfortunately, there's no quick or easy way to determine what special formats are available in PowerShell's built-in formatting files, other than opening them up in Notepad and browsing them. You'll find them in PowerShell's installation folder, each with a .format.ps1xml filename extension.

GroupBy

All the format cmdlets include a parameter called **-GroupBy** that allows you to group output based on a specified property. For example, here is a **Get-Service** expression that groups services by their status such as Running or Stopped. The output below has been edited for brevity.

```
PS C:\> get-service |format-table -groupby status


   Status: Stopped

Status  Name                DisplayName
------  ----                -----------
Stopped Alerter             Alerter
Stopped ALG                 Application Layer Gateway Service
Stopped AppMgmt             Application Management
Stopped aspnet_state        ASP.NET State Service


   Status: Running

Status  Name                DisplayName
------  ----                -----------
Running AudioSrv            Windows Audio
Running Avg7Alrt            AVG7 Alert Manager Server
Running Avg7UpdSvc          AVG7 Update Service
Running AVGEMS              AVG E-mail Scanner


   Status: Stopped

Status  Name                DisplayName
------  ----                -----------
Stopped BAsfIpM             Broadcom ASF IP monitoring service ...
Stopped BITS                Background Intelligent Transfer Ser...
Stopped Browser             Computer Browser
Stopped CiSvc               Indexing Service
Stopped ClipSrv             ClipBook
Stopped clr_optimizatio...  NET Runtime Optimization Service v...
Stopped COMSysApp           COM+ System Application
   Status: Running

Status  Name                DisplayName
------  ----                -----------
Running CryptSvc            Cryptographic Services


   Status: Running

Status  Name                DisplayName
------  ----                -----------
Running wuauserv            Automatic Updates
Running WZCSVC              Wireless Zero Configuration


   Status: Stopped

Status  Name                DisplayName
------  ----                -----------
Stopped xmlprov             Network Provisioning Service

PS C:\>
```

As you can see, grouping helps a little bit. However, this is probably not what you expected, since the cmdlet basically just generates a new group header each time it encounters a new value for the specified property. Because the services weren't first *sorted* on that property, things aren't grouped like you might want them to be. So, the trick, prior to grouping, is to first *sort* them.

By the Way...

Using the -GroupBy parameter is the same as piping objects to the Group-Object cmdlet and then piping the objects to a Format cmdlet. In both cases, you'll want to sort the objects first by using Sort-Object.

Sort-Object: Sorting Objects

The **Sort-Object** cmdlet does exactly what its name implies: it sorts objects based on property values.

```
PS C:\> get-process|sort-object handles
```

Handles	NPM(K)	PM(K)	WS(K)	VM(M)	CPU(s)	Id	ProcessName
0	0	0	16	0		0	Idle
21	1	168	376	4	0.46	776	smss
30	2	1912	2436	29	0.11	1288	cmd
34	2	400	1524	15	0.21	2664	WLTRYSVC
43	2	376	1392	13	0.18	2932	MsPMSPSv
62	3	1820	4404	34	0.21	1456	ApntEx
64	3	1744	5628	37	0.24	324	notepad
65	2	1472	1600	14	0.17	2488	wdfmgr
69	3	632	2044	13	0.10	1580	sqlbrowser
72	3	828	2428	27	0.33	1208	scardsvr
76	2	524	2116	19	0.04	828	avgupsvc
91	5	1284	3184	29	2.16	300	svchost
95	4	1528	5852	39	0.83	844	sqlmangr

...

Here we've taken the output of **Get-Process** and sorted it by the Handles property. The default sort is ascending, but if you prefer, the cmdlet includes a **-descending** parameter:

```
PS C:\> get-process|sort-object handles -descending
```

Handles	NPM(K)	PM(K)	WS(K)	VM(M)	CPU(s)	Id	ProcessName
1290	49	14000	23608	127	38.52	1892	svchost
1076	0	0	220	2	47.18	4	System
817	78	15856	8436	136	15.55	1628	Groove
706	7	1888	4880	28	18.51	868	csrss
616	16	25680	41096	127	100.01	484	explorer
589	12	8076	1508	62	3.24	892	winlogon
538	11	15508	8864	95	126.88	1948	Smc
483	20	38092	63020	223	168.63	2308	WINWORD

...

Let's return to the earlier example in which we tried to group the output of **Get-Service** by status. Now we can pipe the **Get-Service** cmdlet to **Sort-Object**, specifying primary sort on status, and then on name. Next we send the object to **Format-Table** and group by status. Here's the output we get:

```
PS C:\> get-service|sort-object status,name |format-table -groupby status


   Status: Stopped

Status    Name              DisplayName
------    ----              -----------
Stopped   Alerter           Alerter
Stopped   ALG               Application Layer Gateway Service
Stopped   AppMgmt           Application Management
Stopped   aspnet_state      ASP.NET State Service
Stopped   BAsfIpM           Broadcom ASF IP monitoring service ...
Stopped   BITS              Background Intelligent Transfer Ser...
Stopped   Browser           Computer Browser
Stopped   CiSvc             Indexing Service
...
   Status: Running

Status    Name              DisplayName
------    ----              -----------
Running   AudioSrv          Windows Audio
Running   Avg7Alrt          AVG7 Alert Manager Server
Running   Avg7UpdSvc        AVG7 Update Service
Running   AVGEMS            AVG E-mail Scanner
Running   CryptSvc          Cryptographic Services
Running   DcomLaunch        DCOM Server Process Launcher
Running   Dhcp              DHCP Client
Running   Dnscache          DNS Client
Running   EventSystem       COM+ Event System
Running   IISADMIN          IIS Admin
Running   lanmanserver      Server
Running   lanmanworkstation Workstation
...

PS C:\>
```

Again, we've edited the output for brevity, but you get the picture. And, by the way, we should point out that the "Format" cmdlets, discussed earlier, also have a **-groupBy** parameter. Here's an example:

```
PS C:\> get-service | sort status | format-table -groupby status


   Status: Stopped

Status    Name              DisplayName
------    ----              -----------
Stopped   napagent          Network Access Protection Agent
Stopped   Netlogon          Netlogon
Stopped   msvsmon80         Visual Studio 2005 Remote Debugger
Stopped   MSiSCSI           Microsoft iSCSI Initiator Service
Stopped   msiserver         Windows Installer
Stopped   TBS               TPM Base Services
Stopped   odserv            Microsoft Office Diagnostics Service
...


   Status: Running

Status    Name              DisplayName
------    ----              -----------
Running   wudfsvc           Windows Driver Foundation - User-mo...
Running   wuauserv          Windows Update
Running   SSDPSRV           SSDP Discovery
```

```
Running  UleadBurningHelper Ulead Burning Helper
...
```

So, which do you use, **Group-Object** or the -**GroupBy** parameter of a Format cmdlet? Your choice. The **Group-Object** cmdlet has a few other options, such as specifying a case-sensitive grouping and specifying a different culture's sorting rules, but for the most part you'll get the same results, and you should use whichever one you like best.

Getting back to **Sort-Object**: One final parameter is -**Unique**, which not only gives sorted output, but also displays only the unique values:

```
PS C:\> $var=@(7,3,4,4,4,2,5,5,4,8,43,54)
PS C:\> $var|sort
2
3
4
4
4
4
5
5
7
8
43
54

PS C:\> $var|sort -unique
2
3
4
5
7
8
43
54
PS C:\>
```

In the first example, we've defined an array of numbers and first pipe it through a regular **Sort-Object** cmdlet. Compare that to the second expression that uses -**Unique**. Now the output is sorted and only unique objects are returned.

....

Alias Alert
You will probably find it easier to use the alias for Sort-Object, which is Sort, as we did in the last example.

PowerShell also has a **Get-Unique** cmdlet that functions essentially the same as **Sort -Unique**, but without the sorting feature. However, its functionality is limited if you don't sort. Here's the same array piped through **Get-Unique**:

```
PS C:\> $var|get-unique
7
3
4
2
5
4
```

```
8
43
54
PS C:\>
```

The list is not 100% unique, as you'll see the number 4 repeated. This is because **Get-Unique** compares consecutive items and returns the next item only if it is different. This is why you need to sort the object before using **Get-Unique**:

```
PS C:\ > $var | sort | get-unique
2
3
4
5
7
8
43
54
```

This is the same result as with **Sort -Unique**.

By the way, **Sort-Object** is perfectly happy to sort less complicated objects, too. For example:

```
$names = @("Don","Jeff","Alex")
```

The $names variable is now a collection (or array) of three String objects. Asking **Sort-Object** to put these in order is easy—we can even assign the sorted array right back to the same variable:

```
$names = $names | sort
```

Notice that we didn't have to tell **Sort-Object** *what* to sort on; since these are simple objects, it was able to figure it out on its own.

Where-Object: Filtering Objects

In addition to sorting, you may need to limit or filter the output. The **Where-Object** cmdlet is a filter that lets you control what data is ultimately displayed. This cmdlet is almost always used in a pipeline expression where output from one cmdlet is piped to this cmdlet. The **Where-Object** cmdlet requires a code block enclosed in braces that is executed as the filter. Any input objects that match your criteria are passed down the pipeline; any objects that don't match your criteria are dropped.

Here's an expression to get all instances of the Win32_Service class where the State property of each object equals Stopped.

```
Get-WmiObject -class win32_service | where {$_.state -eq "Stopped"}
```

Notice the use of the special **$_** variable, which represents "the current pipeline object." So, that expression reads, "where the current object's State property is equal to the value 'Stopped.'" You may want to further refine this expression and format the output by piping to yet another cmdlet:

```
PS C:\> Get-WmiObject -class win32_service | where {$_.state -eq "Stopped"} | format-wide

Alerter                                    ALG
```

```
AppMgmt                          aspnet_state
BAsfIpM                          Browser
CiSvc                            ClipSrv
clr_optimization_v2.0.50727_32   COMSysApp
CVPND                            dmadmin
dmserver                         ERSvc
FastUserSwitchingCompatibility   GrooveAuditService
GrooveInstallerService           GrooveRunOnceInstaller
helpsvc                          HidServ
NetDDE                           NetDDEdsdm
Netlogon                         NtLmSsp
NtmsSvc                          ose
PDEngine                         Pml Driver HPZ12
...
```

In this example, we've taken the same **Get-WmiObject** expression and piped it through **Format-Wide** to get a nice two-column report.

The key is recognizing that the script block in braces is what filters the object. If nothing matches the filter, then nothing will be displayed.

ForEach-Object: Performing Actions Against Each Object

The **ForEach-Object** cmdlet actually straddles a line between interactive use and scripting. Its alias, **Foreach**, can be seen as a scripting construct, and we'll cover it as such later. However, when used as a cmdlet its syntax is somewhat different, so we'll cover that part here.

In its simplest form, **ForEach-Object** accepts a collection of objects from the pipeline, and then executes a script block that you provide. It executes the script block once for each pipeline object, and within the script block you can use the special **$_** variable to refer to the current pipeline object. For example, this command:

```
Get-WmiObject Win32_LogicalDisk
```

Displays a list of logical disks on your system. If you only wanted the free space on each disk, and if you wanted that value expressed in gigabytes, rather than bytes, you could use **ForEach-Object** as follows:

```
Get-WmiObject Win32_LogicalDisk | ForEach-Object { $_.FreeSpace / 1GB }
```

The script block shown will take the FreeSpace property of the current pipeline object, divide it by the special 1GB variable, and output the result to the pipeline. That script block is actually passed to a parameter named **-process**, which is positional; we don't *need* to supply the parameter name, but the following is functionally identical:

```
Get-WmiObject Win32_LogicalDisk | ForEach-Object -process { $_.FreeSpace / 1GB }
```

Resulting in output much like the following:

```
PS C:\> Get-WmiObject win32_logicaldisk | foreach-object -process { $_.FreeSpace / 1GB }
0
117.766156288
162.83420672
0
27.855847424
```

ForEach-Object has several aliases, including **%**. Condensing this line to use all aliases looks like this:

```
gwmi Win32_LogicalDisk | % -pr { $_.FreeSpace / 1GB }
```

The cmdlet also supports two other parameters: **-begin** and **-end**. These parameters accept script blocks just as **-process** does, but they work slightly differently. The script block given to **-begin** will run only once, before PowerShell processes any pipeline objects. Similarly, the script block given to **-end** will also run only once, but will do so after PowerShell has processed all pipeline objects. Here's an example:

```
PS C:\> gwmi win32_logicaldisk | % -process { $_.FreeSpace / 1GB } -begin { write " '
>> Disk Space Inventory" } -end { Write "Complete" }
>>
>>
Disk Space Inventory
0
117.7658368
162.83420672
0
27.855847424
Complete
```

You can see where the **-begin** and **-end** script blocks executed, displaying their information before and after the **-process** script block executed.

ForEach-Object can seem limited, since it would appear that only a single command can appear within each script block. However, PowerShell uses the **;** character to separate statements that appear on a single physical line. For example, if we wanted our **-process** script block to output the DeviceID property first, we'd do something like this:

```
PS C:\> gwmi Win32_LogicalDisk | % -pr { $_.DeviceID; $_.FreeSpace / 1GB }
```

Now, the **-process** script block contains two actual statements. Although they're contained on a single physical line, PowerShell will treat them, and execute them, independently. The results:

```
A:
0
C:
117.765771264
D:
162.83420672
F:
0
G:
27.855847424
```

But Wait, There's More

The ForEach-Object cmdlet provides functionality similar to a filter or a function, which we cover in the chapter "Script Blocks, Functions, Filters, Snap-ins, and Modules." And, as already mentioned, the cmdlet sort of finds use as the scripting statement foreach, which we cover later.

Select-Object: Choosing Specific Object Properties

Select-Object, or its alias, **Select,** takes a bit of work to understand. First, let's look at what we get when we pass a particular object to **Get-Member** (or its alias, **Gm**), to see what properties and methods the object has:

```
PS C:\> Get-WmiObject win32_bios | gm


   TypeName: System.Management.ManagementObject#root\cimv2\Win32_BIOS

Name                   MemberType  Definition
----                   ----------  ----------
BiosCharacteristics    Property    System.UInt16[] BiosCharacteristics {get;set;}
BIOSVersion            Property    System.String[] BIOSVersion {get;set;}
BuildNumber            Property    System.String  BuildNumber {get;set;}
Caption                Property    System.String  Caption {get;set;}
CodeSet                Property    System.String  CodeSet {get;set;}
CurrentLanguage        Property    System.String  CurrentLanguage {get;set;}
Description            Property    System.String  Description {get;set;}
IdentificationCode     Property    System.String  IdentificationCode {get;set;}
InstallableLanguages   Property    System.UInt16  InstallableLanguages {get;set;}
InstallDate            Property    System.String  InstallDate {get;set;}
LanguageEdition        Property    System.String  LanguageEdition {get;set;}
ListOfLanguages        Property    System.String[] ListOfLanguages {get;set;}
```

Once you know what properties you are interested in, you can use **Select-Object** to limit the results:

```
PS C:\ > Get-WmiObject win32_bios | select Description,Manufacturer,version

Description                         Manufacturer                version
-----------                         ------------                -------
Phoenix ROM BIOS PLUS Version 1.10 A13  Dell Computer Corporation   DELL  - 27d5061e
```

The ability to return selected properties is especially helpful when it comes to exporting information.

Exporting

PowerShell's ability to manipulate objects is pretty formidable. We've seen how PowerShell permits you to control the output format of an expression or cmdlet. However, PowerShell even has the ability to change or export the object into something else.

Export-CSV

A comma-separated value (CSV) file is a mainstay of administrative scripting. It's a text-based database that you can parse into an array or open in a spreadsheet program like Microsoft Excel. The cmdlet requires an input object that is typically the result of a piped cmdlet:

```
Get-process | export-csv processes.csv
```

When you run this command on your system, it creates a text file called processes.csv. When you open the file in a spreadsheet program, you'll be amazed by the amount of information that is available. In fact, it's probably overkill for most situations.

Here's another version of basically the same expression except this time we're using **Select-Object** to specify the properties we want returned:

```
PS C:\> get-process |select-object name,id,workingset,cpu| export-csv processes.csv
PS C:\> get-content processes.csv
#TYPE System.Management.Automation.PSCustomObject
Name,Id,WorkingSet,CPU
acrotray,3996,6574080,0.7110224
ApntEx,1456,4718592,6.5894752
Apoint,1592,7147520,6.0787408
avgamsvr,436,7389184,4.155976
avgcc,1684,12288000,10.4550336
avgemc,860,22593536,9.5036656
avgupsvc,828,3182592,1.6824192
BCMWLTRY,2948,6508544,16.2333424
Client,1084,1019904,140.6121904
cmd,1288,1093632,0.5207488
csrss,868,3440640,82.7790304
cvpnd,4000,8015872,9.6538816
EXCEL,2452,6545408,6.6996336
explorer,484,35528704,801.6427056
firefox,3028,71385088,881.2872288
Groove,2032,11628544,25.3264176
Idle,0,16384,
inetinfo,3012,5357568,1.4420736
Microsoft.Crm.Application.Hoster,1796,28168192,14.7812544
MSASCui,1732,10907648,7.310512
MsMpEng,1832,14114816,107.8951456
MsPMSPSv,2932,1425408,1.0114544
nvsvc32,1788,3522560,2.5236288
powershell,1560,53522432,7.9314048
procexp,588,10452992,86.1438688
PS C:\>
```

This produces a raw data report that we can further process any way we want. For example, if the **Out-File** already exists, it will be overwritten unless you use -**NoClobber**. If you don't want the #TYPE header, which we find distracting, specify -**NoTypeInformation** as part of the **Export-CSV** cmdlet.

On a related note, PowerShell also has an **Import-CSV** cmdlet that reads the contents of the csv file and displays the data as a table. Here's an example with abbreviated output:

```
PS C:\> import-csv processes.csv

Name          Id        WorkingSet    CPU
----          --        ----------    ---
acrotray      3996      6574080       0.7110224
ApntEx        1456      4718592       6.5894752
Apoint        1592      7147520       6.0787408
avgamsvr      436       7389184       4.155976
avgcc         1684      12288000      10.4550336
avgemc        860       22593536      9.5036656
avgupsvc      828       3182592       1.6824192
cmd           1288      1093632       0.5207488
csrss         868       3440640       82.7790304
```

```
cvpnd           4000            8015872         9.6538816
EXCEL           2452            6545408         6.6996336
...
```

By the way, in actuality **Import-CSV** reads a CSV file and assumes that the first line consists of column names. It then creates a collection of objects based upon the contents of the CSV file. For example, if you have a simple text file that looks like this:

```
name,type
notepad,process
calc,process
```

Then **Import-CSV** would create two objects, each with a Name and a Type property. For example:

```
PS C:\> $file = import-csv c:\yserver.txt
PS C:\> $file | gm


   TypeName: System.Management.Automation.PSCustomObject

Name          MemberType    Definition
----          ----------    ----------
Equals        Method        System.Boolean Equals(Object obj)
GetHashCode   Method        System.Int32 GetHashCode()
GetType       Method        System.Type GetType()
ToString      Method        System.String ToString()
name          NoteProperty  System.String name=notepad
type          NoteProperty  System.String type=process
```

As you can see, **$file** is a collection of objects, each of which have a Name and a Type property. You can access this collection like any other:

```
PS C:\> $file[0].name
notepad
PS C:\> $file[1].type
Process
```

Above, we've grabbed the Name property of the first object in the collection, and the Type property of the second.

Import- and Export- other Delimited Data
Both Import-CSV and Export-CSV support a –delimiter parameter, which allows you to specify a data delimiter other than a comma. By using this parameter, you can import and export tab-delimited files (use `t as the delimiter), space-delimited files, pipe-delimited files, or whatever you might need.

Export-CliXML

If you prefer to store results as an XML file, perhaps for processing by other tools, you can use PowerShell's **Export-CliXML** cmdlet. It works much the same way as **Export-CSV**:

```
PS C:\>Get-WmiObject -class win32_processor |export-clixml wmiproc.xml
```

This creates an XML file called wmiproc.xml, which you can import back into PowerShell using **Import-CliXML**:

```
PS C:\> import-clixml wmiproc.xml


AddressWidth                    : 32
Architecture                    : 0
Availability                    : 3
Caption                         : x86 Family 6 Model 9 Stepping 5
ConfigManagerErrorCode          :
ConfigManagerUserConfig         :
CpuStatus                       : 1
CreationClassName               : Win32_Processor
CurrentClockSpeed               : 1598
CurrentVoltage                  : 33
DataWidth                       : 32
Description                     : x86 Family 6 Model 9 Stepping 5
DeviceID                        : CPU0
ErrorCleared                    :
ErrorDescription                :
ExtClock                        : 133
Family                          : 2
InstallDate                     :
L2CacheSize                     : 1024
L2CacheSpeed                    :
LastErrorCode                   :
Level                           : 6
LoadPercentage                  :
Manufacturer                    : GenuineIntel
MaxClockSpeed                   : 1598
Name                            : Intel(R) Pentium(R) M processor 1600MHz
OtherFamilyDescription          :
PNPDeviceID                     :
PowerManagementCapabilities     :
PowerManagementSupported        : False
ProcessorId                     : A7E9F9BF00000695
ProcessorType                   : 3
Revision                        : 2309
Role                            : CPU
SocketDesignation               : Microprocessor
Status                          : OK
StatusInfo                      : 3
Stepping                        : 5
SystemCreationClassName         : Win32_ComputerSystem
SystemName                      : GODOT
UniqueId                        :
UpgradeMethod                   : 6
Version                         : Model 9, Stepping 5
VoltageCaps                     : 2
__GENUS                         : 2
__CLASS                         : Win32_Processor
...
PS C:\>
```

As with the other exporting cmdlets, you can use **-NoClobber** to avoid overwriting an existing file. This can be a useful technique when used with command-line history. First, export it to an XML file:

```
PS C:\> get-history | export-clixml c:\history.xml
```

Later, when you want to re-import that command-line history into the shell, use **Import-CliXML** and pipe the results to **Add-History**:

```
PS C:\> import-clixml c:\history.xml | add-history
```

You can export *most* simple objects into the CliXML format, and then re-import them at a later date to approximately re-create those objects. The technique works best for objects that only have properties, where those properties only contain simple values such as strings, numbers, and Boolean values.

ConvertTo-HTML

Finally, PowerShell includes a cmdlet to convert text output to an HTML table with the **ConvertTo-HTML** cmdlet. At its simplest, you can run an expression like this:

```
PS C:\> Get-Service | ConvertTo-HTML
```

If you execute this expression you'll see HTML code fly across the console, which doesn't do you much good. You can change this by piping the HTML output to a file using **Out-File**, specifying a file name:

```
PS C:\> Get-Service | ConvertTo-HTML |out-file services.html
```

Now when you open services.html in a Web browser, you'll see a pretty complete table of running services and their properties. By default, the cmdlet lists all properties. However, you can specify the properties by name and in whatever order you prefer:

```
PS C:\> Get-Service | ConvertTo-HTML Name,DisplayName,Status | out-file services.html
```

Now when you open services.html, it's a little easier to work with. If you want to dress up the page a bit, **ConvertTo-HTML** has some additional parameters as shown in the following table:

ConvertTo-HTML Optional Parameters

Parameter	Description
Head	Inserts text into the \<head\> tag of the HTML page. You might want to include metadata or style sheet references.
Title	Inserts text into the \<title\> tag of the HTML page. This lets you have a more meaningful title to the page other than the default HTMLTABLE.
Body	Inserts text within the \<body\>\</body\> tag. This lets you specify body formatting like fonts and colors as well as any text you want to appear before the table.
CssUri	Lets you specify the location of a Cascading Style Sheet (CSS) which will be used to apply formatting to the HTML output.
PreContent	Content to be prepended to the final output.
PostContent	Content to be appended to the final output.

Note: Always Read the Help

We're going to be showing you a lot of cmdlets like ConvertTo-HTML, where we only introduce you to some of the things it can do. You should always be reading the help on these cmdlets to see what else they can do. You don't need to memorize the syntax, but knowing what capabilities are in the shell will help you solve real-world problems when the time comes—even if you have to do a bit of research to re-discover something you read about in the past.

Here's a script where we put it all together.

Service2HTML.ps1

```
#Service2HTML.ps1
# a style sheet, style.css, should be in the same directory
# as the saved html file.

$server=hostname
$body="Services Report for "+$server.ToUpper()+"<HR>"
$file="c:\"+$server+"-services.html"

write-host "Generating Services Report for "$server.ToUpper()

 get-service |sort -property status -descending | ConvertTo-HTML '
 Name,DisplayName,Status -Title "Service Report" '
 -Css "style.css" '
 -Body $body | out-file $file

write-host "Report Generation Complete! Open" $file "for results."
```

This script uses the **Get-Service** cmdlet to generate a formatted HTML page. The script starts by defining some variables. First, we want the computer name to use in the report and other variables. Then we define a variable for the **-Body** parameter. If just text is being used, we don't have to bother with this. However, the **ConvertTo-HTML** cmdlet is a little finicky and doesn't handle the results of embedded cmdlets very well. By defining a variable, we can ensure its value is a string. We also specify the location and name of the saved file. We're using the server name as part of the filename.

After a message is sent to the user informing him the report is being generated, the heart of the script is reached. We take the **Get-Service** cmdlet and first pipe it to the **Sort-Object** cmdlet, sorting on service status and returning the results in descending order. This puts Running services at the top of the page and Stopped services at the bottom. Next we pipe that to **ConvertTo-HTML**, specifying the properties we want in the table. We include a **-cssUri** parameter so we can reference a style sheet and then the **-body** parameter using the **$body** variable we defined at the beginning of the script. All of this is piped to **Out-File**, which saves the result to an HTML file. You can see the results in the following figure:

Figure 6-1: HTML output.

Last but not least, **ConvertTo-HTML** allows you to specify a list of properties that you want included in the table, rather than using *all* of the properties. This eliminates the need to first use **Select-Object** to narrow down the property list. Here's how it works:

```
PS C:\> Get-Service | ConvertTo-HTML –property Name,Status,DisplayName | Out-File Services.html
```

The **ConvertTo-HTML** cmdlet is one of your most powerful tools for creating instant management reports right within PowerShell.

Comparing Objects and Collections

Occasionally, you may need to compare complex objects or collections—with text files perhaps being the most common and easily explained example. PowerShell provides a **Compare-Object** cmdlet, which can perform object comparisons. Now, before we get started, we have to remind you: *PowerShell deals in objects, not text.* A text file is technically a *collection* of individual *string objects*; that is, each line of the file is a unique, independent object, and the text file serves to "collect" them together.

When comparing objects, you start with two *sets*: The *reference* set and the *difference* set. In the case of two text files, these would simply be the two files. Which one is the reference and which one is the difference often doesn't matter; **Compare-Object** will show you which objects—that is, which lines of text—exist in one set but not the other, or which are present in both sets but different. That last bit—showing you objects which are present in both sets, but different—can get confusing, so we won't deal with it at first.

To begin, we're going to use two text files named Set1.txt and Set2.txt, which each contain some simple lines of text.

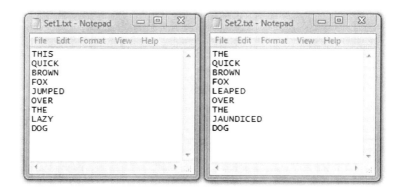

Figure 6-2: Comparing objects.

We'll use **Get-Content** to load each file into a variable, which we'll name $set1 and $set2:

```
PS C:\> $set1 = get-content c:\set1.txt
PS C:\> $set2 = get-content c:\set2.txt
```

And here's our first test:

```
PS C:\> compare-object -reference $set1 -difference $set2

InputObject                    SideIndicator
-----------                    -------------
LEAPED                         =>
THE                            =>
JAUNDICED                      =>
THIS                           <=
JUMPED                         <=
LAZY                           <=
```

The SideIndicator tells us which "side" of the comparison was unequal. The reference set is always thought of as being on the left, while the difference set is thought of as being on the right—exactly as we showed in the screen shot of the two Notepad windows. And remember, we're seeing the *differences* here. So, the first difference is LEAPED, which existed in the right file, but not the left. We also see that THE existed on the right but not the left, along with JAUNDICED. The words THIS, JUMPED, and LAZY appeared on the left, but not in the right. These differences don't appear in the same order as the actual differences within the file, which is important to keep in mind.

And notice, too, how two different lines of text always show as *missing*, rather than *different*. For example, the first lines of the two files are different—THIS and THE—but both THIS and THE are listed separately as "missing" from the other file. That's because the string objects THIS and THE are different objects, so PowerShell can't "match them up" as being the same object with a different property value. Were we to rearrange the text in one file completely, moving different words to different lines, **Compare-Object** would yield the exact same results. For example, these two files:

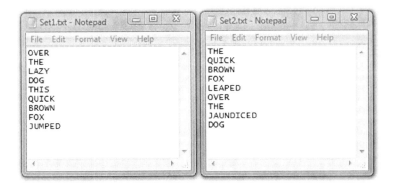

Figure 6-3: Comparing objects again.

Produce exactly the same results:

```
PS C:\> compare-object -reference $set1 -difference $set2

InputObject                     SideIndicator
-----------                     -------------
LEAPED                          =>
THE                             =>
JAUNDICED                       =>
THIS                            <=
JUMPED                          <=
LAZY                            <=
```

This behavior reveals that PowerShell isn't doing a line-by-line comparison. Rather, it's asking itself, "do any of the objects in these files not exist in the other file?" The word THE is the best example of this: Set1 contains the word THE just once; Set2 contains THE twice. So, THE is shown as existing in Set2 at least one time when it doesn't exist somewhere in Set1. Try this: At the bottom of Set2.text, add two more lines containing THE and THE:

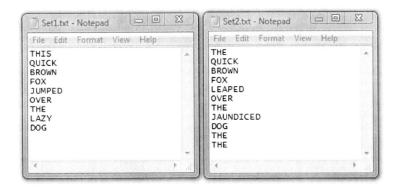

Figure 6-4: Comparing objects one more time.

Once you've made that change, re-run **Compare-Object** and you'll get the *exact same results again.* This type of comparison can be very difficult to understand if you're used to text-based difference utilities, but it's a perfect example of how PowerShell cares about *objects.* That makes **Compare-Object** of limited use for classic text file comparisons, but comparing text files line for line was never really the purpose of this cmdlet.

So, let's focus on what **Compare-Object** is really intended for, as implied by its name: *Objects*. Here's a quick example where we'll query our local computer's Win32_LogicalDisk WMI class into two sets, and then compare them. As expected, when you compare the exact same two things, you get no differences:

```
PS C:\> $set1 = gwmi win32_logicaldisk
PS C:\> $set2 = gwmi win32_logicaldisk
PS C:\> compare-object -ref $set1 -diff $set2
```

So, now we'll change $set2 to be another computer's logical disks:

```
PS C:\> $set2 = gwmi win32_logicaldisk -computer mediaserver
```

Now we'll re-run the comparison. This time we're piping the results to **Format-Table** so that we can use its **-autosize** parameter to generate more easily read results:

```
PS C:\> compare-object -ref $set1 -diff $set2 | ft -auto

InputObject                                          SideIndicator
-----------                                          -------------
\\MEDIASERVER\root\cimv2:Win32_LogicalDisk.DeviceID="A:" =>
\\MEDIASERVER\root\cimv2:Win32_LogicalDisk.DeviceID="C:" =>
\\MEDIASERVER\root\cimv2:Win32_LogicalDisk.DeviceID="D:" =>
\\MEDIASERVER\root\cimv2:Win32_LogicalDisk.DeviceID="E:" =>
\\DON-PC\root\cimv2:Win32_LogicalDisk.DeviceID="A:"      <=
\\DON-PC\root\cimv2:Win32_LogicalDisk.DeviceID="C:"      <=
\\DON-PC\root\cimv2:Win32_LogicalDisk.DeviceID="D:"      <=
\\DON-PC\root\cimv2:Win32_LogicalDisk.DeviceID="F:"      <=
\\DON-PC\root\cimv2:Win32_LogicalDisk.DeviceID="G:"      <=
```

This is showing that our $set2 computer has an A, C, D, and E drive, while our local computer has A, C, D, F, and G. They are indeed different objects, and so they're all listed as such. But now let's have **Compare-Object** only look at a specific object property, rather than the entire object:

```
PS C:\> compare-object -ref $set1 -diff $set2 -property deviceid | ft -auto

deviceid SideIndicator
-------- -------------
E:       =>
F:       <=
G:       <=
```

By adding the **-property** parameter and specifying DeviceID as the property, we're now comparing *just that property* in the two sets. Now, the A, C, and D drives are gone because they're present in both sets. We're left with an E drive in $set2, and an F and G drive in $set1. This is truly showing us the *difference in the logical disk device IDs* between the two computers. But what if we wanted to also see the matching device IDs?

```
PS C:\> compare-object -ref $set1 -diff $set2 -property deviceid -include | ft -auto

deviceid SideIndicator
-------- -------------
A:       ==
C:       ==
D:       ==
```

```
E:          =>
F:          <=
G:          <=
```

Now, the matching properties are also included, with an indicator that they're present in both sets. We accomplished this by adding the -**includeEqual** parameter in the command. Another parameter, -**excludeDifference**, will remove the difference items, leaving just those that are the same in both sets:

```
PS C:\> compare-object -ref $set1 -diff $set2 -property deviceid -include -exclude | ft -auto

deviceid  SideIndicator
--------  -------------
A:          ==
C:          ==
D:          ==
```

Perhaps a more practical example involves the use of the **Get-Process** cmdlet. Try this sometime in the morning:

```
PS C:\> $set1 = Get-Process
```

Leave PowerShell running all day—$set1 will remain in memory. Then, later in the day, run this:

```
PS C:\> $set2 = Get-Process
```

Now you can use **Compare-Object** to see the different processes that were running during the morning and the afternoon. Taken to a more practical level, you could use this as an auditing technique for servers. For example, you could verify that a server is running exactly the processes that it *should* be running all the time:

```
PS C:\> gwmi win32_process -computer mediaserver | export-clixml c:\allowed.xml
```

We've chosen to save this list of "allowed" processes in an XML file, which PowerShell can later use to re-construct the process objects—meaning we don't need to leave the shell running. Now, whenever we want to conduct an audit of the server's processes, we use the following:

```
PS C:\> $allowed = import-clixml c:\allowed.xml
PS C:\> $running = gwmi win32_process -computer mediaserver
PS C:\> compare-object -ref $allowed -diff $running -property name

name                        SideIndicator
----                        -------------
iexplore.exe                =>
notepad.exe                 =>
```

We imported the original "allowed" process objects by using **Import-CliXML**; we then retrieved the current list of processes and compared the two sets by process name, revealing Internet Explorer and Notepad in use. Hey, is someone on that server console surfing the Web?

Chapter 7
Practical Tips and Tricks

Using the Command Line

PowerShell's command line offers a number of shortcuts and features to help make typing faster. After all, just because this is the command line doesn't mean it needs to be primitive! By training yourself to use these shortcuts, you'll become much more efficient.

Command History

Like Cmd.exe and most other command-line environments, PowerShell maintains a history, or "buffer," of commands you've typed (this is different from the command history that the **Get-History** and **Add-History** cmdlets can manipulate). Pressing the Up and Down arrow keys on your keyboard provides access to this history, recalling past commands so that you can either easily run them again, or allowing you to quickly change a previous command and run the new version.

A little-known shortcut is the F7 key, which pops up a command-history window, allowing you to scroll through the window and select the command you want. If you press Enter, the selected command executes immediately. If you press the right or left arrow key, the command will be inserted but not executed. This is helpful when you want to recall a complicated command but need to tweak it. Press Esc to close the window without choosing a command.

By default, PowerShell stores only 50 commands in this buffer. To increase the command buffer, right-click the system menu of your PowerShell window and select Properties. On the Options tab, you can increase the buffer size from the default of 50. While you're at it, make sure the boxes for QuickEdit Mode and Insert Mode are checked. We'll show you how to take advantage of these later. Feel free to change the font size and colors as well.

Finally, one last trick for the command history: Type the beginning of a command that you've recently used, and press F8. PowerShell will fill in the rest of the command, and you can press F8 again to find the next "match" to what you'd typed. This is a quick way to recall a command more conveniently than using the arrow keys.

Line Editing

While PowerShell doesn't provide a full-screen editor (if you need that, then it may be time in investigate a visual development environment that supports PowerShell, such as SAPIEN PrimalScript—www. primalscript.com), it does provide basic editing capabilities for the current line:

- The Left and Right arrow keys move the cursor left and right on the current line.

- Pressing Ctrl+Left arrow and Ctrl+Right arrow moves left and right one word at a time, much as it does in Microsoft Word.

- The Home and End keys move to the beginning and end of the current line, respectively.

- The Insert key toggles between insert and overwrite mode.

- The Delete key deletes the character under the cursor; the Backspace key deletes the character "behind," or to the left of, the cursor.

- The Esc key clears the current line.

Copy and Paste

- If you've enabled QuickEdit and Insert Mode for your PowerShell window, you can easily copy and paste between PowerShell and Windows. To copy from PowerShell, merely use the mouse to select the text, and then press Enter. You can then paste it into another application like Notepad. To paste something into PowerShell, position your cursor in the PowerShell window and right-click. The copied text will be inserted at the command prompt.

Tab Completion

Also called *command completion,* this feature exists to help you complete command names and even parameter values more quickly. Pressing Tab on a blank line will insert an actual tab character; any other time—if you've already typed something on the line, that is—the Tab key kicks in command-completion mode. Here's how it works:

- If you've just typed a period, then command completion will cycle through the properties and methods of whatever object is to the left of the period. For example, if $wmi represents a WMI object, typing **$wmi.** and pressing Tab will call up the first property or method from that WMI object.

- If you've typed a period and one or more letters, pressing Tab will cycle through the properties and methods that *match what you've already typed.* For example, if $wmi is an instance of the Win32_ OperatingSystem WMI class, typing **$wmi.re** and pressing Tab will display "$wmi.Reboot(", which is the first property or method that begins with "re".

- If you've just typed a few characters, and no punctuation other than a hyphen ("-"), command completion will cycle through matching cmdlet names. For example, typing **get-w** and pressing Tab will result in "Get-WmiObject", the first cmdlet that begins with "get-w." Note that this does not work for aliases, only cmdlet names.

- If you've typed a command and a partial parameter name, you can hit Tab to cycle through matching parameter names. For example, you can type **gwmi -comp** and press Tab to get "gwmi -computerName".

- If none of the above conditions is true, then PowerShell will default to cycling through file and folder names. For example, type **cd**, a space, and press Tab. You'll see the first folder or file name in the current folder. Type a partial name, like **cd Doc**, and press Tab to have PowerShell cycle through matching file and folder names. Wildcards work, too: Type **cd pro*files** and press tab to get "cd 'Program Files'", for example.

Instant Expressions

PowerShell can evaluate expressions at the command line. The easiest examples are mathematical expressions:

```
PS C:\> 2 + 2
4
PS C:\> 4 * 4
16
PS C:\> 16 / 16
1
PS C:\> 1 - 1
0
PS C:\>
```

PowerShell recognizes the characters "kb," "mb," "gb," "tb," and "pb" as having special purpose. It uses these characters to represent a *kibibyte*, *mibibyte*, and *gibibyte*, *terabyte*, and *petabyte* units of measurement for computer memory.

....

Kibi-what?
Does kilo equal 1,000 or 1,024? When measuring storage—such as hard drive space—or nearly anything else, kilo means 1,000, while mega means one million and giga means one billion. These three terms have long been used improperly to refer to computer memory measurements, as well. We say "improperly" because a "kilobyte" of computer memory—RAM—is actually 1,024, not an even thousand.

In 2000, the International Electrotechnical Commission (of which the United States' American National Standards Institute is a member) created a new set of measurements specifically for computer memory, ending the 1,000-or-1,024 confusion. The term kilo therefore always means 1,000; since RAM is measured in powers of two, the term kibi was created to represent 1,024. This is all documented in IEEE 1541, a standard of the Institute of Electrical and Electronics Engineers, the European Union legalized these units of measurement in HD60027-2:2003-03.

Technically, the abbreviation kb still means kilobyte; a kibibyte is properly abbreviated as KiB instead. However, PowerShell recognizes kb as meaning 1,024; therefore, it's a kibibyte.

For example, to add one mibibyte to one kibibyte:

```
PS C:\> 1kb + 1mb
1049600
```

These expression evaluation capabilities allow you to quickly perform basic calculations without having to pull up Windows Calculator, and to provide a built-in means of working with binary values. Here's one last example:

```
PS C:\> (gwmi win32_computersystem).TotalPhysicalmemory/1mb
2037.25
PS C:\>
```

The TotalPhysicalMemory property is displayed by default in bytes, but by dividing the value by 1mb, we can represent the value in MB.

Pausing a Script

Use the **Start-Sleep** cmdlet to make your script pause for a specified number of seconds (or milliseconds, if you prefer; seconds is the default measurement):

```
PS C:\> Start-Sleep 10
```

Displaying a Progress Meter

PowerShell's **Write-Progress** cmdlet allows you to display a sort of text-based progress bar in the PowerShell window. During long-running tasks, this can be a useful way of telling the user (or yourself) that PowerShell isn't "locked up," it's just busy. Here's a quick example of how the cmdlet works:

```
for ($i=0; $i -lt 100; $i++) {
    Start-Sleep 1
    Write-Progress -activity "Waiting..." -status "STATUS" -id 1 -percentComplete $i

}
```

This results in a progress bar as shown here:

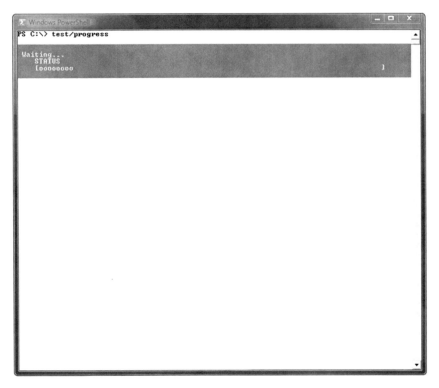

Figure 7-1: Progress bar.

There are a couple of key parameters for **Write-Progress**:

- **-ID** specifies a unique numeric ID number for your progress bar. You can use whatever number you like for this, but you should specify it so that you can refer back to your progress bar.

- **-percentComplete** is the percentage of the bar that should be filled in, on a scale of 1 to 100. In our example, this was easy to provide, because we were using a loop that counted from 1 to 100. If you're using other values, you'll need to divide, multiply, or whatever to ensure that this property receives a value of 1 to 100.

- **-secondsRemaining** is an alternative to **-percentComplete** and simply specifies the number of seconds that the user should expect before the operation will be complete.

- **-activity** and **-status** display text labels, as shown in the example. Typically, the "activity" is whatever broad operation is being conducted, such as "Querying computers." Status is more specified, such as "Querying Server2" or "Querying Server3." You can also specify **-CurrentOperation**, which is even more specific and which appears below the progress bar.

Both **-secondsRemaining** and **-percentComplete** are optional; if you don't specify them, then no progress bar will be displayed. Instead, just the activity and status messages—which are both mandatory—will be displayed.

Here's an extended example. This assumes we have a file named C:\Computers.txt, which contains one computer name per line. Pay close attention to the use of **Write-Progress**: You can see that each time, we're updating the information and, in some cases, displaying a bit more information about what's going on. The current computer name is used for the "status" label, while the current operation—service pack

or logical disk inventory—is displayed for the
-currentOperation parameter.

InventoryProgress.ps1

```
# initial status bar
Write-Progress -activity "Getting inventory" -status "Starting" -id 1

# get computer names
$computers = Get-Content c:\computers.txt

# how many computers?
$qty = $computers | Measure-Object
$currentComputer = 1

foreach ($computer in $computers) {
    # calculate status
    [int]$pct = ($currentComputer / $qty.count) * 100

    # update status bar
    Write-Progress -activity "Getting inventory" -status $computer -id 1 -percent $pct

    # get service pack
    Write-Progress -activity "Getting inventory" -status $computer -id 1 -percent $pct '
        -current "Service Pack"
    $wmi = gwmi win32_operatingsystem -computer $computer
    write 'n
    write $computer
    write "Service Pack: " $wmi.servicepackmajorversion

    # get disks
    Write-Progress -activity "Getting inventory" -status $computer -id 1 -percent $pct '
        -current "Disks"
    $wmi = gwmi win32_logicaldisk -computer $computer
    Write-Host "Logical disks: "
    foreach ($disk in $wmi) {
        write $disk.deviceid
    }

    # next computer...
    $currentComputer++
}
```

Also note that we didn't add any error checking, just to keep this sample clearer. It will result in errors if any of the computer names specified in C:\Computers.txt aren't available, or if we don't have permission to query a computer's WMI information.

When the progress bar finishes, it should automatically go away. If for some reason the progress bar remains on the screen, you can call **Write-Progress –completed $True** to dismiss it.

Keeping a Transcript

Sometimes, it can be useful to keep track of exactly what you're doing in PowerShell. For example, if you're experimenting a bit, going back and reviewing your work can help you spot things that worked correctly. You could then copy and paste those command lines into a script for future use. PowerShell offers a way to keep track of your work through a *transcript*. You start a new one with the **Start-Transcript** cmdlet:

```
PS C:\> Start-Transcript C:\MyWork.txt
```

A transcript is just a simple text file that contains everything shown in the PowerShell console window. A downside to it is that, if you *do* want to copy and paste your work into a script, you first have to edit out all the command prompts, your mistakes, and so forth. Once started, a transcript will continue recording your work until you either close the shell, or run the **Stop-Transcript** cmdlet:

```
PS C:\> Stop-Transcript
```

The **Start-Transcript** has additional parameters (which you can look up by using **Help**) that append to an existing file, force an existing file to be overwritten, and so forth.

Chapter 8
Graphical PowerShell

Windows PowerShell v2.0 ships with a new, "graphical shell" option, as well as a new graphical-based output option.

The Graphical Shell

The graphical shell is a PowerShell hosting application, much like the more familiar console window that you've probably used PowerShell in up to this point. Initially, this new graphical view doesn't seem to provide significant advantages over the console: It offers syntax coloring for the command you're typing, and the area where you type your commands can wrap, allowing long commands to fit more easily; apart from that it works much like the console version of the shell.

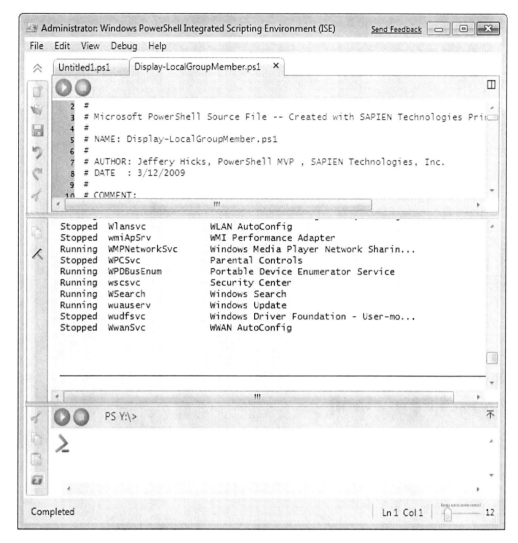

Figure 8-1: The PowerShell ISE.

The Integrated Scripting Environment (ISE) is divided into three resizable sections: a simple script editor, the output pane, and the command pane. Everything is resizable, allowing you to more easily take advantage of larger monitors to display more information without truncating it. Enter a Powershell command at the prompt in the bottom panel and the results are displayed in the center panel. You can also open multiple PowerShell sessions, each in their own runspace by using the Ctrl-T shortcut or selecting File > New PowerShell tab.

In Figure 8-2 we've defined a variable $a.

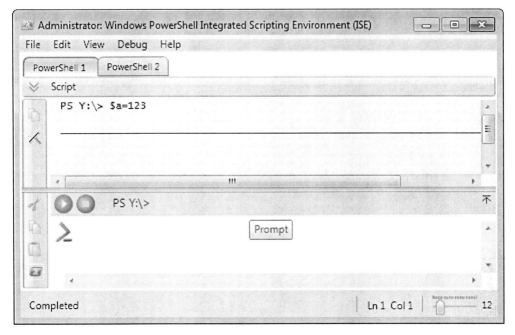

Figure 8-2: PowerShell tabs.

But when we look at the value of $a in the second PowerShell tab as shown in Figure 8-3, you can see it has no value.

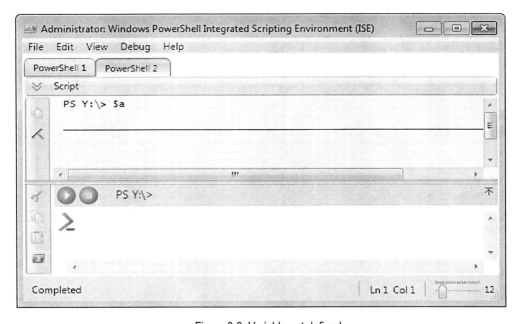

Figure 8-3: Variable not defined.

You can access the graphical shell's entry-level script editor by either opening a .ps1 file or creating a new one from the File menu. This script editor provides syntax highlighting (coloring), and appears in an individual pane just above the shell output window. When you run the script, the ISE places the script's output into the middle output pane. You can still use the lower command-entry area to enter commands and run them ad-hoc—allowing you to quickly test commands—and then paste them into the script above. You can open multiple scripts within each PowerShell session.

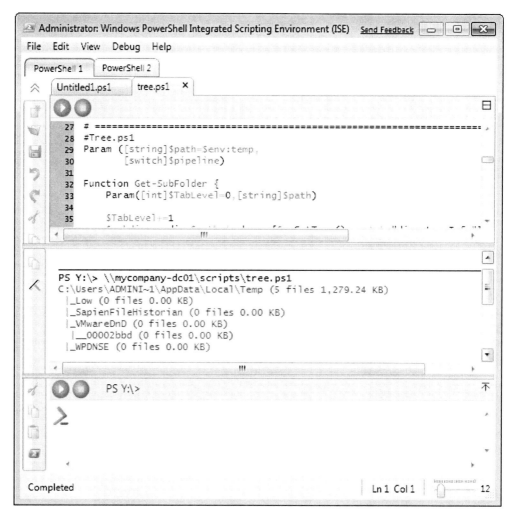

Figure 8-4: The ISE Script Editor.

The graphical shell is not intended to replace more full-featured commercial applications. However, it is a far superior choice to Windows Notepad for script editing, and it offers an enhanced environment for everyday, interactive shell use.

Out-GridView

Another graphical feature of PowerShell v2.0 is the new **Out-GridView** cmdlet. Although this is fully accessible from the text-based console, it works great with the graphical shell, since it offers a more graphical way of viewing table results. Simply pipe objects to **Out-GridView** to use it:

```
PS C:\> gsv | out-gridview
```

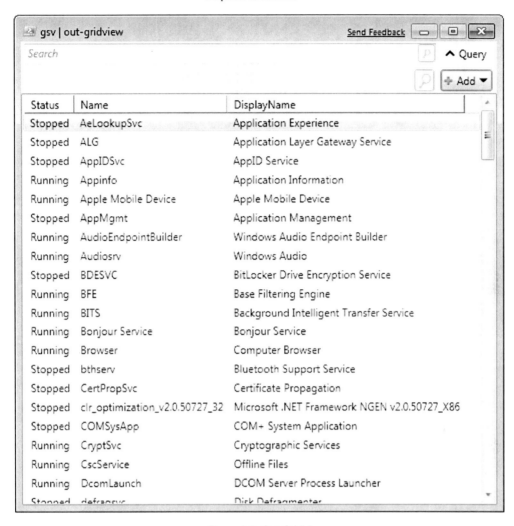

Figure 8-5: Out-GridView.

You can sort the resulting grid on any column by clicking the column header. You can also search for text strings within any column by simply typing your text at the top of the window and pressing Enter; non-matching rows are removed from the display.

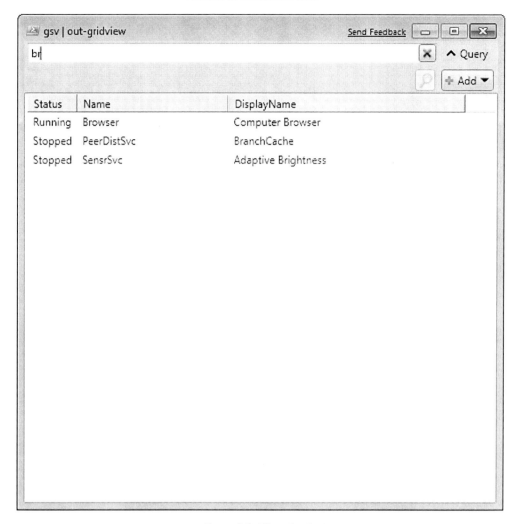

Figure 8-6: Filtered output.

You can also create a complex filter by clicking the Add Filter button. If you don't see it, click Query. Select the properties you want to filter on, click Add, and then modify the filter. You'll notice that the criteria "operator" is underlined. Click on it and select the criteria you would like to use. Add, delete, and edit criteria as needed. Click the magnifying glass icon to apply the filter.

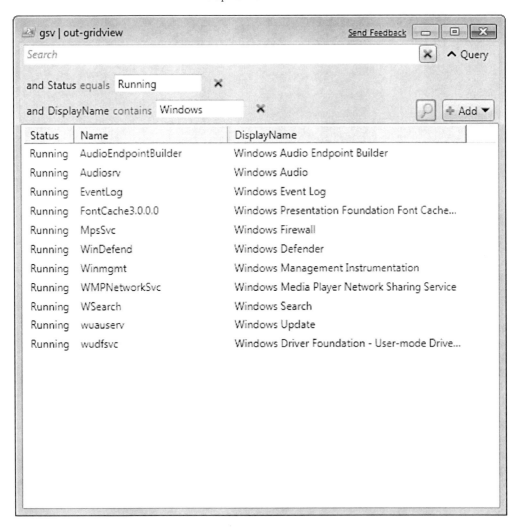

Figure 8-7: Multiple filtering.

You can restore the original, full results by clearing your search text and pressing Enter again or removing all the search criteria.

Out-GridView, which has an alias of **ogv**, is especially useful for reviewing larger result sets in a scrollable, resizable table. Keep in mind that the view is static; it does not continually update. To refresh the grid, you need to close the grid window and re-execute your original command.

Chapter 9
Background Jobs, Remote Jobs, and Remote Shell

In this chapter we'll cover a new set of techniques that Microsoft introduced in Windows PowerShell v2.0, all focused on running tasks in the background and on remote computers. Both provide the ability to run PowerShell commands and scripts in parallel in the background, while you continue to use the shell for other tasks.

Underlying Technology

Both of the features discussed in this chapter rely on WS-MAN, a remote management technology used for the first time in PowerShell v2.0. You need to install this component separately, and PowerShell's installer will actually prompt you to do so if you haven't already.

You also need to configure WS-MAN by running PowerShell *as an administrator* (on Windows Vista, Windows Server 2008, and later, you need to right-click PowerShell's icon and select Run As Administrator), and then running:

```
PS C:\> Set-WSMANQuickConfig
```

Failure to perform this important step will prevent the techniques shown in this chapter from working.

What's in a Name?

You'll also see WS-MAN referred to as WinRM, for Windows Remote Management. Technically, WS-MAN is an industry-standard set of protocols, and WinRM is Microsoft's implementation of WS-MAN for Windows.

By default, WS-MAN sets up on ports 80 and 443. It uses encryption for all traffic, but you do need to ensure that these ports will work. WS-MAN will also not operate on network connections designated as Public. You will see an error like this.

```
Set-WSManQuickConfig : WinRM firewall exception will not work since one of the network connection
types
on this machine is set to Public. Change the network connection type to either Domain or Private
and try again.At line:1 char:21
+ Set-WSManQuickConfig <<<<
    + CategoryInfo          : InvalidOperation: (:) [Set-WSManQuickConfig],
InvalidOperationException
    + FullyQualifiedErrorId : WsManError,Microsoft.WSMan.Management.SetWSManQuickConfigCommand
```

Both techniques discussed in this chapter have the ability to run PowerShell commands on remote computers. In order for this to work, the remote target computers must have both PowerShell v2.0 and WS-MAN installed and properly configured. Also note that, after installation, the WinRM service is not started automatically—you will need to start it in order to begin following along with this chapter.

Another key underlying technology is *object serialization*, the ability of the .NET Framework to create a text-based, XML-formatted representation of objects (a concept we discuss in our chapter on Serialization toward the end of this book). This technology allows objects created on a remote computer to be transmitted across the network as XML, and then reconstructed—or *deserialized*—on your computer, where you can work with them.

Background Jobs

Normally, when you execute a command or run a script in PowerShell, the shell remains unavailable while that execution completes. In other words, the shell is a single-task environment. However, in PowerShell v2.0 you have the ability to run tasks in the background. PowerShell refers to these background tasks as *jobs,* and while they run you have the ability to perform other tasks in the shell.

PowerShell provides six main cmdlets designed to work with jobs—or, as the shell calls them, *PSJobs*:

- **Start-Job** launches a new job.
- **Receive-Job** gets the results of a job into the current shell.
- **Stop-Job** terminates a job.
- **Wait-Job** waits until a job has completed.
- **Get-Job** retrieves a running job.
- **Remove-Job** deletes a job from the system.

PowerShell can start jobs either on the local computer or on a remote computer, which gives you extremely powerful management options.

Starting a Job

You start a job using the **Start-Job** cmdlet. You'll either specify a command, or the path and name of a script. The cmdlet cannot start jobs on remote computers—any job you create will run on the local computer, although the command run by the job may contact remote computers. Once started, you'll see the PowerShell prompt immediately, even though the job continues to run in the background.

In order to maintain separation between jobs and the "foreground" shell, background jobs are executed in their own *runspace*. Roughly, a *runspace* is an instance of the PowerShell engine. So, each background job essentially executes in its own "copy" of the shell. Background runspaces are usually temporary—meaning PowerShell creates them for the background job and they cease to exist when it completes.

At its simplest, you create a new job like this:

```
PS C:\> Start-Job -scriptblock {Get-Service}
Id           Name         State      HasMoreData    Location    Command
--           ----         -----      -----------    --------    -------
1            Job1         Running    True           localhost   get-service


PS C:\>
```

Once you create the background job, it's essentially on its own, meaning you won't see anything from it until you receive the results. For some jobs, that may be okay with you—perhaps you just want them to do something and then go away. If you need results from a job, you'll find it easier if you save the job itself in a variable, otherwise you will need to know the job ID when it comes time to get the results.

```
PS C:\> $job=start-job -scriptblock {get-service}
```

This will enable you to work with the job later via the **$job** variable.

Getting the Results of a Job

Assuming you started the job and saved it into a variable (we'll use **$job** in our examples), you can use the **Receive-Job** cmdlet to retrieve the results of a job into the current shell. This works even if the original job was started on a remote computer:

```
PS C:> Receive-Job -job $job
```

That's it! Whatever objects were produced by the job will be serialized into XML, and then made available via the **Receive-Job** cmdlet. If you need to store the objects in a variable, you can do so:

```
PS C:> $results = Receive-Job -job $job
```

Now if you were following along, when you tried to receive the results the second time you probably didn't get anything. When you receive the results, the job's data is cleared. **Receive-Job** has a handy –**Keep** parameter that instructs PowerShell not to clear out the results.

```
PS C:\> $job=start-job -ScriptBlock {get-process | where {$_.workingset -gt 10mb}}
PS C:\> Receive-Job -job $job -keep
```

```
Handles  NPM(K)    PM(K)     WS(K) VM(M)     CPU(s)     Id ProcessName
-------  ------    -----     ----- -----     ------     -- -----------
    138      11    14456     16580    54              1188 audiodg
    823      30    15812     20416   188   1,014.46    772 csrss
    837      72    97012     68364   340     342.30   1016 explorer
   1286     127   222016    209076   488     412.90   4540 firefox
    438      27    13220     11084   125      18.45   2588 MSASCui
    477      27    28324     34428   160      15.33   1344 mstsc
    204      23    46252     53996   553       6.07   3876 powershell
   1135      51   228412    239620   649      59.64   5996 powershell
    141      21    26044     14072   512       0.19   6120 PresentationFontCache
...
PS C:\
```

Now we can get the results from **$job** as often as necessary.

```
PS C:\> $results=receive-job -job $job -keep
PS C:\> $results.count
33
PS C:\>
```

Remember to always use **–keep** if you think you will want to access job results later. You can also pipe the results of a job to other cmdlets:

```
PS C:> Receive-Job –job $job -keep | Sort Workingset | Select –first 10| Format-Table
```

Waiting for a Job

For longer-running jobs, you may want to get the status of the job from time to time. The **Get-Job** cmdlet allows you to do so:

```
PS C:\> get-job

Id              Name            State         HasMoreData    Location    Command
--              ----            -----         -----------    --------    -------
1               Job1            Failed        False          localhost   get-service
```

Here, you can see that one job has failed. The job was attempting to run **Get-Service**. The "Name" column uses a default name because we didn't specify a name for the job when we created it; the **Start-Job** cmdlet accepts a **–name** parameter where you can specify a name for the job. You can also refer to the job by its ID, also shown in the output of **Get-Job**. For example, to make the current shell wait until job #1 finishes, you would run:

```
PS C:\> Wait-Job -id 1
```

The **Wait-Job** cmdlet can also refer to a job directly by passing a variable (like the **$job** variable we created earlier) by its name, or by its state. By default, the cmdlet will wait until the job completes; you can specify a **–timeout** parameter to have it stop waiting after a specified number of seconds.

Stopping a Job

The **Stop-Job** cmdlet immediately stops a background job. You should be careful when using this, especially if the job is performing sensitive or potentially dangerous operations, as **Stop-Job** doesn't wait for the job to be in any kind of "clean" state, nor does it perform any kind of "graceful" shutdown; it's essentially the same as killing the process using Task Manager. To use it, just refer to the job by providing a session ID number, a job variable, the job's name, or its state:

```
PS C:\> Stop-Job 1
```

You can even pipe an existing job to **Stop-Job**:

```
PS C:\> $job | Stop-Job
```

Or, to stop all jobs:

```
PS C:\> Get-Job | Stop-Job
```

Although **Stop-Job** stops the job from running, it does not remove it from the system. You can still use **Receive-Job** to receive the job's output (if it has produced any prior to being stopped). To completely remove the job from the system, use **Remove-Job**:

```
PS C:\> Remove-Job 1
```

Or perhaps you'd like to clean up all jobs.

```
PS C:\> get-job | remove-job
```

Get-Job has a **–state** parameter that comes in handy here to clean up all completed jobs.

```
PS C:\> get-job -state completed | remove-job
```

Troubleshooting Failed Jobs

Why do jobs fail? We're not talking about an error returned by your scriptblock but a failure for the job itself to run. The reasons are obviously highly variable, but you can find out. Let's start a new job:

```
PS C:\> $job=start-job -ScriptBlock {get-eventlog security -newest 100} -Credential chaos\lucky
PS C:\> get-job

Id            Name        State       HasMoreData       Location      Command
--            ----        -----       -----------       --------      -------
33            Job33       Failed      False             localhost     get-eventlog security ...
```

Our job seems to have failed. To find out why, we'll need to dig a bit into the job object. Each job object will have a collection of child jobs, and the child jobs in turn have a JobStateInfo property that we can check.

```
PS C:\> $job.ChildJobs[0].JobStateInfo.Reason
There is an error launching the background process. Error reported: Logon failure: user account
restriction. Possible reasons are blank passwords not allowed, logon hour restrictions, or a pol-
icy restriction has been enforced.
PS C:\>
```

Not as easy as maybe it could be but we can see that the job failed due to lack of permissions on the credentials we used to run the job.

Background Jobs — Walkthrough

Let's take a look at a successful start-to-finish background job.

We'll start by creating a job:

```
PS C:\> $job = start-job -name "services" -scriptblock {get-service}
```

Next, we'll watch the status of the job. We'll run **Get-Job** twice in succession to see our job go from "Running" to "Completed."

```
PS C:\> get-job
```

Id	Name	State	HasMoreData	Location	Command
--	----	-----	-----------	--------	-------
35	services	Running	True	localhost	get-service

```
PS C:\> get-job
```

Id	Name	State	HasMoreData	Location	Command
--	----	-----	-----------	--------	-------
35	services	Completed	True	localhost	get-service

Now let's get the results for the job (we'll truncate the results to save space):

```
PS C:\> $results = receive-job $job
PS C:\> $results
```

Status	Name	DisplayName
------	----	-----------
Stopped	Alerter	Alerter
Running	ALG	Application Layer Gateway Service
Stopped	AppMgmt	Application Management
Stopped	aspnet_state	ASP.NET State Service
Running	AudioSrv	Windows Audio
Running	BITS	Background Intelligent Transfer Ser...

Now that we're done, let's remove the job:

```
PS C:\> remove-job -name "services"
PS C:\> get-job
```

The last run of **Get-Job** returns no output, confirming that the job was removed. Of course, if you have been running other jobs you'll see those listed, but the "services" job is no longer listed.

Remember… They're *Background* Jobs

Background jobs run entirely in the background, meaning they have no opportunity for user interaction. You should therefore be very careful to not run scripts that contain the **Read-Host** cmdlet. If you do, the job will execute **Read-Host**, but you'll have no way to respond to it. The job will thus hang, forcing you to use **Stop-Job** to stop it.

You should also avoid the use of any **Write-*** cmdlets. While they won't hurt anything, they won't help, either, since there's nobody there to see them. The only exception is **Write-Output**, which you can use to write objects to the success pipeline—objects that become part of the job's output.

Remote Control

Remember, Start-Job can only create background jobs that run on the local computer. However, the job itself can contain commands that target remote computers. We'll look more at this concept of remote control later in this chapter.

Understanding PSSessions

The background job examples we've used so far all create a new runspace, more commonly referred to as a PSSession. When the job is removed, the PSSession is also removed. As we said before, a PSSession is essentially a copy of PowerShell, capable of running commands.

PowerShell has the ability to create new sessions, using the **New-PSSession** cmdlet. Simply running the cmdlet creates a new session on the local computer; you can also create new sessions on a remote computer. When you run **New-PSSession**, you'll specify parameters that define the connection to remote computers:

- **-computerName** accepts a single computer name or an array of computer names. If you specify an array, then one runspace will be created on each computer in the array.

- **-Credential** allows you to specify a user name (you'll be prompted for the password; there's no way to specify it on the command line), which will be used to create the runspace on each computer specified.

- **-Port** allows you to specify a remote port number, which will be used to communicate with WinRM. This defaults to port 80 or, if you specify SSL, to port 443.

- **-UseSSL** specifies that SSL be used for the remote connection. This is not used by default.

- **-ThrottleLimit** lets you specify the maximum number of remote connections in which this command can run concurrently. This defaults to 32, and is useful only if you provided an array of computer names to the **–computerName** parameter.

- **-useBasicAuthentication**. Normally, the cmdlet tells the operating system to use Kerberos (preferred) or NTLMv2 (if Kerberos isn't available) authentication; adding this parameter forces basic (clear-text) authentication.

For example, to connect to three computers and create sessions using the default connection parameters:

```
PS C:\> $sessions = New-PSSession –computer "server1","server2","server3"
```

Or, imagine you have a text file listing one computer name per line. You could connect to all of them like this:

```
PS C:\> $sessions = Get-Content c:\computers.txt | new-PSsession
```

It's important to capture the output into a variable—we've used **$sessions**—so that you have an easy way to refer to the sessions later. You can, of course, use the **Get-PSSession** cmdlet to retrieve previously created sessions; you can optionally specify a computer name to get just a session associated with the specified computer.

You should be aware that maintaining a session does require some local computer resources, as well as some resources on each remote computer you're connected to. This isn't a huge amount of resources, but you don't want to leave sessions sitting around unused for long periods of time. When you're done with a runspace, or a set of sessions, you can remove them by using the **Remove-PSSession** cmdlet:

```
PS C:\> $sessions | Remove-PSSession
```

You can of course see a list of active sessions using **Get-PSSession**, and even close them all at once:

```
PS C:\> Get-PSSession | Remove-PSSession
```

Once you've created a set of sessions, you can use them as the target for sending commands to remote computers—we'll get to that next.

PSSessions and Remote Management

One way to use sessions is with the **Invoke-Command** cmdlet. For example, if you've created a series of sessions and stored them in **$sessions**, you could run a command on each of them very easily:

```
PS C:\> Invoke-Command -scriptBlock { Get-Process } -session $sessions
```

The **Get-Process** command would immediately begin running on the specified sessions. By default, PowerShell throttles to no more than 32 connections, so if more than that are specified, some of them will simply wait until others have completed before beginning their execution. The idea behind this throttle is that you can specify hundred of computers, but control how many will actually run in parallel (the throttle value), thus helping to control network utilization and local computing overhead.

Using **Invoke-Command** submits commands synchronously, meaning you'll have to wait for the command to complete on every session specified before you can do anything else in the shell. However, you can have **Invoke-Command** start a new background job, and then have the job run the specified command on the specified sessions:

```
PS C:\> Invoke-Command -scriptBlock { Get-Process } -session $sessions -AsJob
```

This creates a new PSJob, which you can manage like any other job, as we discussed earlier in this chapter.

Invoke-Command isn't just used to target sessions. If you haven't created sessions, you can specify a single computer name, or an array of computer names, as the target for a command:

```
PS C:\> Invoke-Command -scriptBlock { Get-Process } -computerName "localhost"
```

Or, for several computers:

```
PS C:\> $computers = "server1","server2","server3"
PS C:\> Invoke-Command -script { Get-Process } -computer $computers
```

Of course, you can use the **–AsJob** parameter to start a background job to execute the command, too:

```
PS C:\> $computers = "server1","server2","server3"
PS C:\> Invoke-Command -script { Get-Process } -computer $computers -asjob
```

Something to keep in mind: The script block passed to **Invoke-Command** can contain as complex a script or set of commands as you like. It can also execute a script—although there, you have to be careful: The script must be accessible to each computer that is asked to run it. **Invoke-Command** won't take care of copying the script to the remote computers; you have to do that up front.

Invoke-Command supports a number of additional parameters that govern how it connects to remote computers:

- **-Credential** allows you to specify a user name (you'll be prompted for the password; there's no way to specify it on the command-line), which will be used to create the runspace on each computer specified.

- **-Port** allows you to specify a remote port number, which will be used to communicate with WinRM. This defaults to port 80 or, if you specify SSL, to port 443.

- **-UseSSL** specifies that SSL be used for the remote connection. This is not used by default.

- **-ThrottleLimit** lets you specify the maximum number of remote connections in which this command can run concurrently. This defaults to 32, and is useful only if you provided an array of computer names to the **–computerName** parameter.

You'll notice that these are the same as the parameters used with **New-PSSession**; these parameters are valid if you're specifying computer names (using **–computerName**); they're not valid if you're using the **–session** parameter, because in that case the sessions themselves already have the connection information they need.

....

Invoke-Expression?

You may notice that the Invoke-Expression cmdlet looks remarkably similar to Invoke-Command. Which do you use? Simple: Use Invoke-Expression only for local commands, not for remote commands, and not to start jobs. Invoke-Command is the long-term direction, so get used to using it instead of Invoke-Expression.

You can also use a PSSession interactively, similar to the Secure Shell (SSH) technology used on many *nix operating systems. Assuming **$sessions** contains several PSSessions, you can interactively connect to the first one like this:

```
PS C:\> enter-pssession $sessions[0]
[win2008r2]: PS C:\Users\DonJ\Documents>
```

You'll notice that the normal PowerShell prompt changes, reminding you that you're now commanding a remote PowerShell instance. Everything you type is transmitted to the remote computer for execution, and results are transmitted back to your local copy of PowerShell for display. When you're done working with the remote computer, run **Exit-PSSession** to return to your local shell.

Working with Results from Multiple Remote Computers

It's probably easy to see how you work with the results from a *single* remote computer. For example:

```
PS C:\> Invoke-Command -scriptblock {dir} -computername "win2k801"
```

The output you see is the same as if you just ran **Dir** yourself, except that the results are from a different computer:

```
Directory: C:\Users\administrator.MYCOMPANY\Documents


Mode                LastWriteTime     Length Name                         PSComputerName
----                -------------     ------ ----                         --------------
d----        4/10/2009   10:22 AM            Projects                     win2k801
d----        1/26/2009    1:40 PM            SAPIEN                       win2k801
d----        1/26/2009    1:36 PM            Scripts                      win2k801
d----        4/10/2009   10:22 AM            WindowsPowerShell            win2k801
-a---        2/16/2009   11:13 AM        80  computers.txt                win2k801
-a---        2/16/2009   12:21 PM      14993 ComputerStatusForm.ps1       win2k801
-a---         4/9/2009    4:34 PM     421658 ise01.tif                    win2k801
-a---         4/9/2009    4:41 PM     214050 ise02.tif                    win2k801
-a---         4/9/2009    4:42 PM     214050 ise03.tif                    win2k801
-a---         4/9/2009    4:48 PM     373188 ise04.tif                    win2k801
-a---        2/18/2009   11:36 AM      18470 PerformancePeeker.ps1        win2k801
-a---       12/23/2008    9:39 AM    1806226 Windows6.0-KB950099-x86.msu  win2k801

PS C:\>
```

Notice something, though: This directory is from a particular directory, not the C:\ drive. That's because our command was just **Dir**, and we didn't specify a directory, so we got a directory listing for whatever directory the remote shell defaulted to—which, normally, will be your user profile root folder.

Running this same command against multiple computers will produce output grouped by computer-name. In fact if you have output from multiple remote computers, you easily retrieve information for a specific computer. Again, suppose we have an **Invoke-Command** expression to run a command on multiple computers.

```
PS C:\> invoke-command -ScriptBlock {get-eventlog system -newest 10} -ComputerName $computers
-asjob

Id     Name     State    HasMoreData   Location          Command
--     ----     -----    -----------   --------          -------
16     Job16    Running  True          win2k801,testdesk01  get-eventlog system -n
```

Once the job is finished we'll save the results.

```
PS C:\> $results=receive-job 16 -keep
```

To retrieve results from a single computer, we'll simply filter **$results**.

```
PS C:\> $results | where {$_.pscomputername -match "win2k801"}

Index Time           EntryType   Source           InstanceID Message              PSCompu
----- ----           ---------   ------           ---------- -------              -------
19691 Apr 10 10:21   Information Service Control M... 1073748860 The description for Ev... win2k80
19690 Apr 10 10:21   Information DCOM              3221235501 The description for Ev... win2k80
19689 Apr 10 09:31   Information Service Control M... 1073748860 The description for Ev... win2k80
19688 Apr 10 09:21   Information Service Control M... 1073748860 The description for Ev... win2k80
19687 Apr 10 08:31   Information Service Control M... 1073748860 The description for Ev... win2k80
19686 Apr 10 08:21   Information Service Control M... 1073748860 The description for Ev... win2k80
19685 Apr 10 07:31   Information Service Control M... 1073748860 The description for Ev... win2k80
19684 Apr 10 07:21   Information Service Control M... 1073748860 The description for Ev... win2k80
```

```
19683 Apr 10 06:31 Information Service Control M... 1073748860 The description for Ev... win2k80
19682 Apr 10 06:21 Information Service Control M... 1073748860 The description for Ev... win2k80
```

So that's an overview of how to work with the output produced by running a command on multiple remote computers.

Computer Names vs. PSSessions: Which Do You Use?

Invoke-Command allows you to specify sessions, or you can specify remote computer names, port numbers, throttles, and so forth; why would you do this instead of creating sessions, and then passing those sessions to the cmdlet?

Simple: Re-use. If you plan to run only a single command on a set of computers, then it's often easiest just to specify the computer name and other connection parameters. If you want to run multiple commands throughout the day, it's easier to create a new session first. The session remembers all of your connection preferences, so you can send multiple commands to the remote computers without having to re-specify port numbers and other options each time.

Useful PSSession Tricks

Remember that you can open multiple sessions to a single computer, which allows you—or other administrators—to execute commands in parallel.

Also, if you've painstakingly created a large set of sessions to frequently-managed computers, you can persist them in an external XML file:

```
PS C:\> Get-PSSession | Export-CliXML c:\mysessions.xml
```

When you're ready to re-create those sessions, just import them:

```
PS C:\> Import-CliXML c:\mysessions.xml | New-PSSession
```

You'll doubtless pick up other tricks as you go. We're certain that you'll find PowerShell's background jobs, sessions, and most of all, remote management capabilities to be a significant tool in your administrative tool belt.

Chapter 10
PowerShell Command-line Parsing

In an attempt to be all things to all people, and to maintain backward compatibility with external executables and the way Cmd.exe worked, PowerShell has a rather complex command-line parser. A *parser* is a piece of software that takes the entire command line you've entered, breaks it down, and tries to figure out what you want PowerShell to do. For example, PowerShell's parser looks for spaces as command delimiters, uses hyphens to indicate cmdlet parameters, and uses other standards. Knowing what the parser is doing under the hood can provide some useful insight into why certain commands don't seem to work as expected, and can give you an idea of how to work around any oddities you come across.

Parsing would be simple if it weren't for us humans. For example, nobody wants to type **cd** "\" to change to the root of their hard drive—we just want to type **cd** \. Yet \ is clearly a string (well, a character, in any event), and not a number, and in programming languages, strings are usually enclosed in quotation marks. So, there's a lot of complex stuff under the hood in PowerShell, working to figure out what the heck you mean every time you hit Enter. Fortunately, the eggheads at Microsoft had to write all that complex stuff; you just need to know how it affects you. String handling is a major part of the parser's complexity. The other major part is that the parser can actually operate in one of two distinct modes.

Quotation Marks

Quotation marks are usually used to set off a string of characters that should be treated *just* as a string of characters and not as part of a command or other keyword. For example, consider this:

```
PS C:\> write-host "Hello" -fore cyan
Hello
```

You can't see it, but "Hello" is displayed in the color cyan. You'll have to trust us, because even printing this one page in color would have doubled the price of this book. But that command is very different from:

```
PS C:\> write-host "Hello -fore cyan"
Hello -fore cyan
```

See, the quotation marks are telling PowerShell that "-fore cyan" isn't intended to be a parameter. It's just a string of characters, so PowerShell shouldn't try to interpret it as a command.

PowerShell actually treats single and double quotation marks somewhat differently. Double quotation marks are still subject to a quick review by the parser, to see if any variables are lurking in there. Any variables that PowerShell finds are replaced with their contents. Watch:

```
PS C:\> $hello = "Greeting"
PS C:\> Write-host "What a $hello"
What a Greeting
PS C:\> Write-host 'What a $hello'
What a $hello
```

See the difference between the two? Because PowerShell always looks for spaces to separate different keywords, any string that contains an embedded space needs to be enclosed in *some* kind of quotation mark:

```
PS C:\> cd \program files
Set-Location : A parameter cannot be found that matches parameter name 'files'.
At line:1 char:3
+ cd <<<< \program files
PS C:\> cd "\program files"
PS C:\Program Files>
```

The first command failed, because PowerShell thought "files" was supposed to be a separate parameter, and it couldn't find one named "files," so it got upset. By enclosing everything in quotation marks, we told PowerShell to treat the entire string as a single parameter—the folder we wanted to change to.

PowerShell does support a weird alternative when you only need to quote *one* character, like the space between "Program" and "Files":

```
PS C:\> cd \program' files
PS C:\Program Files>
```

The *backtick*, or *backquote*, is PowerShell's escape character. By "escaping" the space, we're telling PowerShell that the space isn't really a space; it's to be treated literally, as part of a string, not as a keyword separator. But, honestly, that way just looks too strange, and only saves you one keystroke. But that escaping trick works well elsewhere, too. Consider this:

```
PS C:\Program Files> $saying = "Peace"
PS C:\Program Files> write-host "say $saying"
say Peace
PS C:\Program Files> write-host "say '$saying"
say $saying
```

In the second example, by "escaping" the dollar sign, we forced PowerShell to treat it as a literal dollar sign, not as the beginning of a variable name. This prevents PowerShell from "expanding" the variable, even though we used double quotes.

Parsing Modes

PowerShell's parser supports two distinct parsing modes: *Expression mode* and *command mode*. In expression mode, strings must be quoted, numbers aren't quoted, and so forth. In command mode, numbers are still numbers, but anything else is treated as a string unless it starts with $, @, ', ", or (. These are all special characters that denote the start of a variable, array, string, or sub-expression.

Expression mode is active whenever you *don't* type a PowerShell cmdlet name or alias at the start of a line. For example:

```
PS C:\> 2 + 2
4
```

That's expression mode. Command mode kicks in when you *do* start off with a PowerShell cmdlet or alias:

```
PS C:\> Write-Host 2+2
2+2
```

Different output in this case, because you're in command mode and that "+" forces PowerShell to treat "2+2" as a string, and not a number. However, remember that "(" at the start of a string forces expression mode for it:

```
PS C:\> write-host (2+2)
4
```

By forcing into expression mode, "2+2" is evaluated as an expression rather than a string, and you get the output you were probably expecting. The differences between these modes can be subtle, but by remembering these basic rules you'll usually be able to keep yourself out of trouble.

Line Termination

PowerShell needs to know when you've reached the end of a line, so that it can process what you've given it. When you've typed a complete command, a carriage return (technically, a "newline" character) indicates the end of the line. So, if you type something like this, you get a result:

```
PS C:\> write-host "2+2"
2+2
```

However, if you type something that's not *complete*, PowerShell treats the new line character as another form of whitespace, like a tab or space character. At the command line, you'll get a special prompt, telling you that PowerShell is waiting for you to finish:

```
PS C:\> write-host "2+2
>> "
>>
2+2
```

Here, we left off the closing quotation mark, and so PowerShell figured we weren't done yet. It prompted us, and we completed the quotation mark, and hit Enter again to complete the command and display the result. If you purposely want to break a long line and use the nested >> prompt, use the back-tick character at the end of your line:

```
PS C:\ > get-wmiobject win32_computersystem | select-object Caption,Name,Manufacturer, '
>> model | format-list
>>
```

The semicolon is also an "end of line" character. By using it, you can put two logical lines onto a single physical line:

```
PS C:\> 2+2 ; 4+4
4
8
```

Understanding PowerShell's line termination rules can help keep you out of trouble, and help you understand what's going on when you get that strange ">>" prompt.

Chapter 11
Working with the PowerShell Host

Whenever we're using Windows PowerShell interactively, we're working with what's called the *PowerShell hosting application,* or just *PowerShell host.* As we explained in the Architecture and Overview chapter, PowerShell's engine can be *hosted* by many different applications, such as Exchange Server 2007's management GUI, applications like SAPIEN PrimalScript, and more. When using the PowerShell.exe console host, the special variable **$host** provides access to some of this host's unique capabilities.

It is important that you understand the **$host** will vary depending on which application is hosting PowerShell. For many of you, the PowerShell that you downloaded from Microsoft may be the only host you ever work with. To illustrate the concept of different hosts, look at the different values you get for each host. Here is **$host** from a PowerShell session running on Windows Vista:

```
PS C:\ > $host

Name            : ConsoleHost
Version         : 2.0
InstanceId      : 50000e47-cff8-4f72-9239-51831033f89b
UI              : System.Management.Automation.Internal.Host.InternalHostUserInterface
CurrentCulture  : en-US
CurrentUICulture : en-US
PrivateData     : Microsoft.PowerShell.ConsoleHost+ConsoleColorProxy
IsRunspacePushed : False
Runspace        : System.Management.Automation.Runspaces.LocalRunspace
```

We've mentioned that PrimalScript can host PowerShell. Here is the information for that host:

```
Name             : PrimalScriptHostImplementation
Version          : 1.0.0.0
InstanceId       : a92c8ed4-d243-4302-b144-0fe0f677ccb5
UI               : System.Management.Automation.Internal.Host.InternalHostUserInterface
CurrentCulture   : en-US
CurrentUICulture : en-US
PrivateData      :
IsRunspacePushed :
Runspace         :
```

Finally, here is **$host** from Exchange 2007:

```
Name             : ConsoleHost
Version          : 1.0.0.0
InstanceId       : efd45da6-65a4-45ae-b221-ae3317c2b402
UI               : System.Management.Automation.Internal.Host.InternalHostUserInterface
CurrentCulture   : en-US
CurrentUICulture : en-US
PrivateData      : Microsoft.PowerShell.ConsoleHost+ConsoleColorProxy
```

For the most part, these hosts have identical functionality, but that's not to say that some other future host might have additional functionality. One way to check what your host can do is to pipe **$host** to **Get-Member**:

```
PS C:\ > $host | get-member


    TypeName: System.Management.Automation.Internal.Host.InternalHost

Name                   MemberType Definition
----                   ---------- ----------
EnterNestedPrompt      Method     System.Void EnterNestedPrompt()
Equals                 Method     bool Equals(System.Object obj)
ExitNestedPrompt       Method     System.Void ExitNestedPrompt()
GetHashCode            Method     int GetHashCode()
GetType                Method     type GetType()
NotifyBeginApplication Method     System.Void NotifyBeginApplication()
NotifyEndApplication   Method     System.Void NotifyEndApplication()
PopRunspace            Method     System.Void PopRunspace()
PushRunspace           Method     System.Void PushRunspace(runspace runspace)
SetShouldExit          Method     System.Void SetShouldExit(int exitCode)
ToString               Method     string ToString()
CurrentCulture         Property   System.Globalization.CultureInfo CurrentCulture {get;}
CurrentUICulture       Property   System.Globalization.CultureInfo CurrentUICulture {get;}
InstanceId             Property   System.Guid InstanceId {get;}
IsRunspacePushed       Property   System.Boolean IsRunspacePushed {get;}
Name                   Property   System.String Name {get;}
PrivateData            Property   System.Management.Automation.PSObject PrivateData {get;}
Runspace               Property   System.Management.Automation.Runspaces.Runspace Runspace {get;}
UI                     Property   System.Management.Automation.Host.PSHostUserInterface UI {get;}
Version                Property   System.Version Version {get;}
```

You see most of the properties when you invoke **$host**. But what else is there?

Culture Clash

Given that Windows is an international platform, it should come as no surprise that different versions have different regional and language settings. In PowerShell, this is referred to as the Culture, which is a property of **$host**:

```
PS C:\ > $host.currentculture

LCID          Name           DisplayName
----          ----           -----------
1033          en-US          English (United States)
```

You get the same result if you use the **Get-Culture** cmdlet. However, there may be situations where you need to execute a command or expression in another culture setting. Usually, the situation is with non-US users who are running a command or application that fails to execute properly unless they use the EN-US culture. Even though PowerShell has a cmdlet to get the current culture, there are no cmdlets for changing it system wide, which isn't very practical anyway. Culture settings are thread level. But what if you really, really had to change the culture setting temporarily? The PowerShell team at Microsoft posted a function a while ago on their blog. The entry was based on pre-release code so we've updated it a bit:

```
Function Using-Culture {
 Param (
[System.Globalization.CultureInfo]$culture = $(throw "USAGE: Using-Culture -Culture culture
-Script {scriptblock}"),
[String]$script=$(throw "USAGE: Using-Culture -Culture culture -Script {scriptblock}")
)
    $OldCulture = [System.Threading.Thread]::CurrentThread.CurrentCulture
    trap
    {
        [System.Threading.Thread]::CurrentThread.CurrentCulture = $OldCulture
    }
    [System.Threading.Thread]::CurrentThread.CurrentCulture = $culture
    Invoke-Expression $script
    [System.Threading.Thread]::CurrentThread.CurrentCulture = $OldCulture
}
```

Using this function, you can execute any expression or command under the guise of a different culture:

```
PS C:\ > using-culture en-GB {get-date}

10 August 2009 10:54:25
```

The function executes **Get-Date** using the British culture settings, which have a different date format than the United States settings.

Using the UI and RawUI

The **$host** object also gives you access to the underlying user interface (UI). You shouldn't need to access these properties and methods often. There are cmdlets for much of the functionality you are likely to need. Still, there may be situations where you'd like to tweak the PowerShell window or take advantage of a feature that doesn't have a ready cmdlet.

Reading Lines and Keys

The best way to get user input is by using the **Read-Host** cmdlet:

```
PS C:\ > $name=Read-Host "What is your name?"
What is your name?: Jon
PS C:\ > $name
Jon
```

You can use the **ReadLine()** method from $host.ui, but it's a little primitive:

```
PS C:\ > write-host "What is your name?";$name=$host.ui.Readline()
What is your name?
Jon
PS C:\ > $name
Jon
```

The **ReadLine()** method has no provision for a prompt like **Read-Host**, so we used **Write-Host** to display something. The **ReadLine()** method simply waits for the user to type a line and press Enter. Off hand, we can't think of a situation where this would be preferable to using **Read-Host**. But there is another **$host** method that you might find helpful for which there is no PowerShell cmdlet.

The $host.ui.rawui object has a method called **ReadKey()** that works like the **ReadLine()** method, except it only accepts a single key:

```
PS C:\ > $host.ui.rawui.readkey()
y
         VirtualKeyCode            Character        ControlKeyState        KeyDown
         --------------            ---------        ---------------        -------
                     89                    y              NumLockOn           True
PS C:\ >
```

After typing the command, PowerShell will wait for you to press any key. When you do it displays the key. You can fine tune this method by specifying some **ReadKey()** options. You'll likely not need to echo the typed character so we can specify that option along with a few others.

```
PS C:\ > $host.ui.rawui.readkey("NoEcho,IncludeKeyUp,IncludeKeyDown")
```

You should use either IncludeKeyUp or IncludeKeyDown, or both. We always use both. To use this method in a script or function, you'll also need to include the *KeyAvailable* property. This is a Boolean value that indicates whether a keystroke is waiting in the keyboard input buffer.

```
$ESCkey = 27
Write-Host "Press the ESC key to continue"

$Running=$True

while ($Running) {
 if ($host.ui.RawUi.KeyAvailable)
 { $key = $host.ui.RawUI.ReadKey("NoEcho,IncludeKeyUp,IncludeKeyDown")
  if ($key.VirtualKeyCode -eq $ESCkey)
 {
   $Running=$False
 }
 }
}
```

In this code example, we use a While loop that runs until the value of **$Running** is changed to **$False**. The outer If statement checks to see if a key is in the buffer:

```
if ($host.ui.RawUi.KeyAvailable)
```

If so, then the code uses the **ReadKey()** method:

```
{ $key = $host.ui.RawUI.ReadKey("NoEcho,IncludeKeyUp,IncludeKeyDown")
```

If the value of the entered key is 27, which is the key value of the ESC key, then **$Running** is set to **$False** and the next time through the While loop, the code will exit the loop.

Changing the Window Title

You can access the title of your Windows PowerShell window very easily by accessing the *WindowTitle* property:

```
PS C:\ > $host.ui.rawui.WindowTitle
Windows PowerShell
```

You can just as easily change the window title. Here's an example:

Create-ServerReport.ps1

```
function Set-Title {
  Param ([string]$NewTitle)
  $host.ui.rawui.WindowTitle=$NewTitle
}

Set-Alias title Set-Title

function Save-Title {
  $script:SavedTitle=$host.ui.rawui.WindowTitle
}

#call the Save-Title function
Save-Title
$report="report.txt"

#write a line to the report
"REPORT CREATED $(get-date)" | Out-File $report

Get-Content servers.txt | foreach {
#skip blank lines
 if (($_).length -gt 0)
 {
    #create a new variable to make things easier to read and
    #trim off any extra spaces. Make the name upper case
    #while we're at it.
    $server=($_.Trim()).ToUpper()

    $newtitle="Checking $server"
    #set a new title
    title $newtitle

    $server  | Out-File $report -append

    "Operating System" | Out-File $report -append
    Get-WmiObject win32_operatingsystem -computer $server | Out-File $report -append

    "ComputerSystem" | Out-File $report -append
```

```
    Get-WmiObject win32_computersystem -computer $server | Out-File $report -append

    #pause for a few seconds just to show title in action
    #not really required.
    sleep 2
 } #end If
} #end foreach

#revert back to old title
Title $script:savedtitle

#view report
Notepad $report
```

This script processes a list of servers, gets information about each server from WMI and saves the results to a text file. Since this script could run for a long time, we modify the title to reflect what server the script is working on. You can then minimize your PowerShell window yet still be able to monitor the script's progress.

The script defines functions to set the window title as well as save the current one. We also define an alias, or Title, for the Set-Title function. Thus as each server is processed from the list, the window title is changed to reflect the current server:

```
 $newtitle="Checking $server"
    title $newtitle
```

At the end of the script we change the title back to the saved, original window title:

```
Title $script:savedtitle
```

Changing Colors

We can also modify the color settings of PowerShell windows. First, let's look at the current settings:

```
PS C:\ > $host.ui.rawui


ForegroundColor       : DarkYellow
BackgroundColor       : DarkMagenta
CursorPosition        : 0,2999
WindowPosition        : 0,2950
CursorSize            : 25
BufferSize            : 120,3000
WindowSize            : 120,50
MaxWindowSize         : 120,81
MaxPhysicalWindowSize : 160,81
KeyAvailable          : False
WindowTitle           : Windows PowerShell
```

You might prefer something like this:

```
PS C:\ > $host.ui.rawui.backgroundcolor="green"
PS C:\ > $host.ui.rawui.foregroundcolor="black"
```

These changes last only for as long as your PowerShell session is running. If you want a more permanent change, then you will need to add lines like these to your profile script.

Changing Window Size and Buffer

The raw UI also lets you control position and size of your PowerShell windows. To see the current size, you can use this expression:

```
PS C:\ > $host.ui.rawui.Windowsize | format-list


Width  : 120
Height : 50
```

The WindowSize cannot be larger than the value of MaxPhysicalWindowSize. To simplify changing the console window size, you can use this function:

```
Function Set-WindowSize {
   Param([int]$width=$host.ui.rawui.windowsize.width,
         [int]$height=$host.ui.rawui.windowsize.height)

   $size=New-Object System.Management.Automation.Host.Size($width,$height)

   $host.ui.rawui.WindowSize=$size

}
```

Once you've loaded the function, you can use the **Set-WindowSize** command to dynamically change your console window to 60 columns wide by 30 rows high:

```
PS C:\> Set-windowsize 60 30.
```

If you don't specify a width or height value, the function will use the value of the current window size. We can take a similar approach to the console's buffer.

The buffer controls how much of the window can be scrolled either vertically or horizontally. Setting a large vertical buffer lets you see more output from previous commands. If you have a script that will produce a lot of information, you may want to modify the buffer size so you can scroll up to see it all. Here's a function that might help:

```
Function Set-WindowBuffer {
  Param([int]$width=$host.ui.rawui.BufferSize.width,
        [int]$height=$host.ui.rawui.BufferSize.height)

   $buffer=New-Object System.Management.Automation.Host.Size($width,$height)

   $host.ui.rawui.Buffersize=$buffer

}
```

You cannot set a buffer size that is less than the window size. But if your current window and buffer size is 120 x 50, and you run this command:

```
PS C:\ > set-windowbuffer 120 500
```

You'll see a vertical scroll bar appear in your PowerShell window. Now you'll be able to scroll back to see more of your previous commands and output.

Nested Prompts

One of the most interesting features about the console host is its *nested prompts*. This is a bit difficult to see in action, so let's walk through an example. Be *very* careful if you're following along! One wrong keystroke could crash your computer.

First, open several instances of Windows Notepad. Then, in PowerShell, run this:

```
PS C:\> get-process notepad | stop-process -confirm
```

You should see something like this:

```
Confirm
Are you sure you want to perform this action?
Performing operation "Stop-Process" on Target "notepad (2072)".
[Y] Yes [A] Yes to All [N] No [L] No to All [S] Suspend [?] Help (default is "Y"):
```

If you hit **S**, you'll suspend the pipeline operation and enter a *nested prompt*. Your original command is still pending, but you've sort of entered a side conversation with Windows PowerShell. In it, you can do whatever you want—check variables, run cmdlets, and so forth. By default, the PowerShell prompt reflects this nested state:

```
PS C:\>>>
```

Typing **Exit** ends the nested prompt and takes you back up one level:

```
PS C:\>>> exit

Confirm
Are you sure you want to perform this action?
Performing operation "Stop-Process" on Target "notepad (2072)".
[Y] Yes [A] Yes to All [N] No [L] No to All [S] Suspend [?] Help (default is "Y"):
```

Here, you'll see your original command still in action. Select **L** to abort. You can manually create a new nested prompt by running **$host.EnterNestedPrompt()**. There's not much use in this from the command line, perhaps, but when you're writing a script you can have a new prompt created for certain conditions, such as an error occurring. The nested prompt runs "inside" the script, so it'll have access to all the variables and so forth within a script. Again, running **Exit** ends the nested prompt, and would return to your script.

Note that you can't have more than 128 nested prompts (we can't imagine why you'd need even that many, to be honest). A built-in variable, **$NestedPromptLevel**, tells you how deeply you're already nested, and you can check it to see if it's safe to launch a new nested prompt.

By the Way...
Instead of running Exit, you can also run $host.ExitNestedPrompt() to exit a nested prompt.

Quitting PowerShell

Of course, running **Exit** from a non-nested prompt will exit the shell. But you can also run **$host. SetShouldExit(xxx)** to exit the shell, passing a number for *xxx*. This number will be returned as an error code to the Windows environment. This could be useful if running a PowerShell script wrapped up in a batch file or VBScript.

Prompting the User to Make a Choice

The **$host** interface provides some access to PowerShell's underlying user interface capabilities. For example, suppose you want to provide a simple "Yes or No" text prompt. First, you would need to construct the prompt in an array like the one below (we'll discuss arrays in the chapter "Variables, Arrays and Escape Characters".):

```
PS C:\> $no = ([System.Management.Automation.Host.ChoiceDescription]"&No")
PS C:\> $no.helpmessage = "Do not continue"
PS C:\> $yes = ([System.Management.Automation.Host.ChoiceDescription]"&Yes")
PS C:\> $yes.helpmessage = "Continue"
PS C:\> $prompts = ($yes,$no)
```

What we've done is created two new prompts. Use the & character before whichever letter will be the "answer" for that prompt. In other words, in our example, you'd press "N" for "No" and "Y" for "Yes." We also specified a "help message" for each prompt, and then assembled them into an array in the **$prompts** variable. Next, you ask the host to display the prompt:

```
PS C:\> $host.ui.promptforchoice("Continue?","Do you want to continue?",'
>> [System.Management.Automation.Host.ChoiceDescription[]]$prompts,0)
>>

Continue?
Do you want to continue?
[Y] Yes [N] No [?] Help (default is "Y"):
```

Notice that the prompt does not display our "help message" text—that's only displayed if you select? from the prompt. Also, as you can see, you can provide a title, a description, and then your array of choices. Those choices have to be of a specific .NET Framework type, System.Management. Automation.Host.ChoiceDescription, which is why you see that long class name enclosed in square brackets above. The **PromptForChoice()** method will return whatever choice the user made. This is perhaps best wrapped up into a reusable function. Here's a sample script.

Set-ChoicePrompt.ps1

```
Function Set-ChoicePrompt  {
    Param ([string]$caption="Continue?",
          [string]$message="What do you want to do?",
          [System.Management.Automation.Host.ChoiceDescription[]]$choices,
          [int]$default=0)
```

```
        $host.ui.promptforchoice($caption,$message,$choices,$default)
}

#define some variables
$caption="Continue with this operation?"
$message="This is serious stuff. Is your resume up to date? Do you want to continue?"
$yes = ([System.Management.Automation.Host.ChoiceDescription]"&Yes")
$yes.helpmessage = "Continue, I am ready."

$no = ([System.Management.Automation.Host.ChoiceDescription]"&No")
$no.helpmessage = "Do not continue. Get me out of here."
$choices = ($yes,$no)

#show the prompt and set the default to No
[int]$r=Set-ChoicePrompt -caption $caption -message $message -choices $choices -default 1

if ($r -eq 0)
{
    Write-Host "Good Luck" -foregroundcolor Green
}
else
{
    Write-Host "Aborting the mission" -foregroundcolor Yellow
}
```

The script has a relatively simple function to create the choice prompt. All you have to do is assign the values for all the necessary components. In the body of the sample script we've set some of these values and invoked the function. The value returned by the prompt is the index number of the choice. We're setting the default to the prompt with an index value of 1, or the No option. In the script the user is prompted and their choice saved in the variable, **$r**.

```
[int]$r=Set-ChoicePrompt -caption $caption -message $message -choices $choices -default 1
```

Using an If statement to evaluate the value, the script takes appropriate action depending on the choice.

```
PS C:\> .\Set-ChoicePrompt.ps1

Continue with this operation?
This is serious stuff. Is your resume up to date? Do you want to continue?
[Y] Yes  [N] No  [?] Help (default is "N"): n
Aborting the mission
PS C:\>
```

Chapter 12
Security Features

PowerShell has some interesting challenges to meet in terms of security. The last time Microsoft produced a scripting shell, it produced the Windows Script Host (WSH that is commonly used to run VBScript scripts). When WSH was produced, security wasn't much of a concern, which meant that VBScript probably became one of the biggest attack points within Windows. As a result, it was used to write and execute a number of viruses and other malicious attacks. Microsoft certainly didn't want to repeat that with PowerShell, and so a number of security features have been built-in.

Why Won't My Scripts Run?

The first thing you may notice is that files having a .ps1 filename extension don't do anything automatically when double-clicked. The PowerShell window might not even open, since by default the .ps1 filename extension is associated with Notepad! But even if you manually open PowerShell and type a script name, it doesn't run. What good is PowerShell if it can't run scripts?

When Scripts Don't Run

There are two reasons why a PowerShell script might not run. The first is the script's location. PowerShell won't run scripts that are located in the current directory—it's as if it simply can't see them. For example, we created a script named Test.ps1 in a folder named C:\Test. With PowerShell set to that folder, we type the script name—it isn't found:

```
PS C:\test> test
The term 'test' is not recognized as a Cmdlet, function, operable program, or script file.
Verify the term and try again.
At line:1 char:4
+ test <<<<
PS C:\test>
```

This is a security precaution to help prevent a malicious script from intercepting cmdlet and command names and then running. In other words, if we named our script Dir.ps1, it still wouldn't run—the **Dir** command would run instead. So, the only way to run a script is to explicitly refer to that folder:

```
PS C:\test> cd ..
PS C:\> test\test
Ok
PS C:\>
```

By moving up to the C:\ folder on the first line, we are able to run the script by referring to its folder (test) and filename (test, or test\test for the complete relative path).

Actually, you *can* have PowerShell execute scripts in the same directory if you *specify* the directory. For example, running **.\test.ps1** will run the Test.ps1 script in the current directory, which is specified by the .\ part. However, by specifying a directory you're eliminating the possibility of your script being confused for a command or cmdlet, which makes it safer.

The second reason is the most likely reason your script won't run—the execution policy. For security purposes, PowerShell defaults to a very restrictive *execution policy* that says the shell can only be used *interactively*, which occurs when you type in commands directly and have them execute immediately. This helps ensure that PowerShell can't be used to run script-based viruses by default. In order to run scripts, you'll need to change PowerShell to a different execution policy. However, first we need to talk a bit about how PowerShell identifies and decides whether to trust scripts.

Note

When considering security issues, keep in mind that PowerShell is now a core part of Windows and is included with new installations.

Digital Signatures

Digital signatures are an important part of how PowerShell's security works. A digital signature is created by using a code-signing certificate, sometimes referred to as a "Class 3" digital certificate or an Authenticode certificate, which is a Microsoft brand name. These certificates are sold by commercial certification authorities (CA). The certificates can also be issued by a company's own private CA.

The CA is where the trust process starts. All Windows computers have a list of *trusted root CAs* that is configured in the Internet Options control panel applet as shown in the following figure. To access this window, open Internet Options, and then click **Publishers…** on the **Content** tab. Then, select the **Trusted Root Certification Authorities** tab. This list, which is pre-populated by Microsoft and can be customized by administrators, determines the CAs that your computer *trusts*. By definition, your computer will trust any certificates issued by these CAs or any lower-level CA that a trusted CA has authorized. For example, if you trust CA 1, and they authorize CA 2 to issue certificates, then you'll trust certificates issued by CA 1 and by CA 2—your trust of CA 2 comes because it was authorized by the trusted CA 1.

Figure 12-1: Trusted root certificates.

When a CA issues a code-signing certificate, it consists of two halves: a private key and a public key. You usually install the entire certificate on your local computer and use it to digitally sign code including PowerShell scripts. A digital signature is created by calculating a *cryptographic hash*, which is a kind of complex checksum, on the script's contents. The hash is the result of a complex mathematical algorithm that is designed so that no two different scripts can ever produce the same hash value. In other words, the hash acts as a sort of electronic fingerprint for your script. The hash is then encrypted using your certificate's *private* key. This encrypted hash, which is referred to as the *signature*, is appended to the script.

Because the hash portion of the digital signature is unique to your script, it will change if your script changes in the slightest. Even an extra blank line somewhere in your script will invalidate the old checksum and digital signature. After making *any* changes to your script, you'll need to re-sign it. You can configure tools like SAPIEN PrimalScript to automatically sign scripts each time they're saved, which can save *you* a lot of hassle.

Trusted Scripts

When PowerShell tries to run a script, it first looks for a signature. If it doesn't find one, then the script is considered *untrusted*. If PowerShell does find a signature, it looks at the unencrypted part of the signature that contains information about the author of the script. PowerShell uses this information to retrieve the author's *public key*, which is always available from the CA that issued the code-signing certificate that was used to sign the script. If the CA isn't trusted, then the script isn't trusted. In this case, PowerShell doesn't do anything else with the script or signature.

If the CA is trusted, and PowerShell is able to retrieve the public key, then PowerShell tries to decrypt the signature using that public key. If it's unsuccessful, then the signature isn't valid, and the script is untrusted. If the signature can be decrypted, then PowerShell knows the script is *conditionally trusted*, which means it's been digitally signed by a trusted certificate issued by a trusted CA. Finally, PowerShell computes the same hash on the script to see if it matches the previously encrypted hash from the signature. If the two match, then PowerShell knows the script hasn't been modified since it was signed, and then the script is fully trusted. If the hashes do not match, then the script *has* been modified, and the script is untrusted because the signature is "broken."

PowerShell uses the script's status as trusted or untrusted to decide whether it can execute the script in accordance with its current execution policy.

Execution Policies

Within PowerShell, you can run **help about_signing** to learn more about PowerShell's four execution policies that are listed below:

- **AllSigned.** In this mode, PowerShell executes scripts that are trusted, which means they must be properly signed. Malicious scripts can execute, but you can use their signature to track down the author.

- **Restricted.** This is the default policy. The restricted mode means that no scripts are executed, regardless of whether they have been signed.

- **RemoteSigned.** In this mode, PowerShell will run local scripts without them being signed. Remote scripts that are downloaded through Microsoft Outlook, Internet Explorer, and so forth must be trusted in order to run.

- **Unrestricted.** PowerShell runs all scripts, regardless of whether they have been signed. Downloaded scripts will prompt before executing to be sure you really want to run them.

We highly recommend that you sign your scripts since it creates a more secure and trustworthy environment. If you plan to sign your scripts as recommended, then the AllSigned execution policy is appropriate. Otherwise, use RemoteSigned. The Unrestricted policy is overly generous and leaves your computer open to a range of attacks, therefore it shouldn't be used.

Technically, there's a fifth policy called Bypass, which basically allows anything and gives no warnings for any reason. It's designed to be used when PowerShell itself is embedded inside another application, and that application wants to programmatically run PowerShell scripts for some reason. It's expected that the other application would provide a security model, so PowerShell doesn't need to.

To check the current execution policy from within PowerShell, run:

```
PS C:\> Get-executionpolicy
```

You'll get back information about the current execution policy. If it's Restricted, then you'll know why your scripts won't run.

You can change the execution policy within PowerShell. Keep in mind that this is changing a value in the system registry, to which only administrators may have access. Therefore, if you're not an administrator on your computer, then you may not be able to modify the execution policy. To change the execution policy, run the following within PowerShell:

```
PS C:\> set-executionpolicy RemoteSigned
```

This will set the execution policy to RemoteSigned. This change takes effect immediately without restarting PowerShell.

Signing Scripts

Because code-signing certificates can be expensive ($300 per year or more is the current going rate), you may wish to create a *self-signed* certificate for your own local testing purposes. This certificate will be trusted only by your personal computer, but it costs you nothing to create. To create a self-signed certificate, you'll need a program called Makecert.exe that is available in the downloadable Microsoft .NET Framework Software Development Kit (SDK) at http://msdn.microsoft.com/netframework/downloads/updates/default.aspx. This file is also downloadable from the Windows Platform SDK. Documentation, including examples for this utility, can be found at http://msdn2.microsoft.com/en-us/library/aa386968.aspx.

After downloading and installing this file, you can use the Makecert.exe file to create the certificate by running the following from a Cmd.exe shell:

```
C:\> Makecert -n "CN=PowerShell Local Certificate Root" -a sha1
 -eku 1.3.6.1.5.5.7.3.3 -r -sv root.pvk root.cer
 -ss Root -sr localMachine
```

> **Note**
>
> If you have problems running Makecert, run Makecert /? to verify the correct syntax. Different versions of Makecert (a version might be included in your Microsoft Office installation, for example) require slightly different command-line arguments.

Note that this is all one long line of instructions. Next run:

```
C:\> Makecert -pe -n "CN=PowerShell User" -ss MY -a sha1
 -eku 1.3.6.1.5.5.7.3.3 -iv root.pvk -ic root.cer
```

Again, this is all one long line of typed instructions. These lines create two temporary files, root.pvk and root.cer, that you can save as backups. The actual certificate will be installed into your local certificate store where it can be used to sign scripts. Within PowerShell, run:

```
PS C:\> Set-authenticodeSignature "filename.ps1" '
>>@(get-childitem cert:\CurrentUser\My -codesigning)[0]
>>
PS C:\>
```

This is also one long line. This line retrieves your code-signing certificate and signs the file named filename.ps1, which should be an existing, unsigned PowerShell script. You can run **help Set-Authenticodesignature** for additional help with signing scripts. You can also use high-end script development environments, such as SAPIEN's PrimalScript, to sign scripts using a graphical user interface.

We need to emphasize that a certificate made with Makecert is *only* useful for testing on your local computer. If you want to distribute your scripts internally or externally, you'll need to acquire a real code-signing certificate.

Alternate Credentials

Whenever you start a new instance of the PowerShell shell, it runs under your *security context*. This means that PowerShell uses your logon credentials to run whatever scripts and commands you need to run. If your credentials do not have permissions to perform a particular command, such as retrieving a WMI object from a remote computer, then PowerShell will not be able to perform that task. One way to run PowerShell under alternate credentials is to use the Windows **RunAs** command. In this case, PowerShell will run under whatever credentials you provide to **RunAs**. However, sometimes this option might not work for what you need to do. For example, suppose you want to retrieve a WMI object from a computer on which you're not a local administrator. By default, WMI only permits local administrators to access WMI remotely. You *could* launch PowerShell using **RunAs**, if you can provide RunAs with credentials, such as a domain administrator account that is a local administrator on the computer in question. However, if that computer is not a domain member, there is no way to provide **RunAs** with the credentials of *another* computer's local accounts. If this situation arises, it appears that you're stuck.

However, it may only seem that way. Many PowerShell cmdlets support an optional parameter named **-credential**, which allows you to specify an alternate username and password that this one cmdlet will use to execute. For example, the **Get-WmiObject** cmdlet has a **-credential** parameter. Running **Help Get-WmiObject** indicates that the **-credential** parameter takes a value of the type PSCredential. This means you'll need to learn how to make one of those credentials.

The task, then, is to use PowerShell to get something called a *security principal*, which in English is a user or security group. PowerShell provides a cmdlet named **Get-Credential** that does just that. The cmdlet prompts you for the appropriate password and returns a PSCredential object that you can store in a variable. For example:

```
PS:> $cred = get-credential MYDOMAIN\Administrator
```

Note that the user name is specified in the DOMAIN\USER format. For a local computer, use COMPUTER\USER instead. Always specify the short (NetBIOS) domain or computer name rather than the longer DNS domain name. If you prefer, you can also enter the user name in the user@domain format, in which case you'll use the complete DNS domain name.

If you try this, there are two really important things to note:

- A dialog box will pop up, prompting you for the specified user's password.

- PowerShell *does not check the user*. Instead, it prompts you for a password. Keep in mind that it doesn't see if it's correct, and it doesn't check to see if the specified user exists. That's your responsibility.

Now you can run a command like this:

```
PS:> Get-wmiobject -class Win32_Process -computername Client32 -credential $cred
```

This script first utilizes the credential stored in the variable **$cred** to connect to a machine named Client32, and then attempts to retrieve all instances of the WMI Win32_Process class. Note that not *all* cmdlets support the **--credential** parameter as shown here. Run **Help *cmdlet-name*** to view a particular cmdlet's help file to see if it offers this functionality. In many cases, the ability to utilize alternate credentials isn't dependent on whether the cmdlets can accomplish this. Instead, it depends on whether the underlying Windows functionality, which the cmdlet is calling upon, can pass along alternate credentials.

Is PowerShell Dangerous?

The answer is that PowerShell is no more dangerous than any other application. Certainly, PowerShell has the potential for great destruction, since it can delete files, modify the registry, etc. However, so can any other application. If you run PowerShell as a local administrator, then it will have full access to your system—just like any other application. If you follow the *principle of least privilege*, which means you *don't* routinely log on to your computer as a local administrator, and you don't routinely run PowerShell as a local administrator, then its potential for damage is minimized—just like any other application. In fact, when set to its AllSigned execution policy, PowerShell is arguably *safer* than many applications, since you can ensure that only scripts signed by an identifiable author will actually be able to run.

Naturally, much of PowerShell's security begins and ends with *you*. Microsoft has configured it to be *very* safe out-of-the-box. Therefore, anything you do from there can potentially loosen PowerShell's security. For this reason, you need to understand that your actions could have consequences before you do anything.

Safer Scripts from the Internet

One potential danger point is downloading PowerShell scripts from the Internet or acquiring them from other untrusted sources. While these scripts are a great way to quickly expand your scripting skills, they present a danger if you don't know *exactly* what they do. Fortunately, Microsoft has provided the--whatif parameter, which is a very cool way to find out what scripts do.

All PowerShell cmdlets are built from the same basic *class,* or template, which allows them to have a--**whatif** parameter. Not every cmdlet actually implements this, but then not *every* cmdlet does something potentially damaging. Let's look at a good example of how you might use the -**whatif** parameter.

Say you download a script from the Internet, and in it you find the following:

```
PS:> Get-process | stop-process
```

> **Note**
> Did you know that Get-Process, with no other arguments, returns a list of all processes?

This runs the **Get-Process** cmdlet and pipes its output to the **Stop-Process** cmdlet. So, this script will have the effect of *stopping every process* on your computer. Not good. However, if you weren't sure of this output, you could just add--**whatif**:

```
PS:> Get-Process | stop-process -whatif
```

The output listed below is what you'd get, which is a portion of the actual list:

```
What if: Performing operation "stop-process" on Target "acrotray (4092)".
What if: Performing operation "stop-process" on Target "alg (1480)".
What if: Performing operation "stop-process" on Target "ati2evxx (1356)".
What if: Performing operation "stop-process" on Target "ati2evxx (1672)".
What if: Performing operation "stop-process" on Target "BTStackServer (3668)".
What if: Performing operation "stop-process" on Target "BTTray (1252)".
What if: Performing operation "stop-process" on Target "btwdins (168)".
What if: Performing operation "stop-process" on Target "csrss (1084)".
What if: Performing operation "stop-process" on Target "explorer (3380)".
What if: Performing operation "stop-process" on Target "Groove (1232)".
What if: Performing operation "stop-process" on Target "hpqgalry (3260)".
What if: Performing operation "stop-process" on Target "hpqtra08 (1556)".
What if: Performing operation "stop-process" on Target "hpwuSchd2 (3956)".
What if: Performing operation "stop-process" on Target "HPZipm12 (1004)".
```

```
What if: Performing operation "stop-process" on Target "Idle (0)".
What if: Performing operation "stop-process" on Target "inetinfo (236)".
What if: Performing operation "stop-process" on Target "iPodService (1136)".
```

Other than getting this output, nothing would happen. The **--whatif** parameter tells PowerShell (or more specifically, it tells the **Stop-Process** cmdlet) to display what it *would* do, without actually *doing* it. This allows you to see what the downloaded script would have done without taking the risk of running it. That's one way to make those downloaded scripts a bit safer in your environment—or at least see what they'd do. *Most* cmdlets that change the system in some way support **--whatif**, and you can check individual cmdlets' built-in help to be sure.

Note that **-whatif** doesn't take the place of a signature. For example, if your PowerShell execution policy is set to only run trusted (signed) scripts, and you download a script from the Internet that isn't signed, then you'll have to sign the script before you can add **-whatif** and run the script to see what it would do.

> **Our Scripts Aren't Signed!**
>
> We've deliberately not signed any of the sample scripts in this book (which are downloadable from www.SAPIENPress.com). If you decide to run any of our scripts, you need to evaluate them first to make sure they're suitable for you, and then sign them or configure PowerShell to not require a signature on scripts in order to execute them. We don't want you running any of our scripts until you've determined that they're appropriate for your environment, free of typos, and so forth.

You should also bear in mind the differences between the AllSigned and RemoteSigned execution policies. When you download a file with Microsoft Outlook or Microsoft Internet Explorer, Windows "marks" the file as having come from a potentially untrustworthy source, the Internet. Files "marked" in this fashion won't run under the RemoteSigned execution policy unless they've been signed. While we still encourage the use of the AllSigned execution policy, RemoteSigned at least lets you run unsigned scripts that you write yourself, while providing a modicum of protection against potentially malicious scripts you acquire from somewhere else.

The Profile: A Back Door?

Many administrators feel safe in using Windows PowerShell's RemoteSigned execution policy. Their theory is that they're smart enough not to run any scripts without checking them out first, so there's no need to force all scripts to be digitally signed.

However, PowerShell *automatically* executes its profile script *every time the shell opens*. If a malicious piece of software is able to create or modify your profile—which is simply a plain-text file stored in a predetermined location and using a predetermined file name—then the software can insert malicious PowerShell commands, which will execute automatically when the shell opens. The RemoteSigned execution policy provides no protection against this type of attack; only the AllSigned policy does. With AllSigned in effect, your profile has to be signed; an unsigned or modified profile simply won't execute—and, even better, you'll be warned that a problem exists.

Of course, keep in mind that if you've got malware on your computer, you've got bigger problems than what it does to PowerShell. But because it's pretty trivial to change a simple text file like your PowerShell profile, we always feel safer running with the AllSigned execution policy.

Because your profile script lives in your Documents folder, your user account has full access to it, meaning any software that manages to run while you're logged on can modify your profile. The next time you run the shell—bam, you could be executing something like **Del * -recurse**, which would *not* be pleasant. So don't take a chance: Stick with the AllSigned execution policy, obtain a code-signing certificate, and protect your PowerShell environment.

Passwords and Secure Strings

In certain situations, you may need to have a script prompt for a string that you need to keep safe and secure, such as a password. PowerShell provides a special object called SecureString that is designed to securely work with string data. Three cmdlets are available for working with SecureString objects: **Read-Host**, **ConvertFrom-SecureString**, and **ConvertTo-SecureString**.

Read-Host prompts for input and masks whatever is typed. The typed input then returns as the result of the cmdlet that can be stored in a variable. For example:

```
PS C:\> $password = read-host -assecurestring
********
PS C:\>
```

The password is stored in the variable **$password**. However, unlike a regular variable, you can't just display the contents of a SecureString:

```
PS C:\> $password
System.Security.SecureString
PS C:\>
```

As you can see, the contents of **$password** weren't displayed. Instead, the *type* of $password—"System.Security.SecureString"—was displayed. So, how can you get the password? Well, you can't exactly. It's intended to be passed directly to other cmdlets that accept a SecureString as their input.

However, there's another way in which SecureString is useful. You may have already realized that hard-coding passwords within a script is a bad idea. Anyone with permission to run the script also has permission to read it, which means they can read the hard-coded password. SecureString provides a *slight* amount of additional security when you *must* hard-code a password. You start by creating a new SecureString like the ones we've shown you. Then you use **ConvertFrom-SecureString** to export your encrypted password in a format that can be hard-coded into a script:

```
PS C:\> $password = read-host -assecurestring
********

PS C:\> $password = ConvertFrom-SecureString $password
PS C:\> $password
01000000d08c9ddf0115d1118c7a00c04fc297eb010000009c0d9c7fe8c37b439faf
e000000000200000000003660000a80000001000000093aaa18edf6f108b6222559
00000004800000a00000001000000098e4c93b57f59ff35110960a80b248a2180000
10ef82f30674ca4beea5df77c556388e95238b2140000002735d16881363c9c7b385
c7aea529
PS C:\>
```

You can hard-code that string of letters and numbers into your script, assigning them to a variable. When you're ready to actually use the password, such as passing it as a parameter to a cmdlet that accepts a SecureString, then use **ConvertTo-SecureString** to turn the letters and numbers back into a SecureString:

```
PS C:\> $password = read-host -assecurestring
********
```

```
PS C:\> $password = ConvertFrom-SecureString $password
PS C:\> $password
01000000d08c9ddf0115d1118c7a00c04fc297eb010000009c0d9c7fe8c37b439faf
e00000000020000000000003660000a80000001000000093aaa18edf6f108b6222559
000000004800000a00000001000000098e4c93b57f59ff35110960a80b248a2180000
10ef82f30674ca4beea5df77c556388e95238b2140000002735d16881363c9c7b385
c7aea529
PS C:\> $password= ConvertTo-SecureString $password
PS C:\> $password
System.Security.SecureString
PS C:\>
```

The last four lines show **ConvertTo-SecureString** being used. As you can see, once again **$password** is a SecureString. So, here's how this works: You can use a SecureString in your script as a normal variable; only the various "Output" and "Write" cmdlets will be unable to display it. If a cmdlet needs a password, and you send the password in a SecureString, the cmdlet will be able to read the password.

When you need to store a SecureString in a file or in a script, convert it from a SecureString into an encrypted string; convert it back to a SecureString to actually use it.

Here's the only problem—the encryption algorithm used by **CovertFrom-SecureString** is *deterministic*, which means any given input always results in the same output. This makes the encrypted password vulnerable to a dictionary attack, which occurs when the encrypted password is compared to a *huge* list of pre-encrypted passwords. When a match is found, the dictionary knows the clear-text password used to produce that particular encrypted password, which means the password is compromised. You *can* specify an encryption key when you use **CovertFrom-SecureString**; however, that key has to be used with **ConvertTo-SecureString**, and if you store the key in a file or in the script, then the key is essentially compromised and offers no particular security. And, no matter what, the output of **CovertFrom-SecureString** can be cracked by a dictionary attack.

Dictionary attacks are not particularly time-consuming once the dictionary itself is created. Pre-created dictionaries exist that contain every possible character combination for 6-, 7-, and 8-character passwords. A good dictionary will fit on a stack of DVD-ROM discs, and there are places on the Internet where you can buy such a stack—essentially, a ready-to-use, password-cracking tool. If you plan to use this SecureString technique to hard-code passwords into your script, be sure they're *very* long passwords—think pass*phrases*—to help avoid the possibility of an easy dictionary attack.

You should also be aware that a clever .NET developer or PowerShell scripter *can* decrypt the contents of a SecureString and display the clear-text result:

```
PS C:\> $Secret = read-host -assecurestring
********

PS>$Secret
System.Security.SecureString
PS>$BSTR = [System.Runtime.InteropServices.marshal]::SecureStringToBSTR($Secret)
PS>$ClearString = [System.Runtime.InteropServices.marshal]::PtrToStringAuto($BSTR)
PS>[System.Runtime.InteropServices.marshal]::ZeroFreeBSTR($BSTR)
PS>$ClearString
The password
PS>
```

What happened here? A new SecureString was created and stored in the variable **$secret**. This might be a password, for example. Then, .NET's COM interoperability services were used to convert the SecureString to a binary string (BSTR). It is then used to output the clear-text version into the variable **$ClearString**. This isn't exactly the huge security leak it looks like, since it can only be done with the original SecureString object created by **Read-Host**, and only on the computer on which the

SecureString was created. So, really, the only person who could use this trick is the person who typed the password in the first place. In essence, your personal login credentials are used to encrypt the SecureString in memory. So, without those, it can't be decrypted.

Chapter 13
The Microsoft .NET Framework:
An Overview for PowerShell Users

You probably don't *feel* as if you need to know much about the .NET Framework. Or maybe you're just *hoping* that's the case. Well, you're almost right. You certainly don't need to know *much* about the .NET Framework. However, you need to know a little so that all of PowerShell's features make sense to you. The good news is that what you need to know about the .NET Framework is summarized in this short chapter.

Microsoft .NET Framework Essentials

.NET is Microsoft's leading-edge software development framework. Traditional .NET development begins inside a development environment like Microsoft Visual Studio, SAPIEN PrimalScript Enterprise, or even Windows Notepad. After applications are written in languages like Visual Basic .NET or Visual C#, they're compiled to a special language called the Microsoft Intermediate Language (MSIL). This is important, because it's different from how other things such as Visual Basic 6 compiled programs into a native, binary executable.

When you double-click a .NET executable, it doesn't run right away because it contains MSIL, not actual binary code. Instead, Windows fires up the .NET Common Language Runtime (CLR), which is what reads the MSIL and compiles it into executable, binary code that will run on your system. This makes .NET applications inherently portable, since they can (more or less) run on any platform for which a CLR is available. This is all a bit of an oversimplification, but it's more than close enough for Windows administrative work.

The point of all this is that PowerShell is built on .NET, as are the cmdlets you'll be running. .NET is what's called an *object-oriented* framework, which is a fancy way of saying it is kind of template-based. For example, all PowerShell cmdlets start out as copies of a standardized cmdlet *base class* or template. In programmer terms, you'd say that all cmdlets *inherit from* that cmdlet base class. This is important because it's what makes all cmdlets pretty consistent with one another, which allows them to share certain ubiquitous parameters, etc.

The object-oriented stuff plays heavily into how PowerShell works, which is why you need to know a bit more about what an object *is*. At the simplest level, perhaps a level suitable for cocktail parties, an object is a bunch of computer code bundled into a "black box." The black box has buttons you can push to make things happen, and it has little blinking lights to tell you what's going on inside. You don't actually know how the box works—inside it could be anything from a particle accelerator to a cheese sandwich. But that doesn't really matter since the point is that you only interact with the box through its blinking lights and buttons while everything inside remains a big mystery. You can build your own black box that incorporates another black box, which is called *inheritance*. Essentially inheritance occurs when you install box number one inside box number two, so box number two can take full advantage of box number one's functionality without knowing much about what goes on inside.

Everything is an object in .NET and in PowerShell. Every variable you create, every WMI class you return—*everything* is an object. All of these objects have buttons called *methods* and blinking lights called *properties*. For example, when you run the code listed below, the **Get-WmiObject** cmdlet gets all the instances of the Win32_Process WMI class.

```
PS C:\> $stuff = Get-WmiObject -class Win32_Process -namespace root\cimv2
```

Each instance of the Win32_Process WMI class is an object. Together, the instances are bundled into a *collection* of objects that is stored in **$stuff**. The collection *itself* is an object.

> **Note**
> You can think of a collection as a bucket that is an object you can do things to. This bucket can also contain other independent objects. Sometimes a collection is referred to as a list or array.

So, the variable **$stuff** is now a collection of Win32_Process instances. Even a simple string of text "like this one" is really an object—specifically a *string* object—as far as PowerShell and .NET are concerned.

Reflection

Microsoft's Component Object Model (COM) is the pre-PowerShell way of managing Windows, often through a language like VBScript. Part of what made COM so difficult was that objects had to take special steps to define their functionality ahead of time. In other words, when someone at Microsoft created a DLL that allowed your scripts to work with files and folders, they also had to create a little file called a *type library* that explained the capabilities of the DLL. That made COM difficult to extend in certain ways, and certainly made it tough to use.

On the other hand, with .NET there's a nifty feature called *reflection*. Basically, reflection is a way for one application like PowerShell to discover something about an object at runtime without being told in advance what the object can do. Reflection makes PowerShell infinitely extensible because you can add new cmdlets. PowerShell can also, more or less, ask the cmdlets what they do and how they work.

Reflection makes PowerShell easier for you to use. For example, if you don't know what capabilities an object has, just pipe an instance of it to the **Get-Member** cmdlet. This cmdlet uses reflection to display all the known properties and methods of the object within PowerShell.

Assemblies

In .NET, everything eventually gets physically packaged into an *assembly*, which is a fancy word for what we otherwise call an executable, DLL, or some other file-that-contains-executable-code. You'll find assemblies distributed with PowerShell by default in the shell's installation folder.

> **Note**
>
> One assembly can contain or implement multiple objects or interfaces—each one being a separate cmdlet, for example).

For example, System.Management.Automation.Commands.Management.dll is a file containing bunches of different cmdlets.

Classes

The .NET Framework, and also PowerShell, treats almost everything as an object. However, different objects can be expected to have different functionality. For example, a car object has different capabilities than an airplane object. The Framework defines *classes* to distinguish between object types. A class is an abstract description of an object's capabilities. The name of a class is often referred to as its *type*. So, a string variable is more accurately referred to as "an object of the System.String type" or "an object of the System.String class." String objects have some distinct capabilities, such as the ability to return an uppercase version as shown in the following code:

```
PS C:\> $a = "hello"
PS C:\> $a.ToUpper()
HELLO
PS C:\>
```

Or the ability to display their length:

```
PS C:\> $a = "world"
PS C:\> $a.Length
5
PS C:\>
```

> **Don't Forget the ()**
>
> This is a great time to point out a difference between methods and properties. In the above two examples, notice that the method ToUpper() must be executed with parentheses, even though it doesn't have any arguments. The property Length, on the other hand, doesn't use parentheses. If you forget to add the parentheses to a method, it won't run properly. We forget all the time, and it can be very frustrating until you develop the proper typing habits!

The Framework exposes most of Windows' functionality, such as the ability to display graphical dialog boxes as classes. For example, if you create a new instance of the Windows.Forms.Form class, you're creating a new blank window or dialog box. You'll see how to use this in the next section. The important thing to remember right now is that the .NET Framework is comprised entirely of these classes. Knowing how to work with them can give you a lot of capabilities in PowerShell. Even if you don't work with advanced classes like Windows Forms, you can still work with basic classes like String, Int32 that let your scripts manipulate data more easily.

Variables as Objects

Earlier, we mentioned that even variables are objects. In particular, string variables in .NET are extremely robust and have a number of methods. One of them is **Split**, which is a method that takes a string and creates an array (or list) out of it by breaking the list up on some character like a comma or a space. Try this in PowerShell:

```
PS C:\> "1,2,3,4".Split(",")
```

What you're telling PowerShell is "take this string and execute its Split method." Use a comma for the method's input argument. When PowerShell does this, the method returns an array of four elements that each contains a number. PowerShell gets that array and displays it in a textual fashion with one array element per line:

```
1
2
3
4
```

There are other ways to use this technique. For example, we've already referred to **Get-Member**, a cmdlet that displays the methods and variables (which are collectively referred to as *members* in programmer-speak) associated with a given object instance. So, take a string like "Hello, World"—which, remember, is an instance of a String object—and pipe it to the **Get-Member** cmdlet to display information about that String object:

```
PS C:\> "Hello, World" | get-member


   TypeName: System.String

Name          MemberType  Definition
----          ----------  ----------
Clone         Method      System.Object Clone()
CompareTo     Method      int CompareTo(System.Object value), int CompareTo(string strB)
Contains      Method      bool Contains(string value)
CopyTo        Method      System.Void CopyTo(int sourceIndex, char[] destination, int dest...
EndsWith      Method      bool EndsWith(string value), bool EndsWith(string value, System....
Equals        Method      bool Equals(System.Object obj), bool Equals(string value), bool...
GetEnumerator Method      System.CharEnumerator GetEnumerator()
GetHashCode   Method      int GetHashCode()
GetType       Method      type GetType()
GetTypeCode   Method      System.TypeCode GetTypeCode()
IndexOf       Method      int IndexOf(char value), int IndexOf(char value, int startIndex)...
IndexOfAny    Method      int IndexOfAny(char[] anyOf), int IndexOfAny(char[] anyOf, int s...
Insert        Method       string Insert(int startIndex, string value)
IsNormalized  Method      bool IsNormalized(), bool IsNormalized(System.Text.Normalizatio...
LastIndexOf   Method      int LastIndexOf(char value), int LastIndexOf(char value, int sta...
LastIndexOfAny Method     int LastIndexOfAny(char[] anyOf), int LastIndexOfAny(char[] anyO...
Normalize     Method      string Normalize(), string Normalize(System.Text.NormalizationFo...
PadLeft       Method      string PadLeft(int totalWidth), string PadLeft(int totalWidth, ...
PadRight      Method      string PadRight(int totalWidth), string PadRight(int totalWidth,...
Remove        Method      string Remove(int startIndex), string Remove(int count), string Remove(int sta...
Replace       Method      string Replace(char oldChar, char newChar), string Replace(strin...
Split         Method      string[] Split(Params char[] separator), string[] Split(char[] ...
StartsWith    Method      bool StartsWith(string value), bool StartsWith(string value, Sys...
Substring     Method      string Substring(int startIndex), string Substring(int startInde...
```

```
ToCharArray     Method   char[] ToCharArray(), char[] ToCharArray(int startIndex, int le...
ToLower         Method   string ToLower(), string ToLower(System.Globalization.CultureInf...
ToLowerInvariant Method string ToLowerInvariant()
ToString        Method   string ToString(), string ToString(System.IFormatProvider provider)
ToUpper         Method   string ToUpper(), string ToUpper(System.Globalization.CultureInf...
ToUpperInvariant Method string ToUpperInvariant()
Trim            Method   string Trim(Params char[] trimChars), string Trim()
TrimEnd         Method   string TrimEnd(Params char[] trimChars)
TrimStart       Method   string TrimStart(Params char[] trimChars)
Chars           ParameterizedProperty char Chars(int index) {get;}
Length          Property System.Int32 Length {get;}
```

This output is truncated a bit to fit in this book. However, you can see it includes every method and property of the String and correctly identifies "Hello, World" as a "System.String" type, which is the unique *type name* that describes what we informally call a *String object*. You can pipe nearly anything to **Get-Member** to learn more about that particular object and its capabilities.

Variable Types

The fact that PowerShell is built on and around .NET gives PowerShell tremendous power, which isn't always obvious. For example, in the first chapter, we explained that any PowerShell variable can contain any type of data. This occurs because *all* types of data—strings, integers, dates, etc.—are .NET classes that inherit from the base class named Object. A PowerShell variable can contain anything that inherits from Object. However, as in the previous example with a string, PowerShell can certainly tell the difference between different classes that inherit from Object.

You can force PowerShell to treat objects as a more specific type. For example, take a look at this sequence:

```
PS C:\> $one = 5
PS C:\> $two = "5"
PS C:\> $one + $two
10
PS C:\> $one = 5
PS C:\> $two = "5"
PS C:\> $one + $two
10
PS C:\> $two + $one
55
```

In this example, we gave PowerShell two variables: one contained the number five, and the other contained the string character "5". Even though this might look the same to you, it's a big difference to a computer! However, we didn't specify what type of data they were, so PowerShell assumed they were both of the generic Object type. PowerShell also decided it would figure out something more specific when the variables are actually used.

When we added $one and $two, or 5 + "5", PowerShell said, "Aha, this is addition: The first character is definitely not a string because it wasn't in double quotes. The second character one *was* in double quotes, but… well, if I take the quotes away it looks like a number, so I'll add them." This is why we correctly got ten as the result.

However, when we added $two and $one—reversing the order—PowerShell had a different decision to make. This time PowerShell said, "I see addition, but this first operand is clearly a string. The second one is a generic Object. So, let's treat it like a string too and concatenate the two." This is how we got the string "55", which is the first five tacked onto the second five.

But what about:

```
PS C:\> [int]$two + $one
10
```

Same order as the example that got "55", but in this type we specifically told PowerShell that the generic object in $two was an [Int], or integer, which is a type PowerShell knows about. So, this time PowerShell used the same logic as in the first example. When it added the two, it came up with "10".

You can force PowerShell to treat anything as a specific type. For example:

```
PS C:\> $int = [int]"5"
PS C:\> $int | get-member


   TypeName: System.Int32

Name         MemberType   Definition
----         ----------   ----------
CompareTo    Method       System.Int32 CompareTo(Int32 value), System.Int
Equals       Method       System.Boolean Equals(Object obj), System.Boole
GetHashCode  Method       System.Int32 GetHashCode()
GetType      Method       System.Type GetType()
GetTypeCode  Method       System.TypeCode GetTypeCode()
ToString     Method       System.String ToString(), System.String ToStrin
```

Here, the value "5" would normally be either a String object or, at best, a generic Object. But by specifying the type [int], we forced PowerShell to try and convert "5" into an integer before storing it in the variable $int. The conversion was successful, which you can see when we piped $int to **Get-Member** revealing the object's type: System.Int32.

Note that once you apply a specific type to a variable, it stays that way until you specifically change it. For example:

```
PS C:\> [int]$int = 1
```

This creates a variable named $int as an integer and assigns it the value 1. The $int variable will be treated as an integer from now on, even if you don't include the type:

```
PS C:\> $int = 2
```

It is still using $int as an integer because it was already cast into a specific type. Once set up to be an integer, you can't put other types of data into it. Here's an example of an error that occurred when we tried to put a string into a variable that was already specifically cast as an integer:

```
PS C:\> [int]$int = 1
PS C:\> $int = 2
PS C:\> $int = "hello"
Cannot convert value "hello" to type "System.Int32". Error: "Input string was not in a correct
 format."
At line:1 char:5
+ $int <<<< = "hello"
PS C:\>
```

However, you can recast a variable by reassigning a new, specific type:

```
[string]$int = "Hello"
```

That works just fine, and $int will *now* be treated as a string by PowerShell.

PowerShell isn't a miracle worker: For example, if you try to force it to convert something that doesn't make sense, it will complain:

```
PS C:\> $int = [int]"Hello"
Cannot convert "Hello" to "System.Int32". Error: "Input string was not in a correct format."
At line:1 char:13
+ $int = [int]" <<<< Hello"
```

This occurred because "Hello" can't sensibly be made into a number.

This one's even more fun because it illustrates some of the advanced data types:

```
PS C:\> $xml = [xml]"<users><user name='joe' /></users>"
PS C:\> $xml.users.user

name
----
joe
```

In this example we created a string, but told PowerShell it was of the type XML, which is another data type that PowerShell knows. XML data works sort of like an object: We defined a parent object named Users and a child object named User. The child object had an attribute called Name, with a value of Joe. So, when we asked PowerShell to display $xml.users.user, it displays all the attributes for that user. We can prove that PowerShell treated $xml as XML data by using **Get-Member**:

```
PS C:\> $xml | get-member


    TypeName: System.Xml.XmlDocument

Name                        MemberType   Definition
----                        ----------   ----------
ToString                    CodeMethod   static System.Stri
add_NodeChanged             Method       System.Void add_No
add_NodeChanging            Method       System.Void add_No
add_NodeInserted            Method       System.Void add_No
add_NodeInserting           Method       System.Void add_No
add_NodeRemoved             Method       System.Void add_No
add_NodeRemoving            Method       System.Void add_No
AppendChild                 Method       System.Xml.XmlNode
Clone                       Method       System.Xml.XmlNode
CloneNode                   Method       System.Xml.XmlNode
CreateAttribute             Method       System.Xml.XmlAttr
CreateCDataSection          Method       System.Xml.XmlCDat
CreateComment               Method       System.Xml.XmlComm
CreateDocumentFragment      Method       System.Xml.XmlDocu
CreateDocumentType          Method       System.Xml.XmlDocu
CreateElement               Method       System.Xml.XmlElem
CreateEntityReference       Method       System.Xml.XmlEnti
CreateNavigator             Method       System.Xml.XPath.X
CreateNode                  Method       System.Xml.XmlNode
CreateProcessingInstruction Method       System.Xml.XmlProc
...
```

This demonstrates not only that variables *are* objects, but also that PowerShell understands different types of data, and provides different capabilities for the various types of data.

Curious about what object types are available? Here's a quick list of more common types (although there are more than this):

- Array
- Bool (Boolean)
- Byte
- Char (a single character)
- Char[] (Character array)
- Decimal
- Double
- Float
- Int (Integer)
- Int[] (Integer array)
- Long (Long integer)
- Long[] (Long integer array)
- Regex (Regular expression)
- Scriptblock
- Single
- String
- XML

You will learn more about variables in the chapter "Variables, Arrays, and Escape Characters" (where, because repetition is a *good thing* when you're learning, we'll repeat a lot of this information with new examples). We'll also be popping in with details on these other types as appropriate throughout this book. Some of the types aren't frequently used in administrative scripting, so we will not arbitrarily hit you with all of them at once. Instead, we'll cover them in a context where they're accomplishing something useful.

Variable Precautions

One thing to be careful of is PowerShell's ability to change the type of a variable if you haven't explicitly selected a type. For example:

```
Write-host $a.ToUpper()
```

This works fine if **$a** contains a string, as shown here:

```
PS C:\> $a = "Hello"
PS C:\> write-host $a.ToUpper()
HELLO
PS C:\>
```

However, if **$a** was already set to an integer value, you'll get an error:

```
PS C:\> $a = 1
PS C:\> write-host $a.toupper()
Method invocation failed because [System.Int32] doesn't contain a method named 'toupper'.
At line:1 char:22
+ write-host $a.toupper( <<<< )
```

This occurs because, as an integer, **$a** doesn't have a **ToUpper()** method. You need to watch out for this when you're writing scripts that take input from other sources. For example, this might occur with a user or a file, since this type of error can be tricky to troubleshoot. One way around it is to force PowerShell to treat the variable as the string you're expecting it to be:

```
PS C:\> $a = 1
PS C:\> $a = [string]$a
PS C:\> write-host $a.ToUpper()
1
PS C:\>
```

You don't necessarily need to select a type up-front for every variable you use. However, you should be aware of situations that can make a variable contain a type of data other than what you originally expected.

.NET Conclusion

PowerShell is built on and around the .NET Framework, which means everything in PowerShell has a distinctly .NET flavor to it. On one level, you can ignore this and use PowerShell at a more simple level. For example, you can let it treat everything as a generic Object. However, as you grow with PowerShell, and want to leverage more powerful features, you'll find yourself gradually learning more about .NET.

This chapter wasn't meant to be a comprehensive look at .NET—that's another book entirely! Instead, the purpose of this chapter is to provide a rather a quick look at how .NET impacts the way PowerShell is built and the way PowerShell works. You'll see a *lot* more details about these topics, especially variables and their capabilities, throughout the remaining chapters.

Chapter 14
Using WMI in Windows PowerShell

WMI Fundamentals

Like PowerShell, Windows Management Instrumentation (WMI) was created to solve a problem with Windows management: Every different part of Windows made management information available through a different means. WMI is an attempt to make all of that more consistent. As a result, WMI is more or less a "one stop shop" for obtaining management information.

It is important to understand that WMI is completely separate from PowerShell. WMI can be used from within PowerShell, but it can also be used from VBScript, C++, Visual Basic .NET, and nearly any other Windows-based language. There's even **wmic.exe**, a command-line tool that can access WMI from the old Cmd.exe shell.

PowerShell Seeds

You may not be aware of WMIC, many administrators aren't. What you probably also didn't know was that driving force behind WMIC was Jeffrey Snover, the same driving force behind Windows PowerShell. If you have spent any time using WMIC, you can most likely sense the beginnings of Windows PowerShell.

WMI is important to you because, from within PowerShell, you can work with WMI to retrieve and manipulate information related to various aspects of Windows. PowerShell *doesn't* replace WMI, it *uses* it.

WMI Architecture

WMI is built around *classes*, which are abstract descriptions of computer-related things. For example, the Win32_Volume class describes what a logical disk volume looks like. The class includes properties like size and serial number and can perform tasks like defragmenting. However, the class doesn't represent an *actual* volume; it's just a description of what a volume might look like. When you actually have a volume, you have an *instance* of the class. For example, if your computer has two volumes, you have two *instances* of the Win32_Volume class. Actually, only Windows Server 2003 exposes the Win32_Volume class, but we'll discuss this in more detail in a bit. Each instance has properties such as size and name. It might also have methods such as **Defragment()** that you can use to manage that instance.

There are *lots* of WMI classes. Windows itself has hundreds, and Windows Server System products like SQL Server and Microsoft Exchange Server can each add hundreds more. To keep things organized, Microsoft files classes into *namespaces*. The main namespace for the core Windows classes is root\cimv2. Incidentally, most of the core classes' names start with Win32_. Internet Information Services (IIS) 6.0 installs the root\MicrosoftIISv2 namespace, along with lots of classes related to IIS management. You can access the Windows XP SP2 Security Center by the root\SecurityCenter namespace. In fact, nearly any recent Microsoft product installs a WMI namespace and several classes that you can use to manage that product.

WMI Documentation

When you're working with classes, it's useful to know where the documentation is. Fortunately, Microsoft provides it free online. Unfortunately, they change the URLs almost constantly, so it's tough to publish a useful one. Instead, we suggest that you go to http://msdn.microsoft.com/library. In the "Search" box, type **Win32_OperatingSystem**. Make sure the search scope is set to "MSDN Library," then hit the magnifying glass icon. In the search results, one of the first hits should be something like "Win32_OperatingSystem class [WMI]," which is what you want, so click it. Depending on your browser you might to need to synchronize contents. Right above the contents tree view on the left, click the "sync toc" link. This will take you into the WMI Table of Contents. You can browse from there. In other browsers, you might need to click "Up One Level" in the contents—do this twice—to navigate up to where the WMI class documentation starts.

The documentation provides important information. For example, under the Operating System Classes category, locate the Win32_Volume class. You should see something similar to what was shown in the following figure. Notice that the table of contents on the left reveals several methods for this class that are actions you can perform, including **Defrag** and **AddMountPoint**. The main pane includes a brief description of the class, along with a list of its properties such as **DeviceID**, **FreeSpace**, **FileSystem**, and so on. When you scroll all the way to the bottom, you'll see a section labeled **Requirements**. This is where you will find documentation about operating systems, including the one this class exists on—Windows Server 2003 and later. This is important! If you're planning to use this class with a Windows XP computer, you now know that it won't work. From this example you can see why it is important to always check these requirements before you assume a class is universally supported on all versions of Windows. Even within a class, new properties may be added that aren't supported on older versions of Windows as well.

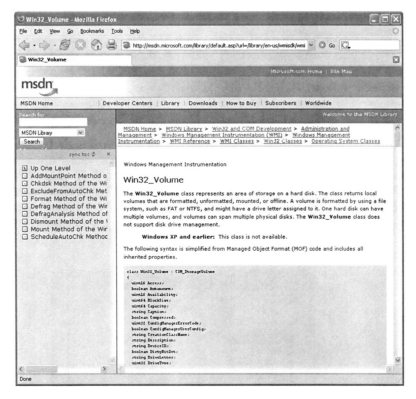

Figure 14-1: MSDN WMI documentation.

Working with WMI Classes

Something you need to keep in mind about WMI is that while its goal is to present management information in a consistent fashion…well, it doesn't, really. The problem is that the actual implementation of WMI in any given Microsoft product is a decision left up to that product's development group. For example, the classes related to the core Windows operating system live in the root\cimv2 namespace. Those classes are all fairly consistent in the way they work: You query classes, the properties are read-only, and you execute methods to make changes. For example, if you query the Win32_Service class, you can examine the **StartMode** and **StartName** properties to determine if the service starts automatically, and to determine the account that the services uses to log on. However, to *change* those items, you execute the **Change()** method, passing parameters with the new information.

There are still inconsistencies. For example, you can connect to a remote computer's WMI service and start a new instance of the Win32_Process class, and that starts a new process running on the remote computer. However, you can't simply create a new instance of the Win32_LogicalDisk class in order to create a new hard disk partition.

Other product teams have taken different approaches. For example, the root\MicrosoftIISv2 namespace contains classes related to Internet Information Services (IIS) 6.0. In that namespace, one set of classes is provided for read-only information; a second set of classes has read-write properties that allow you to make configuration changes. *No* class in root\cimv2, however, has writable properties. This sort of inconsistency in how different products can be managed through WMI is unfortunate, but it's something you'll have to become accustomed to—it's just the way Microsoft built things.

Remote Computers, Security, and WMI

WMI runs as a background service on Windows computers. When you connect to a remote computer, some kind of credentials must be provided so you can connect to the remote computer's WMI service. Normally, *your* credentials are passed along to execute whatever WMI actions you specify. So, if *you* have permission to perform the action, WMI will be able to perform it on your behalf. However, by default, only local administrators have permission to remotely utilize WMI in any way. This is configured in the WMI console. To view it, open a blank Microsoft Management Console (MMC) by running Mmc.exe.

From the File menu, select Add/Remove Snap-In. Click Add and scroll to the bottom to add the WMI Control snap-in. Focus the snap-in on whatever computer you want to view, such as the local computer, and then close the open dialog boxes to go back to the main console. Right-click WMI Control, and then select Properties. If Properties isn't available, left-click WMI Control first, and then right-click it. On the Security tab, select Root and click Security. As shown in the figure below, by default only administrators have the Remote Enable permission, which allows them to remotely utilize WMI on this computer.

Figure 14-2: WMI Security settings.

Caution!
Do not modify the WMI permissions unless you know what you're doing and are being very careful. A number of Microsoft and third-party applications rely on WMI. So, if you change the permissions, those applications might stop working.

Impersonation

Impersonation is an important aspect of WMI security. By default, as we've already described, WMI attempts to pass your credentials to the remote computer, which uses your credentials to execute your query. This is called *impersonation*, and it is WMI's default behavior. However, three other behaviors are possible: *Anonymous* doesn't pass your credentials along at all, *Identify* passes your credentials along but doesn't give the remote computer permission to use them for anything, and *Delegate* not only allows the remote computer to impersonate you, but allows it to pass your credentials along to another computer, which is also permitted to impersonate you. Generally speaking, Anonymous and Identify won't work because of the way WMI's security is configured; Delegate confers excessive permissions and should be avoided. The default setting is sufficient.

Privileges

Another aspect of WMI security is called *privileges*. You can think of these as a sort of safety cover over buttons that perform potentially damaging actions. For example, if you connect to a remote computer and try to clear its security event log using WMI, the action will probably fail—even if you provide Administrator credentials. That's because clearing the security log is a sensitive action, and WMI tries to keep it from being done unintentionally. In order to perform a sensitive action, you have to specify the appropriate *privilege* when connecting to WMI. Essentially, you're removing the safety cover, and then allowing the button to be pushed so that the action is taken.

Using Wbemtest

Windows includes a built-in tool, called Wbemtest.exe, which you can use to test WMI and interactively examine the WMI repository. To run it, select Run from the Start menu, type **Wbemtest**, and then click the OK button.

When the application appears, the first thing you'll do is connect to a computer and a WMI namespace. For example, click the Connect button and type **root\cimv2** to connect to your local computer's root\cimv2 namespace, where the core Windows operating system classes are installed. If you wanted to test a WMI connection to a remote computer you would enter **\\remoteserver\root\cimv2**. Depending on your operating system, the default may already be set to root\cimv2.

Next, you'll issue a WMI query. The easiest type of query takes the pattern **SELECT * FROM <WMI Class Name>**, such as **SELECT * FROM Win32_LogicalDisk**. Click the Apply button to execute the query, and you'll get a window containing the query's results—a collection of WMI instances. You can double-click an instance to examine its properties (when doing so, we always select the Hide System Properties check box to hide the properties that aren't actually very useful). For each instance, you can review the available property names, see the type of data each property holds, and see the property values associated with that particular instance.

The WMI Query Language (WQL) is similar to the Structured Query Language (SQL) used in most relational database management systems like Microsoft SQL Server, Oracle, or MySQL. You can use a WHERE clause to filter results. For example, to only get *local* drives, you'd issue the query **SELECT * FROM Win32_LogicalDisk WHERE DriveType = 3**. If all you cared about was the DeviceID, you could just select that property by issuing **SELECT DeviceID FROM Win32_LogicalDisk**. We'll have some more WQL examples later in the book, but hopefully this gives you an idea of what WQL looks like.

We *strongly* recommend that you play with WMI in Wbemtest before doing so in PowerShell. While PowerShell does make it easy to work with WMI, Wbemtest provides a way of graphically exploring the WMI repository. If you're after a way to *browse* the WMI repository, visit http://www.primaltools.com/downloads/communitytools/ and download the free WMI Explorer. You might also visit http://blog.sapien.com/index.php/2008/09/24/wbemtest-demo/ for a short video demonstration of Wbemtest in action.

So What Can You Do with WMI?

WMI makes all things possible. Well, many things. The challenge with WMI is learning what class will get you the information you need or do the thing you want, and then figuring out which namespace the class lives in. We can't really offer any shortcuts apart from "browse the documentation." Be sure that you scroll to the bottom of a WMI class' documentation page, though, because some classes don't exist in older versions of Windows—each new version of Windows adds new stuff. Even some class properties get added over time, so don't go crazy if a WMI query on Windows Vista has properties that Windows XP doesn't—that's just progress.

If you're totally stuck trying to figure out what WMI class will do what you need, drop on by www. ScriptingAnswers.com and post a question in the Windows PowerShell forum—we'll try and get you pointed in the right direction.

Retrieving WMI Objects

We need to point out that PowerShell actually offers two or three different ways of working with WMI. If you're perusing samples that you find in other books or on the Internet, in fact, you may see some of the other techniques. However, of the various ways PowerShell has to work with WMI, only one way— the way we're going to show you—can do *everything*. That is, we're going to show you the one technique PowerShell has for working with WMI that will do *everything* you'll need.

The first step in working with WMI is to get one or more instances of a WMI class; that is, to get a "WMI object." You might retrieve these instances from your local computer's WMI service, or you might get them from a remote machine's WMI service; either way, what you want is to get a collection of WMI instances (or objects) to work with. PowerShell provides an easy way to do this: The **Get-WmiObject** cmdlet. In its simplest form, you simply tell it which WMI class you want, and it'll retrieve all the instances of that class:

```
PS C:\> Get-WmiObject win32_service
```

If you find that typing **Get-WmiObject** over and over becomes tiresome, try the alias **gwmi** instead:

```
PS C:\> gwmi win32_service
```

Retrieving instances from a remote computer is just as easy:

```
PS C:\> gwmi win32_service -computerName Server2
```

The computer name can be the NETBIOS name, a fully qualified domain name (FQDN) or even an IP address. And, remember, you don't need to type the entire parameter name—you just need to type enough to distinguish the parameter from any others. For example:

```
PS C:\> gwmi win32_service -computer Server2
```

Or even:

```
PS C:\> gwmi win32_service -co Server2
```

PowerShell has tab completion so you can also type –c, and then press the Tab key until you arrive at the desired parameter.

Sometimes, the user credentials you used to run PowerShell won't have the appropriate permissions (generally, local Administrator) on the remote computer. In those cases, the **Get-WmiObject** cmdlet can accept alternate credentials. Note that this *only* works with connections to remote computers! WMI itself is designed to not permit alternate credentials when you're connecting to the local WMI service. There are a couple of ways to specify alternate credentials. This is probably the easiest to type for a quick, one-time connection:

```
PS C:\> gwmi win32_service -computerName Server2 -credential DOMAIN\Username
```

PowerShell will automatically prompt you for the password. However, if you plan to use that same credential over and over, repeatedly typing in the user name and the password can be a pain in the neck. PowerShell does provide a way for you to save the credential in a variable, and then pass that variable to the -**credential** parameter:

```
PS C:\> $cred = get-credential DOMAIN\Username
PS C:\> gwmi win32_service -comp Server2 -cred $cred
```

The **Get-Credential** cmdlet will prompt you for the password, and then securely store the credential in the variable **$cred**. That variable will last for the duration of your PowerShell session and can be passed to the -**credential** parameter of any cmdlet that supports the parameter, including **Get-WmiObject**.

Get-Credential is Not Authentication

The Get-Credential cmdlet is not involved with authentication even though the dialog box looks like a logon. The cmdlet makes no attempt to verify the user name or password. All it does is securely store the information in a PSCredential object. When you pass the object to a cmdlet like Get-WmiObject, it takes the information and passes it to the security subsystem and the typical Windows authentication process continues from there. If you mistyped the password, only then will you get an error.

Impersonation, Privileges, and Authentication Level

By default, **Get-WmiObject** will use impersonation; you can specify the -**impersonation** parameter to force a different behavior. Valid values for this parameter are:

- 0 (Use the registry default, which is usually impersonate or value 3)
- 1 (Anonymous)
- 2 (Identify)
- 3 (Impersonate, the default)
- 4 (Delegate)

You can also specify the level of authentication used by WMI when passing credentials to a remote computer. To do so, use the -**Authentication** parameter, and specify one of the following values:

- 1 (none)
- 2 (connect)
- 3 (call),
- 4 (packet)

- 5 (packet integrity)
- 6 (packet privacy)

Generally, the default—which is selected by your operating system depending upon its version, whether you're in a domain, and other factors—is what you want; to use the default authentication level, simply don't use the -**Authentication** parameter.

Finally, if you want to enable privileges for sensitive operations, querying security logs, or rebooting a server, add the -**EnableAllPrivileges** switch. This parameter enables *all* WMI privileges. PowerShell doesn't currently offer a way to specify individual privileges, but we have yet to see where this is a problem.

Submitting WQL Queries

The techniques we've just shown you assume that you're querying classes from the default root\cimv2 namespace. If you aren't, then you'll need to specify the WMI namespace:

```
PS C:\> gwmi AntiVirusProduct -namespace root\SecurityCenter
```

....
Client Only
Don't expect that example to work on server operating systems; typically, the SecurityCenter namespace is only available on client operating systems, including Windows XP and later.

In the section Using Wbemtest, we made a big deal of using Wbemtest to test your WMI queries before using them in PowerShell. So, where exactly do you use a WQL query? **Get-WmiObject** supports an alternate syntax that accepts a complete WQL query, rather than just a class name:

```
PS C:\> gwmi -query "SELECT * FROM Win32_Service WHERE StartName = 'LocalSystem'"
```

You can use the same -**computerName**, -**credential**, and -**namespace** parameters with this syntax to specify a remote computer to connect to, an alternate set of credentials, and a namespace other than root\cimv2, if necessary.

....
Gotcha!
Don't forget that the operators in a WMI query are the legacy operators you've known and loved for years such as =, >, and <=. Do not use the new PowerShell operators. Also remember to quote any strings you are comparing as we've done in the above example.

An alternative approach is to use the -filter parameter. This parameter, which is available on a number of cmdlets, will filter output. The format depends on the cmdlet. For **Get-WmiObject**, the filter value is the Where component of a WMI query. For example, you could use an expression like this:

```
PS C:\ > gwmi -query "select * from win32_logicaldisk where drivetype=3"
```

```
DeviceID     : C:
DriveType    : 3
ProviderName :
```

```
FreeSpace    : 44984381440
Size         : 80024170496
VolumeName   :
```

Or you can use -filter:

```
PS C:\ > gwmi win32_logicaldisk -filter "drivetype=3"
```

```
DeviceID     : C:
DriveType    : 3
ProviderName :
FreeSpace    : 44984381440
Size         : 80024170496
VolumeName   :
```

The output will be the same in either situation. So, when do you use a filter and when do you use a query? It's really up to you and the situation. If you are only selecting a subset of properties, then a query is more appropriate:

```
PS C:\ > gwmi -query "Select DeviceID,Freespace,Size from win32_logicaldisk where drivetype=3"
```

What you cannot do though is combine **-query** and **-filter**. You can only use one or the other in a **Get-WmiObject** expression.

Get-WmiObject can even help you figure out what classes are available to you. Simply specify the namespace and use the **-list** parameter to list the classes available in that namespace:

```
PS C:\> gwmi -namespace root\securitycenter -list
```

```
__NotifyStatus                          __ExtendedStatus
__SecurityRelatedClass                  __Trustee
__NTLMUser9X                            __ACE
__SecurityDescriptor                    __PARAMETERS
__SystemClass                           __ProviderRegistration
__EventProviderRegistration             __ObjectProviderRegistration
__ClassProviderRegistration             __InstanceProviderRegistration
__MethodProviderRegistration            __PropertyProviderRegistration
__EventConsumerProviderRegistration     __thisNAMESPACE
__NAMESPACE                             __IndicationRelated
__FilterToConsumerBinding               __EventConsumer
__AggregateEvent                        __TimerNextFiring
__EventFilter                           __Event
__NamespaceOperationEvent               __NamespaceModificationEvent
__NamespaceDeletionEvent                __NamespaceCreationEvent
__ClassOperationEvent                   __ClassDeletionEvent
__ClassModificationEvent               __ClassCreationEvent
__InstanceOperationEvent                __InstanceCreationEvent
__MethodInvocationEvent                 __InstanceModificationEvent
__InstanceDeletionEvent                 __TimerEvent
__ExtrinsicEvent                        __SystemEvent
__EventDroppedEvent                     __EventQueueOverflowEvent
__QOSFailureEvent                       __ConsumerFailureEvent
__EventGenerator                        __TimerInstruction
__AbsoluteTimerInstruction              __IntervalTimerInstruction
__Provider                              __Win32Provider
__SystemSecurity                        AntiSpywareProduct
AntiVirusProduct                        FirewallProduct
```

Class names that begin with a double underscore ("__") are *system classes* and you won't usually utilize these directly. Instead, focus on the classes at the end of the list, which don't start with a double underscore.

Advanced WMI Options

The **-amended** switch tells WMI to return objects containing amended information. Normally, this information is localizable data attached to the WMI objects, such as object and property descriptions in localized or localizable formats. Many objects don't return amended information at all, so using this switch often won't make any difference.

The **-locale** switch allows you to specify an alternate locale for WMI objects. You need to know the appropriate locale string, in the format "MS_<LCID>" (such as MS_1033). If you don't specify this, WMI objects will use their default locale.

The **-DirectRead** switch specifies whether direct access to the WMI provider is requested for the class you've specified, without using any super class or derived class information. For many classes, this switch won't make any difference, and in general you shouldn't use it unless you're very familiar with the internal workings of WMI and the WMI provider that you're querying.

Working with WMI Objects

So far, what we've shown you only displays the results of your WMI query. That is, PowerShell retrieves the objects you requested, but since you haven't told it what else to do with them, it converts them into a text list. That's fine if that's all you need, but you can do a lot more. For example, you can pipe those objects to other PowerShell cmdlets to refine and filter your list, such as filtering so that only running services are shown:

```
PS C:\> gwmi win32_service | where { $_.State -eq "Running" }
```

You can further refine that to perhaps list the running services in reverse alphabetical order:

```
PS C:\> gwmi win32_service | where { $_.State -eq "Running" } | sort name -desc
```

This is where the cmdlets introduced in the "Key Cmdlets for Windows Administration" chapter really come in handy to help you further refine that result set. However, you should be aware of one thing: When you run a command line like the one above, PowerShell has to retrieve *all* instances of the specified class. In the case of the Win32_Service class, that's not a big deal because there aren't *that* many. However, it does have to go get them all, and *then* filter them through the **Where-Object** cmdlet. A more efficient technique would be to issue a WQL query that filters the results *at the origin*—that is, on the computer you're connecting to. WQL is capable of filtering results much more quickly than PowerShell, so using the following technique will yield better performance:

```
PS C:\> gwmi -query "SELECT * FROM Win32_Service WHERE State = 'Running'" | sort name -desc
```

Note that we still have to have PowerShell perform the sort, because the WQL language doesn't support any keywords for sorting (there's no equivalent to the SQL language's ORDER BY clause).

All of this, however, still results in PowerShell reaching the end of the pipeline and generating a text list of whatever WMI objects are in the pipeline at that point. Sometimes you might need to place those objects into a variable, so that you can persist your results and actually do other things with them. Here's an example:

```
PS C:\> $wmi = gwmi win32_operatingsystem -computer Server2 -enableAllPrivileges
PS C:\> $wmi.Reboot()
```

This example retrieves the Win32_OperatingSystem class from a remote machine, Server2. It saves the resulting collection (which contains just one instance) in the variable **$wmi**. Because the collection only has one object in it (that particular WMI class can *only* ever return one object), we can just pretend that the **$wmi** variable represents that object directly, and on the second line execute the object's **Reboot()** method—remotely restarting that server. This operation requires special privileges which is why we've included the -**EnableAllPrivileges** parameter.

If your WMI query returns more than one object, however, you have to use a slightly different technique:

```
PS C:\> $wmi = gwmi win32_service
PS C:\> $wmi[0]


ExitCode   : 0
Name       : AcrSch2Svc
ProcessId  : 340
StartMode  : Auto
State      : Running
Status     : OK

PS C:\> $wmi[0].StopService()
```

Here, we've retrieved all instances of Win32_Service and put them into the variable **$wmi**. Next, we display the first instance in the collection—index number zero—by typing **$wmi[0]**. That lets us verify that the first instance is the one we're after by examining its name and other properties. Finally, we take the first instance and execute its **StopService()** method to stop that instance.

....

Wait a Second...
Did we have to use WMI in this example? Couldn't we have just used the Get-Service and Stop-Service cmdlets? Well, yes, in this case—but only because we chose services to work with, and only because we're working with the local machine (unless we create a remote job using these cmdlets). Neither of those cmdlets works with directly remote machines, although WMI does. In addition, WMI works with a broader range of manageable components, although services are a great example. Finally, WMI often provides access to more and better information For example, the information provided by Get-Service doesn't include a service's startup mode and logon user account, although WMI does provide this information.

If you're having trouble figuring out which properties and methods a given WMI class has, remember to consult the documentation—or just ask PowerShell by piping the WMI object to **Get-Member**:

```
PS C:\> gwmi win32_bios | get-member


   TypeName: System.Management.ManagementObject#root\cimv2\Win32_BIOS

Name                MemberType  Definition
----                ----------  ----------
BIOSVersion         Property    System.String[] BIOSVersion {get;set;}
BuildNumber         Property    System.String BuildNumber {get;set;}
```

```
CurrentLanguage        Property   System.String CurrentLanguage {get;set;}
Description            Property   System.String Description {get;set;}
Manufacturer          Property   System.String Manufacturer {get;set;}
Name                  Property   System.String Name {get;set;}
OtherTargetOS         Property   System.String OtherTargetOS {get;set;}
PrimaryBIOS           Property   System.Boolean PrimaryBIOS {get;set;}
ReleaseDate           Property   System.String ReleaseDate {get;set;}
SerialNumber          Property   System.String SerialNumber {get;set;}
SMBIOSBIOSVersion     Property   System.String SMBIOSBIOSVersion {get;set;}
SMBIOSMajorVersion    Property   System.UInt16 SMBIOSMajorVersion {get;set;}
SMBIOSMinorVersion    Property   System.UInt16 SMBIOSMinorVersion {get;set;}
SMBIOSPresent         Property   System.Boolean SMBIOSPresent {get;set;}
SoftwareElementID     Property   System.String SoftwareElementID {get;set;}
SoftwareElementState  Property   System.UInt16 SoftwareElementState {get;set;}
Status                Property   System.String Status {get;set;}
TargetOperatingSystem Property   System.UInt16 TargetOperatingSystem {get;set;}
```

Properties and methods will be listed so that you can see them and figure out what that particular WMI class is capable of doing for you.

Some WMI properties contain multiple values—that is, they're *arrays*. Those can be a bit trickier to work with. For example, the Win32_NetworkAdapterConfiguration class exposes a property named IPAddress, which contains the hardware addresses of a particular network adapter. However, since any given network adapter can have *multiple* IP addresses bound to it, this property must be an array so that it can contain all the possible IP addresses. For the *most part*, PowerShell can just display the property directly. That is, PowerShell detects that the property contains an array and deals with it accordingly. For example:

```
PS C:\> $nics = gwmi win32_networkadapterconfiguration
PS C:\> $nics[4].ipaddress
192.168.4.102
fe80::e468:3091:f2fc:8deb
```

Here you can see that two IP addresses—an IPv4 and IPv6 address (because this was executed on Microsoft Vista)—are returned. If you just wanted *one* of those, you'd treat the IPAddress property like any other PowerShell array or collection:

```
PS C:\> $nics = gwmi win32_networkadapterconfiguration
PS C:\> $nics[4].ipaddress[0]
192.168.4.102
PS C:\> $nics[4].ipaddress[1]
fe80::e468:3091:f2fc:8deb
```

Simply referring to the appropriate array element by its index number allows you to access *just* that element.

Working Directly with Classes

So far, everything we've shown you has been about retrieving and working with instances of WMI classes. But did you know that you can do some cool stuff *directly* with classes, too? For example, let's retrieve a list of WMI classes, and then filter it so that we're just getting the Win32_Process class. We'll format the output in a list form:

```
PS C:\> $class = gwmi -list | where { $_.Name -eq "Win32_Process" }
PS C:\> $class | format-list
```

```
__GENUS           : 1
__CLASS           : Win32_Process
__SUPERCLASS      : CIM_Process
__DYNASTY         : CIM_ManagedSystemElement
__RELPATH         : Win32_Process
__PROPERTY_COUNT  : 45
__DERIVATION      : {CIM_Process, CIM_LogicalElement, CIM_ManagedSystemElement}
__SERVER          : DON-PC
__NAMESPACE       : ROOT\cimv2
__PATH            : \\DON-PC\ROOT\cimv2:Win32_Process
Name              : Win32_Process
```

....

What is All That?

Those WMI properties that start with two underscores (__) are all WMI system properties. They're always included with WMI objects, including the objects returned as the result of WMI functions. You can pretty much ignore them—WMI uses them internally, but they generally don't provide much in the way of useful information for you.

We can see the methods of the class by piping the class itself to **Get-Member**. We'll actually ask that cmdlet to *just* display the methods, so that the list is shorter. Remember, we're not working with any particular running process at this point; we're working with the *class*—the abstract description of what a process looks like this:

```
PS C:\> $class | get-member -membertype method


  TypeName: System.Management.ManagementClass#ROOT\cimv2\Win32_Process

Name      MemberType   Definition
----      ----------   ----------
Create    Method       System.Management.ManagementBaseObject Create(System.String CommandL...
```

In this case, the class has only one method: **Create()**. We're guessing this creates a new process—let's try it:

```
PS C:\> $class.create("calc.exe")


__GENUS           : 2
__CLASS           : __PARAMETERS
__SUPERCLASS      :
__DYNASTY         : __PARAMETERS
__RELPATH         :
__PROPERTY_COUNT  : 2
__DERIVATION      : {}
__SERVER          :
__NAMESPACE       :
__PATH            :
ProcessId         : 4676
ReturnValue       : 0
```

Of course, you can't see it unless you try it, but when we ran this we not only got the output shown, but a new Calculator window also popped up. And remember: If the original **Get-WmiObject()** call had been to a remote computer, *we would be starting the process on that computer.* That doesn't mean the process would be visible to other users on that computer (it normally wouldn't), but you *can* use this technique to start background processes remotely!

There's a quicker way to get a WMI class, using the [WMICLASS] type accelerator:

```
PS C:\> [WMICLASS]$wc = "\\.\root\cimv2:Win32_Process"
```

This retrieves the local computer's (represented by the special computername ".") Win32_Process class. And, by the way, if you're wondering how a particular method works, try running it *without* the (). For example:

```
PS C:\> $wc.create
```

```
MemberType          : Method
OverloadDefinitions : {System.Management.ManagementBaseObject Create(System.String CommandLine,
                      System.String CurrentDirectory, System.Management.Management
                      Object#Win32_ProcessStartup ProcessStartupInformation)}
TypeNameOfValue     : System.Management.Automation.PSMethod
Value               : System.Management.ManagementBaseObject Create(System.String CommandLine,
                      System.String CurrentDirectory, System.Management.Management
                      Object#Win32_ProcessStartup ProcessStartupInformation)
Name                : Create
IsInstance          : True
```

This detailed output shows us that the **Create()** method accepts a string, which is the command line we want to run, another string that is the working directory to set, and then a Win32_ProcessStartup object that contains options for starting the new process. Obviously, all but the first argument is optional, since we were able to use just the first argument in our previous example—you'll need to turn to the documentation, or just recklessly experiment, to see which arguments are required.

Executing WMI Methods

In addition to the previous example, which showed you how to execute a WMI method for a collection of WMI objects, you can also use **Invoke-WmiMethod** to execute a method for a specific class, or to execute a static method of a class—that is, execute a method without actually retrieving an instance of the class. For example, the Win32_Process class has a static **Create()** method. *Static* simply means that the method is available without obtaining an instance of the class—you don't need an actual process in order to create one. The following will run a new instance of Windows Notepad:

```
PS C:\> Invoke-WmiMethod -path Win32_Process -name Create -argumentList Notepad.exe
```

The -**argumentList** parameter accepts an array of arguments, and passes those directly to the method. You'll need to examine the class' documentation in order to see what arguments a given method expects to receive.

The **Invoke-WmiMethod** cmdlet supports most of the same parameters as **Get-WmiObject**, including -**computerName**, -**EnableAllPrivileges**, -**authentication**, and so forth. The following example launches Notepad on three remote computers, by using the -**computerName** parameter:

```
PS C:\> Invoke-WmiMethod -path Win32_Process -name Create -argumentList Notepad.exe '
 -computer "localhost","server2","media1"
```

If you actually try this, you'll notice an interesting limitation with WMI: The launched process doesn't appear on the remote computers' desktops in most instances. That's because Windows inherently supports multiple users on a given system at a single time. Notepad "appears" only to the user account that WMI used to launch it—which isn't necessarily the same account used by the person sitting in front of the computer. So this technique is useful primarily for launching background processes that do not have any kind of GUI and which do not require any kind of user interaction.

Invoke-WmiObject also supports the **-AsJob** parameter, allowing it to execute methods in the background—again, an incredibly useful feature if you're targeting multiple computers with a single command, since it lets you get back to doing other tasks in the shell while the job completes in the background.

Multiple Computers and WMI Background Jobs

PowerShell can easily retrieve WMI objects from multiple computers at once, simply by passing an array of strings into the **-computerName** parameter. For example:

```
PS C:\> $names = "localhost","server2","media1"
PS C:\> gwmi win32_operatingsystem -comp $names
```

In the original version of PowerShell, you could execute methods of the resulting WMI objects only by using the **ForEach-Object** cmdlet to enumerate each object and execute a given method one at a time:

```
PS C:\> $names = "localhost","server2","media1"
PS C:\> gwmi win32_operatingsystem -comp $names -EnableAllPrivileges | foreach-object {
$_.Reboot() }
```

Now, however, the **Invoke-WmiMethod** object makes the syntax somewhat easier:

```
PS C:\> $names = "localhost","server2","media1"
PS C:\> gwmi win32_operatingsystem -comp $names -EnableAllPrivileges | Invoke-WMIMethod Reboot
```

Both examples would reboot the three computers specified. For long-running operations, you can even have PowerShell perform the activity in the background as a job (refer to our chapter on working with background jobs for more information on managing jobs). Note that WMI doesn't utilize PowerShell's remoting subsystem, so you don't need to deploy PowerShell to the target machines in order to use the following technique:

```
PS C:\> $names = "localhost","server2","media1"
PS C:\> gwmi win32_operatingsystem -comp $names -asjob

Id         Name        State     HasMoreData    Location            Command
--         ----        -----     -----------    --------            -------
19         Job19       Running   False          localhost,server2... Get-WMIObject
```

What Runs Where?
The background job is created on the computer where Get-WmiObject was executed. It contacts target computers over the network, using Remote Procedure Calls (RPCs) to connect to each target computer's WMI service. The WMI service executes the actual WMI query and returns the results to Get-WmiObject.

The benefit to running this as a background job is that—especially with larger lists of computer names—you can get back to using the shell for other tasks while your longer-running WMI operation completes in the background. If you'll be using an especially large list of names, you may want to not only run the WMI operation as a background job, but also limit the number of computers that WMI connects to simultaneously. Doing so helps reduce network traffic and helps make sure that PowerShell remains responsive to other commands. To do so, just add the **-throttleLimit** parameter:

```
PS C:\> $names = "localhost","server2","media1"
PS C:\> gwmi win32_operatingsystem -comp $names –asjob –throttleLimit 16

Id          Name        State     HasMoreData   Location    Command
--          ----        -----     -----------   --------    -------
20          Job20       Running   False         localhost,server2...  Get-WMIObject
```

Again, once the job completes you can retrieve its results; our chapter on working with background jobs explains how to do this. Although jobs created by **Get-WmiObject** don't use PowerShell's remoting system, the jobs are managed exactly the same as jobs which *are* created by using the remoting system.

Creating New WMI Instances

Remember that each instance of a WMI object represents a real-world occurrence of a class. For example, each instance of Win32_Environment represents an environment variable; creating a new instance creates a new environment variable. Some common sense needs to apply here: You obviously can't create a new hard drive just by creating a new instance of Win32_DiskDrive. Similarly, some classes, such as Win32_Process, may require you to use a static method of the class itself to create a new instance (as shown in a previous example in this chapter). When possible, though, you can use the **Set-WmiInstance** cmdlet to create new instances of a class.

```
PS C:\> set-wmiinstance -class win32_environment –argument '
@{Name="testvar";VariableValue="testvalue";UserName="<SYSTEM>"}
```

Like most other WMI-related cmdlets, this one accepts -**computerName** and related parameters so that you can perform the operation on a remote computer, or even multiple remote computers; it also accepts -**AsJob** so that the operation can be handled in the background.

Creating a new WMI instance doesn't have a lot of practical uses when you're dealing only with the WMI classes that have to do with the core Windows operating system and your computer system hardware; but when you start working with more complex WMI information—such as the Internet Information Services (IIS) 7.0 WMI provider—you'll find more practical uses for this technique.

Working with WMI Events

Thus far, we've focused on using WMI in what we'll call an on-demand method: We executed methods to make things happen, and retrieved information to store or analyze it. In other words, when we wanted something, we told WMI to do it. But WMI also supports another way of working, where *it* can tell *us* when something happens, allowing us to react to specific events. WMI does this through *WMI events,* which are sort of like notifications that occur when specific things happen within WMI. The easiest way—and we know, this may not look easy at first, but it *is* the easiest way—of working with WMI events is to execute a WMI event query, which is done by using the **Register-WmiEvent** cmdlet. This cmdlet *registers* for an event, and specifies an *action*, in the form of a script block, that we want executed each time the event occurs. Here's what an event registration looks like:

```
PS C:\> $eventQuery = "SELECT * FROM __InstanceModificationEvent WITHIN 2 WHERE '
>> TargetInstance ISA 'Win32_Service' AND TargetInstance.State = 'Stopped'"
>>

PS C:\> $action = { Write-Host "Service Stopped!!" }

PS C:\> Register-WmiEvent -Query $eventQuery -Action $action

Id      Name            State       HasMoreData     Location    Command
--      ----            -----       -----------     --------    -------
39      13200c36-ef5... NotStarted  False                       Write-Host "Service S...


PS C:\>
```

As you can see, the actual registration—performed by **Register-WmiEvent**—isn't that complicated. What's complicated are those WMI event queries!

WMI Event Queries

A WMI event query breaks down into several parts:

- The keyword SELECT.

- A list of properties that you want to retrieve. These are properties of the *event object*, or in other words the object that is generated when the event occurs.

- The keyword FROM.

- The name of the WMI event class that you want to query.

- The keyword WITHIN.

- A time period, in seconds, that determines how often WMI will check to see if the event occurred; this is also called the *polling interval.*

- The keyword WHERE.

- Some criteria to narrow down the event objects returned—in this case, only those events generated by the modification of a Win32_Service object will be returned, and then only if the Win32_Service object's State property was changed to "Stopped."

There are three main event classes that you can query:

- __InstanceCreationEvent

- __InstanceModificationEvent

- __InstanceDeletionEvent

These three events are called *intrinsic* events, which means they're built into WMI and are available for any class. Other events, called *extrinsic* events, may be available for specific classes; the availability of these additional events, as well as details on how they work, will vary widely between classes, so we can't possibly document them or describe them here. You'll need to refer to individual class documentation to see any additional events a particular class offers.

As the intrinsic event names (which start with a *double* underscore, by the way) imply, these events occur whenever a new WMI class instance is created, changed, or deleted. Within the query, the TargetInstance keyword refers to the instance that was created, changed, or deleted. Note that a polling interval is 2 seconds isn't necessarily optimal; values under 30 seconds can, in fact, cause adverse performance, so you need to do a bit of experimentation. However, you don't want too large an interval: If a process is created and finishes within 30 seconds, then a 60-second polling interval might well miss the instance creation event.

Event Actions

The script block passed to the -**Action** parameter of **Register-WmiEvent** is executed each time the event occurs. So, continuing with our example of watching for stopped services using the event query we created earlier:

```
PS C:\> stop-service winrm
PS C:\> Service Stopped!!
```

Press Enter to return to a prompt. Here, you can see that the action was indeed executed when the specified WMI event occurred. Event actions can be as complex as you want, up to and including embedding entire scripts, or even executing a .ps1 script file.

Managing Events

When you register for an event, you create an *event subscriber*. Managing subscribers is easier if you create a friendly name, called a *source identifier*, for each subscriber:

```
PS C:\> Register-WmiEvent -Query $eventQuery –Action $action –SourceIdentifier "MyEvent"
```

If you do so, then you'll be able to unregister the event subscriber easily once you're done using it:

```
PS C:\> Unregister-event "MyEvent"
```

If you don't provide a source identifier, PowerShell will make one up, using a globally unique identifier (GUID), which is a truly lengthy hexadecimal number that you will *not* enjoy typing in. You can see a list of registered event subscribers by running **Get-EventSubscriber**; the output shows the source identifier.

```
PS C:\> get-eventsubscriber


SubscriptionId   : 1
SourceObject     : System.Management.ManagementEventWatcher
EventName        : EventArrived
SourceIdentifier : 13200c36-ef59-489d-8384-823b16abb77a
Action           : System.Management.Automation.PSEventJob
HandlerDelegate  :
SupportEvent     : False
ForwardEvent     : False
```

An easy way to quickly remove all event subscribers is as follows:

```
PS C:\> Get-EventSubscriber | Unregister-Event
```

For more information on managing events, see our chapter, "Working with Events" toward the end of this book.

Practical Uses for WMI Events

Why would you use a WMI event? Focusing just on the core classes in the root\CIMv2 namespace, there are a number of things you might achieve:

- Run a script whenever a new process is created.

- Run a script whenever a service is changed.

- Display an alert whenever a new logical disk is created (e.g., whenever a drive is added—such as a removable flash drive).

The possibilities are pretty limitless. One caveat, however, is that PowerShell *must be running* in order for events to be monitored and actions executed. In other words, PowerShell is receiving the event notifications from WMI and Windows, and then executing your specified actions in response to those events. Close the shell, and all your event monitoring goes away, so no actions will be executed from that point. As with everything else in PowerShell, event subscribers are not persisted between instances of the shell, so if you close and re-open the shell, you'll need to run **Register-WmiEvent** again to register all of your event subscribers anew.

Browsing WMI: There's a Lot to It!

Most of the examples in this chapter have focused on the default root\CIMV2 namespace, which contains most of the WMI classes related to the core Windows operating system and your computer system's hardware. All of the WMI cmdlets support a **-namespace** parameter, which you must specify when working with classes outside the default root\CIMV2 namespace. Consider downloading a tool like the free SAPIEN WMI Explorer (visit the download section of www.primaltools.com), which allows you to see all the namespaces on your computer and browse their classes and instances.

You might wonder how such a short chapter can prepare you to work with WMI in practical situations. The simple fact is that the actual techniques required to work with WMI are pretty simple, and we've shown you just about everything you'll need to use right in these few pages. The difficulty in working with WMI isn't the techniques you have to use, but rather it's the process of finding out which bit of WMI will accomplish whatever task you have in mind. Also, each different product that provides WMI support—Active Directory, DNS, SQL Server, IIS, and so forth—all tend to work slightly differently. Each of them could easily be the subject of a complete book, and we simply can't explain how to work with *all* of them here (we do provide practical examples related to Windows itself in a later chapter, though).

Another difficulty related to WMI is the fact that it's pretty poorly documented. While the core WMI classes—those related to Windows and computer hardware—are pretty well described at http://msdn. microsoft.com/library (we recommend using Google or Bing to search for Win32_Service—that'll get you into the proper section of the MSDN Library quickly), many other WMI classes aren't so well-documented. Documentation on the AD-related classes, for example, can be hard to find, and we've never seen anything documenting the classes in the root\SecurityCenter namespace. If you think that's frustrating—well, all we can do is agree. We try to provide practical, task-specific examples in our online and conference work, and in the ScriptingAnswers.com forums. SAPIEN Press publishes other more product-specific books which often include details on using WMI with that product.

Ultimately, WMI remains difficult to use simply because there's no single, comprehensive reference of everything that's available. You'll need to become proficient at using tools like SAPIEN's WMI Explorer, which at least exposes everything in WMI so that a determined and methodological search can eventually turn up what you need.

Chapter 15
Using ADSI in Windows PowerShell

Before we get started, we need to make sure you have some realistic expectations about ADSI in Windows PowerShell. First, understand that ADSI support was always planned to be a part of PowerShell. Because PowerShell is built on the .NET Framework, it can access the underlying directory service classes. The PowerShell team has provided some type adapters to make working with these classes much easier.

Microsoft Active Directory Cmdlets
As of this writing, the Active Directory team has released a PowerShell solution for managing Active Directory. However, these cmdlets and providers will only work with a Windows 2008 R2 domain controller, although they can also be run from Windows 7. As far as we know there are plans to eventually support Windows 2003 domain controllers and other clients. Full discussion of these cmdlets is outside the scope of this book. Quest Software has created a set of free cmdlets that will work with any Active Directory domain, and the free PowerShell Community Extensions offer a PSDrive provider. But for this chapter, we're sticking with what's built into PowerShell. This information is also important when working with local directory services on member servers and desktops.

ADSI Fundamentals

Active Directory Service Interfaces, or ADSI, is an extremely misleading name. Rather than reading it as "*Active Directory* Service Interfaces," which is what most administrators think it is, you should think of it as "*Active* Directory Service Interfaces." ADSI was named at a time when Microsoft slapped the word "Active" on everything that wasn't bolted down: ActiveX Data Objects, Active Directory, Active

Documents, and more. The thing to remember, though, is that ADSI *isn't just for Active Directory*. It works great with old Windows NT 4.0 domains, and even works with the local security accounts on standalone and member computers running modern versions of Windows.

ADSI is built around a system of *providers*. Each provider is capable of connecting to a particular type of directory: Windows NT (which includes local security accounts on standalone and member computers), Lightweight Directory Access Protocol (LDAP—this is what Active Directory, or AD, uses), and even Novell Directory Services, if you still have that in your environment somewhere.

ADSI Queries

The primary way to access directory objects—that is, users, groups, and so forth—is by issuing an *ADSI query*. A query starts with an ADSI provider, so that ADSI knows which type of directory you're trying to talk to. The two providers you'll use most are **WinNT://** and **LDAP://**—and note that, unlike most things in PowerShell, *these provider names are case-sensitive*, and that *they use forward slashes, not backslashes*. Those two caveats mess us up every time!

The format of an ADSI query depends on the provider. For the WinNT:// provider, queries look something like this:

```
WinNT://NAMESPACE/OBJECT,class
```

The NAMESPACE portion of the query can either be a computer name or a NetBIOS domain name—including AD domains! Remember that AD is backward-compatible with Windows NT, and by using the WinNT:// provider to access AD, you'll be able to refer to directory objects—users and groups—without needing to know what organizational unit (OU) they're in, because Windows NT didn't have OUs. The OBJECT portion of the query is the object name—that is, the user name, group name, or whatever—that you're after. The class part of the query is technically optional, but we recommend always including it: It should be "user" if you're querying a user object, "group" for a group object, and so forth. So, a complete query for our test machine's local Administrator account would look like this:

```
WinNT://TESTBED/Administrator,user
```

An LDAP query is much different. These queries require a *distinguished name* including the ADSI provider. For example, if you need to get the SalesUsers group, which is in the East OU, which is in the Sales OU of the MyDomain.com domain, your query would look like this:

```
LDAP://cn=SalesUsers,ou=East,ou=Sales,dc=MyDomain,dc=com
```

Definitely a bit more complicated. LDAP queries don't directly support wildcards either; you need to know exactly which object you're after (PowerShell does provide a somewhat cumbersome .NET Framework-based means of searching for directory objects, which we'll outline in "Managing Directory Services".

Using ADSI Objects

Once you've queried the correct object, you can work with its properties and methods. Objects queried through the WinNT:// provider generally have several useful properties. Although be aware that if you're accessing an AD object through the WinNT:// provider, you won't have access to all of the object's properties. You'll only see the ones that the older WinNT:// provider "understands." A few methods are available, too, such as **SetPassword()** and **SetInfo()**. The **SetInfo()** method is especially important: You must execute it after you change any object properties, so that the changes you made will be saved back to the directory correctly.

Objects retrieved through the LDAP:// provider don't directly support many properties. Instead, you execute the **Get()** and **GetEx()** methods, passing the property name you want, to retrieve properties. For example, assuming the variable **$user** represented a user object, you'd retrieve the Description property as follows:

```
$user.Get("Description")
```

Get() is used to retrieve properties that have only a single value, such as Description. **GetEx()** is used for properties that can contain multiple values, such as AD's otherHomePhone property. The opposites of these two methods are **Put()** and **PutEx()**, which are used like this:

```
$user.Put("Description","New Value")
```

After you finish all the **Put()** and **PutEx()** calls you want, you must execute the **SetInfo()** method to save the changes back to the directory. As with the WinNT:// provider, security principals retrieved through the LDAP:// provider also have a **SetPassword()** method you can use.

Retrieving ADSI Objects

Unfortunately, there's no built-in "Get-DirectoryObject" cmdlet built into PowerShell, which is a shame. Instead, you have to use the [ADSI] type accelerator to retrieve objects. You'll need to start with an ADSI query string, which we showed you how to build in "ADSI Queries" above. Then, just feed that to the type accelerator:

```
PS C:\> [ADSI]$user = "WinNT://TESTBED/Administrator,user"
```

This will retrieve the local Administrator user account from the computer named TESTBED, using the WinNT:// provider. You can then pipe the resulting object—which we've stored in the **$user** variable—to **Get-Member** (or its alias, **Gm**) to see what properties and methods the object contains:

```
PS C:\> $user | gm
```

```
   TypeName: System.DirectoryServices.DirectoryEntry
```

Name	MemberType	Definition
ConvertDNWithBinaryToString	CodeMethod static	System.String ConvertDNWithBinaryToString…
ConvertLargeIntegerToInt64	CodeMethod static	System.Int64 ConvertLargeIntegerToInt64(P…
AutoUnlockInterval	Property	System.DirectoryServices.PropertyValueCollection…
BadPasswordAttempts	Property	System.DirectoryServices.PropertyValueCollection…
Description	Property	System.DirectoryServices.PropertyValueCollection…
FullName	Property	System.DirectoryServices.PropertyValueCollection…
HomeDirDrive	Property	System.DirectoryServices.PropertyValueCollection…
HomeDirectory	Property	System.DirectoryServices.PropertyValueCollection…
LastLogin	Property	System.DirectoryServices.PropertyValueCollection…
LockoutObservationInterval	Property	System.DirectoryServices.PropertyValueCollection…
LoginHours	Property	System.DirectoryServices.PropertyValueCollection…
LoginScript	Property	System.DirectoryServices.PropertyValueCollection…
MaxBadPasswordsAllowed	Property	System.DirectoryServices.PropertyValueCollection…
MaxPasswordAge	Property	System.DirectoryServices.PropertyValueCollection…

MaxStorage	Property	System.DirectoryServices.PropertyValueCollection...
MinPasswordAge	Property	System.DirectoryServices.PropertyValueCollection...
MinPasswordLength	Property	System.DirectoryServices.PropertyValueCollection...
Name	Property	System.DirectoryServices.PropertyValueCollection...
objectSid	Property	System.DirectoryServices.PropertyValueCollection...
Parameters	Property	System.DirectoryServices.PropertyValueCollection...
PasswordAge	Property	System.DirectoryServices.PropertyValueCollection...
PasswordExpired	Property	System.DirectoryServices.PropertyValueCollection...
PasswordHistoryLength	Property	System.DirectoryServices.PropertyValueCollection...
PrimaryGroupID	Property	System.DirectoryServices.PropertyValueCollection...
Profile	Property	System.DirectoryServices.PropertyValueCollection...
UserFlags	Property	System.DirectoryServices.PropertyValueCollection...

We started with a WinNT:// provider example because these are perhaps the easiest objects to work with: You get nice, clearly defined properties. However, remember in "Using ADSI Objects" above, we said you have to execute the object's **SetInfo()** method whenever you change any properties? Do you see the **SetInfo()** method listed above? Nope. And that's because a major problem with the [ADSI] type accelerator is that it doesn't pass in the object's methods—only its properties. You *can* still use the **SetInfo()** method, though:

```
PS C:\> $user.description = "Local Admin"
PS C:\> $user.SetInfo()
PS C:\> $user.RefreshCache()
PS C:\> $user.description
Local Admin
```

It's just that the method doesn't show up in **Get-Member**, so you'll have to remember the method on your own. Basically, though, that's how you work with objects from the WinNT:// provider: Query the object, view or modify properties, and call **SetInfo()** if you've changed any properties. Use **SetPassword()** to change the password of a user object.

Although it isn't shown in the output of **Get-Member**, you can also use the **Get()**, **Put()**, **GetEx()**, and **PutEx()** methods we discussed in "Using ADSI Objects" above:

```
PS C:\> $user.get("description")
Local Admin
```

This isn't really useful with local computer accounts, since the object has direct properties you can access.

Here, you can see the WinNT:// provider being used to access an AD user named DonJ from the COMPANY domain (note that you have to use the domain's "short," or NetBIOS name, not its full DNS name):

```
PS C:\> [ADSI]$user = "WinNT://COMPANY/DonJ,user"
PS C:\> $user | gm
```

```
   TypeName: System.DirectoryServices.DirectoryEntry
```

Name	MemberType	Definition
----	----------	----------
ConvertDNWithBinaryToString	CodeMethod static	System.String ConvertDNWithBinaryToString...
ConvertLargeIntegerToInt64	CodeMethod static	System.Int64 ConvertLargeIntegerToInt64(P...
AutoUnlockInterval	Property	System.DirectoryServices.PropertyValueCollection...
BadPasswordAttempts	Property	System.DirectoryServices.PropertyValueCollection...
Description	Property	System.DirectoryServices.PropertyValueCollection...
FullName	Property	System.DirectoryServices.PropertyValueCollection...

HomeDirDrive	Property	System.DirectoryServices.PropertyValueCollection...
HomeDirectory	Property	System.DirectoryServices.PropertyValueCollection...
LastLogin	Property	System.DirectoryServices.PropertyValueCollection...
LockoutObservationInterval	Property	System.DirectoryServices.PropertyValueCollection...
LoginHours	Property	System.DirectoryServices.PropertyValueCollection...
LoginScript	Property	System.DirectoryServices.PropertyValueCollection...
MaxBadPasswordsAllowed	Property	System.DirectoryServices.PropertyValueCollectionStr...
MaxPasswordAge	Property	System.DirectoryServices.PropertyValueCollection...
MaxStorage	Property	System.DirectoryServices.PropertyValueCollection...
MinPasswordAge	Property	System.DirectoryServices.PropertyValueCollection...
MinPasswordLength	Property	System.DirectoryServices.PropertyValueCollection...
Name	Property	System.DirectoryServices.PropertyValueCollection...
objectSid	Property	System.DirectoryServices.PropertyValueCollection...
Parameters	Property	System.DirectoryServices.PropertyValueCollection...
PasswordAge	Property	System.DirectoryServices.PropertyValueCollection...
PasswordExpired	Property	System.DirectoryServices.PropertyValueCollection...
PasswordHistoryLength	Property	System.DirectoryServices.PropertyValueCollection...
PrimaryGroupID	Property	System.DirectoryServices.PropertyValueCollection...
Profile	Property	System.DirectoryServices.PropertyValueCollection...
UserFlags	Property	System.DirectoryServices.PropertyValueCollection...

So, where are all the AD-specific properties, like otherHomePhone and sn? Well, perhaps we could use the **Get()** method to retrieve one of them:

```
PS C:\> $user.get("sn")
Exception calling "get" with "1" argument(s): "The directory property cannot be found in
the cache.
"
At line:1 char:10
+ $user.get( <<<< "sn")
```

Nope. It turns out that the WinNT:// provider can't "see" any additional properties from AD; it can only see those properties that are backward-compatible with Windows NT 4.0 domains. So, when you're using the WinNT:// provider to access AD, you're giving up a lot of AD's extended capabilities.

Which brings us to AD's native provider, LDAP://. You'll retrieve objects in pretty much the same way as you did for the WinNT:// provider: Use the [ADSI] type accelerator, and provide an LDAP query string. Take a look:

```
PS C:\> [ADSI]$domain = "LDAP://dc=company,dc=local"
PS C:\> $domain | gm
```

```
   TypeName: System.DirectoryServices.DirectoryEntry
```

Name	MemberType	Definition
----	----------	----------
ConvertDNWithBinaryToString	CodeMethod static	System.String ConvertDNWithBinaryToStr
ConvertLargeIntegerToInt64	CodeMethod static	System.Int64 ConvertLargeIntegerToInt6
auditingPolicy	Property	System.DirectoryServices.PropertyValueCollect
creationTime	Property	System.DirectoryServices.PropertyValueCollect
dc	Property	System.DirectoryServices.PropertyValueCollect
distinguishedName	Property	System.DirectoryServices.PropertyValueCollect
forceLogoff	Property	System.DirectoryServices.PropertyValueCollect
fSMORoleOwner	Property	System.DirectoryServices.PropertyValueCollect
gPLink	Property	System.DirectoryServices.PropertyValueCollect
instanceType	Property	System.DirectoryServices.PropertyValueCollect
isCriticalSystemObject	Property	System.DirectoryServices.PropertyValueCollect
lockoutDuration	Property	System.DirectoryServices.PropertyValueCollect
lockOutObservationWindow	Property	System.DirectoryServices.PropertyValueCollect

lockoutThreshold	Property	System.DirectoryServices.PropertyValueCollect
masteredBy	Property	System.DirectoryServices.PropertyValueCollect
maxPwdAge	Property	System.DirectoryServices.PropertyValueCollect
minPwdAge	Property	System.DirectoryServices.PropertyValueCollect
minPwdLength	Property	System.DirectoryServices.PropertyValueCollect
modifiedCount	Property	System.DirectoryServices.PropertyValueCollect
modifiedCountAtLastProm	Property	System.DirectoryServices.PropertyValueCollect
ms-DS-MachineAccountQuota	Property	System.DirectoryServices.PropertyValueCollect
msDS-AllUsersTrustQuota	Property	System.DirectoryServices.PropertyValueCollect
msDS-Behavior-Version	Property	System.DirectoryServices.PropertyValueCollect
msDs-masteredBy	Property	System.DirectoryServices.PropertyValueCollect
msDS-PerUserTrustQuota	Property	System.DirectoryServices.PropertyValueCollect
msDS-PerUserTrustTombstonesQuota	Property	System.DirectoryServices.PropertyValueCollect
name	Property	System.DirectoryServices.PropertyValueCollect
nextRid	Property	System.DirectoryServices.PropertyValueCollect
nTMixedDomain	Property	System.DirectoryServices.PropertyValueCollect
nTSecurityDescriptor	Property	System.DirectoryServices.PropertyValueCollect
objectCategory	Property	System.DirectoryServices.PropertyValueCollect
objectClass	Property	System.DirectoryServices.PropertyValueCollect
objectGUID	Property	System.DirectoryServices.PropertyValueCollect
objectSid	Property	System.DirectoryServices.PropertyValueCollect
pwdHistoryLength	Property	System.DirectoryServices.PropertyValueCollect
pwdProperties	Property	System.DirectoryServices.PropertyValueCollect
rIDManagerReference	Property	System.DirectoryServices.PropertyValueCollect
serverState	Property	System.DirectoryServices.PropertyValueCollect
subRefs	Property	System.DirectoryServices.PropertyValueCollect
systemFlags	Property	System.DirectoryServices.PropertyValueCollect
uASCompat	Property	System.DirectoryServices.PropertyValueCollect
uSNChanged	Property	System.DirectoryServices.PropertyValueCollect
uSNCreated	Property	System.DirectoryServices.PropertyValueCollect
wellKnownObjects	Property	System.DirectoryServices.PropertyValueCollect
whenChanged	Property	System.DirectoryServices.PropertyValueCollect
whenCreated	Property	System.DirectoryServices.PropertyValueCollect

We've truncated the results a bit, but you can see that we've retrieved the domain object and displayed its properties—but not methods, because those won't be shown—by using the LDAP:// provider and the **Get-Member** cmdlet. We can retrieve the built-in Users container in a similar fashion:

```
PS C:\> [ADSI]$container = "LDAP://cn=users,dc=company,dc=local"
PS C:\> $container | gm


   TypeName: System.DirectoryServices.DirectoryEntry

Name                        MemberType       Definition
----                        ----------       ----------
ConvertDNWithBinaryToString CodeMethod static System.String ConvertDNWithBinaryToString
ConvertLargeIntegerToInt64  CodeMethod static System.Int64 ConvertLargeIntegerToInt64(P
cn                          Property         System.DirectoryServices.PropertyValueCollection
description                 Property         System.DirectoryServices.PropertyValueCollection
distinguishedName           Property         System.DirectoryServices.PropertyValueCollection
instanceType                Property         System.DirectoryServices.PropertyValueCollection
isCriticalSystemObject      Property         System.DirectoryServices.PropertyValueCollection
name                        Property         System.DirectoryServices.PropertyValueCollection
nTSecurityDescriptor        Property         System.DirectoryServices.PropertyValueCollection
objectCategory              Property         System.DirectoryServices.PropertyValueCollection
objectClass                 Property         System.DirectoryServices.PropertyValueCollection
objectGUID                  Property         System.DirectoryServices.PropertyValueCollection
showInAdvancedViewOnly      Property         System.DirectoryServices.PropertyValueCollection
systemFlags                 Property         System.DirectoryServices.PropertyValueCollection
uSNChanged                  Property         System.DirectoryServices.PropertyValueCollection
uSNCreated                  Property         System.DirectoryServices.PropertyValueCollection
```

| whenChanged | Property | System.DirectoryServices.PropertyValueCollection |
| whenCreated | Property | System.DirectoryServices.PropertyValueCollection |

Notice anything similar about the container and the domain? They're both a System.DirectoryServices. DirectoryEntry object, even though they're very different objects. This is one of the things that makes PowerShell's current ADSI support a bit complicated: PowerShell relies on this underlying .NET Framework class, DirectoryEntry, to represent *all* directory objects. Obviously, different types of objects—containers, users, groups, and so forth—have different properties and capabilities, but this class represents them all generically. PowerShell and the Framework try to represent the object's properties as best they can, but they can't always show you *everything* that's available. This becomes especially apparent when you view the *untruncated* output of **Get-Member** for an AD user object:

```
PS C:\> [ADSI]$user = "LDAP://cn=don jones,cn=users,dc=company,dc=com"
PS C:\> $user | gm
```

```
    TypeName: System.DirectoryServices.DirectoryEntry
```

Name	MemberType	Definition
ConvertDNWithBinaryToString	CodeMethod static	System.String ConvertDNWithBinaryToString
ConvertLargeIntegerToInt64	CodeMethod static	System.Int64 ConvertLargeIntegerToInt64(P
accountExpires	Property	System.DirectoryServices.PropertyValueCollection
badPasswordTime	Property	System.DirectoryServices.PropertyValueCollection
badPwdCount	Property	System.DirectoryServices.PropertyValueCollection
cn	Property	System.DirectoryServices.PropertyValueCollection
codePage	Property	System.DirectoryServices.PropertyValueCollection
countryCode	Property	System.DirectoryServices.PropertyValueCollection
displayName	Property	System.DirectoryServices.PropertyValueCollection
distinguishedName	Property	System.DirectoryServices.PropertyValueCollection
instanceType	Property	System.DirectoryServices.PropertyValueCollection
lastLogoff	Property	System.DirectoryServices.PropertyValueCollection
lastLogon	Property	System.DirectoryServices.PropertyValueCollection
logonCount	Property	System.DirectoryServices.PropertyValueCollection
name	Property	System.DirectoryServices.PropertyValueCollection
nTSecurityDescriptor	Property	System.DirectoryServices.PropertyValueCollection
objectCategory	Property	System.DirectoryServices.PropertyValueCollection
objectClass	Property	System.DirectoryServices.PropertyValueCollection
objectGUID	Property	System.DirectoryServices.PropertyValueCollection
objectSid	Property	System.DirectoryServices.PropertyValueCollection
primaryGroupID	Property	System.DirectoryServices.PropertyValueCollection
pwdLastSet	Property	System.DirectoryServices.PropertyValueCollection
sAMAccountName	Property	System.DirectoryServices.PropertyValueCollection
sAMAccountType	Property	System.DirectoryServices.PropertyValueCollection
userAccountControl	Property	System.DirectoryServices.PropertyValueCollection
userPrincipalName	Property	System.DirectoryServices.PropertyValueCollection
uSNChanged	Property	System.DirectoryServices.PropertyValueCollection
uSNCreated	Property	System.DirectoryServices.PropertyValueCollection
whenChanged	Property	System.DirectoryServices.PropertyValueCollection
whenCreated	Property	System.DirectoryServices.PropertyValueCollection

Active Directory Users and Computers uses a dialog box to display user properties and it definitely displays more than these! For example, where is the Description property? Well, it turns out that the particular user we retrieved doesn't *have* a Description property—that is, it was never filled in when the user was created. So, the property isn't shown. We *can* set the property—provided we know the property name already, since **Get-Member** won't show it to us. We'll set the property, use **SetInfo()** to save the change, and then re-query the user to see if the property shows up:

```
PS C:\> $user.put("description","This is a test user.")
PS C:\> $user.setinfo()
PS C:\> $user.RefreshCache()
PS C:\> $user | gm


   TypeName: System.DirectoryServices.DirectoryEntry

Name                        MemberType      Definition
----                        ----------      ----------
ConvertDNWithBinaryToString CodeMethod static System.String ConvertDNWithBinaryToString(
ConvertLargeIntegerToInt64  CodeMethod static System.Int64 ConvertLargeIntegerToInt64(PS
accountExpires              Property        System.DirectoryServices.PropertyValueCollection
badPasswordTime             Property        System.DirectoryServices.PropertyValueCollection
badPwdCount                 Property        System.DirectoryServices.PropertyValueCollection
cn                          Property        System.DirectoryServices.PropertyValueCollection
codePage                    Property        System.DirectoryServices.PropertyValueCollection
countryCode                 Property        System.DirectoryServices.PropertyValueCollection
description                 Property        System.DirectoryServices.PropertyValueCollection
displayName                 Property        System.DirectoryServices.PropertyValueCollection
distinguishedName           Property        System.DirectoryServices.PropertyValueCollection
instanceType                Property        System.DirectoryServices.PropertyValueCollection
lastLogoff                  Property        System.DirectoryServices.PropertyValueCollection
lastLogon                   Property        System.DirectoryServices.PropertyValueCollection
logonCount                  Property        System.DirectoryServices.PropertyValueCollection
name                        Property        System.DirectoryServices.PropertyValueCollection
nTSecurityDescriptor        Property        System.DirectoryServices.PropertyValueCollection
objectCategory              Property        System.DirectoryServices.PropertyValueCollection
objectClass                 Property        System.DirectoryServices.PropertyValueCollection
objectGUID                  Property        System.DirectoryServices.PropertyValueCollection
objectSid                   Property        System.DirectoryServices.PropertyValueCollection
primaryGroupID              Property        System.DirectoryServices.PropertyValueCollection
pwdLastSet                  Property        System.DirectoryServices.PropertyValueCollection
sAMAccountName              Property        System.DirectoryServices.PropertyValueCollection
sAMAccountType              Property        System.DirectoryServices.PropertyValueCollection
userAccountControl          Property        System.DirectoryServices.PropertyValueCollection
userPrincipalName           Property        System.DirectoryServices.PropertyValueCollection
uSNChanged                  Property        System.DirectoryServices.PropertyValueCollection
uSNCreated                  Property        System.DirectoryServices.PropertyValueCollection
whenChanged                 Property        System.DirectoryServices.PropertyValueCollection
whenCreated                 Property        System.DirectoryServices.PropertyValueCollection
```

As you can see, the Description property now appears, because it has a value. This is an important caveat of working with ADSI in PowerShell: You can't rely on **Get-Member** to discover objects' capabilities. Instead, you'll need an external reference such as the MSDN documentation.

Searching for ADSI Objects

Sometimes you need to retrieve an object from Active Directory without knowing exactly where it is or what its distinguishedname is. PowerShell relies on the .NET Framework and the DirectoryServices. DirectorySearcher class. This type of object is used to find objects in a directory service such as Active Directory. Here's a sample function that uses the class to find a user object in Active Directory based on the user's SAM account name:

Find-User Function.ps1

```
Function Find-User {
  Param ($sam=$(throw "you must enter a sAMAccountname"))
  $searcher=New-Object DirectoryServices.DirectorySearcher
```

```
$searcher.Filter="(&(objectcategory=person)(objectclass=user)(sAMAccountname=$sam))"
$results=$searcher.FindOne()
if ($results.path.length -gt 1)
{
  Write $results
}
else
{
  write "Not Found"
}
}
```

You use the **New-Object** cmdlet to create the DirectorySearcher object:

```
$searcher=New-Object DirectoryServices.DirectorySearcher
```

The searcher will by default search the current domain, although you can specify a location such as an OU, which we'll show in a little bit. What you will need to do, however, is specify a LDAP search filter:

```
$searcher.Filter="(&(objectcategory=person)(objectclass=user)(sAMAccountname=$sam))"
```

The filter instructs the searcher to find user objects where the *sAMAccountname* property matches that passed as a function parameter. The function calls the searcher's **FindOne()** method:

```
$results=$searcher.FindOne()
```

Assuming a user is found, the resulting object will be stored in **$results**. The script checks the length of the *Path* property of **$results**. If a user object was found, the *Path* property will be the user's distinguishedname and will have a length greater than 1. Otherwise, the user was not found and the function returns and error message:

```
if ($results.path.length -gt 1)
  {
    write $results
  }
else
  {
    write "Not Found"
  }
```

Here's how you can use the function:

```
PS C:\> find-user jhicks

Path                                                        Properties
----                                                        ----------
LDAP://CN=Jeff Hicks,OU=Employees,DC=company,DC=local       {samaccounttype, countrycode,

PS C:\>
```

The *Path* property shows the user's distinguished name. The *Properties* property is a collection of all the user properties. Here's another way you might use this function:

```
PS C:\> $user=find-user jhicks
PS C:\> $user.properties.description
Company admin
PS C:\> $user.properties.userprincipalname
jhicks@company.local
PS C:\>
```

The results of the Find-User function are stored in the **$user** variable. This means we can access its properties directly, such as *Description* and *UserPrincipalName*. If you want to see all of user's defined properties, simply use:

```
PS C:\> $user.properties
```

You can also use the searcher object to search from a specific container and to find more than one object:

```
PS C:\> $Searcher = New-Object DirectoryServices.DirectorySearcher
PS C:\> $Root = New-Object DirectoryServices.DirectoryEntry '
>> 'LDAP://OU=Sales,OU=Employees,DC=mycompany,DC=local'
>>
PS C:\> $Searcher.SearchRoot = $Root
PS C:\> $searcher.Filter="(&(objectcategory=person)(objectclass=user))"
PS C:\> $searcher.pagesize=100
PS C:\> $Searcher.FindAll()
```

```
Path                                                Properties
----                                                ----------
LDAP://CN=Anne Tern,OU=Sales,OU=Employees,DC=company,DC=...   {company, distinguishedname,...
LDAP://CN=Fiona Thrush,OU=Sales,OU=Employees,DC=company,...   {company, distinguishedname,...
LDAP://CN=George Washington,OU=Sales,OU=Employees,DC=com...   {lastlogon, objectsid, whencr...
LDAP://CN=Roy G. Biv,OU=Sales,OU=Employees,DC=company,DC...   {samaccounttype, lastlogon, g...

PS C:\>
```

In this example, we create a new object type called a DirectoryEntry:

```
PS C:\> $Root = New-Object DirectoryServices.DirectoryEntry '
>> 'LDAP://OU=Sales,OU=Employees,DC=mycompany;DC=local'
>>
```

You can use this object for the *Root* property of the searcher object:

```
PS C:\> $Searcher.SearchRoot = $Root
```

Again, we're going to search for user objects:

```
PS C:\> $searcher.Filter="(&(objectcategory=person)(objectclass=user))"
```

Only this time, we'll use the **FindAll()** method to return all objects that match the search pattern:

```
PS C:\> $Searcher.FindAll()
```

Now all of that may seem like a lot of work, and frankly it is. But we wanted you to know how the DirectorySearcher class works so that you can appreciate and understand the [ADSISearcher] type adapter.

This type adapter simplifies this process.

```
PS C:\> [ADSISearcher]$searcher="(&(objectcategory=person)(objectclass=user))"
PS C:\> $searcher | gm


    TypeName: System.DirectoryServices.DirectorySearcher

Name                        MemberType   Definition
----                        ----------   ----------
CreateObjRef                Method       System.Runtime.Remoting.ObjRef CreateObjRef(Type req
Dispose                     Method       System.Void Dispose()
Equals                      Method       System.Boolean Equals(Object obj)
FindAll                     Method       System.DirectoryServices.SearchResultCollection Find
FindOne                     Method       System.DirectoryServices.SearchResult FindOne()
GetHashCode                 Method       System.Int32 GetHashCode()
GetLifetimeService          Method       System.Object GetLifetimeService()
GetType                     Method       System.Type GetType()
InitializeLifetimeService   Method       System.Object InitializeLifetimeService()
ToString                    Method       System.String ToString()
Asynchronous                Property     System.Boolean Asynchronous {get;set;}
AttributeScopeQuery         Property     System.String AttributeScopeQuery {get;set;}
CacheResults                Property     System.Boolean CacheResults {get;set;}
ClientTimeout               Property     System.TimeSpan ClientTimeout {get;set;}
Container                   Property     System.ComponentModel.IContainer Container {get;}
DerefAlias                  Property     System.DirectoryServices.DereferenceAlias DerefAlias
DirectorySynchronization    Property     System.DirectoryServices.DirectorySynchronization Di
ExtendedDN                  Property     System.DirectoryServices.ExtendedDN ExtendedDN {get;
Filter                      Property     System.String Filter {get;set;}
PageSize                    Property     System.Int32 PageSize {get;set;}
PropertiesToLoad            Property     System.Collections.Specialized.StringCollection Prop
PropertyNamesOnly           Property     System.Boolean PropertyNamesOnly {get;set;}
ReferralChasing             Property     System.DirectoryServices.ReferralChasingOption Refer
SearchRoot                  Property     System.DirectoryServices.DirectoryEntry SearchRoot {
SearchScope                 Property     System.DirectoryServices.SearchScope SearchScope {ge
SecurityMasks               Property     System.DirectoryServices.SecurityMasks SecurityMasks
ServerPageTimeLimit         Property     System.TimeSpan ServerPageTimeLimit {get;set;}
ServerTimeLimit             Property     System.TimeSpan ServerTimeLimit {get;set;}
Site                        Property     System.ComponentModel.ISite Site {get;set;}
SizeLimit                   Property     System.Int32 SizeLimit {get;set;}
Sort                        Property     System.DirectoryServices.SortOption Sort {get;set;}
Tombstone                   Property     System.Boolean Tombstone {get;set;}
VirtualListView             Property     System.DirectoryServices.DirectoryVirtualListView Vi


PS C:\>
```

We generally create the searcher object by defining its filter. The search root defaults to the current domain naming context:

```
PS C:\> $searcher.searchroot


distinguishedName : {DC=company,DC=local}
Path              : LDAP://DC=company,DC=local
```

But of course, you could easily change that. The default search scope is Subtree as well:

```
PS C:\> $searcher.searchscope
Subtree
```

All that you have to do is call either the **FindOne()** or **FindAll()** method:

```
PS C:\> $searcher.findall()

Path                                                        Properties
----                                                        ----------
LDAP://CN=Administrator,CN=Users,DC=company,DC=local        {samaccounttype, lastlogon, l
LDAP://CN=Guest,CN=Users,DC=company,DC=local                {samaccounttype, lastlogon, o
LDAP://CN=SUPPORT_388945a0,CN=Users,DC=company,DC=local     {samaccounttype, lastlogon, o
LDAP://CN=krbtgt,CN=Users,DC=company,DC=local               {samaccounttype, lastlogon, o
LDAP://CN=Jeff Hicks,OU=Employees,DC=company,DC=local       {samaccounttype, countrycode,
LDAP://CN=tuser1,OU=QA,OU=Employees,DC=company,DC=local     {distinguishedname, countryco
LDAP://CN=tuser2,OU=QA,OU=Employees,DC=company,DC=local     {distinguishedname, countryco
LDAP://CN=tuser3,OU=QA,OU=Employees,DC=company,DC=local     {distinguishedname, countryco
LDAP://CN=tuser4,OU=QA,OU=Employees,DC=company,DC=local     {distinguishedname, countryco
LDAP://CN=tuser5,OU=QA,OU=Employees,DC=company,DC=local     {distinguishedname, countryco
LDAP://CN=tuser6,OU=QA,OU=Employees,DC=company,DC=local     {distinguishedname, countryco
LDAP://CN=tuser7,OU=QA,OU=Employees,DC=company,DC=local     {distinguishedname, countryco
LDAP://CN=tuser8,OU=QA,OU=Employees,DC=company,DC=local     {distinguishedname, countryco
LDAP://CN=tuser9,OU=QA,OU=Employees,DC=company,DC=local     {distinguishedname, countryco
LDAP://CN=tuser10,OU=QA,OU=Employees,DC=company,DC=local    {distinguishedname, countryco
LDAP://CN=Roy G. Biv,OU=Sales,OU=Employees,DC=company,DC... {samaccounttype, lastlogon, g
LDAP://CN=Don Jones,OU=Employees,DC=company,DC=local        {samaccounttype, lastlogon, g
LDAP://CN=Amy Admin,OU=Employees,DC=company,DC=local        {samaccounttype, lastlogon, g
LDAP://CN=Charles Dickens,OU=Employees,DC=company,DC=local  {lastlogon, objectsid, whencr
LDAP://CN=Anne Tern,OU=Sales,OU=Employees,DC=company,DC=... {company, distinguishedname,
LDAP://CN=Ben Jay,OU=Finance,OU=Employees,DC=company,DC=... {company, distinguishedname,
LDAP://CN=Charlie Robin,OU=Research,OU=Employees,DC=comp... {company, distinguishedname,
LDAP://CN=David Cardinal,OU=Research,OU=Employees,DC=com... {company, distinguishedname,
LDAP://CN=Ed Nightingale,OU=QA,OU=Employees,DC=company,D... {company, distinguishedname,
LDAP://CN=Fiona Thrush,OU=Sales,OU=Employees,DC=company,... {company, distinguishedname,
LDAP://CN=BettyX,CN=Users,DC=company,DC=local               {samaccounttype, lastlogon, o
LDAP://CN=George Washington,OU=Sales,OU=Employees,DC=com... {lastlogon, objectsid, whencr


PS C:\>
```

We can now slightly re-write our original Find-User function to take advantage of the type adapter:

Find-User Revised.ps1

```
Function Find-User {
  Param ($sam=$(throw "you must enter a sAMAccountname"))

  [ADSISearcher]$searcher="(&(objectcategory=person)(objectclass=user)(sAMAccountname=$sam))"
  $results=$searcher.FindOne()

  if ($results.path.length -gt 1)
    {
    write $results
    }
  else
    {
    write "Not Found"
    }
}
```

Working with ADSI Objects

You've actually already seen a quick example of working with AD objects when we set the Description property of our test user account back in the "Using ADSI Objects" section. Here's how to change a password:

```
PS C:\> $user.setpassword("P@ssw0rd!")
```

Retrieve the object into a variable, and then call its **SetPassword()** method, passing the desired new password as an argument.

Creating new objects is straightforward: You'll need to retrieve the *parent container* that you want the new object created in, and then call the parent's **Create()** method. Doing so will return an object that represents the new directory object; you'll need to set any mandatory properties, and then save the object to the directory. Here's an example:

```
PS C:\> [ADSI]$container = "LDAP://ou=employees,dc=company,dc=local"
PS C:\> $user = $container.create("user","cn=Tim E. Clock")
PS C:\> $user.put("sAMAccountName","tclock")
PS C:\> $user.setinfo()
```

If you're familiar with VBScript, you may be thinking: "Wow! This looks a lot like what we did in VBScript." It sure does—it's almost *exactly* the same, in fact. We'll present additional directory-related tasks in the "Managing Directory Services" chapter, but hopefully this gives you a quick idea of what PowerShell can do with ADSI.

We should show you one more thing before we go on: Some AD properties (like WMI properties) are *arrays*, meaning they contain multiple values. For example, the Member property of an AD group object contains an array of distinguishednames, with each representing one group member. Here's an example of retrieving the distinguishedname of the first member of a domain's Domain Admins group:

```
PS C:\> [ADSI]$group = "LDAP://cn=Domain Admins,cn=Users,dc=company,dc=local"
PS C:\> $group.member[0]
CN=Administrator,CN=Users,DC=company,DC=local
```

Modifying these properties is a bit complicated, since you have to use the **PutEx()** method and pass it a parameter indicating whether you're clearing the property completely, updating a value, adding a value, or deleting a value. The special parameter values are:

- 1: Clear the property.
- 2: Change an existing value within the property.
- 3: Add a new value to the property.
- 4: Delete a value from the property.

So, to add a new user to the Domain Admins group, which we've already retrieved into the **$group** variable, do this:

```
PS C:\> $group.PutEx(3, "member", @("cn=Don Jones,ou=Employees,dc=company,dc=local"))
PS C:\> $group.setinfo()
```

We used the value 3, so we're adding a value to the array. We have to actually add an array, even though we only need to have one item in the array—the user we want to add to the group. So, we use

PowerShell's @ operator to create a new, one-element array containing the distinguishedname of the new group member. You need to use **SetInfo()** to save the information back to the directory.

We hope this quick overview gives you a good start in using ADSI from within PowerShell. As you can see, the actual mechanics of it all aren't that complicated; the tough part is understanding what's going on inside the directory, including the property names that let you view and modify the information you need. We'll return this topic and look at the Quest and Windows Server 2008 R2 cmdlets in the chapter on Managing Directory Services.

Chapter 16
Scripting Overview

With many shells—particularly some *nix shells—using the shell interactively is a very different experience than scripting with the shell. Typically, shells offer a complete scripting language that is *only* available when you're running a script. Not so with PowerShell: The shell behaves exactly the same, and offers exactly the same features and functionality, whether you're writing a script or using the shell interactively. In fact, a PowerShell script is a *true* script—simply a text file listing the things you'd type interactively. The only reason to write a script is because you're tired of typing those things interactively and want to be able to run them again and again with minimal effort.

Script Files

PowerShell recognizes the .PS1 filename extension as a PowerShell script. Notice the "1" in there? That indicates a script designed to work with PowerShell version 1; future versions of PowerShell will presumably be able to use that as an indicator for backward-compatibility. Script files are simple text files; you can edit them with Windows Notepad or any other text editor. In fact, by default, Windows associates the .PS1 filename extension with Notepad, not PowerShell, so double-clicking a script file opens it in Notepad rather than executing it in PowerShell. Of course, we're a bit biased against Notepad as a script editor: Notepad was certainly never designed for that task, and better options exist. We're obviously keen on SAPIEN PrimalScript (www.primalscript.com) because it offers a full visual development environment with PowerShell-specific support, such as the ability to package a PowerShell script in a standalone executable that runs under alternate credentials.

Note that PowerShell v2.0 continues to use the .PS1 filename extension; think of this filename extension as "version 1 of the script file format," rather than having a direct relation to v2.0 of the shell. In fact, v2.0 should run most v1.0 scripts unchanged.

Profiles

PowerShell supports four special scripts called *profiles*. These scripts are physically identical to any other script; what makes them special is that PowerShell looks for them when it starts and, if it finds them, executes them. Think of them as a sort of "auto-run" set of scripts, allowing you to define custom aliases, functions, and so forth. For example, by defining custom aliases in your profile, those aliases will be defined every time PowerShell runs, making your aliases available to you anytime you're using the shell.

PowerShell looks for profiles using a specific path and filename. It looks for them—and executes them, if they're present—in the following order:

- %windir%\system32\WindowsPowerShell\v1.0\profile.ps1
  This applies to all users and to all shells.

- %windir\system32\WindowsPowerShell\v1.0\Microsoft.PowerShell_profile.ps1
  This applies to all users but only to the PowerShell.exe shell.

- %UserDocuments%\WindowsPowerShell\profile.ps1
  This applies to the current user but affects all shells.

- %UserDocuments%\WindowsPowerShell\Microsoft.PowerShell_profile.ps1
  This applies to the current user and only to the PowerShell.exe shell.

By the Way...
%UserDocuments% isn't a valid environment variable; we're using it to represent the user's "Documents" folder. On Windows XP, for example, this would be under %UserProfile%\My Documents; on Windows Vista it's under %UserProfile%\Documents.

Notice the references to "all shells." In this book, we're primarily working with the PowerShell.exe shell. However, other shells exist: The Exchange Management Shell (which ships with Exchange Server 2007) is a different shell. So, if you have things you want defined in *all* the shells you use—such as custom aliases—you'd put them in one of the "all shells" profiles.

A Note on Shells
Note that you don't have to use custom shells. For example, you don't need to use the Exchange Management Shell to manage Exchange Server 2007. Instead, you could simply add the Exchange snap-in to PowerShell.exe, using Add-PSSnapIn. Doing so would give you access to the Exchange cmdlets from the PowerShell.exe shell. This trick allows you to create a shell environment that has all the cmdlets you need to manage all your PowerShell-manageable products.

None of these profile files are created by default. You should also remember that these are *just PowerShell scripts*, so they won't run unless they meet your shell's execution policy—in other words, your profiles need to be signed if your execution policy is AllSigned.

Scripting Basics

In the next several chapters, we'll cover the various elements of PowerShell scripting. These aren't necessarily covered in any particular order; that is, you don't necessarily need to know one thing before another thing. And keep in mind that everything we're covering related to scripting *works fine when you're using the shell interactively*. So, you can use everything we're about to show you even if you're not planning on writing scripts at all. Here's what we'll cover:

- Variables, arrays, and escape sequences, including associative arrays (also called dictionaries or hash tables). We've covered some of this information in earlier chapters, but a review will help you master these concepts, and we'll dive into a bit more depth with them.

- Objects, which are the basis of PowerShell's functionality. Again, we've touched on objects already, but now we'll take the time to completely define them.

- Operators, which allow PowerShell to manipulate and compare data. You've seen some operators in action already, but we'll be covering more operators, and in more depth, than we have previously.

- Regular expressions are a technique used for pattern-matching, and are often used to validate input—for example, making sure an e-mail address *looks like* an e-mail address.

- Loops and decision-making constructs do the following: form the bulk of PowerShell's scripting language, allow your scripts to make decisions based on conditions you specify, and allow you to repeat a given task over and over.

- Error handling is a key skill that allows you to anticipate and deal with errors that occur when your scripts run.

- The PowerShell Debugger provides a simple way to debug scripts by following their execution line by line and examining the contents of variables and object properties as you go.

- Finally, the chapter "PowerShell for VBScript, Cmd.exe, and *nix Users" will introduce PowerShell using concepts familiar to VBScript developers. Think of this as kind of a "jump start" for using PowerShell, where you'll be able to leverage what you already know about VBScript to understand PowerShell more quickly.

Scope

Now that you're going to begin working with scripts, you're going to run up against a concept called *scope*, which is very important in Windows PowerShell. So far, we've just been working interactively in the shell, which is referred to as the *global scope*. When you're just working interactively in the shell, *everything* occurs in the global scope, so it's like there's no scope at all.

However, when you run a script, PowerShell creates a new *script scope*, which contains the script. The script scope is a *child* of the global scope; the global scope is referred to as the script scope's *parent*. Some special rules govern interaction between the two scopes:

- The parent scope cannot see "inside" of the child scope.

- The child scope can *read* elements of the parent scope but can modify them only if a special syntax is used.

- If a child scope attempts to modify a parent scope element *without* using the special syntax, then a new element of the same name is created within the child scope, and the child scope effectively "loses" access to the parent scope element of that name.

Elements, in the above rules, refer primarily to variables and functions. So, to reiterate these rules in a variable-centric sense:

- The parent scope cannot access variables, which are defined in a child scope.

- The child scope can *read* variables defined in the parent scope but can modify them only if a special syntax is used.

- If a child scope attempts to modify a parent scope variable *without* using the special syntax, then a new variable of the same name is created within the child scope, and the child scope effectively "loses" access to the parent scope variable of that name.

When you create a function—either by defining it in the global scope or, more commonly, within a script—the function itself is a *local scope*, and is considered a child of whatever scope it was created in. Here's a quick example—we haven't discussed functions, yet, but this one isn't complicated so we hope it'll help illustrate this scope stuff:

```
1.  $var1 = "Hello"
2.  Function MyFunction {
3.  Write-Host $var1
4.  $var1 = "Goodbye"
5.  Write-Host $var1
6.  }
7.  Write-Host $var1
8.  MyFunction
9.  Write-Host $var1
```

If you were to run this script, here's the output you'd see:

```
Hello
Hello
Goodbye
Hello
```

Why is this true? The first executable line in this script is the first line, which sets the variable **$var1** equal to the value "Hello". Next, a function is defined—but not executed, yet. PowerShell skips over the function definition to line 7, where the contents of $var1 are displayed—our first line of output. Next, line 8 calls MyFunction. This enters the function, which is a child scope of the script scope. Line 3 displays the contents of $var1. Since $var1 hasn't been defined in this scope, PowerShell looks to the parent scope to see if $var1 exists there. It does, and so our second line of output is also "Hello". Line 4 assigns a new value to $var1. Because a scope cannot directly modify its parent's variables, however, line 4 is actually creating a *new* variable called $var1. When line 5 runs, $var1 now exists in the local scope, and so our third line of output is "Goodbye". When we exit the function, its scope is discarded. When line 9 runs, $var1 still contains its original value—the function never modified *this* $var1—and so our last line of output is "Hello" again.

Now take a look at this slight revision:

```
$var1 = "Hello"
Function MyFunction {
 Write-Host $var1
 $script:var1 = "Goodbye"
 Write-Host $var1
}
Write-Host $var1
MyFunction
Write-Host $var1
```

We boldfaced the one line we changed. This time, you'll see:

```
Hello
Hello
Goodbye
Goodbye
```

Inside the function we've used the special syntax that allows a child scope to explicitly modify its parent's variables. When we first look at $var it has a value of "Hello". Then we call the function which reads $var from the parent scope. Then we make our special change using a scope identifier. There are four of these scope identifiers that PowerShell recognizes:

- $global: works with objects in the global scope.

- $script: works with objects in the parent script scope.

- $local: works with objects in the local scope.

- $private: works with objects in a private scope.

When we attempt to read $var again it is now set to "Goodbye". When the script ends, the parent scope has been modified and so $var still equals "Goodbye".

There's another technique, called *dot sourcing*, which impacts scope. Take a look at our original example script, this time with additional modifications:

```
$var1 = "Hello"
Function MyFunction {
 Write-Host $var1
 $var1 = "Goodbye"
$var2 = "I'm new here"Write-Host $var1
}
Write-Host $var1
Write-Host $var2
. MyFunction
Write-Host $var1
```

Write-Host $var2Notice how we're calling the function on the second-to-last line of code? We've typed a period, followed by a space, and then the function name. This is called dot sourcing, and it forces the function to run, not in its own scope but rather *right within the script scope*. In other words, when you run something—a script or a function—using dot sourcing, you tell PowerShell to forgo the step of creating a new scope and to instead run all the commands in the current scope. In this revised example, you should see output like this:

```
Hello

Hello
Goodbye
Goodbye
I'm new here
```

The first "Hello" is the value of $var1 before the function is called. The script then tries to display $var2 which is undefined. In the dot sourced function $var1 is displayed again. Changed to "Goodbye" and displayed. After the function, $var1 has now been changed and because $var2 was defined in the dot sourced function, it now exists in the main script scope.

Dot sourcing is a useful trick. For example, you could write a script that does nothing but define a bunch of utility functions—that is, functions that do some useful tasks that you use from time to time (almost like cmdlets). By dot sourcing that script into the global scope, those functions become defined within the global scope, making them available to you just like a cmdlet or global variable.

We'll touch on scope more as appropriate in the following few chapters; if you're confused about it then, refer back to this chapter and walk through these short examples again to refresh your memory. Scope in PowerShell is actually a lot more expansive than we've covered here; our goal in this chapter was to introduce you to the concept, as it will impact most of your scripts. In the chapter "Scope in Windows PowerShell," we'll dive into scope in much more detail.

Chapter 17
Variables, Arrays, and Escape Characters

PowerShell's power lies in its ability to manipulate objects and command output, parameters, strings, variables, and more. By understanding how PowerShell accomplishes this, you'll be better prepared to manage your systems with PowerShell either straight from the command line or in a PowerShell script. If you're familiar with Microsoft Windows Cmd.exe shell, this power and flexibility will be new and exciting because PowerShell is an object-oriented shell, while Cmd.exe is text-oriented, which makes it much more limited.

Variables

Variables play a key role in PowerShell as they do in most scripting technologies. A *variable* is a place-holder for some value. The value of the placeholder might change based on script actions or intentional changes. In other words, the value is *variable*.

In VBScript, variables are typically set with string values. Consider the following code fragment:

```
Set objNetwork=CreateObject("wscript.network")
strUserName=objNetwork.UserName
wscript.echo "Current user is " & strUsername
```

The variable **strUserName** contains the string value that is returned from the Username property of the objNetwork object. It is often easier to use the variable **strUserName** instead of constantly calling objNetwork.Username. We can use variables in PowerShell the same way.

PowerShell variable names must begin with $:

```
PS C:\> $name="SAPIEN Technologies, Inc."
PS C:\> $name
SAPIEN Technologies, Inc.
PS C:\>
```

In this example, we have created a variable, **$name**, with a value of "SAPIEN Technologies, Inc." We can display the value of the variable by invoking the variable name. This variable will maintain this value until we close the shell or set **$name** to something else.

There are two important things to note in this example.

1. We never had to formally *declare* the variable.

2. We're not writing a script.

PowerShell allows variables to be used "within the shell" or *interactively* without requiring you to write a script. Variables used interactively stay in memory for the duration of the PowerShell session.

Variables can contain numbers as the following example demonstrates:

```
PS C:\> $pi=3.1416
PS C:\> [decimal]$R=Read-host "Enter a radius value"
Enter a radius value: 4
PS C:\> $Area=$pi*($R*$R)
PS C:\> Write-host "The Area of a circle with a radius of $R is $Area" -fore Green
The Area of a circle with a radius of 4 is 50.2656
PS C:\>
```

The example is pretty straightforward. We begin by defining a variable called **$pi**. A value for the radius variable, **$R**, is set by calling **Read-Host**. We specifically cast it as a decimal type otherwise **$R** will be treated as a string, which would cause the mathematical expressions to not be properly interpreted. A variable, **$Area**, is set with the appropriate mathematical formula. Finally, we use **Write-Host** to display the results.

> **Note**
> If you've been coding VBScript for a while, you might get a little confused. PowerShell doesn't require any concatenation symbols like & or + to join strings and variables together. With PowerShell, you simply wrap anything you want displayed in quotes and type out the expression.

If we want to run this again, all we need to do is press the up arrow a few times to reset $R and rerun the **Write-Host** cmdlet. If you're thinking this is a cumbersome method to use variables and repeat code, then you're right! A better approach would be to create a function, which we'll cover in the "Script Blocks, Functions, Filters, Snap-ins, and Modules" chapter.

We can also set a variable to hold the results of a cmdlet:

```
PS C:\> $proc500=get-process | where {$_.handles -gt 500}
PS C:\> $proc500
```

Handles	NPM(K)	PM(K)	WS(K)	VS(M)	CPU(s)	Id	ProcessName
684	7	1680	4580	27	3.96	868	csrss
578	13	26112	38372	104	33.44	2024	explorer
680	76	12024	4896	114	4.39	3916	Groove
1926	54	47988	9536	187	39.28	1228	iTunes
541	12	15092	9892	91	79.01	1896	Smc

```
1228    42    12900    19756    88    15.61   1860   svchost
1141     0        0      220     2    23.15      4   System
 527    21     6716     3488    52     2.04    892   winlogon
PS C:\>
```

In this example, we create a variable called **$proc500**. The value of this variable is created by taking the object output of a **Get-Process** cmdlet and piping it to the **Where** cmdlet. The **Where** cmdlet (technically, **Where** is an alias to **Where-Object**) filters any process with a handle count that is less than or equal to 500 (that is, it "keeps" any processes with a handle count greater than 500). When you type **$proc500** at the next prompt, PowerShell displays the variable's contents in formatted output. It is important to remember that this is not a function or a cmdlet. PowerShell does not reevaluate the value of **$proc500** every time you invoke it.

However, the value of **$proc500** is more than a collection of strings. In fact, it is an object that can be further manipulated. For example, if you run **$proc500.count**, PowerShell returns a value of 8, which is the number of processes in **$proc500**. We'll cover variables as objects in more detail later in this chapter.

PowerShell includes several cmdlets for working with variables that you can see by asking for help:

```
PS C:\> help *var*

Name                     Category  Synopsis
----                     --------  --------
Get-Variable             Cmdlet    Gets the variables in the current console.
New-Variable             Cmdlet    Creates a new variable.
Set-Variable             Cmdlet    Sets the value of a variable. Creates the variable if one w...
Remove-Variable          Cmdlet    Deletes a variable and its value.
Clear-Variable           Cmdlet    Deletes the value of a variable.
Variable                 Provider  Provides access to the Windows PowerShell variables and to ...
about_Automatic_Variables HelpFile  Describes variables that store state information for Window...
about_environment_variables HelpFile Describes how to access Windows environment variables in Wi...
about_preference_variables  HelpFile  Variables that customize the behavior of Windows PowerShell
about_Variables          HelpFile  Describes how variables store values that can be used in W...

PS C:\>
```

Get-Variable

Recall that you can get a variable's value by typing out the variable name. But what if you forgot the variable name? If you can remember at least part of it, you can use **Get-Variable** to list all matching variables and their values:

```
PS C:\> get-variable v*

Name                     Value
----                     -----
var                      9.42
VerbosePreference        SilentlyContinue

PS C:\>
```

In this example, we are finding all the variables that begin with the letter "v". Notice we didn't' need to use $v*. The $ symbol is used in conjunction with the variable name when used in the shell.

Run **Get-Variable** * to see all the defined variables:

```
PS C:\> get-variable *

Name                    Value
----                    -----
Error                   {System.Management.Automation.ParseExce
DebugPreference         SilentlyContinue
PROFILE                 C:\Documents and Settings\admin\My
HOME                    C:\Documents and Settings\admin
Host                    System.Management.Automation.Internal.H
MaximumHistoryCount     64
MaximumAliasCount       4096
pi                      3.1416
input                   System.Array+SZArrayEnumerator
var                     9.42
StackTrace              at System.Number.StringToNumber(Stri
ReportErrorShowSource   1
...
```

The output has been truncated but you will recognize some of these variables from our earlier examples. However, note that variables such as **$MaximumErrorCount** or **$PSHome** are PowerShell's *automatic* variables that are set by the shell. The following table lists these variables. Keep in mind that you should not create a variable that uses one of these default automatic variable names.

PowerShell Automatic Variables

Variable	Description
$$	Contains the last token of the last line received by the shell.
$?	Contains the success/fail status of the last operation.
$^	Contains the first token of the last line received by the shell.
$_	Contains the current pipeline object, used in script blocks, filters, and the Where statement.
$Args	Contains an array of the parameters passed to a function.
$ConsoleFileName	Contains the path of the console file (.psc1) that was most recently used in the session.
$DebugPreference	Specifies the action to take when data is written using Write-Debug in a script, cmdlet or provider.
$Error	Contains objects for which an error occurred while being processed in a cmdlet.
$ErrorActionPreference	Specifies the action to take when data is written using Write-Error in a script. cmdlet or provider.
$Event	Contains a PSEventArgs object that represents the event that is being processed.
$EventSubscriber	Contains a PSEventSubscriber object that represents the event subscriber of the event that is being processed.

Variable	Description
$ExecutionContext	Contains an EngineIntrinsics object that represents the execution context of the Windows PowerShell host.
$False	The Boolean value FALSE.
$foreach	Refers to the enumerator in a foreach loop.
$Home	Specifies the user's home directory. Equivalent of %homedrive%%homepath%.
$Host	Contains an object that represents the current host application for Windows PowerShell.
$Input	Used in script blocks that are in the middle of a pipeline.
$LastExitCode	Contains the exit code of the last Win32 executable execution.
$Matches	Contains the results when using the –match or –notmatch operators.
$MaximumAliasCount	Contains the maximum number of aliases available to the session.
$MaximumDriveCount	Contains the maximum number of drives available, excluding those provided by the underlying operating system.
$MaximumFunctionCount	Contains the maximum number of functions available to the session.
$MaximumHistoryCount	Specifies the maximum number of entries saved in the command history.
$MaximumVariableCount	Contains the maximum number of variables available to the session.
$MyInvocation	Contains an object with information about the current command, such as a script, function, or script block.
$NestedPromptLevel	Contains the current prompt level.
$Null	Contains a NULL or empty value.
$OFS	Output Field Separator, used when converting an array to a string. By default, this is set to the space character. The following example illustrates the default setting and setting OFS to a different value: &{ $a = 1,2,3; "$a"} 1 2 3 &{ $OFS="-"; $a = 1,2,3; "$a"} 1-2-3

Variable	Description
$PID	Contains the process identifier (PID) of the process that is hosting the current Windows PowerShell session.
$Profile	Contains the full path of the Windows PowerShell profile for the current user and the current host application.
$PSBoundParameters	Contains a dictionary of the active parameters and their current values.
$PSCmdlet	Contains an object that represents the cmdlet or advanced function that is being run.
$PSCulture	Contains the name of the culture currently in use in the operating system.
$PSDebugContext	Contains information about the debugging environment.
$PSEmailServer	Contains the name of your SMTP server. Used by default by Send-MailMessage.
$PSHome	Specifies the directory where Windows PowerShell is installed.
$PSScriptRoot	Contains the directory from which the script module is being executed.
$PSVersionTable	Contains a read-only hash table that displays details about the currently running version of Windows PowerShell.
$PSUICulture	Contains the name of the operating system's current user interface (UI) culture.
$PWD	Prints the current working directory.
$ReportErrorShowExceptionClass	When set to TRUE, shows the class names of displayed exceptions.
$ReportErrorShowInnerException	When set to TRUE, shows the chain of inner exceptions. The display of each exception is governed by the same options as the root exception, that is, the options dictated by $ReportErrorShow* will be used to display each exception.
$ReportErrorShowSource	When set to TRUE, shows the assembly names of displayed exceptions.
$ReportErrorShowStackTrace	When set to TRUE, emits the stack traces of exceptions.
$Sender	Contains the object that generated an event.
$ShellID	Contains the identifier of the currently running shell.

Variable	Description
$SourceArgs	Contains objects that represent the event arguments of the event that is being processed.
$StackTrace	Contains detailed stack trace information about the last error.
$This	In a script block that defines a script property or script method, the $This variable refers to the object that is being extended.
$True	The Boolean value TRUE.
$VerbosePreference	Specifies the action to take when data is written using Write-Verbose in a script, cmdlet or provider.
$WarningPreference	Specifies the action to take when data is written using Write-Warning in a script, cmdlet or provider.

Set-Variable

PowerShell has a specific cmdlet for creating variables called **Set-Variable**, which has an alias of **Set**. The syntax is as follows:

```
PS C:\> set-variable var "Computername"
PS C:\> $var
Computername
PS C:>
```

This is the same as typing **$var="Computername"**. This cmdlet has several parameters for which you might find some need. For one thing, you can define a read-only, or constant, variable:

```
PS C:\> set-variable -option "constant" -name pi -value 3.1416
PS C:\> get-variable pi

Name                    Value
----                    -----
pi                      3.1416

PS C:\> $pi=0
Cannot overwrite variable pi because it is read-only or constant.
At line:1 char:4
+ $pi= <<<< 0
PS C:\>
```

By using the **-option** parameter, we specified that we wanted the variable to be a constant. Once set, you cannot change the value or clear or remove the variable. It will exist for as long as your PowerShell session is running. If you close the shell and reopen it, the constant no longer exists.

Variable Already Exists

If you've been following along with the chapter in your own PowerShell session, you may already have a variable called $pi. If so, when you try to run the previous code, you'll get an error that an existing variable cannot be made constant. You can only set the constant option when the variable is first created. In this instance, use Remove-Variable to delete $pi and try to run this code again. It should now work with no errors.

The **-scope** parameter allows you to define the variable's scope or where it can be used. Typically, you will set the scope to global, local, or script.

```
PS C:\>set-variable -scope "global" -name var -value 1
```

Although it is not required, you can create variables with additional parameters, such as **-option** and **-scope**. We also recommend that you use **-name** and **-value**, which help remove any ambiguity about your intentions.

Normally, you can assign the results of a PowerShell expression to a variable:

```
PS C:\>$stoppedServices= get-service |where {$_.status -eq "stopped"}
```

However, if you want to specify additional **Set-Variable** parameters, such as its scope, then you need to use the expression **Set-Variable**:

```
PS C:\> get-service |where {$_.status -eq "stopped"} | set-variable -scope "global" -name
StoppedServices
PS C:\> get-variable stoppedServices

Name                      Value
----                      -----
StoppedServices           {Alerter, ALG, AppMgmt, aspnet_state,...
PS C:\>
```

New-Variable

PowerShell does not have the equivalent of the VBScript **Dim** statement, nor is anything like it required in PowerShell. However, you can use **New-Variable** to explicitly define a variable. This cmdlet is almost identical to **Set-Variable**. You can specify the variable's scope and option as follows:

```
PS C:\> new-variable -option "constant" -name myZip -value 13078
PS C:\> get-variable myzip

Name                      Value
----                      -----
myZip                     13078
```

However, if you attempt to use **New-Variable** again to create the same variable but with a different value, PowerShell will refuse:

```
PS C:\> new-variable myZip 89123
new-variable : A variable with name 'myZip' already exists.
At line:1 char:13
+ new-variable <<<< myZip 89123
```

If you needed to change the variable value, you need to use **Set-Variable**. However, even that will not work in this example because **$myZip** was created as a constant.

You might wonder how you will know when various cmdlets should be used. The answer is that it probably depends on what type of variables you are creating and how they will be used. For example, you may want to create all the empty variables you will need at the beginning of a script with **New-Variable**, and then use **Set-Variable** to define them as needed. Using different cmdlets may help you keep track of what is happening to a variable throughout the script.

Clear-Variable

The process of retaining a variable while changing its value is straightforward:

```
PS C:\> $var="apple"
PS C:\> $var
apple
PS C:\> $var="orange"
PS C:\> $var
orange
PS C:\>
```

This example creates the variable, **$var**, and then sets it to a value. In this case, the value was set to "apple." Changing the value to "orange" is just as easy. If for some reason you want to retain the variable but remove the value, you can use the **Clear-Variable** cmdlet:

```
PS C:\> clear-variable var
PS C:\> $var
PS C:\>
```

Notice we didn't need to use **$var**, just **var**. We also could have set **$var=""**:

```
PS C:\> $var
orange
PS C:\> $var=""
PS C:\> $var

PS C:\>
```

Technically Speaking
Technically, setting $var="" is not the same thing as using the Clear-Variable cmdlet. The cmdlet actually erases the value. The expression $var="" is really setting the value of $var to a string object with a length of 0. In most instances this shouldn't be an issue, but if in doubt, use Clear-Variable.

You can also clear multiple variables with a single command:

```
PS C:\> $var=1
PS C:\> $var2=2
PS C:\> $var3=3
PS C:\> get-variable var*
```

```
Name                    Value
----                    -----
var                     1
var3                    3
var2                    2


PS C:\> clear-variable var*
PS C:\> get-variable var*

Name                    Value
----                    -----
var
var3
var2

PS C:\>
```

In this example, we created variables **$var**, **$var2**, and **$var3**. We used **Get-Variable** to display the values, followed by **Clear-Variable var*** to clear the values of any variables that started with var.

The last item to understand about **Clear-Variable** is that invoking **Clear-Variable** in a child scope has no effect on variables in the parent scope. In fact, this is typically true of most cmdlets. Refer back to the chapter "Scripting Overview" for a refresher on PowerShell scopes.

```
PS C:\> $var=3
PS C:\> &{clear-variable var}
PS C:\> $var
3
PS C:\>
```

The first line of this example is considered the parent scope. Using the ampersand character invokes a child scope and attempts to clear **$var**. But as you can see, that cmdlet had no effect. **$var** remains untouched.

Remove-Variable

When you want to remove the variable and its value, then call the **Remove-Variable** cmdlet. The syntax is essentially the same as **Clear-Variable**. You can remove a single variable:

```
PS C:\> $var="foobar"
PS C:\> $var
foobar
PS C:\> remove-variable var
PS C:\> $var
PS C:\>
```

Alternatively, you can remove multiple variables with a wildcard:

```
PS C:\> get-variable var*

Name                    Value
----                    -----
var                     5
var3                    980
var2                    78
```

```
PS C:\> remove-variable var*
PS C:\> get-variable var*
PS C:\>
```

Environment Variables

Windows has its own set of environment variables, such as %Path% and %Windir%. You can access these variables with the **env** provider in PowerShell. A *provider* acts as an interface between PowerShell and an internal data source. In this case, you can access the environment variables that are stored in the registry. When accessing a variable in expression mode, you type **$env:*variablename***. Don't let this confuse you—we're just using the $ character to prefix the **env:** provider; PowerShell has a built-in variable, $env, which is pre-set to connect to the **env:** provider. Note the colon at the end of the provider name.

Here is an example of how to use the provider:

```
PS C:\> $env:systemroot
E:\WINDOWS
PS C:\> $env:path
C:\Program Files\Windows Resource Kits\Tools\;C:\WINDOWS\system32;C:\WINDOWS;C:\WINDOWS\System32\Wbem;
C:\Program Files\Support Tools\;C:\Program Files\Common Files\GTK\2.0\bin;C:\Program Files\Windows
Power Shell\v1.0\
PS C:\>
```

When used with a cmdlet, you only need to use **env:** instead of **$env:**.

If you want to see all of the current Windows environment variables in PowerShell, type:

```
Get-Childitem env:
```

This is the equivalent of the **SET** command in the traditional Cmd.exe shell. If you want the variables sorted by name use:

```
Get-Childitem env: | sort {$_.key}
```

Variable Types

The fact that PowerShell is built on .NET gives it tremendous versatility that isn't always obvious. Keep in mind that any PowerShell variable can contain any *type* of data. This is true because *all* types of data such as strings, integers, and dates are .NET classes, which means they all inherit from the base class named Object. A PowerShell variable can contain anything that inherits from Object. However, as you saw in earlier examples with a string, PowerShell can tell the difference between different classes that inherit from Object.

You can force PowerShell to treat objects as a more specific type. When you do this, you are asking PowerShell to *cast* a variable to a specific type. We've already done this with the [ADSI] type, in the chapter "Using ADSI in Windows PowerShell." For a simpler example, take a look at this sequence:

```
PS C:\> $one = 5
PS C:\> $two = "5"
PS C:\> $one + $two
10
PS C:\> $two + $one
55
```

Here we give PowerShell two variables. One variable contains the number five, while the other variable contains the string character "5." This might look the same to you, but this is a big difference to a computer! Since we didn't specify what type of data these variables are, PowerShell assumes they are both the generic Object type. This caused PowerShell to decide it would figure out something more specific when the variables are used.

When we added **$one** and **$two** or 5 + "5," PowerShell said, "Aha, this must be addition. The first character is definitely not a string because it's not in double quotes. The second character *is* in double quotes but… Well, if I take the quotes away it looks like a number, so I'll add them." PowerShell's logic correctly gave 10 as the result.

However, when we add **$two** and **$one**, reversing the order, PowerShell has a different decision to make. In this case PowerShell said, "I see addition, but this first operand is clearly a string. The second one is a generic Object, so let's also treat it like a string, and concatenate the two." This PowerShell logic gave us the string "55," which is just the first five tacked onto the second.

But what about:

```
PS C:\> [int]$two + $one
10
```

This is the same order as the example that resulted in "55." However, this time we specifically told PowerShell to cast the generic object in **$two** as an [Int] or integer, which is a type PowerShell knows. So, it used the same logic as in the first example. It added the two to come up with 10.

You can force PowerShell to treat anything as a specific type. For example:

```
PS C:\> [int]$int = "5"
PS C:\> $int.gettype()

IsPublic  IsSerial  Name                          BaseType
--------  --------  ----                          --------
True      True      Int32                         System.ValueType
```

Here the value "5" would normally be either a String object or, at best, a generic Object. However, by specifying the type [int], we forced PowerShell to try to convert "5" into an integer before storing it in the variable **$int**. The conversion was successful because we can see the object's type by invoking the universal **GetType()** method.

Note that once you apply a specific type to a variable, it stays that way until you specifically change it. For example:

```
PS C:\> [int]$int = 1
```

This creates a variable named **$int** as an integer, and assigns it the value 1. PowerShell will treat the **$int** variable as an integer from now on, even if you don't include the type:

```
PS C:\> $int = 2
```

It is still using **$int** as an integer because it was already cast into a specific type. Once set up to be an integer, you can't put other types of data into it. Here's an example of an error because we tried to put a string into a variable that was already specifically cast as an integer:

```
PS C:\> [int]$int = 1
PS C:\> $int = 2
PS C:\> $int = "hello"
Cannot convert value "hello" to type "System.Int32". Error: "Input string was not in a correct
format."
At line:1 char:5
+ $int <<<< = "hello"
PS C:\>
```

However, you can recast a variable by reassigning a new, specific type:

```
PS C:\> [string]$int = "Hello"
```

That works fine, and **$int** will *now* be treated as a string by PowerShell.

PowerShell isn't a miracle worker. For example, PowerShell will complain if you try to force it to convert something that doesn't make sense:

```
PS C:\> [int]$int = "Hello"
Cannot convert "Hello" to "System.Int32". Error: "Input string was not in a correct format."
At line:1 char:13
+ $int = [int]" <<<< Hello"
```

This occurred because "Hello" can't sensibly be made into a number. The next example is even more fun since it illustrates some of the advanced data types:

```
PS C:\> [xml]$xml = "<users><user name='joe' /></users>"
PS C:\> $xml.users.user

name
----
joe
```

Here we created a string, but told PowerShell it was of the type XML, which is another data type with which PowerShell is familiar. XML data works sort of like an object in that we define a parent object named Users, and a child object named User. The child object has an attribute called Name, with a value of Joe. So, when we ask PowerShell to display **$xml.users.user**, it displays all the attributes for that user. We can prove that PowerShell treated **$xml** as XML data by using **Get-Member**:

```
PS C:\> $xml | get-member


   TypeName: System.Xml.XmlDocument

Name                MemberType   Definition
----                ----------   ----------
ToString            CodeMethod   static System.Stri
add_NodeChanged     Method       System.Void add_No
add_NodeChanging    Method       System.Void add_No
add_NodeInserted    Method       System.Void add_No
add_NodeInserting   Method       System.Void add_No
add_NodeRemoved     Method       System.Void add_No
add_NodeRemoving    Method       System.Void add_No
AppendChild         Method       System.Xml.XmlNode
Clone               Method       System.Xml.XmlNode
CloneNode           Method       System.Xml.XmlNode
CreateAttribute     Method       System.Xml.XmlAttr
```

```
CreateCDataSection        Method                System.Xml.XmlCDat
CreateComment             Method                System.Xml.XmlComm
CreateDocumentFragment    Method                System.Xml.XmlDocu
CreateDocumentType        Method                System.Xml.XmlDocu
CreateElement             Method                System.Xml.XmlElem
...
```

This demonstrates not only that variables *are* objects, but also that PowerShell *does* understand different types of data and provides different capabilities for them.

If you're curious about what object types are available, here's a quick list of more common types:

Array	Bool (Boolean)
Byte	Char (a single character)
Char[] (Character array)	Decimal
Double	Float
Int (Integer)	Int[] (Integer array)
Long (Long integer)	Long[] (Long integer array)
Regex (Regular expression)	Single
Scriptblock	String
WMI	XML

There are more types than those listed above. In fact, we'll be popping in with details on the other types as appropriate throughout this book. Some of them aren't frequently used in administrative scripting, so we don't want to arbitrarily hit you with all of them at once. Instead, we'll cover them in a context where they're used for something practical. Just remember that, unlike other scripting languages with which you may be familiar, a PowerShell variable can contain more than a number or string.

Variable Precautions

One thing to be careful of is PowerShell's ability to change the type of a variable if you haven't explicitly selected a type. For example:

```
PS C:\> Write $a.ToUpper()
```

This works fine if **$a** contains a string, as shown here:

```
PS C:\> $a = "Hello"
PS C:\> write $a.ToUpper()
HELLO
PS C:\>
```

However, you'll get an error if **$a** was already set to an integer value:

```
PS C:\> $a = 1
PS C:\> write $a.ToUpper()
Method invocation failed because [System.Int32] doesn't contain amethod named 'ToUpper'.
At line:1 char:22
+ write $a.ToUpper( <<<< )
PS C:\>
```

This occurs because, as an integer, **$a** doesn't have a **ToUpper()** method. Since this type of error can be tricky to troubleshoot, you need to watch out for this when you're writing scripts that take input from other sources, such as a user or a file.

One way around it is to force PowerShell to treat the variable as the string you're expecting it to be:

```
PS C:\> $a = 1
PS C:\> $a = [string]$a
PS C:\> write $a.ToUpper()
1
PS C:\>
```

You don't necessarily need to select a type up front for every variable you use, but you should be aware of situations that can make a variable contain a type of data other than what you originally expected.

You should also take precautions with variable naming. PowerShell is pretty forgiving and will let you use just about anything as a variable name:

```
PS C:\> $$="apple"
PS C:\> $$
apple
PS C:\> ${var}=100
PS C:\> ${var}
100
PS C:\>
PS C:\> $7="PowerShell Scripting"
PS C:\> $7
PowerShell Scripting
PS C:\>
```

However, if you attempt to create a variable with anything other than a number or letter, PowerShell will complain:

```
PS C:\> $(j)="SAPIEN"
Invalid assignment expression. The left hand side of an assignment operator needs to be something
that can be assigned to like a variable or a property.
At line:1 char:6
+ $(j)=" <<<< SAPIEN"
PS C:\>
```

Using these types of variables names isn't very practical or recommended. Instead, you should use variable names that are meaningful to you. So, instead of:

```
PS C:\> $g=Get-Process
```

Use something like:

```
PS C:\> $Processes=Get-Process
```

It may require a bit more typing, but using meaningful variable names will definitely make it easier to troubleshoot and maintain your PowerShell scripts.

Arrays

An *array* is essentially a container for storing things. For almost all administrative scripts, *simple arrays* will suffice. When you think about a simple array, picture an egg carton with a single row. You can make the egg carton as long as you want. With a simple array, you can put numbers, strings, or objects in each compartment. Multi-dimensional arrays exist, but they are beyond the scope of what we want to cover here.

....

Array or Collection

When reading technical material, you may also come across the term collection, which is a type of array that is usually created as the result of some query. For example, you might execute a query to return all instances of logical drives on a remote server using Windows Management Instrumentation (WMI). The resulting object will hold information about all logical drives in a collection. This collection object is handled in the much same way as an array when it comes time to enumerate the contents. For now, remember that when you see the term collection, think array. Or vice-versa; it doesn't really matter which term you use.

You can create an array by defining a variable and specifying the contents as delimited values:

```
PS C:\> $a=9,5,6,3
```

To view the contents of **$a**, all you need to do is type **$a**:

```
PS C:\> $a
9
5
6
3
```

The other technique you are more likely to use is the **ForEach** cmdlet:

```
PS C:\> foreach ($i in $a) {Write-host $i –foregroundcolor Magenta}
9
5
6
3
PS C:\>
```

This cmdlet looks inside the parentheses for what it should process. For every item in the parentheses, the **ForEach** statement does whatever commands are in the curly braces. In the previous example we used a variable name of **$i**. This example instructs the **ForEach** statement that for every **$i** variable in the **$a** variable, our array, it should echo back the value of **$i**.

When we run this command the first time, the cmdlet gets the first value of the array (**$a**) and sets it to **$i**. The cmdlet writes the value of **$i** to the console, and then runs through the array again getting the next array element, 5. This process is repeated until the end of the array is reached.

If you want to create an array with a range of numbers, you should use the range operator (..):

```
PS C:\> $a=2..7
PS C:\> $a
2
3
4
5
6
7
```

```
PS C:\>
```

To create an array with strings, you must enclose each element in quotes:

```
PS C:\> $servers="dc1","app02","print1","file3"
PS C:\> foreach ($c in $servers) {$c}
dc1
app02
print1
file3
PS C:\>
```

If you used **$servers="dc1,app02,print1,file3"** then the only element of the array would be **dc1,app02,print1,file3,** because PowerShell only sees one set of double quotes. Therefore, there would be only one item to make into an array.

PowerShell arrays can also contain objects. Consider this example:

```
PS C:\> $svc=get-service | where {$_.status -eq "running"}
PS C:\> $svc

Status    Name            DisplayName
------    ----            -----------
Running   AudioSrv        Windows Audio
Running   Avg7Alrt        AVG7 Alert Manager Server
Running   Avg7UpdSvc      AVG7 Update Service
Running   AVGEMS          AVG E-mail Scanner
Running   CryptSvc        Cryptographic Services
Running   DcomLaunch      DCOM Server Process Launcher
Running   Dhcp            DHCP Client
Running   Dnscache        DNS Client
Running   Eventlog        Event Log
Running   EventSystem     COM+ Event System
Running   IISADMIN        IIS Admin
Running   iPodService     iPodService
Running   lanmanserver    Server
...
```

We've created an array called **$svc** that contains all running services. We'll work with this more a little later.

When you work with individual elements in an array, the first important thing to remember is that arrays start counting at 0. To reference a specific element the syntax is *$arrayname[index]*:

```
PS C:\> servers[0]
dc1
PS C:\> $servers[3]
file3
PS C:\>
```

You can use the length property of the array to determine how many elements are in the array:

```
PS C:\> $servers.length
4
PS C:\>
```

If you go back and look at the contents, you'll see that file3 is the last element of the array, yet it has an index of [3]. What gives? Remember to start counting at 0.

It's also easy to create an array from an existing source instead of manually typing a list of names. If you already have a list of server names such as Servers.txt, you could read that file with the **Get-Content** cmdlet and populate the array:

```
PS C:\> $Serverlist =get-content servers.txt
PS C:\> $serverlist
Seattle1
Vegas02
XPLAP01
PS C:\>
```

In this example, servers.txt is a simple text file with a list of computer names. We create the array **$serverlist** by invoking **Get-Content**. Invoking **$serverlist** merely displays the array's contents. Armed with this array, it's a relatively simple matter to parse the array and pass the computer name as the parameter for any number of commands:

```
PS C:\> foreach ($srv in $serverlist) {
>> write-host "Examining $srv" –foregroundcolor cyan
>> #calling Get-WmiObject
>> Get-WmiObject -class win32_operatingsystem -computername $srv
>> }
>>
Examining Seattle1


SystemDirectory : C:\WINDOWS\system32
Organization    : MyCompany
BuildNumber     : 3790
RegisteredUser  : MyCompany
SerialNumber    : 69713-640-3403486-45904
Version         : 5.2.3790


Examining Vegas02


SystemDirectory : C:\WINDOWS\system32
Organization    : MyCompany.com
BuildNumber     : 3790
RegisteredUser  :
SerialNumber    : 69723-540-7598465-549822
Version         : 5.2.3790


Examining XPLAP01


SystemDirectory : C:\WINDOWS\system32
Organization    : MyCo
BuildNumber     : 2600
RegisteredUser  : Admin
SerialNumber    : 55274-640-1714466-23528
Version         : 5.1.2600

PS C:\>
```

Using **ForEach**, we enumerate each element of the array and execute two cmdlets. **Write-Host** is called to display a message about what PowerShell is doing. Then we call the **Get-WmiObject** cmdlet to return operating system information from the specified server using WMI.

$OFS

PowerShell has a special variable called **$OFS** which defines the Output Field Separator. By default this is a space. When you convert an array into a string, be default you will get something like this:

```
PS C:\ > $a="Jeff","Don","Chris","Alex"
PS C:\ > [string]$a
Jeff Don Chris Alex
```

However, what if you preferred to separate the values with a comma?

```
PS C:\ > $ofs=","
PS C:\ > [string]$a
Jeff,Don,Chris,Alex
```

Here's another way you might use this:

Get-LargeProcessList.ps1

```
Function Get-LargeProcessList {
  $ps=Get-Process | Where {$_.workingset -ge 50000000}

  $ofs=","
  $results=@()

  foreach ($p in $ps) {
   $results+="$($p.name) ($($p.id))"
  }

  write [string]$results

}
```

This function creates a variable of all processes where the workingset size is greater or equal to 50000000 bytes:

```
$ps=Get-Process | Where {$_.workingset -ge 50000000}
```

The function defines a new Output Field Separator:

```
$ofs=","
```

It also defines an empty array object we'll use a bit later:

```
$results=@()
```

The function then goes through each item in the process collection and populates the **$results** array with the name and process id:

```
foreach ($p in $ps) {
 $results+="$($p.name) ($($p.id))"
}
```

Finally, the function returns a string version of the **$results** array:

```
write [string]$results
```

The end result is something like this:

```
audiodg (1420),avgrssvc (1236),csrss (816),dwm (3720),explorer (3856),firefox
(13480),GROOVE (4248),msnmsgr (3300),OUTOOK (7936),POWERPNT (12284),powershell
(29160),PrimalScript (30332),procexp (1136),SearchIndexer (2708),sidebar (1588), spoolsv
(1996),sqlservr (2204),svchost (1148),svchost (1216),svchost (1252),svchost (1296),svchost
(1604),svchost (172),svchost (2028),TabTip
(3476),WINWORD (12204),WmiPrvSE (19612)
```

Associative Arrays

Associative arrays are special types of arrays. Think of them as a way of relating, or associating, one piece of data with another piece of data. For example, they're useful for performing certain types of data lookup that we'll see in this chapter. You may also see associative arrays referred to as *dictionaries* or *hash tables*.

An associative array is a data structure that stores multiple *key-value* pairs:

Key	Value
Don	Blue
Chris	Pink
Jeffery	Blue

The *key* is usually some piece of well-known or easily obtained information, while the *value* is the data you want to look up. Keys are unique in the array, while values can be repeated as necessary. In our table example, the associative array keys are a person's name, while each corresponding value is the person's favorite color. Notice that the key names are unique while data values can be duplicated.

PowerShell uses the *hash table* data type to store the contents of an associative array because that data type provides fast performance when looking up data. What's really neat about associative arrays is that the individual values can be of different types. In other words, one key might be connected to a string, while another is connected to an XML document. This lets you store any kind of arbitrary data you want in an array.

Creating an Associative Array

The @ operator is used to create an associative array as follows:

```
$aa = @{"Don"="Blue"; "Chris"="Pink"; "Jeffery"="Blue"}
```

This creates an associative array with three keys and three values, exactly as shown in the previous table. Of course, the values don't have to be simple strings. They can be numbers, the output from a cmdlet, or even other associative arrays. We'll take a closer look at this later in the chapter.

By the way, you can also use the @ operator to create a normal array:

```
PS C:\> $a = @(1,2,3,4,5)
PS C:\> $a
1
2
3
4
5
```

The difference is that only values were given to the @ operator; we didn't give it key=value pairs, so it created a normal one-dimensional array for us. Also associative arrays use curly braces {} and regular arrays use parentheses ().

Want to just create an empty hash table so that you can use a script or other process to add data to it?

```
PS C:\> $ht = new-object System.Collections.Hashtable
```

Using an Associative Array

You can display the entire contents of an associative array by calling its name:

```
PS C:\> $aa = @{"Don"="Blue"; "Chris"="Pink"; "Jeffery"="Blue"}
PS C:\> $aa

Name                    Value
----                    -----
Jeffery                 Blue
Chris                   Pink
Don                     Blue


PS C:\>
```

However, normally you'd want to access a single element:

```
PS C:\> $aa."Don"
Blue
PS C:\>
```

Type the associative array variable name, a period, and then the key you want to retrieve. PowerShell will respond by displaying the associated value. Note that keys and values, if the values are strings, can be contained in single or double quotes just like any other string. Keys are always expected to be strings, and so usually need to be enclosed in quotes.

However, the quotes can be omitted if the key doesn't contain any spaces, periods, or other word-breaking characters:

```
PS C:\> $aa.Don
Blue
PS C:\>
```

To check and see what data type a particular key's value is:

```
PS C:\> $aa.Don.GetType()

IsPublic  IsSerial  Name                         BaseType
--------  --------  ----                         --------
True      True      String                       System.Object
```

A single value within an associative array can actually be *another* associative array:

```
PS C:\> $aa2 = @{Key1="Value1"; Colors=$aa}
PS C:\> $aa2.Colors

Name                     Value
----                     -----
Jeffery                  Blue
Chris                    Pink
Don                      Blue


PS C:\> $aa2.Colors.Don
Blue
PS C:\>
```

In this example, a new associative array is named **$aa2**. It has two keys: (1) Key1, which has a value of "Value1"; and (2) Colors, which is assigned the associative array **$aa** we used earlier as its value. Displaying **$aa2.Colors** displays the entire **$aa** associative array, while **$aa2.Colors.Don** accesses a single key within the **$aa** associative array.

Let's take a look at a more practical example. First, we'll demonstrate that an associative array can contain just about any type of value:

```
PS C:\> $systems=@{"XPLAP01"=Get-WmiObject -class win32_computersystem -computername XPLAP01}

PS C:\> $systems

Name                     Value
----                     -----
XPLAP01                  \\XPLAP01\root\cimv2:Win32_ComputerSystem.Name="XPLAP01"


PS C:\> $systems.XPLAP01


Domain              : myit.local
Manufacturer        : Dell Computer Corporation
Model               : Latitude D800
Name                : XPLAP01
PrimaryOwnerName    : Admin
TotalPhysicalMemory : 1609805824
```

Here we've created an associative array called **$systems** with a single element. The key is XPLAP01 and the data value is a WMI object representing an instance of the Win32_Computersystem class. Invoking just the array name displays the contents, which in this case is a single computer. If we want to see the value of the XPLAP01 key we use **$systems.XPLAP01**.

If the key name has a space you will have to use:

```
PS C:\> $myArray.'Test User'
```

Alternatively, you can use:

```
PS C:\> $myArray.['Test User']
```

If we know the name of a specific WMI object attribute, we can return its value with a command like this:

```
PS C:\> $systems.xplap01.totalphysicalmemory
1609805824
PS C:\>
```

This works because the value associated with key XPLAP01 is a WMI object. Therefore, we can use dotted notation to display a specific property value.

Let's add a second system to the array:

```
PS C:\> $systems.DC01=Get-WmiObject -class "win32_computersystem" -computername "MYIT-DC01"
```

We can easily define a new key and value by setting the value for the new key using dotted notation. If you were to run **$systems.count**, it would return a value of 2. How did we know about the Count property? We asked. Pipe an associative array to **Get-Member** to get a complete list of an associative array's methods and properties.

Now that we have more than one item in the array, we can use the **Keys** and **Values** properties to get more than one key or value:

```
PS C:\> $systems.keys
DC01
XPLAP01
PS C:\> $systems.values


Domain               : myit.local
Manufacturer         : MICRO-STAR INTERNATIONAL CO., LTD
Model                : KM400-8235
Name                 : DC01
PrimaryOwnerName     : ADMIN
TotalPhysicalMemory  : 1073168384

Domain               : myit.local
Manufacturer         : Dell Computer Corporation
Model                : Latitude D800
Name                 : XPLAP01
PrimaryOwnerName     : Admin
TotalPhysicalMemory  : 1609805824
PS C:\>
```

Suppose we read a text list of computers and build the associative array. As we've shown, with this type of array, you can get the associated data by specifying the key.

However, if we want to enumerate the array and display only the computer's model as part of a hardware inventory, we would use code like this:

```
PS C:\> $keys=$systems.Get_Keys()
```

This code stores the keys in a yet another array called **$keys**. Technically, **$keys** is a *collection* that is basically a list. We can now use the **ForEach** cmdlet to iterate through the associative array:

```
PS C:\> foreach ($key in $keys) {write-host $key $systems.$key.Model}
DC01 KM400-8235
XPLAP01 Latitude D800
PS C:\>
```

There's a lot going on in this single command, so let's take it apart. We start with the basic **ForEach** cmdlet that says for each item in the **$keys** collection, set it to the **$key** variable. As we loop through, **$key** becomes DC01, XPLAP01, and so on, assuming we had a larger array. Then for each pass, **ForEach** runs the code in the curly braces. The brace code calls the **Write-Host** cmdlet that displays the value of **$key** and the model property from the WMI object value of the corresponding key in **$systems**.

That last part can get a little confusing. Remember, the first time through the value of **$key** is DC01. So, **$systems.$key.model** is the equivalent of typing **$systems.dc01.model**. As we discussed earlier, **$systems.dc01** returns the corresponding value that is a WMI Win32_Computersystem object. Since this is an object, we can get the model property value merely by asking for it. This process is repeated for every item in **$keys**.

In the traditional text-based shell, this type of coding would be complicated and involve a lot of string parsing and manipulation. However, because PowerShell works with objects, even if they are in arrays, we can manipulate the object and let PowerShell display the final results in just about whatever text format we want.

Programmatically Modifying and Enumerating an Associative Array

Even though we haven't covered scripting, yet, we're going to use a script for a quick example—you can always refer back to this later, if you need it. What we want to do is create a new, blank associative array. Next, we want to retrieve a list of local logical disks and add each drive letter as a key to the array, and then add each drive's free space to the array. Finally, we then want to enumerate through the array and display all of that information. Here's the script:

```
$ht = New-Object system.Collections.Hashtable

# add drives to array
$drives = gwmi -query "SELECT * FROM Win32_LogicalDisk WHERE DriveType = 3"
foreach ($drive in $drives) {
   $ht.add($drive.deviceid, $drive.freespace)
}

# enumerate through array
foreach ($key in $ht.keys) {
   Write-Host "$key has..."$ht.item($key) "bytes free"
}
```

We started by creating a new, blank associative array, or hash table. We execute a WMI query (see the chapter "Using WMI in Windows PowerShell" for more information on that) to get a list of local drives (the DriveType restriction in our query eliminates network drives, removable drives, and optical drives). Then, we used the array's **Add()** method to add new elements, simply specifying the key and value as the method's arguments. To enumerate through the array, we chose to enumerate through its **$keys** collection. Each key is a single drive letter; we use the Item property, specifying the key we're interested in, to retrieve that key's value.

Removing a single key works similarly. For example, if we wanted to remove the C: drive from our array, we'd do this:

```
$ht.Remove("C:")
```

We just specify the key we want removed. The **Contains()** method tells us whether the array contains a particular key. For example, if we hadn't removed our C: drive, we could do this:

```
PS C:\> $ht.contains("C:")
True
```

Finally, the **Clear()** method completely empties the array so that we can start over.

Escape Characters

In PowerShell, if you aren't executing a cmdlet, script, or executable, then you are displaying an *expression*. Remember from the "PowerShell Command-line Parsing" chapter that PowerShell parses what you type in either *command mode* or *expression mode*. Numbers are treated as numbers and strings should be placed in quotes. When you enter a string in quotes, PowerShell echoes it back to you:

```
PS C:\> "Hello, Reader"
Hello, Reader
```

If you don't use quotes, PowerShell assumes you are trying to execute something, so it generates an error:

```
PS C:\> Hello,Reader
'Hello' is not recognized as a Cmdlet, function, operable program, or script file.
At line:1 char:6
+ Hello, <<<< Reader
```

You can also use **Write-Host** to echo what you've typed back to the console. See if you can spot the subtle differences in these two expressions:

```
PS C:\> write-host "Hello, Reader"
Hello, Reader
PS C:\> write-host Hello, Reader
Hello Reader
PS C:\>
```

In the first expression, the phrase "Hello, Reader" is written to the console screen exactly as you typed it into the expression. In the second expression, PowerShell is smart enough to figure out that Hello and Reader are both strings. However, it only writes back the two strings. Notice what's missing. PowerShell thinks the comma is a separator, so it writes back the two strings, which at first glance looks like the first expression. We think you'll be better served, though, if you use quotes for strings that you want to display. It will make it easier to separate text you have specified versus cmdlet results or expressions.

Occasionally you may want to display a *literal* value in a string, such as the quotes. To accomplish this, you need to insert a special escape character, the backward apostrophe, before the quote characters so they are treated as literal values. The backward apostrophe is technically known as the grace accent but often referred to as a back tick.

```
PS C:\> write-host '"Hello', Reader'"
"Hello, Reader"
```

In this example, we also escaped the comma since that's part of the string expression and not a PowerShell character. You are more likely to use this technique with folder paths. If you try to run this:

```
PS C:\ > get-childitem program files
```

You'll get an error. Now, you could enclose the folder name in quotes, "program files", or you can use the escape character:

```
PS C:\ > get-childitem program' files
```

Which method you use is up to you. If you need something special, such as a beep or a tab, simply use one of PowerShell's escape characters shown in this table:

Escape Characters

Sequence	Result
`0	(null)
`a	(alert)
`b	(backspace)
`f	(form feed)
`n	(new line)
`r	(carriage return)
`t	(tab)
`v	(vertical quote)

To see how this works, open a PowerShell window and run the following command:

```
PS C:\> Write-Host 'a
```

Depending on your computer's configuration, a beep should be emitted.

Reference Variables

Thus far, all of the variables we've discussed are standard, *value* variables. That is, each variable holds a unique object (or set of objects). For example, if you create a variable **$a**, and then create a new variable **$b** as a copy of **$a**, such as this:

```
PS C:\> $a = 5
PS C:\> $b = $a
```

The **$b** variable is literally a *copy* of **$a**; any changes to **$b** will not affect **$a** at all:

```
PS C:\> $b = 6
PS C:\> $a
5
PS C:\> $b
6
```

However, PowerShell also supports *reference variables*. A reference variable is one which refers to another variable, rather than being a copy of it. Changes to the reference variable affect the original variable. In some ways, you can think of a reference variable as being an alias to another variable, because it ultimately refers to the original variable.

Reference variables are most often used in the input arguments of functions. This allows objects to be passed into a function, and allows the function to *modify the original objects* without having to pass them back out as output. Here's an example:

....

Flash Forward
We're getting a bit ahead of ourselves by discussion functions, but we'll keep this example simple and explain what we're doing. The point here is just to demonstrate what it is that reference variables do, and what they're used for.

```
Function MyFunction {
  Param([ref]$var1, $var2)
  $var1.value = $var1.value + $var1.value
  $var2 = $var2 + $var2
}

$myvalue1 = 10
$myvalue2 = 10
MyFunction ([ref]$myvalue1) $myvalue2
```

Here, we've defined variables **$myvalue1** and **$myvalue2**. Both have been set to contain an integer object with the value of 10. Each is passed into the function MyFunction. You can see in the declaration of MyFunction that the first parameter is a reference variable, declared using the [ref] type. The second is not, so it's a standard "value" parameter.

Inside the function, **$var1** and **$var2** are both doubled by simply adding them to themselves. When modifying the referenced variable you must use the value property. Otherwise you are attempting to add two System.Management.Automation.PSReference objects together, which don't have any concept of addition, but their value being an integer does.

What's important is what happens *after* the function completes. This function does not produce any output or return any values. However, after the function runs, **$myvalue1** contains 20. That's because it was passed *by reference* into the function; the parameter **$var1** became a pointer to **$myvalue1** rather than containing a copy of it. However, **$myvalue2** still contains 10, because it was *copied* into the parameter **$var2**. Although **$var2** was modified and eventually contained 20, that change was never made to **$myvalue2**.

Notice some important things about how this works:

- The function specifically declares incoming reference parameters with a [ref] type.

- When the function is called, any reference variables must be passed in as we have done: ([ref]$*variable_name*). Non-reference parameters are passed in by simply providing the variable name.

Reference variables are useful for very specific situations, such as when you need to modify or use an object within a function, and then pass the original object back out again. However, many people go their entire careers without once using a reference variable—so if you don't personally see any immediate need for one, that's okay.

Chapter 18
Objects

An object is essentially a black box that a developer has designed to fill a certain need. The Microsoft Windows operating system contains hundreds of objects. From an administrative scripting or automation perspective, you can exploit many of these objects through scripting.

We've stressed many times that PowerShell is an object-oriented shell based on .NET. This means you will manipulate objects in the shell and in PowerShell scripts.

Properties

All objects have properties. Some objects have more properties than other objects. The properties depend on the object. Consider an automobile as an object. For many people, an automobile is essentially a "black box." Many people don't fully understand how it works, but they do know how to use it. An automobile "object" may have properties such as model, color, horsepower, and maximum speed. These properties will have values such as Ferrari, red, 450, and 180.

Object properties that you can change are called *read-write* properties. In the automobile example, the color property might be read-write because you can change the color of the car by painting it. Other properties that the user can't change are considered *read-only* properties. In the automobile object example, horsepower and maximum speed are read-only properties because the user can't change them.

Methods

An object's methods are actions that the object can take. Depending on the object, some methods are executed from the object, while other methods are executed on the object, usually to make a change to the object.

Continuing with the automobile object, it may have an **Accelerate()** method that makes it do something. Or it may have a **ChangeTire()** method that makes a change to the object itself. Some methods can take parameters to fine tune what the method will do. For example, the automobile's **Accelerate()** method may require two parameters: (1) a start speed; and (2) an end speed.

Generally, you specify an object's methods and properties by using dotted notation. Let's say we created a car object called objMyCar. We could set some properties using dotted notation:

> objMyCar.color="blue"

> objMyCar.horsepower=300

> objMyCar.MaxSpeed=120

Calling a method can be as simple as:

> objMyCar.Accelerate(0,60)

This pseudo-command calls the **Accelerate()** method of the car object with a start speed parameter of 0 and an end speed parameter of 60.

That's all fine with a metaphorical object, but you are probably wondering how this applies to things you care about, like WMI or file system objects. So, let's begin by discussing how you find out about the properties and methods of objects. One way is to review the online documentation from Web sites such as MSDN or by using solid reference books.

With the addition of .NET, PowerShell reflection can make this even easier. Now you can use the **Get-Member** cmdlet to ask the object what it can do and how you can configure it. Once you have a reference to an object, pass it to **Get-Member** through a pipeline:

```
PS C:\> $var=123
PS C:\> $var | get-member


   TypeName: System.Int32

Name        MemberType Definition
----        ---------- ----------
CompareTo   Method     int CompareTo(System.Object value), int CompareTo(int value)
Equals      Method     bool Equals(System.Object obj), bool Equals(int obj)
GetHashCode Method     int GetHashCode()
GetType     Method     type GetType()
GetTypeCode Method     System.TypeCode GetTypeCode()
ToString    Method     string ToString(), string ToString(string format), string ToString(System.IForma...

PS C:\>
```

If you only want to see an object's properties, you can use **Get-Member -membertype properties**. You still may need to refer to documentation to fully understand what all the output means. However, at least you have an idea of what you're looking for when you read the documentation.

Here's a clever trick to see all the properties and their values for a given object:

```
PS C:\> get-service winrm | select *


Name                : winrm
RequiredServices    : {RPCSS, HTTP}
CanPauseAndContinue : False
CanShutdown         : True
```

```
CanStop            : True
DisplayName        : Windows Remote Management (WS-Management)
DependentServices  : {}
MachineName        : .
ServiceName        : winrm
ServicesDependedOn : {RPCSS, HTTP}
ServiceHandle      : SafeServiceHandle
Status             : Running
ServiceType        : Win32ShareProcess
Site               :
Container          :

PS C:\>
```

In this example, we piped a single service object to **Select-Object** using a wildcard to instruct it to return all properties.

Variables as Objects

Earlier we mentioned that PowerShell variables are actually objects. In .NET, string variables are extremely robust and have a number of methods and properties. For example, take **Split()**, which is a method that takes a string and creates an array (or list) by breaking the list on some character such as comma or a space. Try this in PowerShell:

```
PS C\:> "1,2,3,4".Split(",")
```

This tells PowerShell to "take this string and execute its **Split()** method. Use a comma for the method's input argument." When PowerShell executes this command, the method returns an array of four elements, each element containing a number. PowerShell displays the array in a textual fashion, with one array element per line:

```
1
2
3
4
```

There are other ways to use this. For example, PowerShell has a cmdlet called **Get-Member** that displays the methods and variables associated with a given object instance. Taking a string like "Hello, World", which is a String object, and piping it to the **Get-Member** cmdlet, displays information about that String object:

```
PS C:\> "Hello, World" | get-member


   TypeName: System.String
Name         MemberType           Definition
----         ----------           ----------
Clone        Method               System.Object Clone()
CompareTo    Method               System.Int32 CompareTo(Object v
Contains     Method               System.Boolean Contains(String
CopyTo       Method               System.Void CopyTo(Int32 source
EndsWith     Method               System.Boolean EndsWith(String
Equals       Method               System.Boolean Equals(Object ob
IndexOf      Method               System.Int32 IndexOf(Char value
IndexOfAny   Method               System.Int32 IndexOfAny(Char[]
```

```
Insert           Method                    System.String Insert(Int32 star
LastIndexOf      Method                    System.Int32 LastIndexOf(Char v
LastIndexOfAny   Method                    System.Int32 LastIndexOfAny
PadLeft          Method                    System.String PadLeft(Int32 tot
PadRight         Method                    System.String PadRight(Int32 to
Remove           Method                    System.String Remove(Int32 star
Replace          Method                    System.String Replace(Char oldC
Split            Method                    System.String[] Split(Params Ch
StartsWith       Method                    System.Boolean StartsWith(Strin
Substring        Method                    System.String Substring(Int32 s
ToCharArray      Method                    System.Char[] TSystem.Char[] To
ToLower          Method                    System.String ToLower(), System
ToString         Method                    System.String ToString(), Syste
ToUpper          Method                    System.String ToUpper(), System
Trim             Method                    System.String Trim(Params Char[
TrimEnd          Method                    System.String TrimEnd(Params Ch
TrimStart        Method                    System.String TrimStart(Params
Chars            ParameterizedProperty     System.Char Chars(Int32 inde
Length           Property                  System.Int32 Length {get;}
```

Even though this output is truncated a bit to fit in this book, you can see that it includes every method and property of the String. It also correctly identifies "Hello, World" as a "System.String" type, which is the unique *type name* that describes what we informally call a String object. You can pipe nearly *anything* to **Get-Member** to learn more about that particular object and its capabilities.

One of the most frequently used object variables is the **$_** variable. We've used it repeatedly in our examples. **$_** is an automatic variable that stands for the current object. Here's an example:

```
PS C:\> get-process | where {$_.workingset -gt 1MB}

Handles  NPM(K)    PM(K)     WS(K) VS(M)   CPU(s)     Id ProcessName
-------  ------    -----     ----- -----   ------     -- -----------
    604      14    23856     37308   112    32.26   2236 explorer
    114       5     6540     12380    52     3.12   2444 i_view32
    617      10    56252     52784   172     7.02    632 PS
    246       5     8672     12300    45     3.02   1512 MsMpEng
    201      12    11528     19400    71     1.24   3452 Skype
    198       6    26016     12816  1584     1.07    544 sqlservr
   1416      49    17768     26312   131     5.25   1556 svchost
    405      14    37140     58236   287   111.07   3900 WINWORD
```

This pipes the output of **Get-Process** to the **Where** cmdlet and only displays those processes where the workingset property of the current object (**$_**) is greater than 1MB. We use dotted notation to define the object and property: **$_.workingset**.

....

How Did We Know That?

The output of the Get-Process cmdlet is a System.Diagnostic.Process object. One of this object's properties is workingset. You can find the properties yourself by running:

```
PS C:\> get-process | get-member -membertype property
```

Let's go back and look at the array of service objects we created earlier in this chapter. We used the following expression to create the object:

```
PS C:\> $svc=get-service | where {$_.status -eq "running"}
```

Since we know the array contains service objects, it might help to know more about these objects. Let's look at the first element of the array:

```
PS C:\> $svc[0]

Status    Name           DisplayName
------    ----           -----------
Running   AudioSrv       Windows Audio
```

We know the first running service in the array is Windows Audio. We're going to learn about this object using this service as an example, even if we're not interested in that specific service. We'll pass the first element of the array to **Get-Member** and display the object's properties.

```
PS C:\> $svc[0] |get-member -membertype properties


   TypeName: System.ServiceProcess.ServiceController

Name                   MemberType      Definition
----                   ----------      ----------
Name                   AliasProperty   Name = ServiceName
CanPauseAndContinue    Property        System.Boolean CanPauseAndCont
CanShutdown            Property        System.Boolean CanShutdown {ge
CanStop                Property        System.Boolean CanStop {get;}
Container              Property        System.ComponentModel.IContain
DependentServices      Property        System.ServiceProcess.ServiceC
DisplayName            Property        System.String DisplayName {get
MachineName            Property        System.String MachineName {get
ServiceHandle          Property        System.Runtime.InteropServices
ServiceName            Property        System.String ServiceName {get
ServicesDependedOn     Property        System.ServiceProcess.ServiceC
ServiceType            Property        System.ServiceProcess.ServiceT
Site                   Property        System.ComponentModel.ISite Si
Status                 Property        System.ServiceProcess.ServiceC
```

Not every property is necessarily populated, nor is it of interest. However, we want to show you where this information comes from and how it is connected to the object.

The easier way to learn property names is by sending the output of the array element to **Format-List**:

```
PS C:\> $svc[0] |format-list


Name                : AudioSrv
DisplayName         : Windows Audio
Status              : Running
DependentServices   : {}
ServicesDependedOn  : {RpcSs, PlugPlay}
CanPauseAndContinue : False
CanShutdown         : False
CanStop             : True
ServiceType         : Win32ShareProcess
```

As you can see, *everything* in PowerShell is an object, with properties and methods that you can use directly—you don't necessarily need a cmdlet to do everything, since many objects have their own built-in capabilities that you can call upon. If an object is stored in a variable, then the variable *represents* that object and has the same properties and methods as the object itself.

Chapter 19
Operators

As with any shell or scripting language, you need a set of operators to do stuff. You need to be able to compare objects, perform arithmetic operations, perform logical operations, and more.

Assignment Operators

PowerShell uses assignment operators to set values to variables. We've been using the equals sign, but there are many other operators as well. The following table lists PowerShell assignment operators:

PowerShell Assignment Operators

Operator	Description
=	Sets the value of a variable to the specified value.
+=	Increases the value of a variable by the specified value or appends to the existing value.
-=	Decreases the value of a variable by the specified value.
*=	Multiplies the value of a variable by the specified value or appends to the existing value.
/=	Divides the value of a variable by the specified value.
%=	Divides the value of a variable by the specified value and assigns the remainder (modulus) to the variable.

In addition to the traditional uses of =, in PowerShell this operator has a few extra bells and whistles that might be of interest to you. First, when you assign a hexadecimal value to a variable, it is stored as its decimal equivalent:

```
PS C:\> $var=0x10
PS C:\> $var
16
PS C:\>
```

You can also use a type of shorthand to assign a variable a multiple byte value. By using **kb**, **mb**, **gb**, **tb** and **pb** which are known as numeric constants, you store actual kilobyte, megabyte, gigabyte, terabyte, and petabyte values respectively:

```
PS C:\> $var=10KB
PS C:\> $var
10240
PS C:\> $var=2MB
PS C:\> $var
2097152
PS C:\> $var=.75GB
PS C:\> $var
805306368
PS C:\> $var=2TB
PS C:\> $var
2199023255552
PS C:\> $var=1PB
PS C:\> $var
1125899906842624
PS C:\>
```

In the first example, we set **$var** to 10KB or 10 kilobytes. Displaying the contents of **$var** shows the actual byte value of 10 kilobytes. We repeat the process by setting **$var** to 2 megabytes, .75 gigabytes, 2 terabytes, and 1 petabyte. In each example, we display the value of **$var**.

The += operator increases the value of a given variable by a specified amount:

```
PS C:\> $var=7
PS C:\> $var
7
PS C:\> $var+=3
PS C:\> $var
10
PS C:\>
```

The variable **$var** begins with a value of 7. We then use += to increment it by 3, which changes the value of **$var** to 10.

The -= operator decreases the value of a given variable by a specified amount. Let's continue with the previous example:

```
PS C:\> $var-=3
PS C:\> $var
7
PS C:\>
```

$var starts out with a value of 10. Using the -= operator, we decrease its value by 3, which returns us to 7.

What if we want to multiply a variable value by a specific number? This calls for the *= operator. Let's continue with the same **$var** that currently has a value of 7:

```
PS C:\> $var*=3
PS C:\> $var
21
PS C:\>
```

We can also divide by using the /= operator:

```
PS C:\> $var/=7
PS C:\> $var
3
PS C:\>
```

Finally, we can use %= to divide the variable value by the assigned value and return the modulus or remainder:

```
PS C:\> $var=9
PS C:\> $var%=4
PS C:\> $var
1
PS C:\>
```

In this example, we start with a **$var** value of 9. Using the modulus assignment operator with a value of 4 means we're dividing 9 into 4. The remainder value is then assigned to **$var**, which in this example is 1.

You need to be careful with assignment operators and variable values. Remember PowerShell does a pretty good job at deciding if what you typed is a number or a string. If you put something in quotes, PowerShell treats it as a string. If you're not careful, you can get some odd results:

```
PS C:\> $var="3"
PS C:\> $var+=7
PS C:\> $var
37
PS C:\>
```

In this example, we think we set **$var** to 3 and increased it by 7 using the += operator. However, "3" is a string, so the += operator simply concatenates instead of adds, which is why we end up with a **$var** value of 37. If you are ever unsure about what type of object you're working with, you can use the **GetType()** method:

```
PS C:\> $var.gettype()

IsPublic  IsSerial  Name                    BaseType
--------  --------  ----                    --------
True      True      String                  System.Object

PS C:\>
```

One final comment on assignment operators: It is possible to assign values to multiple variables with a single statement:

```
PS C:\> $varA,$varB,$varC="Apple",3.1416,"Windows"
PS C:\> get-variable var?
```

```
Name                    Value
----                    -----
varC                    Windows
varB                    3.1416
varA                    Apple
```

PS C:\>

The assigned values are set to their respective variables. If you have more values than variables, then the extra values are assigned to the last variable:

```
PS C:\> $varA,$varB,$varC="Apple",3.1416,"Windows","Linux"
PS C:\> get-variable var?
```

```
Name                    Value
----                    -----
varC                    {Windows, Linux}
varB                    3.1416
varA                    Apple
```

PS C:\>

Our recommendation is to be careful with this type of statement because you can end up with unintentional variable values. PowerShell will wait, so set and modify variables one at a time.

Arithmetic Operators

Arithmetic operators allow you to perform mathematical calculations with numeric values from variables or parameters. With these operators, you can add, subtract, multiply, and divide. You can then pass the result as a parameter to another process or cmdlet. The following table lists these operators.

PowerShell Arithmetic Operators

Operator	**Description**	**Example**
+	Adds two values together.	PS C:\> 5+4 9
−	Subtracts one value from another.	PS C:\> 134-90 44
−	Changes a value to a negative number.	PS C:\>-6 -6
*	Multiplies two values together.	PS C:\> 3*4.5 13.5
/	Divides one value by another.	PS C:\> 6/4 1.5
%	Returns the remainder from a division. This is also known as the modulus.	PS C:\> 6%4 2

As you see from the examples in the table, results are not limited to integer values. In fact, you can obtain some pretty detailed results:

```
PS C:\> 3.1416*3
9.4248
PS C:\> 3.1416/12345
0.000254483596597813
PS C:\>
```

··

Extra Credit

In PowerShell, you also have access to the .NET Framework Math class. If you need more sophisticated mathematical operations such as square root or raising a number to a power, you can invoke those methods like this:

```
PS C:\> [system.math]::pow(2,16)
65536
```

```
PS C:\> [system.math]::sqrt(5)
2.23606797749979
```

See http://msdn.microsoft.com/en-us/library/system.math_methods.aspx for a full list of available methods for the Math class.

Precedence

As you probably learned in elementary school, there is an order for evaluating arithmetic operators. Suppose you have an expression like 5+1/2*3. Would you be surprised that the answer is 6.5? Take a moment and look at the order of precedence:

- - (for a negative number)
- *, /, %
- +, - (for subtraction)

Expressions are evaluated left to right following the order above. So, when 5+1/2*3 is evaluated, 1 divided by 2 is first, which equals .5. This value is then multiplied by 3, which equals 1.5. Next, 1.5 is added to 5 for a result of 6.5.

We use parentheses to override the precedence. In this case, (5+1)/(2*3) will equal 1. Parenthetical elements are evaluated first, and then the rest of the expression is evaluated. In the new example, 5+1=6 and 2*3=6, then 6 divided by 6 equals 1.

Variables

Using arithmetic operators with variables is no different from using numbers, as long as the variable contains a number:

```
PS C:\> $var1="Windows"
PS C:\> $var2=100
PS C:\> $var1+var2
You must provide a value expression on the right-hand side of the '+' operator.
```

```
At line:1 char:7
+ $var1+v <<<< ar2
PS C:\>
```

In this example, we set two variables, but one of them is a string. When we try to use the + operator, PowerShell throws an error. Here is a valid example:

```
PS C:\> $var1=5
PS C:\> $var2=1
PS C:\> $var3=2
PS C:\> $var4=3
PS C:\> ($var1+$var2)/($var3*$var4)
1
PS C:\>
```

This is essentially the same example we used earlier, except that we substituted variables. Here's a more practical example:

```
PS C:\> $proc=Get-process
PS C:\> $total=0
PS C:\> foreach ($p in $proc) {$total+=$p.workingset}
PS C:\> $total
584568832
PS C:\>
```

This example gets the total number of bytes for all running processes allocated to the working sets of each processes. First we send the output of the **Get-Process** cmdlet to a variable and initialize the total variable to zero. We then use a simple **ForEach** loop and add the working set size of each process object to the running total. Finally, we display the value of **$total**. Since the value of **$total** is in bytes, we might want to display it in KB or MB:

```
PS C:\> $total/1KB
570868
PS C:\> $total/1MB
557.48828125
PS C:\>
```

Be careful when trying to mix numbers and text, such as when using the **Write-Host** cmdlet. This cmdlet will expand variables but not perform any arithmetic operations:

```
PS C:\> write-host "Total working set size=$total/1KB KB"
Total working set size= 584568832/1KB KB

PS C:\>
```

That's not really what we're after. By enclosing **$total/1KB** in parenthesis, the expression is evaluated and written to the screen as expected:

```
PS C:\> write-host "Total working set size= $($total/1KB) KB"
Total working set size= 570868 KB
PS C:\> write-host "Total working set size= $($total/1MB) MB"
Total working set size= 557.48828125 MB
PS C:\>
```

Technically we are creating a sub-expression using **$($total/1KB)**. PowerShell evaluates the code within the parentheses, and then treats the result as a variable so that the **Write-Host** cmdlet does the proper variable expansion.

Unary Operators

A subtype of the arithmetic operator is a unary operator, which is used to increment or decrement a variable's value. PowerShell uses **++** to increase a value by one and **--** to decrease it:

```
PS C:\> $var=10
PS C:\> $var++
PS C:\> $var
11
PS C:\> $var--
PS C:\> $var
10
PS C:\>
```

$var starts with a value of 10. Using the **++** operator doesn't appear to do anything, but it actually increased the value of **$var** by 1. Using the **--** operator decreases the value by 1.

Logical Operators

PowerShell logical operators are used to test or validate an expression. Typically, the result of these operations is TRUE or FALSE. Here are the operators:

PowerShell Logical Operators

Operator	Description	Example
-and	All expressions must evaluate as TRUE.	(1 -eq 1) -and (2 -eq 2) returns TRUE
-or	At least one expression must evaluate as TRUE.	(1 -eq 1) -or (2 -eq 4) returns TRUE
-not	Evaluates the inverse of one of the expressions.	(1 -eq 1) -and -not (2 -gt 2) returns TRUE
!	The same as -not.	(1 -eq 1) -and ! (2 -gt 2) returns TRUE

You should use logical operators when you want to evaluate multiple conditions. While you can evaluate several expressions, your scripts and code will be easier to debug or troubleshoot if you limit the operation to two expressions:

```
PS C:\> $varA=5
PS C:\> $varB=5
PS C:\> if (($varA -eq $varB) -and ($varB -gt 20))
>>{
>>Write-Host "Both conditions are true." -foregroundcolor green
>>}
>>else
>>{
>>Write-Host "One or both conditions are false." -foregroundcolor red
>>}
>>
```

```
One or both conditions are false.
PS C:\>
```

Here's the same example using -**or**:

```
PS C:\> if (($varA -eq $varB) -or ($varB -gt 20))
>> {
>> Write-Host "At least one condition is true." –foregroundcolor green
>> }
>> else
>> {
>> Write-Host "Both conditions are false." –foregroundcolor red
>> }
>>
At least one condition is true.
PS C:\>
```

We get a different result if we change **$varA** to 20:

```
PS C:\> $varA=20
PS C:\> if (($varA -eq $varB) -or ($varB -gt 20))
>> {
>> Write-Host "At least one condition is true." –foregroundcolor green
>> }
>> else
>> {
>> Write-Host "Both conditions are false." –foregroundcolor red
>> }
>>
Both conditions are false.
PS C:\>
```

Bitwise Operators

If you find yourself needing binary or bitwise operations, PowerShell has the requisite operators as shown:

PowerShell Bitwise Operators

Operator	Definition
-band	binary and
-bor	binary or
-bnot	binary not

The underlying binary math is beyond the scope of this book. However, here are some examples if you need to perform a bitwise comparison:

```
PS C:\> 255 -band 255
255
PS C:\> 255 -band 150
150
PS C:\> 32 -bor 16
48
PS C:\>
```

In each case, the value that is returned from the comparison is the digital equivalent of the underlying bitwise operation.

String Operators

String operators are designed to manipulate string values in some fashion. PowerShell supports two string operators, **-split** and **–join**. They serve complementary purposes: **-split** is designed to take a delimited list and turn it into an array, where **–join** takes an array and turns it into a flat, delimited list.

For example, beginning with a three-element array:

```
$arr = 1,2,3
```

The **–join** operator will turn this into a flat, delimited string. You can select the delimiter character; for illustration purposes we'll use the ^ character:

```
PS C:\> $arr
1
2
3
PS C:\> $arr -join "^"
1^2^3
```

Here, we're looking at the contents of **$arr** first. PowerShell defaults to displaying each element of the array on a new line, proving that this is in fact an array of three elements. Next, the **–join** operator joins them into a single string, with each element separated by the ^ character. This is a convenient way to make an array of values into a comma-delimited list, for example, which can be easily written out to a CSV file.

The **-split** operator goes the other direction:

```
PS C:\> "1,2,3,4,5" -split ","
1
2
3
4
5
```

Here, a comma-separated string has been split on the commas, so that each value becomes an element in an array. This is a convenient way to read in, for example, a line from a CSV file, and then split that line into array elements so that each value can be accessed independently. The operator defaults to turning each value in the string into an array element; you can change that by specifying how many total elements to create. This example turns the first two elements into array elements, and then creates a third element containing the remainder of the string:

```
PS C:\> "1,2,3,4,5" -split ",",3
1
2
3,4,5
```

The result is a total of three array elements, which is what we specified. The first two elements contain individual values, while the remaining element contains whatever was left in the original string.

The **–split** operator can also work with a script block. Each character in the input string is passed into the script block one at a time; the script block accesses these through the **$_** variable, and if the script block returns **$True**, then the **–split** operator considers that character to be a delimiter, and splits the string accordingly. Here's a quick example:

```
PS C:\test> "testtesttestest" -split { if ($_ -eq "t") { $True } }
```

es

es

es
es

Here, the script block is testing to see if the input character is a "t." If it is, it returns **$True**. This results in the "t" being the delimiter character, and the output reflects that. A good practical use of this technique is to use a regular expression (which we discuss in the chapter, "Regular Expressions") to allow a number of different characters to become delimiters:

```
PS C:\test> "Monday,Tuesday^Wednesday/Thursday.Friday" -split { $_ -match "[,\^/\.]" }
Monday
Tuesday
Wednesday
Thursday
Friday
```

Here, the regex accepted the characters, ^ / and . as delimiters, returning **$True** whenever one of those characters was passed into **$_**.

Special Operators

PowerShell has several special operators that are capable of specialized tasks that can't be easily accomplished any other way.

Splat Operator

The "splat" operator is the "at" sign, or **@**. It's designed to take a collection of items (that is, a list) and assign them to the input arguments of a function. An illustration makes this a bit easier to understand.

Imagine you have a function defined as follows:

```
Function MyFunction  {
  Param ($a, $b, $c)
  # some code here
}
```

This function accepts three input arguments: **$a**, **$b**, and **$c**. One way to call the function would be to simply specify a value for each argument:

```
$result = MyFunction 1 2 3
```

Note that input arguments are delimited by a space, not by commas; if you did this:

```
$result = MyFunction 1,2,3
```

PowerShell would pass an array of three elements to argument **$a**, and arguments **$b** and **$c** would receive nothing. Similarly, if you created a regular array and passed that as an input argument, the entire array would go to **$a**, while **$b** and **$c** got nothing:

```
$arr = 1,2,3
$result = MyFunction $arr
```

The splat operator (the origin of that name, by the way, is lost in the mists of *nix history) is designed to take an array, expand it out into individual elements, and then pass each element as a single input argument to a function:

```
$arr = 1,2,3
$result = MyFunction @arr
```

This way, **$a** gets the value 1, **$b** gets 2, and **$c** gets 3—each value is extracted from the array and passed to an individual argument. Notice that the operator, **@**, replaces the **$** in the variable name. Here's another example.

Splat-Foo.ps1

```
Function Splat-Foo {
 Param($computername,$namespace,$class,$report)

 Write-Host "Getting WMI data for $computername" -foregroundcolor cyan
 $wmi=Get-WmiObject -Namespace $namespace -Class $class -computername $computername
 Write-Host "Saving results to $report" -foregroundcolor cyan
 $wmi | select * | Out-File $report

}

$data="godot7","root\cimv2","win32_operatingsystem","c:\WMIReport.txt"
Splat-Foo @data
Get-Content $data[-1]
```

The main function has several parameters that are used to retrieve WMI information and save it to a text file. The **$data** variable contains values we want to pass to the function. The function is called and the values splatted to the function.

```
$data="godot7","root\cimv2","win32_operatingsystem","c:\WMIReport.txt"
Splat-Foo @data
```

When using this technique you must ensure that all your values are in the correct order.

Replace Operator

You can use the **-replace** operator to substitute characters in a string. The operator essentially uses pattern matching to find a target string or character. If it is found, the substitution is made. The **-replace** syntax is:

```
"String-to-search" -replace "Search-for","Replace-with"
```

You can search and replace a single character or part of a word:

```
PS C:\> "PowerShell" -replace "e","3"
Pow3rSh3ll
PS C:\> "PowerShell" -replace "shell","tool"
Powertool
PS C:\> "PowerShell" -replace "k","m"
PowerShell
PS C:\>
```

In the first example, all instances of the letter e are replaced with the number 3. In the second, the string "shell" is replaced with "tool". The last example shows that if no successful match is made, the string remains untouched. You can use the **-replace** operator with variables, but be careful:

```
PS C:\> $var="PowerShell"
PS C:\> $var -replace "p","sh"
showerShell
PS C:\> $var
PowerShell
PS C:\>
```

The **-replace** operator doesn't change the original variable—instead, it only displays the replaced result. When we look at **$var** again, we see it hasn't changed. If you want to change the variable value, you should use something like this:

```
PS C:\> $var=$var -replace "p","sh"
PS C:\> $var
showerShell
PS C:\>
```

All we need to do is redefine **$var** by setting its value to the output of the **-replace** operation. The operator can also make replacements within collections and arrays:

```
PS C:\> $var=@("aaa","bbb","abab","ccc")
PS C:\> $var
aaa
bbb
abab
ccc
PS C:\> $var=$var -replace "a","z"
PS C:\> $var
zzz
bbb
zbzb
ccc
PS C:\>
```

We start with a simple array, then redefine **$var** using the **-replace** operator to change all occurrences of a to z.

There's really no limit when using this operator. You can even use it to make changes to text files:

```
PS C:\> $var=get-content "boot.ini"
PS C:\> $var -replace "windows","WIN"
[boot loader]
timeout=15
default=multi(0)disk(0)rdisk(0)partition(2)\WIN
[operating systems]
multi(0)disk(0)rdisk(0)partition(2)\WIN="Microsoft WIN XP Professional" /fastdetect /
```

```
NoExecute=OptIn
multi(0)disk(0)rdisk(0)partition(1)\WIN="WIN Server 2003, Enterprise" /noexecute=optout /
fastdetect
C:\CMDCONS\BOOTSECT.DAT="Microsoft WIN Recovery Console" /cmdcons
PS C:\>
```

Here we dumped the contents of our boot.ini file to **$var**, and then replaced all instances of "Windows" with "WIN". Granted, this may not be the best production-oriented example, but it demonstrates the point.

Keep in mind that the **-replace** operator is case-insensitive. However, if you want to use this operator to make a case-sensitive search and replace, you can use the **-creplace** operator. The next table lists the **-replace** special operators.

PowerShell Replace Operators

Operator	Definition	Example
-replace	Replace.	"PowerShell" -replace "s","$"
-ireplace	Case-insensitive replace. Essentially the same as -replace.	"PowerShell" -ireplace "s","$"
-creplace	Case-sensitive replace.	"PowerShell" -creplace "p","t"

When using **-creplace**, the replacement is only made when a case-sensitive match is made:

```
PS C:\> "PowerShell" -creplace "p","t"
PowerShell
PS C:\> "PowerShell" -creplace "P","t"
towerShell
PS C:\>
```

In the first example, since no lower case "p" is found, no replacement is made. However, in the second example a match is made, so the operator replaces "P" with "t".

In the "Regular Expressions" chapter we will discuss how you can also use regular expressions for matching and replacing.

Type

If you've been following along, by now you surely know that PowerShell is an object-oriented shell. As such, we may need to check if a variable is a particular type of object. PowerShell includes three type operators, as shown:

PowerShell Type Operators

Operator	Definition	Example
-is	Checks if object IS a specific type.	$var -is [string]
-isnot	Checks if object IS NOT a specific type.	$var -isnot [string]
-as	Converts object to specified type.	3.1416 -as string

The operation result will be either TRUE or FALSE for -**is** and -**isnot**.

```
PS C:\> $now=get-date
PS C:\> $now -is [datetime]
True
PS C:\> 1024 -is [int]
True
PS C:\> "Microsoft" -isnot [string]
False
PS C:\>
```

In the first example, we create the variable **$now** from the output of the **Get-Date** cmdlet. Now we can use -**is** to validate that it is a **DateTime** object. We do the same thing by verifying that 1024 is an integer. Both operations return TRUE. In the last example, we checked to see if "Microsoft" is not a string. Since it is a string, the operation returns FALSE.

The -**as** operator converts the object to the specified type:

```
PS C:\> $var=get-date
PS C:\> $var.gettype()

IsPublic  IsSerial  Name                    BaseType
--------  --------  ----                    --------
True      True      DateTime                System.ValueType


PS C:\> if ($var -isnot [string]) {
>> $var=$var -as [string]
>> $var.gettype()
>> $var.PadLeft(25)
>> }
>>

IsPublic  IsSerial  Name                    BaseType
--------  --------  ----                    --------
True      True      String                  System.Object
    5/21/2006 7:53:02 PM
PS C:\>
```

In this example, we created a **DateTime** object. To do this, we called the **GetType()** method to show we have nothing hidden up our sleeves. However, we want to call the **Padleft()** method of the **string** object. We check to see if **$var** is not a string. If so, then we use the -**as** operator to recreate **$var** as a **string** object. Again, we call the **GetType()** method to show the successful change, and then finally call the **Padleft()** method.

ToString
It is easier to convert an object to a string by using the **ToString()** method. Most objects have this method. The end result is essentially the same as using the -**as** operator.

Range Operator (..)

You use the range operator (**..**) is used to indicate a range of values. Keep in mind that you must specify the beginning and end points of the range:

```
PS C:\> $var=@(1..5)
PS C:\> $var
1
2
3
4
5
PS C:\>
```

Here, we created an array variable whose contents are 1 through 5 inclusive. The range operator only works with integer values. If you try this with string characters, PowerShell will complain:

```
PS C:\> $var=@("a".."j")
Cannot convert value "a" to type "System.Int32". Error: "Input string
was not in a correct format."
At line:1 char:13
+ $var=@("a".." <<<< j")
PS C:\>
```

Call Operators (&)

You use call operators (**&**) when you want to execute a command. Sometimes PowerShell can't tell if what you typed is a command. To force PowerShell to execute a statement, use the ampersand (**&**) character. For example, we might want to execute all PowerShell scripts in the current directory:

```
PS C:\> $all=get-childitem *.ps1
PS C:\> foreach ($s in $all) {&$s}
PS C:\> #each Powershell script executes
```

You can also use the call operator to create a variable that holds the results of a cmdlet:

```
PS C:\> $j=get-process | where {$_.workingset -gt 5000000}
PS C:\> &$j
PS C:\> #an array of all processes with a workingset size greater than 5000 is returned.
```

In this example, when we force **$j** to run, the output is a little unfriendly. We can get a nicer output from **$j** by using a command like this:

```
PS C:\> foreach ($item in $j) {$item.name}
```

In both of these examples, the variable we are creating is the output of the cmdlet we ran. In a significant manner, this is slightly different than the following:

```
PS C:\> $j="get-process"
PS C:\> $j
get-process
PS C:\> &$j | where {$_.workingset -gt 5000000}
```

Handles	NPM(K)	PM(K)	WS(K)	VM(M)	CPU(s)	Id	ProcessName
209	6	3696	6768	56	25.65	416	avgcc
873	21	34840	16820	161	1,282.25	1256	explorer
1056	24	97188	116708	464	247.16	4972	firefox
806	81	16636	21764	143	17.18	5264	Groove

```
 659    20   28224     5284   264     75.64   1488  iexplore
 234    10   10912     6116    68     17.09   1420  mmc
 251     5    9308     4920    47    251.73   1552  MsMpEng
  63     3    1696     5604    37      0.54   1372  notepad
1772    69  112832    31536   712    200.94   2304  OUTLOOK
 553    11   49156    48388   163      7.16    532  powershell
 393    61   15164     9952    89     94.55    596  Skype
 559    12   16192    12808    97  5,118.91   1676  Smc
 298    13   14816     6464    88    177.96    576  StatBar
1549    51   24640    15220   166    366.55   1596  svchost
 351    30   14612   551216   653  3,497.73   5412  vmware-vmx
 446    17   33656    53764   282     25.21   2600  WINWORD
 592    21   21564    15984   106     11.52   4636  wmplayer

PS C:\>
```

In this instance, we set **$j** to a string of a cmdlet name. When we use the call operator, the value of **$j** is evaluated and executed. Notice that we added our workingset filter to the line where **$j** is executed. This is because the **$_** variable doesn't exist until the cmdlet is run. All we've really done here is essentially create another alias for the **Get-Process** cmdlet.

Don't get too hung up on this operator. The only time you are likely to use it is when calling a PowerShell command from outside of PowerShell:

```
C:\powershell "&c:\scripts\showservices.ps1"
```

This command is run from a Windows Cmd.exe prompt. Using the **&** operator tells PowerShell to execute c:\scripts\showservices.ps1. This is one way you can integrate your PowerShell scripts into your Cmd.exe environment.

Format Operator (-f)

The PowerShell format operator (**-f**) let's you format strings using the .NET string object format method. The syntax is a little backwards compared to what we've worked with so far:

```
PS C:\ > FormatString -f "string to format"
```

.NET formatting is a way of specifying the format of a particular object. For example, a **DateTime** object could be formatted as a short date (5/22/2007) or a long date (Monday, May 22, 2007). You can format a number as currency, number, or percent. To get the most out of this operator, you need to become very familiar with .NET formatting, most of which is outside the scope of this book. However, we'll provide a few examples that you will find useful.

```
PS C:\ > $now=get-date
PS C:\> $now

Friday, August 28, 2009 12:35:58 PM


PS C:\> "{0:d}" -f $now
8/28/2009
PS C:\> "{0:D}" -f $now
Friday, August 28, 2009
PS C:\> "{0:t}" -f $now
12:35 PM
```

```
PS C:\> "{0:T}" -f $now
12:35:58 PM
PS C:\>
```

In this example, we created the variable **$now** that holds the current date and time. We can format this variable in a number of ways. First, we can use the format pattern {0:d} to display **$now** as a short date. Alternatively, we can use {0:D} to format **$now** as a long date. This is another example where PowerShell is case-sensitive. Using {0:t} or {0:T} will format for short or long time, respectively. Let's look at the examples of numeric formatting that are included below:

```
PS C:\> $var=12345.6789
PS C:\> "{0:N}" -f $var
12,345.68
PS C:\> "{0:N3}" -f $var
12,345.679
PS C:\> "{0:F}" -f $var
12345.68
PS C:\> "{0:F3}" -f $var
12345.679
PS C:\>
```

The numeric variable is being formatted in these examples. In the first example, the formatting patter {0:N} formats the variable as a number with a thousands separator. The default for this formatter for most English language systems is to specify two decimal places. You can change this default by using a precision modifier. In the second example, {0:N3} instructs PowerShell to format **$var** as a number to three decimal places. Using the **F** formatting string tells PowerShell to format the number in a fixed format. {0:F} is practically the same as {0:N}, except there is no thousands separator. We can also specify a precision modifier, such as {0:F3}, to control the number of decimals. Here's a practical example:

```
PS C:\> $proc=get-process | where {$_.workingset -gt 5MB}
PS C:\> $proc | select Name,@{name="WS(MB)";expression={"{0:N4}" -f ($_.workingset/1MB) }}

Name                                    WS(MB)
----                                    ------
audiodg                                 15.6055
cmd                                      6.2148
csrss                                    5.0898
csrss                                   20.7383
dllhost                                  5.8320
dwm                                      7.1328
explorer                                65.0430
firefox                                220.3633
igfxsrvc                                 7.1875
lsass                                    5.6484
mdm                                      5.4609
PS C:\>
```

In this example, we piped **$proc** to the **Select-Object** cmdlet, selecting the process name and creating a custom property that displayed the workingset size in MB to four decimal places.

So, exactly how does the formatting operator work? Or, more specifically, how do these .NET Framework formatting strings work?

The examples we've used so far all look something like "{0:N4}", which is composed of two distinct parts: The *argument number*, and the *formatting directive*. Essentially, this example says, "take the argument in the first position, and format it according to the N4 style." N4 means numeric, with 4 digits after the decimal. The first position is numbered zero, which is where the zero comes from in the formatting string. Here's another example:

```
PS C:\> $v1 = 1.23456
PS C:\> $v2 = 6.54321
PS C:\> "{0:N4} {1:N3}" -f $v1,$v2
1.2346 6.543
```

Here, we've created two variables, each with decimal values. This time, our formatting string is taking the first item and formatting it in the N4 style, and the second item is being numbered in the N3 style—that is, numeric, with three digits after the decimal. After the **-f** operator, we've provided a comma-separated list (technically, an array) with our two values. And, as you can see in the output, each was formatted according to the strings: Position one (index number zero) has four decimal places, and position two (index number one) has three.

So, if the first part of a formatting directive indicates which input value is to be formatted, and the second indicates what type of formatting to use, then what types of formatting are available? Here's a list of common formats:

Numeric Formats

- C or c—Currency; C2 would include two digits after the decimal.

- D or d—Decimal; D2 would indicate at least two digits, with zeros added to the beginning if necessary.

- E or e—Scientific notation; E2 indicates two digits after the decimal.

- F or f—Fixed-point; F2 indicates two digits after the decimal.

- G or g—Uses the most compact available method—either fixed-point or scientific notation.

- N or n—Basic number; N2 indicates two digits after the decimal.

- P or p—Percentage; P2 indicates two digits after the decimal.

- R or r—Round-trip; only supported for [single] and [double] numbers.

- X or x—Hexadecimal; H2 indicates a minimum of 2 digits in the output; the case (X or x) determines the case of the output.

Date and Time Formats

- d—Short date

- D—Long date

- f—Full date/time (short)

- F—Full date/time (long)

- g—General date/time (short)

- G—General date/time (long)

- M —Month- pattern (MM)

- m –Minute pattern (mm)

- o—Round-trip day/time

- R or r—RFC1123 date (ddd, dd MMM yyyy HH:mm:ss GMT)

- s—Sortable (ISO 8601)

- t—Short time

- u—Universal sortable date/time (no timezone conversion)

- U—Universal sortable date/time (uses Coordinated Universal Time, or UTC)

- Y or y—Year-month pattern (yyyy MMMM)

You can combine these patterns to create a date pattern like this:

```
PS C:\> "{0:yyyy/MM/dd hh:mm:ss}" -f (get-date)
2009/09/10 10:37:03
```

Note that the "round trip" formats are intended to produce output that can be successfully converted back into its original non-string data type. In the case of a date, for example, it includes a time zone indicator. Also note that these are just the standard formats; it's possible to create custom formats, but doing so generally requires specialized .NET Framework programming and is beyond the scope of this book.

Online Help
Microsoft's official documentation on .NET formatting is available at http://msdn2.microsoft.com/en-us/library/26etazsy.aspx.

Comparison Operators

PowerShell has several types of comparison operators that you can use to evaluate expressions. These operators are listed in the following table.

PowerShell Comparison Operators

Operator	Description	Algebraic Equivalent
-eq	Equals	A=B
-ne	Not equal	A<>B
-gt	Greater than	A>B
-ge	Greater than or equal to	A>=B
-lt	Less than	A<B
-le	Less than or equal to	A<=B

Note
These operators are all case-insensitive, meaning that "HELLO" is the same as "hello", as far as PowerShell is concerned. Case-sensitive operators are available: -ceq, -cne, -cgt, -cge, -clt, and -cle all perform case-sensitive comparisons when you're comparing strings.

You are probably familiar with most of these operators or at least their algebraic equivalent. In PowerShell, these operators are used to evaluate an expression and return either TRUE or FALSE.

```
PS C:\> $varA=100
PS C:\> $varB=200
```

```
PS C:\> $varA -eq $varB
False
PS C:\> $varA -ne $varB
True
PS C:\> $varA -lt $varB
True
PS C:\>
```

After we define some variables, we compare them with a few of the comparison operators that return either TRUE or FALSE.

These comparison operators work just fine for simple numeric comparisons. For string comparisons we can use **-like** and **-match**. If your comparison needs are simple, the **-like** operator may be all you need:

```
PS C:\> "10.10.10.1" -like "10.10.10.*"
True
PS C:\> "10.10.10.25" -like "10.10.10.*"
True
PS C:\> "10.10.11.1" -like "10.10.10.*"
False
PS C:\>
```

....

Note
The -like and -match operators are also case-insensitive; -clike and -cmatch are their case-sensitive counterparts.

In this example, we're comparing an IP address (10.10.10.1) to a pattern that uses the wildcard character (*). This comparison returns the Boolean value TRUE. The second comparison also matches, but the third fails. The operator returns FALSE because the third octet no longer matches the pattern.

Depending on the logic of your script, you may want to check the inverse. In other words, you may want to determine whether the address is not like the pattern. For an inverse type of comparison, use the **-notlike** operator.

```
PS C:\> "10.10.11.1" -notlike "10.10. 10.*"
True
PS C:\>
```

This is essentially the same comparison, except this operator returns TRUE because 10.10.11.1 is not like 10.10.10.*.

The asterisk is a multiple character wildcard that can be used if we need something more granular. For example, we can use the "?" operator if we want to match any subnet of 10.10.10.x to 10.10.19.x.

```
PS C:\> "10.10.11.1" -like "10.10.1?.*"
True
PS C:\> "10.10.15.1" -like "10.10.1?.*"
True
PS C:\> "10.10.25.1" -like "10.10.1?.*"
False
PS C:\>
```

In this example, you can see the first two comparisons are TRUE, but the last one does not meet the pattern so it returns FALSE.

Text Comparison Only
Make sure you understand the IP address comparisons are merely looking at the IP address string.
We are not calculating or comparing network address with subnet masks or the like.

Let's look at some text comparison examples.

```
PS C:\> "sapien" -like "SAPIEN"
True
PS C:\> "sapien" -like "sap*"
True
PS C:\> "sapien" -like "sap?"
False
PS C:\> "sapien" -like "sapie[a-p]"
True
PS C:\>
```

The first example is a pretty basic comparison that also demonstrates that the **-like** operator is case-insensitive. The second example uses the wildcard character, which means it will return TRUE for a string like "sapien". However, it will also return TRUE for "sapsucker" and "sapling". The third example returns FALSE because the "?" character means any single character after "sap". The last example is a bit different. We can use brackets to denote a range of characters with which to compare. In this case, the **-like** operator will return TRUE for anything that starts with "sapie" and ends with any character between "a" and "p".

The **-like** operator limits your comparisons essentially to a few wildcards. If you need something that will compare a pattern, then use the **-match** operator. This operator also returns TRUE if the string matches the specified pattern.

At its simplest, **-match** returns TRUE if any part of the string matches the pattern:

```
PS C:\> $var="XPDesktop01"
PS C:\> $var -match "XP"
True
PS C:\> $var -match "desk"
True
PS C:\> $var -match "01"
True
PS C:\>
```

In this example, we set a variable to the value "XPDesktop01" and compared it with a variety of patterns using **-match**. As you can see, they all return TRUE because pattern such as "desk" exist somewhere in the string. However, sometimes we need to be more particular such as only returning TRUE if the name starts with "XP". In this case, we can use "^" to indicate we want to match the beginning characters:

```
PS C:\> $var -match "^XP"
True
PS C:\> $var -match "^Win2K"
False
PS C:\>
```

If we want to match something at the end of the string, then we use the **$** character:

```
PS C:\> $var -match "01$"
True
```

```
PS C:\> $var -match "02$"
False
PS C:\>
```

In the first example, we get a positive match because **$var**, which is XPDesktop01, ends in 01. The second attempt is FALSE because **$var** does not end in 02.

Other times, we may be looking for something in between such as a range of characters. In this case, we can use brackets and match anything that falls within the range:

```
PS C:\> "hat" -match "h[aeiou]t"
True
PS C:\> "hit" -match "h[aeiou]t"
True
PS C:\> "hyt" -match "h[aeiou]t"
False
PS C:\>
```

In this example, "hat" and "hit" match the pattern because the middle character is included in the bracketed set. The last example fails to match because "y" is not in the set.

One final comment on **-match** is that the matching results are automatically stored in an array called **$matches**:

```
PS C:\> "CHI-SRV-02" -match "^chi"
True
PS C:\> $matches

Name                      Value
----                      -----
0                         CHI
PS C:\> "NYD-SRV-03" -match "^NY[a-d]"
True
PS C:\> $matches

Name                      Value
----                      -----
0                         NYD
PS C:\>
```

In the first example, the match pattern is looking for a string that begins with "chi". Since the string includes "chi", it returns TRUE. The **$matches** array is automatically populated with the matching text. In the second example, we're looking for something that starts with NY and the third character can be a, b, c, or d. The **$matches** array shows us that NYD matched.

The 0 element of the array always returns the matched string. However, it is also possible to group results and save them as named groups:

```
PS C:\> "Computer system=XPDesk02" -match "^comp.*=(?<sysname>.*)"
True
PS C:\> $matches

Name                      Value
----                      -----
sysname                   XPDesk02
0                         Computer system=XPDesk02
PS C:\> $matches.sysname
XPDesk02
```

```
PS C:\>
```

In this example, we have a string, "Computer system=XPDesk02" that is being matched against a pattern that will match up with "Computer system=". To create a named group, we enclose the name of our group in parentheses. In this case, sysname and a matching pattern (.*) will be enclosed in parentheses. The syntax for defining the named group is **?<*name*>**. If we have a match, then the **$matches** array will not only have element 0, but also our named element sysname. Until we use **-match** again, this array remains intact, and we can get the sysname property with dotted notation as we did with **$matches.sysname** in the example above.

Almost all of our examples have been fairly basic and theoretical. Here's an example of how we might use **-match** in a production setting:

```
PS C:\> $sys=Get-WmiObject -class "win32_computersystem"
PS C:\> $sys.name
XPDESK01
PS C:\> if ($sys.name -match "^xp") {
>> write-host "Running audit code"
>> #audit code can run here
>> }
>> else
>> {
>> write-host "Skipping system"
>> }
>>
Running audit code
PS C:\>
```

This code could be part of a larger script. Essentially, it sets the variable **$sys** to an instance of the Win32_ComputerSystem WMI object. We're displaying the object's name property so you'll understand how the rest of the code works. Next we build an IF statement that says, "If the name property starts with XP, then display a message and run something. Otherwise, just display a message that the system is being skipped". At this point, do not be concerned about understanding the IF statement since it will be covered in the chapter "Loops and Decision-making Constructs." As you see, the name matches so the appropriate message is displayed.

The **-match** operator is also used with regular expressions, which will be discussed in the "Regular Expressions" chapter.

Note

And, in case you haven't guessed, **-match** and **-notlike** are case-insensitive. **-cmatch** and **-cnotlike** are their case-sensitive versions. This is the case for most comparison operators: Put a "c" between the dash and the operator to make it case-sensitive.

Chapter 20
Regular Expressions

How often have you tried searching through log files looking for a particular piece of information or searching for all information that meets a certain format like an IP address? A regular expression is a text pattern that you can use to compare against a string of text. If the string of text matches the pattern, then you've found what you're looking for. For example, we know that an IP address has the format *xxx.xxx.xxx.xxx*. We don't know how many integers each octet has, only that there should be four sets of three numbers that are separated by periods. Conceptually, *xxx.xxx.xxx.xxx* is our pattern, and if it's found in the string we are examining, a match is made. Regular expressions can be very complex and confusing at first. We don't have space in this chapter for an exhaustive review of this topic, but we will give you enough information to use basic regular expressions in your PowerShell scripts.

Up to this point, pattern matching has been pretty simple and straightforward. But what if we want to validate that a string was in a particular format such as a UNC path or an IP address? In this case, we can use regular-expression special characters to validate a string. The following table lists several of the more common special characters:

Regular-expression Special Characters

Character	Description
\w	Matches a word (alpha-numeric and the underscore character).
\d	Matches any digit (0-9).
\t	Matches any tab.
\s	Matches any whitespace, tab, or newline.

There are additional special characters, but these are the ones you are most likely to use. By the way, each of these characters has an inverse option you can use simply by using the capital letter version. For example, if you want to match a pattern for anything that was *not* a digit, you would use \D. This is an example of when PowerShell is case-sensitive.

PowerShell supports the qualifiers available in .NET regular expressions, as shown in the next table:

Regular-expression Qualifiers

Format	Description
Value	Matches exact characters anywhere in the original value.
.	Matches any single character.
[value]	Matches at least one of the characters in the brackets.
[range]	Matches at least one of the characters within the range; the use of a hyphen (-) allows specification of contiguous characters.
[^]	Matches any character except those in brackets.
^	Matches the beginning characters.
$	Matches the end characters.
*	Matches zero or more instances of the preceding character.
?	Matches zero or more instances of the preceding character.
\	Matches the character that follows as an escaped character.
+	Matches repeating instances of the specified pattern such as abc+.
{n}	Specifies exactly n matches.
{n,}	Specifies at least n matches.
{n,m}	Specifies at least n, but no more than m, matches.

By combining pattern matching characters with these qualifiers, it is possible to construct some very complex regular expressions.

Writing Regular Expressions

Let's look at some simple, regular-expression examples:

```
PS C:\> "SAPIEN Press" -match "\w"
True
PS C:\> $matches

Name                      Value
----                      -----
0                         S


PS C:\> "SAPIEN Press" -match "\w*"
True
PS C:\> $matches

Name                      Value
----                      -----
0                         SAPIEN

PS C:\> "SAPIEN Press" -match "\w+"
```

```
True
PS C:\> $matches

Name                    Value
----                    -----
0                       SAPIEN


PS C:\> "SAPIEN Press" -match "\w* \w*"
True
PS C:\> $matches

Name                    Value
----                    -----
0                       SAPIEN Press


PS C:\>
```

The first example compares the string "SAPIEN Press" to the pattern \w. Recall that comparison results are automatically stored in the **$matches** variable. As you can see, \w matches "S". Why doesn't it match "SAPIEN" or "SAPIEN Press"? The \w pattern means any word, even a single-character word. If we want to match a complete word, then we need to use one of the regular-expression qualifiers. For example, you can see the second and third examples use \w* and \w+ respectively. In this particular example, these patterns return the same results.

If we want to match a two word phrase, then we would use an example like the last one using \w* \w*. If we were testing a match for "SAPIEN Press PowerShell", then we'd use something like this:

```
PS C:\> "SAPIEN Press PowerShell" -match "\w* \w*"
True
PS C:\> $matches

Name                    Value
----                    -----
0                       SAPIEN Press


PS C:\>
```

This also matches, but as you can see it only matches the first two words. If we want to specifically match a two-word pattern, then we need to qualify our regular expression so it starts and ends with a word:

```
PS C:\> "SAPIEN Press PowerShell" -match "^\w* \w*$"
False
PS C:\> "SAPIEN Press" -match "^\w* \w*$"
True
PS C:\>
```

The recommended best practice for strict, regular-expression evaluation is to use the ^ and $ qualifiers to denote the beginning and end of the matching pattern.

Here's another example:

```
PS C:\> "1001" -match "\d"
True
PS C:\> $matches
```

```
Name                    Value
----                    -----
0                       1
```

```
PS C:\> "1001" -match "\d+"
True
PS C:\> $matches
```

```
Name                    Value
----                    -----
0                       1001
```

```
PS C:\>
```

In the first example, we used the digit-matching pattern to get a TRUE result. However, **$matches** shows it only matched the first digit. Using **\d+** in the second example returns the full value. If we want the number to be four digits, then we can use a qualifier like this:

```
PS C:\> "1001" -match "\d{4,4}"
True
PS C:\> "101" -match "\d{4,4}"
False
PS C:\>
```

The qualifier {4,4} indicates that we want to find a string with at least four matches. In this case, that would be an integer (\d) and no more than 4. When we use the regular expression to evaluate 101, it returns TRUE.

The following example shows a regular expression that is evaluating a simple UNC path string:

```
PS C:\> "\\file01\public" -match "^\\\\\w*\\\w*$"
True
PS C:\> $matches
```

```
Name                    Value
----                    -----
0                       \\file01\public
```

```
PS C:\>
```

This example looks a little confusing, so let's break it apart. First, we want an exact match so we're using **^** and **$** to denote the beginning and end of the regular expression. We know the server name and path will be alphanumeric words, so we can use **\w**. Because we want the entire word, we'll use the ***** qualifier. All that's left are the \\ and \ characters in the UNC path. Remember that \ is a special character in regular expressions. If we want to match the \ character itself, then we need to "escape" it using another \ character. In other words, each \ will become \\. So, the elements of the regular expression break down to:

^ (beginning of expression)

\\   becomes \\\\

\w* (servername)

\   becomes \\

268

\w* (sharename)

$ (end of expression)

Putting this all together, we end up with ^\\\\\w*\\\w*$. As you can see in the example, this is exactly what we get.

Notice that **$matches** indicates the match at index 0, which is fine assuming we want a complete match. But we can also use regular expressions to match individual components by grouping each pattern:

```
PS C:\> "\\server01\public" -match "(\\\\\w*)\\(\w*)"
True
PS C:\> $matches

Name                    Value
----                    -----
2                       public
1                       \\server01
0                       \\server01\public
```

You're probably thinking, "So what?" Well, regular expressions in PowerShell support a feature called *named captures*. This allows us to define a name for the capture instead of relying on the index number. The format is to use "?<capturename>" inside parentheses of each pattern.

```
PS C:\> "\\server01\public" -match "(?<server>\\\\\w*)\\(?<share>\w*)"
True
PS C:\> $matches

Name                    Value
----                    -----
server                  \\server01
share                   public
0                       \\server01\public
```

We still have the complete match at index 0, but notice there are now names associated with the other matches. Now I can reference these elements directly by name:

```
PS C:\> $matches.server
\\server01
PS C:\> $matches.share
public
```

Using named captures makes it much easier to work with the **$matches** variable. One final note on this particular pattern is that it will not match a longer UNC like \\File01\Public\Scripts.

Let's look at another example. Here's a regular-expression pattern to match an IP address:

```
PS C:\> "192.168.100.2" -match "^\d+\.\d+\.\d+\.\d+$"
True
PS C:\> $matches

Name                    Value
----                    -----
0                       192.168.100.2
```

```
PS C:\> "192.168.100" -match "^\d+\.\d+\.\d+\.\d+$"
```

```
False
PS C:\>
```

This should begin to look familiar. We're matching digits and using the \ character to escape the period character, since the period is a regular-expression special character. By using the beginning and end of regular-expression characters, we also know that we'll only get a successful match on a string with four numbers that are separated by periods. Of course, there's more to an IP address than four numbers. Each set of numbers can't be greater than three digits long. Here's how we can construct a regular expression to validate that:

```
PS C:\> "192.168.100.2" -match "^\d{1,3}\.\d{1,3}\.\d{1,3}\.\d{1,3}$"
True
PS C:\> "172.16.1.2543" -match "^\d{1,3}\.\d{1,3}\.\d{1,3}\.\d{1,3}$"
False
PS C:\>
```

The first example matches because each dotted octet is between 1 and 3 digits. The second example fails because the last octet is 4 digits.

PowerShell regular expressions also support named character sets, using a named character set:

```
PS C:\> "powershell" -match "\p{Ll}"
True
PS C:\> $matches

Name                    Value
----                    -----
0                       p
```

The named character set syntax is to use **\p** and the set name, in this case {Ll} to indicate all lowercase letters. This is functionally the same as:

```
PS C:\> "powershell" -match "[a-z]"
```

This may not seem like much of an improvement, but using character classes can simplify your regular expressions:

```
PS C:\> "PowerShell" -match "\p{L}+"
True
PS C:\> $matches

Name                    Value
----                    -----
PowerShell
```

The {L} character class indicates any uppercase or lowercase character. We could get the same result with this:

```
PS C:\> "PowerShell" -match "[a-zA-z]+"
```

The character set requires a little less typing. As your expressions grow in length and complexity, you will appreciate this.

You can use any of these Unicode character sets:

Regular-expression, Unicode Character Sets

Character Set	Description
Cc	Other, Control
Cf	Other, Format
Cn	Other, Not Assigned (no characters have this property)
Co	Other, Private Use
Cs	Other, Surrogate
Ll	Letter, Lowercase
Lm	Letter, Modifier
Lo	Letter, Other
Lt	Letter, Titlecase (e.g., Microsoft Windows)
Lu	Letter, Uppercase
Mc	Mark, Spacing Combining
Me	Mark, Enclosing
Mn	Mark, Nonspacing
Nd	Number, Decimal Digit
Nl	Number, Letter
No	Number, Other
Pc	Punctuation, Connector
Pd	Punctuation, Dash
Pe	Punctuation, Close
Pf	Punctuation, Final quote
Pi	Punctuation, Initial quote
Po	Punctuation, Other
Ps	Punctuation, Open
Sc	Symbol, Currency
Sk	Symbol, Modifier
Sm	Symbol, Math
So	Symbol, Other
Zl	Separator, Line
Zp	Separator, Paragraph
Zs	Separator, Space

The .NET Framework also provides other grouping categories for the character sets shown above.

Additional Regular-expression Groupings

Character Set	Grouping
C	All control characters Cc, Cf, Cs, Co, and Cn.

Character Set	**Grouping**
L	All letters Lu, Ll, Lt, Lm, and Lo.
M	All diacritical marks Mn, Mc, and Me.
N	All numbers Nd, Nl, and No.
P	All punctuation Pc, Pd, Ps, Pe, Pi, Pf, and Po.
S	All symbols Sm, Sc, Sk, and So.
Z	All separators Zs, Zl, and Zp.

You might have to experiment with these sets because they may not all be self-evident. For example:

```
PS C:\> "<tag>" -match "\p{P}"
```

Will return FALSE because < is not considered punctuation but rather a symbol:

```
PS C:\> "<tag>" -match "\p{S}"
PS C:\> $matches
```

```
Name                     Value
----                     -----
0                        <
```

This expression will return TRUE.

Select-String

PowerShell includes a pattern matching cmdlet called **Select-String**. The intent is that you'll be able to select strings from text files that match the pattern. The pattern can be as simple as "ABC" or a regular expression like "\d{1,3}\.\d{1,3}\.\d{1,3}\.\d{1,3}". This cmdlet is like the *grep* and *findstr* commands found in other shells.

For example, you might have an audit file of user activity and you want to find all lines that include the user account for Tybald Rouble:

```
PS C:\> get-content audit.txt | select-string -pattern "mydomain\trouble"
```

PowerShell will display every line with the pattern "mydomain\trouble".

When used with the **Get-ChildItem** cmdlet, you can quickly search an entire directory of files for specific strings. Jeff finds this especially useful. Despite his best efforts, Jeff's script library is a little disorganized. Often, Jeff will know he has code to do something but can't remember what script or scripts might include it. Using a command like this, he can quickly find what scripts include the code snippet he's after:

```
PS C:\> dir  s:\ | Select-String "Security_.AuthenticationLevel"
```

PowerShell will display a list of every script and line number, including the matching text. PowerShell stores these results in a **MatchInfo** object:

```
TypeName: Microsoft.PowerShell.Commands.MatchInfo
```

Name	MemberType	Definition
Equals	Method	System.Boolean Equals(Object obj)
GetHashCode	Method	System.Int32 GetHashCode()
GetType	Method	System.Type GetType()
get_Filename	Method	System.String get_Filename()
get_IgnoreCase	Method	System.Boolean get_IgnoreCase()
get_Line	Method	System.String get_Line()
get_LineNumber	Method	System.Int32 get_LineNumber()
get_Path	Method	System.String get_Path()
get_Pattern	Method	System.String get_Pattern()
RelativePat h	Method	System.String RelativePath(String directory)
set_IgnoreCase	Method	System.Void set_IgnoreCase(Boolean value)
set_Line	Method	System.Void set_Line(String value)
set_LineNumber	Method	System.Void set_LineNumber(Int32 value)
set_Path	Method	System.Void set_Path(String value)
set_Pattern	Method	System.Void set_Pattern(String value)
ToString	Method	System.String ToString(), System.String ToString(String directory)
Filename	Property	System.String Filename {get;}
IgnoreCase	Property	System.Boolean IgnoreCase {get;set;}
Line	Property	System.String Line {get;set;}
LineNumber	Property	System.Int32 LineNumber {get;set;}
Path	Property	System.String Path {get;set;}
Pattern	Property	System.String Pattern {get;set;}

Knowing the outgoing object allows us to accomplish tasks like this:

```
PS C:\> dir s:\| Select-String "Security_.AuthenticationLevel" '
| select filename,LineNumber | format-table -auto
```

Filename	LineNumber
CompSysClass.vbs	15
DiskClass.vbs	84
DiskUsagetoXML.vbs	95
GetEventsLogsAsynch-Msg.vbs	39
GetEventsLogsAsynch.vbs	23
GetPercentFreeDrive.vbs	25
MailstoreFileSizeReport.vbs	151
ScriptFunctionLibrary.vbs	30
ScriptFunctionLibrary.vbs	60
wmiphysicalmemquery-v2.vbs	26

Now Jeff can open each file and jump right to the line with his "missing" code sample. But if you look at the results closely, you'll see that one file made two matches. For a short example like this, it is trivial, but it might make a difference when searching thousands of lines of text in a directory. The **Select-String** cmdlet has a **-List** parameter that will stop searching a file at the first match. This is very handy when you don't need every match in the file.

By the way, if you're using PrimalScript, you don't need to use this technique because the "Find In Files" feature returns the same type of results. What about something more administrative?

```
PS C:\> get-eventlog -logname system -newest 100 | select message,timewritten '
>> |select-string -pattern "Windows Installer"
```

This example will search the local event log for the last 100 events and display those with the pattern "Windows Installer" in the message.

The **Select-String** cmdlet can also use regular-expression patterns:

```
PS C:\> cat c:\iplist.txt | select-string "(172.16.)\d{2,3}\.\d{1,3}"
```

This regular-expression will select all strings from IPList.txt that start with 172.16 and where the third octet has either two or three digits. This pattern will match on strings like 172.16.20.124, but not on 172.16.2.124.

Regex Object

When you use the -**match** operator, even with a regular-expression pattern, the operation only returns the first match found:

```
PS C:\> $var="Sapien Press PowerShell TFM"
PS C:\> $var -match "\w+"
True
PS C:\> $matches

Name                     Value
----                     -----
0                        Sapien
PS C:\>
```

To match all instances of the pattern, you need to use the -**Regex** object. In this example, notice that the **Matches()** method returns all matches in **$var**:

```
PS C:\> $regex=[regex]"\w+"
PS C:\> $regex.matches($var)

Groups    : {Sapien}
Success   : True
Captures  : {Sapien}
Index     : 0
Length    : 6
Value     : Sapien

Groups    : {Press}
Success   : True
Captures  : {Press}
Index     : 7
Length    : 5
Value     : Press

Groups    : {PowerShell}
Success   : True
Captures  : {PowerShell}
Index     : 13
Length    : 10
Value     : PowerShell

Groups    : {TFM}
Success   : True
Captures  : {TFM}
Index     : 24
Length    : 3
Value     : TFM
PS C:\>
```

We create an object variable called **$regex** and cast it to a -**Regex** object using [regex], specifying the regular-expression pattern. We can now call the **Matches()** method of the -**Regex** object using **$var** as a parameter. The method returns all instances where the pattern matches, as well as where they were found in **$var**. A more direct way to see all the matches is to use the Value property:

```
PS C:\> foreach ($i in $regex.matches($var)) {$i.value}
Sapien
Press
PowerShell
TFM
PS C:\>
```

The results of **$regex.matches($var)** is a *collection*. Using a **ForEach** loop, we can enumerate the collection and display the Value property for each item in the collection. The -**Regex** object has several methods and properties with which you will want to become familiar:

```
PS C:\> $regex|get-member
```

```
   TypeName: System.Text.RegularExpressions.Regex

Name                   MemberType    Definition
----                   ----------    ----------
Equals                 Method        System.Boolean Equals(Object obj)
get_Options            Method        System.Text.RegularExpressions.RegexOpt
get_RightToLeft        Method        System.Boolean get_RightToLeft()
GetGroupNames          Method        System.String[] GetGroupNames()
GetGroupNumbers        Method        System.Int32[] GetGroupNumbers()
GetHashCode            Method        System.Int32 GetHashCode()
GetType                Method        System.Type GetType()
GroupNameFromNumber    Method        System.String GroupNameFromNumber(Int32
GroupNumberFromName    Method        System.Int32 GroupNumberFromName(String
IsMatch                Method        System.Boolean IsMatch(String input), S
Match                  Method        System.Text.RegularExpressions.Match Ma
Matches                Method        System.Text.RegularExpressions.MatchCol
Replace                Method        System.String Replace(String input, Str
Split                  Method        System.String[] Split(String input), Sy
ToString               Method        System.String ToString()
Options                Property      System.Text.RegularExpressions.RegexOpt
RightToLeft            Property      System.Boolean RightToLeft {get;}
```

```
PS C:\>
```

In order to see the current value of **$regex**, we need to use the **ToString()** method:

```
PS C:\> $regex.ToString()
\w+
PC C:\>
```

IsMatch() will return either TRUE or FALSE if any match is made:

```
PS C:\> if ($regex.IsMatch($var)) {
>> write-host "found" ($regex.Matches($var)).Count "matches"
>> }
>>
found 4 matches
PS C:\>
```

In this example, we check to see if **IsMatch()** is TRUE. If it is TRUE, PowerShell will display the number of matches found in the string. By the way, the **Count()** method is not a property of the -**Regex** object, but the result of evaluating **$regex.Matches($var)**, which returns a collection object:

```
PS C:\> ($regex.Matches($var)).gettype()

IsPublic  IsSerial  Name                              BaseType
--------  --------  ----                              --------
True      True      MatchCollection                   System.Object


PS C:\>
```

You can also use regular expressions to perform a find and replace operation. Simple operations can be done with the **Replace** operator:

```
PS C:\> $text="The quick brown fox jumped over the lazy cat"
PS C:\> $text=$text -replace "cat","dog"
PS C:\> $text
The quick brown fox jumped over the lazy dog
```

In this example, we've replaced all patterns of "cat" with "dog". We can also use this operator with the -**Regex** object:

```
PS C:\> [regex]$regex="timeout=\d{1,3}"
PS C:\> $boot=get-content c:\boot.ini
PS C:\> $boot -match $regex
timeout=30
PS C:\> $boot=$boot -replace $regex,"timeout=10"
```

In this example, our regular-expression pattern is looking for the phrase "timeout=", followed by 1 to 3 digits. To see how this might work, we save the contents of boot.ini to **$boot** and attempt a regular-expression match.

```
PS C:\> $boot -match $regex
timeout=30
```

There is a match on the line "timeout=30". Now we can replace that line with a new line:

```
PS C:\> $boot=$boot -replace $regex,"timeout=10"
```

$Boot will now have an updated version of my boot.ini, which we could then write back to a file.

But this example doesn't' really take advantage of the -**Regex** object because there was only one match. Consider this:

```
PS C:\> [regex]$regex="[\s:]"
PS C:\> $c=(get-date).ToLongTimeString()
PS C:\t > $c
3:20:07 PM
PS C:\> $d=$regex.replace($c,"_")
PS C:\> $d
3_20_07_PM
```

The regular-expression pattern is searching for any space character or colon (:). We're going to use it against a variable that holds the result of **Get-Date**. The idea is that we want to use the time stamp as a filename, but this means we need to replace the colon character with a legal filename character. For the sake of consistency, we'll replace all instances with the underscore character:

```
PS C:\> $d=$regex.replace($c,"_")
```

You can now use the value of **$d** as part of a filename.

With regular expressions it is critical that you are comparing apples to apples. In order for a regular-expression pattern to match, it must match the pattern but also *not* match something else. For example, consider this variable:

```
PS C:\> $a="Windows 2003 PowerShell 101"
```

Suppose we want to match a number:

```
PS C:\> [regex]$regex="\d+"
```

The **-Regex** object will match all numbers in **$a**:

```
PS C:\> $regex.matches($a)
```

```
Groups    : {2003}
Success   : True
Captures  : {2003}
Index     : 8
Length    : 4
Value     : 2003

Groups    : {101}
Success   : True
Captures  : {101}
Index     : 24
Length    : 3
Value     : 101
```

But if the only number we want to match is at the end, then we need a more specific, regular-expression pattern like this:

```
PS C:\> [regex]$regex="\d+$"
PS C:\> $regex.matches($a)
```

```
Groups    : {101}
Success   : True
Captures  : {101}
Index     : 24
Length    : 3
Value     : 101
```

Now, we are only obtaining a match at the end of the string. Let's go through one more example to drive this point home. Here's a regular-expression pattern that matches a domain credential:

```
PS C:\> [regex]$regex="\w+\\\w+"
```

This will return TRUE for expressions like these:

```
PS C:\> $regex.IsMatch("sapien\jeff")
True
PS C:\> $regex.IsMatch("sapien\jeff\oops")
True
```

Clearly the second string is not a valid credential. To get a proper match we need a regular expression like this:

```
PS C:\> [regex]$regex="^\w+\\\w+$"
PS C:\> $regex.IsMatch("sapien\jeff")
True
PS C:\> $regex.IsMatch("sapien\jeff\oops")
False
```

Now the match is more accurate because the pattern uses **^** to match at the beginning of the string and **$** to match at the end.

Regular-expression Examples

Before we wrap up this quick introduction to regular expressions, let's review the regular expressions that you're likely to need and use.

E-mail Address

It's not unreasonable that you might want to search for a string of text that matches an e-mail address pattern. Here is one such regular expression:

```
^([\w-]+)(\.[\w-]+)*@([\w-]+\.)+[a-zA-Z]{2,7}$
```

The selection is a sequence consisting of:

- A start anchor (^).
- The expression ([\w-]+) that matches any word string and the dash character.
- The expression (\.[\w-]+)* that matches a period, and then any word string and the dash.
- The @ character.
- The expression ([\w-]+\.)+ that matches any word string that ends in a period.
- The expression [a-zA-Z]{2,7} that matches any string of letters and numbers at least two characters long and no more than seven. This should match domain names like .ca and .museum.
- An end anchor ($).

There's More than One Way
There are many, different, regular-expression patterns for an e-mail address. Even though this particular pattern should work for just about any address, it is not 100% guaranteed. We used this pattern because it is relatively simple to follow.

Here's how we might use this regular expression:

```
PS C:\> $regex=[regex]"^([\w-]+)(\.[\w-]+)*@([\w-]+\.)+[a-zA-Z]{2,7}$"
PS C:\> $var= ("j.hicks@sapien.com","oops@ca","don@sapien.com","alex@dev.sapien.com")
PS C:\> $var
j.hicks@sapien.com
oops@ca
don@sapien.com
alex@dev.sapien.com
PS C:\> $var -match $regex
j.hicks@sapien.com
don@sapien.com
alex@dev.sapien.com
PS C:\> $var.count
4
PS C:\>
```

We start by creating a **-Regex** object with our e-mail pattern and define an object variable with some e-mail names to check. We've introduced one entry that we know will fail to match. The easiest way to list the matches is to use the **-match** operator that returns all the valid e-mail addresses.

If you try expressions like these:

```
PS C:\> $regex.matches($var)
PS C:\> $regex.IsMatch($var)
False
PS C:\>
```

You will see that nothing or FALSE is returned. This occurs because **$var** is an array. We need to enumerate the array and evaluate each element against the regular-expression pattern:

```
PS C:\> foreach ($item in $var) {
>> if ($regex.IsMatch($item)) {
>> write-host $item "is a valid address"
>> }
>> else {
>> write-host "$item is NOT a valid address" }
>> }
>>
j.hicks@sapien.com is a valid address
oops@ca is NOT a valid address
don@sapien.com is a valid address
alex@dev.sapien.com is a valid address
PS C:\>
```

In this example we're enumerating each item in **$var**. If the current variable item matches the regular-expression pattern, then we display a message confirming the match. Otherwise, we display a non-matching message.

String with No Spaces

Up to now, we've been using regular expressions to match alphanumeric characters. However, we can also match whitespaces such as a space, tab, new line, or the lack of whitespace. Here's a **-Regex** object that uses **\S** that is looking to match non-whitespace characters:

```
PS C:\> $regex=[regex]"\S"
PS C:\> $var="The-quick-brown-fox-jumped-over-the-lazy-dog."
PS C:\> $var2="The quick brown fox jumped over the lazy dog."
PS C:\>
```

In this example, we have two variables—one with whitespaces and the other without. Which one will return TRUE when evaluated with the **IsMatch()** method?

```
PS C:\> $regex.IsMatch($var)
True
PS C:\> $regex.IsMatch($var2)
True
PS C:\>
```

Actually, this is a trick question because both return TRUE. This happens because **\S** is looking for any non-whitespace character. Since each letter or the dash is a non-whitespace character, the pattern matches. If our aim is to check a string to find out if it contains any spaces, then we really need to use a different regular expression and understand that a finding of FALSE is what we're seeking:

```
PS C:\> $regex=[regex]"\s{1}"
PS C:\> $regex.Ismatch($var)
False
PS C:\> $regex.Ismatch($var2)
True
PS C:\>
```

The regular expression **\s{1}** is looking for a whitespace character that occurs only one time. Evaluating **$var** with the **IsMatch()** method returns FALSE because there are no spaces in the string. The same execution with **$var2** returns TRUE because there are spaces in the string. So, if we wanted to take some action based on this type of negative matching, we might use something like this:

NegativeMatchingTest.ps1

```
$var="The-quick-brown-fox-jumped-over-the-lazy-dog."
$var2="The quick brown fox jumped over the lazy dog."
$regex=[regex]"\s{1}"
$var
if (($regex.IsMatch($var)) -eq "False")
{
write-host "Expression has spaces"
}
else
{
write-host "Expression has no spaces" }

$var2
if (($regex.IsMatch($var2)) -eq "False")
{
write-host "Expression has spaces"
}
```

```
else
{
write-host "Expression has no spaces" }
```

This action produces the following output:

```
The-quick-brown-fox-jumped-over-the-lazy-dog.
Expression has no spaces
The quick brown fox jumped over the lazy dog.
Expression has spaces
PS C:\>
```

The purpose of this example is to illustrate that there may be times when you want to match on something that is missing or a negative pattern.

Domain Credential

Let's look at a regular-expression example to match a Windows domain name that is in the format *Domain\username*:

```
PS C:\> $regex=[regex]("\w+\\\w+")

PS C:\> $var=@("sapien\jeff","sapien\don","sapien\alex")
PS C:\> $regex.matches($var)


Groups    : {sapien\jeff}
Success   : True
Captures  : {sapien\jeff}
Index     : 0
Length    : 11
Value     : sapien\jeff

Groups    : {sapien\don}
Success   : True
Captures  : {sapien\don}
Index     : 12
Length    : 10
Value     : sapien\don

Groups    : {sapien\alex}
Success   : True
Captures  : {sapien\alex}
Index     : 23
Length    : 11
Value     : sapien\alex


PS C:\>
```

Again, we create our **-Regex** object and an object variable with some domain names. Invoking the **Matches()** method shows the results. As we've demonstrated earlier, you can display the match values in at least two different ways:

```
PS C:\> foreach ($m in $regex.matches($var)) {$m.value}
sapien\jeff
sapien\don
```

```
sapien\alex

PS C:\> $var -match $regex
sapien\jeff
sapien\don
sapien\alex
PS C:\>
```

Which method you choose will depend on what you want to do with the information.

Telephone Number

Matching a phone number is pretty straightforward. We can use the pattern **\d{3}-\d{4}** to match any basic phone number without the area code:

```
PS C:\> $regex=[regex]"\d{3}-\d{4}"
PS C:\> "555-1234" -match $regex
True
PS C:\> $matches

Name                    Value
----                    -----
0                       555-1234

PS C:\> "5551-234" -match $regex
False
PS C:\> $regex.IsMatch("abc-defg")
False
PS C:\> $regex.IsMatch("123-0987")
True
PS C:\>
```

We hope these examples are looking familiar. First, we defined a regular-expression object, and then we tested different strings to see if there was a match. You can see that only three digits (\d{3}) plus a dash (-) plus four digits (\d{4}) make a match.

IP Address

For our final example, let's look at a likely use for a regular expression. We want to examine a Web log and pull out all the IP addresses. Here's the complete set of commands. We'll go through them at the end:

```
PS C:\Logs> $var=get-content "ex060211.log"
PS C:\Logs> $regex=[regex]"\d{1,3}\.\d{1,3}\.\d{1,3}\.\d{1,3}"
PS C:\Logs> $regex.Matches($var)
Groups    : {192.168.10.1}
Success   : True
Captures  : {192.168.10.1}
Index     : 15679
Length    : 12
Value     : 192.168.10.1

Groups    : {217.58.174.3}
Success   : True
Captures  : {217.58.174.3}
Index     : 15728
Length    : 12
```

```
Value     : 217.58.174.3

PS C:\Logs> $regex.Matches($var)| select-object -unique -property "value"

Value
-----
192.168.10.1
69.207.16.195
61.77.118.73
69.207.43.227
59.16.161.193
221.248.23.251
202.196.222.222
216.127.66.128
64.252.96.72
213.97.113.25
85.124.110.222
59.11.81.103
59.13.34.109
220.195.3.86
38.119.239.197
217.58.174.3
220.135.88.151
69.241.39.66
213.152.142.15


PS C:\Logs>
```

The first thing we do is dump the contents of the log file to the variable **$var**. Next we create an object variable that will be a regular-expression object by casting it as type [regex] and specifying the matching pattern.

```
PS C:\Logs> $regex=[regex]"\d{1,3}\.\d{1,3}\.\d{1,3}\.\d{1,3}"
```

Remember, we need to use a regular-expression object because the -**match** operator only checks for the first instance of a match. In an IIS log, the first IP listed is usually the host Web server and we want the visitor's IP address that comes second. Everything we've covered up to now about patterns and regular expressions is still valid. We're just going to use an object with built-in, regular-expression functionality. You'll also notice that our IP address pattern does not use ^ and **$**. That's because the IP addresses we're looking for don't start or end each line of the log file.

Invoking the **Matches()** method of the -**Regex** object essentially takes our matching pattern and compares it to the contents of **$var**:

```
PS C:\Logs> $regex.Matches($var)
```

Whenever a match is found, it will be displayed. We've edited the output to only show a few representative examples.

Alone that might be sufficient. But we'll take this one step further and send the output of the **Matches()** method to the **Select-Object** cmdlet.

```
PS C:\Logs> $regex.Matches($var)| select-object -unique -property "value"
```

With this cmdlet we can select only the value property of each regular-expression match and also return a list of unique values.

Regular-expression Reference

We've only scratched the surface on regular expressions. This is a very complex topic that extends well beyond the scope of this book. Even so, we want to make sure you know where you can go to quench your thirst for more information on regular expressions.

In PowerShell, you can run `Help about_regular_expression` to view PowerShell's documentation on the topic. If you'd like a book recommendation, *Mastering Regular Expressions* by Jeffrey Friedl (O'Reilly) is considered by many to be a definitive reference.

As you might expect, there are many excellent online resources. Here is a short list of our favorites:

- The official Microsoft documentation can be found at http://msdn.microsoft.com/en-us/library/hs600312.aspx

- Regexlib.com has an online, regular-expression tester and a terrific one page "cheat sheet".

- Wikipedia has a great article on regular expressions including historical background at http://en.wikipedia.org/wiki/Regular_expression.

- http://www.regular-expressions.info offers some nice tutorials and general information about regular expressions.

Finally, there are a number of free tools you can download that will help you evaluate and test regular expressions:

- Regex Coach (http://weitz.de/regex-coach/)

- Regular Expression Workbench 3.1 (http://code.msdn.microsoft.com/RegexWorkbench)

- Expresso (http://www.codeproject.com/dotnet/expresso.asp)

- RegEx Buddy (http://www.regexbuddy.com)—this is a commercial tool, meaning you'll have to purchase it if you like it.

Chapter 21
Loops and Decision-Making Constructs

One advantage PowerShell has over the traditional Cmd.exe shell is that you can create loops and logic structures directly from the console. If you've read this book from the beginning, you've seen examples like this:

```
PS C:\> foreach ($i in (1,2,3,4,5)) {
>> write-host "Current value is "$i
>> }
>>
Current value is 1
Current value is 2
Current value is 3
Current value is 4
Current value is 5
PS C:\>
```

The curly brace { at the end of the first line tells PowerShell there is more to the **ForEach** command. When we press Enter, PowerShell changes the prompt to >>, which indicates it is waiting for the rest of command. Once we enter the last element and press Enter for a new line, PowerShell parses and executes the command.

We mention this because many of our examples in this chapter are presented as PowerShell scripts. The benefit is that it is easier to edit and re-run a script than to retype an entire logic construct, since that provides another opportunity for you to make a typing mistake.

Let's start our exploration with the logic construct we just used.

If

The **If** statement executes a block of code if some condition is met. However, this construct can also execute a block of code if the condition is not met. For this reason, **If** is more of a decision-making construct instead of a looping one:

```
if (<condition>)
  {<code_block1>}
[else
  {<code_block2>}]
```

The **Else** section is optional. Here's a quick one-line example:

```
PS C:\> $i=1
PS C:\> if ($i -le 10) {write-host "less than 10"}
less than 10
PS C:\>
```

This example says that if the condition contained within the parentheses is TRUE, then execute the code in the braces. Since **$i** is less than 10, the code is executed.

If we want a block of code to run if the condition is not TRUE, then we introduce the **Else** operator.

```
PS C:\> $i=11
PS C:\> if ($i-le 10) {
>> "Less than 10"
>. }
>> else
>. {
>>"Greater than 10"
>> }
>>
```

In simple English, if **$i** is less than 10, then execute the first block of code; otherwise, execute the second block of code. By the way, you are very likely to see code snippets where the **If Else** statement is all on a single line like this:

```
PS C:\> $var=Get-WmiObject -class win32_logicaldisk | '
>> where {$_.deviceid -eq "C:"}
>>
PS C:\> if ($var.freespace -le 5GB) {"Low space"} else {"OK"}
Low space
PS C:\> if ($var.freespace -le 1GB) {"Low space"} else {"OK"}
OK
PS C:\>
```

The **If** statement in this example is checking if the free space on drive C:, which we obtained through WMI, is less than some value. If so, then a "Low Space" message is displayed. Otherwise, an "OK" message is displayed.

Formatting the Expression

As long as you have the proper syntax with parentheses and braces, it is up to you on how you format the expression. You can either break it into different lines as we did in IfTest.ps1 or stick to a single line as we did in the example above. If you have several lines of code or commands that you want to execute, you'll find it easier to write and troubleshoot by breaking the statement into multiple lines.

But what about a situation where if a condition is not true you want it to check for other conditions before resorting to an **Else** statement? PowerShell supports an **ElseIf** component to the **If** statement:

```
if (<condition>)
  {<code_block1>}
Elseif (<condition2>)
  {<code_block2>)
else
  {<code_block3>}
```

Here, our previous example is expanded to demonstrate:

```
PS C:\> $i=45
PS C:\> if ($i -le 10) {
>> write-host "Less than 25"
>> }
>> elseif ($i -le 50)
>> {
>> write-host "Less than 50"
>> }
>> else
>> {
>> write-host "Greater than 50"
>>}
>>
```

The logic of this example is that if **$i** is less than 10, then execute the first block of code. If it is not, then the **ElseIf** condition is evaluated. If this condition is TRUE, then the second block of code is executed. If even this condition is FALSE, then the last **Else** statement is reached and the last block of code is run.

You can have as many **ElseIf** statements as you want. However, from a practical perspective more than one or two will make your code a little harder to troubleshoot. If you want to evaluate multiple conditions, a better operator to use is **Switch**, which is discussed below.

Finally, even though it may not be technically required, if you include **ElseIf**, you should end your **If** statement with an **Else** clause. Let's look at a practical example that combines several logic constructs in a single script. The script checks the CPU time for each running process. If the CPU time is less than 300 seconds, the script displays the process name and CPU time in green. If the CPU time is greater than 301 and less than 1000, the process displays the information with no color coding. Otherwise, the process information is displayed in red:

ProcessCPU.ps1

```
#ProcessCPU.ps1
$process=get-process
$low=0 #counter for low cpu processes
```

```
$med=0 #counter for medium cpu processes
$high=0 #counter for high cpu processes
foreach ($p in $process) {
[int]$cpuseconds="{0:F0}" -f $p.cpu

 if ($cpuseconds -le 300) {
 write-host $p.name $cpuseconds "seconds" -foregroundcolor "Green"
 $low++
 }
 elseif (($cpuseconds -ge 301) -AND ($cpuseconds -le 1000)) {
 write-host $p.name $cpuseconds "seconds"
 $med++
 }
 else
 {
 write-host $p.name $cpuseconds "seconds" -foregroundcolor "Red"
 $high++
 }
}
#display a summary message
write-host 'n"Process Summary"
write-host "-->" $low "low CPU processes"
write-host "-->" $med "medium CPU processes"
write-host "-->" $high "high CPU processes"
```

This script uses a number of PowerShell elements that we've covered up to this point. The script begins by initializing some variables, including one that holds the output of the **Get-Process** cmdlet. We then use **ForEach** to enumerate each element of the **$process** object. Remember, it is a collection. Within this construct, we use **If** and **ElseIf** statements to evaluate a condition as follows. Determine whether the value of **$cpuseconds** is greater or less than some value. For example, if the value of **$cpuseconds** is less than or equal to 300, then we display a message in green and increase the **$low** variable by one. If that isn't true, then the **ElseIf** statement is evaluated. If this condition is true, then the number of CPU seconds is between 301 and 1000, which means the process information is displayed. Otherwise, the **Else** clause is reached and the number of CPU seconds is greater than 1000, so we display the message in red.

....

Formatting Details
We want to point out some special characters that were used in the `ProcessCPU.ps1` script. First, we specifically cast **$cpuseconds** as an integer type by using [int]. We did this so that our comparisons with **-le** and **-ge** would work as expected. We also used **-f** to format the value of **$p.cpu** that contains the number of seconds, and then format it to a fixed type with no decimal places. This changes a value like 180.7899632 to 181. Finally, the `n instructs PowerShell to write a blank line to the console. It helps separate the summary section from the rest of the output.

Here's an excerpt of the script's output:

```
svchost 73 seconds
svchost 47 seconds
svchost 1133 seconds
svchost 27 seconds
svchost 261 seconds
svchost 24 seconds
System 5645 seconds
wcescomm 12747 seconds
wdfmgr 9 seconds
winlogon 55 seconds
```

```
WINWORD 71 seconds
WISPTIS 4 seconds
WLTRAY 168 seconds
WLTRYSVC 9 seconds
wmiapsrv 654 seconds

Process Summary
--> 42 low CPU processes
--> 4 medium CPU processes
--> 15 high CPU processes
PS C:\>
```

You'll have to run the full script on your system to see the actual colorized output.

Switch

If you find yourself needing to check multiple conditions or otherwise create a lengthy **If** and **ElseIf** statement, then you need to use PowerShell's **Switch** statement. This statement acts like many **If** statements. If you have experience with VBScript, you'll recognize this construct as a Select Case statement. By default, **Switch** is not case-sensitive. Here's a quick example:

```
PS C:\> $var=5
PS C:\> switch ($var) {
>> 1 {"Option 1"}
>> 2 {"Option 2"}
>> 3 {"Option 3"}
>> 4 {"Option 4"}
>> 5 {"Option 5"}
>> }
>>
Option 5
PS C:\>
```

The **Switch** statement evaluates the contents contained within parentheses, and then the condition or value is matched against a set of expressions contained within braces. Each expression has a corresponding block of code in braces. If the expression matches, then command processing *switches* to the corresponding code.

In this example, PowerShell executes the code that corresponds to the matching expression since the value of **$var** is 5. If there is no match, then nothing will be displayed. However, you can use **default** at the end of the **Switch** statement to execute code in the event that no other matches are made:

```
PS C:\> $var=5
PS C:\> switch ($var) {
>> 1 {"Option 1"}
>> 2 {"Option 2"}
>> 3 {"Option 3"}
>> Default {"No match"}
>> }
>>
No match
PS C:\>
```

In this variation, PowerShell executes the default code block since there is no matching expression for the value of **$var**.

Typically, you will write out **Switch** statements on separate lines to make it easier to read and troubleshoot. However, you could just as easily write a statement like this:

```
Switch ($i) {1 {"Option 1"} 2 {"Option 2"} 3{"Option 3"}}
```

This statement will evaluate **$i** by looking for 1, 2, or 3, and then executing the corresponding code.

The **Switch** statement also supports additional options that are outlined in the following table:

Switch Options

Option	Description
-casesensitive	If the match clause is a string, modifies it to be case-sensitive. If the variable to be evaluated is not a string, ignores this option.
-exact	Indicates that if the match clause is a string, it must match exactly. Use of this parameter disables -wildcard and -regex. If the variable to be evaluated is not a string, ignores this option.
-file	Takes input from a file (or representative) rather than a statement. If multiple -file parameters are provided, it uses the last one. Each line of the file is read and passed through the switch block.
-regex	Indicates that the match clause, if a string, is treated as a regular expression string. Using this parameter disables -wildcard and -exact. If the variable to be evaluated is not a string, this option is ignored.
-wildcard	Indicates that if the match clause is a string, it is treated as a -wildcard string. Use of this parameter disables -regex and -exact. If the variable to be evaluated is not a string, this option is ignored.

The complete **switch** syntax can be one of the following:

```
switch [-regex|-wildcard|-exact][-casesensitive] ( pipeline )
```

or

```
switch [-regex|-wildcard|-exact][-casesensitive] -file filename {
"string"|number|variable|{ expression } { statementlist }
default { statementlist
}
```

Let's look at a quick example.

```
PS C:\> $var="PowerShell123","PowerShell","123","PowerShell 123"
PS C:\> Switch -regex ($var) {
>> "^\w+[a-zA-Z]$" {write-host $_" is a word"}
>>"^\d+$" {write-host $_" is a number"}
>>"\s" {write-host $_" has a space"}
>>Default {write-host "No match found for"$_}
>>}
>>
```

In this script, we set a variable with several different values. The **Switch** statement uses the regex option, which tells PowerShell we will be matching based on regular expressions. A different message is displayed, depending on the match:

```
No match found for PowerShell123
PowerShell is a word
123 is a number
PowerShell 123 has a space
PS C:\>
```

If a **Switch** statement will result in multiple matches, then each matched block of code will be executed. If this is not your intention, then you need to use the **Break** or **Continue** keywords, which are covered below.

For

The **For** loop is similar to the **ForEach** loop. With this statement, we can keep looping while some condition is met and execute a block of code each time through the loop. The condition could be a counter. For example, we might need a loop that says, "Start counting at one and execute some block of code each time until you reach ten." Or we might need a loop that says, "As long as some statement is true, keep looping and execute a block of code each time."

If you've used the **For** loop in VBScript, conceptually PowerShell's implementation is no different. However, the syntax of PowerShell's **For** loop may confuse you at first:

```
for (<init>; <condition>; <repeat>) {<command block>}
```

This syntax essentially instructs PowerShell that *for (some set of conditions) {do this block of commands}.*

Let's break this down. The <init> element is one or more sets of commands that are separated by commas. These commands are run before the loop begins. Typically, this is where you initialize a variable with some starting value. This variable is usually checked by some statement or code, <condition>, that returns a Boolean value of TRUE or FALSE. If the condition is TRUE, then PowerShell executes the code in the command block code that is enclosed in braces, <command block>. The <repeat> element is one or more sets of commands that are separated by commas, and are run each time through the loop.

Traditionally, these commands are used to modify the init variable. Each element in parentheses is separated by a semicolon or a carriage return. Thus, you could have a **For** statement that looks like this:

```
for (<init>
    <condition>
    <repeat>){
    <command_block>
    }
```

Here's a very basic example:

```
PS C:\> for ($i=1;$i -le 10;$i++) {write-host "loop #"$i}
loop # 1
loop # 2
loop # 3
loop # 4
loop # 5
loop # 6
loop # 7
loop # 8
loop # 9
loop # 10
PS C:\>
```

The initial command sets **$i** to a value of 1. The condition that PowerShell checks each time is to see if **$i** is less than 10. If it is, then we use the **Write-Host** cmdlet to display a message. Each time the loop is executed, **$i** is incremented by 1 by using $i++.

This is a very complete example. However, it's possible to reference other variables from within the same scope. The following command is essentially the same, except **$i** is defined outside of the **For** statement.

```
PS C:\> $i=1
PS C:\> for (;$i -le 10;$i++) {write-host "loop #"$i}
loop # 1
loop # 2
loop # 3
loop # 4
loop # 5
loop # 6
loop # 7
loop # 8
loop # 9
loop # 10
PS C:\>
```

Notice the **For** statement's condition, which is the portion in parentheses, has an empty init value. Even so, we still include the semi-colon delimiter.

....

Runaway Loop
Be careful with the **For** syntax. If you do not properly specify an expression to evaluate each time through the loop, it will run an infinite number of times until you press Ctrl-Break or Ctrl-C, or kill the PowerShell process.

While

The **While** statement is similar to the **For** statement. This logical construct also executes a block of code as long as some condition is TRUE:

```
while (<condition>){<command_block>}
```

However, the syntax is a little more direct. Here's essentially the same loop as we used before, only we rewrote it to use the **While** operator:

```
PS C:\> $i=1
PS C:\> while ($i -le 10)
>> {
>> write-host "loop #"$i
>> $i++
>> }
>>
loop # 1
loop # 2
loop # 3
loop # 4
loop # 5
loop # 6
loop # 7
```

```
loop # 8
loop # 9
loop # 10
PS C:\>
```

In this example, we've broken the **While** operation into separate lines to make it easier to follow. However, we could have written this as one line:

```
while ($i -le 10){write-host "loop #"$i;$i++}
```

Do While

A variation on **While** is **Do While**. In the **While** operation, PowerShell checks the condition at the beginning of the statement. In the **Do While** operation, PowerShell checks it at the end:

```
PS C:\> $i=0
PS C:\> do {
>> $i++
>> write-host "`$i="$i
>> }
>> while ($i -le 5)
>>
$i= 1
$i= 2
$i= 3
$i= 4
$i= 5
$i= 6
PS C:\>
```

In this example, you can see what happens when you check at the end. The loop essentially says, "Increase **$i** by one and display the current value as long as **$i** is less than or equal to 5."

However, notice that we end up with a sixth pass. This occurs because when **$i=5**, the While condition is still TRUE, so the loop repeats, including running the increment and display code. But now when PowerShell evaluates the While clause, it is FALSE, which causes the loop to end. This is not necessarily a bad thing. This type of loop will always run at least once until the While clause is evaluated. It will continue looping for as long as the condition is TRUE.

Do Until

A similar loop is **Do Until**. Like **Do While**, PowerShell evaluates the expression at the bottom of the loop. This construct will keep looping *until* the expression is TRUE:

```
PS C:\> do {
>> $i++
>> write-host "`$i="$i
>> }
>> until ($i -ge 5)
>>
$i= 1
$i= 2
$i= 3
$i= 4
$i= 5
PS C:\>
```

This is almost the same code block that we used with **Do While**. However, the conditional expression uses **-ge** instead of **-le**. The advantage of using **Do Until** is that the loop ends when we expect it to, because when one **$i** equals 5, the loop exits. Again, we want to stress that there is nothing wrong with using **Do** loops instead of **While**. It all depends on what you are trying to achieve.

ForEach

You use the **ForEach** statement for stepping through a collection of objects. Usually, PowerShell executes some block of code for each step when you use the **ForEach** statement. In other words, "take these steps for each thing in the collection of things." Here's the syntax for this statement:

```
foreach ($<item> in $<collection>){<command_block>}
```

This statement is expecting a variable and a collection in parentheses. PowerShell will execute the command block that is contained in the braces for each variable, each time it goes through the collection. The command block can be as simple as something like this:

```
PS C:\> $var=("apple","banana","pineapple","orange")
PS C:\> foreach ($fruit in $var) {$fruit}
apple
banana
pineapple
orange
PS C:\>
```

We first create an array of fruits. Remember that an array is a collection. The **ForEach** statement says that for each fruit variable in the fruit collection (**$var**), display the value of the fruit variable.

Here's a slightly more involved example:

ForEachFruit.ps1

```
#ForEachFruit.ps1
$var=("apple","banana","pineapple","orange")
foreach ($fruit in $var) {
$i++ #this is a counter that is incremented by one each time through
write-host "Adding" $fruit
}
write-host "Added" $i "pieces of fruit"
```

When this script is run, it produces the following output:

```
Adding apple
Adding banana
Adding pineapple
Adding orange
Added 4 pieces of fruit
PS C:\>
```

We can even nest other logic constructs within a **ForEach** statement:

ForEachFile.ps1

```
#ForEachFile.ps1
set-location "C:\"
$sum=0
foreach ($file in get-childitem) {
#$file.GetType()
 if (($file.GetType()).Name -eq "FileInfo") {
  write-host $file.fullname 't $file.length "bytes"
  $sum=$sum+$file.length
  $i++
  }
}
write-host "Counted" $i "file for a total of" $sum "bytes."
```

In this script, we're using the **Get-ChildItem** cmdlet to return all items in C:\. We can do this because the results of the **Get-ChildItem** cmdlet return a collection object. So, even though we don't know the contents of the collection, we can still enumerate on the fly. For each **$file** variable in the collection, if the object type name is FileInfo, then we display the name and file size (using the length property). We've also added code to calculate a running total of the sum of all the files using **$sum**, and we use **$i** as a counter that increases by one each time.

When the script is run, it generates the following output:

```
C:\AUTOEXEC.BAT        0 bytes
C:\AVG7QT.DAT    12283633 bytes
C:\COMLOG.txt    0 bytes
C:\CONFIG.SYS    0 bytes
C:\docs.csv      24938 bytes
C:\DVDPATH.TXT   55 bytes
C:\EventCombMT_Debug.log        854 bytes
C:\hpfr5550.xml         488 bytes
C:\IALog.txt     271 bytes
C:\log.csv       10734 bytes
C:\Log.txt       72 bytes
C:\mtaedt22.exe         2650696 bytes
C:\netdom.exe    142848 bytes
C:\new-object.txt        10240 bytes
C:\out-grid.ps1         811 bytes
C:\out-propertyGrid.ps1         1330 bytes
C:\processes.html        118828 bytes
C:\servers.txt   19 bytes
C:\showprocessinfo.ps1   710 bytes
C:\showservices.ps1      477 bytes
C:\test.ps1      88 bytes
C:\txt.csv       22995 bytes
Counted 22 file for a total of 15270087 bytes.
PS C:\>
```

Alias Alert
The **ForEach** statement is also an alias for the **ForEach-Object** cmdlet. We're pointing this out in case you find examples using the cmdlet, because this particular alias works a bit differently than the cmdlet. PowerShell has a special parsing mode that detects the alias and lets you use it as we're showing. If you were to simply replace "foreach" in the examples above with "foreach-object", the script wouldn't run.

Typically, you'll use **ForEach** (the alias) in a script and **ForEach-Object** (the cmdlet) in a one-liner at the command line.

To make things more confusing, PowerShell defines another alias, **%** (just the percent sign). It is interchangeable with the **ForEach-Object** cmdlet, but not with **ForEach**. For that reason, we'll often refer to **ForEach** as a statement rather than a cmdlet—but you'll see other folks refer to it however they prefer, so be prepared.

Break

The **Break** statement very simply terminates just about any logic construct we've covered in this chapter, including **For, ForEach, While,** and **Switch.** When a **Break** statement is encountered, PowerShell exits the loop and runs the next command in the command block or script:

```
PS C:\> $i=0
PS C:\> $var=10,20,30,40
PS C:\> foreach ($val in $var)
>> {
>> $i++
>> if ($val -eq 30){break}
>> }
>> write-host "found a match at item $i"

found a match at item 3
PS C:\>
```

In this example, we're searching an array of numbers for 30. When it is found, we want to stop looking, exit the **ForEach** loop, and then display the message. Even though the **Switch** statement is not a loop, **Break** also is used within a code block to force an exit from the entire **Switch** statement.

Continue

The **Continue** statement is essentially the opposite of **Break.** When the **Continue** statement is encountered, PowerShell returns immediately to the beginning of a loop like **For, ForEach,** and **While.** You can also use **Continue** with **Switch.**

Here's a script that doesn't use **Continue**:

SwitchNoContinue.ps1

```
#SwitchNoContinue.ps1
$var="PowerShell123","PowerShell","123","PowerShell 123"
```

```
Switch -regex ($var) {
"\w" {write-host $_" matches \w"}
"\d" {write-host $_" matches \d"}
"\s" {write-host $_" matches \s"}
Default {write-host "No match found for"$_ }
}
```

When you run this script, PowerShell runs all matching code blocks, since there are multiple possible matches:

```
PowerShell123 matches \w
PowerShell123 matches \d
PowerShell matches \w
123 matches \w
123 matches \d
PowerShell 123 matches \w
PowerShell 123 matches \d
PowerShell 123 matches \s
PS C:\>
```

If we want the switch statement to only run code after the first match, then we can use **Continue**, which will keep processing eachelement in **$var**:

SwitchContinue.ps1

```
#SwitchContinue.ps1
$var="PowerShell123","PowerShell","123","PowerShell 123"
Switch -regex ($var) {
"\w" {write-host $_" matches \w" ;
     continue}
"\d" {write-host $_" matches \d" ;
     continue}
"\s" {write-host $_" matches \s" ;
     continue}
Default {write-host "No match found for"$_ ;
     }
}
```

This is the same script except with the addition of **Continue**. When run, the script produces the following output:

```
PowerShell123 matches \w
PowerShell matches \w
123 matches \w
PowerShell 123 matches \w
PS C:\ >
```

Because each element of **$var** matches the \w regular expression, PowerShell executes only the block of code associated with that part of the **Switch** statement.

Chapter 22
Script Blocks, Functions, Filters, Snap-ins, and Modules

Modularization is generally thought of as a way to break code down into discrete, more or less self-contained segments. These segments, or *modules*, can be transported between scripts so they can be reused again and again with minimal modification. In this chapter, we'll look at some of the ways you can modularize PowerShell code.

Script Blocks

A *script block* is a series of PowerShell statements enclosed in curly braces. You can assign a script block to a variable as shown here:

```
PS C:\> $sb = {
>> $x = 10
>> $y = 10
>> $x * $y }
>>
```

Note that this script was typed interactively. When it saw the { character, PowerShell knew we were typing a script block. The special >> prompt indicated that PowerShell was waiting for additional input. Pressing Enter on a blank >> prompt ended the input. You can prove that the script block text is in the **$sb** variable by checking it as follows:

```
PS C:\> $sb
$x = 10
$y = 10
$x * $y
```

```
PS C:\>
```

You can execute the script block with the invoke, or call, operator, which is an ampersand "**&**":

```
PS C:\> &$sb
100
PS C:\>
```

When invoked as part of a pipeline, a script block has access to a special variable called *$input* that contains all of the objects passed through the pipeline. For example, the **Get-Process** cmdlet returns an object for each running process. PowerShell stores all these objects in **$input** and you can enumerate them with a **foreach** construct:

```
PS C:\> $sb = {
>> foreach ($process in $input ) {
>> $process.ProcessName }
>> }
>>
PS C:\> get-process | &$sb
acrotray
alg
ati2evxx
ati2evxx
BTSTAC~1
BTTray
btwdins
csrss
dllhost
explorer
firefox
Groove
Hpqgalry
```

Again, this was all typed interactively. Notice that when you call the **Get-Process** cmdlet, PowerShell pipes its output to **$sb**, which was invoked using the & operator. This may be clearer in the following script:

Blocktest.ps1

```
$sb = {
 foreach ($process in $input) {
   $process.ProcessName
 }
}

get-process | &$sb
```

Running this script produces the same output:

```
PS C:\> test\blocktest
acrotray
alg
ati2evxx
ati2evxx
BTSTAC~1
BTTray
```

```
btwdins
csrss
dllhost
explorer
firefox
Groove
Hpqgalry
```

Script blocks are a simple way to modularize code and allow it to be reused. However, script blocks become more important when used in conjunction with other modularization techniques, such as functions and filters.

Functions

Functions are a construct common to most programming languages that provide the basic modularization programmers have used for decades. PowerShell allows you to create a function by *declaring* it as follows:

1. Use the **Function** keyword.

2. Provide the name of your function.

3. Enclose the function's code within {curly braces}.

A very basic function might look like this:

```
function myFunction {
 write-host "Hello"
}
```

Functions are nearly identical to script blocks except for two differences: (1) functions are explicitly declared using the **Function** keyword, and (2) functions have a name. Otherwise, functions are practically the same as a script block.

This particular function doesn't accept any input arguments, nor does it really return any kind of value. It simply displays "Hello" on the screen. In languages like VBScript, this function might have been written as a Sub, since functions typically return some value in VBScript. However, in PowerShell, there is not a separate construct if a value isn't being returned. Instead, you simply have the function not return anything if you don't need it to.

Note that you can interactively declare functions without writing a script. Try typing the following into PowerShell at the prompt:

```
PS C:\> function myFunction { write-host "Hello" }
```

This is the same function as the first example, but it is declared all on one line. Because it was entered into the command prompt within PowerShell, this function becomes available globally. In other words, it lives within the global *scope*. Scope controls the availability of functions, and it applies to the availability of variables (we covered scope for the first time in the chapter "Scripting Overview"). With myFunction declared globally, any child scopes such as scripts will be able to call the function. However, if you declare a function within a script, then only that script and *its* child scopes will be able to "see" the function and use it.

You can also nest functions:

```
Function Outer1 {
 Function Inner1 {
   #code A here
 }
 Function Inner2 {
   #code B here
 }
 #code C here
}
Function Outer2 {
 Function Inner3 {
   #code D here
 }
 Function Inner4 {
   #code E here
 }
 #code F here
}
```

If this were included in a script, then the entire script would be able to call either Outer1 or Outer2. However, the script would not be able to directly call any of the Inner functions, since those exist within the Outer functions' private scopes. Any code within Outer1 (code C) is able to call Inner1 and Inner2. However, the code within Outer2 (code F) is not able to access Inner1 and Inner2 because those two functions are contained within the private scope of Outer1.

Input Arguments

Functions have two ways of accepting input arguments. Here's the first:

```
Function add2 {
 [int]$args[0] + [int]$args[1]
}
```

This could be called like this:

```
PS C:\> Add2 10 20
30
```

This output shows that the two input arguments, 10 and 20, were successfully added. Inside the function these arguments were accessed by using the special **$args** variable. The **$args** variable is an array in which each element in the array represents one argument passed to the function. Even though this is a fairly informal technique for accepting input arguments, it may be difficult to follow when you read the script months later. A more formal, easier-to-maintain way to work with input arguments looks like this:

```
Function add2 ([int]$x, [int]$y) {
 $x + $y
}
```

You would call this in exactly the same way. Up front, it defines that two input arguments of the Integer type are required.

A third way to declare this function is as follows:

```
Function add2 {
 Param ([int]$x, [int]$y)
 $x + $y
}
```

This is the same idea; however, you must define the parameters in a special **Param** section that must be the first line of code in the function, instead of defining the arguments as a part of the function declaration itself.

Once again, you can call the function as follows:

```
PS C:\> Add2 10 20
30
```

However, when you specifically define and name arguments using either of the above techniques, you can also call the function by naming the arguments as you pass them in:

```
PS C:\> Add2 -x 10 -y 20
30
```

This passes the value 10 specifically to the **$x** argument and 20 to the **$y** argument. It does not make a difference in the math, but for more complex functions, this technique provides more control and allows you to pass in arguments out of order, if necessary.

You can also declare a default value for an argument. In this case, if you call the function without a value for the argument, the function may be able to proceed using a default value:

```
Function add2 {
 Param ([int]$x = 10, [int]$y = 10)
 $x + $y
}
```

Calling the function with no input arguments results in a value:

```
PS C:\> Add2
20
```

Returning a Value

Returning a value from a function is fairly easy—whatever the function outputs *to the default output stream* (typically using the **Write-Output** cmdlet) is also its return. So, really, all of the sample functions we've looked at so far *have* returned a value. For example:

```
PS C:\> $result = add2 10 10
PS C:\> $result
20
```

Here, we called our Add2 function with 10 and 10 as input arguments. PowerShell stored the result of the function in **$result**. *Anything* output from the function becomes part of its result, not just the last thing it outputs. For example:

Functiontest.ps1

```
$a = "Hello"

function foo ($b) {
 $b.ToUpper()
 $b.ToLower()
}
$x = foo $a
$x
```

The function foo outputs both the uppercase and lowercase versions of the input argument. **$x** is set equal to foo's output. Notice that the function doesn't explicitly use the **Write-Output** cmdlet; instead, it's simply allowing the default cmdlet to write to the default output stream. The result of this is:

```
PS C:\> test\functiontest
HELLO
Hello
```

This shows that **$x** contains both pieces of information output by the function.

You can also use the **Return** keyword to explicitly return a value:

```
$a = "Hello"

function foo ($b) {
 return $b.ToUpper()
 $b.ToLower()
}
$x = foo $a
$x
```

There's a caveat, though: Once you use **Return**, the function exits immediately. So, in the above example, **$b.ToLower()** would never execute, because it comes *after* the **Return**.

If a function produces output and uses **Return**, the value on the **Return** line is simply appended to any other output. Consider this function:

```
$a = "Hello"

function foo ($b) {
 $b.ToUpper()
 Return $b.ToLower()
}
$x = foo $a
$x
```

The result is identical to the first version of this function:

```
PS C:\> test\functiontest
HELLO
Hello
```

The idea of having a function return *anything* output from that function is neat, but it can also be confusing. We recommend that you concatenate all of your intended output into a variable and use the **Return** keyword to return that value from the function. That way your function is only returning data through one technique, and it's a technique that's easy to spot when you're reviewing the code later.

Piping to Functions

The examples you've seen so far in this chapter have demonstrated that you can call functions outright. However, you can also pipe the output of other commands into a function. When you do this, PowerShell stores the piped-in data in the special **$input** variable. If you pipe multiple objects to a function, then the function is called only once. In this case, PowerShell places all of the objects into **$input** at the same time. Here's a very simple example of a function that simply outputs whatever's piped in:

```
function foo {
 $input
}
```

Piping this function generates the same output for the **Get-Process** cmdlet as the **Get-Process** cmdlet generates by itself:

```
PS C:\> get-process | foo
```

Handles	NPM(K)	PM(K)	WS(K)	VM(M)	CPU(s)	Id	ProcessName
37	3	1080	3624	31	0.05	2208	acrotray
104	5	1144	3384	32	0.02	492	alg
61	2	548	2136	19	0.52	1076	ati2evxx
90	3	1152	4664	31	0.72	3960	ati2evxx
228	7	6316	8688	65	0.64	3216	BTSTAC~1
182	5	4004	7420	56	98.94	2216	BTTray
55	3	2060	3044	31	0.16	1508	btwdins
1093	9	2020	3964	31	51.44	816	csrss
218	5	2896	7716	45	0.30	5836	dllhost
697	15	18696	7036	108	160.30	604	explorer

However, consider this revised function:

```
function foo {
 $input | get-member
}
```

The function is now piping its input to the **Get-Member** cmdlet, which changes the output as follows:

```
PS C:\> get-process | foo


   TypeName: System.Diagnostics.Process
```

Name	MemberType	Definition
Handles	AliasProperty	Handles = Handlecount
Name	AliasProperty	Name = ProcessName

Even though this output is truncated, it shows that PowerShell recognized **$input** as an object of the **System.Diagnostics.Process** type.

Here's another example:

```
function foo {
 foreach ($i in $input) {
   $i.ProcessName
 }
}
```

Below is the partial output from this function when you pipe the **Get-Process** cmdlet to it:

```
PS C:\> get-process | foo
acrotray
alg
ati2evxx
ati2evxx
BTSTAC~1
BTTray
btwdins
csrss
dllhost
```

The function takes the output of the **Get-Process** cmdlet into the **$input** variable. It then goes through each object in **$input** and displays just the ProcessName property of each.

Function Phases

Functions can include up to three special script blocks that execute during different phases of execution. When we discuss filters in the next section, you'll see this applies to filters also. These script blocks use special names to identify themselves:

- **Begin:** PowerShell executes this script block only once when you first call the function or filter.

- **Process:** If you pass multiple objects into the function or filter through the pipeline, PowerShell executes this script block once for each object.

- **End:** PowerShell executes this script block after the Process script block deals with all the pipeline objects.

Understanding how these script blocks work might take a little time. With a function, you normally lump together everything in the pipeline into the **$input** variable. However, if the function contains a Process block, then **$input** is null. Instead, the Process block uses the special **$_** variable to access the current pipeline object. Here's an example:

```
function foo {
 Begin {
   "Running processes:"
 }
 Process {
   $_.ProcessName
 }
 End {
   "Complete"
 }
}
```

This produces the following output when you pipe the **Get-Process** cmdlet to it:

```
PS C:\> get-process | foo
Running processes:
```

```
acrotray
alg
ati2evxx
ati2evxx
BTSTAC~1
BTTray
btwdins
csrss
dllhost
explorer
firefox
Groove
hpqgalry
hpqtra08
hpwuSchd2
HPZipm12
Complete
```

The Begin block runs first. For each object in the pipeline, PowerShell executes Process once, and puts the current object into the **$_** variable. Then it executes End when it has processed all objects. Note that when using any of these blocks, *no code can appear outside a block*. Any code within the function that's not within a block will result in an error. For example:

```
function foo {
 "Starting function foo"
 Begin {
   "Running processes:"
 }
 Process {
   $_.ProcessName
 }
 End {
   "Complete"
 }
}
```

Results in this:

```
PS C:\> get-process | foo
Starting function foo
'begin' is not recognized as a cmdlet, function, operable program,
or script file.
At C:\test\blocktest.ps1:3 char:8
+  Begin <<<< {
Get-Process : Cannot evaluate parameter 'Name' because its argument
is specified as a script block and there is no input. A script
block cannot be evaluated without input.
At C:\test\blocktest.ps1:6 char:10
+  Process <<<< {
'end' is not recognized as a cmdlet, function, operable program,
or script file.
At C:\test\blocktest.ps1:9 char:6
+  End <<<< {
PS C:\>
```

This occurs because code exists outside a script block when script blocks are in use.

Filters

Filters are *essentially* the same as functions. The big differences are that: (1) you declare filters using the **Filter** keyword, and (2) when you pipe objects to a filter, the filter executes one time for each object in the pipeline, rather than just one time for the entire pipeline. Basically, a filter is like a function that contains only a Process script block.

Filters make use of the special **$_** variable that represents the current pipeline object. Here's an example:

```
filter foo {
    $_.ProcessName
}
```

When you pipe the output of the **Get-Process** cmdlet to this filter, the filter executes one time for each object that the **Get-Process** cmdlet produces. You can see how this differs from a function, which gets *all* of the objects in one big chunk through the **$input** variable. You can use the filter just like you might use a function:

```
PS C:\> get-process | foo
acrotray
alg
ati2evxx
ati2evxx
BTSTAC~1
BTTray
btwdins
```

Because the filter only gets one object at a time from the pipeline, it doesn't need to use a **foreach** construct the way our earlier function example did.

Functions vs. Filters

The differences between a function and a filter can be summarized as follows:

- When you pipe something to a function, the piped data goes into the special **$input** variable and PowerShell executes the function once.

- When you pipe something to a filter, PowerShell executes the filter one time for each object in the piped data. The current object is available in the special **$_ variable**, and there's no **$input** variable.

One thing that can make it difficult to understand these differences is that you can write functions that behave exactly the same way filters behave. For example, consider this filter:

```
filter ext {
    $_.Extension
}
```

Now, use the **Get-ChildItem** cmdlet to retrieve the child items (files) of the C: drive, and pipe the child items (files) to the newly created **Ext** filter:

```
PS C:\> get-childitem c: | ext
.wsf
.sql
.BAT
.txt
```

```
.SYS
.pdf
.log
.xml
.Log
.wsf
.log
.wsf
.log
.txt
```

As you can see, the **Get-ChildItem** cmdlet returns several child objects—all files—that were piped to **Ext**. The **Ext** filter executed *one time* for each item in the pipeline. For each item in the pipeline, **Ext** displayed its **Extension** property.

Let's try the exact same thing with a function:

```
function ext2 {
    $_.Extension
}
```

Now run it the same way:

```
PS C:\> get-childitem c: | ext2
PS C:\>
```

Why is there no output? The answer is because it's a function, so it's executed only *one time*. It's not passed to each child item one at a time. Instead, it's passed to an entire *collection* of child objects in one big chunk. So, using **$_** to access the pipeline object is really accessing that collection, which doesn't have an **Extension** property.

With this in mind, let's revise our function:

```
function ext2 {
 foreach ($file in $input) {
   $file.Extension
 }
}
```

Now we'll get the same output as with the original filter:

```
PS C:\> get-childitem c: | ext2
.wsf
.sql
.BAT
.txt
.SYS
.pdf
.log
.xml
.Log
.wsf
.log
.wsf
.log
.txt
```

This time the function is taking **$input** and going through each item *inside the function.*

Here's another way to write the function to get the exact same result:

```
function ext2 {
 Process {
   $_.Extension
 }
}
```

This time the function is using the special Process script block, which means the function *itself* is called only once:

```
PS C:\> get-childitem c: | ext2
.wsf
.sql
.BAT
.txt
.SYS
.pdf
.log
.xml
.Log
.wsf
.log
.wsf
.log
.txt
```

The special Process script block automatically takes **$input** and executes the script block one time for each object within **$input**, making each object accessible via the **$_** variable, which is exactly the same as a filter would do.

So, you may be wondering how to know when you should write a filter and when you should use a function that uses script blocks. Really, it's up to you. Whatever is easier for you to understand and use, then that's the one you should use. A function containing a Process script block is functionally identical to a filter.

OK, Let's Be Honest
Really, filters shouldn't be in PowerShell at all. You can do everything they do—and more—with functions. Microsoft added filters early in PowerShell's development, and never removed them—even when they'd basically been rendered redundant by more powerful functions. We never use filters.

Cmdlets and Snap-ins

Cmdlets are the basic commands available within PowerShell. As such, they encapsulate code that performs useful work. This code is normally written by Microsoft. Cmdlets are normally written in a higher-level .NET Framework language such as Visual Basic .NET or C#. For example, the PowerShell documentation provides this C# example of a cmdlet that generates a random number:

```
using System;
using System.Management.Automation;
```

```
// GetRandom.cs
/// <summary>
/// an implementation of a random number generator
/// </summary>
[Cmdlet("get", "random")]
public class GetRandomCommand : Cmdlet
{
    protected override void EndProcessing()
    {
        Random r = new Random();
        WriteObject(r.Next());
    }
}
```

You would then compile this code using **Csc.exe**, which is the C# compiler provided with the .NET Framework Software Development Kit (SDK). Once compiled, you would call it from within PowerShell as follows:

```
PS C:\> (new-object random).next()
```

As explained in the first chapter, snap-ins are more or less collections of cmdlets. In a base installation of PowerShell, you can see which snap-ins, if any, are available but not active by running the **Get-PSSnapin** cmdlet and using the **-registered** parameter. Nothing will be shown because only the core PowerShell snap-ins exist that were loaded into the shell by default. However, if you've installed third-party snap-ins, they'll be displayed. You can subsequently load them into the shell using the **Add-PSSnapIn** cmdlet:

```
PS C:\> Add-pssnapin MySnapInName
```

Creating new snap-ins is fairly complex and typically requires a high-level .NET language, such as Visual Basic .NET or C#. It's beyond the scope of this book to cover cmdlet or snap-in creation. However, we've provided these examples so you can see a bit of what goes into them and how they're used to encapsulate more complex, high-level code for use within PowerShell.

Modules

While it's useful to have script blocks, functions, and filters available for copying and pasting between scripts, you may want to consider PowerShell's *modules* feature as a way of packaging and re-using your code more easily. A *module* is essentially a specialized PowerShell script with a .psm1 extension, which may be bundled with a snap-in DLL that you can add into the shell as a single unit.

To create a simple module, simply create a regular .ps1 script file containing one or more functions. In order for the shell to find the module, you need to place it into a specific path. For modules—or *packages,* to use another term—intended to be available to all users of a computer, you'll open the folder $pshome/modules, create a new folder that uses your module's name, and then place your .psm1 file in that folder. Your .psm1 file name also needs to use your module's name. So, if you decide to name your module MyModule, your file would be:

```
$pshome/Modules/MyModule/MyModule.psm1
```

For packages intended only for your own personal use, you create a folder named WindowsPowerShell within your Documents folder ("My Documents" on Windows XP or Windows Server 2003). In that, create the Packages folder, your module folder, and your module file:

`/Users/`*`username`*`/Documents/WindowsPowerShell/Modules/MyModule/MyModule.psm1`

To load your module into the shell, run this:

```
PS C:\> Import-Module MyModule
```

PowerShell searches the machine-wide modules path first, and then searches your user-specific path next. The practical effect of adding a .psm1 file as a module is that any function defined within the .psm1 file becomes available from within the scope where you executed the **Import-Module** cmdlet. In other words, if you run the **Import-Module** cmdlet at the main shell prompt, the functions inside the .psm1 file will become globally available within the shell.

Module Files

A .psm1 file is actually the simplest form of module. In reality, when you run the **Import-Module** cmdlet, it searches your module's folder for the following files, in this order (these examples assume your module name is MyModule):

- MyModule.psd1
- MyModule.psm1
- MyModule.dll

A .psd1 file is a special type of file, usually referred to as a *manifest*, used to provide metadata about an imported module. This file must have the same name as the .psm1 file and reside in the same directory. A .psm1 file is a true PowerShell module file, and we'll discuss how to use that in a moment. A .dll file is expected to be a Windows PowerShell snap-in: By adding the snap-in using the **Import-Module** cmdlet, instead of the **Add-PSSnapin** cmdlet, you don't have to register the snap-in in advance with the .NET Framework; you can simply add it on the fly.

PowerShell only loads a single file for a module: If a .psm1 file and a .dll file exist, PowerShell will only load the .psm1 file, in accordance with the priority order listed here.

Managing Modules

PowerShell supports the **Get-Module** cmdlet, which lists currently loaded modules, and the **Remove-Module** cmdlet, which removes a module and any functions it loaded.

Once you load a module, if you try to reload it with the **Import-Module** cmdlet, you likely won't see an error but also nothing will really happen. If you modify the module and want to reload it so the changes take effect use the **–force** parameter.

PSM1 Modules

A .psm1 file lets you really leverage module features. This file starts out as a standard .ps1 file, just with a different file-name extension. For example, here's a .psm1 file that contains two functions, named Mod1 and Mod2. Also notice that it contains a script-level variable named **$counter**.

```
$counter = 0
function Mod1 {
  Mod2
  Write $counter
}
function Mod2 {
```

```
    $script:counter++
}
```

This script uses some less-than-wonderful practices, which we'll discuss in a moment, but our point is to demonstrate some unique features of .psm1 modules. To begin, the **$counter** variable is initialized to zero. The function Mod1, when executed, calls Mod2 (this is technically a poor practice since Mod2 is defined outside Mod1, not within it). Mod1 then outputs the current value of **$counter**. Mod2 simply increments **$counter** by one (also a bad practice—functions shouldn't modify variables from outside their own scope).

If we were to add this module to the shell, both Mod1 and Mod2 would be "seen" as functions within the shell. In other words, once you loaded the module, you could type this at the shell to run Mod1 and Mod2:

```
PS C:\>Mod1
PS C:\>Mod2
```

However, since this is a .psm1 file, and not a .ps1 file, we have an additional capability that we're going to utilize:

```
$counter = 0
function Mod1 {
  Mod2
  Write $counter
}
function Mod2 {
  $script:counter++
}
Export-ModuleMember Mod1
```

The **Export-ModuleMember** statement changes what happens when you add the module into the shell. Now, rather than adding both Mod1 and Mod2 to the shell, only Mod1 will be visible. Mod2 remains *private*, meaning that Mod1—which lives in the same module script—can access Mod2, but Mod2 will be "hidden" from anything outside the module script, including the shell itself.

In addition, variables within the .psm1 file will *persist*. In other words, the **$counter** variable will retain its value for the remainder of the shell session. Any modifications to **$counter** made from within the module script will "stick around." So, assuming we save this in …\Documents\WindowsPowerShell\Modules\TestMod\TestMod.psm1, we can do the following:

```
PS C:\>Import-Module TestMod
PS C:\>Mod1
1
PS C:\>Mod1
2
PS C:\>$counter
PS C:\>
```

We used the **Import-Module** cmdlet to add TestMod to the shell. We then called Mod1. Internally, it called Mod2, which incremented **$counter** to 1, and then displayed $counter. We called Mod1 again, which internally incremented $counter to 2, proving that $counter is maintaining its value between executions of the module script. We then attempted to display $counter directly. However, the $counter contained in the module file is *private* to the module, meaning the shell can't see it directly. So the shell didn't display any value, because as far as the shell is concerned, the variable $counter doesn't exist.

Uses for Modules

Modules are a great way to consolidate several useful functions, or even script cmdlets, into a single file that's easy to add to the shell and use. Your script can include supporting functionality, which is hidden from the shell and available only to code running within the module itself. If you were to create a .psm1 file full of script cmdlets, you would essentially be creating a script-based snap-in which behaves much as a regular, compiled snap-in that is distributed in a DLL file.

Chapter 23
Error Handling

Error handling is sort of proactive debugging: Using special techniques, you build scripts that anticipate certain errors and deal with them on the fly, instead of just crashing. PowerShell divides errors into two categories:

- **Terminating:** Causes your script or command to stop executing.

- **Non-terminating:** Even though a problem still exists, the script or command is allowed to continue running.

When an error occurs, the error itself is represented by an object called **ErrorRecord**. This object contains an *exception*, which is essentially a fancy word for *error*. An exception also includes other information about why and where the error occurred. Like any other object, **ErrorRecord** has properties that you can examine:

- **Exception:** This is the error that occurred. It's an object in and of itself. For example, Exception.Message contains an English description of the error.

- **TargetObject:** This is the object that was being operated when the error occurred. This may be Null if there was no particular object involved.

- **CategoryInfo:** This divides all errors into a few dozen broad categories.

- **FullyQualifiedErrorId:** This property identifies the error more specifically. In fact, it is the most specific identifier.

- **ErrorDetails:** May be Null, but when present contains additional information. It's actually a sub-object called ErrorDetails.Message. One of its properties is the most-specific-possible English description of the error.

- **InvocationInfo:** Tells you the context in which the error occurred, such as a cmdlet name or script line. May be Null.

PowerShell uses a special variable, **$error**, to store the most recent **ErrorRecord** objects. In fact, by default it stores the most recent 256 errors. The $error variable is an array. For example, $error[0] contains the most recent error and $error[1] is the one before that. Each element of $error is an ErrorRecord object. For example, to see the error text for the most recent error, you would examine:

```
PS C:\> $error[0].Exception.Message
```

When an error occurs, you can examine **$error** to determine whether your script can do anything about the error. However, before your script has the opportunity to do so, you will have to *trap* the error.

Error Actions

Most cmdlets support the ubiquitous -**ErrorAction** argument, which is aliased as just -**EA**. This argument specifies what should happen if the cmdlet encounters a non-terminating error. The default behavior is Continue, which means the cmdlet displays the error and tries and continue executing the cmdlet or script. Other options include:

- **Stop:** Makes the cmdlet stop executing.

- **Inquire:** Asks the user what to do.

- **SilentlyContinue:** Continues without displaying any clues as to what went wrong.

Here's an example of Stop:

```
PS C:\> $a = Get-WmiObject Win32_OperatingSystem -ea stop
```

This executes the **Get-WmiObject** cmdlet. If something goes wrong, it will stop rather than continue. However, if you've defined a *trap handler*, which we'll discuss next, then the trap handler will still execute after the cmdlet stops. Essentially, the -**ea stop** parameter is telling the cmdlet: "Hey, if an error occurs, raise an exception for me." This exception is the key to making error trapping work: When an exception is raised, PowerShell will look for a trap handler that's set up to handle that particular type of exception. If it finds one, it will execute the handler. So, without an exception, you can't trap errors in PowerShell.

Note that if you tell a cmdlet to "SilentlyContinue" or "Continue," then no exception is raised when a problem occurs. Without an exception, PowerShell won't try to look for a trap handler, and you'll never be able to "handle" the problem.

Let's emphasize that: **The only way to trap an error and deal with it yourself is to set an ErrorAction of Stop.** Anything else might write an error message to the console, but it won't generate an exception; only Stop generates exceptions, and only exceptions can be trapped.

To complicate matters slightly, PowerShell defines a built-in variable called **$ErrorActionPreference**. This variable has the same possible settings as the -ErrorAction parameter; if you don't specify -ErrorAction, then the value of $ErrorActionPreference governs the shell's behavior. Because $ErrorActionPreference is a variable, you can define it in any scope: A script, the shell, a function, and so forth. The shell's default value for this variable is "Continue." We'll see in a bit how this plays into error trapping.

Trapping Errors

Trapping in PowerShell can be fairly complicated. When an error occurs in a script, an exception is "thrown" or "raised." PowerShell delivers that exception to an exception handler, which is also called the *trap handler*. Following the execution of the handler, PowerShell checks the session state established by **ErrorPolicy** settings to determine whether the script should continue running. If you have not defined a specific trap handler, PowerShell will simply deliver the exception to the output mechanism. This usually means the exception will be displayed and the script will halt. If you have defined a trap handler, it may reset the **ErrorPolicy**, which determines whether the script will continue after you resolve the error.

Let's briefly summarize how this works. If you have defined a *trap handler*, PowerShell executes the handler when an error occurs. The handler has access to **$error** to see what went wrong. It can also set the **ErrorPolicy** to determine whether the script continues. Defining the trap handler looks a bit like this:

```
Trap [ExceptionType] {
 # statements go here
 # $_ represents the ErrorRecord that was thrown
 break | continue
}
```

The **[ExceptionType]** is the type of exception you want to trap. This allows you to define a different trap handler for different types of errors or exceptions. However, you do not *have* to include [ExceptionType]. If you don't, the trap handler will handle any exceptions that occur. You can actually define multiple traps for the same exception. If that exception occurs, all of the traps will execute in the order in which they're defined.

Within the trap handler, the special **$_** variable represents the **ErrorRecord** that caused the trap handler to be executed in the first place.

At the end of the trap handler, you have two options:

- **Continue:** This causes script execution to continue at the line of code following the line that caused the error—*in the same scope as the trap handler itself.* In other words, if an error occurred inside a function, but you didn't trap the error in the function, then PowerShell passes the error up to the function's parent scope. If you've trapped the error there, and the trap ends with Continue, then the script will not re-enter the function. Instead, it will resume on the line of code following the function call—staying in the same scope in which the trap exists.

- **Break:** This causes the current scope to stop executing.

Because the trap is cconsidered a scriptblock, you can also use the Return keyword and specify an argument. This value will be passed on to the pipeline. If multiple trap handlers are executed, then the Continue/Break/Return of the *last-executed handler* is the one that takes effect.

Understanding how these options work requires you to understand a bit about trap scope. If you don't specify any of these three options, then the trap handler will exit returning **$_**, which is the error that caused the trap handler to be called in the first place.

Trap Scope

Remember that PowerShell supports *scopes* (which we discussed in the chapter "Scripting Overview"). Essentially, the shell is the global scope. Running a script begins a new scope in which the script itself runs. In addition, each function that's executed has a unique scope. You can define a unique trap handler within each of these scopes. Scripts can have trap handlers, while functions can have self-contained trap handlers that are private to the function. When an exception is thrown, PowerShell executes a trap handler in the *current scope* if one is available. For example, if an error occurs in a script, PowerShell looks for a trap handler defined within the script. If it can't find one, the error is raised to the parent scope, and PowerShell looks for a trap handler there.

When you exit a trap handler using **Continue**, PowerShell executes the next line of code *in the same scope as the trap handler.* The **Break** keyword exits the current scope and goes up one level to the parent scope, passing the exception up to the parent scope. If you've defined another trap handler in the parent scope, it can be called at this point.

It's also important to know that within the trap *itself* is a unique, private scope—meaning the trap can't easily modify variables from outside itself. You *can* do that, if you need to—for example, to change the value of a status variable or some other operation. The trap's own scope is scope zero; the scope which contains the trap (in other words, the trap's parent) is scope 1, and so forth. So using the **Set-Variable** cmdlet lets you modify these scopes explicitly:

```
Set-Variable –name MyVar –scope 1 –value $true
```

This would set the variable **$MyVar**, contained in the trap's parent, to **$true**.

Some Trap Examples

The interaction of errors, exceptions, and traps is exceedingly complicated, and we think it's often easier to see it in action. So consider this example:

```
Function MyFunction {
  Trap {
    Write-Host "FUNCTION TRAPPED" –foregroundcolor magenta
  }
  Get-WmiObject Win32_Service –computerName "Server2"
}

Trap {
  Write-Host "SCRIPT TRAPPED" –foregroundcolor magenta
}

MyFunction
```

This is a very simplistic script. It contains a function named MyFunction, which simply executes a **Get-WmiObject** operation, attempting to connect to a computer which, for the purposes of our example, doesn't exist. We've defined two trap handlers. When we run this script, we get the following output:

```
ERROR: Get-WmiObject : The RPC server is unavailable. (Exception from HRESULT: 0x80070
ERROR: 6BA)
ERROR: At line:5 char:16
ERROR: +   Get-WmiObject  <<<< Win32_Service -computerName "Server2"
```

Here's what happened:

- The function was called.

- An error occurred with the **Get-WmiObject** cmdlet.

- The function did not define **$ErrorActionPreference**, so the shell followed the normal rules for accessing items like variables and looked for the variable in the parent scope, which is the script. The script also did not define $ErrorActionPreference, so the shell went up one last level to the shell, where $ErrorActionPreference was at the default of **Continue**.

- The **Continue** value meant no exception was raised, so no trap executed. However, the **Continue** value allowed an error message to be written to the console, so that's what we saw.

Let's make one minor change:

```
$ErrorActionPreference="SilentlyContinue"
Function MyFunction {
  Trap {
    Write-Host "FUNCTION TRAPPED" -foregroundcolor magenta
  }
  Get-WmiObject Win32_Service -computerName "Server2"
}

Trap {
  Write-Host "SCRIPT TRAPPED" -foregroundcolor magenta
}

MyFunction
```

This time, our script returns no output. Here's why:

- The function was called.

- An error occurred with the **Get-WmiObject** cmdlet.

- The function did not define **$ErrorActionPreference**, so the shell followed the normal rules for accessing items like variables and looked for the variable in the parent scope, which is the script. The script did define $ErrorActionPreference to **SilentlyContinue**, so that's what the shell used.

- The **SilentlyContinue** value means that no exception was raised, so no trap was executed. However, the error message was also suppressed, so we saw no output.

Time for another change:

```
$ErrorActionPreference="SilentlyContinue"
Function MyFunction {
  Trap {
    Write-Host "FUNCTION TRAPPED" -foregroundcolor magenta
  }
  Get-WmiObject Win32_Service -computerName "Server2" -ea stop
}

Trap {
  Write-Host "SCRIPT TRAPPED" -foregroundcolor magenta
}

MyFunction
```

The only change here was to add **-EA Stop** to the **Get-WmiObject** cmdlet. Now, our script's output is this:

```
FUNCTION TRAPPED
```

Here's why:

- The function was called.

- An error occurred with the **Get-WmiObject** cmdlet. The cmdlet specified an **ErrorAction** of **Stop**, so PowerShell generated an exception *and wrote an error message.*

- A trap existed in the function's scope, which is where the error occurred, so the trap executed—resulting in the output we saw.

- The function didn't define **$ErrorActionPreference**, but its parent scope did; the value of **SilentlyContinue** suppressed the error message written by the **Get-WmiObject** cmdlet.

- The trap didn't specify an exit action, so **Continue** was assumed. Because there was no further code within the function, the function exited.

So let's throw in some more lines of code to really follow the flow:

```
$ErrorActionPreference="SilentlyContinue"
Function MyFunction {
  Trap {
    Write-Host "FUNCTION TRAPPED" –foregroundcolor magenta
    Continue
  }
  Get-WmiObject Win32_Service -computerName "Server2" -ea stop
  Write-Host "END OF FUNCTION" –foregroundcolor green
}

Trap {
  Write-Host "SCRIPT TRAPPED" –foregroundcolor magenta
  Continue
}

MyFunction
Write-Host "END OF SCRIPT" –foregroundcolor green
```

This time, we get the following output:

```
FUNCTION TRAPPED
END OF FUNCTION
END OF SCRIPT
```

- The function was called.

- An error occurred with the **Get-WmiObject** cmdlet. The cmdlet specified an **ErrorAction** of **Stop**, so PowerShell generated an exception *and wrote an error message.*

- A trap existed in the function's scope, which is where the error occurred, so the trap executed—resulting in the output we saw.

- The function didn't define **$ErrorActionPreference**, but its parent scope did; the value of **SilentlyContinue** suppressed the error message written by the **Get-WmiObject** cmdlet.

- The trap explicitly specified **Continue**, so the line of code following the exception executed, which was in the same scope, resulting in "END OF FUNCTION" being displayed.

- The function exited, and the script executed its last line of code.

OK, one last change:

```
$ErrorActionPreference="SilentlyContinue"
Function MyFunction {
  Trap {
```

```
    Write-Host "FUNCTION TRAPPED" -foregroundcolor magenta
    Break
  }
  Get-WmiObject Win32_Service -computerName "Server2" -ea stop
  Write-Host "END OF FUNCTION" -foregroundcolor green
}

Trap {
  Write-Host "SCRIPT TRAPPED" -foregroundcolor magenta
  Continue
}

MyFunction
Write-Host "END OF SCRIPT" -foregroundcolor green
```

This time, we get the following output:

```
FUNCTION TRAPPED
SCRIPT TRAPPED
END OF SCRIPT
```

And here's why that occurred:

- The function was called.

- An error occurred with the **Get-WmiObject** cmdlet. The cmdlet specified an **ErrorAction** of **Stop**, so PowerShell generated an exception *and wrote an error message.*

- A trap existed in the function's scope, which is where the error occurred, so the trap executed—resulting in the output we saw.

- The function didn't define **$ErrorActionPreference**, but its parent scope did; the value of **SilentlyContinue** suppressed the error message written by the **Get-WmiObject** cmdlet.

- The trap explicitly specified **Break**. This forced the function to exit, and passed the exception up to the parent scope.

- The parent scope also defined a trap, which trapped the exception that was passed up from the function. That's why "SCRIPT TRAPPED" was displayed.

- The script's trap handler exited with **Continue**, so the script resumed execution *on the next line of code within the same scope*. Because the function passed up an exception, the script "saw" the function as causing the exception. Therefore, the following line of code was "END OF SCRIPT," which appeared in our script's output.

Hopefully this walkthrough demonstrates the complexity of traps and exceptions in PowerShell, and helps you understand how to follow the flow of events.

Throwing Your Own Exceptions

You can use the **Throw** keyword to throw an exception. This is basically the same thing that happens when a line of script causes an error, except you're sort of causing the error on purpose. You can use this to pass the error up to a parent scope for handling. For example:

Script1.ps1

```
trap {
 write-host "YIKES!!!"
 throw $_
}
script2
```

Script2.ps1

```
trap {
 write-host "In Script2"
 break
}
$a = get-content C:\nofile.txt -erroraction stop
```

Here, Script1 calls Script2. Script2 defines a trap handler, and then attempts to get the content of a nonexistent file. Note that the **Get-Content** cmdlet is run with the -**ErrorAction** argument, specifying that should an error occur, the cmdlet should **Stop**. The default action is to **Continue**. Other choices would be **SilentlyContinue** or **Inquire** (e.g., ask the user what to do). So, when an error occurs, since C:\nofile.txt doesn't exist, an exception is thrown by the **Get-Content** cmdlet. It stops running, and the exception is picked up by the trap handler in Script2. This trap handler outputs "In Script2," and then breaks. This break causes the execution of Script2 to stop, and the execution to return to the parent scope, which is Script1.

The **Break** keyword passes the exception up to Script1, which has its own trap handler defined. It outputs "YIKES!!!," and then throws an exception. The exception it throws is **$_**, which is the exception that caused the trap handler to run. Throwing an exception is kind of like using **Break**—the current scope exits and the specified exception is passed to the calling scope. Assuming Script1 was launched interactively from within PowerShell, then the global scope is the calling scope and will receive the exception in **$_**.

The output looks like this:

```
PS C:\> script1
In Script2
YIKES!!!
The path 'nofile.txt' does not exist.

At c:\ps\scripts\script2.ps1:6 char:17
+ $a = get-content <<<< C:\nofile.txt -erroraction stop
```

You can see where we executed Script1 from a PowerShell prompt. Script2 was called, and its trap handler output "In Script2" before passing the exception back to Script1. Script1's trap handler outputs "YIKES!!!" before passing the exception back up the line to the global scope. PowerShell's behavior is to display the error: "The path 'nofile.txt' does not exist," and then list the original location where the error occurred.

You can also use the **Throw** keyword to throw a text error:

```
Throw "this is my error"
```

Make sure **$ErrorActionPreference** is set to **Continue**. PowerShell constructs an actual **ErrorRecord** object out of this. The exception is a generic RuntimeException, the **ErrorID** is the string you provided (which will also go into the exception's Message property), the **ErrorCategory** is **OperationStopped**, and the targetObject property is the string you provided.

If you just call the **Throw** keyword with no argument, the **ErrorRecord's** exception is **RuntimeException**. The **ErrorID** is "ScriptHalted," which also goes into the exception's Message property. The **ErrorCategory** is **OperationStopped**, and the targetObject property is Null.

Tips for Error Trapping

Take a look at TrapTest.ps1:

TrapTest.ps1

```
function CheckWMI {
 Param($computer)

 trap {
    Write-Host "An error occured: "
    write-host "ID: " $_.ErrorID
    Write-Host "Message: "$_.Exception.Message
    throw "Couldn't check $computer"
 }

 $a = Get-WmiObject Win32_OperatingSystem  -property "ServicePackMajorVersion" '
-computer $computer -ea stop
 write-host "$computer : " $a.ServicePackMajorVersion

}

write-host "Service Pack Versions:"
CheckWMI $env:computername
CheckWMI "FOO"
```

The first time the function is called we pass the value from **$env:computername**, which is the PowerShell equivalent of the %computername% environment variable for the local computer. Computer FOO doesn't exist. This produces the following output:

```
PS C:\> test\traptest
Service Pack Versions:
GODOT7 : 0
An error occured:
ID:
Message: The RPC server is unavailable. (Exception from HRESULT: 0x800706BA)
Line 10: Couldn't check FOO
```

Notice that we specified **-ea stop** for the cmdlet, ensuring that it would stop execution and allow the trap to execute. Let's make one small change to the original script: Remove the **-ea** argument, allowing the default of Continue to take place.

Here's the revised output:

```
PS C:\> test\traptest
Service Pack Versions:
GODOT7 : 0
ERROR: Get-WmiObject : The RPC server is unavailable. (Exception from HRESULT: 0x800706BA)
ERROR: At line:12 char:20
ERROR: + $a = Get-WmiObject <<<<  Win32_OperatingSystem  -property "ServicePackMajorVersion"
```

```
-computer $computer
ERROR:      + CategoryInfo          : InvalidOperation: (:) [Get-WmiObject], COMException
ERROR:      + FullyQualifiedErrorId : GetWMICOMException,Microsoft.PowerShell.Commands.
GetWmiObjectCommand
ERROR:
FOO :
PS C:\>
```

See the difference? The trap didn't get to execute in this case—the error occurred right at the cmdlet. So, whenever possible, make sure you're executing cmdlets with an appropriate **ErrorAction** argument, and defining a trap to handle whatever errors might crop up.

Easier Error Handling

If all of this business with traps and exceptions is making your head spin—well, we couldn't agree more. Fortunately, PowerShell v2.0 introduced a new and easier way to detect and deal with errors, called a **Try…Catch…Finally** block. Here's an example:

```
Try {
    Get-WmiObject Win32_Service -ComputerName Server2 -EA Stop
} Catch {
    Write-Host "Couldn't contact Server2" –foregroundcolor red
}
```

You start by using the keyword **Try**, and then following with the command or commands that you think might cause an error. Keep in mind that, as with the techniques discussed earlier, PowerShell can only detect exceptions, meaning you need to have an **ErrorAction** of **Stop** in order for this to work. Next, you include a **Catch** block, which contains the code you want executed if an exception occurs within the **Try** block. It's that simple! Note that PowerShell may still write error messages, and you can still suppress them by starting out with **$ErrorActionPreference = "SilentlyContinue,"** just as we demonstrated earlier in this chapter.

Optionally, you can include a **Finally** block, which contains code that will execute regardless of whether an exception occurs:

```
Try {
    Get-WmiObject Win32_Service -ComputerName Server2 -EA Stop
} Catch {
    Write-Host "Couldn't contact Server2" –foregroundcolor red
} Finally {
    Write-Host "ALL DONE!" –foregroundcolor green
}
```

We think this is a *much* easier was to detect and handle problems that may occur in your scripts. However, PowerShell v2.0 still supports the other techniques we've outlined in this chapter, and you're free to use them. You should make an effort to understand how both techniques work, so that you can easily follow the flow of scripts that someone else may have written. We recommend that as you write new scripts that will only execute on PowerShell v2.0 to use the **Try…Catch**.

We'll wrap up the chapter with a more practical example:

UptimeReport.ps1

```
#requires -version 2.0

#define the parameters
param (
    [Parameter(
     ValueFromPipeline=$True,
     Position=0,
     Mandatory=$True,
     HelpMessage="Enter the name of a text file with servernames to query.")]
     [String[]]$File
     )
try {
  #verify file exists
  $servers=Get-Content $File -ea stop
  Write-Host "Processing computernames in $file" -foregroundcolor green
  foreach ($server in $servers) {
     try {
       $wmi=Get-WmiObject win32_operatingsystem -computername $server -ea Stop
       $wmi | select @{name="Computer";Expression={$_.CSName}},'
       @{name="LastBoot";Expression={$_.ConvertToDateTime($_.lastbootuptime)}},'
       @{name="Uptime";Expression={((get-date) - ($_.ConvertToDateTime($_.lastbootuptime)))}}

     }# end inner Try
     catch {
       Write-Warning "Failed to connect to $server"
     }

  } #end foreach
} #end outer try
catch {
 Write-Warning "Failed to find or open $file"
}
finally {
  Write-Host "exiting the script" -foregroundcolor green
}
```

This script will only run on PowerShell v2.0. The script takes the name of a text file that contains all the computers you want to work with. The script's goal is to show when a computer last booted and how long it has been up. The main body of the script consists of a **Try...Catch** construct.

The first **Try** expression is to verify that the file exists and that it can be read:

```
try {
  #verify file exists
  $servers=Get-Content $File -ea stop
```

If there was any sort of error, then the code within the **Catch** scriptblock executes:

```
catch {
 Write-Warning "Failed to find or open $file"
}
```

Assuming the file is okay, PowerShell saves the contents to a variable and we use a **ForEach** loop to enumerate each computer name. Now we have a second **Try...Catch** block:

```
Write-Host "Processing computernames in $file" -foregroundcolor green
foreach ($server in $servers) {
  try {
    $wmi=Get-WmiObject win32_operatingsystem -computername $server -ea Stop
```

If we can't connect to the remote computer, PowerShell displays a warning message:

```
  catch {
    Write-Warning "Failed to connect to $server"
  }
```

Assuming no problems, PowerShell writes the computer's information to the pipeline:

```
  $wmi | select @{name="Computer";Expression={$_.CSName}},'
  @{name="LastBoot";Expression={$_.ConvertToDateTime($_.lastbootuptime)}},'
  @{name="Uptime";Expression={((get-date) - ($_.ConvertToDateTime($_.lastbootuptime)))}}}
```

Regardless of whether there were any errors, the **Finally** script block executes at the script's conclusion:

```
finally {
  Write-Host "exiting the script" -foregroundcolor green
}
```

One final point to keep in mind is that *all* of the code within the **Try** script block must be able to execute without error. If any expression fails, then PowerShell will execute the **Catch** script block.

Chapter 24
The PowerShell Debugger and Debugging Techniques

Debugging is the process of removing bugs, or errors, from your script. There are really two types of errors: Simple *syntax errors*, which are usually just typos, and *logic errors*, which mean your script won't behave like you think it should—even though it might not actually give you any error messages. In this chapter, we'll show you a few different types of errors, and walk you through a methodology that helps locate the error quickly, so that you can fix it and move on.

The Debugging Process

Debugging can be tricky. The best way to debug is to have a thorough understanding of what your script is doing and how PowerShell is executing it. Let's work with an example: Without actually *running* this script, can you predict where the error will occur?

TrickyDebugging.ps1

```
1. $foo = "this is the original text"
2.
3.  function f1($str)
4.  {
5.  "Calling f1..."
6.  $str.toUpper()
7.  }
8.
9.  function f2($value)
10. {
11. "Calling f2... what is value?"
12. $value | get-member
```

```
13. ""
14. "Before f1 value is: " + $value
15. "Before f1 foo is: " + $script:foo
16. $script:foo = f1 $value
17. "after f1 value is: " + $value
18. "after f1 foo is: " + $script:foo
19. }
20.
21. ""
22. "BEFORE PASS 1, WHAT IS FOO?"
23. $foo | get-member
24. ""
25.
26. "PASS 1"
27. f2 $foo
28.
29. ""
30. "AFTER PASS 1, WHAT IS FOO?"
31. $foo | get-member
32. ""
33.
34. ""
35. "PASS 2"
36. f2 $foo
37.
38. ""
39. "global value"
40. $foo
```

Here's What We Do

When we're trying to follow a script like this, we take a piece of paper and a pen, and a printout of the script, and start reading. We use the paper to keep track of the values inside variables, in much the same way that PowerShell keeps track of them in memory. Usually, a methodical approach like that reveals the bug in no time.

After you read through this script, try running it in PowerShell. Then, load the script into an editor like PrimalScript that offers line numbering, and let's walk through *exactly* what's happening. This is the process you'll have to do anytime you want to debug something.

First, we assign a value to the variable, **$foo**. This occurs in the script's scope, which is a child of the shell's global scope. Then, we define but don't yet execute two functions, F1 and F2.

The action starts on line 21, where two literal strings are the output and we pipe $foo to the **Get-Member** cmdlet. This displays the type of object **$foo** is. If you've run the script, you'll see that it's a **System.String**. Remember this piece of information.

Next, the script outputs a blank line on line 24. On line 27, we pass **$foo** to the F2 function. We defined that function on line 9; you can see it's accepting input—whatever was in **$foo**—into the variable **$value**. Line 12 passes **$value** to the **Get-Member** cmdlet. Notice anything? The **$value** variable isn't recognized as a string since it's a generic **System.Object**. On line 14, the script outputs **$value** and the script-level **$foo** variable. You'll notice in the script's output that these two match. This is exactly what should occur at this point.

The script calls the F1 function, passing **$value** as its input argument. The function places that input into the **$str** variable. It outputs "Calling f1…", and then outputs the result of $str.toUpper. We didn't check, but we can expect that **$str** was received as a System.Object, but that PowerShell was able to coerce it into being a System.String so the **ToUpper()** method would work. *Everything* output by function F1 becomes its "return value," which is placed into the script-level **$foo** variable back on line 16. Lines 17 and 18 confirm that **$value** and **$foo** are now different, since we have replaced **$foo** with an uppercase version of **$value**.

So far so good. However, on line 31, the output indicates that **$foo** isn't a **System.String** anymore; it's now a **System.Object**. Line 36 repeats the whole process, but gets an error on line 6 when the script calls F1 a second time, because **$str** is now an Object that can't be coerced into a String. As such, it has no **ToUpper()** method to call, which is what the error indicates if you run the script.

So, the problem is that at some point PowerShell stopped coercing **$str** into a String and left it as an Object. Why? The answer is on the *first call* to F1. Remember, F1's output was "Calling f1..." followed by a carriage return, followed by the result of **$str.toUpper**. That carriage return is the culprit since it prevents PowerShell from recognizing a string. Instead the carriage return causes it to recognize an *array* of two strings. This means the second time we call F1, **$str** appears to contain an array, which doesn't have a **ToUpper()** method.

The *proper* way to have a function output text without having that text become part of the function's return value is to use the **Write-Host** cmdlet. Modify line 5 as follows:

```
Write-Host "Calling f1..."
```

When you run the script again, you'll see it works fine! That's because the output of F1 never contains a carriage return, which allows the string to be recognized as a System.String by PowerShell.

Another fix would be to modify line 1 as follows:

```
[string]$foo = "this is the original text"
```

Again, *just* this change makes the script work because the decision on whether the string is a String or an Object is no longer PowerShell's choice. In fact, we declared **$foo** explicitly as a String and it stays that way throughout. Strings *can* contain carriage returns. However, keep in mind when something is not specifically declared as a String that contains a carriage return, it will be interpreted as an Object.

This is just one example of how nitty-gritty you need to get when you're debugging. Walk through every line of code. As in this example, add extra code to help you figure out what's what, such as when we used the **Get-Member** cmdlet to see how data type variables were being treated. This isn't to say that debugging is *simple*. However, the best way to debug is by following your script one line at a time and *seeing* what PowerShell is doing.

> **Please, Believe Us**
> Nobody believes us when we say, "walk through your script one line at a time." Invariably, we'll watch administrators struggle with a script, glancing at it, thinking they know what the problem is, and making a change that doesn't help. You can't debug like that—we call it "shotgun debugging," because your "fixes" are all over the place, and you wind up blasting holes in your script. Trust us, a methodical, line-by-line approach might seem more time-consuming, but in the end, it isn't.

Debug Mode and Tracing

As the previous debugging example illustrated, it's critical to understand what your script is doing and with what data it's working. The contents of variables change as your script jumps in and out of functions. So, knowing exactly what's going on allows you to mentally follow the script's progress and spot the problems that are causing bugs. Unfortunately, PowerShell v1.0 lacks a full debugger. In fact, v1.0 lacks any means for a third-party debugger to "plug in" and help you. That means you're more or less on your own when it comes to figuring out what your scripts are doing.

Fortunately, PowerShell *does* include a "debug mode" that gives you some ability to see what's going on inside your script. Your primary tool is the **Set-PSDebug** cmdlet that allows you to trace the execution of your script. This means that by writing status information throughout the script, you can see what's happening as your script executes.

The **Set-PSDebug** cmdlet is a fairly complicated cmdlet that allows you to control the *trace level* of script execution. It also allows you to turn on line-by-line script execution, pausing execution after each line so you can examine the contents of variables to see what your script is doing. We'll use the DebugTest.ps1 script in the following example to see how this works:

DebugTest.ps1

```
function F1 {
 param ($n, $a)
 if (F2($a)) {
   "$n is old enough to vote"
 } else {
   "$n is too young to vote"
 }
}

function F2 {
 param ($var)
 if ($var -gt 17) {
   $true
 } else {
   $false
 }
}

[string]$name = "Joe"
[int]$age = 25

F1 $name, $age
```

Looking at this script, you'd expect it to display "Joe is old enough to vote." Walk through the script in your head to make sure you agree with that before you proceed.

However, running the script produces this output:

```
PS C:\> test\debugtest
Joe 25 is too young to vote
```

Clearly this output is not correct. So, what went wrong? The best way to find out is to start debugging in order to find out what's in the variables and what execution path the script is taking.

We'll start by running the **Set-PSDebug** cmdlet and specifying a trace level. We'll also turn on step-by-step execution. There are three possible trace levels:

- **0:** No tracing.

- **1:** Trace script lines as they execute.

- **2:** Also trace variable assignments, function calls, and scripts.

Level 2 is the most detailed, which is what we want. Actually, specifying the **-Step** argument implies **-Trace 1**, so we'll need to explicitly specify **-Trace 2** to get the detail we want. After running the **Set-PSDebug** cmdlet, we'll run our script.

As you can see, PowerShell now asks on a line-by-line basis if we're ready to execute that line:

```
PS C:\> set-psdebug -trace 2 -step
PS C:\> test\debugtest

Continue with this operation?
  1+ test\debugtest
[Y] Yes [A] Yes to All [N] No [L] No to All [S] Suspend [?] Help
(default is "Y"):
```

If you're following along, hit "Y" for each of the following lines as we move through this script one line at a time:

- You'll notice that the first three lines are merely asking for permission to execute the script itself, and to recognize the two functions. Press Enter three times ("Y" is the default) to move to line 19 of the script.

- After setting a variable, PowerShell confirms the value that's gone into the variable. This is shown by default in yellow text after the line of script is run:

```
Continue with this operation?
 19+ [string]$name = "Joe"
[Y] Yes [A] Yes to All [N] No [L] No to All [S] Suspend [?] Help
(default is "Y"):
DEBUG:  19+ [string]$name = "Joe"
DEBUG:    ! SET $name = 'Joe'.

Continue with this operation?
 20+ [int]$age = 25
[Y] Yes [A] Yes to All [N] No [L] No to All [S] Suspend [?] Help
(default is "Y"):
```

- We then set the **$age** variable, which is confirmed.

- Next we call the F1 function.

- Now we're on line 3 inside of function F1, which calls function F2.

- This is a good point to see what actually got passed into F1 for input arguments. Press "S" and hit Enter to suspend the script. Notice that PowerShell drops to a special prompt so we can examine the values of the **$n** and **$a** variables. Notice that **$n** contains "Joe," a carriage return, and "25," which is not what we expected. Also notice that **$a** does not contain anything, which is why our script isn't working properly:

```
Continue with this operation?
  3+   if (F2($a)) {
[Y] Yes [A] Yes to All [N] No [L] No to All [S] Suspend [?] Help
(default is "Y"):S
PS C:\>>> $n
Joe
25
PS C:\>>> $a
```

```
PS C:\>>>
```

- Since we've spotted a problem, there's no point in continuing until this problem is fixed. We'll enter EXIT to return to the script, and then reply with "L" to abandon execution of further lines of code:

```
PS C:\>>> exit

Continue with this operation?
  3+  if (F2($a)) {
[Y] Yes [A] Yes to All [N] No [L] No to All [S] Suspend [?] Help
(default is "Y"):1
WriteDebug stopped because the DebugPreference was 'Stop'.
At C:\test\debugtest.ps1:22 char:1
+ F <<<< 1 $name, $age
PS C:\>
```

So, our problem is that both the name and age are being passed into the **$n** argument of function F1, while **$a** isn't getting a value at all. The problem? Our initial call to F1:

```
F1 $name, $age
```

PowerShell doesn't use a comma to separate arguments. This line should be:

```
F1 $name $age
```

After making this modification, let's debug the script again. To begin, hit Enter at the debug prompts until you get to line 3 again. Then, hit S to suspend the script and check the values in **$n** and **$a**:

```
PS C:\> test\debugtest

Continue with this operation?
  1+ test\debugtest
[Y] Yes [A] Yes to All [N] No [L] No to All [S] Suspend [?] Help
(default is "Y"):
DEBUG:   1+ test\debugtest
DEBUG:    ! CALL script 'debugtest.ps1'

Continue with this operation?
  1+ function F1 {
[Y] Yes [A] Yes to All [N] No [L] No to All [S] Suspend [?] Help
(default is "Y"):
DEBUG:   1+ function F1 {

Continue with this operation?
 10+ function F2 {
[Y] Yes [A] Yes to All [N] No [L] No to All [S] Suspend [?] Help
(default is "Y"):
DEBUG:  10+ function F2 {

Continue with this operation?
 19+ [string]$name = "Joe"
[Y] Yes [A] Yes to All [N] No [L] No to All [S] Suspend [?] Help
(default is "Y"):
DEBUG:  19+ [string]$name = "Joe"
DEBUG:    ! SET $name = 'Joe'.
```

```
Continue with this operation?
 20+ [int]$age = 25
[Y] Yes [A] Yes to All [N] No [L] No to All [S] Suspend [?] Help
(default is "Y"):
DEBUG:  20+ [int]$age = 25
DEBUG:   ! SET $age = '25'.

Continue with this operation?
 22+ F1 $name $age
[Y] Yes [A] Yes to All [N] No [L] No to All [S] Suspend [?] Help
(default is "Y"):
DEBUG:  22+ F1 $name $age
DEBUG:    ! CALL function 'F1' (defined in file 'C:\test\debugtest.ps1')

Continue with this operation?
  3+  if (F2($a)) {
[Y] Yes [A] Yes to All [N] No [L] No to All [S] Suspend [?] Help
(default is "Y"):s
PS C:\>>> $n
Joe
PS C:\>>> $a
25
PS C:\>>>
```

Now we can see that **$n** contains "Joe" and **$a** contains "25", which is what we want. We'll type EXIT to return to the script, and then hit A to execute all remaining lines without stopping one line at a time:

```
PS C:\>>> exit

Continue with this operation?
  3+  if (F2($a)) {
[Y] Yes [A] Yes to All [N] No [L] No to All [S] Suspend [?] Help
(default is "Y"):a
DEBUG:   3+  if (F2($a)) {
DEBUG:    ! CALL function 'F2' (defined in file 'C:\test\debugtest.ps1')
DEBUG:  12+  if ($var -gt 17) {
DEBUG:  13+     $true
DEBUG:   4+    "$n is old enough to vote"
Joe is old enough to vote
PS C:\>
```

You can see that the script still outputs trace messages for each line of code that executes, but we're not prompted to run each line. Line 3 calls function F2, which starts on line 12. We can see that the If construct was true because it executed line 13, which returned the value **$true**. That resulted in a true comparison for line 3, which resulted in line 4 executing, and that produced our script's output. We'll disable tracing by running:

```
Set-PSDebug -off
```

Tracing Your Work

PowerShell also provides the **Trace-Command** cmdlet, which is pretty complicated but provides insight into PowerShell's internal workings. Because it provides such a deep view of PowerShell, it requires significant programming experience to use and understand. Therefore, we will not cover it, since we consider it a bit beyond the scope of this book.

One good technique for using the **Set-PSDebug** cmdlet is to either have a printed copy of your script or have your script running in a script development environment, such as SAPIEN PrimalScript, as you execute the script line by line. That way you can see each line of script code in the context of the full script, which allows you to follow PowerShell's execution of your script one line at a time. As you debug, keep a piece of scratch paper handy so you can jot down variables' contents. You'll also frequently suspend the script to check variables' contents. When PowerShell displays each line of code prior to executing it, ask yourself what *should* happen. That way, when you hit Enter to execute that line, you'll either get the result you expected indicating all is well, or you won't, meaning you'll know where the problem occurred.

Advanced Debugging

PowerShell v2.0 introduced new debugging capabilities, including the ability to set *breakpoints*. A breakpoint is a predefined point in your script where PowerShell will stop and either wait for you to tell it to continue or perform some predefined action that you've specified. PowerShell allows you to set breakpoints in a variety of places:

- At a specific line of your script.

- At a specific column of your script.

- When a function runs.

- When a command runs.

- When a variable changes.

When you reach a breakpoint, PowerShell can either run a script block that you provide—which might write debugging information to the console or a log file—or it can open a *nested prompt*. A nested prompt is exactly the same thing you get when you debug the script manually, as we described earlier in this chapter, and select the option to Suspend the script. Within the nested prompt, you can access the script's variables, and you can run the Exit command to allow the script to continue running to the next breakpoint. Within the nested prompt you can also execute **Step-*** cmdlets, which tell PowerShell what line of code to execute next, allowing you to execute one line of code at a time.

You manage breakpoints by using a set of cmdlets:

- **Set-PSBreakpoint:** creates a new breakpoint.

- **Get-PSBreakpoint:** retrieves an existing breakpoint.

- **Enable-PSBreakpoint:** makes a breakpoint active.

- **Disable-PSBreakpoint:** makes a breakpoint inactive.

- **Remove-PSBreakpoint:** removes a breakpoint.

Managing Breakpoints

To create a new breakpoint, use the **Set-PSBreakpoint** cmdlet. You have the option of providing a script block to the -**Action** parameter; if you do, the breakpoint will run that script block. If you don't, the breakpoint will open a nested prompt.

Note that you can define breakpoints in the shell itself; part of the breakpoint's definition is which script will trigger the breakpoint. This allows you to set breakpoints for multiple scripts, and have PowerShell remember them. Like anything else you define in the shell, breakpoints cease to exist when you close the shell. However, you can persist breakpoints in an XML file, and then re-import them:

```
PS C:\> Get-PSBreakpoint | Export-CliXML c:\breakpoints.xml
PS C:\> Import-CliXML c:\breakpoints.xml | Set-PSBreakpoint
```

This technique allows you to save and re-load a set of breakpoints after closing and re-opening the shell; we cover importing and exporting objects in more detail in the chapter, "Object Serialization."

To create a breakpoint that stops when a given function or command is run:

```
PS C:\> Set-PSBreakpoint -command MyFunction -script c:\test\test.ps1
```

Or, if you want to specify a script block to run when the breakpoint is hit:

```
PS C:\> $sb { Write-Debug $var }
PS C:\> Set-PSBreakpoint -command MyFunction -script c:\test\test.ps1 -action $sb
```

You *must* specify a script for the breakpoint, unless you're already in a nested prompt opened by a breakpoint. Within a nested prompt, you can omit the -**script** parameter to set an additional breakpoint inside the script that's currently running.

Note that PowerShell permits wildcards in the command specification. Note that you can only set breakpoints for commands inside of scripts; you can't set a breakpoint for commands that are run interactively within the shell.

Breakpoint Tip
If you want to have multiple different actions occur for a particular breakpoint, simply create multiple breakpoints for the same condition.

To set a breakpoint on a variable, you need to decide if you want the breakpoint to occur when the variable is read, written, or both. You'll specify one parameter: -**Mode**, with a value of "Read", "Write" (default), or "ReadWrite." You have to be a bit careful with these. For example, this code:

```
$var = $var + 1
```

Is both reading and writing the variable **$var**. So is this:

```
$var += 1
```

Make sure you select an appropriate breakpoint mode so that you're getting the results you need. To set the breakpoint:

```
PS C:\> Set-PSBreakpoint -Mode Read -Script c:\test\test.ps1 -Variables "var,var2,myvar"
```

Note that variable names do not need a **$** with this cmdlet, and you can provide a list of variables for a single breakpoint.

Finally, your last option is to create a breakpoint for a specific line, or line/column combination:

```
PS C:\> Set-PSBreakpoint -ColumnNumber 5 -LineNUmber 52 -script c:\test\test.ps1
PS C:\> Set-PSBreakpoint -LineNumber 53 -script c:\test\test.ps1
```

And you can of course specify the **-action** parameter with any of these examples to run a script block instead of opening a nested prompt.

> **Breakpoint Tip**
> It's easier to set line and column breakpoints if you have an editor that displays line/column infor-mation, such as the graphical PowerShell tool or SAPIEN PrimalScript.

To see a list of currently defined breakpoints, run the **Get-PSBreakpoint** cmdlet. The shell assigns all breakpoints an ID number; you can remove breakpoints one at a time using the **Remove-PSBreakpoint** cmdlet and providing the desired ID number. You can also remove all breakpoints by running:

```
PS C:\> Get-PSBreakpoint | Remove-PSBreakpoint
```

Additionally, you may want to temporarily disable a breakpoint by using the **Disable-PSBreakpoint** cmdlet. For example, to globally disable all currently defined breakpoints:

```
PS C:\> Get-PSBreakpoint | Disable-PSBreakpoint
```

The corresponding **Enable-PSBreakpoint** cmdlet allows you to re-enable a disabled breakpoint.

Within the Nested Prompt

If you've chosen to have your breakpoints open a nested prompt when they're hit, you have a few com-mands you can work with that are specific to debugging within the nested prompt. The four commands are:

- **Step-Into:** Executes the next line of code, and then returns to the nested prompt. When it returns to the prompt, the cmdlet displays a preview of the *next* line of code, but doesn't execute it. That way, you can see what's coming up.

- **Step-Over:** Works like **Step-Into** except that when you execute a function call or script invo-cation, it doesn't step through the code inside the function or script. Instead, it simply runs the function or script, and then returns to the nested prompt.

- **Step-Out:** Works a bit differently depending on where you script it. Within a function or an invoked script, **Step-Out** will finish executing the function or script unless it runs into another breakpoint. It will then return to the nested prompt once back in the calling scope—essentially, "stepping out" of the function or script, and then breaking again. When used within the main script, it will resume execution of the script until it reaches the end or another breakpoint.

- **Get-PSCallStack:** Displays the *call stack* at that point. The call stack is simply a list of functions and scripts that are executing. For example, a call stack like this one indicates that you're at a nested prompt, which was triggered by a breakpoint at the command **Gcm**, which was run with the argument "get-content":

```
2: prompt
1: gcm: $args=["get-content"]
0: prompt: $args=[]
```

Learning to use these commands is a key task to effective debugging. Of course, within the nested prompt, you can also access variables—either directly or through the **$PSDrive** variable—evaluate expressions, and indeed do anything that you could normally do at a PowerShell prompt. Just keep in mind that the nested prompt is "inside" your script, meaning it acts within your script's scope.

> **Note: Commands, not Cmdlets**
>
> The **Step-*** commands aren't like traditional cmdlets; for example, you won't find help for them, although they are described in **help about_debuggers**. They're only useful when you're stopped at a breakpoint in the special debugging prompt.

Debugging Techniques

In addition to knowing how to use the debugger, there's a lot to be said for having some good debugging tricks up your sleeve. In the next few sections, we'll share some of our favorite tips for making debugging go a bit smoother.

Remember that our goal with debugging is *always* to get a better idea of what our script *is actually doing*, and then compare that to our expectations. If you don't have any expectations for your script, then you won't know if it's doing anything wrong! Always follow this basic methodology:

1. Print your script. Seriously, this seems archaic today, but until you get to be a really skilled debugger, this is a huge help.

2. Next to each line of the script, jot down a note about what the line does. For example, "queries two classes from WMI." Be specific. If you've already put these types of comments into your script—good for you! See how much time it saves, now that you're debugging?

3. Walk through your script *one line at a time* and predict what each will do. Keep two pieces of scratch paper: One for variables, and one for output. On each, write down what you think PowerShell will do. This lets you keep track of variables' values, and predict the output.

With the above pieces of paper in hand, you're ready to start debugging. In many cases, you can use the built-in debugger and compare its line-by-line results to your own to see if there's any difference (difference = bug). In other cases, you may wish to "beef up" your script by using some of the following techniques. For each of these, we're going to be starting with the following script:

```
#Test-Debug.ps1
$computers = Get-Content c:\computers.txt
foreach ($computer in $computers) {
    Write-Output 'n$computer
    $wmi = gwmi -query "select * from win32_logicaldisk where drivetype=3" '
     -computer $computer
    foreach ($drive in $wmi) {
        $device = $drive.deviceid
        $space = $drive.freespace / 1MB
        Write-Output "$device has $space MB free"
```

```
        }
}
```

As is, this script produces output like this:

```
LOCALHOST
C: has 113432.03515625 MB free
D: has 155298.8046875 MB free
G: has 32439.875 MB free


MEDIASERVER
C: has 136600.62109375 MB free
D: has 194455.5390625 MB free
```

Writing Verbose Information

Our short sample script above produces useful information: an inventory of free drive space on local drives for a list of computers. However, if something goes wrong, then we just get error messages mixed into the output and may have to guess at the cause. Sometimes, having the option to see more detailed information—that is, more *verbose* information—is useful. PowerShell's **Write-Verbose** cmdlet gives us this capability. For example, consider this revision:

```
#Test-Debug.ps1
$computers = Get-Content c:\computers.txt
$qty = $computers | Measure-Object
$qty = $qty.count
Write-Verbose "Inventorying $qty computers"

foreach ($computer in $computers) {
    Write-Output 'n$computer
    Write-Verbose "Connecting..."
    $wmi = gwmi -query "select * from win32_logicaldisk where drivetype=3" '
     -computer $computer

     Write-Verbose "Free space on local drives..."
    foreach ($drive in $wmi) {
        $device = $drive.deviceid
        $space = $drive.freespace / 1MB
        Write-Output "$device has $space MB free"
    }
}
```

You can see in the beginning of the script that we've actually calculated information specifically to be written "verbosely:" the number of computers in the list. When we run this, here's what we get:

```
LOCALHOST
C: has 113432.015625 MB free
D: has 155298.8046875 MB free
G: has 32439.875 MB free


MEDIASERVER
C: has 136577.55859375 MB free
D: has 194455.5390625 MB free
```

Um, wait a minute… that's the same thing. The trick to the **Write-Verbose** cmdlet, you see, is that it writes to the *verbose* pipeline—which, by default, is turned off. We can turn it on by setting the **$VerbosePreference** variable from its default value of **SilentlyContinue** to **Continue**, and then rerunning our script:

```
PS C:\> $verbosepreference = "Continue"
PS C:\> .\test-debug.ps1
VERBOSE: Inventorying 3 computers


LOCALHOST
VERBOSE: Connecting...
VERBOSE: Free space on local drives...
C: has 113431.640625 MB free
D: has 155298.8046875 MB free
G: has 32439.875 MB free


MEDIASERVER
VERBOSE: Connecting...
VERBOSE: Free space on local drives...
C: has 136573.43359375 MB free
D: has 194455.5390625 MB free
```

Of course, you can't see it here, but the verbose information it not only prefaced by "VERBOSE:" but also displayed in an alternate color so that it stands out. Now we can watch our script run with a lot more detail about what's happening at each step. This is also useful when you're not necessarily debugging, just to help track down exactly what's going on in the script.

Writing Debugging Information

Debugging information is often much less attractively formatted, and typically includes "inside" information. Here's a modified script that includes this information, using the **Write-Debug** cmdlet:

```
#Test-Debug.ps1
$computers = Get-Content c:\computers.txt
$qty = $computers | Measure-Object
Write-Debug "'$qty is $qty"

$qty = $qty.count
Write-Debug "'$qty is $qty"
Write-Verbose "Inventorying $qty computers"

foreach ($computer in $computers) {
    Write-Debug "'$computer is $computer"
    Write-Output 'n$computer

    Write-Verbose "Connecting..."
    $wmi = gwmi -query "select * from win32_logicaldisk where drivetype=3" '
    -computer $computer

    $wmi | Measure-Object | write-debug

    Write-Verbose "Free space on local drives..."
    foreach ($drive in $wmi) {
        $device = $drive.deviceid
        Write-Debug "'$device is $device"

        $space = $drive.freespace / 1MB
        Write-Debug "'$space is $space"
```

```
        Write-Output "$device has $space MB free"
    }
}
```

Our strategy is to put a **Write-Debug** cmdlet after every variable assignment or change, outputting the new variable value. This lets us keep close tabs on what the script is doing. You'll notice that we wrote strings like "`$qty is $qty" a lot. PowerShell will display the first $qty literally, because we've *escaped* the dollar sign. The second $qty will be replaced with the variable's actual value.

The **Write-Debug** cmdlet writes to PowerShell's *debug* pipeline, and the **$DebugPreference** variable controls whether that pipeline is on or off. By default, it's set to **SilentlyContinue**, which means "don't display." We'll set it to **Continue** to see our debug output:

```
PS C:\> $debugpreference = "continue"
PS C:\> .\test-debug.ps1
DEBUG: $qty is Microsoft.PowerShell.Commands.GenericMeasureInfo
DEBUG: $qty is 3
VERBOSE: Inventorying 3 computers
DEBUG: $computer is LOCALHOST


LOCALHOST
VERBOSE: Connecting...
DEBUG: Microsoft.PowerShell.Commands.GenericMeasureInfo
VERBOSE: Free space on local drives...
DEBUG: $device is C:
DEBUG: $space is 113431.625
C: has 113431.625 MB free
DEBUG: $device is D:
DEBUG: $space is 155298.8046875
D: has 155298.8046875 MB free
DEBUG: $device is G:
DEBUG: $space is 32439.875
G: has 32439.875 MB free
DEBUG: $computer is MEDIASERVER


MEDIASERVER
VERBOSE: Connecting...
DEBUG: Microsoft.PowerShell.Commands.GenericMeasureInfo
VERBOSE: Free space on local drives...
DEBUG: $device is C:
DEBUG: $space is 136542.49609375
C: has 136542.49609375 MB free
DEBUG: $device is D:
DEBUG: $space is 194455.5390625
D: has 194455.5390625 MB free
```

Wow! That's a lot of extra information. As you can see, it's a bit poorly formatted, but that's okay because this information is just for us, so we can follow our script. We can now see "inside" the script, looking at every value as it changes and following the script's execution with great precision.

The *best* part about the **Write-Debug** cmdlet and the **Write-Preference** cmdlet is that you can use them in your script from the very start, before you ever have to debug. By default, their output isn't displayed, but you can turn them on whenever you need them and turn them off again when you're finished. You can see a *really* cool part about these cmdlets in a development environment like PrimalScript: If you set the **$DebugPreference** variable *in your script*, say as the first line, then PrimalScript captures this debug information to a separate pane, which allows you to review the debug information separately from your script's primary output.

Using Nested Prompts

We talked about nested prompts first in the chapter "Working with the PowerShell Host." A *nested prompt* is one which occurs inside an existing pipeline. For debugging purposes, it's pure gold: You can have your script "pause" in mid-execution, open a new nested prompt, and then use the shell interactively *inside your script's scope*. That means all your script variables and so forth will be completely available. We're going to go back to our original example script and throw in a nested prompt:

```
#Test-Debug.ps1
$computers = Get-Content c:\computers.txt
foreach ($computer in $computers) {
    Write-Output 'n$computer
    $wmi = gwmi -query "select * from win32_logicaldisk where drivetype=3" '
     -computer $computer
    $host.EnterNestedPrompt()
    foreach ($drive in $wmi) {
       $device = $drive.deviceid
       $space = $drive.freespace / 1MB
       Write-Output "$device has $space MB free"
    }
}
```

Important!
Keep in mind that the capabilities of the **$Host** variable are typically available only within the PowerShell.exe console host. If you're running your script from PrimalScript, configure it to not capture script output. This will launch your script in a new instance of PowerShell.exe.

When we run this script, as soon as it hits the $Host.EnterNestedPrompt() line, a new nested prompt is opened. We can then examine variables, such as the **$wmi** variable we just created, to see if they contain what we expect. When we're done, entering **Exit** will exit the nested prompt, returning control to the script. Here's what it looks like from the shell:

```
PS C:\> .\test-debug.ps1


LOCALHOST
PS C:\>>> $wmi


DeviceID     : C:
DriveType    : 3
ProviderName :
FreeSpace    : 118939058176
Size         : 250056704000
VolumeName   :

DeviceID     : D:
DriveType    : 3
ProviderName :
FreeSpace    : 162842599424
Size         : 250056704000
VolumeName   : Storage

DeviceID     : G:
DriveType    : 3
ProviderName :
```

```
FreeSpace    : 34015674368
Size         : 163913347072
VolumeName   : Backup


PS C:\>>> exit
C: has 113429.125 MB free
D: has 155298.8046875 MB free
G: has 32439.875 MB free


MEDIASERVER
PS C:\>>>
```

You can use nested prompts to "break" or "pause" your script at a specific point, let you examine and change things, and then pick right back up where you left off—an invaluable debugging technique.

Keep Your Eye on the Goal

Remember that the primary goal of debugging is to find out what values and objects are inside your script's variables. Almost all logical errors within a script are the result of you expecting one thing to be in your variables, but PowerShell finding something else. By figuring out what's really going on, and comparing that to your intentions and expectations, you'll be able to quickly spot inconsistencies and correct them.

Chapter 25
The PowerShell Data Language and Internationalization

If you've written a PowerShell script—or indeed, written a script or program in any other language or environment—you're probably accustomed to incorporating string data into your code. For example, the following wouldn't be out of place in a PowerShell script:

```
$un = Read-Host "Enter a user name"
```

However, this combination of code and strings can make your scripts more difficult to manage. If the time comes when you need to—for whatever reason—change "user name" to "network ID," you have to scan through all of your scripts, do a search and replace, and so forth. It's tedious.

PowerShell provides a way to separate data and code through the use of a built-in data language, introduced in PowerShell v2.0. A major use of this feature is to make your scripts easier to localize into other languages; by separating the string literals from your code, a person can more easily translate the string literals into other languages, giving your scripts a more worldly flair.

The DATA Section

The foundation for separating strings and code is PowerShell's DATA section. Note that this is a PowerShell v2.0 feature; scripts using this won't run under earlier versions. You should use a #REQUIRES comment (which we introduced in the chapter, "What's New in Windows PowerShell v2.0") to document scripts as requiring v2.0, and to prevent unpredictable behavior or errors under prior versions.

The DATA section (and a script can have more than one, if needed) contains a specified subset of the PowerShell scripting language. At its simplest, a DATA section consists of the **Data** keyword, a variable name (without the $), and then simple string data. For example:

```
Data PromptUserName {
  "Enter a user name"
}
```

Once defined, simply use the variable **$PromptUserName** (in this example) to access the contents. By placing DATA sections at the beginning of your script (this is required; they must appear before you can use them), you make it easier for translators or other individuals to access this string data, and they're able to easily modify it without touching your code.

Of course, with an example this simplistic, you might wonder why you can't just define a bunch of variables in the usual way:

```
$PromptUserName = "Enter a user name"
```

And you could, for an example this simple. But the DATA section can do a lot more because it can contain not just string data, but a subset of the PowerShell scripting language:

- All operators, except **-match**.
- If, ElseIf, and Else statements.
- Certain automatic variables: $Culture, $UICulture, $True, $False, and $Null.
- Comments.
- Pipelines.
- Statements separated by semicolons.
- Literal values (strings, numbers, arrays, and more).
- Specific cmdlets, such as **ConvertFrom-StringData**.
- Any cmdlet you explicitly permit in the DATA section by using the section's **-supportedCommand** parameter. You can permit any cmdlet that produces only data—that is, fairly simple values. You can also allow functions that produce only data. Use the parameter as follows:

```
Data -supportedCommand Format-XML,Out-String { # Data goes here }
```

ConvertFrom-StringData

A key player in the data language is the **ConvertFrom-StringData** cmdlet, which converts a string that contains one or more "Name=Value" pairs into a hash table. It's specifically designed to be used within DATA sections. You start by defining some string data, in "Name=Value" format, with one pair per line:

```
$sample = @"
Msg1 = This is message one
Msg2 = This is message two
Msg3 = This is message three
"@
```

Notice the use of the @ signs, and the fact that the name=value pairs appear with a single pair per line. With this string data stored in the **$sample** variable, you'd use it like this:

```
ConvertFrom-StringData -stringdata $sample
```

....

It's a Here-String

The syntax we're using—with the @ signs—creates what PowerShell calls a here-string. A here-string can, as we've shown, span multiple lines, and the shell interprets quotation marks within the here-string literally, so that you don't have to escape them or do anything special. PowerShell expands variables within a double-quotation mark here-string, just like with regular strings; in single quotes, it treats variable names literally.

Of course, this is more useful if the resulting hash table is stored in a variable:

```
$hash = ConvertFrom-StringData -stringdata $sample
```

You can then access individual strings using their name:

```
$hash.Msg1
```

So how does this work in a DATA section?

```
Data Prompts {
 ConvertFrom-StringData -stringdata @"
  Prompt001 = The user name is invalid.
  Prompt002 = Please enter a user name.
  Prompt003 = No user name was entered.
"@
}
```

You would then be able to access these prompts using syntax like this:

```
$Prompts.Prompt001
```

This is much more efficient than the first DATA section example, because it permits you to place multiple strings—indeed, all the strings your script might need—in a single DATA section, and then access them via a single variable.

Logic in Data Sections

DATA sections can include basic logical decision-making capability, primarily for the purpose of localization. By checking the value of the built-in **$Culture** variable, you can define different messages based on the language that Windows is currently configured for:

```
Data Prompts {
 If ($culture -eq "en-us") {
  ConvertFrom-StringData @"
   Msg001 = This is message one
   Msg002 = This is message two
  "@
 } elseif ($culture -eq "de-de") {
  ConvertFrom-StringData @"
  Msg001 = Das ist Nachricht eins
```

```
  Msg002 = Das ist Nachricht zwei
 "@
 }
}
```

Accessing Prompts.Msg001 would return "This is message one" on a U.S. English system and "Das ist Nachrict eins" on a German system. This technique is useful when you have only a small number of languages that you need to support—perhaps two or three, to accommodate people working in different offices. Using this technique allows the script to be entirely self-contained; however, a large number of languages (or strings) will cause the script to become pretty large and unwieldy, and harder to maintain in the long term. If you have a larger number of languages or strings to support, consider full-scale internationalization, which we'll cover next.

Full-Scale Internationalization

Internationalization is the concept of creating scripts that have default string values, which you can override by using localized (translated) versions of those strings. Start by defining your script's strings in a data section, using the **ConvertFrom-StringData** cmdlet and Name=Value pairs, as we demonstrated earlier. You should include a comment on a line by itself to indicate what the default language is.

```
Data msgs {
 # culture="en-US"
 ConvertFrom-StringData @"
  Msg001 = This is message one
  Msg002 = This is message two
"@
}
```

For this running example, we'll assume that the script name is Global.ps1. That's important, because now you'll create .ps1d files that contain localized versions of these strings. You'll need to set up a directory structure; assuming Global.ps1 is located in C:\Test, then:

- C:\Test\de-de\Global.ps1d contains German translations.

- C:\Test\ar-SA\Global.ps1d contains Arabic (Saudi Arabia) translations.

And so forth. Each Global.ps1d file contains just the DATA section, with translated strings. For example:

```
Data msgs {
 # culture="de-de"
 ConvertFrom-StringData @"
  Msg001 = Das ist Nachricht eins
  Msg002 = Das ist Nachricht zwei
"@
}
```

To retrieve the correct language when your script runs, you'll use two built-in PowerShell variables and the **Import-LocalizedData** cmdlet. Actually, the cmdlet is smart enough to check the built-in **$UICulture** variable and load the correct file; you basically just need to give it the variable name from your DATA section:

```
Import-LocalizedData –bindingVariable msgs
```

When the script runs, it will examine Windows' current culture information and attempt to locate the correct .ps1d file. If the correct file can't be found, then the default strings included in the script (the English language strings, in our example) will be used.

A downside of this technique is that your script is no longer standalone: You have to distribute a set of .ps1d files with it, and those have to be in the correct folders in order to work. However, for larger scripts that need to support a broader variety of languages, or which use a large number of strings, this technique is easier to maintain in the long term. In addition, companies specializing in string translation are accustomed to receiving and working with files like this, so you'll facilitate the actual translation process.

Tips for the Data Language

Try to get into the habit of using the data language for any script you write that will have a long life—that is, which you'll be keeping and using again and again. If you set up your strings using the **ConvertFrom-StringData** cmdlet as we've shown, you can easily add internationalization at any time, simply by adding the appropriate .ps1d files and calling the **Import-LocalizedData** cmdlet at the start of your script. This makes your scripts more easily shared between international divisions or offices within your organization, and helps give your scripts a longer, more useful life.

Chapter 26
PowerShell for VBScript, Cmd.exe, and *nix Users

PowerShell can seem intimidating for VBScript users and familiar for *nix users—and both types of user would be wrong, in a way! In reality, PowerShell's a lot more like VBScript than you might think (well, in some ways, at least), and although it's definitely inspired by *nix shells, its differences are significant and profound. In this chapter, we'll try to address some of the most common "migration points" that come up as folks start to learn PowerShell.

If You're Used to VBScript...

Let's quickly clear up a potential point of confusion: There's no easy, set way to convert a VBScript to a PowerShell script. But why would you want to? If the VBScript works, keep it! After all, VBScript isn't going anywhere. However, in this chapter we will present a sort of "jump-start" guide to PowerShell using VBScript as a basis. That way, if you *do* know VBScript, you'll be able to start writing *new* scripts in PowerShell a bit more quickly. So, this chapter is about converting *you* to PowerShell, not your scripts.

Let's begin by acknowledging that PowerShell is *very* different from VBScript. You *will* need to learn new technologies and concepts to use PowerShell effectively. However, there are some similarities, especially in PowerShell's scripting language, that can be a bit easier to learn if you see them side by side with their VBScript counterparts. So, in this chapter we'll cover the similarities between PowerShell and VBScript.

As we begin, keep in mind that PowerShell is a *management* shell. It isn't intended for logon scripts (although it can definitely be used as a logon script processor), so there are a lot of topics, such as mapping drives and checking for group membership, that we will not cover in this chapter. PowerShell's best use is not as a logon script processor. For the time being, stick with VBScript or KiXtart for those scripts.

Perhaps most importantly is that PowerShell works in a way that is radically different from VBScript. So, we don't want you to try and "convert" your VBScript code to PowerShell. In fact if your VBScript tools work you can continue to use them. But if you feel you must rework them, *rewrite* these scripts from scratch using PowerShell's unique, and often easier, way of doing things.

Variables

PowerShell variables do *not* need to be declared up front. That's true in VBScript, except VBScript *does* give you the option of doing so, while PowerShell does not. However, explicit variable declaration is *always* optional in PowerShell.

Variables in PowerShell, like those in VBScript, can contain any type of data. In VBScript, this is done by making all variables the Variant type. In PowerShell, variables are the more generic Object type. Unlike in VBScript, you can tell PowerShell to force a variable to be of a certain type:

```
[string]$var = "hello"
```

This creates a new variable, **$var**, and forces it to be a string. Notice that all variable names being with **$**. Apart from that, PowerShell variable naming rules are similar to the rules in VBScript.

Variable naming in VBScript typically uses Hungarian notation, where a three-letter prefix such as obj, str, or int is used to denote the type of data the variable is intended to hold. PowerShell does not require this. In fact, when working with PowerShell this isn't considered a best practice. However, you're welcome to name your variables in this fashion if you're accustomed to doing so.

COM Objects

If you've used VBScript, KiXtart, or any similar scripting language for Windows administration, at some point you've almost certainly used a Component Object Model (COM) component. Windows is built on COM, and COM objects provide significant functionality for files, folders, WMI, and much more. Scripting without COM would be almost unthinkable.

However, PowerShell isn't built on COM; instead it's built on the .NET Framework. The Framework replaces *much* of the functionality you may have used COM for, but not *all*. As a result, there's often still a need to utilize an old COM component. Sometimes, that need might simply be that you know how to do something using a particular COM component and you don't have time to learn an alternative way in PowerShell. Fortunately, PowerShell includes an adaptation layer that permits you to utilize COM components.

Instantiating Objects

If you've used VBScript, you may be familiar with syntax like this:

```
Dim objFSO
Set objFSO = CreateObject("Scripting.FileSystemObject")
```

In VBScript, this statement instantiates a COM component having the ProgID Scripting. FileSystemObject. When executed, VBScript asks Windows to instantiate the component. In turn, Windows looks up the ProgID in the registry to locate the actual DLL involved, loads the DLL into memory, and plugs it into the script. The variable **objFSO** represents the running DLL, providing an interface for working with it.

PowerShell can do nearly the same thing:

```
$fso = new-object -COM Scripting.FileSystemObject
```

Using the same ProgID, PowerShell can instantiate the COM object and assign it to a variable so you can work with it. Notice the **-COM** parameter, which is easy to forget. However, if you don't include it, PowerShell will not be able to "find" the COM object and instantiate it for you.

Using Objects

Once instantiated, using a COM object's properties and methods is straightforward:

```
$file = $fso.OpenTextFile("C:\file.txt",8,True)
```

You can even pipe the COM object to the **Get-Member** cmdlet to see the available properties and methods of a COM object:

```
PS C:\> $fso | get-member
```

```
  TypeName: System.__ComObject#{2a0b9d10-4b87-11d3-a97a-00104b365c9

Name                    MemberType  Definition
----                    ----------  ----------
BuildPath               Method       string BuildPath (string, string)
CopyFile                Method       void CopyFile (string, string, bool)
CopyFolder              Method       void CopyFolder (string, string, bool
CreateFolder            Method       IFolder CreateFolder (string)
CreateTextFile          Method       ITextStream CreateTextFile (string, b
DeleteFile              Method       void DeleteFile (string, bool)
DeleteFolder            Method       void DeleteFolder (string, bool)
DriveExists             Method       bool DriveExists (string)
FileExists              Method       bool FileExists (string)
FolderExists            Method       bool FolderExists (string)
GetAbsolutePathName     Method       string GetAbsolutePathName (string)
GetBaseName             Method       string GetBaseName (string)
GetDrive                Method       IDrive GetDrive (string)
GetDriveName            Method       string GetDriveName (string)
GetExtensionName        Method       string GetExtensionName (string)
GetFile                 Method       IFile GetFile (string)
GetFileName             Method       string GetFileName (string)
GetFileVersion          Method       string GetFileVersion (string)
GetFolder               Method       IFolder GetFolder (string)
GetParentFolderName     Method       string GetParentFolderName (string)
GetSpecialFolder        Method       IFolder GetSpecialFolder (SpecialFold
GetStandardStream       Method       ITextStream GetStandardStream (Standa
GetTempName             Method       string GetTempName ()
MoveFile                Method       void MoveFile (string, string)
MoveFolder              Method       void MoveFolder (string, string)
OpenTextFile            Method       ITextStream OpenTextFile (string, IOM
Drives                  Property    IDriveCollection Drives () {get}
```

However, there's an important caveat here. PowerShell creates this list by looking at the COM object's type library that is either embedded in the DLL or included in a separate TLB file. If PowerShell can't find the type library, then *it can't use the COM component*. Most COM components come with type libraries, especially the COM components written by Microsoft. However, some COM components don't have a type library, or if they do, the type library isn't properly registered with Windows. In these cases, the COM component won't be usable within PowerShell.

In addition, if a type library is *wrong*, which happens occasionally, PowerShell may not be able to utilize the entire COM object. For example, the Microsoft-supplied type library for the WshController COM object provides an incorrect spelling for the Execute method. This makes the object difficult to use properly. However, in the case of this particular object, there's little reason to use it inside PowerShell.

GetObject

Another way you may have used COM in VBScript was with the **GetObject()** method, which often connects to an existing object or service. In VBScript, you could do this:

```
Set objUser = GetObject("WinNT://don-pc/administrator,user")
```

This example uses the ADSI WinNT provider to retrieve the local administrator user.

Using the **GetObject()** method in PowerShell is a bit more difficult. Unfortunately, PowerShell doesn't have a cmdlet that does exactly this. In fact, PowerShell doesn't even provide a cmdlet for ADSI; instead, as outlined in the "Using ADSI in Windows PowerShell" chapter, you use the [ADSI] type accelerator, which works similarly to **GetObject()** in VBScript. Had this **GetObject()** example been for WMI, we could use the **Get-WmiObject** cmdlet instead. In some cases, WMI offers an alternative to what you were doing in ADSI (especially with member and standalone computers), although certainly not always (as with domain controllers).

Comments

VBScript uses a single quote (') to begin a comment, while PowerShell uses the hash (#) symbol.

Loops and Constructs

As illustrated in the following table, there's nearly a one-to-one correspondence between VBScript and PowerShell constructs:

In VBScript...	In PowerShell...
Exit Do, Exit For	Break
For...Next	For
For Each...Next	Foreach
Function	Function
Sub	(no equivalent; use Function)
If...Then	If
If...ElseIf...Else	If, ElseIf, and Else
Select...Case	Switch
Do...Loop Until, Do Until...Loop	Do...until, Do until
Do...Loop While, Do While...Loop	Do...While, While

Refer to the chapter "Loops and Decision-making Constructs" to review the discussion of these loops and constructs.

Type Conversion

VBScript provides a number of specific functions to convert between data types including **CStr()**, **CInt()**, and **CDate()**. PowerShell uses a single operator, **-as**, to do the same thing:

```
$var = $var2 -as [string]
```

This example attempts to convert **$var2** into a string and store the result in **$var**. Refer to the "Variables, Arrays, and Escape Characters" chapter for more information on variables and types.

Operators and Special Values

In many cases, PowerShell uses different operators than VBScript, and it uses some operators differently. The following table provides a summary of these operators:

In VBScript...	Purpose...	In PowerShell...
=	Assignment	=
=	Equality test	-eq
>	Greater than	-gt
<	Less than	-lt
>=	Greater than or equal to	-ge
<=	Less than or equal to	-le
True	Boolean True	$true
False	Boolean False	$false
AND	Boolean AND	-and
NOT	Boolean NOT	-not
OR	Boolean OR	-or
AND	Binary AND	-band
OR	Binary OR	-bor
NOT	Binary NOT	-bnot
&, +	String concatenation	+

Refer to the chapter "Operators" to review the discussion of the additional operators offered in PowerShell.

Functions and Subs

VBScript and PowerShell declare functions similarly. Here's a function in VBScript that returns TRUE if the input parameter is more than 5; otherwise, it returns FALSE:

```
Function IsMoreThan5 (intValue)
  If intValue > 5 Then
    IsMoreThan5 = True
  Else
    IsMoreThan5 = False
  End if
End Function
```

Notice that VBScript returns a value by setting the function name equal to the return value. PowerShell works similarly:

```
Function IsMoreThan5 {
 Param([int]$value)
 If ($Value -gt 5) {
   Return $true
 } Else {
   Return $false
 }
}
```

Notice that PowerShell uses the **Return** keyword to return the function's value. In fact, PowerShell will append *any* output of the function to the return value. The following is functionally identical:

```
Function IsMoreThan5 {
 Param([int]$Value)
 If ($Value -gt 5) {
   $true
 } Else {
   $false
 }
}
```

This example shows that outputting **$true** or **$false** into the pipeline makes those values the function's return value. You don't need to use the Return key word at all. Refer to the "Script Blocks, Functions, Filters, Snap-ins, and Modules" chapter to review the discussion of how functions have significantly expanded capabilities in PowerShell.

PowerShell does not provide a separate Sub construct as VBScript does. However, a Function that returns no value is essentially the same as a Sub.

Error Handling

VBScript uses its **On Error Resume Next** statement, and the corresponding **On Error Goto 0** statement, to implement error handling. Essentially, you execute **On Error Resume Next** before any operation that may result in an error, and then check the special **Err** object to see if an error did indeed occur. VBScript's error handling is actually quite primitive, while PowerShell's is much more advanced.

In brief, you declare a *trap*, which is what PowerShell executes when an error occurs (or an *exception* is *thrown*). You do whatever you need to do within the trap, and then tell PowerShell to either **continue**, which resumes execution on the line following whatever line caused the exception, or **break**, which halts execution. For example:

```
Trap {
 # handle error here
 Continue
}
```

Refer to the "Error Handling" chapter to review the discussion of how to define different trap handlers for different types of exceptions.

Windows Management Instrumentation

This is an easy point of conversion. Any time you used **GetObject()** or some other means of retrieving WMI information, just use the **Get-WmiObject** cmdlet or its convenient alias, **Gwmi**, in PowerShell. However, notice that just running it with a class name won't return every property of the class by default:

```
PS C:\> gwmi win32_operatingsystem
```

```
SystemDirectory : C:\WINDOWS\system32
Organization    : SAPIEN Technologies, Inc.
BuildNumber     : 2600
RegisteredUser  : Don Jones
SerialNumber    : 76487-338-1820253-22242
Version         : 5.1.2600
```

Notice that this doesn't return every property for the class. Instead, the properties shown are defined by a special *view* within PowerShell. While you can update that view to list more properties, you can also use the -**Property** parameter if there's a specific property you need:

```
PS C:\> gwmi win32_operatingsystem -property buildnumber
```

```
BuildNumber      : 2600
__GENUS          : 2
__CLASS          : Win32_OperatingSystem
__SUPERCLASS     :
__DYNASTY        :
__RELPATH        :
__PROPERTY_COUNT : 1
__DERIVATION     : {}
__SERVER         :
__NAMESPACE      :
__PATH           :
```

If necessary, you can assign that to a variable. However, notice that you get back a collection of multiple instances that you can refer to individually by number, as shown here:

```
PS C:\> $obj = gwmi win32_logicaldisk
PS C:\> $obj[0]
```

```
DeviceID     : A:
DriveType    : 2
ProviderName :
FreeSpace    :
Size         :
VolumeName   :
```

```
PS C:\> $obj[1]
```

```
DeviceID     : C:
DriveType    : 3
ProviderName :
FreeSpace    : 91841773568
Size         : 153006624768
VolumeName   :
```

If you just need a specific property from an instance:

```
PS C:\> $obj[1].DriveType
3
```

355

Run **Help Gwmi** to get a comprehensive list of parameters.

Active Directory Services Interface

It's unfortunate that PowerShell doesn't come with a built-in "Get-ADSIObject" cmdlet. You *can* use WMI to perform some ADSI queries. You *can* also use the underlying .NET Framework directory services classes, and the [ADSI] type accelerator to manipulate AD. There are two chapters you can review for some examples of what you *can* do in PowerShell with ADSI: "Using ADSI in Windows PowerShell" and "Managing Directory Services." For now, however, you may want to continue using VBScript for more complex ADSI-related tasks.

Common Tasks in VBScript

You are probably familiar with the VBScript items listed below. Therefore, we'll quickly point out how to do nearly the same thing in PowerShell:

- **WScript.Echo:** For producing output to the command line, use the **Write-Host** cmdlet.

- **MsgBox(), InputBox():** No direct analog in PowerShell, since it's intended to be entirely command-line driven. Use the **Read-Host** cmdlet to accept input from the command line.

- **WMI:** Use **Get-WmiObject**.

- **Working with text files:** Refer to the "Managing Files and Folders" chapter. Several PowerShell cmdlets are available to manipulate text files. The basic technique is to read the entire file into an object, and then enumerate through each line of the file as a child object.

- **ADSI:** Tricky because there's not a direct equivalent in PowerShell. However, refer to the discussion earlier in this book for information on how to work with ADSI. You'll primarily use the [ADSI] type accelerator, which will accept the same ADSI queries that you used with **GetObject()** in VBScript.

- **Working with the registry:** Review the "Managing the Registry" chapter for more information. PowerShell provides a registry "drive" and cmdlets for working with the registry.

PowerShell Paradigm Change

Probably the biggest mental leap you can make when moving from VBScript to PowerShell is that PowerShell is intended to deal with *objects* and not text. That's all well and good in theory, but it can be a confusing concept to implement until you get used to it. For example, look at ServicePack.vbs, which is a VBScript script that reads a list of names from C:\Computers.txt (one name per line) and uses WMI to display the service pack version for each:

ServicePack.vbs

```
Dim strFile
strFile = "C:\computers.txt"

Dim objFSO, objTS, strComputer
Set objFSO = CreateObject("Scripting.FileSystemObject")
If objFSO.FileExists(strFile) Then
    Set objTS = objFSO.OpenTextFile(strFile)
    Do Until objTS.AtEndOfStream
        strComputer = objTS.ReadLine

        Dim objWMI
```

```
        Set objWMI = GetObject("winmgmts:\\" & strComputer & _
        "\root\cimv2")

        Dim colResults, objResult, strWMIQuery

        strWMIQuery = "SELECT * FROM Win32_OperatingSystem"
        Set colResults = objWMI.ExecQuery(strWMIQuery)
        For Each objResult In colResults
            WScript.Echo strComputer & ":" & _
             objResult.ServicePackMajorVersion
        Next

    Loop
End If

objTS.Close
WScript.Echo "Complete"
```

As mentioned previously, you're probably familiar enough with VBScript to follow what this script is doing. However, take time to notice the methodology. Each time through the **Do** loop, the script reads a line from the text file, which is assumed to be a computer name. VBScript creates a WMI connection to that computer and retrieves the Win32_OperatingSystem class. For each instance of the class, a loop displays the ServicePackMajorVersion property.

Now look at ServicePack.ps1, which does the same thing:

ServicePack.ps1

```
$names = get-content "c:\computers.txt"
foreach ($name in $names) {
 $wmi = Get-WmiObject win32_operatingsystem -property servicepackmajorversion  -computer $name
 $sp = $wmi.servicepackmajorversion
 write-host "$name : $sp"
}
```

First of all, notice how much shorter this is! It actually could be shorter, but we wrote it more for clarity than brevity. Again, the *real* thing to notice is the methodology. You use the **Get-Content** cmdlet to retrieve the entire contents of the text file into **$names**, all in one step. A **ForEach** loop goes through each child item (or line) of the text file, pulling each child item into **$name**. The **Get-WmiObject** cmdlet retrieves just the desired property, placing the class instance into **$wmi**. You use the **$sp** variable to hold the actual property in which we're interested. You use the **Write-Host** cmdlet to output the information to the screen.

Keep in mind that, where VBScript typically requires something to be done in a particular way, PowerShell is a lot more flexible. ServicePack2.ps1 demonstrates the same script, from a different approach:

ServicePack2.ps1

```
filter getversion {
 $wmi = Get-WmiObject win32_operatingsystem -property servicepackmajorversion -computer $_
 $sp = $wmi.servicepackmajorversion
 write-host "$_  : $sp"
}

get-content "c:\computers.txt" | getversion
```

Here, you pipe the content of the text file to "getversion", which is a custom filter. This filter is called once for each object or line of text in the text file. The special **$_** variable refers to the current object, which would be a single computer name. ServicePack3.ps1 simplifies this even further:

ServicePack3.ps1

```
filter getversion {
 $wmi = Get-WmiObject win32_operatingsystem -property servicepackmajorversion -computer $_
 write-host "$_ : " $wmi.servicepackmajorversion
}
get-content "c:\computers.txt" | getversion
```

All that's been done here is to remove the **$sp** variable. We did this because **$wmi.servicepackmajorversion** is now output directly, which removes a line of code. You could simplify this even further. However, the VBScript example we started with has been simplified about as much as possible.

Getting used to PowerShell's way of working with objects takes some time. However, if you make the effort, these examples have demonstrated how much more quickly you can produce usable administrative scripts.

If You're Used to Cmd.exe

By and large, almost everything you know and do in Cmd.exe works the same in Windows PowerShell, so jump right in and start working! There are, of course, exceptions, which can be frustrating as you're getting started.

First, remember that PowerShell uses a space to separate elements of a command. So, consider this command from Cmd.exe:

```
C:\Test\> cd..
```

It isn't legal in PowerShell. Instead, you have to use this syntax, with a space between the command (or rather, the alias) and the argument:

```
PS C:\> cd ..
```

Spaces in file and folder paths can be frustrating, too. Simply remember to enclose them in quotes using one of the following methods:

- Enclose portions of a path that contain a space in quotation marks, as in cd \"program files"\ sapien.

- Use a backtick to escape the spaces, as in cd \program` files\sapien.

- Enclose the entire path in quotation marks, as in cd "\program files\sapien".

Which method you use is up to you. Also remember that whenever PowerShell sees a space followed by a dash, it assumes that you're giving it a command-line argument. That can be a problem sometimes, so you may need to enclose things in quotation marks to force PowerShell to behave in a certain way.

Perhaps the most useful utility for troubleshooting comes with the free PowerShell Community Extensions (http://www.codeplex.com/PowerShellCX): Echoargs.exe. This handy external utility will accept a command line and tell you how PowerShell interpreted it. Be sure to check it out if you're having difficulty getting a particular Cmd.exe-style command line to run properly from PowerShell.

For

In the CMD.exe shell, you can use the FOR command to process a text file or the results of a command. As an example, you might have an expression like this:

```
C:\>for /f %s in (servers.txt) do @wmic /node:%s os get csname,caption
```

This expression will go through the servers.txt file, presumably a list of server names, and then use Windows Management Instrumentation Command Line (WMIC) to return the caption from OS, which is an alias for the Win32_OperatingSystem class and the server name.

In PowerShell, you will use the **ForEach-Object** cmdlet. In this particular scenario, you will also use the **Get-WmiObject** cmdlet:

```
PS C:\>foreach ($s in (get-content servers.txt)) {
>> Get-WmiObject win32_operatingsystem -computer $s | format-table CSName,Caption -auto
>> }
>>
```

This will work, but in PowerShell you can simplify this further:

```
PS C:\>Get-WmiObject win32_operatingsystem -computer (get-content servers.txt) |
>> Format-Table CSName,Caption -auto
```

In this example, the **ForEach** cmdlet is implied by:

```
(get-content servers.txt)
```

PowerShell understands that the **Get-Content** cmdlet is returning an array of strings and will automatically enumerate the array when used in this context.

Often, administrators need to parse out files:

```
C:\>for /f "tokens=1,2 delims=," %t in (tasks.csv) do @echo %t= %u
```

This example gets the first and second element of each line in tasks.csv, using the comma as the delimiter. In PowerShell, you would achieve the same result with an expression like this:

```
PS C:\> foreach ($line in (get-content tasks.csv)) {$a=$line.split(",");$a[0]+" = "+$a[1]}
```

As we did earlier, we're getting each line of the file, but instead of displaying it, we're using the **Split()** method, specifying the comma as the delimiter to create a temporary array:

```
{$a=$line.split(",")
```

In PowerShell, the first array element starts at 0, so to display the first two elements we use code like this:

```
$a[0]+" = "+$a[1]
```

Working with Environment Variables

Not only does PowerShell have its own variables, but it can also access environment variables through the Environment provider. To retrieve all environment variables in a CMD.exe shell, you would type:

```
C:\> set
```

In PowerShell, you can use the **DIR** command because the Environment provider presents the variables as a drive:

```
PS C:\> dir env:
```

To reference a specific environment variable, use syntax like this:

```
PS C:\> $env:windir
C:\WINDOWS
```

You can modify the environment variables or even add new ones, but they won't change environment variables in your CMD.exe shell nor will they be seen outside of PowerShell. You need to modify the registry if you want to make permanent changes. Once your PowerShell session terminates, environment variable changes will also terminate.

"If" Comparisons

In the CMD.exe shell, the **If** statement is used frequently, especially in batch files. PowerShell also has an **If** statement that is not too dissimilar. Let's look at some of the ways you use **If** in a CMD.exe shell and the corresponding PowerShell equivalent.

One common usage in a CMD.exe session is to check for the existence of a file:

```
C:\> if exist %windir%\notepad.exe echo Found Notepad
```

In PowerShell:

```
PS C:\> if (dir $env:windir\notepad.exe) {write-host "Found Notepad"}
```

If the **Dir** command is successful, the If statement will be TRUE and PowerShell will execute the **Write-Host** script block.

In the CMD.exe shell, you might also have taken this to the next step:

```
C:\>if exist %windir%\notepad.exe (echo Found Notepad) ELSE echo Notepad not found
```

The PowerShell syntax is very similar:

```
PS C:\> if (dir $env:windir\notepad.exe) {write-host "Found Notepad"
>> } else {
>> write-host "Notepad not found"
>> }
>>
```

This code works fine when Notepad.exe exists, but if it doesn't, PowerShell will generate an error and the last part of the If statement will never run. To instruct PowerShell to continue so that your error handling will work, run this command first:

```
PS C:\> $erroractionpreference="SilentlyContinue"
```

This instructs PowerShell to ignore any error and continue. To change back to PowerShell's default, use this command:

```
PS C:\> $erroractionpreference="Continue"
```

There is more information on using If in PowerShell "Loops and Decision-making Constructs" chapter.

If You're Used to *nix

UNIX and Linux variants are *so* geared to text-based operations that they can take an act of will to wrench your mind out of the text-based way of doing things. The two most common questions we're asked from *nix administrators is whether PowerShell has something like grep or awk—two text-parsing utilities that every *nix administrator relies upon as heavily as they do the oxygen they breathe. PowerShell does *not* have these utilities, because it does not *need* these utilities; PowerShell offers a profoundly better way of performing tasks that doesn't require text parsing. Because PowerShell often "looks" so much like a *nix shell (PowerShell was, after all, inspired by shells like Bash), *nix administrators subconsciously start applying their *nix know-how to the tasks they need to accomplish in PowerShell. If you find yourself doing that, stop and think about the *PowerShell* way to accomplish the task—using objects.

For example, we're often asked if there's a way to grep the output of the **Get-Alias** cmdlet in order to locate all the available aliases for a given cmdlet. That's a classically *nix way of attacking the problem: You have a command that produces a list of aliases and their corresponding cmdlets, so you parse that text output looking for a specific cmdlet name—thus, locating all the aliases in the process.

But remember that things are different in PowerShell. An alias or a cmdlet, creates an object, complete with properties and methods. The output of the **Get-Alias** cmdlet *is not text:* It is a collection of Alias objects. Piping one to the **Get-Member** cmdlet reveals its properties:

```
PS C:\> get-alias | get-member


   TypeName: System.Management.Automation.AliasInfo

Name                   MemberType   Definition
----                   ----------   ----------
Equals                 Method       System.Boolean Equals(Object obj)
GetHashCode            Method       System.Int32 GetHashCode()
GetType                Method       System.Type GetType()
get_CommandType        Method       System.Management.Automation.CommandTypes get_Com...
get_Definition         Method       System.String get_Definition()
get_Description        Method       System.String get_Description()
get_Name               Method       System.String get_Name()
get_Options            Method       System.Management.Automation.ScopedItemOptions ge...
get_ReferencedCommand  Method       System.Management.Automation.CommandInfo get_Refe...
get_ResolvedCommand    Method       System.Management.Automation.CommandInfo get_Reso...
set_Description        Method       System.Void set_Description(String value)
set_Options            Method       System.Void set_Options(ScopedItemOptions value)
ToString               Method       System.String ToString()
```

```
CommandType          Property       System.Management.Automation.CommandTypes Command...
Definition           Property       System.String Definition {get;}
Description          Property       System.String Description {get;set;}
Name                 Property       System.String Name {get;}
Options              Property       System.Management.Automation.ScopedItemOptions Op...
ReferencedCommand    Property       System.Management.Automation.CommandInfo Referenc...
ResolvedCommand      Property       System.Management.Automation.CommandInfo Resolved...
ResolvedCommandName  ScriptProperty System.Object ResolvedCommandName {get=$this.Reso...
```

Hmm, the ResolvedCommandName property might contain the name of the cmdlet that the alias resolves to. Let's test it by examining an alias to see what that property contains:

```
PS C:\> $aliases = get-alias
PS C:\> $aliases[0].resolvedcommandname
Add-Content
```

Sure enough! So, if we're looking for aliases of the **Get-ChildItem** cmdlet, for example, we could simply filter on the ResolvedCommandName property as follows:

```
PS C:\> get-alias | where { $_.ResolvedCommandName -eq "Get-ChildItem" }

CommandType    Name            Definition
-----------    ----            ----------
Alias          gci             Get-ChildItem
Alias          ls              Get-ChildItem
Alias          dir             Get-ChildItem
```

Easy enough, and we didn't have to parse any text at all. Instead, we just used the objects' native properties.

Some *nix admins may wonder: What if I needed to find every instance of an object—say, a service—where one of the properties contains a specific substring? I don't know if what I'm looking for will be in the Name or DisplayName properties, for example, and I don't know the complete string I'm after, only a substring. Still not a problem—and still no need for something like grep:

```
PS C:\> get-service | where { $_.Name -like "*Wind*" -or $_.DisplayName -like "*Wind*" }

Status  Name              DisplayName
------  ----              -----------
Running AudioEndpointBu... Windows Audio Endpoint Builder
Running Audiosrv          Windows Audio
Running Eventlog          Windows Event Log
Stopped FontCache3.0.0.0  Windows Presentation Foundation Fon...
Stopped idsvc             Windows CardSpace
Running MpsSvc            Windows Firewall
Stopped msiserver         Windows Installer
Stopped QWAVE             Quality Windows Audio Video Experience
Stopped SDRSVC            Windows Backup
```

It's unlikely that you'd ever need to do a search like this across *all* of an object's properties; bear in mind how many different properties exist, and how few of them actually contain text strings like this. In addition, because we're not just working with text, the output of the above command *is actual Service objects*, meaning they have methods like Stop and Start. So, once you've got the services you want, you don't have to re-parse the output of grep to do something to those services: You've already got the actual services to work with!

In general, anytime you're approaching a problem and thinking: "How can I parse this text to get what

I want?" Stop yourself and instead ask: "What's an object-oriented way to do this so that I don't have to parse any text at all?" As you educate yourself about more and more of PowerShell's abilities, you're likely to discover easier and more efficient ways to accomplish many tasks (at least on Windows-based systems).

Chapter 27
Best Practices for Scripting

Now we come to the "Best Practices" chapter, a chapter that no self-respecting book on coding can be without. Please understand that, in administrative scripting, there are no points (or at least very few points) for style; that said, these best practices are intended to help make your scripts easier to read, easier to write, easier to maintain, and easier to debug. Feel free to use, modify, or disregard these practices as desired!

Script Formatting

Apart from PowerShell's own basic formatting requirements—primarily that functions must appear in your script *before* you can call those functions—we simply recommend that you keep your scripts neat-looking. Here's how we recommend that you format functions, loops, and other constructs for clarity:

```
If ($x -eq 5) {
        # code
        # code
}
```

Notice that we've put the construct's starting { curly brace on the same line as the construct's opening keyword; the code within the construct is indented, and the construct's closing } curly brace is on its own line, vertically aligned with the start of the construct's opening keyword.

This formatting technique helps you visually identify constructs, the code within the construct, and visually verify that the construct has been properly closed.

We also recommend including a blank line before each construct's first line. This helps to visually separate the construct and makes your script easier to read.

Comments

PowerShell uses the # character to start a comment line, and we *strongly* recommend commenting your scripts. We offer the following recommendations:

- Start your script with several comments that provide your name, the version of the script, and its overall purpose.

- Place a comment before each construct, indicating what the construct is doing. In multi-part constructs, including a comment within each part indicating what that part does. For example:

```
# Check to see if $x contains the key value 5
If ($x -eq 5) {

        # $x does contain 5
        # more code goes here
} else {

        # $x does not contain 5
        # more code goes here
}
```

- Place a comment before each cmdlet used, indicating in a general sense what you're doing. For example:

```
# Retrieve the logical disk WMI class
$wmi = Get-WmiObject win32_logicaldisk
```

Proper use of comments can make your scripts easier to read for someone else—or for *you*, several months later, when you've forgotten exactly why you wrote the script the way you did.

Internal Documentation

PowerShell provides a way for your scripts to internally document any dependencies, using a special #REQUIRES comment. It should be the first line in your script, and looks something like this:

```
#REQUIRES -version 2.0
#REQUIRES -pssnapin pscx
# Your code begins here
```

The #REQUIRES comment allows you to specify the version of the shell that your script was written for—v2.0 in this example—as well as any PSSnapIns that are required for your script to run—here, we've specified the PowerShell Community Extensions by specifying their snap-in name, "pscx." You can even specify a specific version of a snap-in:

```
#REQUIRES -version 2.0
#REQUIRES -pssnapin pscx -version 1.1
# Your code begins here
```

Note that you can include as many #REQUIRES comments as necessary to document your script's dependencies. This is a great idea, and you should make a habit of using it in *all* of your scripts—even those which only require core PowerShell snap-ins. Other administrators will be able to easily see what snap-ins and shell versions are needed, and if necessary can look up the snap-ins in the cmdlet directory at www.PowerShellCommunity.org to find out where to obtain a needed snap-in.

Script and Function Naming

Although we don't follow this suggestion in many of the examples in this book (primarily for clarity when we're trying to make a quick point), we do agree with the PowerShell team's overall recommendation that scripts and functions follow cmdlet-style naming conventions. That is, use a *verb-noun* naming syntax, where nouns are singular ("Get-Process", not "Get-Processes"), and where verbs are selected from the official verb list:

Common Verbs

- **Add:** Adds a resource to a container or attaches an element to another element (use with Remove).
- **Clear:** Removes all elements from a container.
- **Copy:** Copies a resource to another name or another container.
- **Get:** Retrieves data (use with Set).
- **Hide:** Makes not visible (use with Show).
- **Invoke:** Introduces or puts into operation.
- **Join:** Joins two or more resources (use with Split).
- **Lock:** Locks a resource (use with Unlock).
- **Move:** Moves a resource.
- **New:** Creates a new resource.
- **Remove:** Removes a resource from a container (use with Add).
- **Rename:** Renames a resource.
- **Select:** Identifies a subset of resources.
- **Set:** Places some data (use with Get).
- **Show:** Makes visible (use with Hide).
- **Split:** Splits a resource (use with Join).
- **Unlock:** Unlocks a resource (use with Lock).
- **Wait:** Remains inactive until something expected happens.

Communications Verbs

- **Connect:** Connects to a resource (use with Disconnect).
- **Disconnect:** Detaches from a resource (use with Connect).
- **Read:** Reads from a connected resource (use with Write).
- **Receive:** Acquires information from a connected resource (use with Send).
- **Send:** Writes information to a destination (use with Receive).
- **Write:** Writes information to a target (use with Read).

Data Verbs

- **Backup:** Backs up data.

- **Checkpoint:** Creates a snapshot of the current state or configuration (use with Restore).

- **Compare:** Compares two resources and shows a set of differences.

- **Convert:** Changes data into a specific format or encoding.

- **ConvertFrom:** Changes data from one format to another, where the source format is described by the noun (e.g., ConvertFrom-Unicode); use Import if the data will be copied from a persistent storage form such as a file.

- **ConvertTo:** Changes data from one format to another, where the destination format is described by the noun (e.g., ConvertTo-HTML); use Export if the data will be copied to a persistent storage form such as a file.

- **Dismount:** Detaches an entity from a path.

- **Export:** Copies a set of resources to a persistent data store, such as a file.

- **Import:** Creates a set of resources from a persistent data store, such as a file.

- **Initialize:** Prepares a resource for use.

- **Limit:** Limits the consumption of or applies a constraint to a resource.

- **Merge:** Combines resources into a single unit.

- **Mount:** Attaches an entity to a path.

- **Out:** Sends data out of the environment.

- **Publish:** Makes known to another (use with Unpublish).

- **Restore:** Rolls back the data state to a predefined set of conditions (use with Checkpoint).

- **Unpublish:** Makes unknown to another (use with Publish).

- **Update:** Updates or refreshes a resource.

Diagnostic Verbs

- **Debug:** Examines an operation or diagnoses a problem.

- **Measure:** Retrieves statistics or identifies resources consumption.

- **Ping:** Determines if a resource is responding to requests.

- **Resolve:** Translates a shorthand name into its proper, full name.

- **Test:** Verifies an operation or consistency.

- **Trace:** Tracks activity.

Lifecycle Verbs

- **Disable:** Makes something unavailable (use with Enable).

- **Enable:** Makes something available or active (use with Disable).

- **Install:** Places resources in a location and initializes them (use with Uninstall).

- **Restart:** Resumes operation (use with Suspend).

- **Start:** Starts an activity (use with Stop).

- **Stop:** Stops an activity (use with Start).

- **Suspend:** Pauses an operation (use with Resume).

- **Uninstall:** Removes resources and de-initializes them (use with Install).

Security Verbs

- **Block:** Prevents access to a resource (use with Unblock).

- **Grant:** Allows access to a resource (use with Revoke).

- **Revoke:** Removes access to a resource (use with Grant).

- **Unblock:** Permits access to a resource (use with Block).

Stay Up-to-Date!
The official list of allowed verbs is published in the PowerShell Software Development Kit, located at http://msdn2.microsoft.com/en-us/library/ms714428.aspx.

Parameter Declaration

Although PowerShell is fairly flexible in how you declare parameters (arguments) for functions, we definitely prefer the use of a Param() block. For example, rather than this:

```
Function MyFunction($arg1, $arg2) {
}
```

We suggest:

```
Function MyFunction {
    Param (
        [int]$arg1 = 5,
        [string]$arg2 = "Hello"
        )
}
```

There are several reasons for this. First and foremost, this is the *only* way to declare input parameters for a *script* (and the Param() block must begin on the script's first line), and so using this technique for functions provides better consistency. Second, we think this method is easier to read, making functions more self-documenting.

You'll notice that we also provided a specific data type for each argument, and provided a default value for each—two additional best practices that can save you a great deal of debugging time, and which we heartily recommend that you *always* follow.

Functions vs. Filters

A filter really isn't that different from a function. For example, this:

```
Filter Test1 {
    $_.Name
```

```
}
```

is functionally identical to this:

```
Function Test1 {
      PROCESS {
              $_.Name
              }
}
```

We prefer using a function with a PROCESS script block over filters. Our first reason is that functions can provide additional capabilities in the form of BEGIN and END blocks; filters cannot. Our second reason is that since you can get all the functionality you need from a function, why not just use them consistently for everything? We also think the use of the PROCESS script block is visually clearer, and is equivalent to the syntax of the **ForEach-Next** cmdlet (which uses **-process**, **-begin**, and **-end** parameters to accomplish something similar). Again, visual clarity and consistency are driving forces behind many of our best practices recommendations.

Variable Naming

PowerShell doesn't enforce many restrictions on variable names, and in a simple script, you probably don't need to either. Use variable names which are visually meaningful—**$computername**, for example, rather than **$c**—but otherwise, don't worry much about the names.

In more complicated scripts, however, you might find a naming convention that provides a clue as to a variable's scope to be useful. For example, a short prefix on each variable name can help make script- and function-scope variables more visually obvious, and help prevent you from accidentally using the exact same variable name in a nested scope (which, as we discussed in the "Scripting Overview" chapter, can cause unexpected behavior). For example:

- $s_computername represents a script-level variable.

- $l_computername represents a variable declared within a script's child scope, such as a function or filter.

- $l2_computername might be a variable that exists within a nested function—that is, a function nested within another function.

There are no formal rules for this, and you should definitely adopt a naming practice that works for you. Having *some* kind of system in place can make it easier to keep track of what variables go where.

Similarly, it can be useful to develop a naming scheme that indicates what type of data a variable holds. Here are some suggestions:

- $s_computername is a script-level variable that hasn't been assigned a specific type.

- $s_intComputerNumber is a script-level variable that has been specifically cast to the [int] type.

- $l_strUserName is a function's local variable, which has been set as a [string] type.

You get the idea. If you decide to take this approach, you can consider using the Hungarian-notation type prefixes, which were popularized in VBScript:

- Str for [string]

- Int for [int]

- Bol for [Boolean]

- Dat for [datetime]

- Xml for [xml]

- Sng for [single]

- Dbl for [double]

And so forth. While this form of notation is no longer popular amongst developers working in languages like C# or VB, that's primarily because those languages strongly enforce data types; if you try to put the wrong type of data into a variable, you get an error, so there's less need to remind yourself which type of data is "supposed" to be in a variable. PowerShell is less strict about enforcing types, unless you explicitly cast a variable as a specific type; using notations like this may help you keep track of variables' types more easily. It's your decision.

Use Source Control

You've taken the time to write a script, debug it, and get it working—why would you not put it somewhere safe? This is especially true if you're working with other administrators on the same scripts. Source control solutions let you "check in" a script, retrieve read-only copies to run, and "check out" scripts for editing. When you "check in" a script, your version replaces the old version as the "newest," but you can still retain and retrieve old versions—in case you suddenly realize that some of the changes in the new version are incorrect.

SAPIEN PrimalScript integrates with popular source-control solutions like Microsoft Visual SourceSafe (and compatible solutions), as well as open-source systems like CVS/Subversion. You might also be interested in SAPIEN's own source control program ChangeVue (www.primaltools.com). There are even free, "personal" source control products that are SourceSafe-compatible, so you don't need to spend money to take advantage of these features. In many cases, the source control repository or database can be located on another computer, providing an additional level of backup in case the computer where you're working crashes.

Chapter 28
Managing Files and Folders

File and directory management is a pretty common administrative task. Here are some ways to accomplish typical tasks using PowerShell.

Creating Text Files

We've already discussed how you can use console redirection to send output to a text file and how to using the **Out-File** cmdlet, so we won't go into detail. Instead, we'll provide a few examples for creating text files. First, let's look at a line of code that redirects output to a text file:

```
PS C:\> Get-WmiObject win32_share > myshares.txt
```

Remember > sends output to the specified file, overwriting an existing file with the same name. Use >> to append to an existing file. The file will be created if it doesn't already exist.

Here's the same expression, but using the **Out-File** cmdlet:

```
PS C:\> Get-WmiObject win32_share | out-file myshares.txt -noclobber
```

We used the **-NoClobbe**r parameter to prevent the **Out-Fil**e cmdlet from overwriting myshares.txt, if it already exists.

Finally, you can also use the **New-Item** cmdlet to create a file and even add some content to it:

```
PS C:\> $now=get-date
PS C:\> new-item audit.log -type File -value "Created $now" -force


   Directory: Microsoft.PowerShell.Core\FileSystem::C:\


Mode                LastWriteTime     Length Name
----                -------------     ------ ----
-a---         6/16/2008 10:40 AM        30 audit.log


PS C:\> get-content audit.log
Created 6/16/2008 10:40:30 AM
PS C:\>
```

In this example, we used the **New-Item** cmdlet to create a file called audit.log and give it some content.

Reading Text Files

Reading text files is pretty straightforward with the **Get-Content** cmdlet:

```
PS C:\> get-content boot.ini
[boot loader]
timeout=15
default=multi(0)disk(0)rdisk(0)partition(2)\WINDOWS
[operating systems]
multi(0)disk(0)rdisk(0)partition(2)\WINDOWS="Microsoft Windows XP
Professional"
 /fastdetect /NoExecute=OptIn
multi(0)disk(0)rdisk(0)partition(1)\WINDOWS="Windows Server 2003,
Enterprise" /
noexecute=optout /fastdetect
C:\CMDCONS\BOOTSECT.DAT="Microsoft Windows Recovery Console" /cmdcons
PS C:\>
```

We can use the **-TotalCount** parameter to display a specified number of lines from a text file:

```
PS C:\> get-content ADOXEXCEPTION.LOG -TotalCount 5
CADOXCatalog Error
        Code = 80040e4d
        Code meaning = IDispatch error #3149
        Source = Microsoft OLE DB Provider for SQL Server
        Description = Login failed for user 'scriptaccess'.
PS C:\>
```

In this example, the first five lines of a log file are displayed. You can get the same result with this expression:

```
PS C:\> get-content ADOXEXCEPTION.LOG |select-object -first 5
```

An advantage to this approach is that the **Select-Object** cmdlet also has a **-Last** parameter that you can use to display a specified number of lines from the end of the file.

Parsing Text Files

While PowerShell might be a highly object-oriented shell, that doesn't mean *you* don't need to work with pure text now and again. Log files and INI files are perhaps two of the most common examples of text files Windows administrators need to work with on a regular basis.

Typically, in a text file, you are looking to extract pieces of information. PowerShell offers several techniques. The simplest approach is to use the -**Match** operator:

```
PS C:\ > (get-content foo.txt) -match "bar"
```

More complicated parsing and matching might require regular expressions and the regex object:

```
PS C:\ > [regex]$regex="\d{1,3}\.\d{1,3}\.\d{1,3}\.\d{1,3}"
PS C:\ > $regex.Matches((get-content ex070517.log))|select value

Value
-----
172.16.10.1
172.16.10.101
172.16.10.1
172.16.10.2
```

You might also use the **Select-String** cmdlet to extract complete lines from a text file:

```
PS C:\ > gc C:\temp\teched.txt | select-string "server 2008"
```

If you need a refresher, take a look back at the chapter "Regular Expressions."

Parsing IIS Log Files

Using **Select-String**, it is very easy to extract information from IIS log files. Suppose you want to find all the 404 errors that occurred during May 2008. You could use an expression like this:

```
get-childitem ex0805* | select-string " - 404"
```

You'll see a listing of every matching line. Use console redirection or the **Out-File** cmdlet to save the results:

```
get-childitem ex0805* | select-string " - 404" | out-file May08-404.txt
```

Let's take this a step further and find the IP addresses for the computers that received the 404 error. To accomplish this, we will use a combination of the **Select-String** cmdlet and a regular expression:

```
PS C:\system32\LogFiles\W3SVC1 > [regex]$regex="\d{1,3}\.\d{1,3}\.\d{1,3}\.\d{1,3}"
PS C:\system32\LogFiles\W3SVC1 > $(foreach ($found in (get-childitem ex0705* | '
>> select-string " - 404")) {
>> ($regex.matches($found.ToString()))[1].value} ) | select -unique
>>
64.34.179.85
69.207.43.227
69.207.92.234
69.207.4.215
```

```
71.98.99.72
207.36.196.127
210.253.120.121
203.17.208.78
```

We'll break this apart from the inside out so you can see what is happening. First, we know that an expression like this:

```
get-childitem ex0705* | select-string " - 404"
```

will return all the strings from log files that start with ex0705 that match on " - 404". We want to examine each matched line, so we'll nest the previous command in a **ForEach** construct:

```
Foreach($found in (get-childitem ex0705* | select-string " - 404"))
```

For every line in the file, we first need to convert it into a string:

```
$found.ToString()
```

We have a regex object, with a pattern that should match an IP address:

```
[regex]$regex="\d{1,3}\.\d{1,3}\.\d{1,3}\.\d{1,3}"
```

The **Matches()** method of the Regex object will return all matching instances in the line:

```
$regex.matches($found.ToString())
```

But we only need to see the value of the second match. The first match will be the Web server's IP address:

```
($regex.matches($found.ToString()))[1].value
```

If we ran what we have so far:

```
PS c:\system32\LogFiles\W3SVC1 > foreach ($found in (get-childitem ex0705* | '
>> select-string " - 404")) {($regex.matches($found.ToString()))[1].value}
```

Every client IP address would be listed, probably in duplicate. Because this is PowerShell, we'll add one final tweak by piping the output of this command to the **Select-Object** cmdlet, specifying the **-Unique** parameter:

```
PS C:\system32\LogFiles\W3SVC1 > $(foreach ($found in (get-childitem ex0705* | '
>> select-string " - 404")) {
>> ($regex.matches($found.ToString()))[1].value} ) | select -unique
```

Notice that we've enclosed the main filtering expression in parentheses and preceded it by a $ sign. This indicates that PowerShell should treat it as an expression and execute it in its entirety. We then piped the results of that expression to the **Select-Object** cmdlet, leaving us with a list of unique IP addresses.

Parsing INI Files

Another common administrative task is parsing information from ini files like this:

```
;MyApp.ini
;last updated 2:28 PM 6/13/2008
[Parameters]
Password=P@ssw0rd
Secure=Yes
Encryption=Yes
UseExtendedSyntax=No

[Open_Path]
path=\\server01\files\results.txt

[mail]
server=MAIL01
from=admin@mycompany.com

[Win2003]
foo=bar
```

If all the settings are unique in the entire file, you can use the **Select-String** cmdlet to extract the value for a particular setting with a PowerShell one-liner:

```
PS C:\ > ((cat myapp.ini | select-string -pattern "password=").ToString()).Split("=")[1]
P@ssword
```

Here's how this works. First, this example is using **cat**, which is an alias for the **Get-Content** cmdlet, which keeps a long expression from having to be any longer. Piping the contents of myapp.ini to the **Select-String** cmdlet will return a MatchInfo object when PowerShell finds a match:

```
cat myapp.ini | select-string -pattern "password="
```

However, we need to convert the result to a string object, so we use the **ToString()** method:

```
(cat myapp.ini | select-string -pattern "password=").ToString()
```

If we were to look at the returned value thus far, we would get:

```
Password=P@ssw0rd
```

Since we now have a string, we can use the **Split()** method to split the string at the = sign:

```
((cat myapp.ini | select-string -pattern "password=").ToString()).Split("=")
```

This expression results in a small 0-based array, meaning the first element has an index number of 0. All that remains is to display the second array element, which has an index number of 1:

```
((cat myapp.ini | select-string -pattern "password=").ToString()).Split("=")[1]
```

In our sample ini file, this technique would work since all of our values are unique. But what about situations where we need a specific value under a specific heading? This is a little more complicated, but you can achieve it with some extra parsing. Here's a function we wrote to retrieve the value from a particular section of an ini file:

```
Function Get-INIValue {

# $ini is the name of the ini file
# $section is the name of the section head like [Mail]
# Specify the name without the brackets
# $prop is the property you want under the section
# sample usage: $from=Get-inivalue myapp.ini mail from

Param ([string]$ini,[string]$section,[string]$prop)

#get the line number to start searching from
$LineNum=(Get-Content myapp.ini | Select-String "\[$section\]").Linenumber
$limit=(Get-Content myapp.ini).length #total number of lines in the ini file

for ($i=$LineNum;$i -le $limit;$i++) {
 $line=(Get-Content myapp.ini)[$i]
     if ($line -match $prop+"=") {
       $value=($line.split("="))[1]
       return $value
       Break
       }
   }
return "NotFound"
}
```

The function is expecting the name of the ini file, the section name, and the name of the value. Once PowerShell loads this file, you can use it like this:

```
PS C:\ > $smtp=Get-inivalue myapp.ini mail server
```

The function will return the value the "server" setting under the [Mail] section of myapp.ini. The function first obtains the number of the line in the ini file that contains the section heading:

```
$LineNum=(Get-Content myapp.ini | Select-String "\[$section\]").Linenumber
```

The function also gets the total number of lines in the ini file that it will use later:

```
$limit=(Get-Content myapp.ini).length #total number of lines in the ini file
```

Now that we know where to start searching, we can loop through each line of the ini file until we reach the end:

```
for ($i=$LineNum;$i -le $limit;$i++) {
```

Because the ini file will be treated as a 0-based array, the value of **$LineNum** will actually return the first line after the heading:

```
 $line=(Get-Content myapp.ini)[$i]
```

The function examines each line using the -**Match** operator to see if it contains the property value we are seeking:

```
  if ($line -match $prop+"=") {
```

If not, the function will keep looping until it reaches the end of the file, at which point the function will return "NotFound".

When PowerShell makes a match, it splits the line at the = sign and returns the second item (index number of 1):

```
  $value=($line.split("="))[1]
```

The function returns this value, and since there's no longer any need to keep looping through the ini file, the function stops by using the **Break** statement:

```
  return $value
  Break
```

Copying Files

Copying files in PowerShell is not much different than copying files in Cmd.exe. In fact, by default PowerShell uses the alias **Copy** for the **Copy-Item** cmdlet:

```
PS C:\> copy *.ps1 c:\temp
PS C:\> get-childitem c:\temp


    Directory: Microsoft.PowerShell.Core\FileSystem::C:\temp


Mode                LastWriteTime     Length Name
----                -------------     ------ ----
-a---         5/17/2008   8:31 PM        863 brace.ps1
-a---         5/29/2008  12:18 PM         15 demo.txt
-a---         2/11/2008   6:26 PM      19817 ex060211.log
-a---         5/29/2008  10:58 AM         16 .txt
-a---         5/23/2008   1:03 PM        811 out-grid.ps1
-a---         5/23/2008   1:06 PM       1330 out-propertyGrid.ps1
-a---         5/19/2008  11:17 AM        710 showprocessinfo.ps1
-a---         5/19/2008  11:04 AM        477 showservices.ps1
-a---          5/1/2008   8:10 PM         88 test.ps1


PS C:\>
```

This example copies all ps1 files in C: to C:\temp. You can also recurse and force files to be overwritten:

```
PS C:\>copy-item C:\Logs C:\Backup -recurse -force
```

This expression copies all files and subdirectories from C:\Logs to C:\Backup, overwriting any existing files and directories with the same name.

As you work with PowerShell, you'll discover that not every command you can execute in Cmd.exe is valid in PowerShell. For example, the following is a valid command in Cmd.exe:

```
C:\logs> copy *.log *.old
```

When you try this in PowerShell, you'll get a message about an invalid character. It appears the **Copy-Item** cmdlet works fine when copying between directories, but it can't handle a wildcard copy within the same directory.

Here's a workaround:

BulkCopy.ps1

```
#BulkCopy.ps1
Set-Location "C:\Logs"

$files=Get-ChildItem |where {$_.extension -eq ".log"}

foreach ($file in $files) {
 $filename=($file.FullName).ToString()
 $arr=@($filename.split("."))
 $newname=$arr[0]+".old"

 Write-Host "copying "$file.Fullname "to"$newname
 copy $file.fullname $newname -force
}
```

With this script, we first define a variable that contains all the files we want to copy by extension. Next we iterate through the variable using the **ForEach** construct. Within the loop, we break apart the filename using the **Split** method so we can get everything to the left of the period. We need this name so we can define what the new filename will be with the new extension, including the path. Then it's a matter of calling the **Copy-Item** cmdlet. Notice that in the script, we're using the **copy** alias.

....

Provider Alert

If you look through the Help for the Copy-Item cmdlet and some of the other Item cmdlets, you will see a -Credential parameter. This might lead you to believe that you could use the -Credential parameter to copy files to a network and share and specify alternate credentials. Unfortunately, in the current version of PowerShell, the file system and registry providers do not support this parameter. Hopefully, this will change in later versions of PowerShell. In the meantime, start a PowerShell session using the RunAs command if you need to specify alternate credentials.

Deleting Files

The **Remove-Item** cmdlet has aliases of **del** and **erase**, and functions essentially the same as these commands in Cmd.exe:

```
PS C:\> remove-item c:\temp\*.txt
```

The cmdlet comes in handy when you want to recurse through a directory structure or exclude certain files:

```
PS C:\> remove-item c:\backup\*.* - recurse -exclude 2008*.log
```

This expression will recurse through c:\backup, deleting all files except those that match the pattern 2008*.log. Like the **Copy-Item** cmdlet, you can also use **-Include** and **-Credential**.

Renaming Files

Renaming files is also very straightforward:

```
PS C:\Temp> rename-item foo.txt bar.txt
```

This cmdlet has aliases of **rni** and **ren**, and like the other item cmdlets, it lets you specify credentials and force an overwrite of an existing file. You have to be a little more creative if you need to rename multiple files:

BulkRename.ps1

```
#BulkRename.ps1
Set-Location "C:\Logs"

$files=get-childitem -recurse |where {$_.extension -eq ".Log"}

foreach ($file in $files) {
 $filename=($file.name).ToString()
 $arr=@($filename.split("."))
 $newname=$arr[0]+".old"

 Write-Host "renaming"$file.Fullname "to"$newname
 ren $file.fullname $newname -force
}
```

This is a legitimate command in Cmd.exe:

```
C:\ ren *.log *.old
```

Since this doesn't work in PowerShell, we use something like the BulkRename script instead. This is a variation on our BulkCopy script from above. Instead of **copy**, we call **ren**. By the way, as the script is written above, it will recurse through subdirectories starting in C:\Logs, renaming every file it finds that ends in .log to .old.

File Attributes and Properties

Earlier in this chapter, we worked with file attributes to work around some issues copying files in PowerShell. Often times, you may need to know if a file is marked as ReadOnly or set as such. You can easily accomplish this by checking the **IsReadOnly** property of the file object:

```
PS C:\ > (Get-childitem file.txt).IsReadonly
False
```

You can enable ReadOnly by calling the **Set-ReadOnly()** method:

```
PS C:\ > (Get-childitem file.txt).Set_IsReadonly($TRUE)
PS C:\ > (Get-childitem file.txt).IsReadonly
True
```

Specify **$TRUE** to enable it and **$FALSE** to turn it off:

```
PS C:\ > (Get-childitem file.txt).Set_IsReadonly($False)
PS C:\ > (Get-childitem file.txt).IsReadonly
False
```

To display other attributes, you can use the **Attributes** property:

```
PS C:\ > (get-childitem boot.ini -force).Attributes
Hidden, System, Archive
```

We use the **-Force** parameter so that the **Get-ChildItem** cmdlet will ignore the Hidden attribute and display file information. To set other file attributes you can use the **Set_Attributes()** method:

```
PS C:\ > (get-childitem file.txt).Attributes
Archive
PS C:\ > (get-childitem file.txt).Set_Attributes("Archive,Hidden")
PS C:\ > (get-childitem file.txt -force).Attributes
Hidden, Archive
```

In this snippet, you can see the file.txt only has the Archive attribute set. Using **Set_Attributes()**, we set the file attributes to Archive and Hidden, which is confirmed with the last expression. This is also another way of setting the ReadOnly attribute.

Setting the file attributes to Normal will clear all basic file attributes:

```
PS C:\ > (get-childitem file.txt -force).Set_Attributes("Normal")
PS C:\ > (get-childitem file.txt -force).Attributes
Normal
PS C:\ > attrib file.txt
        C:\file.txt
PS C: \ >
```

Because everything is an object in PowerShell, working with file properties such as when a file was created or last modified is very simple. Here's an abbreviated output that gets all files from F:\SAPIEN and displays when the file was created, last accessed, and last modified:

```
PS C:\ > get-childitem f:\sapien | Select Name,CreationTime,LastAccessTime,LastWriteTime `
>>| format-table -auto
>>

Name                     CreationTime         LastAccessTime       LastWriteTime
----                     ------------         --------------       -------------
Add2LocalAdmin.bat        6/12/2008 1:17:34 PM 6/15/2008 9:04:01 AM 6/12/2008 1:20:23 PM
Add2LocalAdmin.txt        6/14/2008 9:28:43 PM 6/15/2008 9:04:01 AM 6/12/2008 1:20:23 PM
AddToGroup.txt            6/14/2008 9:28:43 PM 6/15/2008 9:04:01 AM 6/12/2008 1:22:38 PM
AddToGroup.Wsf            6/12/2008 1:21:43 PM 6/15/2008 9:04:02 AM 6/12/2008 1:22:38 PM
AddUsertoGroup.txt        6/14/2008 9:28:43 PM 6/15/2008 9:04:02 AM 6/12/2008 4:18:54 PM
AddUsertoGroup.vbs        6/12/2008 4:18:54 PM 6/15/2008 4:29:51 PM 6/12/2008 4:18:54 PM
```

It Isn't Necessarily What You Think
The LastAccessTime property will indicate the last time a particular file was accessed, but this doesn't mean by a user. Many other processes and applications, such as anti-virus programs and defragmentation utilities, can affect this file property. Do not rely on this property as an indication of the last time a user accessed a file. You would need to enable auditing to obtain that information.

PowerShell makes it very easy to change the value of any of these properties. This is similar to the Touch command:

```
PS C:\ > (get-childitem file.txt).Set_LastAccessTime("12/31/2008 01:23:45")
PS C:\ > (get-childitem file.txt).Set_LastWriteTime("12/31/2008 01:23:45")
PS C:\ > (get-childitem file.txt).Set_CreationTime("12/31/2008 01:23:45")
PS C:\ > get-childitem file.txt |select Name,CreationTime,LastWriteTime,LastAccessTime | '
>> format-table -auto
>>

Name       CreationTime            LastWriteTime           LastAccessTime
----       ------------            -------------           --------------
file.txt   12/31/2008 1:23:45 AM   12/31/2008 1:23:45 AM   12/31/2008 1:23:45 AM
```

Here, we've set all the time stamps to 12/31/2008 1:23:45 AM. Obviously, use this power with caution.

Another property that you can easily set from the console is file encryption. You accomplish this by using the **Encrypt()** method:

```
PS C:\ > (get-childitem file.txt).Attributes
Archive
PS C:\ > (get-childitem file.txt).Encrypt()
PS C:\ > (get-childitem file.txt).Attributes
Archive, Encrypted
```

You can still open the file because PowerShell encrypted it with your private key, but anyone else attempting to open the file will fail. To reverse the process, simply use the **Decrypt()** method:

```
PS C:\ > (get-childitem file.txt).Decrypt()
PS C:\ > (get-childitem file.txt).Attributes
Archive
```

Proceed with Caution
Before you get carried away and start encrypting everything—stop. Using the encrypting file system requires some serious planning and testing. You have to plan for recovery agents, lost keys, and more. This is not a task to undertake lightly. You will need to research the topic and test thoroughly in a non-production environment.

What about compression? Even though compression can be indicated as file attribute, you cannot compress a file simply by setting the attribute. Nor does the .NET file object have a compression method. The easy solution is to use Compact.exe to compress files and folders.

The other approach is to use **WMI**:

```
PS C:\ > $wmifile=Get-WmiObject -query "Select * from CIM_DATAFILE where name='c:\\file.txt'"
PS C:\ > $wmifile
```

```
Compressed : False
Encrypted  : False
Size       :
Hidden     : False
Name       : c:\file.txt
Readable   : True
System File :
Version    :
Writeable  : True
```

You would think all you need to do is set the Compressed property to TRUE:

```
PS C:\ > $wmifile.Compressed=$TRUE
PS C:\ > $wmifile.Compressed
True
```

It looks like it works, but when you examine the file in Windows Explorer, you'll see that it isn't actually compressed:

```
PS C:\ > (get-childitem file.txt).Attributes
Archive
```

You need to use the **Compress()** method:

```
PS C:\ > $wmifile.Compress()
```

```
__GENUS          : 2
__CLASS          : __PARAMETERS
__SUPERCLASS     :
__DYNASTY        : __PARAMETERS
__RELPATH        :
__PROPERTY_COUNT : 1
__DERIVATION     : {}
__SERVER         :
__NAMESPACE      :
__PATH           :
ReturnValue      : 0
```

```
PS C:\ > (get-childitem file.txt).Attributes
Archive, Compressed
```

You can also confirm this in Windows Explorer. To reverse the process, use the **Uncompress()** method:

```
PS C:\ > $wmifile.Uncompress()
```

Working with Paths

When working with folders in PowerShell, you are also working with paths. A path, as the name suggests, is the "direction" to reach a particular destination. For a short path and likely known path like C:\

Windows, working with paths isn't critical. But as your scripts grow in complexity or you are dealing with path variables, you'll want to be familiar with PowerShell's path cmdlets. These cmdlets work with any provider that uses paths, such as the registry and certificate store.

Test-Path

Adding error handling to a script is always helpful, especially when dealing with folders that may not exist. You can use the **Test-Path** cmdlet to validate the existence of a given path. The cmdlet returns TRUE if the path exists:

```
PS C:\ > test-path c:\windows
True
```

You can also use this cmdlet to verify the existence of registry keys:

```
PS C:\ > test-path hklm:\software\Microsoft\Windows\CurrentVersion
True
PS C:\ > test-path hklm:\software\MyCompany\MyApp\Settings
False
```

Convert-Path

Before PowerShell can work with paths, they also need to be properly formatted. The **Convert-Path** cmdlet will take paths or path variables and convert them to a format PowerShell can understand. For example, the ~ character represents your user profile path. Using the **Convert-Path** cmdlet will return the explicit path:

```
PS C:\ > convert-path ~
C:\Documents and Settings\jhicks
```

Here are some other ways you might use this cmdlet:

```
PS C:\windows\system32 > convert-path .
C:\windows\system32
PS C:\windows\system32 > convert-path hklm:\system\currentcontrolset
HKEY_LOCAL_MACHINE\system\currentcontrolset
PS C:\windows\system32 > convert-path ..\
C:\windows
PS C:\windows\system32 > convert-path ..\..\
C:\
PS C:\windows\system32 >
```

You could also achieve the last two examples by using **Split-Path**.

Split-Path

This cmdlet will split a given path into its parent or leaf components. You can use this cmdlet to display or reference different components of a given path. The default is to split the path and return the parent path component:

```
PS C:\ > split-path c:\folderA\FolderB
c:\folderA
```

This cmdlet also works with other providers such as the registry:

```
PS C:\ > split-path hklm:\system\currentcontrolset
hklm:\system
```

The **Split-Path** cmdlet will include the specified path's qualifier, which is the provider path's drive such as D:\ or HKLM:. If you wanted to get just the qualifier, in essence the root, use the -**Qualifier** parameter:

```
PS C:\ > split-path f:\folderA\FolderB\FolderC -qualifier
f:
```

You can use -**NoQualifier** to return a path without the root:

```
PS C:\ > split-path f:\folderA\FolderB\FolderC -noqualifier
\folderA\FolderB\FolderC
PS C:\ > split-path hklm:\system\currentcontrolset -noqualifier
\system\currentcontrolset
```

However, if you need the last part of the path and not the parent, use the -**Leaf** parameter:

```
PS C:\ > split-path c:\folderA\FolderB -leaf
FolderB
```

You're not limited to folder paths. You can use the -**Leaf** parameter to parse out a file name from a path:

```
PS C:\ > split-path "C:\program files\SAPIEN\PrimalScript 2008 Enterprise\PrimalScript.exe" '
>>-leaf
PrimalScript.exe
```

When using path variables, you may need to include the -**Resolve** parameter to expand the variable to its full path:

```
PS C:\ > split-path $pshome\*.xml -leaf -resolve
microsoft.powershell.commands.management.dll-help.xml
microsoft.powershell.commands.utility.dll-help.xml
microsoft.powershell.consolehost.dll-help.xml
microsoft.powershell.security.dll-help.xml
PshX-SAPIEN.dll-Help.xml
system.management.automation.dll-help.xml
```

This parameter is also useful in confirming that a path component exists:

```
PS C:\ > split-path C:\Windows\system33 -leaf -resolve
Split-Path : Cannot find path 'C:\Windows\system33' because it does not exist.
At line:1 char:11
+ split-path <<<< C:\Windows\system33 -leaf -resolve
```

PowerShell also has a specific cmdlet for resolving path names.

Resolve-Path

The **Resolve-Path** cmdlet is primarily intended to resolve wildcards or variables that might be part of a path:

```
PS C:\ > resolve-path $env:windir

Path
----
C:\WINDOWS
```

The cmdlet's output is a PathInfo object. This object provides additional PowerShell information about the path:

```
PS C:\ > resolve-path $env:windir | format-list


Drive        : C
Provider     : Microsoft.PowerShell.Core\FileSystem
ProviderPath : C:\WINDOWS
Path         : C:\WINDOWS
```

You can also use the cmdlet with wildcards:

```
PS C:\ > resolve-path c:\windows\*.exe

Path
----
C:\windows\dbplugin.exe
C:\windows\explorer.exe
C:\windows\hh.exe
C:\windows\IsUninst.exe
C:\windows\notepad.exe
C:\windows\regedit.exe
C:\windows\slrundll.exe
C:\windows\TASKMAN.EXE
C:\windows\twunk_16.exe
C:\windows\twunk_32.exe
C:\windows\winhelp.exe
C:\windows\winhlp32.exe
```

Join-Path

Occasionally, you need to construct a path from disparate elements, and the **Join-Path** cmdlet will create a PowerShell-ready path:

```
PS C:\ > join-path -path c:\scripts -childpath "My PowerShell Projects"
c:\scripts\My PowerShell Projects
```

The -**Path** and -**Childpath** parameters are positional, so you don't need to specify the parameter names. You can get the same result as the example above like this:

```
PS C:\ > join-path c:\scripts "My PowerShell Projects"
c:\scripts\My PowerShell Projects
```

The path name doesn't have to be explicit. You can also use variables like this:

```
PS C:\ > join-path $env:userprofile "Scripts\PowerShell"
C:\Documents and Settings\jhicks\Scripts\PowerShell
```

The cmdlet can also work with wildcards and the **-Resolve** parameter to expand the wildcard and create a complete path:

```
PS C:\ > join-path c:\prog* "microsoft*" -resolve
C:\Program Files\Microsoft ActiveSync
C:\Program Files\Microsoft CAPICOM 2.1.0.2
C:\Program Files\Microsoft Expression
C:\Program Files\microsoft frontpage
C:\Program Files\Microsoft IntelliPoint
C:\Program Files\Microsoft Money
C:\Program Files\Microsoft Office
C:\Program Files\Microsoft SQL Server
C:\Program Files\Microsoft Visual Studio
C:\Program Files\Microsoft Visual Studio 8
C:\Program Files\Microsoft Works
C:\Program Files\Microsoft.NET
```

Creating Directories

Creating directories in PowerShell is nearly the same as it is in Cmd.exe:

```
PS C:\Temp> mkdir "NewFiles"
```

Alternatively, you can use the **New-Item** cmdlet that offers a few more features:

```
PS C:\Temp> new-item -type directory \\File01\public\sapien
```

The cmdlet also creates nested directories. In other words, like **mkdir** in Cmd.exe, it creates any intermediate directories:

```
PS C:\Temp> new-item -type directory c:\temp\1\2\3


    Directory: Microsoft.PowerShell.Core\FileSystem::C:\temp\1\2


Mode                LastWriteTime     Length Name
----                -------------     ------ ----
d----         6/16/2006  1:56 PM          3
PS C:\Temp> tree /a
Folder PATH listing for volume Server2003
Volume serial number is 0006EEA4 34AB:AD37
C:.
+---1
|   \---2
|       \---3
+---jdh
+---sapien
\---temp2
PS C:\Temp>
```

Listing Directories

Even though you can use dir in PowerShell to list directories and files, it is really an alias for the **Get-**

ChildItem cmdlet. However, you can specify files to include or exclude in the search and also recurse through subdirectories:

```
PS C:\> dir -exclude *.old -recurse
```

Remember: even though PowerShell is displaying text, it is really working with objects. This means you can get creative in how you display information:

```
PS C:\Temp> dir -exclude *.old,*.bak,*.tmp -recurse | select-object '
>>FullName,Length,LastWriteTime | format-table -auto
>>
FullName                      Length   LastWriteTime
--------                      ------   -------------
C:\Temp\1                              6/16/2008  1:56:45 PM
C:\Temp\1\2                            6/16/2008  1:56:45 PM
C:\Temp\1\2\3                          6/16/2008  1:56:45 PM
C:\Temp\jdh                            6/16/2008  1:09:41 PM
C:\Temp\sapien                         6/16/2008  1:05:41 PM
C:\Temp\temp2                          6/16/2008 12:48:44 PM
C:\Temp\temp2\bar.Log             11   6/16/2008 11:09:27 AM
C:\Temp\showservices.ps1         477   5/19/2008 11:04:29 AM
C:\Temp\test.abc                  88   5/01/2008  8:10:10 PM
C:\Temp\test.Log                  88   5/01/2008  8:10:10 PM
C:\Temp\test.ps1                  88   5/01/2008  8:10:10 PM


PS C:\Temp>
```

This expression recurses from the starting directory, listing all files that don't end in .old, .bak, or .tmp. Using the **dir** alias, we piped the output from the **Get-ChildItem** cmdlet to the **Select-Object** cmdlet because we wanted to display only certain information formatted as a table.

Deleting Directories

Deleting a directory is essentially the same as deleting a file. You can use the **rmdir** alias for the **Remove-Item** cmdlet:

```
PS C:\Temp> rmdir sapien
```

PowerShell gives you a warning if you attempt to remove a directory that isn't empty:

```
PS C:\Temp> rmdir files

Confirm
The item at C:\Temp\files has children and the -recurse parameter was
not specified. If you continue, all children will be removed with the
item. Are you sure you want to continue?
[Y] Yes [A] Yes to All [N] No [L] No to All [S] Suspend [?] Help
(default is "Y"):n
PS C:\Temp>
```

As you can see, the solution is to use the **-Recurse** parameter:

```
PS C:\Temp> rmdir files -recurse
PS C:\Temp>
```

Chapter 29
Managing Systems by Using WMI

Using WMI in administrative scripts is a common practice. WMI is an extremely powerful way to manage just about every aspect of a system including hardware, software, and configuration. You can also use it to remotely manage systems.

PowerShell has the **Get-WmiObject** cmdlet that acts as an interface to WMI. This cmdlet lets you access any WMI class in any WMI namespace. For our purposes, we'll stick to the default namespace of Root\Cimv2 and the Win32 classes, since you'll use these classes in 95% of your scripts.

Retrieving Basic Information

At its simplest, all you have to do is specify a class and run the **Get-WmiObject** cmdlet in order for the cmdlet to find all instances of that class and return a page of information:

```
PS C:\> Get-WmiObject win32_share

Name                 Path                 Description
----                 ----                 -----------
E$                   E:\                  Default share
IPC$                                      Remote IPC
downloads$           e:\downloads
ADMIN$               E:\WINDOWS           Remote Admin
C$                   C:\                  Default share


PS C:\>
```

In this example, we asked PowerShell to display WMI information about all instances of the Win32_ Share class on the local computer. With this particular class, there are other properties that by default are not displayed. Depending on the class, you might get different results. For example, the following expression displays a long list of properties and values:

```
PS C:\> Get-WmiObject win32_Processor
```

Listing Available Classes

You're probably saying: "That's great, but how do I find out what Win32 classes are available?" All you have to do is ask. The **Get-WmiObject** cmdlet has a **-List** parameter you can invoke. Open a PowerShell prompt and try this:

```
PS C:\> Get-WmiObject -list | where {$_.name -like "win32*"}
```

You should get a long, two-column list of all the available Win32 classes. You can query any of these classes using the **Get-WmiObject** cmdlet.

The **Get-WmiObject** cmdlet defaults to the root\CIMv2 namespace, but you can query available classes in any namespace:

```
PS C:\> Get-WmiObject -namespace root\securitycenter -list

__SystemClass                        __thisNAMESPACE
__InstanceOperationEvent             __MethodInvocationEvent
__InstanceCreationEvent              __InstanceModificationEvent
__InstanceDeletionEvent              __ExtrinsicEvent
__SystemEvent                        __EventDroppedEvent
__ConsumerFailureEvent               __QOSFailureEvent
__EventQueueOverflowEvent            __ClassOperationEvent
__ClassModificationEvent             __ClassCreationEvent
__ClassDeletionEvent                 __TimerEvent
__AggregateEvent                     __EventConsumer
__FilterToConsumerBinding            __TimerNextFiring
__EventFilter                        __ProviderRegistration
__EventProviderRegistration          __EventConsumerProviderRegistratio
__PropertyProviderRegistration       __ObjectProviderRegistration
__ClassProviderRegistration          __InstanceProviderRegistration
__MethodProviderRegistration         __SystemSecurity
__SecurityRelatedClass               __NTLMUser9X
__PARAMETERS                         __NotifyStatus
__ExtendedStatus                     FirewallProduct
AntiVirusProduct
PS C:\>
```

Note

All those classes starting with __ are WMI system classes; you can't really hide them, but you're not going to really use them either. You want the classes that don't start with __.

Here we've queried for a list of classes in the Root\SecurityCenter namespace.

Listing Properties of a Class

The next question most of you are asking is: "How can I find out the properties for a given class?" As we discussed previously, you can use the **Get-Member** cmdlet to list all the properties for a WMI object. Take a look at the following script:

List-WMIProperties.ps1

```
#List-WMIProperties.ps1
$class=Read-Host "Enter a Win32 WMI Class that you are interested in"

$wmi=get-WMIObject -class $class -namespace "root\Cimv2"
$wmi | get-member -membertype properties | where {$_.name -notlike "__*"} | select name
```

This script prompts you for a Win32 WMI class and defines a variable using the **Get-WmiObject** cmdlet for that class. We define a second variable that is the result of piping the first variable to the **Get-Member** cmdlet. Finally we pipe the class object to the **Get-Member** cmdlet selecting only Properties. Because this will likely include system properties, we'll filter those out as well. Here's what you get when you run the script:

```
Enter a Win32 WMI Class that you are interested in: win32_logicaldisk

Name
-------
Access
Availability
BlockSize
Caption
Compressed
ConfigManagerErrorCode
ConfigManagerUserConfig
CreationClassName
Description
DeviceID
DriveType
ErrorCleared
ErrorDescription
ErrorMethodology
FileSystem
FreeSpace
InstallDate
LastErrorCode
MaximumComponentLength
MediaType
...
PS C:\>
```

Usually, there are only a handful of properties in which you are interested. In this case, you can use the **-Property** parameter to specify which properties you want to display:

```
PS C:\> Get-WmiObject -class win32_processor -property name,caption,L2CacheSize
>>

__GENUS          : 2
__CLASS          : Win32_Processor
__SUPERCLASS     :
__DYNASTY        :
```

```
__RELPATH           :
__PROPERTY_COUNT    : 3
__DERIVATION        : {}
__SERVER            :
__NAMESPACE         :
__PATH              :
Caption             : x86 Family 6 Model 9 Stepping 5
L2CacheSize         : 1024
Name                : Intel(R) Pentium(R) M processor 1600MHz


PS C:\>
```

Here, we've asked for the Win32_Processor class, and specifically the name, caption, and L2CacheSize properties. Unfortunately, the cmdlet also insists on displaying system properties, such as __Genus. Since you don't care about those properties most of the time, a neater approach is something like this:

```
PS C:\> Get-WmiObject -class win32_processor | select-object name,caption,L2CacheSize | format-list


name         : Intel(R) Pentium(R) M processor 1600MHz
caption      : x86 Family 6 Model 9 Stepping 5
L2CacheSize  : 1024


PS C:\>
```

Here, we're calling the same cmdlet, except we use the **Select-Object** cmdlet to pick the properties in which we're interested.

Examining Existing Values

As you learn to work with WMI, it's helpful to look at what information is populated on a system. This is a great way to learn the different properties and what values you can expect. The more you work with WMI, you'll realize that not every property is always populated. There's no reason to spend time querying empty properties. With this in mind, we've put together a helpful script that enumerates all the properties for all the instances of a particular WMI class. However, the script only displays properties with a value and it won't display any of the system class properties like __Genus:

List-WMIValues.ps1

```
#List-WMIValues.ps1
$class=Read-Host "Enter a Win32 WMI Class that you are interested in"
$wmi=get-WMIObject -class $class -namespace "root\CimV2"

$properties=$wmi | Get-Member -membertype Property
Write-Host "Properties for $($Class.ToUpper())" -foregroundcolor yellow
# if more than one instance was returned then $wmi will be an array
# and we need to loop through it
$i=0

if ($wmi.Count -ge 2) {
 do {
 foreach ($property in $properties) {
 #only display values that aren't null and don't display system
```

```
#properties that start with __
  if ($wmi[$i].($property.name) -ne $Null -AND '
$property.name -notlike "__*") {
   write-Host -foregroundcolor "Green" '
$property.name"="$wmi[$i].($property.name)
  }
 } #end foreach

 Write-Host "**********************************"

#divider between instances
 $i++
 }while($i -le ($wmi.count-1))
} #end if
# else $wmi has only one instance
else {
 foreach ($property in $properties) {
  if ($wmi.($property.name) -ne $Null -AND '
$property.name -notlike "__*") {
   write-Host -foregroundcolor "Green" '
$property.name"="$wmi.($property.name)
  } #end if
 } #end foreach
} #end else
```

This script is based on our earlier **List-WMIProperties** script. Once we have the variable with all the properties, we iterate through all the instances of the specified WMI class. If the property value isn't null and the property name is not like __*, then the property name and its value are displayed. We've even thrown in a little color to spice up the display. You can also use an expression like this:

```
PS C:\> get-wmobject win32_logicaldisk | Select *
```

But that will show you all properties, including system properties, regardless of whether they have a value.

Remote Management

Now that you know about WMI classes and properties, we'll take a closer look at what you do with it. While you can make some system configuration changes with WMI, most of the WMI properties are read-only, which makes for terrific management reports. The **Get-WmiObject** cmdlet even has two parameters that make this easy to do on your network.

You *can* use the -**Computername** parameter to specify a remote computer that you want to connect to and the -**Credential** parameter to specify alternate credentials. However, you *can't* use alternate credentials when querying the local system. Here's an example:

```
PS C:\> Get-WmiObject win32_operatingsystem -computer dc01 -credential (get-credential)

SystemDirectory : C:\WINDOWS\system32
Organization    : SAPIEN Press
BuildNumber     : 3790
RegisteredUser  : Staff
SerialNumber    : 69713-640-3403486-45904
Version         : 5.2.3790


PS C:\>
```

This example connects to computer DC01 and gets information on the Win32_Operatingsystem WMI object. For alternate credentials, we call the **Get-Credential** cmdlet that presents what looks like a standard Windows authentication box. Except the **Get-Credential** cmdlet doesn't authenticate the user or verify the password. It simply stores this information securely in a PSCredential object.

VBScript Alert
If you have a library of WMI scripts written in VBScript, don't delete them yet! With a little tweaking, you can take the essential WMI queries from your VBScripts and put them into PowerShell scripts. Use the Where cmdlet for your WMI queries. For example, you may have a WMI query like:

```
Select deviceID,drivetype,size,freespace from Win32_LogicalDisk
where drivetype='3'
```

In PowerShell you could rewrite this as:

```
Get-WmiObject win32_logicaldisk | Select deviceid,drivetype,size,
freespace | where {drivetype -eq 3}
```

But the better approach is to simply pass the original WQL query to Get-WmiObject by using its -query parameter.

```
Get-WmiObject -query "Select deviceid,drivetype,size,freespace
from win32_logicaldisk where drivetype=3"
```

Once you have the core query, you can tweak your PowerShell script and use the filtering, formatting, sorting, and exporting options that are available in PowerShell. If you don't have a script library, there are many, many WMI scripts available on the Internet that you can leverage and turn into PowerShell scripts.

The **Get-WmiObject** cmdlet does not allow you to specify multiple classes. So, if you want information from different Win32 classes, you'll have to call the cmdlet several times and store information in variables:

WMIReport.ps1

```
#WMIReport.ps1
$OS=Get-WmiObject -class win32_operatingsystem -property Caption,CSDVersion

#select fixed drives only by specifying a drive type of 3
$Drives=Get-WmiObject -class win32_logicaldisk -filter "DriveType = 3"

Write-Host "Operating System:" $OS.Caption $OS.CSDVersion

Write-Host "Drive Summary:"
Write-Host "Drive"'t"Size (MB)"'t"FreeSpace (MB)"
```

```
foreach ($d in $Drives) {
 $free="{0:N2}" -f ($d.FreeSpace/1MB -as [int])
 $size="{0:N0}" -f ($d.size/1MB -as [int])
 Write-Host $d.deviceID 't $size 't $free
} #end foreach
```

This script reports system information from two WMI Win32 classes. We first define a variable to hold operating system information, specifically the Caption and CSDVersion, which is the service pack. The second class, Win32_LogicalDisk, is captured in **$Drives**. Since we're only interested in fixed drives, we use the filter parameter to limit the query by drive type.

Once we have this information we can display it any way we choose. Here's what you might see when the script runs:

```
Operating System: Microsoft(R) Windows(R) Server 2003, Enterprise Edition Service Pack 1
Drive Summary:
Drive  Size (MB)       FreeSpace (MB)
C:      8,095          2,417
E:     15,006          4,696
PS C:\>
```

The [WMI] Type

If you prefer a different approach to working with WMI and have some experience working with it, you may prefer to use PowerShell's [WMI] type:

```
PS C:\> [WMI]$srv="root\cimv2:win32_computersystem.Name='Godot'"
PS C:\> $srv


Domain               : WORKGROUP
Manufacturer         : Dell Computer Corporation
Model                : Latitude D800
Name                 : Godot
PrimaryOwnerName     : Administrator
TotalPhysicalMemory  : 1609805824
```

By creating a new object of type [WMI], we can directly access the WMI instance. PowerShell returns a pre-defined subset of information when you call an object as we did above. However, you have access to all the WMI properties, which you can see by piping the object to the **Get-Member** cmdlet:

```
PS C:\> $srv | Get-Member
```

If we want additional information, all we have to do is check the object's properties:

```
PS C:\> $srv.Status
OK
PS C:\> $srv.Roles
LM_Workstation
LM_Server
SQLServer
Print
NT
PS C:\>
```

While you can't specify alternate credentials using the [WMI] type, you can specify a remote system like this:

```
PS C:\> [WMI]$srv="\\DC01\root\cimv2:win32_computersystem.Name='DC01'"
```

To use the [WMI] type, you must create a reference to a specific instance of a WMI object. For example, you can't create a WMI object to return all instances of Win32_LogicalDisk:

```
PS C:\> [WMI]$disk="root\cimv2:win32_logicaldisk"
Cannot convert value "root\cimv2:win32_logicaldisk" to type "System.Management.ManagementObject".
Error: "Specified argument was out of the range of valid values.
Parameter name: path"
At line:1 char:11
+ [WMI]$disk= <<<< "root\cimv2:win32_logicaldisk"
PS C:\>
```

Instead, you must specify a single instance by using the WMI object's primary key and querying for a certain value:

```
PS C:\> [WMI]$disk="root\cimv2:win32_logicaldisk.DeviceID='C:'"
PS C:\> $disk


DeviceID     : C:
DriveType    : 3
ProviderName :
FreeSpace    : 2797834240
Size         : 15726702592
VolumeName   : Server2003


PS C:\>
```

That's great, but how do you figure out an object's primary key? The easiest way is to run Wbemtest and query for a Win32 class. The results are the format you need to use with the [WMI] type in PowerShell:

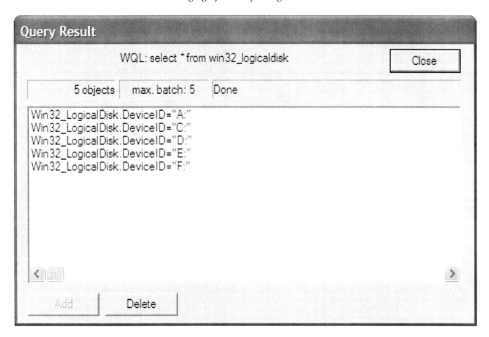

Figure 29-1: Wbemtest query result.

In this screen shot you can see that we've queried for all instances of the Win32_logicaldisk class. PowerShell displays each instance by using the default key, which in this case is DeviceID. Here's another example:

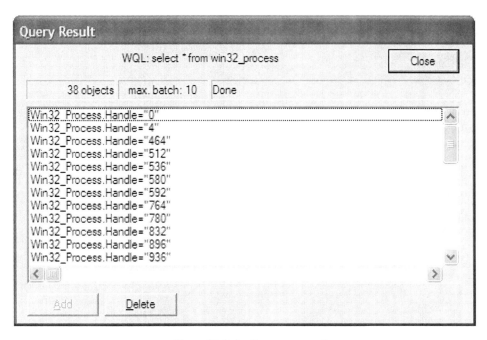

Figure 29-2: Another query result.

We can tell from this screenshot that the default key is Handle. The Handle is the same as the ProcessID. If you need a refresher on Wbemtest, see the earlier chapter, "Using WMI in Windows PowerShell."

Once we know this piece of information, we can write PowerShell code like this:

```
PS C:\> [wmi]$ps="root\cimv2:win32_process.handle='4536'"
PS C:\> $ps | Select Name,VirtualSize,WorkingSetSize,PageFileUsage,ExecutablePath


Name            : WINWORD.EXE
VirtualSize     : 451452928
WorkingSetSize  : 89120768
PageFileUsage   : 74940
ExecutablePath  : C:\Program Files\Microsoft Office\Office14\WINWORD.EXE
```

The [WMISearcher] Type

Finally, PowerShell also has a [WMISearcher] type. This allows you to submit a query to WMI and return a collection of objects:

```
PS C:\> [WMISearcher]$d = "Select * from Win32_Logicaldisk where drivetype = 3"
PS C:\> $d.get()


DeviceID     : C:
DriveType    : 3
ProviderName :
FreeSpace    : 3007844352
Size         : 15726702592
VolumeName   : Server2003

DeviceID     : E:
DriveType    : 3
ProviderName :
FreeSpace    : 3738099712
Size         : 24280993792
VolumeName   : XP
```

The object, $d, is a collection of all Win32_LogicalDisk instances where drive type is equal to 3. To access the collection, we call the **Get()** method. This technique is very helpful when you want to find dynamic information that might include multiple instances of a given WMI class:

```
PS C:\> [WMISearcher]$s="Select * from win32_Service where StartMode='Disabled'"
PS C:\> $s.Get() | format-table -autosize

ExitCode Name                            ProcessId StartMode State   Stat
-------- ----                            --------- --------- -----   --
    1077 Alerter                                 0 Disabled  Stopped OK
    1077 ALG                                     0 Disabled  Stopped OK
    1077 ClipSrv                                 0 Disabled  Stopped OK
    1077 FastUserSwitchingCompatibility          0 Disabled  Stopped OK
    1077 HidServ                                 0 Disabled  Stopped OK
    1077 Irmon                                   0 Disabled  Stopped OK
    1077 Messenger                               0 Disabled  Stopped OK
    1077 msvsmon80                               0 Disabled  Stopped OK
    1077 NetDDE                                  0 Disabled  Stopped OK
    1077 NetDDEdsdm                              0 Disabled  Stopped OK
    1077 RemoteAccess                            0 Disabled  Stopped OK
    1077 RemoteRegistry                          0 Disabled  Stopped OK
    1077 SCardSvr                                0 Disabled  Stopped OK
    1077 SharedAccess                            0 Disabled  Stopped OK
```

```
 1077 TermService                       0  Disabled  Stopped  OK
 1077 TlntSvr                           0  Disabled  Stopped  OK
 1077 WMDM PMSP Service                 0  Disabled  Stopped  OK

PS C:\>
```

If you want to query a remote system, you need to take an extra step to modify the management scope path:

```
PS C:\> $s.scope.path.path=\\server01\root\cimv2
PS C:\> $s.Get() | format-table -autosize
```

So, when should you use the **Get-WmiObject** cmdlet and when should you use the WMI type? If you know exactly the WMI object and instance you want to work with, and don't need to specify alternate credentials, then WMI type is the best and fastest approach. Otherwise, use the **Get-WmiObject** cmdlet.

Invoking WMI Methods

In PowerShell v1.0, calling a method of a WMI object was a little cumbersome. We had to resort to using a **ForEach** loop like this, even if there was only a single instance:

```
PS C:\> gwmi win32_process -filter "name='notepad.exe'" | foreach {$_.terminate()}
```

PowerShell v2.0 introduces the **Invoke_WmiMethod** cmdlet. This cmdlet shares many of the same parameters as **Get-WmiObject.** There are several ways you can use the cmdlet, depending on the method and objects you need to work with. Here's a simpler solution for our previous command:

```
PS C:\> gwmi win32_process -filter "name='notepad.exe'" | invoke-wmimethod -name terminate
```

Even if there are multiple instances of Notepad, they will all be terminated. You can also specify a particular WMI object, even on a remote computer. Let's change the Browser service on DC01 to have a startmode value of manual:

```
PS C:\> invoke-wmimethod -ComputerName dc01 -Credential $cred -path "win32_service.name='browser'" '
>>-name ChangeStartMode -argumentList "manual"
```

As you can see, we can include alternate credentials as we've done using a previously created PSCredential object. The path parameter is the WMI path to the object you want to manage, in this case the browser server. The name of the method we're invoking is **ChangeStartMode()** which takes an argument indicating the new start mode. The WMI method returns a results object. A return value of 0 generally indicates success. Any other value means something went wrong. You'll need to turn to the WMI documentation for the class and method on MSDN to interpret these values.

Practical Examples

Let's look at a few practical examples of using WMI and PowerShell. If you are like most administrators, you have a list or two of server names. Often, you want to obtain information from all of the servers in a list or perform some action against each of them, such as restarting a service. There are a few ways you can "process" multiple computers from a list. Here's one approach:

```
foreach ($server in (get-content servers.txt)) {
  # do something else to each computer
  Get-WmiObject <WMIClass or query> -computer $server
  }
```

With this approach, you can run multiple commands on each server, passing the server name as the **-computer** parameter for the **Get-WmiObject** cmdlet. Here's how this might look in a script:

```
foreach ($server in (get-content servers.txt)) {
  Write-Host $server.ToUpper() -fore Black -back Green
  Get-WmiObject Win32_Operatingsystem -computer $server |
   Format-Table Caption,BuildNumber,ServicePackMajorVersion
  Get-WmiObject Win32_Computersystem -computer $server |
   Format-Table Model,TotalPhysicalMemory
  }
```

The code snippet takes each computer name from servers.txt using the **Get-Content** cmdlet. Each time through the list, the computer name is assigned to the **$server** variable and first displayed by using the **Write-Host** cmdlet:

```
Write-Host $server.ToUpper() -fore Black -back Green
```

Then we execute two different **Get-WmiObject** expressions and pipe the results of each to the **Format-Table** cmdlet. The end result is information about each operating system, including its name and service pack version, as well as information about the server model and the total amount of physical memory.

If you are only executing a single command for each server, a more efficient approach is something like this:

```
Get-WmiObject <WMI Query or Class> -computer (Get-Content servers.txt)
```

You can use whatever syntax variation you want for the **Get-WmiObject** cmdlet. The trick here is that PowerShell will implicitly process the result of the **Get-Content** command as if you were using **ForEach**. Here's a variation on something we tried above:

```
PS C:\> Get-WmiObject Win32_Computersystem -computer (Get-Content servers.txt) |
>> Format-Table Model,TotalPhysicalMemory
>>
```

We will get a table with hardware model and total physical memory for each computer in the list. But if you run this yourself, you'll notice something is missing. How you can tell what information belongs to which computer? Easy. Have WMI tell you. Most WMI classes have a property, usually CSName, that will return the name of the computer. Testing your WMI expression will let you know what you can use. If nothing else, you can always use the __SERVER property. This is always populated. Here's our previous example revised to include the server name:

```
PS C:\> Get-WmiObject Win32_Computersystem -computer (Get-Content servers.txt) |
>> Format-Table __Server,Model,TotalPhysicalMemory
>>
```

Now you will get a more meaningful report.

Here's one more slightly complex example, but something you are likely to need. This code sample could be used in a script to return drive utilization information:

```
Get-WmiObject -query "Select * from win32_logicaldisk where drivetype=3" '
-computer (Get-Content servers.txt) -credential $cred | '
Format-Table @{Label="Server";Expression={$_.SystemName}},DeviceID,'
@{Label="Size (MB)";Expression={"{0:N2}" -f ($_.Size/1MB)}}, '
@{Label="Free (MB)";Expression={"{0:N2}" -f ($_.FreeSpace/1MB)}}
```

The **Get-WmiObject** cmdlet is using the query parameter to return all logical disks of drive type 3, which indicates a fixed local disk. The example runs this query against each computer listed in servers. txt. Our example also passes a stored set of alternate credentials, which has been saved ahead of time in the **$cred** variable.

We then pipe the results of the query to the **Format-Table** cmdlet, which creates a few custom table headers. Because the query returned the Size and FreeSpace properties in bytes, we'll format them to megabytes by using the format operator, **-f,**. The result is a table showing every server name, its fixed drives, and their size and free space in MB to two decimal places.

WMI Events and PowerShell

A particularly useful feature of WMI is the ability to subscribe to Windows events and execute code in response to each event. For example, you could run a WMI script that would check every five seconds to verify that a specific service had not stopped. Or you might need to monitor a folder and be notified when a new file is created. WMI events are used to meet these needs. PowerShell v2.0 includes cmdlets for working with WMI events.

Register-WmiEvent

The **Register-WmiEvent** cmdlet creates a WMI subscriber for a defined WMI event. You can define the monitored event several ways. The easiest way is to specify a WMI trace class. Use this expression to see the available classes:

```
PS C:\> gwmi -list | where {$_.name -match "trace"} | Select Name
```

For example, suppose you want to watch for when a new process is started. We'll use the Win32_ProcessStartTrace class:

```
PS C:\> register-wmiEvent -class 'Win32_ProcessStartTrace' -sourceIdentifier "NewProcess"
```

We also assign an identifier for this event which will come in handy later. If you run this command it appears that nothing happens. But in the background, we created a WMI subscriber and any time a new process is launched and a corresponding event is fired, the subscriber captures it. Even though our examples are for the local machine, you can monitor events on remote computers as well using the -computername parameter.

Get-Event

Assuming you've started some processes or launched applications, you can run the **Get-Event** cmdlet to see the results:

```
PS C:\> get-event
```

```
ComputerName    :
RunspaceId      : dc988f63-1ecd-4875-8023-7b96f754c0ab
EventIdentifier : 1587
Sender          : System.Management.ManagementEventWatcher
SourceEventArgs : System.Management.EventArrivedEventArgs
SourceArgs      : {System.Management.ManagementEventWatcher, System.Management.
EventArrivedEventArgs}
SourceIdentifier : NewProcess
TimeGenerated   : 4/14/2009 3:34:26 PM
MessageData     :

ComputerName    :
RunspaceId      : dc988f63-1ecd-4875-8023-7b96f754c0ab
EventIdentifier : 1588
Sender          : System.Management.ManagementEventWatcher
SourceEventArgs : System.Management.EventArrivedEventArgs
SourceArgs      : {System.Management.ManagementEventWatcher, System.Management.
EventArrivedEventArgs}
SourceIdentifier : NewProcess
TimeGenerated   : 4/14/2009 3:34:30 PM
MessageData     :
```

This will return all events. If you have multiple event subscribers, use the -sourceidentifier parameter:

```
PS C:\> get-event -sourceidentifier "NewProcess"
```

What is not easy is to figure out what process was started. The information is buried and hopefully will be easier to retrieve in future versions. Let's look at how to do it for a single event:

```
PS C:\> $p=(get-event)[0]
```

PowerShell embedded the process in the NewEvent property of the SourceEventArgs property:

```
PS C:\> $p.SourceEventArgs.NewEvent
```

```
__GENUS             : 2
__CLASS             : Win32_ProcessStartTrace
__SUPERCLASS        : Win32_ProcessTrace
__DYNASTY           : __SystemClass
__RELPATH           :
__PROPERTY_COUNT    : 8
__DERIVATION        : {Win32_ProcessTrace, Win32_SystemTrace, __ExtrinsicEvent, __Event...}
__SERVER            :
__NAMESPACE         :
__PATH              :
PageDirectoryBase   : 0
ParentProcessID     : 2932
ProcessID           : 7500
ProcessName         : notepad.exe
SECURITY_DESCRIPTOR :
SessionID           : 1
Sid                 : {1, 5, 0, 0...}
TIME_CREATED        : 128842112669259213
```

Armed with this information it's simple to pull new process event information:

```
PS C:\> get-event -SourceIdentifier "newProcess" | Select TimeGenerated,@{
>> name="Process";Expression={ ($_.SourceEventArgs.NewEvent).processname}}
>>
```

```
TimeGenerated                                          Process
-------------                                          -------
4/14/2009 3:34:26 PM                                   notepad.exe
4/14/2009 3:34:30 PM                                   calc.exe
4/14/2009 3:36:16 PM                                   more.com
4/14/2009 3:37:28 PM                                   SearchProtocolHost.exe
4/14/2009 3:37:28 PM                                   SearchFilterHost.exe
4/14/2009 3:39:36 PM                                   dllhost.exe
4/14/2009 3:39:38 PM                                   SearchProtocolHost.exe
4/14/2009 3:39:38 PM                                   SearchFilterHost.exe
4/14/2009 3:40:49 PM                                   notepad.exe
4/14/2009 3:41:09 PM                                   more.com
4/14/2009 3:41:12 PM                                   more.com
4/14/2009 3:41:48 PM                                   notepad.exe
4/14/2009 3:42:32 PM                                   notepad.exe
4/14/2009 3:42:55 PM                                   taskeng.exe
4/14/2009 3:42:56 PM                                   mcupdate.exe
```

Remove-Event

The event queue will fill up pretty quickly. You can use the **Remove-Event** cmdlet to remove specific events or all events associated with a source identifier:

```
PS C:\> remove-event -SourceIdentifier "newprocess"
```

Unregister-Event

Even though you may have removed the event, this does not prevent additional events from queuing as they are fired. Doing so will require system resources, so if you no longer need to monitor the start process event use **Unregister-Event**:

```
PS C:\> Unregister-Event -SourceIdentifier "NewProcess"
```

This snippet is only removing the NewProcess event subscription. If other subscriptions are defined, they will remain.

Querying for Specific Events

If you need a more refined approach, you can also use a WMI query with the **Register-WmiEvent** cmdlet:

```
PS C:\> register-wmiEvent -query "Select * from win32_ProcessStartTrace where
processname='notepad.exe'" -sourceIdentifier "New Notepad"
```

This creates a new event subscription that will only fire when Notepad is launched. The **Register-WmiEvent** cmdlet also has an -**Action** parameter, which will execute a defined script block when a targeted event fires instead of sending it to the queue. Let's create an event subscription that watches for when Notepad.exe ends:

```
PS C:\> register-wmiEvent '
>> -query "Select * from win32_ProcessStopTrace where processname='notepad.exe'" '
>> -sourceIdentifier "Close Notepad" -action {("{0} Notepad has terminated" -f (get-date)) |
>. Add-content c:\log.txt}
>>

Id        Name            State        HasMoreData   Location    Command
--        ----            -----        -----------   --------    -------
1         Close Notepad   NotStarted   False                     ("{0} Notepad has term...
```

This expression is watching for events where Notepad.exe is terminated. When the event fires, the action script block instructs PowerShell to write information to a log file. This will continue until you unregister the "Close Notepad" event.

Watching Services

Let's look at another scenario and another technique. You may want to watch for when a mission-critical service stops. There are no trace classes for service objects, but there are other classes we can use. WMI has several system classes that we can take advantage of:

- __InstanceCreationEvent

- __InstanceModificationEvent

- __InstanceDeletionEvent

The names should give you a good idea of what to expect. These are very broad events so we need to build a more refined query. When one of these events fires, a new object, the *targetinstance*, is also created as a returned property. In our situation the target instance will be a Win32_service object. Let's further stipulate we want to watch for changes to the Secondary Logon service. We might come up with a query like this:

```
Select * from __InstanceModificationEvent where TargetInstance ISA 'win32_service' and
name='seclogon'
```

In practice though, we probably don't need to be constantly checking for when an event fires. Instead we will use a *polling* interval to tell WMI to check every *x* number of seconds. Here's the revised query:

```
$query="Select * from __InstanceModificationEvent within 10 where TargetInstance ISA 'win32_ser-
vice' and Targetinstance.name='seclogon'"
```

Now let's use it with the **Register-WmiEvent** cmdlet:

```
PS C:\> Register-WmiEvent -Query $query -SourceIdentifier "Service Change" -ComputerName "CHAOS"
```

If we modify the service in some way, the event will fire and we can retrieve it with the **Get-Event** cmdlet:

```
PS C:\> get-event -SourceIdentifier "Service Change"


ComputerName    :
RunspaceId      : dc988f63-1ecd-4875-8023-7b96f754c0ab
EventIdentifier : 1616
Sender          : System.Management.ManagementEventWatcher
```

```
SourceEventArgs  : System.Management.EventArrivedEventArgs
SourceArgs       : {System.Management.ManagementEventWatcher, System.Management.
EventArrivedEventArgs}
SourceIdentifier : Service Change
TimeGenerated    : 4/14/2009 5:07:50 PM
MessageData      :
```

Using our technique from earlier yields slightly different results:

```
PS C:\> (get-event -SourceIdentifier "Service Change").SourceEventArgs.newEvent


__GENUS            : 2
__CLASS            : __InstanceModificationEvent
__SUPERCLASS       : __InstanceOperationEvent
__DYNASTY          : __SystemClass
__RELPATH          :
__PROPERTY_COUNT   : 4
__DERIVATION       : {__InstanceOperationEvent, __Event, __IndicationRelated, __SystemClass}
__SERVER           : CHAOS
__NAMESPACE        : //./root/CIMV2
__PATH             :
PreviousInstance   : System.Management.ManagementBaseObject
SECURITY_DESCRIPTOR :
TargetInstance     : System.Management.ManagementBaseObject
TIME_CREATED       : 128842168700235873
```

We already know what service was changed. But suppose we didn't'? We also can't tell from this what change was made. Notice the TargetInstance property? There is also a PreviousInstance property that holds the object's previous state. Comparing the two objects isn't too difficult, although it does require a little finesse:

```
PS C:\> $event=(get-event -SourceIdentifier "Service Change").SourceEventArgs.newEvent
PS C:\> $previous=$event.previousinstance
PS C:\> $target=$event.targetinstance
PS C:\> foreach ($property in ($previous.psbase.properties)) {
>>    if ($previous.($property.name) -ne $target.($property.name))
>>    {
>>       $obj=New-Object PSObject
>>       $obj | Add-Member Noteproperty "Property" $property.name
>>       $obj | Add-Member Noteproperty "Previous" $previous.($property.name)
>>       $obj | Add-Member Noteproperty "Target" $target.($property.name)
>>       write $obj
>>    }
>>
>> }
>>

Property                          Previous                          Target
--------                          --------                          ------
State                             Paused                            Running


PS C:\>
```

This could probably be written more concisely but we didn't want to sacrifice the clarity. We first create a variable for the event object. Remember, this has previous and target instance properties, which we also save to variables. The **ForEach** construct enumerates the properties of the previous instance, which should be identical in name, but not value, to the target instance. Within the enumeration, we compare the property on both objects. If they are different, we create a custom object and add some properties so we can see what properties changed between the two objects.

Watching Files and Folders

We'll wrap up our discussion of WMI Events with another common request we've seen: notification when a folder changes. Usually the requirement is to watch for new files and take action when they are detected. Here's how we might solve this problem.

We will use a WMI query for the __InstanceCreationEvent class where the target instance is a CIM_DATAFILE. This class can be tricky to work with and in our experience the more specific you can make your query the better:

```
PS C:\> $computername="CHAOS"
PS C:\> $drive="c:"
PS C:\> #folder path must escape the \ with another \
PS C:\> $folder="\\test\\files\\"
PS C:\> $poll=10
PS C:\> $query="Select * from __InstanceCreationEvent Within $poll where TargetInstance ISA 'CIM_
datafile' AND TargetInstance.drive='$drive' AND TargetInstance.Path='$folder'"
PS C:\> Register-WmiEvent -Query $query -SourceIdentifier "New File" -MessageData "File Created"
-computername $computer
```

When the script creates a new file in C:\test\files, it fires an event that the event subscriber receives:

```
PS C:\> get-event


ComputerName     :
RunspaceId       : 186e078f-b685-40dc-955f-12ad1eb0f17f
EventIdentifier  : 1
Sender           : System.Management.ManagementEventWatcher
SourceEventArgs  : System.Management.EventArrivedEventArgs
SourceArgs       : {System.Management.ManagementEventWatcher, System.Management.
EventArrivedEventArgs}
SourceIdentifier : New File
TimeGenerated    : 4/15/2009 9:08:32 AM
MessageData      : File Created
```

As before, we need to dig a little to get information about the target instance:

```
PS C:\> get-event -SourceIdentifier "New File" | foreach {
>>   $_.sourceEventArgs.NewEvent.TargetInstance
>> }
>>


__GENUS          : 2
__CLASS          : CIM_DataFile
__SUPERCLASS     : CIM_LogicalFile
__DYNASTY        : CIM_ManagedSystemElement
__RELPATH        : CIM_DataFile.Name="c:\\test\\files\\data20.txt"
__PROPERTY_COUNT : 33
__DERIVATION     : {CIM_LogicalFile, CIM_LogicalElement, CIM_ManagedSystemElement}
__SERVER         : CHAOS
__NAMESPACE      : root\CIMV2
__PATH           : \\CHAOS\root\CIMV2:CIM_DataFile.Name="c:\\test\\files\\data20.txt"
AccessMask       : 18809343
```

```
Archive                 : True
Caption                 : c:\test\files\data20.txt
Compressed              : False
CompressionMethod       :
CreationClassName       : CIM_LogicalFile
CreationDate            : 20090415090831.728186-240
CSCreationClassName     : Win32_ComputerSystem
CSName                  : CHAOS
Description             : c:\test\files\data20.txt
Drive                   : c:
EightDotThreeFileName   : c:\test\files\data20.txt
Encrypted               : False
EncryptionMethod        :
Extension               : txt
FileName                : data20
FileSize                : 18648
FileType                : Text Document
FSCreationClassName     : Win32_FileSystem
FSName                  : NTFS
Hidden                  : False
InstallDate             : 20090415090831.728186-240
InUseCount              :
LastAccessed            : 20090415090831.728186-240
LastModified            : 20090415090831.974211-240
Manufacturer            :
Name                    : c:\test\files\data20.txt
Path                    : \test\files\
Readable                : True
Status                  : OK
System                  : False
Version                 :
Writeable               : True


PS C:\>
```

Use the standard PowerShell cmdlets to filter, select, or sort the output.

The **Register-WmiEvent** cmdlet has a handy parameter for this specific situation: -Action. You might want to add code to copy the new file or perhaps send an e-mail notification. The possibilities are limited only by your creativity.

....

Read More About It

Our book, Advanced VBScript for Microsoft Windows Administrators (Microsoft Press 2006), has a chapter devoted to scripting events with WMI. Even though the topic is covered from a VBScript point of view, it should still give you some helpful information. You should be able to use the examples as starting points for your PowerShell script development.

Chapter 30
Managing Services

PowerShell offers several cmdlets that make managing Windows servers a breeze. We briefly discuss the cmdlets you will use most often in the following sections.

Listing Services

We've used the **Get-Service** cmdlet in many examples throughout this book. The **Get-Service** cmdlet with no parameters will display some information about the services on your computer. Usually you want to filter out services. Here's a standard expression to list all running services:

```
PS C:\> get-service | Where {$_.status -eq "Running"}
```

We'll omit results as you can easily run this command yourself. The **Get-Service** cmdlet also supports wildcards, useful when you aren't sure of the exact service name. The cmdlet's alias is **gsv**:

```
PS C:\> gsv sp*

Status    Name          DisplayName
------    ----          -----------
Running   Spooler       Print Spooler
Stopped   sppsvc        Software Protection
Stopped   sppuinotify   SPP Notification Service
```

Or if you only know services by their display name, the **-DisplayName** parameter will come in handy. It too, supports wildcards:

```
PS C:\> gsv -DisplayName Microsoft*

Status     Name                DisplayName
------     ----                -----------
Stopped    clr_optimizatio...  Microsoft .NET Framework NGEN v2.0....
Stopped    MSiSCSI             Microsoft iSCSI Initiator Service
Stopped    swprv               Microsoft Software Shadow Copy Prov...
```

PowerShell v2.0 also made it easier to identify required services, that is, services that the specified service relies on:

```
PS C:\>  gsv winrm -RequiredServices

Status     Name                DisplayName
------     ----                -----------
Running    RPCSS               Remote Procedure Call (RPC)
Running    HTTP                HTTP
```

This means that in order for the WinRM service to function, the RPCSS and HTTP services must be running.

We can also look at this from the other end and see what services depend on a specific service:

```
PS C:\> gsv http -DependentServices

Status     Name                DisplayName
------     ----                -----------
Running    WMPNetworkSvc       Windows Media Player Network Sharin...
Running    WinRM               Windows Remote Management (WS-Manag...
Stopped    Wecsvc              Windows Event Collector
Stopped    upnphost            UPnP Device Host
Stopped    Mcx2Svc             Media Center Extender Service
Running    SSDPSRV             SSDP Discovery
Running    Spooler             Print Spooler
Stopped    RemoteAccess        Routing and Remote Access
Stopped    PeerDistSvc         BranchCache
Stopped    HomeGroupProvider   HomeGroup Provider
Running    FDResPub            Function Discovery Resource Publica...
Stopped    IPBusEnum           PnP-X IP Bus Enumerator
Stopped    fdPHost             Function Discovery Provider Host
```

These are all the services that rely on the HTTP service. Notice WinRM in the list?

....

Elevated Sessions

You may find on some platforms such as Windows 7 or Windows Server 2008 that you can't get detailed information for some services. If that is the case, make sure you have started PowerShell with elevated credentials, even if you are logging on as an administrator.

Here's a short script that recursively calls itself to get the required services for a given service:

Get-Required.ps1

```
#requires -version 2.0

param (
```

```
  [Parameter(
   ValueFromPipeline=$false,
   Position=0,
   Mandatory=$True,
   HelpMessage="Enter a service name like spooler.")]
   [String]$service,

   [Parameter(
   ValueFromPipeline=$false,
   Position=1,
   Mandatory=$false,
   HelpMessage="Enter a computername. The default is the local computer.")]
   [String]$computername=$env:computername
   )

#make sure you run this in an elevated PowerShell session

function Get-Required {
#requires -version 2.0
  Param([string]$name,[string]$computername)

  $errorActionPreference="SilentlyContinue"

  Get-Service -Name $name -computername $computername -requiredServices  | foreach {
  #write the service name to the pipeline
   write $_
   Get-Required $_.name $computername
   #filter out duplicates based on displayname
  } | select displayname -unique | foreach {
  #then get the re-get the service object
   Get-Service -DisplayName $_.displayname -computername $computername
  }

 } #end function

#main script body
try {
 Get-Service -Name $service -computername $computername -ea stop | Out-Null
 Get-Required $service $computername
}
catch {
 Write-Warning "Failed to find service $service on $computername"
}
Finally {}
```

The script takes a service and computer name as parameters. If you don't specify a computer name, the script defaults to the local computer. The purpose of the script is to display all services required for a given service to start. For example, the BITS service requires the RPCSS service, which in turn requires DcomLaunch and RpcEptMapper. The Get-Required.ps1 script calls the Get-Required function which uses the **Get-Service** cmdlet to get the required services:

```
 Get-Service -Name $name -computername $computername -requiredServices  | foreach {
```

Each required service is then passed to the function again:

```
 ...| foreach {
 #write the service name to the pipeline
  write $_
  Get-Required $_.name $computername
```

It is likely that some services may have the same requirements, so we need a little sleight of hand to filter out the duplicates:

```
#filter out duplicates based on displayname
} | select displayname -unique | foreach {
#then get the re-get the service object
 Get-Service -DisplayName $_.displayname -computername $computername
}
```

When executed, you have a list of all services necessary for a given service to run. Here are all the required services for BITS:

```
PS C:\> c:\scripts\Get-Required.ps1 bits

Status    Name                DisplayName
------    ----                -----------
Running   EventSystem         COM+ Event System
Running   RpcSs               Remote Procedure Call (RPC)
Running   DcomLaunch          DCOM Server Process Launcher
Running   RpcEptMapper        RPC Endpoint Mapper
```

Starting Services

It should come as no surprise that PowerShell uses the **Start-Service** cmdlet to start a service. You can specify the service by its real name:

```
PS C:\> start-service -name "spooler"
```

Alternatively, you can specify the service by its display name:

```
PS C:\> start-service -Displayname "Print spooler"
```

Be sure to use quotes for the display name, since it usually contains spaces. Because the cmdlet doesn't display a result unless there is an error, you can use the **-Passthru** parameter to force the cmdlet to pass objects down the pipeline:

```
PS C:\> start-service -displayname "print spooler" -passthru

Status    Name                DisplayName
------    ----                -----------
Running   Spooler             Print Spooler


PS C:\>
```

Stopping Services

Stopping services is just as easy. Everything we discussed about starting services applies to stopping services. The only difference is, we use the **Stop-Service** cmdlet:

```
PS C:\> stop-service webclient -passthru
```

```
Status  Name           DisplayName
------  ----           -----------
Stopped WebClient      WebClient


PS C:\>
```

Suspending and Resuming Services

You can suspend or pause some services. This doesn't stop the service completely; it only prevents it from doing anything. Be aware that not all services support suspension:

```
PS C:\> suspend-service spooler
Suspend-Service : Service 'Print Spooler (Spooler)' cannot be suspended because the service does
not support being suspended or resumed.
At line:1 char:16
+ suspend-service <<<< spooler
PS C:\>
```

If you can suspend a service, you'll see something like this:

```
PS C:\> suspend-service w3svc -passthru

Status  Name           DisplayName
------  ----           -----------
Paused  W3SVC          World Wide Web Publishing


PS C:\>
```

Use the **Resume-Service** cmdlet to resume a suspended service:

```
PS C:\> resume-service w3svc -passthru

Status  Name           DisplayName
------  ----           -----------
Running W3SVC          World Wide Web Publishing


PS C:\>
```

Restarting Services

If you want to restart a service, you could use the combination of the **Stop-Service** and **Start-Service** cmdlets. But the simpler approach would be to use the **Restart-Service** cmdlet:

```
PS C:\> restart-service spooler
WARNING: Waiting for service 'Print Spooler (Spooler)' to finish starting...
PS C:\> get-service spooler

Status  Name           DisplayName
------  ----           -----------
Running Spooler        Print Spooler
```

For services with dependencies, you'll need to use the **-Force** parameter, otherwise PowerShell will object:

```
PS C:\> restart-service lanmanserver
Restart-Service : Cannot stop service 'Server (lanmanserver)' because it has dependent services.
It can only be stopped if the Force flag is set.
At line:1 char:16
+ restart-service <<<< lanmanserver
PS C:\> (get-service lanmanserver).DependentServices

Status  Name            DisplayName
------  ----            -----------
Running Browser         Computer Browser
```

The solution is to use the **-Force** parameter:

```
PS C:\> restart-service lanmanserver -force -passthru

Status  Name            DisplayName
------  ----            -----------
Running lanmanserver    Server
```

Managing Services

Use the **Set-Service** cmdlet to change a service's start mode, say from Auto to Manual. You can either specify the service by name or display name:

```
PS C:\> set-service -name spooler -StartupType Manual
```

You can change the Startup Type to Automatic, Manual, or Disabled. Unfortunately, there are no provisions in the **Get-Service** cmdlet to see the start-mode. You'll need to use WMI.

The **Set-Service** cmdlet also allows you to modify the current status of the service, and even allows you to pipe in services (retrieved with the **Get-Service** cmdlet) or service names from a text file. For example:

```
PS C:\> Get-Service | Set-Service -status "Running"
```

Be careful—that'll attempt to start every service on your computer! The **Set-Service** cmdlet has several other capabilities, including:

- An **-include** and **-exclude** parameter, which allow you to filter the services affected by the cmdlet.

- A **-passThru** parameter, which outputs whatever services the **Set-Service** cmdlet modifies so that additional cmdlets can do something with them.

- Parameters for **-Name**, **-DisplayName**, and **-Description** that allow you to modify the settings of services.

- A **-Computername** parameter for managing services on remote computers.

PowerShell has no built-in method for changing the service account or its password; instead, you'll have to use WMI—the Win32_Service class has much broader capabilities—to perform these and additional service-related tasks. If you need to work with services on remote systems, then this is the only way you can accomplish these tasks.

Get Service Information with Get-WmiObject

Here is the basic command:

```
PS C:\> Get-WmiObject win32_service
```

This will provide a list of service information on the local system. There are several ways to filter WMI information. Here's one approach:

```
PS C:\> Get-WmiObject win32_service -filter "state='running'"| Select Name,State,StartMode
```

```
Name                State       StartMode
----                -----       ---------
AcrSch2Svc          Running     Auto
ALG                 Running     Manual
AppMgmt             Running     Manual
AudioSrv            Running     Auto
Avg7Alrt            Running     Auto
Avg7UpdSvc          Running     Auto
AVGEMS              Running     Auto
BITS                Running     Manual
CryptSvc            Running     Auto
DcomLaunch          Running     Auto
Dhcp                Running     Auto
Dnscache            Running     Auto
```

We've truncated the output to save space. Because we can't do it with the basic service cmdlets, let's find services where the startup type is not **Auto**:

```
PS C:\> Get-WmiObject win32_service -filter "StartMode != 'Auto'"| Select Name,StartMode |
>> sort StartMode | format-table
>>
```

```
Name                            StartMode
----                            ---------
MSSQLServerADHelper             Disabled
NetDDE                          Disabled
Messenger                       Disabled
FastUserSwitchingCompatibility  Disabled
Irmon                           Disabled
SQLBrowser                      Disabled
TlntSvr                         Disabled
RemoteAccess                    Disabled
NetDDEdsdm                      Disabled
NetTcpPortSharing               Disabled
Alerter                         Disabled
ClipSrv                         Disabled
ALG                             Manual
SCardSvr                        Manual
SSDPSRV                         Manual
SwPrv                           Manual
SysmonLog                       Manual
RasMan                          Manual
RasAuto                         Manual
Pml Driver HPZ12                Manual
```

Again, we've truncated the output. One thing to be aware of is that even though we are working with services, there are two different objects. The objects returned by the **Get-Service** cmdlet are

417

ServiceController objects and the objects from the **Get-WmiObject** cmdlet are Win32_Service objects. Each object may have a different name for the same property. For example, the ServiceController object's property name is "State" while it is "Status" for the Win32_Service. But both will indicate whether a service is running, stopped, or whatever. But this doesn't mean we can't combine the best of both worlds:

```
PS C:\> Get-WmiObject win32_service -filter "StartMode = 'Disabled'" |

>> set-service -startuptype Manual -whatif
>>

What if: Performing operation "Set-Service" on Target "Media Center Extender Service (Mcx2Svc)".
What if: Performing operation "Set-Service" on Target "Net.Tcp Port Sharing Service (NetTcpPortSharing)".
What if: Performing operation "Set-Service" on Target "Routing and Remote Access (RemoteAccess)".
What if: Performing operation "Set-Service" on Target "Internet Connection Sharing (ICS) (SharedAccess)".
What if: Performing operation "Set-Service" on Target "Telnet (TlntSvr)".
```

This snippet takes the output of the **Get-WmiObject** cmdlet that will return all disabled services and pipes it to the **Set-Service** cmdlet, which changes the startup type to **Manual**. We've also added the **-Whatif** parameter, which displays what would have happened.

Change Service Logon Account

To change the logon account for a service requires WMI. Suppose you want to change the logon account for the Search service. We'll start by creating an object for the Search service:

```
PS C:\> [wmi]$svc=Get-wmiobject -query "Select * from win32_service where name='wsearch'"
```

We can check the StartName property to see the current service account:

```
PS C:\> $svc.StartName
LocalSystem
```

To change the service configuration requires us to invoke the **Change()** method. Reading the MSDN documentation for this method http://msdn.microsoft.com/en-us/library/aa384901(VS.85).aspx, we see that the method requires multiple parameters:

```
Change(DisplayName, PathName, ServiceType, ErrorControl, StartMode,
DesktopInteract, StartName, StartPassword, LoadOrderGroup,
LoadOrderGroupDependencies, ServiceDependencies)
```

Even though we only want to change the **StartName** and **StartPassword** parameters, we still have to provide information for the other parameters. In PowerShell, we can pass **$Null**. This will keep existing settings for the service:

```
PS C:\> $svc.Change($Null,$Null,$Null,$Null,$Null,$Null,"MyDomain\svcAccount","P@ssw0rd123")
```

We use **$Null** for the first six parameters, and then specify the new account and password. We don't have to specify the service parameters after the password since they aren't changing. They will assumed to be $Null. If you are successful, WMI will return a value of 0:

```
__GENUS          : 2
__CLASS          : __PARAMETERS
__SUPERCLASS     :
__DYNASTY        : __PARAMETERS
__RELPATH        :
__PROPERTY_COUNT : 1
__DERIVATION     : {}
__SERVER         :
__NAMESPACE      :
__PATH           :
ReturnValue      : 0
```

If you get any other errors, check the MSDN documentation for the error code.

....

What About Invoke-WMIMethod?

Theoretically you should also be able to use the Invoke-WMIMethod cmdlet to make this change. However, we have not had any success. We suspect the cmdlet is getting hung up on all the $Null values we're passing. For methods with one or two parameters, this cmdlet should work just fine.

Of course, the new settings won't take effect until you restart the service:

```
PS C:\> restart-service "wsearch"
```

Because we are using the **Get-WmiObject** cmdlet, you could also do this for services on remote computers:

```
PS C:\> [wmi]$svc=Get-wmiobject -query "Select * from win32_service where name='Alerter'" '
>> -computer "FILE01" -credential "mydomain\administrator"
>>
PS C:\>
```

From this point, everything else is the same, except for restarting the service. For that we can use the **Invoke-WMIMethod** cmdlet against the remote computer.

```
PS C:\> invoke-wmimethod -path "\\file01\root\cimv2:win32_service.name='alerter'" -name stopservice '
>>-credential "mydomain\administrator"
>>
```

```
__GENUS          : 2
__CLASS          : __PARAMETERS
__SUPERCLASS     :
__DYNASTY        : __PARAMETERS
__RELPATH        :
__PROPERTY_COUNT : 1
__DERIVATION     : {}
__SERVER         :
__NAMESPACE      :
__PATH           :
ReturnValue      : 0
```

```
PS C:\> invoke-wmimethod -path "\\file01\root\cimv2:win32_service.name='alerter'" -name startservice '
>>-credential "mydomain\administrator"
```

```
>>


__GENUS          : 2
__CLASS          : __PARAMETERS
__SUPERCLASS     :
__DYNASTY        : __PARAMETERS
__RELPATH        :
__PROPERTY_COUNT : 1
__DERIVATION     : {}
__SERVER         :
__NAMESPACE      :
__PATH           :
ReturnValue      : 0



PS C:\>
```

Controlling Services on Remote Computers

To control services on remote computers, such as starting, stopping, or pausing, you can't use the PowerShell cmdlets. You will have to use the WMI methods. WMI does not have a restart method, but we can achieve the same result by using the WMI service object, **$svc**:

```
PS C:\> $svc.StopService()
PS C:\> $svc.StartService()
```

You would use these commands at the end of our change service account process. In fact, there's no reason you couldn't use them for managing services on the local system as well. If you want to pause or resume a service, the methods are **PauseService()** and **ResumeService()**. In case you are jumping around, be sure to look at the examples above for how to use the **Invoke-WMIMethod** cmdlet.

Change Service Logon Account Password

Changing the service account password uses essentially the same approach as changing the **Startname** parameter. The only service parameter that is changing is **StartPassword**:

```
PS C:\> [wmi]$svc=Get-wmiobject -query "Select * from win32_service where name='Alerter'"
PS C:\> $rc=$svc.Change($Null,$Null,$Null,$Null,$Null,$Null,$Null,"N3wP@ssw")
PS C:\> if ($rc -eq 0) {restart-service "Alerter"} else {
>> write-host -foreground "RED" "Changing password failed with a return value of $rc."}
>>
PS C:\>
```

As we did with changing the service account on a remote computer, you can use the same techniques for changing the service account password as well, by specifying a remote computer name and alternate credentials.

Note

The WMI Win32_Service class isn't compatible with cmdlets like Stop-Service and Start-Service. That is, you can't get a bunch of Win32_Service objects and pipe them to the Start-Service cmdlet; the *-Service cmdlets only accept service objects generated by the Get-Service cmdlet.

Chapter 31
Managing Permissions

Managing file permissions with scripting has always been a popular and challenging task. Even though PowerShell provides new ways to access and work with access-control lists (ACLs), you still may find more familiar command-line utilities—Cacls.exe, Xcacls.exe, Dsacls.exe, and forth—easier to use. And the good news is that you can use them right from within PowerShell! In this chapter, we'll also look at PowerShell's native abilities to work with permissions.

Viewing Permissions

You can use the **Get-Acl** cmdlet to obtain security descriptor information for files, folders, printers, registry keys, and more. By default, all information is displayed in a table format:

```
PS C:\> get-acl $env:systemroot\regedit.exe


    Directory: C:\Windows


Path                    Owner                          Access
----                    -----                          ------
regedit.exe             NT SERVICE\TrustedInstaller    NT AUTHORITY\SYSTEM Allow
ReadAndE...

PS C:\>
```

The problem is that some of the information is truncated. Therefore, you'll probably prefer to use something like this:

```
PS C:\> get-acl $env:systemroot\regedit.exe |format-list

Path    : Microsoft.PowerShell.Core\FileSystem::C:\Windows\regedit.exe
Owner   : NT SERVICE\TrustedInstaller
Group   : NT SERVICE\TrustedInstaller
Access  : NT AUTHORITY\SYSTEM Allow  ReadAndExecute, Synchronize
          BUILTIN\Administrators Allow  ReadAndExecute, Synchronize
          BUILTIN\Users Allow  ReadAndExecute, Synchronize
          NT SERVICE\TrustedInstaller Allow  FullControl
Audit   :
Sddl    : O:S-1-5-80-956008885-3418522649-1831038044-1853292631-2271478464G:S-1-5-80-956008885-3418522649-
          1831038044-1853292631- 271478464D:PAI(A;;0x1200a9;;;SY)(A;;0x1200a9;;;BA)(A;;0x1200a9;;;BU)(A;;F
          A;;;S-1-5-80-956008885-3418522649-1831038044-1853292631-2271478464)


PS C:\>
```

The **Get-Acl** cmdlet writes an object to the pipeline that is part of the System.Security.AccessControl .NET class. Access information is presented as a System.Security.AccessControl.FileSystemAccessRule object which you can vie via the Access property.

```
PS C:\> (get-acl $env:systemroot\regedit.exe).Access


FileSystemRights  : ReadAndExecute, Synchronize
AccessControlType : Allow
IdentityReference : NT AUTHORITY\SYSTEM
IsInherited       : False
InheritanceFlags  : None
PropagationFlags  : None

FileSystemRights  : ReadAndExecute, Synchronize
AccessControlType : Allow
IdentityReference : BUILTIN\Administrators
IsInherited       : False
InheritanceFlags  : None
PropagationFlags  : None

FileSystemRights  : ReadAndExecute, Synchronize
AccessControlType : Allow
IdentityReference : BUILTIN\Users
IsInherited       : False
InheritanceFlags  : None
PropagationFlags  : None

FileSystemRights  : FullControl
AccessControlType : Allow
IdentityReference : NT SERVICE\TrustedInstaller
IsInherited       : False
InheritanceFlags  : None
PropagationFlags  : None
```

Or, you may prefer output that is more like Cacls.exe, which you can get by looking at the AccessToString property:

```
PS C:\> (get-acl $env:systemroot\regedit.exe).AccessToString
NT AUTHORITY\SYSTEM Allow  ReadAndExecute, Synchronize
BUILTIN\Administrators Allow  ReadAndExecute, Synchronize
BUILTIN\Users Allow  ReadAndExecute, Synchronize
NT SERVICE\TrustedInstaller Allow  FullControl
```

The **Get-Acl** cmdlet also works for directories:

```
PS C:\> get-acl $pshome | format-list

Path    : Microsoft.PowerShell.Core\FileSystem::C:\Windows\System32\WindowsPowerShell\v1.0
Owner   : NT SERVICE\TrustedInstaller
Group   : NT SERVICE\TrustedInstaller
Access  : CREATOR OWNER Allow  268435456
          NT AUTHORITY\SYSTEM Allow  268435456
          NT AUTHORITY\SYSTEM Allow  Modify, Synchronize
          BUILTIN\Administrators Allow  268435456
          BUILTIN\Administrators Allow  Modify, Synchronize
          BUILTIN\Users Allow  -1610612736
          BUILTIN\Users Allow  ReadAndExecute, Synchronize
          NT SERVICE\TrustedInstaller Allow  268435456
          NT SERVICE\TrustedInstaller Allow  FullControl
Audit   :
Sddl    : O:S-1-5-80-956008885-3418522649-1831038044-1853292631-2271478464G:S-1-5-80-956008885-3418522649-
          1831038044-1853292631-1271478464D:PAI(A;OICIIO;GA;;;CO)(A;OICIIO;GA;;;SY)(A;;0x1301bf;;;SY)(A;OIC
          IIO;GA;;;BA)(A;;0x1301bf;;;BA)(A;OICIIO;GXGR;;;BU)(A;;0x1200a9;;;BU)(A;CIIO;GA;;;S-1-5-80-9560088
          85-3418522649-1831038044-1853292631-2271478464)(A;;FA;;;S-1-5-80-956008885-3418522649-1831038044-
          1853292631-2271478464)

PS C:\>
```

It will even work on registry keys:

```
PS C:\> get-acl HKLM:\software\microsoft\windows\CurrentVersion\run|format-list

Path    : Microsoft.PowerShell.Core\Registry::HKEY_LOCAL_MACHINE\software\microsoft\windows\
CurrentVersi...
Owner   : BUILTIN\Administrators
Group   : BUILTIN\Administrators
Access  : BUILTIN\Users Allow  ReadKey
          BUILTIN\Users Allow  -2147483648
          BUILTIN\Administrators Allow  FullControl
          BUILTIN\Administrators Allow  268435456
          NT AUTHORITY\SYSTEM Allow  FullControl
          NT AUTHORITY\SYSTEM Allow  268435456
          CREATOR OWNER Allow  268435456
Audit   :
Sddl    : O:BAG:BAD:AI(A;ID;KR;;;BU)(A;CIIOID;GR;;;BU)(A;ID;KA;;;BA)(A;CIIOID;GA;;;BA)(A;ID;KA;;;SY)
          (A;CIIOID;GA;;;SY)(A;CIIOID;GA;;;CO)

PS C:\>
```

Notice that the cmdlet returns the owner. You can create a **Get-Acl** expression to display just that information:

```
PS C:\> get-acl c:\files\*.exe | format-table PSChildName,Owner -autosize

PSChildName                                           Owner
-----------                                           -----
ActiveRolesManagementShellforActiveDirectoryx64_12.exe  MYCOMPANY\adeco
ActiveRolesManagementShellforActiveDirectory_12.exe   MYCOMPANY\adeco
ChromeSetup.exe                                       MYCOMPANY\File Admins
helpshop(1).exe                                       MYCOMPANY\File Admins
hmsetup.exe                                           MYCOMPANY\File Admins
htmlhelp.exe                                          MYCOMPANY\File Admins
```

```
IE8-WindowsVista-x64-ENU.exe                          MYCOMPANY\File Admins
IE8-WindowsVista-x86-ENU.exe                          MYCOMPANY\File Admins
jing_setup.exe                                        MYCOMPANY\File Admins
linkd.exe                                             MYCOMPANY\File Admins
LiveMesh.exe                                          MYCOMPANY\File Admins
LiveMesh32.exe                                        MYCOMPANY\File Admins
msicuu2.exe                                           BUILTIN\Administrators
PrimalPad.exe                                         BUILTIN\Administrators
registry-defrag-setup.exe                             BUILTIN\Administrators
VMware-Vim4PS-1.5.0-142961.exe                        BUILTIN\Administrators
WindowsServer2003.WindowsXP-KB926141-x64-ENU.exe      BUILTIN\Administrators
WindowsXPMode_en-us.exe                               O:S-1-5-21-2704478247-3271226993-
4103978002-1112
wpilauncher.exe                                       BUILTIN\Administrators
wwhelp_rt.exe                                         BUILTIN\Administrators
...
```

We've truncated and edited the output to fit the page, but you get the idea.

....

What about Active Directory?
PowerShell itself does include anyr Active Directory cmdlets or providers. Windows Server 2008
R2 does ship with an Active Directory module that does include cmdlets, but even here there is
nothing designed to work with Active Directory permissions. The best approach is to continue using
command-line tools like Dsacls.exe.

Viewing Permissions for an Entire Object Hierarchy

The **Get-Acl** cmdlet doesn't have a **Recurse()** method, but we won't let that slow us down. If you want a report to show owners for a directory structure, you can use a script like this:

GetOwnerReport.ps1

```
#GetOwnerReport
$report="C:\OwnerReport.csv"
$StartingDir=Read-Host "What directory do you want to start at?"
Get-ChildItem $StartingDir -recurse |Get-Acl | select Path,Owner | Export-Csv $report
-NoTypeInformation

#send two beeps when report is finished
write-Host 'a 'a 'n"Report finished. See $report"
```

The script prompts you for a starting directory. It then uses the **Get-ChildItem** cmdlet to pass every item to the **Get-Acl** cmdlet and recurse through subdirectories. You'll notice that we piped output to the **Select-Object** cmdlet to get just the Path and Owner properties. Finally, we send the data to a CSV file. The script beeps a few times to let you know it is finished and displays a message.

Changing Permissions

Getting access-control lists is half the job. You might still want to reset permissions through PowerShell. To be honest, this is not the easiest task to do in PowerShell, mainly because permissions in Windows are *complicated*, and there's only so much a shell can do to simplify that situation.

To get really detailed with permissions, you need to understand .NET security objects and NTFS security descriptors. However, we're going to start with some simpler examples. Setting an access-control rule is a matter of bit-masking access rights against a security token. The bits that match a security principal's account determine whether you can view a file, make changes to a file, or take ownership.

You can use the **Set-Acl** cmdlet to update an object's access rule. However, you first have to construct a .NET security descriptor, or get the security descriptor from an existing object, modify the security descriptor appropriately, and then apply it to the desired object. This is not an insurmountable task, just very tedious. The script ChangeACL.ps1 takes a simplified approach and grants permissions you specify to the specified security principal on all objects in the specified starting directory and subdirectories:

ChangeACL.ps1

```
$Right="FullControl"

#The possible values for Rights are
# ListDirectory
# ReadData
# WriteData
# CreateFiles
# CreateDirectories
# AppendData
# ReadExtendedAttributes
# WriteExtendedAttributes
# Traverse
# ExecuteFile
# DeleteSubdirectoriesAndFiles
# ReadAttributes
# WriteAttributes
# Write
# Delete
# ReadPermissions
# Read
# ReadAndExecute
# Modify
# ChangePermissions
# TakeOwnership
# Synchronize
# FullControl

$StartingDir=Read-Host " What directory do you want to start at?"
$Principal=Read-Host " What security principal do you want to grant" '
"$Right to? 'n Use format domain\username or domain\group"

#define a new access rule
#the $rule line has been artificially broken for print purposes
#It needs to be one line. The online version of the script is properly
#formatted.
$rule=new-object System.Security.AccessControl.FileSystemAccessRule($Principal,$Right,"Allow")

foreach ($file in $(Get-ChildItem $StartingDir -recurse)) {
 $acl=get-acl $file.FullName
 #display filename and old permissions
 write-Host -foregroundcolor Yellow $file.FullName
 #uncomment if you want to see old permissions
 #write-Host $acl.AccessToString 'n

 #Add this access rule to the ACL
 $acl.SetAccessRule($rule)

 #Write the changes to the object
 set-acl $File.Fullname $acl
```

```
#display new permissions
$acl=get-acl $file.FullName
Write-Host -foregroundcolor Green "New Permissions"
Write-Host $acl.AccessToString `n
} #end foreach file
```

This script creates a simple access rule that allows a specific right. If you can use a broad right, such as Modify or Full Control, you'll find it easy to work with the script. We've hard coded in the **$Right** variable. The script prompts you for directory path and the name of the security principal to which you wish to apply the right.

The real work of the script is creating a new FileSystemAccess rule object. Creating the object requires that we specify the name of the security principal, the right to be applied, and whether to allow or deny the right. With this rule, we can recurse through the file system starting at the specified directory. For each file, we get the current access-control list using the **Get-Acl** cmdlet:

```
$acl=get-acl $file.FullName
```

Next we add the new access control rule to the ACL:

```
$acl.SetAccessRule($rule)
```

Now we call the **Set-Acl** cmdlet to write the new and modified ACL back to the object:

```
set-acl $File.Fullname $acl
```

The script finishes the loop by displaying the new ACL so you can see the changes.

Automating Cacls.exe to Change Permissions

As you've seen, using the **Set-Acl** cmdlet is not simple, especially if you have complex permissions. Therefore, you may find it easier to use Cacls.exe from within a PowerShell script:

SetPermswithCACLS.ps1

```
#SetPermsWithCACLS.ps1
# CACLS rights are usually
# F = FullControl
# C = Change
# R = Readonly
# W = Write

$StartingDir=Read-Host " What directory do you want to start at?"
$Right=Read-Host " What CALCS right do you want to grant? Valid choices are F, C, R or W"
Switch ($Right) {
 "F" {$Null}
 "C" {$Null}
 "R" {$Null}
 "W" {$Null}
 default {
   Write-Host -foregroundcolor "Red" '
   'n $Right.ToUpper() "is an invalid choice. Please Try again."'n
   exit
 }
```

```
}

$Principal=Read-Host " What security principal do you want to grant" '
"CACLS right"$Right.ToUpper()"to?" 'n '
"Use format domain\username or domain\group"

$Verify=Read-Host 'n "You are about to change permissions on all" '
"files starting at"$StartingDir.ToUpper() 'n "for security"'
"principal"$Principal.ToUpper() '
"with new right of"$Right.ToUpper()"."'n '
"Do you want to continue ? [Y,N]"

if ($Verify -eq "Y") {

 foreach ($file in $(Get-ChildItem $StartingDir -recurse)) {
 #display filename and old permissions
 write-Host -foregroundcolor Yellow $file.FullName
 #uncomment if you want to see old permissions
 #CACLS $file.FullName

 #ADD new permission with CACLS
 CACLS $file.FullName /E /P "${Principal}:${Right}" >$NULL

 #display new permissions
 Write-Host -foregroundcolor Green "New Permissions"
 CACLS $file.FullName
 }
}
```

This script first prompts you for a starting directory and the permission rights you want to grant. We've used a **Switch** statement to make sure a valid parameter for Cacls.exe is entered. As long as the user has entered F, C, W, or R, the script continues and prompts you for the name of a security principal you want to add to the access-control list. Because this is a major operation, we've included a prompt using the **Read-Host** cmdlet to provide a summary of what the script is about to do. If anything other than Y is entered, the script ends with no changes being made. Otherwise, the script executes the **ForEach** loop.

Within this **ForEach** loop, we use the **Get-ChildItem** cmdlet to enumerate all the files in the starting directory path and recurse through all subdirectories. The script displays the current file as a progress indicator, and then calls Cacls.exe. Because of the way PowerShell processes Win32 commands such as Cacls.exe, we need to enclose the program's parameters in quotes. You'll also notice that instead of using:

```
CACLS $file.FullName /e /p "$Principal:$Right"
```

we used:

```
CACLS $file.FullName /e /p "${Principal}:${Right}"
```

PowerShell treats an expression like Foo:Bar as <namespace>:<name>, which is like $global:profile or $env:windir. In order for PowerShell to treat the Cacls.exe parameter as a command-line parameter, we must delimit the variable name using braces, as we've done in this example. The script finishes by displaying the new access-control permissions for each file.

If you've used Cacls.exe before, you may have noticed that we used /E /P to assign permissions. According to Cacls.exe's Help screen, you use /P to modify permissions for an existing entry. You would use /G to grant permissions to a new user. In Cmd.exe, either /G or /P will work regardless of whether the user already existed in the access-control list.

This is not the case in PowerShell. PowerShell actually appears to enforce the Cacls.exe parameters. You can use /G if a user does not exist in the file's access-control list. However, you must use /P if the user already exists. When you attempt to use /G to modify an existing user's permission, Cacls.exe will run, but no change will be made.

So, how do you know if you should use /P or /G without checking every file first? Not to worry. You can use /P regardless of whether the user exists in the access-control list, which is what we've done here. The moral is, don't assume that every single Cmd.exe tool and command works identically in PowerShell. Most should, but if it doesn't, you have to look at how PowerShell is interpreting the expression.

One final note about the script: we could have used /T with Cacls.exe to change permissions on all files and subdirectories. The end result would have been the same, but then we couldn't have demonstrated some of PowerShell's output features.

Complex Permissions in PowerShell

By now you've seen that you can manage permissions with PowerShell, although it is not for the faint of heart. That said, let's look at a few more situations where you can use PowerShell.

Get Owner

We showed you earlier how you can use the **Get-Acl** cmdlet to display the owner of a file. You may prefer to create a function that takes a file name as a parameter:

```
Function Get-Owner {
param([string]$file)

 try {
  Get-Item $file -ea stop | Out-Null
  write (Get-Acl $file).Owner
  }
  catch {
   Write-Warning "Failed to find $file"
   }
  finally {}
}
```

With this function loaded, you can use an expression like:

```
PS C:\> Get-Owner c:\file.txt
```

To return the owners on a group of files, you have to enumerate the file collection like this:

```
dir c:\files\ | select fullname,@{name="Owner";Expression={Get-Owner $_.fullname}}
```

Because we are leveraging the pipeline, you can accomplish something like this:

```
PS C:\> dir c:\files -recurse | select fullname,@{name="Owner";Expression={Get-Owner $_.fullname}}
|
>> group owner | format-table Name,Count -autosize
>>
```

```
Name                                               Count
----                                               -----
BUILTIN\Administrators                               777
MYCOMPANY\adeco                                        6
MYCOMPANY\File Admins                                 10
O:S-1-5-21-2704478247-3271226993-4103978002-1112       1
```

Set Owner

Unfortunately, PowerShell does not provide a mechanism for setting the owner of a file to other than an administrator or the Administrators group. Even though Windows 2003 now allows you to assign ownership, you cannot do it through PowerShell. Use this technique to set a new owner on a file:

```
PS C:\> [System.Security.Principal.NTAccount]$newOwner="Administrators"
PS C:\> $file=get-childitem c:\file.txt
PS C:\> $acl=$file.GetAccessControl()
PS C:\> $acl.SetOwner($NewOwner)
PS C:\> $file.SetAccessControl($acl)
```

The important step is to cast the **$NewOwner** variable as a security principal:

```
PS C:\> [System.Security.Principal.NTAccount]$newOwner="Administrators"
```

After we get the current access-control list, we call the **SetOwner()** method, specifying the new owner:

```
PS C:\> $acl.SetOwner($NewOwner)
```

This change will not take effect until we call the **SetAccessControl()** method on the file and apply the modified access-control list with the new owner:

```
PS C:\> $file.SetAccessControl($acl)
```

Retrieving Access Control

We showed you at the beginning of the chapter how to use the **Get-Acl** cmdlet to retrieve file permissions. One approach you might take is to wrap the code into a function:

```
Function Get-Access {
param([string]$file)
   write $file.ToUpper()
   write (Get-Acl $file).Access
 }
```

Once you've loaded it into your PowerShell session or script, you can use it to quickly get the access control for a given file:

```
PS C:\test>  get-access $env:systemroot\system32\cmd.exe
C:\WINDOWS\SYSTEM32\CMD.EXE


FileSystemRights  : ReadAndExecute, Synchronize
AccessControlType : Allow
```

```
IdentityReference : NT AUTHORITY\SYSTEM
IsInherited       : False
InheritanceFlags  : None
PropagationFlags  : None

FileSystemRights  : ReadAndExecute, Synchronize
AccessControlType : Allow
IdentityReference : BUILTIN\Administrators
IsInherited       : False
InheritanceFlags  : None
PropagationFlags  : None

FileSystemRights  : ReadAndExecute, Synchronize
AccessControlType : Allow
IdentityReference : BUILTIN\Users
IsInherited       : False
InheritanceFlags  : None
PropagationFlags  : None

FileSystemRights  : FullControl
AccessControlType : Allow
IdentityReference : NT SERVICE\TrustedInstaller
IsInherited       : False
InheritanceFlags  : None
PropagationFlags  : None
```

The downside to this approach is that you can't easily use it in the pipeline. Take an expression like this:

```
PS C:\> get-childitem c:\files\*.txt | get-access | format-table
```

It will fail to enumerate all the files. A better approach is a filtering function:

Get-AccessControlFilter.ps1

```
Filter Get-AccessControl {
 [string]$file=$input
 $access=(Get-Acl $file).Access
 $obj=New-Object PSObject

 Add-Member -inputobject $obj -membertype Noteproperty -Name FileName -value $file.ToUpper()
 Add-Member -inputobject $obj -membertype Noteproperty -Name AccessControl -value $access

 write $obj
}
```

We've used the **New-Object** cmdlet to create a custom object to return file and access information. Because the AccessControl property of our custom object is a collection of access rules, you need to use an expression like this in order to expand them:

```
PS C:\> (get-childitem c:\file.txt | Get-AccessControl).AccessControl
```

Or use this to examine a group of files:

```
dir c:\files | foreach {
   write-host $_.fullname -foregroundcolor Green
  ($_.fullname | get-AccessControl).AccessControl
 }
```

But what if you want to find a particular security principal? Use this function to enumerate the AccessControl property, searching for the particular user or group:

Get-PrincipalFilter.ps1

```
Filter Get-Principal {
Param([string]$Principal)

foreach ($rule in $_.AccessControl) {
   if ($rule.IdentityReference -eq $Principal) {
     $_.filename,$rule
    } #end if
  } #end foreach
} #end filter
```

Use this filter in conjunction with the **Get-AccessControl** cmdlet to display files and access rules that apply to a given user:

```
PS C:\> dir c:\files\*.exe | get-accesscontrol | get-principal "mycompany\file admins
C:\FILES\ACTIVEROLESMANAGEMENTSHELLFORACTIVEDIRECTORYX64_12.EXE


FileSystemRights  : FullControl
AccessControlType : Allow
IdentityReference : MYCOMPANY\File Admins
IsInherited       : True
InheritanceFlags  : None
PropagationFlags  : None

C:\FILES\ACTIVEROLESMANAGEMENTSHELLFORACTIVEDIRECTORY_12.EXE
FileSystemRights  : FullControl
AccessControlType : Allow
IdentityReference : MYCOMPANY\File Admins
IsInherited       : True
InheritanceFlags  : None
PropagationFlags  : None

C:\FILES\CHROMESETUP.EXE
FileSystemRights  : FullControl
AccessControlType : Allow
IdentityReference : MYCOMPANY\File Admins
IsInherited       : True
InheritanceFlags  : None
PropagationFlags  : None
...
```

Removing a Rule

Removing access for a user or group is relatively straightforward:

```
$file="file.txt"
[System.Security.Principal.NTAccount]$principal="mycompany\rgbiv"
$acl=Get-Acl $file
$access=(Get-Acl $file).Access
$rule=$access | where {$_.IdentityReference -eq $principal}
$acl.RemoveAccessRuleSpecific($rule)
Set-Acl $file $acl
```

Obviously, we need to know what file and user or group we are working with:

```
$file="file.txt"
[System.Security.Principal.NTAccount]$principal="mycompany\rgbiv"
```

As we did when adding a rule, we need to use the **Get-Acl** cmdlet to retrieve the current access control list:

```
$acl=Get-Acl $file
```

To find a specific access control rule, we need to filter the existing rules with the **Where-Object** cmdlet:

```
$access=(Get-Acl $file).Access
$rule=$access | where {$_.IdentityReference -eq $principal}
```

The **$rule** variable will hold all the rules that apply to the specified security principal. To remove the rule, we call the **RemoveAccessRuleSpecific()** method:

```
$acl.RemoveAccessRuleSpecific($rule)
```

Finally, to apply the new access control list, we call **Set-Acl**:

```
Set-Acl $file $acl
```

Chapter 32
Managing Event Logs

PowerShell has a terrific cmdlet in **Get-Eventlog** that makes it easy to find information in a system's event log. Since different systems may have different event logs, one of the first commands you'll want to use is this:

```
PS C:\> get-eventlog -list
```

```
Max(K) Retain OverflowAction        Entries Log
------ ------ ---------------        ------- ---
20,480      0 OverwriteAsNeeded       47,615 Application
   512      7 OverwriteOlder              0 DFS Replication
20,480      0 OverwriteAsNeeded           0 HardwareEvents
   512      7 OverwriteOlder              0 Internet Explorer
20,480      0 OverwriteAsNeeded           0 Key Management Service
 8,192      0 OverwriteAsNeeded        2,858 Media Center
16,384      0 OverwriteAsNeeded           0 ODiag
16,384      0 OverwriteAsNeeded         886 OSession
20,480      0 OverwriteAsNeeded       42,564 Security
20,480      0 OverwriteAsNeeded       39,604 System
15,360      0 OverwriteAsNeeded       14,919 Windows PowerShell
```

```
PS C:\>
```

If you run something like the following script, every single entry in the log will scroll by:

```
Get-Eventlog "Windows Powershell"
```

That's probably not very practical, unless you're dumping the contents to another file.

Fortunately, the cmdlet has a parameter, **-Newest**, that will display the last (or newest) number of log entries that you specify:

```
PS C:\> get-eventlog "windows powershell" -newest 5


  Index Time          EntryType    Source         InstanceID Message
  ----- ----          ---------    ------         ---------- -------
  14919 Apr 15 08:57  Information  PowerShell            400 Engine state is changed from None....
  14918 Apr 15 08:57  Information  PowerShell            600 Provider "Certificate" is Starte. ...
  14917 Apr 15 08:57  Information  PowerShell            600 Provider "Variable" is Started. ...
  14916 Apr 15 08:57  Information  PowerShell            600 Provider "Registry" is Started. ...
  14915 Apr 15 08:57  Information  PowerShell            600 Provider "Function" is Started. ...


PS C:\>
```

The default table format usually ends up truncating the event message. If that happens, you can try something like:

```
PS C:\> get-eventlog "windows powershell" -newest 5 |format-list
```

Alternatively, you can try something like this:

```
PS C:\> Get-EventLog "windows powershell" -newest 5 |
>> select EntryType,TimeGenerated,EventID,Message |
>> format-list
>>


EntryType     : Information
TimeGenerated : 4/15/2009 8:57:01 AM
EventID       : 400
Message       : Engine state is changed from None to Available.

                Details:
                    NewEngineState=Available
                    PreviousEngineState=None

                    SequenceNumber=18

                    HostName=PrimalScriptHostImplementation
                    HostVersion=1.0.0.0
                    HostId=9345e558-7b34-40c3-90d2-7b35a5e154ed
                    EngineVersion=2.0
                    RunspaceId=de94a631-4aaa-4dd9-8b0a-c3f02a1ee55d
                    PipelineId=
                    CommandName=
                    CommandType=
                    ScriptName=
                    CommandPath=
                    CommandLine=
...
```

We've truncated the output, but you get the idea. If you're interested in a specific event ID, use the **Where-Object** cmdlet. Here, we're looking for event log entries with an EventID of 7036:

```
PS C:\> get-eventlog System -newest 5 |where {$_.EventID -eq 7036}

Index Time          Type Source              EventID Message

 Index Time          EntryType  Source              InstanceID Message
 ----- ----          ---------  ------              ---------- -------
 108990 Apr 15 09:05 Information Service Control M... 1073748860 The description for Event ID '1073...
 108989 Apr 15 09:04 Information Service Control M... 1073748860 The description for Event ID '1073...
 108988 Apr 15 08:57 Information Service Control M... 1073748860 The description for Event ID '1073...
 108987 Apr 15 08:43 Information Service Control M... 1073748860 The description for Event ID '1073...
 108986 Apr 15 08:43 Information Service Control M... 1073748860 The description for Event ID '1073...


PS C:\>
```

As of PowerShell v2.0, the **Get-EventLog** cmdlet offers some additional capabilities for filtering the events you see:

- Use the **-index** parameter to get a specific event by its index number:

```
PS C:\> get-eventlog System -index 108990

 Index  Time         EntryType  Source              InstanceID Message
 -----  ----         ---------  ------              ---------- -------
 108990 Apr 15 09:05 Information Service Control M... 1073748860 The description for Event ID '1073...
```

- Use the **-entryType** parameter to get just specific types of entries, such as SuccessAudit entries from the Security log. Valid parameter values are Error, Information, FailureAudit, SuccessAudit, and Warning:

```
PS C:\> Get-EventLog Security -entryType "SuccessAudit"
```

- Use the **-Source** parameter to get just entries from specific sources, such as "Microsoft-Windows-Security-Auditing:"

```
PS C:\> get-eventlog System -Source DCOM

 Index Time          EntryType  Source      InstanceID Message
 ----- ----          ---------  ------      ---------- -------
 108983 Apr 15 08:43 Information DCOM        3221235501 The description for Event ID '-107...
 108981 Apr 15 08:43 Information DCOM        3221235501 The description for Event ID '-107...
 108862 Apr 15 08:24 Information DCOM        3221235501 The description for Event ID '-107...
 108821 Apr 15 08:20 Error       DCOM        3221235482 The description for Event ID '-107...
 108377 Apr 15 07:57 Information DCOM        3221235501 The description for Event ID '-107...
```

- Use the **-list** parameter (by itself) to get a list of available logs:

```
PS C:\> Get-EventLog -list
```

To see that same list as a string, rather than a set of objects:

```
PS C:\> Get-EventLog -list -asstring
```

- Use the **-Before** and **-After** parameters to filter by date:

```
PS C:\> get-eventlog system -before 3/1/2009 -after 2/1/2009 -EntryType Error
```

This expression will return all Error events in the System event log that occurred between 2/1/2009 and 3/1/2009.

- Use the **-Message** parameter to find events that contain a particular string. Wildcards are permitted:

```
PS C:\> get-eventlog system -Message "*spooler*" -EntryType Error
```

Use the **-Username** parameter to find events for a specific user. Not all events will populate this field:

```
PS C:\> get-eventlog application -username mycompany\administrator
```

Curious about where all your errors are coming from? Try something like this:

```
PS C:\> get-eventlog -log system | group source | Select Count,Name | sort count |format-table
-auto

Count Name
----- ----
    1 Application Popup
    1 bowser
    1 PlugPlayManager
    1 Microsoft-Windows-BitLocker-Driver
    1 Ntfs
    2 VDS Dynamic Provider
    3 Print
    3 Microsoft-Windows-Diagnostics-Networking
    4 yukonx64
    4 Server
    4 RasSstp
    4 MRxDAV
    5 netbt
    6 WPDClassInstaller
    6 RemoteAccess
    6 Microsoft-Windows-DriverFrameworks-UserMode
   10 Microsoft-Windows-Power-Troubleshooter
   11 Microsoft-Windows-Kernel-Power
   15 WPDMTPDriver
   15 VMnetDHCP
   21 Virtual Disk Service
   25 Microsoft-Windows-ResourcePublication
   40 disk
   52 WinRM
   52 BROWSER
   53 WMPNetworkSvc
   56 Microsoft-Windows-TBS
   63 HTTP
   96 VMnetAdapter
  103 Microsoft-Windows-Kernel-General
  107 Microsoft-Windows-WLAN-AutoConfig
  109 USER32
  120 Microsoft-Windows-Kernel-Processor-Power
  120 Microsoft-Windows-FilterManager
  120 VMnetuserif
  129 Microsoft-Windows-WindowsUpdateClient
  140 volsnap
  143 Dhcp
```

```
  144 W32Time
  152 Microsoft-Windows-User-PnP
  153 inic1620_amd64
  309 WinDefend
  323 EventLog
  448 Tcpip
  512 DCOM
 7171 Service Control Manager
28740 Microsoft-Windows-Servicing
```

Every event log includes a source indicating where the event originated. All we've done is look at the System event log, grouping the event records by the Source property, piping that result to **Select-Object** so that we only get the Count and Name properties, which in turn are sorted by the **Sort-Object** cmdlet, and finally PowerShell presents the results by using the **Format-Table** cmdlet. This is a terrific example of leveraging the pipeline. You can use the same technique to get a summary breakdown of error types:

```
PS C:\> get-eventlog -log system | group EntryType | Select Count,Name | sort count |format-table
-auto

Count Name
----- ----
 167 Error
 262 Warning
2159 Information
```

If you want results for all logs, it takes a little more finesse:

```
foreach ($log in (Get-EventLog -list)) {
    #only display logs with records
    if ($log.Entries.Count -gt 0) {
      Write-Host -background DarkGreen -foreground Black $log.log
      Get-EventLog -log $log.log | group EntryType | Select Count,Name | sort count '
      | Format-Table -auto
    }
}
```

This snippet uses the **ForEach** cmdlet to get every event log on the local system. If the number of entries in each log is greater than 0:

```
if ($log.Entries.Count -gt 0) {
```

Then we'll display the log name, and then use the same code from earlier to return a count of each error type.

Let's combine both of our efforts and get a listing of event types for each source from every event log with records:

```
foreach ($log in (Get-EventLog -list)) {
    #only display logs with records
    if ($log.Entries.Count -gt 0) {
      Write-Host -background DarkGreen -foreground Black $log.log
      Get-EventLog -log $log.log | group source,entrytype | sort count | '
      select Count,Name |format-table -auto
    }
}
```

We'll get a listing like this for every event log:

```
Application

Count Name
----- ----
    1 Windows Product Activation, Warning
    1 WSH, 0
    1 Winlogon, Information
    1 MPSampleSubmission, Information
    1 WmdmPmSp, Information
    1 Windows Product Activation, Information
    1 WLTRYSVC, Information
    1 SceCli, Information
    2 NTBackup, Error
    2 WSH, Information
    2 WmdmPmSN, Information
    2 MsiInstaller, Error
    2 ESENT, Error
    2 Userenv, Information
    3 ASP.NET 2.0.50727.0, Warning
    3 System.ServiceModel.Install 3.0.0.0, Information
    3 MSDTC, Information
    4 HHCTRL, Information
    4 COM+, Information
    4 crypt32, Information
    5 MPSampleSubmission, Error
    6 ASP.NET 2.0.50727.0, Information
    9 System.ServiceModel.Install 3.0.0.0, Warning
    9 DrWatson, Information
   10 NTBackup, Information
   14 usnjsvc, 0
   14 VMware Virtual Mount Service Extended, Information
   14 WinMgmt, Warning
```

Vista and Later

The **Get-Eventlog** cmdlet is designed to work with the classic logs like System, Application, and Security. This is actually true for any *-Eventlog cmdlet. To manage the newer event logs introduced in Windows Vista, we need to use the **Get-WinEvent** cmdlet. This cmdlet also requires that you have at least .NET Framework version 3.5 installed. You can also manage classic event logs with this cmdlet, so you may prefer to use it for all your event-log management.

Let's begin by finding out what logs are available:

```
PS C:\> get-winevent -ListLog *
```

The -**Listlog** parameter requires a value or a wildcard. If you run this on a Vista or later computer you might be surprised by the number of logs. Classic logs are usually listed first. Why don't we look at a specific log in more detail:

```
PS C:\> $log=get-winevent -ListLog "Windows PowerShell"
PS C:\> get-winevent -ListLog $log.logname | select *
```

```
FileSize               : 13701120
IsLogFull              : False
```

```
LastAccessTime                      : 8/18/2008 1:26:01 PM
LastWriteTime                       : 4/15/2009 8:50:36 AM
OldestRecordNumber                  : 1
RecordCount                         : 14919
LogName                             : Windows PowerShell
LogType                             : Administrative
LogIsolation                        : Application
IsEnabled                           : True
IsClassicLog                        : True
SecurityDescriptor                  : O:BAG:SYD:(A;;0xf0007;;;SY)(A;;0x7;;;BA)(A;;0x7;;;SO)
(A;;0x3;;;IU)(A;;0
                                      x3;;;SU)(A;;0x3;;;S-1-5-3)(A;;0x3;;;S-1-5-33)
(A;;0x1;;;S-1-5-32-573)
LogFilePath                         : %SystemRoot%\System32\Winevt\Logs\Windows PowerShell.evtx
MaximumSizeInBytes                  : 15728640
LogMode                             : Circular
OwningProviderName                  :
ProviderNames                       : {PowerShell}
ProviderLevel                       :
ProviderKeywords                    :
ProviderBufferSize                  : 64
ProviderMinimumNumberOfBuffers      : 0
ProviderMaximumNumberOfBuffers      : 64
ProviderLatency                     : 1000
ProviderControlGuid                 :
```

Now we can easily retrieve events:

```
PS C:\> Get-WinEvent -LogName $log.logname
```

This code snippet returns a number of entries. Fortunately the **Get-WinEvent** cmdlet has some parameters to filter. We might use the **-MaxEvents** parameter to return only 10 events:

```
PS C:\> Get-WinEvent -LogName $log.logname -MaxEvents 10
```

By default the cmdlet returns newest events first. But you can use the **-Oldest** parameter to reverse that:

```
PS C:\> Get-WinEvent -LogName $log.logname -MaxEvents 10 -oldest
```

The **Get-WinEvent** cmdlet offers several filtering techniques. You could pipe output to the **Where-Object** cmdlet:

```
PS C:\> get-winevent -LogName $log.logname | Where {$_.id -eq 400 -and '
>> $_.TimeCreated -gt [datetime]"4/10/2009" -and $_.timeCreated -lt [datetime]"4/11/2009"}
```

But a better approach is to use the **-FilterHashTable** parameter and supply a hash table of properties to filter:

```
PS C:\> get-winevent -FilterHashtable @{LogName=$log.logname;id=400;StartTime="4/10/2009"}
```

When using a hash table you must provide a logname, providername, or path. You are also limited to these parameters:

- LogName
- ProviderName

- Path

- Keywords

- ID

- Level

- StartTime

- EndTime

- UserID

- Data

You can create XML filters, although they are a little more complicated:

```
PS C:\> get-winevent -FilterXML "<QueryList><Query><Select Path='Windows PowerShell'>*[System[(Eve
ntID=400)]]</Select></Query></QueryList>"
```

We recommend you use the EventViewer management console, create a query, and then copy and paste the XML into your PowerShell code.

A variety of providers write Windows event logs and often you need to filter based on a given provider. First, use the **-ListProvider** parameter to see all providers:

```
PS C:\> get-winevent -listprovider *
```

If you noticed earlier, providers are also part of the log file's properties. Here's an easy way to list them:

```
PS C:\> (get-winevent -listlog System).providernames
```

To learn more about a specific provider, all we have to do is ask:

```
PS C:\> get-winevent -listprovider *firewall | select *


ProviderName       : Microsoft-Windows-Firewall
Name               : Microsoft-Windows-Firewall
Id                 : e595f735-b42a-494b-afcd-b68666945cd3
MessageFilePath    : %SystemRoot%\System32\mpssvc.dll
ResourceFilePath   : %SystemRoot%\System32\mpssvc.dll
ParameterFilePath  :
HelpLink           : http://go.microsoft.com/fwlink/events.asp?CoName=Microsoft
Corporation&ProdName=
                     Microsoft® Windows® Operating System&ProdVer=6.0.6001.18000&FileName=mpssvc.
dll&
                     FileVer=6.0.6001.18000
DisplayName        : Microsoft-Windows-Firewall
LogLinks           : {System}
Levels             : {win:Error}
Opcodes            : {win:Info}
Keywords           : {}
Tasks              : {}
Events             : {6400}
```

Finally to find events associated with a specific provider, use the **-ProviderName** parameter:

```
PS C:\> get-winevent -ProviderName "user32"
```

Working with Remote Event Logs

If you have computers running Windows Vista or later that are also running .NET Framework version 3.5 or later, you can use the **Get-WinEvent** cmdlet to manage their event logs just as if they were local. You can use the -**Computername** and -**Credential** parameters:

```
PS C:\> get-winevent -ListLog * -computer win2k801 -Credential $cred | Where {$_.RecordCount -gt 0} |
>> Sort Recordcount -descending | Select Logname,RecordCount,LastWriteTime,IsLogFull | format-table -auto
>>
```

LogName	RecordCount	LastWriteTime		IsLogFull
Security	39707	4/09/2009	5:08:18 AM	False
Microsoft-Windows-TaskScheduler/Operational	28247	4/09/2009	5:08:18 AM	False
System	20011	4/09/2009	5:08:08 AM	False
Microsoft-Windows-GroupPolicy/Operational	9214	4/09/2009	5:08:19 AM	False
Microsoft-Windows-WinRM/Operational	3814	4/09/2009	5:10:45 AM	False
Microsoft-Windows-ReliabilityAnalysisComponent/Operational	2221	4/09/2009	5:23:16 AM	False
Application	747	4/09/2009	5:08:17 AM	False
Microsoft-Windows-Bits-Client/Operational	558	4/09/2009	5:10:45 AM	False
Microsoft-Windows-WindowsUpdateClient/Operational	486	4/09/2009	5:11:37 AM	False
Windows PowerShell	310	4/09/2009	10:23:56 AM	False
Microsoft-Windows-PowerShell/Operational	79	4/10/2009	10:07:41 AM	False
Microsoft-Windows-LanguagePackSetup/Operational	30	4/09/2009	5:23:14 AM	False
Microsoft-Windows-Diagnosis-DPS/Operational	27	4/09/2009	10:19:49 AM	False
Microsoft-Windows-Kernel-WHEA	23	4/09/2009	5:08:17 AM	False
Microsoft-Windows-Resource-Exhaustion-Detector/Operational	22	4/09/2009	5:18:07 AM	False
Microsoft-Windows-ServerManager/Operational	13	2/12/2009	3:07:17 AM	False
Microsoft-Windows-MUI/Operational	11	12/17/2008	1:32:00 PM	False
Microsoft-Windows-CodeIntegrity/Operational	8	4/09/2009	10:20:32 AM	False
Microsoft-Windows-RestartManager/Operational	8	3/09/2009	1:15:16 PM	False
Setup	7	12/30/2008	12:41:36 PM	False
Microsoft-Windows-TerminalServices-PnPDevices/Admin	6	4/09/2009	10:19:44 AM	False
Microsoft-Windows-Help/Operational	4	12/17/2008	2:17:50 PM	False
Microsoft-Windows-Forwarding/Operational	1	4/15/2009	3:18:15 PM	False

The -**Credential** parameter accepts a standard PSCredential. The **$cred** variable is a saved PSCredential object.

You can use just about all the expressions we showed you earlier with remote computers; for example, using a hash table filter:

```
PS C:\> get-winevent -FilterHashtable @{LogName="System";Level=2} -computer Win2k801 -max 10
```

You can still manage logs on legacy systems remotely using the **Get-Eventlog** cmdlet. It too now has a -**Computername** parameter, but unfortunately no credential parameter:

```
PS C:\> get-eventlog -list -ComputerName "xp01"
```

Max(K)	Retain	OverflowAction	Entries	Name
512	7	OverwriteOlder	402	Application
512	7	OverwriteOlder	0	Internet Explorer
16,384	0	OverwriteAsNeeded	0	ODiag

```
16,384        0 OverwriteAsNeeded          86 OSession
   512        7 OverwriteOlder              0 Security
   512        7 OverwriteOlder          2,412 System
15,360        0 OverwriteAsNeeded       3,656 Windows PowerShell
```

It's just as easy to filter event logs remotely. Here's one example:

```
PS C:\> get-eventlog -ComputerName "XP01" -after "4/13/2009" -LogName "System"

  Index Time          EntryType   Source          InstanceID Message
  ----- ----          ---------   ------          ---------- -------
   2412 Apr 13 18:35  Information Service Control M...  1073748860 The Windows Installer ser
   2411 Apr 13 18:30  Error       DCOM              3221235481 DCOM was unable to commun
   2410 Apr 13 18:29  Error       DCOM              3221235481 DCOM was unable to commun
   2409 Apr 13 18:20  Information Service Control M...  1073748860 The Windows Installer ser
   2408 Apr 13 18:20  Information Service Control M...  1073748859 The Windows Installer ser
```

Here's another:

```
PS C:\> get-eventlog -ComputerName "XP01" -LogName "System" -EntryType "Error" -newest 50
```

While we think PowerShell should be all you need, the EventViewer management console that ships with Windows Vista is a considerable improvement over the legacy MMC. PowerShell v2.0 includes the **Show-EventLog** cmdlet that will launch the EventViewer.

```
PS C:\> show-eventlog
```

You can also use the **-Computername** parameter to connect to a remote computer.

Configuring Event Logs

PowerShell v2.0 offers a few cmdlets for configuring event logs themselves. For example, suppose you want to change the Windows PowerShell log to have a size limit of 10 MB:

```
PS C:\> Limit-EventLog -LogName "Windows PowerShell" -MaximumSize 10mb
```

Perhaps you also want to change the log so that it overwrites as needed and retains records for no longer than 14 days. Here's how:

```
PS C:\> Limit-EventLog -LogName "Windows PowerShell" -OverflowAction "overwriteolder"
-RetentionDays 14
```

Configure logs on remote servers using the **-Computername** parameter:

```
PS C:\> get-content servers.txt | foreach {limit-eventlog -logname System -computer $_
-MaximumSize 25MB}
```

Backup Event Logs

Unfortunately there still are no cmdlets for backing up classic event logs in PowerShell v2.0. However, backing up event logs is relatively straightforward in PowerShell. If you use the [WMI] type adapter, you'll have access to the **BackupEventLog()** method:

```
PS C:\> [wmi]$syslog=Get-WMiobject -query "Select * from win32_NTEventLogFile where '
>> LogFileName='system'" -enableAllPrivileges
>>
PS C:\> $backup=(get-date -format yyyyMMdd)+"_"+$syslog.CSName+"_"+$syslog.logfilename+".evt"
PS C:\> $syslog.backupeventlog("F:\backups\$backup")


__GENUS             : 2
__CLASS             : __PARAMETERS
__SUPERCLASS        :
__DYNASTY           : __PARAMETERS
__RELPATH           :
__PROPERTY_COUNT    : 1
__DERIVATION        : {}
__SERVER            :
__NAMESPACE         :
__PATH              :
ReturnValue         : 0


PS C:\>
```

Here's how this works. In this example, we going to back up the System event log on the local computer:

```
PS C:\> [wmi]$syslog=Get-WMiobject -query "Select * from win32_NTEventLogFile where '
>> LogFileName='system'"
```

We need a name for the backup file, which we calculate using the current date, the name of the computer, and the log file name:

```
PS C:\> $backup=(get-date -format yyyyMMdd)+"_"+$syslog.CSName+"_"+$syslog.logfilename+".evt"
```

This expression will return a value like 20090422_XPDESK01_System.evt. The advantage to using the CSName property is that if we back up a remote server, we can automatically capture the name.

In order to back up event logs, you need to specify the Backup privilege. If you don't, you'll get an Access Denied message when you try to back up the log. That's why we include the **-EnableAllPrivileges** parameter.

With privileges enabled, we can now back up the event log:

```
PS C:\> $syslog.backupeventlog("F:\backups\$backup")
```

Location, Location, Location
There is a very subtle but important detail about the BackupEventLog() method, especially when using the Get-WmiObject cmdlet to access event logs on remote computers. Even though you are running a script and remotely accessing a computer, the backup method is actually executing on the remote system. This means that the path you specify is relative to the remote system. If you back up the event log to drive C:\, it will be backed up to drive C:\ of the remote computer, not the computer where you are executing the script. Verify that the destination folder is accessible from the remote computer and you won't have any surprises.

If you want to back up all event logs, you can use code like this:

```
$path="F:\Backups"
foreach ($log in (Get-WmiObject win32_nteventlogfile -enableallprivileges)) {
    $backup=(Get-Date -format yyyyMMdd)+"_"+$log.CSName+"_"+$log.logfilename+".evt"
    Write-Host "Backing up"$log.LogFileName"to $path\$backup"
    $rc=$log.backupeventlog($path+"\"+$backup)
    if ($rc.ReturnValue -eq 0) {
        Write-Host -foreground GREEN "Backup successful" }
        else {
        Write-Host -foreground RED '
        "Backup failed with a return value of"$rc.ReturnValue
    }
}
```

The **$path** variable is the backup directory we want to use. Using a **ForEach** loop, we get every event log on the computer, enabling all privileges:

```
foreach ($log in (Get-WmiObject win32_nteventlogfile -enableAllPrivileges)) {
```

As we did before, we define a backup file name:

```
$backup=(Get-Date -format yyyyMMdd)+"_"+$log.CSName+"_"+$log.logfilename+".evt"
Write-Host "Backing up"$log.LogFileName"to $path\$backup"
```

When we call the **BackupEventLog()** method, we save the results to a variable:

```
$rc=$log.backupeventlog($path+"\"+$backup)
```

With this variable, we can check if the backup was successful or not. If it wasn't, we display the ReturnValue property:

```
if ($rc.ReturnValue -eq 0) {
    Write-Host -foreground GREEN "Backup successful" }
    else {
    Write-Host -foreground RED '
    "Backup failed with a return value of"$rc.ReturnValue
}
```

One thing to be aware of is that if the backup file already exists, it will not be overwritten and you will get a return value of 183.

Clearing Event Logs

Clearing an event log is very easy in PowerShell v2.0 using the **Clear-EventLog** cmdlet:

```
PS C:\> clear-eventlog -LogName "Windows Powershell"
```

There is a slight caveat: this only works with classic logs; however, you can use the **-Computername** parameter and clear logs on remote computers. We're not aware of any PowerShell solutions for backing up or clearing the newer event-log types that shipped with Windows Vista and later.

Let's wrap up our exploration of backing up and clearing event logs by using a PowerShell script. The Backup-EventLog.ps1 script uses WMI to back up and clear event logs on any computer in your domain:

Backup-EventLog.ps1

```
<#
.Synopsis
    Back up a computer event log with an option to clear.
.Description
    This function will back up the specified event log on a given computer
    to the specified path. Each log will be backed up to a file named
    YYYYMMDD_computername_logname.evt. You can only back up event logs
    to a local drive, relative to the remote computer. You'll need a
    separate process to copy or move the file to a network share. If
    you are running this on the local machine, then you can specify a mapped
    drive or UNC.

    If you specify -clear, each backed up log will also be cleared.
.Parameter Computername
    What is the name of the computer to back up? The default is the local computer.
.Parameter Logname
    What is the name of the event log to back up? The backup will fail if the
    file already exists.
.Parameter Filepath
    What is the path for the backup file? This path is relative to the remote
    computer and must be a local drive.
.Parameter Clear
    Clear the event log if it successfully backed up
.Example
    PS C:\> Backup-Eventlog -computername CHAOS -logname "Windows PowerShell" -Filepath "d:\backups"
-clear

    This backups up the Windows PowerShell log to the D:\Backups drive on CHAOS.
    The log will be cleared if the backup is successful.
.Example
    PS C:\> get-eventlog -list -AsString | foreach { .\Backup-EventLog.ps1 -logname $_ -filepath q:\
backup}

    This gets all event logs on the local computer and backs them up to Q:\backup
.Example
    PS C:\> get-content servers.txt | foreach {.\backup-eventlog.ps1 -computer $_ -log Security -file-
path c:\ -clear}

    This command will process the list of server names. Each name is piped to Foreach which connects
    to the remote computer, backs up the Security event log to the local C: drive and then clears the
log
    if successful.

.ReturnValue
```

```
      None
.Link
    Get-WMIObject
    Get-Eventlog
    Clear-Eventlog

.Notes
 NAME:      Backup-EventLog
 VERSION:   1.0
 AUTHOR:    Jeffery Hicks
 LASTEDIT:  4/16/2009 5:00:00 PM

#requires -version 2.0
#>

[CmdletBinding(
    SupportsShouldProcess=$False,
    SupportsTransactions=$False,
    ConfirmImpact="None",
    DefaultParameterSetName="")]

param(
[Parameter(Position=0, Mandatory=$False, ValueFromPipeline=$false,
 HelpMessage="What is the name of the computer to back up?")]
[string]$computername=$env:computername,

[Parameter(Position=1, Mandatory=$true, ValueFromPipeline=$false,
 HelpMessage="Enter an event log name like System")]
[string]$logname,

[Parameter(Position=2, Mandatory=$true, ValueFromPipeline=$false,
 HelpMessage="Enter the path for the backup log.")]
[string]$filepath,

[Parameter(Position=3, Mandatory=$false, ValueFromPipeline=$false)]
[switch]$Clear
   )

#main script body
$log=Get-WmiObject -Class win32_NTEventLogFile -computername $computername -authentication
PacketPrivacy -enableAllPrivileges -filter "logfilename='$logname'"

if ($log) {
  $backupfile="{0}_{1}_{2}.{3}" -f (Get-Date -format yyyyMMdd),$computername,$logname.replace("
 ",""),$log.extension
  $backup=Join-Path $filepath $backupfile

  Write-Host "Backing up $($log.name) on $computername to $backup" -foreground Cyan

  $rc=$log.BackupEventLog($backup)

  switch ($rc.ReturnValue) {
    0 { #success
        Write-Host "Backup successful." -foreground Green
        if ($clear) {
          $rc=$log.ClearEventLog()
          if ($rc.returnvalue -eq 0) {
            Write-Host "Event log cleared" -foreground Green
          }
          else {
            Write-Warning "Failed to clear event log.Return code $($rc.ReturnValue)" -foreground
Green

        }
```

```
      } #end if $clear
      } #end 0
    3 {
        Write-Warning "Backup failed. Verify $filepath is accessible from $computername"
      }
    5 {
          Write-warning "Backup failed. There is likely a permission or delegation problem."
      }
    8 {
          Write-warning "Backup failed. You are likely missing a privilege."
      }

   183 {
        Write-Warning "Backup failed. A file with the same name already exists."
        }
    Default {
         Write-Warning "Unknown Error! Return code $($rc.ReturnValue)"
        }
  }#end switch

}
else {
  Write-Warning "Failed to find $logname on $computername"
}
```

The script takes advantage of new scripting features in PowerShell v2.0. The first section defines script metadata that you can use with the Help feature:

```
PS C:\> help .\backup-eventlog.ps1

NAME
    C:\backup-eventlog.ps1

SYNOPSIS
    Back up a computer event log with an option to clear.


SYNTAX
    C:\backup-eventlog.ps1 [[-computername] [<String>]] [[-logname] [<String>]] [[-filepath]
[<String>
    ommonParameters>]


DETAILED DESCRIPTION
    This function will back up the specified event log on a given computer
    to the specified path. Each log will be backed up to a file named
    YYYYMMDD_computername_logname.evt. You can only back up event logs
    to a local drive, relative to the remote computer. You'll need a
    separate process to copy or move the file to a network share. If
    you are running this on the local machine, then you can specify a mapped
    drive or UNC.

    If you specify -clear, each backed up log will also be cleared.


RELATED LINKS
    Get-WMIObject
    Get-Eventlog
    Clear-Eventlog

REMARKS
    To see the examples, type: "get-help C:\backup-eventlog.ps1 -examples".
```

449

```
For more information, type: "get-help C:\backup-eventlog.ps1 -detailed".
For technical information, type: "get-help C:\backup-eventlog.ps1 -full".
```

As you can see, the script takes a computer and log file name as parameters. You must also specify a location for the backed up event log. This directory is relative to the remote computer and must be a local drive. If you are running the script on your computer you can specify a networked drive or UNC.

The script uses the **Get-WmiObject** cmdlet to retrieve the event log:

```
$log=Get-WmiObject -Class win32_NTEventLogFile -computername $computername -authentication
PacketPrivacy
-enableAllPrivileges -filter "logfilename='$logname'"
```

The script constructs the backup file name if it finds a log file:

```
if ($log) {
  $backupfile="{0}_{1}_{2}.{3}" -f (Get-Date -format yyyyMMdd),$computername,$logname.replace("
","")),$log.extension
  $backup=Join-Path $filepath $backupfile
```

The script removes spaces from the log file name. The backup file name will be something like 20090418_XP01_WindowsPowerShell.evt. The backup file will use the same file extension as the log file. You join this file name to the file path by using the **Join-Path** cmdlet to create a complete file name.

PowerShell then uses the file name as a parameter for the **BackupEventLog()** method:

```
$rc=$log.BackupEventLog($backup)
```

This method returns an object and we can use its ReturnValue to determine whether the backup was successful. A Switch construct will display different warning messages depending on the return value.

Assuming a successful backup, if you used the -**Clear** parameter, then PowerShell clears the log by using the **ClearEventLog()** method. Again, we capture the return object so we can tell whether this was successful:

```
switch ($rc.ReturnValue) {
  0 { #success
      Write-Host "Backup successful." -foreground Green
      if ($clear) {
        $rc=$log.ClearEventLog()
        if ($rc.returnvalue -eq 0) {
          Write-Host "Event log cleared" -foreground Green
        }
        else {
          Write-Warning "Failed to clear event log.Return code $($rc.ReturnValue)" -foreground
Green

        }
      } #end if $clear
    } #end 0
```

Here are some ways you might use this script:

```
PS C:\> Backup-Eventlog -computername CHAOS -logname "Windows PowerShell" -Filepath "d:\backups" -clear
```

This expression will back up the Windows PowerShell log on CHAOS to the D:\Backups folder. PowerShell will clear the log if the backup is successful:

```
PS C:\> get-eventlog -list -AsString | foreach { .\Backup-EventLog.ps1 -logname $_ -filepath q:\backup}
```

In this example, we are getting all event logs on the local computer and backing them up to Q:\backup:

```
PS C:\> get-content servers.txt | foreach {.\backup-eventlog.ps1 -computer $_ -log Security -filepath c:\ -clear}
```

This command will process the list of server names in servers.txt. We pipe each name to the **Foreach** loop, which connects to the remote computer, backs up the Security event log to the remote computer's C:\ drive, and then clears the log if successful.

Chapter 33
Managing Processes

If you've been with us from the beginning, you're familiar with the **Get-Process** cmdlet. This cmdlet lists the status of all current processes on your system:

```
PS C:\> get-process

Handles NPM(K)    PM(K)      WS(K) VM(M)   CPU(s)     Id ProcessName
------- ------    -----      ----- -----   ------     -- -----------
     33      2      800       3128    23     0.44   3580 ApntEx
     79      3     1768       5668    36     4.61   3852 Apoint
    128      4     2388       5752    45     1.40   1732 avgamsvr
    180      6     3500      10852    53     3.65   4016 avgcc
    168      7     2084       6708    50     2.29   1760 avgemc
     77      2      536       2128    20     0.48   1748 avgupsvc
    155      4     2700       6288    47     6.77   1604 BCMWLTRY
...
```

If you're interested in a specific process, you can reference it by name or by ID:

```
PS C:\> get-process winword

Handles NPM(K)    PM(K)      WS(K) VM(M)   CPU(s)     Id ProcessName
------- ------    -----      ----- -----   ------     -- -----------
    403     16    34340      53644   188    10.77   3032 WINWORD
PS C:\> get-process -id 3032
```

```
Handles NPM(K)    PM(K)      WS(K) VM(M)  CPU(s)     Id ProcessName
------- ------    -----      ----- -----  ------     -- -----------
    408     17    34384      53788   188   13.46   3032 WINWORD
```

```
PS C:\>
```

As you can see, either expression returns the same information. The reason you need to know either the process name or ID is so you can terminate the process with the **Stop-Process** cmdlet, which has an alias of **kill**:

```
PS C:\> notepad
PS C:\> get-process notepad
```

```
Handles NPM(K)    PM(K)      WS(K) VM(M)  CPU(s)     Id ProcessName
------- ------    -----      ----- -----  ------     -- -----------
     33      3     1180       3812    32    0.11   3868 notepad
```

```
PS C:\> kill 3868
```

We started Notepad and found the process ID with the **Get-Process** cmdlet. Once we identified the process ID, we called the **Stop-Process** cmdlet to kill it. Yes, there are more efficient ways to accomplish this but all we're doing is demonstrating the **Stop-Process** cmdlet.

Because the **Get-Process** cmdlet produces objects like all other cmdlets, you can use it in the pipeline. Here's one example:

```
PS C:\> get-process | where {$_.handles -gt 1000} | sort handles -descending
```

```
Handles NPM(K)    PM(K)      WS(K) VM(M)   CPU(s)     Id ProcessName
------- ------    -----      ----- -----   ------     -- -----------
   4218     25   163156      57408   406  5,073.57   4832 firefox
   3111     17   130808     144644   363    808.68   1284 thunderbird
   2344     33    41108      19944   191     48.27   3700 msnmsgr
   1882     90    56308      12332   285    330.66   3084 GROOVE
   1858     65    34520      45848   176    115.58   1180 svchost
   1507     14    80784      20948   249     58.50   2972 powershell
   1462     28    63000      82512   302     21.70   9448 PrimalScript
   1092     14     2276       5624    39      4.91   1064 svchost
```

This expression takes the output of the **Get-Process** cmdlet and filters it with the **Where-Object** cmdlet looking for processes with a handle count greater than 1000. PowerShell then pipes the results to the **Sort-Object** cmdlet, which sorts the output by the Handles property in descending order.

You can use the **-computerName** parameter to retrieve processes from a remote computer. The remote computer does not have to be running PowerShell, but you will need access via RPC and DCOM:

```
PS C:\> Get-Process -computer "Server2"
```

Detailed Process Information

When you're working with local processes (as opposed to those from a remote computer), you can retrieve additional useful information. For example, if you'd like to see a list of all modules that each process has loaded, add the **-module** parameter:

```
PS C:\> Get-Process -module
```

The resulting list will be very long—you might prefer to limit it to a single process that you're interested in. The **Get-Process** cmdlet has an alias of **ps**:

```
PS C:\> ps notepad -mod| ft -auto

Size(K) ModuleName    FileName
------- ----------    --------
    160 notepad.exe   C:\Windows\system32\notepad.exe
   1180 ntdll.dll     C:\Windows\system32\ntdll.dll
    876 kernel32.dll  C:\Windows\system32\kernel32.dll
    792 ADVAPI32.dll  C:\Windows\system32\ADVAPI32.dll
    780 RPCRT4.dll    C:\Windows\system32\RPCRT4.dll
    300 GDI32.dll     C:\Windows\system32\GDI32.dll
    628 USER32.dll    C:\Windows\system32\USER32.dll
    680 msvcrt.dll    C:\Windows\system32\msvcrt.dll
    460 COMDLG32.dll  C:\Windows\system32\COMDLG32.dll
    352 SHLWAPI.dll   C:\Windows\system32\SHLWAPI.dll
   1656 COMCTL32.dll  C:\Windows\WinSxS\x86_microsoft.windows.common-controls...
  11324 SHELL32.dll   C:\Windows\system32\SHELL32.dll
    264 WINSPOOL.DRV  C:\Windows\system32\WINSPOOL.DRV
   1296 ole32.dll     C:\Windows\system32\ole32.dll
    564 OLEAUT32.dll  C:\Windows\system32\OLEAUT32.dll
    120 IMM32.DLL     C:\Windows\system32\IMM32.DLL
    800 MSCTF.dll     C:\Windows\system32\MSCTF.dll
     36 LPK.DLL       C:\Windows\system32\LPK.DLL
    500 USP10.dll     C:\Windows\system32\USP10.dll
    252 UxTheme.dll   C:\Windows\system32\UxTheme.dll
```

You can also have the cmdlet display file version information for processes. Again, you can do this for all processes, or limit things down to one or more processes that you're interested in. Just use the **-fileVersionInfo** parameter:

```
PS C:\> ps "calc","notepad" -fileversion

ProductVersion    FileVersion      FileName
--------------    -----------      --------
6.0.6000.16386    6.0.6000.1638... C:\Windows\system32\calc.exe
6.0.6000.16386    6.0.6000.1638... C:\Windows\system32\notepad.exe
```

Starting a Process

On the local system, the easiest and most obvious way to start a process is to simply run a program. You can also run commands as jobs, which will put processes in the background.

Stopping Local Processes

We can kill a process with the **Stop-Process** cmdlet by specifying the ID:

```
PS C:\> stop-process 1676
```

If we didn't know the process ID, we can also use:

```
Stop-process -name notepad
```

Because terminating a process could have a significant effect on your system, you may want to take advantage of the **-Confirm** parameter to verify you're killing the correct process:

```
PS C:\> stop-process 1676 -confirm

Confirm
Are you sure you want to perform this action?
Performing operation "Stop-Process" on Target "schedul2 (1676)".
[Y] Yes [A] Yes to All [N] No [L] No to All [S] Suspend [?] Help (default is "Y"):
```

We'll explain how to stop processes on remote servers a little bit later. Note that PowerShell won't normally stop processes that aren't owned by your user account; if you try to do so, it'll prompt you before actually stopping the processes.

Waiting on a Process

Sometimes, you might want to launch a process, and then have PowerShell—or your script—wait until that process completes before continuing. The **Wait-Process** cmdlet can do just that. You provide it with an **-ID** or **-Name** parameter, plus either a process ID or name, and it will wait until that process completes before continuing execution.. Here's an example:

```
Write-Host "Please edit the file and close Notepad when you are done."
Notepad c:\test.ps1
Wait-Process -Name Notepad
Write-Host "Thank you for closing Notepad." -foregroundcolor green
```

You can optionally specify a **-timeout** parameter, in seconds, to have execution continue after that amount of time even if the process hasn't ended. If the process does not terminate in the time allotted then an exception is raised.

```
PS C:\> wait-process -Name notepad -Timeout 5
Wait-Process : This command stopped execution because process "notepad (3136)" is not terminated
in the specified Timeout.
At line:1 char:13
+ wait-process <<<<  -Name notepad -Timeout 5
    + CategoryInfo          : CloseError: (System.Diagnostics.Process (notepad):Process) [Wait-
Process], TimeoutException
    + FullyQualifiedErrorId : ProcessNotTerminated,Microsoft.PowerShell.Commands.WaitProcessCommand
```

Process Tasks

Here are some examples of using PowerShell for common process-management tasks.

Find Top 10 Processes by CPU Usage

```
PS C:\> Get-process | sort cpu -desc | select -first 10

Handles NPM(K)    PM(K)     WS(K) VM(M)   CPU(s)      Id ProcessName
------- ------    -----     ----- -----   ------      -- -----------
   3951     31   304104    208512   571  3,822.30   4832 firefox
    305      9    35384      6328  1496    601.85   1888 sqlservr
   1419     29    62120     41964   307    549.94   4520 PrimalScript
   1880     17   118824    132564   364    499.01   1284 thunderbird
```

```
 365      9    1908     4520    32    480.17      796 services
 294      8   21304    26324    73    442.37     3560 procexp
 796      0       0      220     2    361.70        4 System
 786     22   33384    23772   149    286.46     2528 explorer
1816     90   52576    17280   264    232.18     3084 GROOVE
 340      8    8832    14912    76    211.08     3536 xfilter
```

Here's another example of leveraging the pipeline. The CPU property sorts the **Get-Process** cmdlet output in descending order. It then pipes that output to the **Select-Object** cmdlet, which only returns the first 10 items in the list.

Find Top 10 Processes by Memory Usage

To find the top 10 processes with the largest working set, we can use a similar expression as above:

```
PS C:\> Get-Process | sort workingset -desc | select -first 10

Handles NPM(K)    PM(K)     WS(K) VM(M)   CPU(s)      Id ProcessName
------- ------    -----     ----- -----   ------      -- -----------
   3948     31   304092    208512   570 3,828.01    4832 firefox
   1879     17   118828    132568   364   499.05    1284 thunderbird
    671     14    64684     70508   224    20.16    2972 powershell
   1425     29    62120     41968   307   550.99    4520 PrimalScript
   1788     65    30316     41632   174    65.83    1180 svchost
    724     21    43384     33896   258   176.05    2900 WINWORD
    294      8    21304     26324    73   442.52    3560 procexp
    786     22    33384     23772   149   286.74    2528 explorer
   1841     33    40888     22572   191    36.65    3700 msnmsgr
    270      7    19080     21904    63   147.00    1136 MsMpEng
```

The only difference from the previous example is that we are sorting on the Workingset property.

Find Top 10 Longest-running Processes

```
PS C:\> Get-process | where {($_.name -ne "System") -and ($_.name -ne "Idle")} `
>> | sort starttime | select -first 10
>>

Handles NPM(K)    PM(K)     WS(K) VM(M)   CPU(s)      Id ProcessName
------- ------    -----     ----- -----   ------      -- -----------
     21      1      172       388     4    0.44     600 smss
    824      9     3356      5708    69   47.87     724 csrss
    583     74     8172      2808    63    1.69     748 winlogon
    366      9     1908      4520    32  487.66     796 services
    552     11     5176      1092    46    3.66     808 lsass
    221      6     3440      5432    63    1.08     960 svchost
    626     14     2256      5604    39    2.69    1064 svchost
    276      8    19128     21932    64  147.06    1136 MsMpEng
   1788     65    30292     41624   174   65.88    1180 svchost
    111      6     1732      4236    32    0.96    1292 svchost
```

This example is a little more complex because we want to filter out the Idle and System processes by using the **Where-Object** cmdlet:

```
where {($_.name -ne "System") -and ($_.name -ne "Idle")}
```

This expression is a compound filter using the **-And** operator to return process objects where the name is not "System" and not "Idle". PowerShell uses the StartTime property to sort the remaining process objects. **Select-Object** finally returns the first 10 objects in the list.

How did we know about the **StartTime** property? We used the **Get-Member** cmdlet to see all the possible **Process** object properties:

```
PS C:\> get-process | get-member
```

Find Process Details

Once you know what type of process information you can get, you can execute expressions like this:

```
PS C:\> get-process | Select Name,ID,Company,FileVersion,Path


Name        : alg
Id          : 1380
Company     : Microsoft Corporation
FileVersion : 5.1.2600.2180 (xpsp_sp2_rtm.040803-2158)
Path        : C:\WINDOWS\System32\alg.exe

Name        : ApntEx
Id          : 3432
Company     : Alps Electric Co., Ltd.
FileVersion : 5.0.1.13
Path        : C:\Program Files\Apoint\Apntex.exe

Name        : Apoint
Id          : 2960
Company     : Alps Electric Co., Ltd.
FileVersion : 5.4.101.113
Path        : C:\Program Files\Apoint\Apoint.exe
…
```

In addition to the Name and ID properties, we've selected the Company, FileVersion, and Path information for each process. Now you can be better informed about exactly what is running on your server.

Find Process Owners

Another piece of process information you might find valuable is the process owner. Unfortunately, the **Get-Process** cmdlet doesn't provide access to this information. But we can use the **Get-WmiObject** cmdlet:

```
PS C:\> $n=Get-wmiobject -query "Select * from win32_process where name='notepad.exe'"
PS C:\> $n.GetOwner().user
PS C:\> jeff
```

This **Get-WmiObject** expression creates a WMI object that has a **GetOwner()** method. The method returns an object with properties of Domain and User. Once you understand the concept, you can put this together as a one-line expression:

```
PS C:\> (Get-WmiObject -query "Select * from win32_process where '
>> name='notepad.exe'").GetOwner().User
>>
```

jeff

We've broken the expression up for printing, but you can type it as one line. Here's an example of how to show the owners of all running processes:

```
PS C:\> Get-WmiObject -query "Select * from win32_Process" | '
Select ProcessID,Name,@{Name="Owner";Expression={$_.GetOwner().User}}'
|sort owner | Format-Table ProcessID,Name,Owner -autosize
```

This example is pretty straightforward until we get to the **Select-Object** cmdlet. In addition to selecting the ProcessID and Name properties, we're also defining a custom property called Owner. The value will be the result of calling the **GetOwner()** method of the current object in the pipeline:

```
Expression={$_.GetOwner().User}
```

You can pass this property through the pipeline to the **Sort** cmdlet, which in turn sends the output to the **Format-Table** cmdlet for presentation. We'll let you run this on your own to see the results.

Remote Processes

As with most PowerShell cmdlets, the process management tools only work on the local system. The exception being the **Get-Process** cmdlet, which returns processes from a remote computer, but offers no way to pass alternate credentials. Although you could establish a remote session with alternate credentials, and then use the **Get-Process** cmdlet. Of course there's nothing wrong with continuing to use WMI to manage processes on remote systems:

```
PS C:\> Get-wmiobject -class win32_process -computer DC01 -credential $cred |
>> select Name,Handle,VirtualSize,WorkingSetSize | format-table -autosize
>>

Name                 Handle VirtualSize WorkingSetSize
----                 ------ ----------- --------------
System Idle Process  0                0          28672
System               4          1916928          57344
smss.exe             356        3624960          57344
csrss.exe            488       28372992        1503232
winlogon.exe         512       80613376        7442432
services.exe         564       32690176        3039232
lsass.exe            576       44298240        3260416
svchost.exe          736       68718592        1839104
svchost.exe          820       39534592        2166784
svchost.exe          884      151957504       12713984
svchost.exe          932       30928896        1507328
svchost.exe          964       38674432        1667072
mdm.exe              1208      25915392        1175552
netdde.exe           1220      27979776          69632
VMwareService.exe    1296      32428032         913408
alg.exe              1636      33574912         147456
csrss.exe            384       19238912         204800
winlogon.exe         284       41697280         184320
rdpclip.exe          1292      37167104        1671168
...
```

This example assumes we've defined the **$cred** variable earlier with the **Get-Credential** cmdlet. When using the **Get-WmiObject** cmdlet, you'll get back some additional WMI properties like __Class that generally aren't needed, so use **Select-Object** or choose properties with the **Format-Table** cmdlet to present only the information you want. It is also possible, by using the **Get-WmiObject** cmdlet, to query for specific processes:

```
PS C:\> Get-WmiObject -query "Select * from win32_process where workingsetsize > '
>> 10248000" -computer "DESK61"| >> format-table Name,ProcessID,WorkingSetSize -autosize
>>

Name           ProcessID  WorkingSetSize
----           ---------  --------------
MsMpEng.exe         1136        21778432
svchost.exe         1180        47415296
explorer.exe        2528        30642176
xfilter.exe         3536        15269888
procexp.exe         3560        28946432
msnmsgr.exe         3700        20414464
SnagIt32.exe        2472        15695872
powershell.exe      2972        17870848
thunderbird.exe     1284       146759680
firefox.exe         4832        58589184
WINWORD.EXE         9588        83107840
PrimalScript.exe    9448        90677248
```

After using the **Get-Process** cmdlet for a while, you may come to expect the same results when querying a remote computer by using the **Get-WmiObject** cmdlet. You can get the same information with an expression like this:

```
Get-WmiObject -Query "Select * from win32_process" | '
Format-Table HandleCount,QuotaNonPagedPoolUsage,PageFileUsage,'
WorkingSetSize,VirtualSize,KernelModeTime,ProcessID,Name | '
Format-Table -autosize
```

But if you execute this code, you'll see the formatting isn't quite what you might expect. This is because PowerShell has defined a default view for the **Get-Process** cmdlet that handles all the formatting. You can achieve a similar result with an expression like this:

```
Get-WmiObject -Query "Select * from win32_process" | sort Name | Format-Table '
@{Label="Handles";Expression={$_.HandleCount}},'
@{Label="NPM(K)";Expression={"{0:F0}" -f ($_.QuotaNonPagedPoolUsage/1KB)}},'
@{Label="PM(K)";Expression={"{0:F0}" -f ($_.PageFileUsage/1KB)}},'
@{Label="WS(K)";Expression={"{0:F0}" -f ($_.WorkingSetSize/1KB)}},'
@{Label="VM(M)";Expression={"{0:F0}" -f ($_.VirtualSize/1MB)}},'
@{Label="CPU(s)";Expression={"{0:N2}" -f (($_.KernelModeTime/10000000)+($_.
UserModeTime/10000000))}},'
@{Label="ID";Expression={$_.ProcessID}},'
@{Label="ProcessName";Expression={$_.Name}} '-autosize
```

PowerShell sorts the results of the **Get-WmiObject** cmdlet, and then sends them to the **Format-Table** cmdlet. We then define custom labels and values by using script blocks that will give us the same results as the **Get-Process** cmdlet. The added benefit is that we can specify a remote computer. Since this is a lot to type each time you want to use it, we recommend creating a script block:

```
$pswmi={Get-WmiObject -Query "Select * from win32_process" | sort Name | '
Format-Table '
@{Label="Handles";Expression={$_.HandleCount}},'
@{Label="NPM(K)";Expression={"{0:F0}" -f ($_.QuotaNonPagedPoolUsage/1KB)}},'
```

```
@{Label="PM(K)";Expression={"{0:F0}" -f ($_.PageFileUsage/1KB)}},'
@{Label="WS(K)";Expression={"{0:F0}" -f ($_.WorkingSetSize/1KB)}},'
@{Label="VM(M)";Expression={"{0:F0}" -f ($_.VirtualSize/1MB)}},'
@{Label="CPU(s)";Expression={"{0:N2}" -f (($_.KernelModeTime/10000000)+($_.
UserModeTime/10000000))}},'
@{Label="ID";Expression={$_.ProcessID}},'
@{Label="ProcessName";Expression={$_.Name}} -autosize}
```

Any time you want to run this, simply type:

```
&$pswmi
```

An even better approach would be to add the -**Computer** parameter:

```
$pswmi={Get-WmiObject -Query "Select * from win32_process" -computer $computer '
 | sort Name | Format-Table '
@{Label="Handles";Expression={$_.HandleCount}},'
@{Label="NPM(K)";Expression={"{0:F0}" -f ($_.QuotaNonPagedPoolUsage/1KB)}},'
@{Label="PM(K)";Expression={"{0:F0}" -f ($_.PageFileUsage/1KB)}},'
@{Label="WS(K)";Expression={"{0:F0}" -f ($_.WorkingSetSize/1KB)}},'
@{Label="VM(M)";Expression={"{0:F0}" -f ($_.VirtualSize/1MB)}},'
@{Label="CPU(s)";Expression={"{0:N2}" -f (($_.KernelModeTime/10000000)+($_.
UserModeTime/10000000))}},'
@{Label="ID";Expression={$_.ProcessID}},'
@{Label="ProcessName";Expression={$_.Name}} -autosize}
```

As long as we have defined the **$computer** variable, we can successfully run this script block. Finally, here's one more approach:

Get-PS.ps1

```
Function Get-PS {
Param([string]$computer=$env:computername,[System.Management.Automation.PSCredential]$credential)

if ($credential)
{#use alternate credentials if supplied

 Get-WmiObject -Query "Select * from win32_process" -computer $computer '
 -credential $credential | sort Name | Format-Table '
 @{Label="Handles";Expression={$_.HandleCount}},'
 @{Label="NPM(K)";Expression={"{0:F0}" -f ($_.QuotaNonPagedPoolUsage/1KB)}},'
 @{Label="PM(K)";Expression={"{0:F0}" -f ($_.PageFileUsage/1KB)}},'
 @{Label="WS(K)";Expression={"{0:F0}" -f ($_.WorkingSetSize/1KB)}},'
 @{Label="VM(M)";Expression={"{0:F0}" -f ($_.VirtualSize/1MB)}},'
 @{Label="CPU(s)";Expression={"{0:N2}" -f (($_.KernelModeTime/10000000)+'
 ($_.UserModeTime/10000000))}},'
 @{Label="ID";Expression={$_.ProcessID}},'
 @{Label="ProcessName";Expression={$_.Name}} '
 -autosize

    }

else
{

 Get-WmiObject -Query "Select * from win32_process" -computer $computer '
 | sort Name | Format-Table '
 @{Label="Handles";Expression={$_.HandleCount}},'
 @{Label="NPM(K)";Expression={"{0:F0}" -f ($_.QuotaNonPagedPoolUsage/1KB)}},'
```

```
@{Label="PM(K)";Expression={"{0:F0}" -f ($_.PageFileUsage/1KB)}},'
@{Label="WS(K)";Expression={"{0:F0}" -f ($_.WorkingSetSize/1KB)}},'
@{Label="VM(M)";Expression={"{0:F0}" -f ($_.VirtualSize/1MB)}},'
@{Label="CPU(s)";Expression={"{0:N2}" -f (($_.KernelModeTime/10000000)+'
($_.UserModeTime/10000000))}},'
@{Label="ID";Expression={$_.ProcessID}},'
@{Label="ProcessName";Expression={$_.Name}} '
 -autosize
 }
}
```

This function takes parameters for the computer name and alternate credentials:

```
Get-PS file02 (get-credential SAPIEN\administrator)
```

If a computer name is not passed, the default will be the value of the %computername% environment variable:

```
Param([string]$computer=$env:computername,
```

If the user passes an alternate credential object, then PowerShell will call a version of the **Get-WmiObject** script block that uses **-Credential** parameter:

```
Get-WmiObject -Query "Select * from win32_process" -computer $computer '
 -credential $credential | sort Name | Format-Table '
```

Otherwise, the function executes the **Get-WmiObject** cmdlet with the current credentials:

```
Get-WmiObject -Query "Select * from win32_process" -computer $computer '
```

There are many variations on this you might want to consider. The right approach will depend on your needs.

Creating a Remote Process

For a remote machine, you can easily create a remote process by using WMI and the **Invoke-WmiMethod** cmdlet:

```
PS C:\> invoke-wmimethod –comp XP01 -path win32_process -name create -argumentlist notepad.exe
```

We can check whether the command was successful by examining the ReturnValue property. Remember that any process you start on a remote system is not necessarily interactive with any logged on user. This technique is only useful when you want to start some background process on a remote computer that does not require any user intervention. Of course, if you have remote sessions set up with computers, you can simply start a new process by running a command.

Stopping Remote Process

To stop a remote process you will need to use WMI. Begin by obtaining a reference to it by using the **Get-WmiObject** cmdlet:

```
PS C:\> $calc=Get-Wmiobject -query "Select * from win32_Process where name='calc.exe'" -computer
FILE02
PS C:\> $calc.Terminate()
```

This expression will terminate the Windows calculator running on FILE02. As with starting processes, the **Terminate()** method will return an object with a ReturnValue property. A value of 0 will indicate success. You can execute this command as a one-liner as well:

```
(Get-Wmiobject -query "Select * from win32_Process where name='calc.exe'" -computerFILE02).
Terminate()
```

You can use the **Invoke-WmiMethod** cmdlet, but you'll need to know the process ID in order to construct the right path. You should be able to find the process ID by using either the **Get-Process** cmdlet or the **Get-WmiObject** cmdlet if you need alternate credential support. Once obtained, you can kill the process like this:

```
PS C:\> Invoke-WmiMethod -path "\\dc01\root\cimv2:win32_process.handle=3536" -name terminate
```

This command terminates the Notepad process running on DC01. PowerShell also supports using alternate credentials.

Chapter 34
Managing the Registry

One of the great features in Windows PowerShell is its ability to treat the registry like a file system. Now you can connect to the registry and navigate it just as you would a directory. This is because PowerShell has a **Registry** provider that presents the registry as a drive. That shouldn't come as too much of a surprise because the registry is a hierarchical storage system much like a file system. So, why not present it as such?

In fact, PowerShell accomplishes this feat for other hierarchical storage types. If you run the **Get-PSDrive** cmdlet, you can see the available "drives" and their providers:

```
PS C:\> get-psdrive

Name      Used (GB) Free (GB) Provider      Root                CurrentLocation
----      --------- --------- --------      ----                ---------------
Alias                         Alias
C             57.64     54.05 FileSystem    C:\
cert                          Certificate   \
D                             FileSystem    D:\
E             64.82      9.71 FileSystem    E:\
Env                           Environment
F            272.27     25.82 FileSystem    F:\
Feed                          FeedStore
Function                      Function
G                             FileSystem    G:\
Gac                           AssemblyCache Gac
H            151.06     81.82 FileSystem    H:\                 datastore1
HKCU                          Registry      HKEY_CURRENT_USER
HKLM                          Registry      HKEY_LOCAL_MACHINE  system\
CurrentControlSet
```

```
Variable                        Variable
WSMan                           WSMan
```

You can use the **Set-Location** cmdlet or its alias **cd** to change to any of these PSDrives just as if they were another hard drive in your computer:

```
PS C:\> cd HKLM:System
PS HKLM:\System> dir


   Hive: HKEY_LOCAL_MACHINE\system


SKC  VC Name                    Property
---  -- ----                    --------
  5   0 ControlSet001           {}
  5   0 ControlSet002           {}
  0  25 MountedDevices          {\DosDevices\C:, \DosDevices\D:, \DosDevices\E:, \DosDevices\F:...}
  0   2 RNG                     {ExternalEntropyCount, Seed}
  0   4 Select                  {Current, Default, Failed, LastKnownGood}
  8  11 Setup                   {OsLoaderPath, RestartSetup, SetupType, SystemPartition...}
 11   0 WPA                     {}
  5   0 CurrentControlSet       {}

PS HKLM:\> cd currentcontrolset\services\tcpip
PS HKLM:\system\currentcontrolset\services\tcpip> dir

   Hive: HKEY_LOCAL_MACHINE\system\currentcontrolset\services\tcpip


SKC  VC Name                    Property
---  -- ----                    --------
  0   3 Linkage                 {Bind, Route, Export}
  5  21 Parameters              {ICSDomain, SyncDomainWithMembership, DataBasePath, NameServer...}
  0   5 Performance             {Close, Collect, Library, Open...}
  0   7 ServiceProvider         {Class, DnsPriority, HostsPriority, LocalPriority...}
  0   3 Enum                    {0, Count, NextInstance}

PS HKLM:\system\currentcontrolset\services\tcpip>
```

For example, if we want to see the keys in our current registry location, we would use an expression like this using **Get-ItemProperty**:

```
PS HKLM:\system\currentcontrolset\services\tcpip> get-itemproperty .


PSPath          : Microsoft.PowerShell.Core\Registry::HKEY_LOCAL_MACHINE\system\
                  currentcontrolset\services\tcpip
PSParentPath    : Microsoft.PowerShell.Core\Registry::HKEY_LOCAL_MACHINE\system\
                  currentcontrolset\services
PSChildName     : tcpip
PSDrive         : HKLM
PSProvider      : Microsoft.PowerShell.Core\Registry
BootFlags       : 1
DisplayName     : @%SystemRoot%\system32\tcpipcfg.dll,-50003
Group           : PNP_TDI
ImagePath       : System32\drivers\tcpip.sys
ErrorControl    : 1
Start           : 0
Tag             : 3
```

```
Type               : 1
NdisMajorVersion   : 6
NdisMinorVersion   : 20
Description        : @%SystemRoot%\system32\tcpipcfg.dll,-50003


PS HKLM:\system\currentcontrolset\services\tcpip>
```

In fact, you have to use the **Get-ItemProperty** cmdlet to retrieve any registry keys. You can use this cmdlet without even having to change your location to the registry:

```
PS C:\> get-itemproperty HKLM:\software\microsoft\windows\currentversion\run


PSPath            : Microsoft.PowerShell.Core\Registry::HKEY_LOCAL_MACHINE\software\microsoft\
                    windows\currentversion\run
PSParentPath      : Microsoft.PowerShell.Core\Registry::HKEY_LOCAL_MACHINE\software\microsoft\
                    windows\...
PSChildName       : run
PSDrive           : HKLM
PSProvider        : Microsoft.PowerShell.Core\Registry
BCSSync           : "C:\Program Files\Microsoft Office\Office14\BCSSync.exe" /DelayServices
iTunesHelper      : "C:\Program Files\iTunes\iTunesHelper.exe"
nwiz              : nwiz.exe /installquiet
QuickTime Task    : "C:\Program Files\QuickTime\QTTask.exe" -atboottime
vmware-tray       : "C:\Program Files\VMware\VMware Workstation\vmware-tray.exe"
NvCplDaemon       : RUNDLL32.EXE C:\Windows\system32\NvCpl.dll,NvStartup
SunJavaUpdateSched : "C:\Program Files\Java\jre6\bin\jusched.exe"
```

This expression lists registry keys that indicate what programs are set to run when the computer starts up. We didn't have to change our location to the registry; we only had to specify the registry location as if it were a folder.

You can also create a variable for an item's properties. Here we get the registry keys for **Parameters** from our current location by using the **Get-ItemProperty** cmdlet:

```
PS HKLM:\system\currentcontrolset\services\tcpip> $ipparams=get-itemproperty Parameters
PS HKLM:\system\currentcontrolset\services\tcpip>$ipparams


PSPath                     : Microsoft.PowerShell.Core\Registry::HKEY_LOCAL_MACHINE\system\
                             currentcontrolset\services\tcpip\Parameters
PSParentPath               : Microsoft.PowerShell.Core\Registry::HKEY_LOCAL_MACHINE\system\
                             currentcontrolset\services\tcpip
PSChildName                : Parameters
PSDrive                    : HKLM
PSProvider                 : Microsoft.PowerShell.Core\Registry
ICSDomain                  : mshome.net
SyncDomainWithMembership   : 1
DataBasePath               : C:\Windows\System32\drivers\etc
NameServer                 :
ForwardBroadcasts          : 0
IPEnableRouter             : 0
Domain                     : mycompany.local
SearchList                 :
UseDomainNameDevolution    : 1
EnableICMPRedirect         : 1
DeadGWDetectDefault        : 1
DontAddDefaultGatewayDefault : 0
EnableWsd                  : 1
```

```
QualifyingDestinationThreshold : 3
HostName                       : WIN7DESK01
NV HostName                    : WIN7DESK01
IPAutoconfigurationSubnet      : 0.0.0.0
IPAutoconfigurationMask        : 0.0.0.0
NV Domain                      : mycompany.local
DhcpNameServer                 : 172.16.10.1 172.16.10.2
DhcpDomain                     : mycompany.local


PS HKLM:\system\currentcontrolset\services\tcpip> $ipparams.dhcpnameserver
172.16.10.1 172.16.10.2
PS HKLM:\system\currentcontrolset\services\tcpip>
```

We defined the **$ipparams** variable to hold the registry keys from HKLM\System\CurrentControlSet\Services\Tcpip\Parameters. Invoking the **$ipparams** variable lists all the keys and their values. Alternatively, we can get a specific key and value by using a property name:

```
$ipparams.dhcpnameserver
```

We can set a registry value using the **Set-ItemProperty** cmdlet. Say you want to change the RegisteredOrganization registry entry. Here's the current value:

```
PS C:\> get-itemproperty "hklm:\software\microsoft\windows nt\currentversion\" '
>> -Name registeredorganization
>>


PSPath                 : Microsoft.PowerShell.Core\Registry::HKEY_LOCAL_MACHINE\software\micro
                         soft\windows nt\currentversion\
PSParentPath           : Microsoft.PowerShell.Core\Registry::HKEY_LOCAL_MACHINE\software\micro
                         soft\windows nt
PSChildName            : currentversion
PSDrive                : HKLM
PSProvider             : Microsoft.PowerShell.Core\Registry
RegisteredOrganization :
```

Now let's change it by using the **Set-ItemProperty** cmdlet:

```
PS C:\> set-itemproperty "hklm:\software\microsoft\windows nt\currentversion\" '
>> -Name registeredorganization -value "MyCompany" –passthru
>>


PSPath                 : Microsoft.PowerShell.Core\Registry::HKEY_LOCAL_MACHINE\software\microsoft\
                         windows nt\currentversion\
PSParentPath           : Microsoft.PowerShell.Core\Registry::HKEY_LOCAL_MACHINE\software\microsoft\
                         windows nt
PSChildName            : currentversion
PSDrive                : HKLM
PSProvider             : Microsoft.PowerShell.Core\Registry
registeredorganization : MyCompany
```

By default, the **Set-ItemProperty** cmdlet doesn't write anything to the pipeline so you wouldn't normally see anything. We've added the -**passthru** parameter to force the cmdlet to write to the pipeline so we can see the result. To properly use the **Set-ItemProperty** cmdlet, you need to specify a path. You can use a period to indicate the current directory, or specify a complete path as in the example above.

Because accessing the registry in PowerShell is like accessing a file system, you can recurse through it, search for specific items, or do a massive search and replace. You can use the **New-Item** and **New-ItemProperty** cmdlets to create new registry keys and properties. Let's change our location to HKEY_Current_User and look at the current items in the root:

```
PS HKCU:\> dir


    Hive: HKEY_CURRENT_USER


SKC  VC Name                       Property
---  -- ----                       --------
  2   0 AppEvents                  {}
  0  36 Console                    {ColorTable00, ColorTable01, ColorTable02, ColorTable03...}
 13   0 Control Panel              {}
  0   3 Environment                {TEMP, TMP, PATH}
  5   0 EUDC                       {}
  1   6 Identities                 {Identity Ordinal, Migrated7, Last Username, Last User ID...}
  3   0 Keyboard Layout            {}
  2   0 Network                    {}
  4   0 Printers                   {}
 31   0 Software                   {}
  1   0 System                     {}
  0   1 Typewriter Preference      {FontName}
  1   8 Volatile Environment       {LOGONSERVER, USERDOMAIN, USERNAME, USERPROFILE...}


PS HKCU:\>
```

Creating Registry Items

In PowerShell it is very easy to create new registry keys and values. We'll create a new subkey called PowerShell TFM under HKCU by using the **New-Item** cmdlet:

```
PS HKCU:\> new-item "PowerShell TFM"


  Hive: Microsoft.PowerShell.Core\Registry::HKEY_CURRENT_USER

SKC VC Name                      Property
--- -- ----                      --------
  0  0 PowerShell TFM            {}


PS HKCU:\> cd "PowerShell TFM"
PS HKCU:\PowerShell TFM>
```

The **New-Item** cmdlet creates the appropriate type of object because it realizes we are in the registry. To create registry values, we use the **New-ItemProperty** cmdlet:

```
PS HKCU:\PowerShell TFM> new-itemproperty –path . -name "Pub" -value "SAPIEN"

PSPath        : Microsoft.PowerShell.Core\Registry::HKEY_CURRENT_...
PSParentPath  : Microsoft.PowerShell.Core\Registry::HKEY_CURRENT_USER
PSChildName   : PowerShell TFM
PSDrive       : HKCU
```

```
PSProvider   : Microsoft.PowerShell.Core\Registry
Pub          : SAPIEN


PS HKCU:\PowerShell TFM>
```

We now have a String entry called Pub with a value of SAPIEN. The default property type is String. If you want to create a different registry entry, such as a DWORD, use the **-PropertyType** parameter:

```
PS HKCU:\PowerShell TFM> new-itemproperty -path . -PropertyType DWORD -name "Recommend" -value 1

PSPath       : Microsoft.PowerShell.Core\Registry::HKEY_CURRENT_USE...
PSParentPath : Microsoft.PowerShell.Core\Registry::HKEY_CURRENT_USER
PSChildName  : PowerShell TFM
PSDrive      : HKCU
PSProvider   : Microsoft.PowerShell.Core\Registry
Recommend    : 1


PS HKCU:\PowerShell TFM>
```

Removing Registry Items

To remove an item, we call the **Remove-ItemProperty** cmdlet:

```
PS HKCU:\PowerShell TFM> remove-itemproperty -path . -name Recommend
```

We use the **Remove-Item** cmdlet to remove the subkey we created:

```
PS HKCU:\> remove-item "PowerShell TFM"
```

> **Standard Registry Rules Apply**
> Since PowerShell takes a new approach to managing the registry, take great care in modifying the registry. Be sure to test your registry editing skills with these new expressions and cmdlets on a test system before even thinking about touching a production server or desktop. Also don't forget to use the -whatif or -confirm parameters with these cmdlets to avoid surprises.

Searching the Registry

Searching the registry for information is not that much different from searching any other file system. However, because there is so much information, you'll want to filter it in some way. Here's one example:

```
PS HKLM:\software> dir sapien*


    Hive: HKEY_LOCAL_MACHINE\software


SKC  VC Name                     Property
---  -- ----                     --------
  4   0 SAPIEN Technologies, Inc.   {}
```

```
PS HKLM:\software>
```

From the current location, we're searching for any child keys that match the word "Sapien". We could take this a step further and enumerate all the matching registry keys:

```
PS HKLM:\software> dir sapien* -rec | select name

Name
----
HKEY_LOCAL_MACHINE\software\SAPIEN Technologies, Inc.\PrimalForms
HKEY_LOCAL_MACHINE\software\SAPIEN Technologies, Inc.\PrimalForms\2009
HKEY_LOCAL_MACHINE\software\SAPIEN Technologies, Inc.\PrimalScript
HKEY_LOCAL_MACHINE\software\SAPIEN Technologies, Inc.\PrimalScript\2009
HKEY_LOCAL_MACHINE\software\SAPIEN Technologies, Inc.\PrimalScript\2009\Settings
HKEY_LOCAL_MACHINE\software\SAPIEN Technologies, Inc.\PrimalSQL
HKEY_LOCAL_MACHINE\software\SAPIEN Technologies, Inc.\PrimalSQL\2009
HKEY_LOCAL_MACHINE\software\SAPIEN Technologies, Inc.\PrimalXML
HKEY_LOCAL_MACHINE\software\SAPIEN Technologies, Inc.\PrimalXML\2009
```

As you work with the registry in PowerShell, you will realize that you need to use the **Get-ChildItem** cmdlet to enumerate child keys and the **Get-ItemProperty** cmdlet to retrieve values; sometimes, you need to combine the two cmdlets:

```
PS HKLM:\software> dir sapien* -rec| foreach {
>>    Write-Host $_.name -foregroundcolor green
>>    Get-ItemProperty -path $_.pspath | select * -exclude PS*
>>  }| Format-List
>>
HKEY_LOCAL_MACHINE\software\SAPIEN Technologies, Inc.\PrimalForms
HKEY_LOCAL_MACHINE\software\SAPIEN Technologies, Inc.\PrimalForms\2009


(default) : C:\Program Files\SAPIEN Technologies, Inc\PrimalForms 2009\PrimalForms.exe

HKEY_LOCAL_MACHINE\software\SAPIEN Technologies, Inc.\PrimalScript
HKEY_LOCAL_MACHINE\software\SAPIEN Technologies, Inc.\PrimalScript\2009
(default) : C:\Program Files\SAPIEN Technologies, Inc\PrimalScript 2009\PrimalScript.exe
Path      : C:\Program Files\SAPIEN Technologies, Inc\PrimalScript 2009\PrimalScript.exe

HKEY_LOCAL_MACHINE\software\SAPIEN Technologies, Inc.\PrimalScript\2009\Settings
Company : MyCompany
Name    : Administrator

HKEY_LOCAL_MACHINE\software\SAPIEN Technologies, Inc.\PrimalSQL
HKEY_LOCAL_MACHINE\software\SAPIEN Technologies, Inc.\PrimalSQL\2009
(default) : C:\Program Files\SAPIEN Technologies, Inc\PrimalSQL 2009\PrimalSQL.exe

HKEY_LOCAL_MACHINE\software\SAPIEN Technologies, Inc.\PrimalXML
HKEY_LOCAL_MACHINE\software\SAPIEN Technologies, Inc.\PrimalXML\2009
(default) : C:\Program Files\SAPIEN Technologies, Inc\PrimalXML 2009\PrimalXML.exe


PS HKLM:\software>
```

Here's what is going on. From the current directory we recursively look for all keys that start with SAPIEN:

```
PS HKLM:\software> dir sapien* -rec| foreach {
```

For each key that we find, PowerShell writes the path to the console in green:

```
>>     Write-Host  $_.name -foregroundcolor green
```

Then we call the **Get-ItemProperty** cmdlet by using the PSPath property of the current object. The cmdlet creates additional properties similar to PSPath, which we want to filter out so we pipe to the **Select-Object** cmdlet to exclude these properties:

```
>>     Get-ItemProperty -path $_.pspath | select * -exclude PS*
```

At the end, to make the output easier to read we pipe to the **Format-List** cmdlet, and you can see the results.

Finally, suppose you recall part of a registry value but are not sure of the exact location. We might use a process like this:

```
PS HKLM:\software\microsoft> dir "windows*"-recurse -ea silentlycontinue | foreach {
>> if ( (get-itemproperty $_.pspath -name "RegisteredOwner" -ea silentlycontinue).RegisteredOwner
) {
>>     $_.name
>>     (Get-ItemProperty $_.pspath -name "RegisteredOwner").RegisteredOwner
>>     Break
>>    } #end if
>>   } #end foreach
>>
```

We start by recursively searching from the current location. We're using the cmdlet's **ErrorAction** parameter to turn off the error pipeline. Otherwise we'll get a lot of errors about non-existing keys. For each item, we'll call the **Get-ItemProperty** cmdlet and check for the **RegisteredOwner** value. If it exists, then we write the name of the registry key and the RegisteredOwner value. Finally, we use the **Break** keyword to stop the pipeline and discontinue searching. This is not necessarily a speedy solution, but it appears to be the best we can do with the registry **PSDrive** provider.

Managing Remote Registries with WMI

To access remote registries, the easiest approach is to use a remote session and the registry PSDrives. If that is not an option, you can use WMI and the **StdReg** provider:

```
PS C:\> [WMIClass]$Reg = "root\default:StdRegProv"
```

This will connect you to the local registry via WMI. We recommend you test things locally first. When you are ready, you can connect to a remote registry by specifying a computer name in the path:

```
PS C:\> [WMIClass]$Reg = "\\Computername\root\default:StdRegProv"
```

You must be running PowerShell with credentials that have administrative rights on the remote computer. There is no mechanism to specify alternate credentials. Once you have this object, you can use its methods as shown in the following table:

StdRegProv Class

Name	MemberType
CheckAccess()	Method
CreateKey0	Method
DeleteKey()	Method
DeleteValue()	Method
EnumKey()	Method
EnumValues()	Method
GetBinaryValue()	Method
GetDWORDValue()	Method
GetExpandedStringValue()	Method
GetMultiStringValue()	Method
GetStringValue()	Method
SetBinaryValue()	Method
SetDWORDValue()	Method
SetExpandedStringValue()	Method
SetMultiStringValue()	Method
SetStringValue()	Method
ConvertFromDateTime()	ScriptMethod
ConvertToDateTime()	ScriptMethod
CreateInstance()	ScriptMethod
Delete()	ScriptMethod
GetRelatedClasses()	ScriptMethod
GetRelationshipClasses()	ScriptMethod
GetType()	ScriptMethod
Put()	ScriptMethod

You can get this same information by piping the **$reg** variable to the **Get-Member** cmdlet.

To use the WMI object, almost all the methods will require you to specify a hive constant. Add these commands to your profile or any remote registry scripts:

```
$HKLM=2147483650
$HKCU=2147483649
$HKCR=2147483648
$HKEY_USERS=2147483651
```

Due to the WMI architecture and security, you cannot access the HKEY_CURRENT_USER hive on a remote machine. We've included it here for any PowerShell scripts you plan to run locally that will use WMI to access the registry. Most of your remote registry commands will use the constant for HKEY_LOCAL_MACHINE.

Enumerating Keys

Use the **EnumKey()** method to enumerate registry keys, starting from a given key:

```
PS C:\> $reg.EnumKey($HKLM,"Software")
```

```
__GENUS            : 2
__CLASS            : __PARAMETERS
__SUPERCLASS       :
__DYNASTY          : __PARAMETERS
__RELPATH          :
__PROPERTY_COUNT   : 2
__DERIVATION       : {}
__SERVER           :
__NAMESPACE        :
__PATH             :
ReturnValue        : 0
sNames             : {A bootable USB, Acro Software Inc, Adobe, Apple Computer, Inc....}
```

You need to specify the hive constant and the name of the registry key. In this example, we are enumerating the keys directly in HKEY_LOCAL_MACHINE\Software. PowerShell stores the returned values as an array in the sNames property:

```
PS C:\> $reg.EnumKey($HKLM,"Software").snames
```

If you wanted to recurse through subkeys, you would need an enumeration function. We'll show you one later.

Enumerating Values

To enumerate values for registry keys, use the **EnumValues()** method:

```
PS C:\> $regpath="SOFTWARE\Microsoft\Windows\CurrentVersion\Run"
PS C:\> $values=$reg.EnumValues($HKLM,$RegPath)
PS C:\test> $values.snames
BCSSync
iTunesHelper
nwiz
QuickTime Task
vmware-tray
NvCplDaemon
SunJavaUpdateSched
PS C:\>
```

As with the **EnumKeys()** method, you need to specify a hive and registry path. PowerShell stores the returned values in the sNames property, which is why we enumerate them like an array.

In this particular example, we are returning the values of the registry keys in HKEY_LOCAL_ MACHINE\ SOFTWARE\Microsoft\Windows\CurrentVersion\Run. The semantics Microsoft chose are a little misleading. Even though we're getting values for registry keys, we don't know the data associated with each key. In the above example, the value may be sufficient. But what about something like this:

```
PS C:\> $regpath="SOFTWARE\Microsoft\Windows NT\CurrentVersion"
PS C:\> $values=$reg.EnumValues($HKLM,$RegPath)
PS C:\> $values.snames
CurrentVersion
CurrentBuild
SoftwareType
CurrentType
InstallDate
SystemRoot
InstallationType
```

```
EditionID
ProductName
ProductId
DigitalProductId
DigitalProductId4
CurrentBuildNumber
BuildLab
BuildLabEx
BuildGUID
CSDBuildNumber
PathName
RegisteredOrganization
RegisteredOwner
PS C:\>
```

We need the associated data for each of these key values. The registry provider has several methods for getting key data. But you need to know what type of data is in each key. We'll show you one way to get the type information a little bit later.

In our example above, we know that all the data are strings, so we will use the **GetStringValue()** method:

```
PS C:\> $values.snames | foreach {
>> write ("{0} = {1}" -f $_,($reg.getstringvalue($HKLM,$regpath,$_).svalue))
>>
>>
CurrentVersion = 6.1
CurrentBuild = 7600
SoftwareType = System
CurrentType = Multiprocessor Free
InstallDate =
SystemRoot = C:\Windows
InstallationType = Client
EditionID = Ultimate
ProductName = Windows 7 Ultimate
ProductId = 00426-292-0111684-85702
DigitalProductId =
DigitalProductId4 =
CurrentBuildNumber = 7600
BuildLab = 7600.win7_rtm.090713-1255
BuildLabEx = 7600.16385.x86fre.win7_rtm.090713-1255
BuildGUID = e331ce24-377a-47bd-86de-92ae1aa1ae65
CSDBuildNumber = 1
PathName = C:\Windows
RegisteredOrganization = MyCompany
RegisteredOwner = Jeff
PS C:\>
```

The method requires the registry hive, the path, and the value to get. In our example the value is the sNames value coming from the pipeline:

```
"+$reg.GetStringValue($HKLM,$regpath,$_)
```

The code is getting each value and passing it to the **GetStringValue()** method. You could manually get the value for a single value like this:

```
PS C:\> $reg.GetStringValue($hklm,"software\microsoft\windows nt\currentversion","RegisteredOwner
")
```

```
__GENUS              : 2
__CLASS              : __PARAMETERS
__SUPERCLASS         :
__DYNASTY            : __PARAMETERS
__RELPATH            :
__PROPERTY_COUNT     : 2
__DERIVATION         : {}
__SERVER             :
__NAMESPACE          :
__PATH               :
ReturnValue          : 0
sValue               : Jeff
```

Searching the Registry

To search the registry with WMI requires a little fancy footwork. You have to get each key and its values, and then repeat the process for every subkey. We've put together a few functions in the following script to make this easier:

Get-RegistryPath.ps1

```
Function Get-RegistryPath {

Param([Management.ManagementObject]$Reg,[int64]$Hive,[string]$regpath)

#$reg must previously defined
#[WMIClass]$Reg = "root\default:StdRegProv"
# or
#[WMIClass]$Reg = "\\servername\root\default:StdRegProv"
#$Hive is a numeric constant
# $HKLM=2147483650
# $HKCU=2147483649

    Function Get-RegistryValue {

    Param([Management.ManagementObject]$Reg,
          [int64]$Hive,
          [string]$regitem,
          [string]$value,
          [int32]$iType)

    #$reg must previously defined
    #$Reg = [WMIClass]"root\default:StdRegProv"
    # or
    # $Reg = [WMIClass]"\\servername\root\default:StdRegProv"
    # $Hive is a numeric constant
    # $HKLM=2147483650
    # $HKCU=2147483649

    # $regitem is a registry path like "software\microsoft\windows nt\currentversion"
    # $Value is the registry key name like "registered owner

    # iType is a numeric value that indicates what type of data is stored in the key.
    # Type 1 = String
    # Type 2 = ExpandedString
    # Type 3 = Binary
```

```
    # Type 4 = DWord
    # Type 7 = MultiString
    # sample usage:
    # $regPath="software\microsoft\windows nt\currentversion"
    # $regKey="RegisteredOwner"
    # Get-RegistryValue $reg $hklm $regPath $regKey 1

        $obj=New-Object PSObject

        switch ($iType) {
            1 {
                $data=($reg.GetStringValue($Hive,$regitem,$value)).sValue
            }
            2 {
                $data=($reg.GetExpandedStringValue($Hive,$regitem,$value)).sValue
            }
            3 {
                $data="Binary Data"
            }
            4 {
                $data=($reg.GetDWordValue($Hive,$regitem,$value)).uValue
            }
            7 {
                $data=($reg.GetMultiStringValue($Hive,$regitem,$value)).sValue
            }
            default {
                $data="Unable to retrieve value"
            }
        } #end switch

        Add-Member -inputobject $obj -membertype "NoteProperty" -name Key -value $value
        Add-Member -inputobject $obj -membertype "NoteProperty" -name KeyValue -value $data
        Add-Member -inputobject $obj -membertype "NoteProperty" -name RegPath -value $regitem
        Add-Member -inputobject $obj -membertype "NoteProperty" -name Hive -value $hive
        Add-Member -inputobject $obj -membertype "NoteProperty" -name KeyType -value $iType
        write $obj

    } #end Get-RegistryValue function

#get values in root of current registry key
 $values=$Reg.enumValues($Hive,$regpath)
 if ($values.snames.count -gt 0) {
     for ($i=0;$i -lt $values.snames.count;$i++) {
         $iType = $values.types[$i]
         $value = $values.snames[$i]
         Get-RegistryValue $Reg $Hive $regpath $value $iType
     }
 }

$keys=$Reg.EnumKey($Hive,$regpath)

# enumerate any subkeys
if ($keys.snames.count -gt 0) {
   foreach ($item in $keys.snames) {

        #recursively call this function
        Get-RegistryPath $Reg $hive "$regpath\$item"

   }
 }
}
```

The **Get-RegistryPath** function takes parameters for the WMI registry object, the hive constant, and the starting registry path:

```
Get-RegistryPath $reg $HKLM "Software\Microsoft\Windows NT\CurrentVersion"
```

The **Get-RegistryPath** function calls the nested **Get-RegistryValue** function, which returns key data for any keys in the starting location. Then it enumerates any subkeys. If the count is greater than 0, the function recurses and calls itself. In this way, the function recursively enumerates the entire registry key.

This second function requires a registry provider, hive constant, registry path, key name, and data type as parameters. These are passed from the **Get-RegistryPath** function:

```
$values=$Reg.enumValues($Hive,$regpath)
 if ($values.snames.count -gt 0) {
    for ($i=0;$i -lt $values.snames.count;$i++) {
       $iType = $values.types[$i]
       $value = $values.snames[$i]
       Get-RegistryValue $Reg $Hive $regpath $value $iType
    }
 }
```

The **Get-RegistryPath** function checks the collection of values to see if there are any. Assuming there are values, the collection is enumerated. The **$values** variable actually has two properties. The sNames property is every key name and the Types property is the corresponding data type. The WMI registry provider doesn't have a good mechanism for discovering what type of data might be in a given key. So, we have to match up the data type with the key name. We then pass these values to the **Get-RegistryValue** function.

This function evaluates the data type with the **Switch** statement and uses the appropriate method to read the data. It skips binary data and returns a message instead. We then use a custom object to return information. The advantage is that we can use these object properties in formatting the output:

```
PS C:\> Get-RegistryPath $reg $hklm "software\microsoft\windows nt\currentversion" |'
>> Select Key,Keyvalue,RegPath
>>
```

Or you can run a command like this:

```
PS C:\> Get-RegistryPath $reg $hklm "software\microsoft\windows nt\currentversion" | '
>> where {$_.key -match "registeredowner"}
>>
```

Enumerating or searching the registry with WMI is a slow process. Over the network to a remote computer will be even slower. So if this is your business requirement, don't expect blazing results.

Modifying the Registry

Creating a registry key with the WMI provider is pretty simple:

```
PS C:\> $reg.CreateKey($HKCU,"PowerShellTFM")
```

This will create a key called "PowerShellTFM" under HKEY_CURRENT_USER. You can even create a hierarchy with one command:

```
PS C:\> $reg.CreateKey($HKCU,"PowerShellTFM\Key1\Key2")
```

The command will create Key1 and Key2. What about adding values to keys? It depends on the type of data you need to store:

```
#create a string value
PS C:\> $reg.SetStringValue($HKCU,"PowerShellTFM\Key1","SampleKey","I am a string")

#create a dword
PS C:\> $reg.SetDWORDValue($HKCU,"PowerShellTFM\Key1","Sample Dword",1024)

#create an expanded string value
PS C:\> $reg.SetExpandedStringValue($HKCU,"PowerShellTFM\Key1\Key2",'
>> "Sample Expandable","%Username%")
>>

#create multistring value
PS C:\> $reg.SetMultiStringValue($HKCU,"PowerShellTFM\Key1\Key2",'
>> "Sample Multi",(get-content c:\file.txt))
>>
PS C:\>
```

When creating a multistring value, you can't have any blank lines. The WMI method will let you insert blank lines, but when you edit the value with Regedit.exe, it will remove them. Make sure you have no blank lines to begin with, and you should be fine. In all cases, you can check the Return value to verify success. A value of 0 indicates the value was successfully written to the registry.

To delete a value, specify the hive, the registry path, and the key name:

```
PS C:\> $reg.DeleteValue($HKCU,"PowerShellTFM\Key1","SampleKey")
```

To delete a key, specify the hive and key path:

```
PS C:\> $reg.DeleteKey($HKCU,"PowerShellTFM\Key1\Key2")
```

You delete a key with values, but you can't delete a key with subkeys. If we had used this command instead:

```
PS C:\> $reg.DeleteKey($HKCU,"PowerShellTFM\Key1")
```

you would get a return value of 5, which tells you there are subkeys that you must remove first. In this case, that would be Key2. So, to cleanly delete the keys, we would first need to remove Key2, and then remove Key1.

Working with remote registries via WMI is possible, but it is not the easiest management task you'll face. Write functions and scripts to make it a little easier, but don't expect snappy performance.

Managing Remote Registries with the .NET Framework

Another remote registry management alternative is to use the .NET Framework registry classes. You'll find some similarities with the WMI approach. First we connect to a specific remote registry hive:

```
PS C:\> $computer="GODOT7"
PS C:\> $regbase=[Microsoft.Win32.RegistryKey]::OpenRemoteBaseKey("localmachine",$computer)
```

The first parameter for the **OpenRemoteBaseKey()** method is the hive name, which will probably always by HKLM. Use the **OpenSubKey()** method to, well, open a subkey:

```
PS C:\> $key="software\microsoft\windows nt\currentversion"
PS C:\> $cv=$regbase.OpenSubKey($key)
```

We always like to pipe new objects to the **Get-Member** cmdlet to discover that they can do:

```
PS C:\> $cv | gm

    TypeName: Microsoft.Win32.RegistryKey

Name                        MemberType Definition
----                        ---------- ----------
Close                       Method     System.Void Close()
CreateObjRef                Method     System.Runtime.Remoting.ObjRef CreateObjRef(type requestedType)
CreateSubKey                Method     Microsoft.Win32.RegistryKey CreateSubKey(string subkey),
                                       Microsoft.Win32.RegistryKey CreateSubKey(string subkey...
DeleteSubKey                Method     System.Void DeleteSubKey(string subkey), System.Void
                                       DeleteSubKey(string subkey, bool throwOnMissingSubKey)
DeleteSubKeyTree            Method     System.Void DeleteSubKeyTree(string subkey)
DeleteValue                 Method     System.Void DeleteValue(string name), System.Void
                                       DeleteValue(string name, bool throwOnMissingValue)
Equals                      Method     bool Equals(System.Object obj)
Flush                       Method     System.Void Flush()
GetAccessControl            Method     System.Security.AccessControl.RegistrySecurity GetAccessControl(),
GetHashCode                 Method     int GetHashCode()
GetLifetimeService          Method     System.Object GetLifetimeService()
GetSubKeyNames              Method     string[] GetSubKeyNames()
GetType                     Method     type GetType()
GetValue                    Method     System.Object GetValue(string name), System.Object GetValue(string
                                       name, System.Object defaultValue), System.Ob...
GetValueKind                Method     Microsoft.Win32.RegistryValueKind GetValueKind(string name)
GetValueNames               Method     string[] GetValueNames()
InitializeLifetimeService Method       System.Object InitializeLifetimeService()
OpenSubKey                  Method     Microsoft.Win32.RegistryKey OpenSubKey(string name, bool writable),
SetAccessControl            Method     System.Void SetAccessControl(System.Security.AccessControl.
                                       RegistrySecurity registrySecurity)
SetValue                    Method     System.Void SetValue(string name, System.Object value), System.Void
                                       SetValue(string name, System.Object value, ...
ToString                    Method     string ToString()
Name                        Property   System.String Name {get;}
SubKeyCount                 Property   System.Int32 SubKeyCount {get;}
ValueCount                  Property   System.Int32 ValueCount {get;}
```

We can use the **GetValueNames()** method to list all the values and the **GetValue()** method to return the corresponding value:

```
PS C:\> $cv.GetValueNames() | sort | foreach {
>>     "{0} = {1}" -f $_,$cv.GetValue($_)
>>   }
>>
BuildGUID = e331ce24-377a-47bd-86de-92ae1aa1ae65
BuildLab = 7600.win7_rtm.090713-1255
BuildLabEx = 7600.16385.x86fre.win7_rtm.090713-1255
CSDBuildNumber = 1
CurrentBuild = 7600
CurrentBuildNumber = 7600
CurrentType = Multiprocessor Free
```

```
CurrentVersion = 6.1
DigitalProductId = System.Byte[]
DigitalProductId4 = System.Byte[]
EditionID = Ultimate
InstallationType = Client
InstallDate = 1250446001
PathName = C:\Windows
ProductId = 00426-292-0111684-85702
ProductName = Windows 7 Ultimate
RegisteredOrganization = MyCompany
RegisteredOwner = Jeff
SoftwareType = System
SystemRoot = C:\Windows
```

We can also enumerate subkeys:

```
PS C:\> $key="software\sapien technologies, inc."
PS C:\> $cv=$regbase.OpenSubKey($key)
PS C:\> $cv.GetSubKeyNames()
PrimalForms
PrimalScript
PrimalSQL
PrimalXML
```

Retrieving registry values is also not especially difficult. You need a subkey object:

```
PS C:\> $k=$regbase.OpenSubKey("Software\RegisteredApplications")
```

Use the **GetValueNames()** method to enumerate it:

```
PS C:\> $k.getValuenames()
Windows Address Book
Paint
Windows Search
Windows Disc Image Burner
Windows Photo Viewer
Windows Media Player
Wordpad
Internet Explorer
Windows Media Center

Firefox
Google Chrome
iTunes
Microsoft Office Outlook
QuickTime
Skype
Thunderbird
Thunderbird (News)
WindowsLive.PhotoGallery.14.0
WinRAR
ImgBurn
```

Now get the value by using the **GetValue()** method:

```
PS C:\> $k.getvaluenames() | foreach {write ("{0} = {1}" -f $_, $k.GetValue($_))}

Windows Address Book = Software\Clients\Contacts\Address Book\Capabilities
```

```
Paint = SOFTWARE\Microsoft\Windows\CurrentVersion\Applets\Paint\Capabilities
Windows Search = Software\Microsoft\Windows Search\Capabilities
Windows Disc Image Burner = Software\Microsoft\IsoBurn\Capabilities
Windows Photo Viewer = Software\Microsoft\Windows Photo Viewer\Capabilities
Windows Media Player = Software\Clients\Media\Windows Media Player\Capabilities
Wordpad = Software\Microsoft\Windows\CurrentVersion\Applets\Wordpad\Capabilities
Internet Explorer = SOFTWARE\Microsoft\Internet Explorer\Capabilities
Windows Media Center = Software\Clients\Media\Windows Media Center\Capabilities
 =
Firefox = Software\Clients\StartMenuInternet\FIREFOX.EXE\Capabilities
Google Chrome = Software\Clients\StartMenuInternet\Google Chrome\Capabilities
iTunes = Software\Clients\Media\iTunes\Capabilities
Microsoft Office Outlook = Software\Clients\Mail\Microsoft Outlook\Capabilities
QuickTime = SOFTWARE\Clients\Media\QuickTime\Capabilities
Skype = SOFTWARE\Clients\Internet Call\Skype\Capabilities
Thunderbird = Software\Clients\Mail\Mozilla Thunderbird\Capabilities
Thunderbird (News) = Software\Clients\News\Mozilla Thunderbird\Capabilities
WindowsLive.PhotoGallery.14.0 = Software\Microsoft\Windows Live\Photo Gallery\Capabilities
WinRAR = Software\WinRAR\Capabilities
ImgBurn = SOFTWARE\ImgBurn\Capabilities
```

The blank entry is from the (DEFAULT) value. The method will work with any data type from String to DWORD to MultiString and automatically format the results.

Because of security, creating and modifying registry entries can be a little tricky. Depending on the operating system and credentials, the following may or may not work for you. Everything is pretty much as we've already shown, with the addition of the **Set-Value()** method. The default value is a string, but you can also create other values such as DWORD. If you enter the wrong value type, the error message will give you the correct values so don't worry too much about making mistakes:

```
PS C:\> $lm=[Microsoft.Win32.RegistryKey]::OpenRemoteBaseKey("localcomputer",$computer)
PS C:\> $lm.CreateSubKey("MYCOMPANY")

SKC  VC Name                         Property
---  -- ----                         --------
  0   0


PS C:\> $lm.setValue("Office","Las Vegas")
PS C:\> $lm.setValue("Updated",1,"DWORD")
PS C:\> $lm.getvaluenames()
Office
Updated
PS C:\> $cu.getvaluenames() | foreach {$cu.getValue($_)}
Las Vegas
1
```

As you can see, working with the registry, locally or remote, takes a bit of work and some actual scripting. We're hoping at some point to have a set of cmdlets that will make this a much easier administrative task.

Chapter 35
Managing Directory Services

As we described in earlier chapters, Windows PowerShell's current support for ADSI is pretty limited. The Active Directory team at Microsoft has released a PowerShell solution for Active Directory, but it is only supported on Windows Server 2008 R2. The expectation is that eventually it will be supported by Windows 2003 domains as well. Full coverage of those cmdlets is outside the scope of this book, although we will give you a small sampling to whet your appetite. We also encourage you to look at *Managing Active Directory with Windows PowerShell: TFM* (SAPIEN Press 2008) for detailed information that you can use today on managing directory services with PowerShell on any Active Directory domain. This chapter will be focused on managing directory services by using the .NET Framework DirectoryService classes, which you can access by using the **New-Object** cmdlet:

```
$Root = New-Object DirectoryServices.DirectoryEntry "LDAP://DC=MyCompany,dc=local"
```

However, the PowerShell team realized most administrators won't have experience programming in .NET Framework, so they developed an ADSI type adapter, which we cover in more detail a bit later in the chapter. This type adapter abstracts the underlying .NET Framework classes and makes it a little bit easier to work with Active Directory objects.

As you work with the ADSI type adapter, you'll realize there are limitations. Fortunately, Quest Software has developed a free set of cmdlets for managing Active Directory users and computers. These cmdlets can create and modify common Active Directory objects, such as users, groups, and computers. Finally, we covered PSDrives earlier in the book. Wouldn't it be nice to mount your Active Directory store like any other file system? PowerShell itself does not ship with a directory services provider, but the free PowerShell Community Extensions includes one. The AD cmdlets shipping with Windows Server 2008 R2 also include a **PSDrive** provider. When installed, the provider will create a new PSDrive that is mapped to the root of your Active Directory domain. You can then navigate Active Directory just like any other drive. This **PSDrive** provider is compatible with the Quest cmdlets.

Depending on your needs, there are several approaches to working with Active Directory without resorting to third-party extensions. We'll show you several example tasks in this chapter. After working with these examples, you'll realize how valuable the third-party extensions are.

Working with Users by Using the [ADSI] Type Adapter

The PowerShell team introduced the ADSI type adapter in version 1.0 and improved it in version 2.0. This type adapter makes it easier to create, modify, display, and delete Active Directory objects such as users, groups, and computers. In order to use the type adapter, you need to know the distinguished name of the object:

```
PS C:\> [ADSI]$admin="LDAP://CN=Administrator,CN=Users,DC=MyCompany,DC=local"
PS C:\> $admin
PS C:\scripts> $admin


distinguishedName : {CN=Administrator,CN=Users,DC=MyCompany,DC=local}
Path              : LDAP://CN=Administrator,CN=Users,DC=MyCompany,DC=local

PS C:\> $admin.memberof
CN=Group Policy Creator Owners,CN=Users,DC=MyCompany,DC=local
CN=Domain Admins,CN=Users,DC=MyCompany,DC=local
CN=Enterprise Admins,CN=Users,DC=MyCompany,DC=local
CN=Schema Admins,CN=Users,DC=MyCompany,DC=local
CN=Administrators,CN=Builtin,DC=MyCompany,DC=local
PS C:\> $admin.WhenChanged

Tuesday, November 17, 2007 12:18:27 PM
```

Piping the **$admin** variable to the **Get-Member** cmdlet will list what appear to be all the available ADSI properties of the object. If you are familiar with ADSI, you'll realize that some properties are missing. The **Get-Member** cmdlet only displays properties with defined values. You can modify other properties as long as you already know the property name, which we'll show you later. One other important reminder is that when you create an object, PowerShell stores the property values in a local cache. If a user modifies the object in Active Directory, you won't see the changes locally unless you refresh the cache. Here's how we would do it with our previous example:

```
$admin.refreshcache()
```

We can also use the ADSI type accelerator to create an object in Active Directory. Take a look at the CreateUser.ps1 script:

CreateUser.ps1

```
#specify the OU where you want to create the account
[ADSI]$OU="LDAP://OU=Employees,DC=MyCompany,DC=Local"

#Add the user object as a child to the OU
$newUser=$OU.Create("user","CN=Jack Frost")
$newUser.Put("sAMAccountName","jfrost")

#commit changes to Active Directory
```

```
$newUser.SetInfo()

#set a password
$newUser.SetPassword("P@ssw0rd")

#Define some other user properties
$newUser.Put("DisplayName","Jack Frost")
$newUser.Put("UserPrincipalName","jfrost@mycompany.com")
$newUser.Put("GivenName","Jack")
$newUser.Put("sn","Frost")

#enable account = 544
#disable account = 546
$newUser.Put("UserAccountControl","544")

$newUser.Put("Description","Created by PowerShell $((get-date).ToString())")

#commit changes to Active Directory
$newUser.SetInfo()

#flag the account to force password change at next logon
$newUser.Put("pwdLastSet",0)
$newUser.SetInfo()
```

Before you can create an object, you first must create an object for the parent container. In this example, we're using the Employees organizational unit. To create a new user object, we simply invoke the parent object's **Create()** method and specify the type of child object and its name:

```
$newUser=$OU.Create("user","CN=Jack Frost")
```

To define properties, we'll use the **Put()** method. When you create a user account, you have to also define the sAMAccountname:

```
$newUser.Put("sAMAccountName","jfrost")
```

Before we can set any other properties, you need to write the object from the local cache to Active Directory. You can accomplish this by calling the **SetInfo()** method:

```
$newUser.SetInfo()
```

To set the user's password, there is a **SetPassword()** method that takes the new password as a parameter:

```
$newUser.SetPassword("P@ssw0rd")
```

Once this is accomplished, we can define some additional properties by using the **Put()** method, as you can see in the remainder of the script.

To modify an existing user, it is merely a matter of creating an ADSI user object and using the **Put()** method to define user attributes. Don't forget to call the **SetInfo()** method, or none of your changes will be committed to Active Directory:

```
PS C:\> [ADSI]$user="LDAP://CN=Bill Shakespeare,OU=Employees,DC=MyCompany,dc=local"
PS C:\> $user.put("Title","Playwright")
PS C:\> $user.Setinfo()
```

```
PS C:\> $user.RefreshCache()
PS C:\> $user.Title
Playwright
PS C:\>
```

To delete a user, we create an object for the parent container, typically an organizational unit, and then simply call the **Delete()** method:

```
PS C:\> [ADSI]$ou="LDAP://OU=Sales,OU=Employees,DC=MyCompany,DC=local"
PS C:\> $ou.Get_Children()


distinguishedName : {OU=Agents,OU=Sales,OU=Employees,DC=MyCompany,DC=local}
Path              : LDAP://OU=Agents,OU=Sales,OU=Employees,DC=MyCompany,DC=local

distinguishedName : {CN=Anne Tern,OU=Sales,OU=Employees,DC=MyCompany,DC=local}
Path              : LDAP://CN=Anne Tern,OU=Sales,OU=Employees,DC=MyCompany,DC=local

distinguishedName : {CN=Fiona Thrush,OU=Sales,OU=Employees,DC=MyCompany,DC=local}
Path              : LDAP://CN=Fiona Thrush,OU=Sales,OU=Employees,DC=MyCompany,DC=local

distinguishedName : {CN=George Washington,OU=Sales,OU=Employees,DC=MyCompany,DC=local}
Path              : LDAP://CN=George Washington,OU=Sales,OU=Employees,DC=MyCompany,DC=

distinguishedName : {CN=Roy G. Biv,OU=Sales,OU=Employees,DC=MyCompany,DC=local}
Path              : LDAP://CN=Roy G. Biv,OU=Sales,OU=Employees,DC=MyCompany,DC=local

distinguishedName : {CN=Sales Managers,OU=Sales,OU=Employees,DC=MyCompany,DC=local}
Path              : LDAP://CN=Sales Managers,OU=Sales,OU=Employees,DC=MyCompany,DC=loc


PS C:\> $ou.Delete("User","CN=Fiona Thrush")
PS C:\> $ou.refreshCache()
PS C:\> $ou.Get_Children()


distinguishedName : {OU=Agents,OU=Sales,OU=Employees,DC=MyCompany,DC=local}
Path              : LDAP://OU=Agents,OU=Sales,OU=Employees,DC=MyCompany,DC=local

distinguishedName : {CN=Anne Tern,OU=Sales,OU=Employees,DC=MyCompany,DC=local}
Path              : LDAP://CN=Anne Tern,OU=Sales,OU=Employees,DC=MyCompany,DC=local

distinguishedName : {CN=George Washington,OU=Sales,OU=Employees,DC=MyCompany,DC=local}
Path              : LDAP://CN=George Washington,OU=Sales,OU=Employees,DC=MyCompany,DC=

distinguishedName : {CN=Roy G. Biv,OU=Sales,OU=Employees,DC=MyCompany,DC=local}
Path              : LDAP://CN=Roy G. Biv,OU=Sales,OU=Employees,DC=MyCompany,DC=local

distinguishedName : {CN=Sales Managers,OU=Sales,OU=Employees,DC=MyCompany,DC=local}
Path              : LDAP://CN=Sales Managers,OU=Sales,OU=Employees,DC=MyCompany,DC=loc


PS C:\>
```

There is no need in this situation to call the **SetInfo()** method. As soon as you invoke the **Delete()** method, the object is gone. You can use this method to delete any object. All you have to do is specify the object class and its name.

Getting Password Age

The easiest way to obtain the password age for a user or a computer is to use the **WinNT** provider and look at the PasswordAge property:

```
PS C:\> [ADSI]$user="WinNT://MyCompany/aSample,user"
PS C:\> $user.passwordage[0]/86400 -as [int]
78
PS C:\>
```

The first step is to create an ADSI object for the user employing the **WinNT** provider. In this example, we are getting the user object for Ann Sample in the MyCompany domain. Her SAMAccountname is asample.

PowerShell stores the password age in the password property, but returns it as a single element array. Therefore, we reference it with an index number of 0. The value is in seconds, so we divide it by 86400 to obtain the number of days and cast the result as an integer, which in effect rounds the value. As you can see, her password was last changed 78 days ago.

You can use the password age for a computer account to identify obsolete computer accounts. If the password has not changed in, say, 45 days, it is very likely the computer account is no longer active:

```
PS C:\> [ADSI]$server="WinNT://company/NTFile07$"
PS C:\> $server.passwordage[0]/86400 -as [int]
368
PS C:\>
```

The only difference with this code, compared to the code for a user account, is that we must specify the SAMAccountname of the computer, which should be the computer's NetBIOS name appended with the $ sign. The remaining code is the same. In this example, it is very clear that server NTFile07 is likely obsolete and no longer in use, since its password age is over a year old.

Deleting Users

Deleting a user is a very straightforward task. All you need is the distinguished name of the container or organizational unit and the Active Directory name of the user object:

```
PS C:\> [ADSI]$ou="LDAP://OU=employees,DC=MyCompany,dc=local"
PS C:\> $ou.Delete("user","CN=Sam Hamm")
```

The first line creates an ADSI object that represents the parent container—in this case, the Employees OU. The second line calls the **Delete()** method, which requires the type of object and its canonical name.

Bulk-creating Users

With a little extra effort, we can expand the previous example to create a group of users in bulk. The following script will create a group of users based on information stored in a comma-separated value file:

Import Users.ps1

```
#Import-Users.ps1

$data="newusers.csv"
$imported=Import-Csv $data

#retrieve list of csv column headings
#Each column heading should correspond to an ADSI user property name

$properties=$imported |Get-Member -type noteproperty |
where {$_.name -ne "OU" -and $_.name -ne "Password" '
-and $_.name -ne "Name" -and $_.name -ne "sAMAccountName"}

 for ($i=0;$i -lt $imported.count;$i++) {
   Write-Host "Creating User"$imported[$i].Name "in" $imported[$i].OU

   [ADSI]$OU="LDAP://"+$imported[$i].OU

   $newUser=$OU.Create("user","CN="+$imported[$i].Name)
   $newUser.Put("sAMAccountName",$imported[$i].samAccountname)
   #commit changes to Active Directory
   $newUser.SetInfo()
   #set a password
   $newUser.SetPassword($imported[$i].Password)
   $newUser.SetInfo()

      foreach ($prop in $properties) {
       #set additional properties
       $value=$imported[$i].($prop.name)
       if ($value.length -gt 0) {
          #only set properties that have values
          $newUser.put($prop.name,$value)
          }
      }
   $newUser.SetInfo()
 }
```

Our script assumes the CSV file will have required column headings of OU, Name, SAMAccountname, and Password. The OU column will contain the distinguished name of the organizational unit where PowerShell will create the new user account, such as OU=Employees,DC=MyCompany,DC=Local. The Name property will be the user's Active Directory name and the SAMAccountname property will be the user's down-level logon name. You can have as many other entries as you want. Each column heading must correspond to an ADSI property name. For example, use SN for the user's last name and GivenName for the user's first name. The script begins by using the **Import-CSV** cmdlet to import the CSV file:

```
$data="newusers.csv"
$imported=Import-Csv $data
```

Because the CSV file will likely contain column headings for additional user properties, we'll create an object to store those property names. We'll exclude the required columns by selecting all property names that don't match the required names:

```
$properties=$imported | Get-Member -type noteproperty | '
where {$_.name -ne "OU" -and $_.name -ne "Password" '
-and $_.name -ne "Name" -and $_.name -ne "sAMAccountName"}
```

Armed with this information, we can now run through the list of new user information using the **For** construct:

```
for ($i=0;$i -lt $imported.count;$i++) {
    Write-Host "Creating User" $imported[$i].Name "in" $imported[$i].OU
```

The **$imported** variable is an array, so we can access each array member by using the array index. We'll first create an object for the OU where the user will be created, using the ADSI type adapter:

```
[ADSI]$OU="LDAP://"+$imported[$i].OU
```

Now we can create the new user by referencing the required imported user properties:

```
$newUser=$OU.Create("user","CN="+$imported[$i].Name)
$newUser.Put("sAMAccountName",$imported[$i].samAccountname)
#commit changes to Active Directory
$newUser.SetInfo()
```

At this point, we can add any other user properties that are defined in the CSV file. We accomplish this by enumerating the property list object:

```
    foreach ($prop in $properties) {
```

For each property name, we'll get the corresponding value from the current user:

```
    $value=$imported[$i].($prop.name)
```

For example, if the property name is Title, then the script sets the **$value** variable to the value of $imported[$i].Title. We put the **$prop.name** variable in parentheses to instruct PowerShell to evaluate the expression, so it will return Title in this example.

As written, this script can only set single-valued properties that accept strings. The script checks the length of the **$value** variable. A length of 0 means there is no value and there's no reason to attempt to set the property. So, if the length of **$value** is greater than 0, we know there is a value, and we'll set the user property with it:

```
    if ($value.length -gt 0) {
        #only set properties that have values
        $newUser.put($prop.name,$value)
        }
```

After you have set all the properties, we call the **SetInfo()** method to write the new information to Active Directory:

```
$newUser.SetInfo()
```

We repeat this process for every user imported from the CSV file.

Working with Computers

Creating a new computer account is very similar to creating a new user account, and, in many ways, it's much easier because there are very few properties you have to define. Here's a function you can use to create a new computer account:

CreateNewComputer.ps1

```
Function New-Computer {
    Param([string]$name=$(Throw "You must enter a computer name."),
    [string]$Path="CN=computers,DC=MyCompany,DC=Local",
    [string]$description="Company Server",
    [switch]$enabled)

    [ADSI]$OU="LDAP://$Path"
    #set name to all uppercase
    $name=$name.ToUpper()

    $computer=$OU.Create("computer","CN=$name")
    $computer.Put("SamAccountName",$name)
    $computer.put("Description",$description)

    if ($enabled) {
        $computer.Put("UserAccountControl",544)
        } else {
        $computer.Put("UserAccountControl",546)
    }

    $computer.SetInfo()
} #end function
```

The function requires the name of the new computer object and, optionally, the organizational unit path, a description, and whether the account should be enabled. It is disabled by default unless you use the **-Enabled** parameter. Default values are specified for the optional parameters.

The function creates an ADSI object for the OU or container where you want to create the computer object:

```
[ADSI]$OU="LDAP://$Path"
```

The function next creates the computer object in the container specifying the Active Directory name and the SAMAccountname:

```
$computer=$OU.Create("computer","CN=$name")
$computer.Put("SamAccountName",$name)
```

The function defines the description:

```
$computer.put("Description",$description)
```

By default, PowerShell disables the computer account, but you can specify to create the accounts as enabled. The UserAccountControl property defines this setting:

```
if ($enabled) {
    $computer.Put("UserAccountControl",544)
    } else {
    $computer.Put("UserAccountControl",546)
}
```

Finally, we call the **Setinfo()** method to write the new account to the Active Directory database:

```
$computer.SetInfo()
```

Delete Computer Accounts

Deleting a computer is essentially the same as with user accounts. All you need are the distinguished name of the container or organizational unit and the Active Directory name of the computer object:

```
PS C:\> [ADSI]$ou="LDAP://OU=Desktops,DC=MyCompany,dc=local"
PS C:\> $ou.Delete("computer","CN=XPDesk81")
```

The first line creates an ADSI object that represents the parent container—in this case, the Desktops OU. The second line calls the **Delete()** method, which requires the type of object and its canonical name.

Working with Groups

Creating a group is very similar to creating a user:

```
PS C:\> [ADSI]$OU="LDAP://OU=SAPIEN,DC=MyCompany,dc=local"
PS C:\> $newGroup=$OU.Create("group","CN=SAPIEN Authors")
PS C:\> $newGroup.Put("sAMAccountName","SAPIEN-Authors")
PS C:\> $newGroup.Put("Description","Contract Writers")
PS C:\> $newGroup.SetInfo()
PS C:\>
```

Modifying group membership is not especially difficult. If you are familiar with this task in ADSI, it's not too different conceptually in PowerShell. As with ADSI, you need a DirectoryEntry object for the group. You also need to know the distinguished name of the user object you want to add. Armed with that information, it's a matter of adding the user's distinguished name to the object's Member property. Here's a script that demonstrates how to modify group membership:

AddToGroup.ps1

```
#AddToGroup.ps1

[ADSI]$Grp="LDAP://CN=SAPIEN Authors,OU=SAPIEN,DC=MyCompany,DC=local"
$NewUserDN="CN=Jeffery Hicks,OU=IT,OU=Employees,DC=MyCompany,DC=local"

#create an array object from current group members
$grpMembers=@($Grp.Member)

#display current group membership
Write-Host "There are currently $($grpMembers.Count) members in $($Grp.Name)" -foregroundcolor
cyan
foreach ($user in $grpMembers) {$user}

Write-Host 'n; Write-Host "Adding $NewUserDN" -foregroundcolor cyan
($grp.Member).add($NewUserDN) > $NULL

#commit changes to Active Directory
$Grp.SetInfo()
```

```
#refresh object and display new membership list
$Grp.refreshCache()
$grpMembers=@($grp.Member)

#display new membership
Write-Host "There are now $($grpMembers.Count) members in $($grp.Name)" -foregroundcolor cyan
foreach ($user in $grpMembers) {
 if ($user -eq $NewUserDN) {
 Write-Host $user -foregroundcolor Green
 }
 else
 {
 write-Host $user -foregroundcolor Yellow
 }
}
```

This script creates an ADSI object for the SAPIEN Authors group and also creates an object for the current membership list that is displayed using the **ForEach** loop. Adding the new user appears a little confusing at first:

```
($grp.Member).add($NewUserDN) > $NULL
```

What we need to do is to call the **Add()** method for the group's Member property, which is a collection, and specify the user's distinguished name. By the way, if we wanted to nest another group, we would specify that group's distinguished name. The reason we redirect output to the **$Null** variable is purely cosmetic. Without the redirection, the expression returns the number of members currently in the group. In the course of running the script, displaying that number here serves no purpose and is distracting. We eliminate it by redirecting any output to **$Null**.

None of this work means anything until we commit the change to Active Directory by using the **SetInfo()** method. The script finishes by refreshing the local cache and listing its new members, indicating the new users in a green font and existing users in yellow.

Moving Objects

PowerShell and the .NET Framework use a slightly different method for moving objects in Active Directory. You should be able to call the **MoveTo()** method like this:

```
PS C:\> [ADSI]$obj="LDAP://CN=Desk61,CN=Computers,DC=MyCompany,dc=local"
PS C:\> $obj.MoveTo("LDAP://OU=Desktops,DC=MyCompany,dc=local")
```

All you have to do is specify the container where the object should be moved to. You can also use the Active Directory **PSDrive** provider in the PowerShell Community Extensions. Because the provider allows you to navigate your Active Directory domain as if it were a file system, you can use the **Move** command much the same way you would move a file:

```
PS COMPANY:\computers> move XPDesk02 company:\desktops
```

WinNT:// Provider

Even though we've been showing you how to use the ADSI type with the **LDAP://** provider and Active Directory, it will also work with the **WinNT://** provider. You can use this provider if you want a flat view of your domain or if you are working with member servers and desktops:

```
[ADSI]$member="WinNT://$env:computername"
$member.Children | where {$_.schemaclassname -eq "user"} | select Name
```

This script will list every object from the local computer that is of the user schema class and display the user name. If you substitute the computername with the flat name of your domain, you will get a list of all user accounts, regardless of what organizational unit they might belong to. The displayed name will be the SAMAccountname.

Searching for Users

We'll wrap up this chapter by showing you how easy it is to search in Active Directory with PowerShell. Because PowerShell is based on the .NET Framework, it can create a DirectorySearcher object using the [ADSISearcher] type adapter. Here's a short script that will return the distinguished name of every user account in an Active Directory domain:

SearchForAllUsers.ps1

```
#SearchForAllusers.ps1
[ADSISearcher]$searcher="(&(objectcategory=person)(objectclass=user))"

#enable paged searching
$searcher.pagesize=50
$users=$searcher.FindAll()

#display the number of users
Write-Host "There are $($users.count) users in this domain." -foregroundcolor cyan
#display each user's distinguishedname
foreach ($user in $users) {
 Write-Host $user.properties.distinguishedname -foregroundcolor green
}
```

We use the [ADSISearcher] type adapter to create a DirectorySearcher object. It is just as easy to specify the filter when creating the object. The filter is an LDAP query string. In this case, we want to find all objects that are basically user accounts. The DirectorySearcher object has two methods you are most likely to use: **FindAll()** and **FindOne()**. The former will return all objects that match the query, and the latter will only return the first one it finds. In this script, we create a new object to hold the query results. We can then use the **For-Each** construct to display the distinguishedname property of each user in the result collection.

....

Fun with LDAP Filters

You don't have to have extensive knowledge about LDAP to build a complex query. If you are running Windows 2003 or later, you already have a tool that will do it for you. In Active Directory Users and Computers, there is a Saved Queries feature. When you create a query, Active Directory creates an LDAP query string. All you need to do is copy the string and use it as the directory searcher filter. For example, we created a saved query to find all disabled users that created an LDAP query string of (&(objectCategory = person) (objectClass = user) (userAccountControl:1.2.840.113556.1.4.803: = 2)). When we substitute this string for the filter in SearchForAllUsers. ps1, we get a list of every disabled user. The tool is pretty powerful and can create some very complex query strings. Now, you can also use them in your PowerShell scripts.

There is a subtle but important fact to remember when using the DirectorySearcher object. The objects returned by the query aren't really the Active Directory objects but are more like pointers. The search result can give you some property information like distinguishedname, but if you want more specific object information, you need to get the object itself. This script is slightly modified from SearchForAllUsers.ps1:

SearchForAllUsersAdvanced.ps1

```
#SearchForAllUsersAdvanced.ps1
[ADSISearcher]$searcher="(&(objectcategory=person)(objectclass=user))"
$searcher.pagesize=50
$users=$searcher.FindAll()

#display the number of users
Write-Host "There are $($users.count) users in this domain." -foregroundcolor cyan

#display user properties
foreach ($user in $users) {
 foreach ($user in $users) {
 $entry= $user.GetDirectoryEntry()
 $entry |Select displayname,samaccountname,description,distinguishedname
 }
}
```

In the **ForEach** loop, we create a new variable called **$entry** by invoking the **GetDirectoryEntry()** method of the object that the query returned. This object gives us access to all the properties in Active Directory. In this script, we selected to show DisplayName, SAMAccountName, Description, and DistinguishedName. When executed we get a result like this:

```
displayname               samaccountname        description                 disting
-----------               --------------        -----------                 -------
{}                        {Administrator}       {Built-in account for admi... {CN=Adm
{}                        {Guest}               {Built-in account for gues... {CN=Gue
{CN=Microsoft Corporation,... {SUPPORT_388945a0}    {This is a vendor's accoun... {CN=SUP
{}                        {krbtgt}              {Key Distribution Center S... {CN=krb
{Jeff Hicks}              {jhicks}              {Demo Account}              {CN=Jef
{Test User1}              {tuser1}              {Sample Test Users}         {CN=tus
{Test User2}              {tuser2}              {Sample Test Users}         {CN=tus
{Test User3}              {tuser3}              {Sample Test Users}         {CN=tus
{Test User10}             {tuser10}             {Sample Test Users}         {CN=tus
{Roy G. Biv}              {rgbiv}               {}                          {CN=Roy
{Don Jones}               {djones}              {Created by PowerShell 7/3... {CN=Don
{Amy Admin}               {aadmin}              {Company help desk admin}   {CN=Amy
{Anne Tern}               {ATern}               {}                          {CN=Ann
{Ben Jay}                 {BJay}                {}                          {CN=Ben
{Charlie Robin}           {CRobin}              {}                          {CN=Cha
{David Cardinal}          {DCardinal}           {}                          {CN=Dav
{Ed Nightingale}          {ENightingale}        {}                          {CN=Ed
```

Output has been truncated but the Distinguishedname property is the last column. We mentioned that the DirectorySearcher object also has a **FindOne()** method. This is very useful when you know there is only one result, such as finding the distinguishedname of a user when all you know is the user's SAMAccountname:

FindUserDN.ps1

```
#FindUserDN.ps1
$sam=Read-Host "What user account do you want to find?"
[ADSISearcher]$searcher="(&(objectcategory=person)(objectclass=user)(sAMAccountname=$sam))"
```

```
$searcher.pagesize=50
$results=$searcher.FindOne()

if ($results.path.length -gt 1)
  {
    write $results.path
  }
else
  {
   Write-Warning "User $sam was not found."
}
```

This script is very similar to the other searching scripts. The primary difference is that the search filter is looking for user objects where the SAMAccountname is equal to a value specified by the user with the **Read-Host** cmdlet. Since we know there will only be one result, the searcher can stop as soon as it finds a match. We've added some error checking in the script. If the script finds a match, then the length of the path property will be greater than one and we can display it. Otherwise, there is no path, which means the script found no match and we can display a message to that effect.

The [ADSI] and [ADSISearcher] type adapters are merely wrappers for .NET Framework directory service objects. They abstract much of the underlying functionality, making them easy to use. You can create PowerShell scripts that directly create and manipulate the .NET Framework objects, but in our opinion that process is more like systems programming than scripting.

....

Read More About It

These are very rich classes and we've only touched upon all the functionality. To learn more you will want to consult the MSDN documentation for the bjects and the System.DirectoryServices. Namespace at: http://msdn.microsoft.com/en-us/library/system.directoryservices.aspx.

Quest Active Directory Cmdlets

You also have seen that we did not discuss any cmdlets related to Active Directory. We had to write our own functions and scripts. We believe you'll find it much easier to manage Active Directory with the free, third-party snap-ins from Quest Software. These cmdlets use the same .NET Framework classes, but because they are cmdlets they are easier to use, especially in a pipelined expression. Here are some examples.

First, after you've installed the cmdlets, you'll need to add the PSSnapin to your session:

```
PS C:\> add-pssnapin quest.activeroles.admanagement
```

All of the cmdlets preface the noun portion of the name with QAD so you can easily get help:

```
PS C:\> help *qad*
```

The cmdlets have full help and examples; we only have room to give you a sampling. Let's begin by finding a user account with the **Get-QADUser** cmdlet:

```
PS C:\> get-qaduser rbiv
Name                        Type            DN
----                        ----            --
Roy Biv                     user            CN=Roy Biv,OU=IT,OU=Employees,DC=MYCOMPANY,DC=LOCAL
```

The cmdlet also makes it easier to find users based on some criteria like department:

```
PS C:\> get-qaduser -department sales | select name,title,telephonenumber

Name                             Title                    telephonenumber
----                             -----                    ---------------
Sales User1                      Sales Executive          555-2222
Sales User2                      Sales Executive          555-2222
Sales User3                      Sales Executive          555-2222
Sales User4                      Sales Executive          555-2222
Sales User5                      Account Rep              555-2222
Sales User6                      Account Rep              555-2222
Sales User7                      Account Rep              555-2222
Sales User8                      Account Rep              555-2222
Sales User9                      Account Rep              555-2222
Sales User10                     Sales Executive          555-2222
```

You'll notice we've also selected some user properties. Next, let's change the phone number for these people:

```
PS C:\> get-qaduser -department sales | set-qaduser -telephonenumber 555-3333 -whatif
What if: Performing operation "Set-QADUser" on Target "CN=Sales User1,OU=Sales,OU=Employees,DC=MYCOMPAN...
What if: Performing operation "Set-QADUser" on Target "CN=Sales User2,OU=Sales,OU=Employees,DC=MYCOMPAN...
What if: Performing operation "Set-QADUser" on Target "CN=Sales User3,OU=Sales,OU=Employees,DC=MYCOMPAN...
What if: Performing operation "Set-QADUser" on Target "CN=Sales User4,OU=Sales,OU=Employees,DC=MYCOMPAN...
What if: Performing operation "Set-QADUser" on Target "CN=Sales User5,OU=Sales,OU=Employees,DC=MYCOMPAN...
What if: Performing operation "Set-QADUser" on Target "CN=Sales User6,OU=Sales,OU=Employees,DC=MYCOMPAN...
What if: Performing operation "Set-QADUser" on Target "CN=Sales User7,OU=Sales,OU=Employees,DC=MYCOMPAN...
What if: Performing operation "Set-QADUser" on Target "CN=Sales User8,OU=Sales,OU=Employees,DC=MYCOMPAN...
What if: Performing operation "Set-QADUser" on Target "CN=Sales User9,OU=Sales,OU=Employees,DC=MYCOMPAN...
What if: Performing operation "Set-QADUser" on Target "CN=Sales User10,OU=Sales,OU=Employees,DC=MYCOMPA...
```

We piped the user objects to the **Set-QADUser** cmdlet to modify the telephone number. The cmdlet even supports **-WhatIf** and **-Confirm** parameters. Here's one more example. We're going to create a new user, force the user to change passwords at next logon, and then add him to a group with a one-line PowerShell expression:

```
PS C:\> new-qaduser -parent "OU=Employees,DC=mycompany,DC=local" -name "Art Deco" '
>> -samaccountname "adeco" -displayname " Art Deco" -firstname "Art" -lastname "Deco" '
>> -description "Created by PowerShell" -userprincipalname "adeco@mycompany.com '
>>" -userpassword "P@ssw0rd" |
>> Set-QADUser -UserMustChangePassword $True |
>> Add-QADGroupMember "Alpha Users"
>>

Name                   Type        DN
----                   ----        --
Art Deco               user        CN=Art Deco,OU=Employees,DC=mycompany,DC=local
```

We pipe the output from the **New-QADUser** cmdlet to the **Set-QADUser** cmdlet to force the password change, and then pipe the object to the **Add-QADGroupMember** cmdlet to add the user to the Alpha Users group. Remember, no scripts were used or harmed in this example. We think this is a terrific example of why you should be excited and eager to get PowerShell going in your organization.

There is so much more that you can accomplish with these cmdlets. Download them from Quest Software and try them out. You will also want to pick up a copy of *Managing Active Directory with Windows PowerShell: TFM* (SAPIEN).

Microsoft Active Directory Cmdlets

With the release of Windows Server 2008 R2 (abbreviated as R2 for the rest of this chapter), Microsoft has finally released a PowerShell solution for managing Active Directory. This requires PowerShell v2.0 and an R2 domain controller. It's our understanding that support will extend eventually to legacy Active Directory domains. Again, full coverage is outside the scope of this book but we want to give you an idea of what to expect.

First we need to load the Active Directory cmdlets. Where we've used PSSnapins before, R2 delivers these cmdlets via a module, so the first step is to import the module into our PowerShell session. In fact, we'll even do this via a remote session:

```
PS C:\> enter-pssession researchdc -Credential research\administrator
[researchdc]: PS C:\Users\Administrator\Documents> cd \
[researchdc]: PS C:\>
[researchdc]: PS C:\> Import-Module ActiveDirectory
```

The module ships with 76 cmdlets. Here are a few:

```
[researchdc]: PS C:\> get-command -module ActiveDirectory | select Name -first 5

Name
----
Add-ADComputerServiceAccount
Add-ADDomainControllerPasswordReplicationPolicy
Add-ADFineGrainedPasswordPolicySubject
Add-ADGroupMember
Add-ADPrincipalGroupMembership
```

How about creating a new user account? With the R2 cmdlets we will use the **New-ADUser** cmdlet. The cmdlet will require that you pass the password as a secure string so we'll first get one using the **Read-Host** cmdlet:

```
[researchdc]: PS C:\> $userpwd=read-host "Enter default password" -asSecureString
WARNING: A script or application on the RESEARCHDC remote computer is sending a Prompt request.
When prompted, enter sensitive information like your credentials or password only if you trust the
remote computer and the application or script requesting it.
Enter default password: ********
```

We can use this variable in an expression like this:

```
[researchdc]: PS C:\> new-aduser -name "Huck Finn" -AccountPassword $userpwd '
>> -ChangePasswordAtLogon $True -enabled $True  -givenname "Huck" -surname "Finn" '
>> -samaccountname "hfinn" -userprincipalname "hfinn@research.mycompany.com" -department "Chemistry"
'
>> -path "OU=Staff,DC=Research,DC=MyCompany,DC=local" -passthru


DistinguishedName : CN=Huck Finn,OU=Staff,DC=Research,DC=MyCompany,DC=local
Enabled           : True
GivenName         : Huck
Name              : Huck Finn
ObjectClass       : user
ObjectGUID        : f52230f6-0b8d-4ca9-9919-e154d36696c7
SamAccountName    : hfinn
SID               : S-1-5-21-2704478247-3271226993-4103978002-1107
Surname           : Finn
```

```
UserPrincipalName : hfinn@research.mycompany.com
```

If you don't specify a distinguished name for the path property, PowerShell will create the account in the default USERS container. By default the cmdlet doesn't write anything to the pipeline, so we used the **-PassThru** parameter to see the results. This is the same information we would see if we had used the **Get-ADUser** cmdlet:

```
[researchdc]: PS C:\> get-aduser hfinn


DistinguishedName : CN=Huck Finn,OU=Staff,DC=RESEARCH,DC=MYCOMPANY,DC=LOCAL
Enabled           : True
GivenName         : Huck
Name              : Huck Finn
ObjectClass       : user
ObjectGUID        : f52230f6-0b8d-4ca9-9919-e154d36696c7
SamAccountName    : hfinn
SID               : S-1-5-21-2704478247-3271226993-4103978002-1107
Surname           : Finn
UserPrincipalName : hfinn@research.mycompany.com
```

But we forgot a few things, so let's modify the account by using the **Set-ADUser** cmdlet:

```
[researchdc]: PS C:\> get-aduser hfinn | set-aduser -Title "Lab Technician" '
>> -DisplayName "Huckleberry Finn"
```

Unlike the Quest cmdlets and even ADSI, if you want to see specific properties, you have to ask for them:

```
[researchdc]: PS C:\> get-aduser hfinn -properties Department,Title,Displayname |
>> Select Name,Displayname,Department,Title
```

Name	Displayname	Department	Title
Huck Finn	Huckleberry Finn	Chemistry	Lab Technician

We should probably also add our new user to a group:

```
[researchdc]: PS C:\> add-adgroupmember "Chemistry Users" "hfinn"
[researchdc]: PS C:\> get-adgroupmember "chemistry users" | select Name

Name
----
Huck Finn
Robert Boyle
Amedeo Avogadro
Antoine Lavoisier
```

As you can see, using cmdlets is not that difficult. The most time consuming part is studying the help and examples for these new cmdlets.

One last new R2 feature we want to at least bring to your attention is the Active Directory PSDrive. When you import the Active Directory module, R2 creates a new PSDrive called AD:

```
[researchdc]: PS C:\> cd AD:
[researchdc]: PS AD:\> dir
```

Name	ObjectClass	DistinguishedName
Configuration	configuration	CN=Configuration,DC=MYCOMPANY,DC=LOCAL
Schema	dMD	CN=Schema,CN=Configuration,DC=MYCOMPANY,DC=LOCAL
ForestDnsZones	domainDNS	DC=ForestDnsZones,DC=MYCOMPANY,DC=LOCAL
RESEARCH	domainDNS	DC=RESEARCH,DC=MYCOMPANY,DC=LOCAL
DomainDnsZones	domainDNS	DC=DomainDnsZones,DC=RESEARCH,DC=MYCOMPANY,DC=LOCAL

To change "directories" use the object's distinguished name:

```
[researchdc]: PS AD:\> cd "dc=research,dc=mycompany,dc=local"
[researchdc]: PS AD:\dc=research,dc=mycompany,dc=local> dir
```

Name	ObjectClass	DistinguishedName
Builtin	builtinDomain	CN=Builtin,DC=RESEARCH,DC=MYCOMPANY,DC=LOCAL
Computers	container	CN=Computers,DC=RESEARCH,DC=MYCOMPANY,DC=LOCAL
Domain Controllers	organizationalUnit	OU=Domain Controllers,DC=RESEARCH,DC=MYCOMPANY,DC=LOCAL
ForeignSecurityPr...	container	CN=ForeignSecurityPrincipals,DC=RESEARCH,DC=MYCOMPANY,DC=LOCAL
Infrastructure	infrastructureUpdate	CN=Infrastructure,DC=RESEARCH,DC=MYCOMPANY,DC=LOCAL
LostAndFound	lostAndFound	CN=LostAndFound,DC=RESEARCH,DC=MYCOMPANY,DC=LOCAL
Managed Service A...	container	CN=Managed Service Accounts,DC=RESEARCH,DC=MYCOMPANY,DC=LOCAL
NTDS Quotas	msDS-QuotaContainer	CN=NTDS Quotas,DC=RESEARCH,DC=MYCOMPANY,DC=LOCAL
Program Data	container	CN=Program Data,DC=RESEARCH,DC=MYCOMPANY,DC=LOCAL
System	container	CN=System,DC=RESEARCH,DC=MYCOMPANY,DC=LOCAL
Users	container	CN=Users,DC=RESEARCH,DC=MYCOMPANY,DC=LOCAL

Let's look at our user objects by changing to the Staff organizational unit and getting a "directory" listing:

```
[researchdc]: PS AD:\dc=research,dc=mycompany,dc=local> cd OU=Staff
[researchdc]: PS AD:\OU=STaff,dc=research,dc=mycompany,dc=local> dir
```

Name	ObjectClass	DistinguishedName
Amedeo Avogadro	user	CN=Amedeo Avogadro,OU=Staff,DC=RESEARCH,DC=MYCOMPANY,DC=LOCAL
Antoine Lavoisier	user	CN=Antoine Lavoisier,OU=Staff,DC=RESEARCH,DC=MYCOMPANY,DC=LOCAL
Huck Finn	user	CN=Huck Finn,OU=Staff,DC=RESEARCH,DC=MYCOMPANY,DC=LOCAL
Robert Boyle	user	CN=Robert Boyle,OU=Staff,DC=RESEARCH,DC=MYCOMPANY,DC=LOCAL
Tom Sawyer	user	CN=Tom Sawyer,OU=Staff,DC=RESEARCH,DC=MYCOMPANY,DC=LOCAL

The items you see are merely pointers to the full AD user object, so we need to still use the **Get-ADUser** cmdlet to retrieve useful information:

```
[researchdc]: PS AD:\OU=STaff,dc=research,dc=mycompany,dc=local> dir | get-aduser -properties * |
>> Select Name,Title, Department
>>
```

Name	Title	Department
Amedeo Avogadro	Senior Chemist	Chemistry
Antoine Lavoisier	Senior Chemist	Chemistry
Huck Finn	Lab Technician	Chemistry
Robert Boyle	Senior Chemist	Chemistry
Tom Sawyer		Physics

The full management experience with PowerShell and these cmdlets will take a period of adjustment, but once you understand the basics from this book your learning time for the R2 AD cmdlets, or any other PowerShell solution, should be shortened.

Chapter 36
Scope in Windows PowerShell

In the chapter "Scripting Overview," we touched on the concept of scope in Windows PowerShell. In that chapter, we were primarily concerned with variables and functions, the two elements of PowerShell where scope is of most concern. But scope in PowerShell is much more flexible and functional than we let on in that earlier chapter, so we're taking the time in this chapter to explain it in all its gory detail.

First, the term *scope* is defined in the dictionary as "extent or range of view, outlook, application, effectiveness, etc." That's a good definition for our purposes, because PowerShell's scope does define the range of effectiveness for a number of elements, including variables, functions, aliases, and more.

Types of Scope

PowerShell starts with one top-level scope: The *global* scope. This is the only scope that is not contained within any other scope; you can think of it as the ultimate "parent" scope, or the "root" scope. The command line itself exists within the global scope, and any variables, PSDrives, aliases, or functions that you define interactively all exist in the global scope.

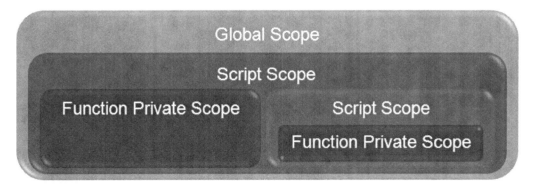

Whenever you run a script, PowerShell creates a new scope to contain the script. This *script scope* is a child of the scope that ran the script. In other words, if you run a script in the global scope, the new script scope is a child of the global scope. If one script runs another, then the second script's scope is a child of the first script's scope, and so forth. It's essentially a hierarchy, not unlike the file system's hierarchy of folders and subfolders.

The inside of a function, script block, or filter is a private scope as well, and it is a child of whatever scope contains it. A function within a script has a scope that is a child of the script's scope—again, similar to the hierarchy of folders on the file system.

Scope-aware Elements

Several elements of PowerShell are scope-aware:

- Variables
- Functions
- Aliases
- PSDrives

Those last two may be surprising, but, in fact, you can define an alias within a script—which has its own scope—and that alias *will exist only within that scope*. This plays directly into PowerShell's scoping rules, which we'll discuss next.

Scope Rules

PowerShell's rules regarding scopes are simple: When you try to access an element, PowerShell first looks to see if it's defined in the current scope. If it is, then you'll be able to access it for both reading and writing—meaning you'll be able to *use* the element and *change* the element, if desired.

If the specified element isn't available in the current scope, then PowerShell starts looking up the hierarchy, starting with the parent of the current scope, then its parent, then its parent, and so forth, up to the top-level global scope. If PowerShell finds the specified element at some point, then you'll have access to *use* it, but not *change* it—at least, not without using a special technique. A simple script is probably the easiest way to illustrate this:

```
function test1 {
 write-host $example    # line 2
 $example = "Two"       # line 3
 write-host $example    # line 4
}
```

```
$example = "One"        # line 7
Write-host $example     # line 8
test1                   # line 9
write-host $example     # line 10
```

This produces the following output:

```
One
One
Two
One
```

On line 7, the script places the value "One" into the **$example** variable. Line 8 writes this, resulting in the first line of output. Line 9 then calls the function, which is a new scope. Line 2 writes the current value of $example. This variable doesn't exist in the function's scope, so PowerShell looks up one scope to the function's parent, which is the script itself. PowerShell finds the $example variable, and then line 2 outputs it—resulting in our second line of output. Line 3 changes the value of the $example variable. However, by default a scope cannot *change* elements from its parent. Therefore, PowerShell creates a *new* $example variable *within the current scope*. Line 4 attempts to access $example, and *now* it does exist in the current scope, resulting in our third line of output. With the function complete, we execute line 10. Our last line of output is "One," because that's still the value of $example *within the current scope*. Parent scopes—the script, in this case—cannot "see" inside their child scopes; they cannot see the function.

The same thing applies to functions, aliases, and PSDrives. Here's another example:

```
function test1 {
 new-psdrive Z filesystem c:\test
 dir z:
}

test1
dir Z:
```

Try running this (assuming you have a folder named C:\Test). The function maps a new drive, Z:, to the C:\Test folder, and returns a directory listing. After the function exits, the script tries to get a directory listing of Z: and fails because the Z: mapping *only exists* inside the function's scope.

Aliases work the same way:

```
function test1 {
 new-alias plist get-process
 plist
}

test1
plist
```

Again, the function defines a new alias, and then uses it; the script is unable to use that alias because the alias definition only exists within the function's scope.

Specifying Scope

When you look at these four elements—functions, aliases, PSDrives, and variables—you'll find that three of them have specific cmdlets used to create new elements:

- **New-Alias** is used to create new aliases.

- **New-Variable** is used to create new variables.

- **New-PSDrive** is used to create new PSDrives.

Each of these three cmdlets supports a **-scope** parameter, which allows you to create a new element *in a scope other than the current one.* The **Set-Variable** cmdlet, which allows you to change an existing variable, also has a **-scope** parameter, which allows you to change the value of a variable in a scope other than the current one.

> **By the Way...**
> Other cmdlets used to deal with aliases, variables, and PSDrives also support a -scope parameter, such as Remove-Alias and New-PSDrive.

All of these **-scope** parameters can accept one of several values:

- "Global" references the global scope.

- "Script" references the first script that is a parent of the current scope.

- "Local" references the current scope.

- A numeric value, with 0 representing the current scope, 1 representing the current scope's parent, and so forth.

As a general rule, it's considered a poor practice to have one scope modify anything in its parent or parents. That's because, as you move around and re-use an element—such as a script or function—in different ways, you can't be sure what the state of the parent scope will be. Modifying a parent scope involves a risk that you'll impact some other process or operation. However, sometimes it's necessary, which is why the **-scope** parameter exists. For example, to create a function that defines a new alias in the global scope, you'd do something like this:

```
Function test1 {
 New-Alias plist get-process -scope global
}
```

Or, to change the value of a global variable named $example:

```
Set-Variable $example "New Value" -scope global
```

Variables provide a shortcut reference, which may be easier to remember:

```
$global:example = "New Value"
```

Again, you can use the keywords Global, Local, and Script with this syntax.

Best Practices for Scope

As we've already mentioned, avoid modifying parent scopes unless there's absolutely no other way to accomplish what you need. Functions are a good example: A function should *never* do this:

```
Function example {
 $script:var = "New Value"
}

$var = "Old value"
example
```

Why? Well, for one, if you ever re-use this function in a different script, $var might not be the right variable name. By tying the function to this script, we've limited the function's reusability. Instead, functions should output their return values or collections:

```
Function example {
 return "New Value"
}

$var = "Old value"
$var = example
```

This way, you can easily drop the function into any script, or even the global shell, and use it safely.

Our second recommendation is to *always* assign a value to a variable before using it in the current scope. Consider this sample function:

```
Function sample {
 $var = $input1 + $input2
 Return $var
}
```

What will the function return? Well, we've no idea—it depends on what the **$input1** and **$input2** variables contain. The script that this function lives in might have defined those variables, or it might not have. Instead, use variables only after they've been explicitly assigned a value in the current scope:

```
Function sample {
 $input1 = 1
 $input2 = 2
 $var = $input1 + $input2
 Return $var
}
```

Or, in the case of a function, define them as input arguments with default values:

```
Function sample ($input1 = 1, $input2 = 2) {
 $var = $input1 + $input2
 Return $var
}
```

This ensures that the function won't "pick up" a variable from a parent scope by accident. Another way to look at this best practice is that functions should *never* rely on a variable from a parent scope. If you need to use information inside of a function, pass it into the function via arguments. So, the only way data gets *in* a function is via arguments, and the only way data gets *out* of a function is by being returned from the function. This makes functions self-contained and self-reliant, and you won't need to worry about their parent scope.

Forcing Best Practices

PowerShell comes with a cmdlet called **Set-Strict**, which is designed to enforce specific best practices. When you violate those best practices in a given scope, the shell will return an error. When running the **Set-Strict** cmdlet, it *only affects the scope in which it is run*, as well as any child scopes that do not run **Set-Strict** on their own.

First, you should know how to turn off strict mode:

```
Set-Strict -off
```

When you turn on strict mode, you have two choices: Version 1 and Version 2:

```
Set-Strict -version 1
```

Version 1 will throw an exception if you use a variable in the current scope without first assigning a value to that variable within the current scope. In other words, it prevents the current scope from searching its parents for the variable:

```
Set-Strict -version 2
```

Version 2 will also throw an exception for un-initialized variables. In addition, if you attempt to refer to non-existent properties of an object, or try to use certain invalid forms of syntax (such as calling functions using parentheses and commas with the parameters), Version 2 will throw an exception. With strict mode off, these operations are allowed, but will typically return unexpected results. For example, assume you have a function named **MyFunction**, which accepts two input parameters. With strict mode off, the following is legal:

```
$result = MyFunction(1,2)
```

This syntax is something you'd find in a language like VBScript, where it works fine; in PowerShell it passes an array of two elements to the function's first input parameter, while leaving the second parameter blank. This usually isn't what was intended, and so strict mode prohibits this syntax entirely, preventing the unexpected behavior which would otherwise result.

Dot Sourcing

Dot sourcing is a clever technique that tells PowerShell to execute something—usually a script—in the current scope, rather than creating a new scope. For example, consider the following script, which we'll pretend is named Sample.ps1:

```
New-Alias PList Get-Process
PList
```

This simple script defines a new alias, and then uses it. Just run this script:

```
PS C:\> test\sample
```

PowerShell defines the alias, executes the script, and then discards the script scope when the script ends, so the alias no longer exists. However, if you *dot source* the script:

```
PS C:\> . test\sample
```

Now the script runs *without creating a new scope*. Since it was run from the shell, which is the global scope, the script's commands all execute within the global scope. Now the PList alias will *remain* defined after the script runs, because we executed the **New-Alias** cmdlet within the global scope.

Dot sourcing can be a useful technique for "including" a script library file. For example, suppose you have a script file named Library.ps1, which contains a function named **Ping-Computer**. You can easily reuse that across multiple scripts. Here's an example of a script that "includes" Library.ps1:

```
# include library functions
. path\library

# use library function
Ping-computer localhost
```

The script shown *dot sources* Library.ps1, so Library.ps1 executes in *this script's scope,* rather than launching in a new child scope. Therefore, everything defined in Library.ps1, including the **Ping-Computer** function, is now defined inside this script's scope, making those functions available for use. PowerShell doesn't include a dedicated "include" statement simply because dot sourcing provides that functionality already.

> ....
> **By the Way...**
> PowerShell follows its execution policy when dot sourcing scripts. For example, if we had located Library.ps1 on a network folder and accessed it via a UNC path, then Library.ps1 would have to be digitally signed and the execution policy in PowerShell would need to be set to RemoteSigned. If both of those conditions weren't true, PowerShell would pause the script execution and prompt you for permission to run Library.ps1.

Nested Prompts

Earlier, we introduced you to the concept of nested prompts. A nested prompt exists *in the same scope as it was created*. In other words, imagine we have a script like this:

```
Function Test1 {
    $var = 3
    Function Test2 {
        $var = 5
        $host.EnterNestedPrompt()
    }
    Test2
}
$var = 1
Test1
```

When we run this, the script sets the **$var** variable to 1, and calls the **Test1** function. It then sets $var to 3, creating a new $var in this scope, and calls the **Test2** function. Test2 sets $var to 5, creating yet another version of $var in the local scope. Test2 then opens a nested prompt. If, within that nested prompt, we examined the value of $var, we would find it to be 5:

```
PS C:\> test\demo1
PS C:\>>> $var
5
PS C:\>>> exit
PS C:\>
```

This behavior ensures that nested prompts remain a useful debugging technique: The nested prompt exists *within* the scope in which the prompt is called, so it has access to all of that scope's PSDrives, variables, aliases, functions, and so forth.

Tracing Complicated Nested Scopes

Dealing with scopes can become complicated when they're very deeply nested—in fact, that complication is just one more reason to observe our two main best practices: Don't use one scope to mess with another, and don't use variables without assigning them a value inside the current scope. Consider the following example, and assume that the script Library.ps1 (referred to in the example) contains a function named **Four**:

```
function One {
    $var1 = "One"

    function Two {
        $var2 = "Two"

            function Three {
                $var3 = "Three"
                test/ExternalScript
                . test/Library
              }

        $host.EnterNestedPrompt()
    }
}
$var = "Zero"
```

Here are some statements regarding this code:

- The **$var** variable exists in the script scope, which is a child of the global scope.

- The **$var2** variable exists in the scope of function **Two**, which is a child of function **One**, which is a child of the script, which is a child of the global scope—that means $var2 is four levels deep.

- Function **Four**, which we said Library.ps1 defines, exists five levels deep: We dot sourced it into function **Three**. Inside function Four is a new scope, which is six levels deep.

- ExternalScript is running in its own scope, because it wasn't dot sourced. The script scope for ExternalScript is six levels deep: It's a child of function **Three**, which is a child of function **Two**, which is a child of function **One**, which is a child of the script, which is a child of the global scope.

- Function **Two** creates a nested prompt, which is in the same scope—four levels deep—as function Two itself.

PowerShell doesn't provide any built-in means of determining how deeply nested the current scope is, so you have to pay close attention to scopes as you're writing and working with scripts. You have to remember the rules for scope use and dot sourcing, and keep track of these things—on a piece of paper, if necessary!

Chapter 37
Working with COM Objects

Just because Windows PowerShell is based on the .NET Framework doesn't mean you can't use older Component Object Model (COM) components in your scripts. For example, using the **Add-PSDrive** cmdlet to map a network drive in PowerShell *doesn't* add the drive mapping to Windows Explorer; however, you can still use the WshNetwork COM component to perform this task. You'll use the **New-Object** cmdlet to instantiate the COM component, and then call its methods or access it properties much as you may have done in VBScript or some other language. Here's an example:

```
PS C:\> $network = new-object -com "WScript.Network"
PS C:\> $network.MapNetworkDrive("z:","\\localhost\c$")
PS C:\> z:
PS Z:\>
```

You'll need to know the unique ProgID ("WScript.Network," in this case) of the COM component you want to use. You'll notice that PowerShell's tab completion (which we covered in the "Practical Tips and Tricks" chapter) works for many COM components as well.

....

Oops...
Don't forget to add the -comObject parameter to the New-Object cmdlet (we've used a shortened version of the parameter name). If you do forget, the New-Object cmdlet won't work properly.

There's an incredible amount of trickery going on under the hood when PowerShell instantiates a COM component, and it can get complicated. For example, sometimes a COM component has what's called an *interop assembly,* which is a special .NET Framework assembly that connects complex COM com-

509

ponents to the .NET Framework—and, thus, to PowerShell. Other COM components don't have an interop assembly available. Sometimes, when you try to instantiate a COM component that *does* have an interop assembly, PowerShell winds up "connected" to that interop assembly and not the actual COM component, which means you won't have access to the properties and methods you need.

To force PowerShell to throw an error in this condition, you can add the **-strict** parameter to the **New-Object** cmdlet:

```
PS C:\> $network = new-object -com "WScript.Network" -strict
```

This way, if PowerShell "sees" an interop assembly, it will raise an exception that you can trap (read the "Error Handling" chapter for details), and your script will "know" that it has to work differently. This particular error still returns the COM component, but lets you know that you might have to take different steps to use it, because you'll actually be working with the interop wrapper. This technique is especially important when you're deploying a script to different machines. Some machines may have an interop assembly for your COM component, while other machines might not; the **-strict** parameter lets your script detect machines that do have an interop assembly and at least fail somewhat more gracefully.

Working with COM components can be frustrating sometimes, because in many cases, the COM components don't expose the full functionality available from a given piece of Windows. For example, the WshNetwork object gives you access to the current computer, user, and domain name, but not the site name or forest name. For that information, you'll have to use a different COM component, ADSysInfo. However, *that* component won't map drives—you'll still need WshNetwork for that. So, COM scripting becomes a patchwork exercise, an exercise that PowerShell was actually designed to improve by having *all* functionality exposed through cmdlets. However, until that happy day arrives, we're left with COM for many tasks.

A complete review of all the COM components available in Windows is far beyond the scope of this book—there are literally thousands. However, Bruce Payette's book, *Windows PowerShell in Action* (we're firm believers that you can't have too many PowerShell books), provides a number of fun examples for using COM to automate Internet Explorer, Windows Explorer, Microsoft Word, and other common applications. You can also pick up a copy of Don Jones' *VBScript, WMI, and ADSI Unleashed* (SAMS), which covers a number of COM components that are useful for scripting.

Finally, don't forget that if you want to learn more about a particular COM object, first create it in PowerShell, and then pipe the object to the **Get-Member** cmdlet. Most of the properties should be self-explanatory.

Practical Examples of Using COM

We'd like to share a few valuable COM components that you may have use for in your administrative scripts. None of these examples are long or complicated, which means you can put them to use right away.

Mapping Network Drives and Printers

When you use the **New-PSDrive** cmdlet to add a mapped drive—that is, a local drive mapped to a shared folder—to the shell, you're *only* adding that mapped drive to PowerShell. It won't show up in Windows Explorer at all, which means the **New-PSDrive** cmdlet isn't such a good technique for mapping drives in a logon script. But you do have two alternatives: First, you could simply run the **Net Use** command, the same command you'd run in Cmd.exe to map a drive. Or, you could use a COM object:

```
PS C:\> $net = new-object -com "WScript.Network"
$net.MapNetworkDrive("Z:\","\\Server\Share")
```

This is essentially the same thing you'd do to accomplish this task in VBScript, which brings up an excellent point: *PowerShell can do many of the same things as VBScript, in the exact same way.* So, you don't necessarily have to learn a new technique for everything; while the "VBScript way" might not be the most efficient use of PowerShell, many times it'll still work.

Accessing Local Domain, Site, Forest, and Logon Information

This is another task example where PowerShell doesn't contribute a lot of specific functionality, but where an old VBScript-style technique can address the problem perfectly. For example, to access the name of the local computer, the logged-on user, or the user's logon domain, do this:

```
PS C:\> $net = new-object -com "WScript.Network"
PS C:\> $net.UserName
JJones
PS C:\> $net.UserDomain
SAPIEN
PS C:\>$net.ComputerName
XPDESK02
PS C:\>
```

The WScript.Network object, however, is relatively old, and doesn't provide Active Directory-specific information. The ADSysInfo COM object could help with that; however, the object appears to be lacking a means of interoperating with the .NET Framework. You can get this COM object to work in PowerShell, but it's frankly not worth the effort. This is another reminder that not all COM objects are readily usable in PowerShell.

Automating Internet Explorer

One of our favorite uses for COM is to pop up an Internet Explorer window and direct it to a particular Web site. For example, if your company has an intranet Web server, you could post a "message of the day" Web page there. Then, in a PowerShell logon script, you could pop up Internet Explorer and navigate it to that page each time a user logs on. It's a great way to convey important information. Here's how to do it from the PowerShell command line:

```
PS C:\> $ie = new-object -com "InternetExplorer.Application"
PS C:\> $ie.navigate("www.microsoft.com")
PS C:\> $ie.visible = $true
```

Of course, doing this in a script uses exactly the same commands.

Controlling an Interactive Character

This is another fun trick that might find its way into a logon script you write. PowerShell architect Jeffrey Snover uses this at the beginning of his talks on Windows PowerShell, and it's very attention-getting! The idea is to instantiate a Microsoft Agent character—a little cartoon person not unlike the old Office Assistant characters—and get it to say something. Here's how to do it:

```
PS C:\> $agent = new-object -com "Agent.Control.2"
PS C:\> $agent.connected = $true
PS C:\> $character = join-path $env:windir "msagent\chars\merlin.acs"
```

```
PS C:\> [void]$agent.characters.load("merlin",$character)
PS C:\> $merlin = $agent.characters.item("merlin")
PS C:\> $action = $merlin.moveto(100,100)
PS C:\> $action = $merlin.show()
PS C:\> $action= $merlin.speak("Hello, there, everybody!")
PS C:\> $action = $merlin.hide()
PS C:\> $agent.connected = $false
```

You can use the Agent's **MoveTo()**, **Show()**, **Hide()**, and **Speak()** methods to control it. Notice that each of these methods returns a status code, which is why we've assigned the result of the method to the **$action** variable—we don't *need* the status code, but if we don't put it into a variable, PowerShell will try and display it. Merlin is the only character we found on our Windows Vista computer; Robbie the Robot, Peedy the Parrot, and Genie characters might be available on your system—check the folder we referenced above for the appropriate .ACS files.

Making Your Computer Talk

In the previous example, we showed you an example of controlling Microsoft Agent, an interactive character that includes speech synthesis capabilities. But what if you *just* want the speech, without the cartoon character? No problem:

```
PS C:\> $voice = new-object -com "SAPI.SPVoice"
PS C:\> $voice.speak("This PowerShell stuff rocks!")
```

Feed it any text you like, and it'll say it. Not always the best pronunciation, perhaps, but usually comprehensible.

Issues with COM in PowerShell

COM is not completely trouble free when used in PowerShell. For one, you cannot successfully adapt every COM component into PowerShell; sometimes, you'll have to figure out some strange techniques in order to get things to work properly. This is primarily due to the way the .NET Framework deals with COM components—that is, not always very well.

COM component threading also causes some issues. PowerShell is what's called a *multithreaded apartment* application, or MTA application. Many COM components won't work unless the application using them is *single-threaded*, or STA, so the PowerShell COM adapter basically tries to fake it if need be. There's a workaround for COM components that don't work properly because of this threading issue, but it essentially requires .NET Framework programming. It's pretty hardcore, and frankly we don't understand it very well—it's a bit beyond the purview of a systems administrator.

Chapter 38
Working with XML Documents

Windows PowerShell has a very powerful and intuitive way of allowing you to work with complex XML documents. Essentially, PowerShell *adapts* the structure of the XML document itself into an object hierarchy, so that working with the XML document becomes as easy as referring to object properties and methods.

What PowerShell Does with XML

When PowerShell converts text into XML, it parses the XML's document hierarchy and constructs a parallel object model. For example, take the following XML document (which you can type into a text file that has an XML file name extension):

```
<Pets>
 <Pet>
 <Breed>Ferret</Breed>
 <Age>3</Age>
 <Name>Patch</Name>
 </Pet>
 <Pet>
 <Breed>Bulldog</Breed>
 <Age>5</Age>
 <Name>Chesty</Name>
 </Pet>
</Pets>
```

You can load that XML into PowerShell as follows:

```
PS C:\> [xml]$xml = get-content c:\pets.xml
```

PowerShell then constructs the object hierarchy. For example, you could access the breed of the first pet as follows:

```
PS C:\> $xml.pets.pet[0].breed
Ferret
```

The **$xml** variable represents the XML document itself. From there, you simply specify the document elements as properties: The top-level <Pets> element, the first <Pet> element (indicated by pet[0], just like an array), and then the <Breed> element. If you don't specify a sub-element, PowerShell treats sub-elements as properties. For example, to view *all* of the properties—sub-elements, that is—of the second pet, you'd do this:

```
PS C:\> $xml.pets.pet[1]

Breed                    Age                      Name
-----                    ---                      ----
Bulldog                  5                        Chesty
```

This is a pretty creative way of working with XML and doesn't require you to use any of the more complex mechanisms that software developers usually have to deal with. Let's move on to a more complex example.

Basic XML Manipulation

As an example, we went to our own blog's RSS feed—RSS just being an XML application, after all—located at http://feeds2.feedburner.com/SapienBlog, and saved the RSS XML as a local file so that we could work with it:

```
PS C:\> $webclient.DownloadFile("http://feedproxy.google.com/SapienBlog?format=xml",'
"c:\test\sapienblog.xml")
```

The following page includes an excerpt; the remainder of the file just has additional <Item> nodes containing more blog entries. With this XML in a local file, our first step is to get this loaded into PowerShell and recognized as XML:

```
PS C:\> [xml]$rss = get-content c:\test\sapienblog.xml
```

Simple enough: By specifically casting $rss as an [xml] type, we've let PowerShell know that some XML is coming its way. The **Get-Content** cmdlet loads the text from the file, and then PowerShell does the rest. You can view the file in Notepad if you'd like. We won't take space here to display it.

What is $rss?

```
PS C:\> $rss

xml                              xml-stylesheet                          rss
---                              --------------                          ---
version="1.0" encoding="UTF-8"   {type="text/xsl" media="screen" href... rss
```

If you have the file opened in a text editor, you'll realize these three properties are the first set of tags.

Let's drill down:

```
PS C:\> $rss.rss
```

```
content     : http://purl.org/rss/1.0/modules/content/
wfw         : http://wellformedweb.org/CommentAPI/
dc          : http://purl.org/dc/elements/1.1/
atom        : http://www.w3.org/2005/Atom
sy          : http://purl.org/rss/1.0/modules/syndication/
feedburner  : http://rssnamespace.org/feedburner/ext/1.0
version     : 2.0
channel     : channel
```

What you're looking at here is the <rss> element of the **$rss** variable, our XML document, and you're seeing the *attributes* of the <rss> tag—go back and refer to the XML excerpt, and you'll see where these values came from. We didn't have to do anything special to access them—PowerShell just knew how.

Underneath the <rss> tag is a <channel> tag, and underneath that is a <title> tag. We can access the feed's title as follows:

```
PS C:\> $rss.rss.channel.title
```

```
        SAPIEN Technologies
```

In other words, the object hierarchy—rss.channel.title—mirrors the hierarchy of tags in the XML document. Underneath the <channel> tag we'll also find multiple <item> tags, each one representing a blog posting. Each <item> tag has various sub-tags, including a <title> tag, which is the title of that blog posting. Because PowerShell will find more than one <item> section, it will create a collection out of them. So, to access the title of the first blog post:

```
PS C:\> $rss.rss.channel.item[0].title
```

```
        Patch Tuesday
```

What if we want to see the post titles for the first six entries? All we need to do is select the Title property for each item object:

```
PS C:\> $rss.rss.channel.item[0..5] | select Title
```

```
title
-----
Patch Tuesday
Up another PowerShell Tree
DEADLINE: PowerShell Special Forces Training
April One-Liner
Out-CSV
Get ServiceAccount Name with ADSI
```

For the sake of illustration, perhaps we want to change the title of the second post:

```
PS C:\> $rss.rss.channel.item[1].title = "Alternate title"
```

We could, of course, invoke the XML object's **Save()** method to write the XML to a file:

```
PS C:\> $rss.Save("c:\test\revised.xml")
```

Working with XML in PowerShell is fairly straightforward.

Our little example here illustrates how easily you can work with a basic XML file; more complicated files simply create a deeper object hierarchy—they don't really change how things work. It's beyond the scope of this book to get into really complicated XML operations like XPath queries and so forth. However, we hope this quick look at XML has given you an idea of what PowerShell can do and offered some possibilities for parsing XML files that you may have in your environment.

A Practical Example

So, what good is all this XML stuff? Let's look at a real-world example—one that will also introduce you to additional XML techniques. We're going to start with a basic XML file that contains computer names. We'll call this Inventory.xml:

```
<Computers>
 <Computer Name="DON-LAPTOP" />
 <Computer Name="LOCALHOST" />
 <Computer Name="SERVER2" />
</Computers>
```

We want to inventory some basic information from these computers (of course, you could add more to your list, if you wanted to), including their Windows build number, service pack version, and the amount of free space on their local disk drives. We want our final result to look something like this:

```
<Computers>
 <Computer Name="DON-LAPTOP">
   <Status>Complete</Status>
   <OS BuildNumber="6000" ServicePack="0" />
   <Disks>
       <Disk DeviceID="C:" FreeSpace="10MB" />
       <Disk DeviceID="E:" FreeSpace="22MB" />
   </Disks>
 </Computer>
 <Computer Name="LOCALHOST">
   <Status>Complete</Status>
   <OS BuildNumber="6000" ServicePack="0" />
   <Disks>
       <Disk DeviceID="C:" FreeSpace="10MB" />
       <Disk DeviceID="E:" FreeSpace="22MB" />
   </Disks>
 </Computer>
 <Computer Name="SERVER2">
   <Status>Unreachable</Status>
 </Computer>
</Computers>
```

Our goal is to build a PowerShell script not only capable of retrieving the necessary information, but also capable of putting it into this XML format and saving it all back to disk. We'll start by defining a **GetStatus** function, which we'll use to ensure WMI connectivity to a remote computer. This function simply makes an attempt to query a WMI class from the specified computer; its -**ErrorAction** parameter is set to SilentlyContinue, so that in the event of an error, no error message will be shown. The built-in **$?** variable contains a TRUE or FALSE value, depending on whether the previous command completed successfully, so we're simply outputting that variable as the result of the function:

```
function GetStatus([string]$computer) {
    gwmi win32_operatingsystem -computer $computer -ea silentlycontinue
    Write-Output $?
}
```

Next, we write out a status message and load our inventory XML file from disk. Notice that we're explicitly declaring the **$xml** variable as an [XML] data type, forcing PowerShell to parse the text file as XML:

```
Write-Host "Beginning inventory..."

# load XML
[xml]$xml = gc c:\files\inventory.xml
```

Next, we're going to repeat a large block of code once for each <computer> node found in the XML. We start by pulling the Name attribute of the <computer> tag into the **$name** variable. Be careful here because XML is case-sensitive. Make sure the attribute you are calling is the same case as the XML file:

```
for ($i=0; $i -lt $xml.computers.computer.count; $i++) {
    # get computername
    $name = $xml.computers.computer[$i].getattribute("Name")
```

We create a new XML node named <Status>. Notice that the main XML document, stored in the **$xml** variable, has the capability of creating new nodes—we're specifically creating an *element*, which is basically an XLM tag. We're then executing our **GetStatus** function, passing it the current computer name to test:

```
    # create status node and get status
    $statusnode = $xml.CreateNode("element","Status","")
    $status = GetStatus $name
```

If the status comes back as FALSE—that is, not TRUE, as indicated by the ! operator—we set the <Status> node's inner text—the text appearing between <Status> and </Status>—to "Unreachable." Otherwise, we set the inner text to "Complete" and continue with the rest of our script:

```
    if (! $status) {
        $statusnode.set_innertext("Unreachable")
    }
      else {
        $statusnode.set_innertext("Complete")
```

If our status check was successful, we'll query the Win32_OperatingSystem class from the remote computer. We're also submitting a WMI query to retrieve all instances of Win32_LogicalDisk where the DriveType property is equal to 3, indicating a local disk. We issued the query this way because it'll actually be processed by the remote computer; we *could* have queried all instances of Win32_LogicalDisk and piped them to the **Where-Object** cmdlet to filter for the ones with a DriveType of 3, but that would have brought all the remote disks' data over to our computer first. This way, we're filtering out what we don't want right at the source:

```
# get OS info
$os = gwmi win32_operatingsystem -computer $name

# get local disks
$disks = gwmi -computer $name -query '
"select * from win32_logicaldisk where drivetype=3" '
```

We'll ask the XML document in the **$xml** variable to create <OS> and <Disks> elements. We'll continue working with these elements to populate them with inventory data:

```
# create os node, disks node
$osnode = $xml.CreateNode("element","OS","")
$disksnode = $xml.CreateNode("element","Disks","")
```

Since we have the operating system build number and service pack information available, we can add those attributes to the <OS> element:

```
# append OS attrs to node
$osnode.setattribute("BuildNumber",$os.buildnumber)
$osnode.setattribute("ServicePack", '
$os.servicepackmajorversion)
```

Now we append the complete <OS> element to the current <Computer> node. Notice that we're piping the output of the **AppendChild()** method to the **Out-Null** cmdlet. That's because **AppendChild()** normally displays the node it just finished appending; that output looks messy when we run our script, so we're sending the output to the **Out-Null** cmdlet to get rid of it:

```
# append OS node to Computer node
$xml.computers.computer[$i].appendchild($osnode)  | Out-Null
```

Now it's time to enumerate through the logical disks we retrieved from WMI. We start by creating a new XML element named <Disk>, which will store our device ID and free space information:

```
# go through the logical disks
foreach ($disk in $disks) {
    # create disk node
    $disknode = $xml.CreateNode("element","Disk","")
```

Next we create the DeviceID attribute on the <Disk> node. We also convert the free space to megabytes, rather than bytes, by dividing the FreeSpace property by 1MB. We then use the .NET Framework's System.Math class to round the megabyte measurement to the nearest megabyte, so that we don't wind up with a decimal value. Finally, we convert the numeric free space measurement to a string, and concatenate the letters "MB" to provide a unit of measurement in our inventory file. We set the <Disk> node's FreeSpace attribute equal to our megabyte measurement:

```
#create deviceid and freespace attribs
$disknode.setattribute("DeviceID",$disk.deviceid)
$freespace = $disk.freespace / 1MB
$freespace = [system.math]::round($freespace)
$freespace = $freespace.tostring() + "MB"
$disknode.setattribute(,"FreeSpace",$freespace)
```

We're now ready to append the current <Disk> node to the overall <Disks> node. After completing all of the available logical disks, we append the completed <Disks> node to the current <Computer> node. Again, we're using the **Out-Null** cmdlet to keep the output from the **AppendChild()** method from displaying:

```
        # append Disk node to Disks node
        $disksnode.appendchild($disknode) | Out-Null
    }

    # append disks node to Computer node
    $xml.computers.computer[$i].appendchild($disksnode) |          Out-Null }
```

We've reached the end of our If/Else construct, which had checked the result of our **GetStatus** function. We can, therefore, append the <Status> node, which will either contain "Complete" or "Unreachable," to the <Computer> node. Again, we're piping the output of the **AppendChild()** method to the **Out-Null** cmdlet in order to suppress the output text:

```
    # append status node to Computer node
    $xml.computers.computer[$i].appendchild($statusnode) | out-null
}
```

At this point, we've reached the end of our original **For** loop. We're ready to delete any existing output file and write our modified XML to a new filename, complete with all the inventory information we've added:

```
# output XML
del "c:\test\inventory-out.xml" -ea silentlycontinue
$xml.save("c:\test\inventory-out.xml")

Write-Host "...Inventory Complete."
```

You can open and view the saved XML file in Internet Explorer or any other application that knows how to read XML files. Here's the full, final script:

XMLInventory.ps1

```
function GetStatus([string]$computer) {
    gwmi win32_operatingsystem -computer $computer '
     -ea silentlycontinue
    Write-Output $?
}

Write-Host "Beginning inventory..."

# load XML
[xml]$xml = gc c:\test\inventory.xml

for ($i=0; $i -lt $xml.computers.computer.count; $i++) {

    # get computername
    $name = $xml.computers.computer[$i].getattribute("Name")

    # create status node and get status
    $statusnode = $xml.CreateNode("element","Status","")
    $status = GetStatus $name
    if (! $status) {
        $statusnode.set_innertext("Unreachable")
```

```
    }
    else {
        $statusnode.set_innertext("Complete")

        # get OS info
        $os = gwmi win32_operatingsystem -computer $name

        # get local disks
        $disks = gwmi -computer $name -query '
         "select * from win32_logicaldisk where drivetype=3" '

        # create OS node, disks node
        $osnode = $xml.CreateNode("element","OS","")
        $disksnode = $xml.CreateNode("element","Disks","")

        # append OS attrs to node
        $osnode.setattribute("BuildNumber",$os.buildnumber)
        $osnode.setattribute("ServicePack", '
         $os.servicepackmajorversion)

        # append OS node to Computer node
        $xml.computers.computer[$i].appendchild($osnode) | Out-Null

        # go through the logical disks
        foreach ($disk in $disks) {
            # create disk node
            $disknode = $xml.CreateNode("element","Disk","")

            #create deviceid and freespace attribs
            $disknode.setattribute("DeviceID",$disk.deviceid)
            $freespace = $disk.freespace / 1MB
            $freespace = [system.math]::round($freespace)
            $freespace = $freespace.tostring() + "MB"
            $disknode.setattribute("FreeSpace",$freespace)

            # append Disk node to Disks node
            $disksnode.appendchild($disknode) | Out-Null
        }

        # append Disks node to Computer node
        $xml.computers.computer[$i].appendchild($disksnode) | Out-Null
    }

    # append status node to Computer node
    $xml.computers.computer[$i].appendchild($statusnode)| out-null

}

# output XML
del "c:\test\inventory-out.xml" -ea silentlycontinue
$xml.save("c:\test\inventory-out.xml")

"Write-Host "...Inventory Complete."
```

Turning Objects into XML

PowerShell also supports the **ConvertTo-XML** cmdlet. By piping objects to this cmdlet, you can have PowerShell automatically construct an XML document based on those objects' properties. You can then manipulate the resulting XML document as described in this chapter. For example:

```
[xml]$xml = Get-Process | ConvertTo-XML
```

This cmdlet is a useful way of taking complex data represented by objects and turning it into a form that can be more easily manipulated and used for other purposes. Be aware that this XML file is different than what you get when you use the **ExportTo-Clixml** cmdlet. The **ConvertTo-XML** cmdlet is creating traditional XML:

```
PS C:\> $xml

xml                                          Objects
---                                          -------
version="1.0"                                Objects

PS C:\> $xml.objects.object[0]

Type                                         Property
----                                         --------
System.Diagnostics.Process                   {__NounName, Name, Handles, VM...}

PS C:\> $xml.objects.object[0].property | Select Name,'#text

Name                                         #text
----                                         -----
__NounName                                   Process
Name                                         audiodg
Handles                                      106
VM                                           54407168
WS                                           16338944
PM                                           13717504
NPM                                          7552
Path
Company
CPU
FileVersion
ProductVersion
Description
Product
BasePriority                                 8
ExitCode
HasExited
ExitTime
Handle
HandleCount                                  106
Id                                           1180
MachineName                                  .
MainWindowHandle                             0
MainWindowTitle
MainModule
MaxWorkingSet
MinWorkingSet
Modules
NonpagedSystemMemorySize                     7552
NonpagedSystemMemorySize64                   7552
PagedMemorySize                              13717504
PagedMemorySize64                            13717504
PagedSystemMemorySize                        86152
PagedSystemMemorySize64                      86152
PeakPagedMemorySize                          14839808
PeakPagedMemorySize64                        14839808
PeakWorkingSet                               17604608
PeakWorkingSet64                             17604608
PeakVirtualMemorySize                        59498496
PeakVirtualMemorySize64                      59498496
PriorityBoostEnabled
```

```
PriorityClass
PrivateMemorySize                               13717504
PrivateMemorySize64                             13717504
PrivilegedProcessorTime
ProcessName                                     audiodg
ProcessorAffinity
Responding                                      True
SessionId                                       0
StartInfo                                       System.Diagnostics.ProcessStartInfo
StartTime
SynchronizingObject
Threads
TotalProcessorTime
UserProcessorTime
VirtualMemorySize                               54407168
VirtualMemorySize64                             54407168
EnableRaisingEvents                             False
StandardInput
StandardOutput
StandardError
WorkingSet                                      16338944
WorkingSet64                                    16338944
Site
Container
```

As you see, we can work with this object like any other XML object.

Chapter 39
The PowerShell Extensible Type System

As you've no doubt picked up by now, Windows PowerShell is entirely object-oriented. The objects that PowerShell works with are each of a particular *type*. That is, what we've loosely been calling a "string object" or "Process object" is more correctly referred to as "an object of the String type," or "an object of the Process type." Actually, even more specifically, we'd use the *complete* type name: System.String, or System.Diagnostic.Process.

While all of these types come straight from the .NET Framework, PowerShell doesn't expose us directly to them in most cases. Instead, it *adapts* the Framework objects into something a bit more administrator-friendly. For example, run:

```
PS C:\> Get-Process | Get-Member
```

You'll notice that the end of the member listing includes several items called a "ScriptProperty." These properties don't exist in the actual System.Diagnostic.Process type; rather, they're added, or adapted, onto the type by PowerShell. For example, the CPU ScriptProperty gives us an easier property name—CPU—to work with than the underlying type does. In other cases, PowerShell will create AliasProperties, perhaps substituting the property name "Count" for the less consistent "Length" that some Framework types use.

Most of PowerShell's additions, changes, and so forth are defined in Types.ps1xml, a file that's installed along with PowerShell, in the same folder as the PowerShell.exe console application. This XML-formatted file doesn't contain *every* type that PowerShell can use; rather, it contains those types that PowerShell's programmers wanted to extend, modify, or otherwise adapt for our ease of use.

Types.ps1xml is digitally signed using a Microsoft certificate; modifying the file would break the signa-

523

ture and render the entire file unusable. Fortunately, however, PowerShell's *extensible type system* permits us to create *our own* type extension files, using the same format and capabilities as Types.ps1xml. We can then import our files into PowerShell and take advantage of whatever capabilities we've built into our extended types.

In this chapter, we'll introduce you to several type extension features:

- Creating an AliasProperty.

- Creating a ScriptProperty.

- Creating a NoteProperty.

- Creating a ScriptMethod.

- Defining a set of default properties—the properties used by the **Format-List** cmdlet if you don't specify any properties.

There are other capabilities in the type extension system, but most of them require a deeper understanding of .NET Framework programming than we can cover in this book.

....

Type Trivia
If you browse around the Types.ps1xml file included with PowerShell, you'll notice that many types, especially WMI classes, have a "PSStatus" property set defined, and you might wonder what this is for. During PowerShell's development, this property set was originally part of a concept to provide task-specific views—for example, a "status" view, a "capacity" view, and so forth, and these "PSStatus" property sets were to define the properties that would comprise a "status" view. Although the idea never made it further than defining these property sets for a few types, the concept is still a good one. Perhaps it will make a comeback in a future version of PowerShell!

The Basic Type Extension File

The basic type extension file is simple—no more than three lines:

```
<?xml version="1.0" encoding="utf-8" ?>
<Types>
</Types>
```

You will insert all of your type extensions between the <Types> and </Types> tags.

....

Don't Forget!
All editions of PrimalScript provide good support for XML editing, including tag color-coding, auto-indentation, and so forth. Enterprise editions of PrimalScript also include a Visual XML Editor, which provides a graphically based, XML-editing experience that some users greatly prefer.

Creating Type Extensions

Within the <Types> and </Types> tags of your file, you'll place <Type> sections—one for each type that you're extending. A simple <Type> section looks like this:

```
<Type>
    <Name>type name</Name>
    <Members>
    </Members>
</Type>
```

Within the <Name> and </Name> tags, you'll place the *entire* .NET Framework type name of the type you're extending. The easiest way to find the type name is to retrieve one or more instances of the type and pipe them to the **Get-Member** cmdlet:

```
PS C:\> get-item test | gm


   TypeName: System.IO.DirectoryInfo
```

The **Get-Member** cmdlet's output will clearly list the TypeName, as shown here—simply copy it into the <Name> tag and you're done. Your actual type extensions, which we'll cover in the next several sections, will go within the <Members> and </Members> tags. That's an important convention to take note of.

....

Remember!
Every type extension we show you in the next section is intended to be inserted within the <Member> and </Member> tags, unless we explicitly state otherwise at the time.

Keep in mind that each new <Type> you define can have *as many* of the following extensions as you need, in any combination.

AliasProperty

An AliasProperty extension simply assigns a new name to one of a type's existing properties. For example, if you find the built-in property name PerformanceOverOneHour to be too cumbersome, you could make an AliasProperty named POOH, and PowerShell would let you use the new property name. The original property name would be suppressed within PowerShell, not even showing up in the **Get-Member** cmdlet's output. Here's how to do it:

```
<AliasProperty>
    <Name>property</Name>
    <ReferencedMemberName>original</ReferencedMemberName>
</AliasProperty>
```

You'd replace *property* with your new property name, and *original* with the original property name.

ScriptProperty

A ScriptProperty extension allows you to create a new property *that contains PowerShell script code*. This means you're essentially creating a dynamically valued property! Here's what one looks like:

```
<ScriptProperty>
    <Name>property</Name>
    <GetScriptBlock>
        code
    </GetScriptBlock>
```

```
</ScriptProperty>
```

You'd replace *property* with your new property name, and ***code*** indicates where your PowerShell script code would go. This code can use a special **$this** variable to refer to the current object instance. For example, suppose you have an object that has a TotalSpace and a FreeSpace property—not unlike the Win32_LogicalDisk class, perhaps. You decide you want to create a new PercentFree property, which will contain the percentage of free space, something which would need to be calculated based on the TotalSpace and FreeSpace values. Here's how it might look:

```
<ScriptProperty>
    <Name>PercentFree</Name>
    <GetScriptBlock>
        [system:math]::round($this.FreeSpace / $this.TotalSpace)
    </GetScriptBlock>
</ScriptProperty>
```

Remember that this script code works *exactly* as if you were in the PowerShell console or writing a script. Because we haven't started the line with a cmdlet—we just launched straight into our math expression—the **Write-Output** cmdlet is implied, meaning that PowerShell writes the output to the success pipeline. Anything that your script outputs to the success pipeline will become the value for your ScriptProperty.

A ScriptProperty is a very valuable and powerful way to extend PowerShell's capabilities by using script code that's simpler to write than full .NET Framework code.

By the way: Notice that a <GetScriptBlock> tag pair contains the script code? That's important. PowerShell runs this script whenever someone tries to *read* the property value. That is, if we're trying to display PercentFree, the script calls the <GetScriptBlock>. It wouldn't make sense to be able to put a value into PercentFree; we can't change the amount of free disk space just by sticking a new number into a property (although we sure wish we could, sometimes)! In theory, you could create a ScriptProperty that was *writable*—that is, which allowed changes to be made to the property. However, because you won't usually have a means of passing that property change through to the underlying .NET Framework type, there's not much use for such a capability.

NoteProperty

A NoteProperty extension is an odd duck: It's essentially a property with a fixed, static value. Here's an example:

```
<NoteProperty>
    <Name>property</Name>
    <Value>value</Value>
</NoteProperty>
```

You'd replace ***property*** with the name for your NoteProperty, and replace ***value*** with the static value that you want the property to contain. PowerShell primarily uses specially named NoteProperties to contain fixed metadata values, such as the serialization depth of certain types of objects; we haven't thought of a good use for NoteProperty in a type extension file, but if we do, we'll make a point of blogging about it at http://blog.sapien.com (search the blog for NoteProperty to see if we've come up with anything since publishing this book).

ScriptMethod

A ScriptMethod extension is a bit like a ScriptProperty extension. In fact, in many instances there isn't a great distinction between them. In programmer-speak, though, a property simply returns some value, such as our ScriptProperty example, which returned a value that was calculated from two other existing properties. In other words, our ScriptProperty didn't *do* anything. A method, on the other hand, is expected to carry out some action, although it may also return a value as the result of that. Here's what a ScriptMethod looks like:

```
<ScriptMethod>
    <Name>property</Name>
    <Script>
       code
    </Script>
</ScriptMethod>
```

You'd replace **property** with your new property name, and **code** indicates where your PowerShell script code would go. That code can use a special **$this** variable to refer to the current object instance, just as you did with a ScriptProperty. And, as with ScriptProperty, anything output to the success pipeline becomes a return value for your method.

Default Property Set

When you use the **Format-List** cmdlet to format a set of objects—or when PowerShell automatically chooses **Format-List** according to its formatting rules—PowerShell will list *all* properties for the objects, unless you've registered a type extension that defines a *default property set*. If you've defined a default property set, then PowerShell will only include those properties in the list, unless you explicitly use the **Format-List** cmdlet and specify a different set of properties for inclusion. A default property set is easy to create:

```
<MemberSet>
    <Name>PSStandardMembers</Name>
    <Members>
       <PropertySet>
           <Name>DefaultDisplayPropertySet</Name>
           <ReferencedProperties>
               <Name>property</Name>
               <Name>property</Name>
               <Name>property</Name>
           </ReferencedProperties>
       </PropertySet>
    </Members>
</MemberSet>
```

You would, of course, replace our **property** placeholders with the property names you want. You can include as many <Name> tag sets as desired within the <ReferencedProperties> section. Remember that each property you specify *must be an actual property of the type*; you can't just make up words! If you want to see a list of available properties, pipe an instance of the type to the **Get-Member** cmdlet and review the output.

Importing Your Type Extensions

When you've finished your type extension file, you need to tell PowerShell to use it. To do so, you'll run the **Update-TypeData** cmdlet. You have the choice of having your extensions loaded *in front* of

PowerShell's built-in extensions, or *after* the built-in ones; in case of a conflict, PowerShell uses the first type extension definition it finds, so having your extensions loaded first will let them "win" over PowerShell's built-in extensions.

- To load your extensions in front of PowerShell's, run **Update-TypeData -prependPath** *filename*.

- To load your extensions after PowerShell's, run **Update-TypeData -appendPath** *filename*.

In both instances, of course, provide the complete path and file of your .ps1xml type extension file. Your changes take effect immediately and last until you close the shell; there is no cmdlet for unloading a type data file. You also can't reload a file once it's been loaded into a PowerShell session. You have to exit and restart PowerShell. To have your changes take effect each time you open a new shell, add the **Update-TypeData** cmdlet's commands to your PowerShell profile.

A Practical Example

For an example, we've decided to extend the System.String type. We're going to add an AliasProperty that renames the String's Length property to HowLong, and we're going to add a ScriptMethod that assumes the String contains a computer name or IP address and tells you if it can ping that address. We'll also add a ScriptProperty that returns a TRUE or FALSE, depending on whether the String's contents look like a Universal Naming Convention (UNC) path. These are perhaps not the *most* practical examples, but they will let us show you the breadth of the type extension system using a common, easy-to-experiment-with type.

Because the type extensions themselves are relatively simple and are well-described in the preceding sections, we're just going to show you the entire type extension file all at once. We'll import this by using the **Update-TypeData** cmdlet and its **-prependPath** parameter, and then walk you through a test:

StringTypeExtension.ps1xml

```
<?xml version="1.0" encoding="utf-8" ?>
<Types>
 <Type>
   <Name>System.String</Name>
   <Members>
     <AliasProperty>
       <Name>HowLong</Name>
       <ReferencedMemberName>Length</ReferencedMemberName>
     </AliasProperty>
     <ScriptProperty>
       <Name>IsUNC</Name>
       <GetScriptBlock>
        $this -match "^\\\\\w+\\\w+"
       </GetScriptBlock>
     </ScriptProperty>
     <ScriptMethod>
       <Name>CanPing</Name>
       <Script>
        $wmi = gwmi -query "select * from win32_pingstatus where address = '$this'"
        If ($wmi.statuscode -eq 0) { $true } else { $false }
       </Script>
     </ScriptMethod>
   </Members>
 </Type>
</Types>
```

For our ScriptProperty, we're using a regular expression (which we covered beginning on page 223), and the regular expression **-match** operator. Because the operator already returns a TRUE or FALSE value, we're just letting that output become the value of our ScriptProperty. Our ScriptMethod isn't much more complicated: It uses the Win32_PingStatus WMI class to ping whatever's in the String (which we reference by using the **$this** variable). If the resulting StatusCode property is zero, we output the Boolean $true value; if not, we output $false.

Let's see our new type extension in action:

```
PS C:\test> Update-TypeData -pre sample.ps1xml
PS C:\test> [string]$s = "localhost"
PS C:\test> $s.canping()
True
PS C:\test> $s = "\\Server\Share"
PS C:\test> $s.isunc
True
PS C:\test> $s.howlong
14
PS C:\test>
```

Perfect results!

Chapter 40
Creating Custom Objects

Why in the world would you need to create a custom object? Surely there are enough objects in the world already, right? Even a function returns objects. But usually there are limitations. Consider this example:

PingFunction.ps1

```
function Ping-Computer {
    PROCESS {
        $wmi = gwmi -query "SELECT StatusCode FROM Win32_PingStatus WHERE Address = '$_'"
        foreach ($result in $wmi) {
            if ($result.statuscode -eq 0) {
                Write-Output $_
            }
        }
    }
}

Get-Content c:\computers.txt | Ping-Computer
```

When we run this script, it'll read computer names from a file named C:\Computers.txt, and then pipe those to the **Ping-Computer** function. That function has a Process script block (which we discussed in the chapter "Script Blocks, Functions, Filters, Snap-ins, and Modules"), which processes the names one at a time. For each name, it attempts to ping it using the Win32_PingStatus WMI class. If the ping is successful (a StatusCode of zero), the script block outputs the computer name back to the pipeline.

This is a useful function… but it's of *minimal* usefulness. For example, the Win32_PingStatus class can return other information, such as the address that the destination computer used to reply, or the resolved address, or the response time. Unfortunately, if we're just returning simple values from our function, we can't return *all* of that data—we're stuck with just returning the names of the computers we could ping.

And that's why we might want to create a custom object. For example, suppose we make up a PingResult object. That's the object's *type name*, and we'll give it several properties:

- **Address:** the address or computer name we attempted to ping.
- **ProtocolAddress:** the address the destination used to reply.
- **ResponseTime:** the time elapsed to handle the request.
- **Status:** the English text that corresponds to the StatusCode.
- **StatusCode:** a numeric code indicating whether the ping succeeded.

Windows PowerShell allows us to create such an object on the fly. We can reprogram our **Ping-Computer** function to output these PingResult objects, allowing us to output a richer type of information than merely a list of successful computer names.

Custom Object Creation

Creating a new object is straightforward: Use the **New-Object** cmdlet, and ask it to create a new generic object—that is, an object of the generic Object type:

```
PS C:\> $obj = New-Object Object
```

From there, you can add *members*—properties, in this case—to the object. We're going to work with a special type of property called a *NoteProperty*, which is something PowerShell can add to almost any type of object, and which you can use to store simple values like strings, numbers, and so forth. To add a member to our object, we'll pipe our object to the **Add-Member** cmdlet, telling **Add-Member** what type of member to add, the name we want for the new member, and the value we want the member set to:

```
PS C:\> $obj | Add-Member NoteProperty MyProperty -value "Hello"
```

And that's it. We can pipe the **$obj** variable to the **Add-Member** cmdlet again and again to add as many properties as we need.

Using Custom Objects

So, let's get back to our **Ping-Computer** function example. Here's a revised version of the function that utilizes custom objects:

CustomObjectPing.ps1

```
function ping-computer {
    PROCESS {
        $wmi = gwmi -query "SELECT * FROM Win32_PingStatus WHERE Address = '$_'"
        foreach ($result in $wmi) {
            $pingresult = New-Object object
            $pingresult | Add-Member noteproperty ResponseTime -value $result.responsetime
            $pingresult | Add-Member noteproperty StatusCode -value $result.StatusCode
            $pingresult | Add-Member noteproperty ProtocolAddress -value $result.ProtocolAddress
```

```
        $pingresult | Add-Member noteproperty Address -value $result.Address
        switch ($result.statuscode) {
            0     { $status = "Success" }
            11001 { $status = "Buffer too small" }
            11002 { $status = "Dest net unreachable" }
            11003 { $status = "Dest host unreachable" }
            11004 { $status = "Dest protocol unreachable" }
            11005 { $status = "Dest port unreachable" }
            11006 { $status = "No resources" }
            11007 { $status = "Bad option" }
            11008 { $status = "Hardware err" }
            11009 { $status = "Packet too big" }
            11010 { $status = "Request timed out" }
            11011 { $status = "Bad request" }
            11012 { $status = "Bad route" }
            11013 { $status = "TTL expired transit" }
            11014 { $status = "TTL expired reass'y" }
            11015 { $status = "Paramater err" }
            11016 { $status = "Source quench" }
            11017 { $status = "Option too big" }
            11018 { $status = "Bad dest" }
            11032 { $status = "Negot IPSEC" }
            11050 { $status = "Failure" }
            default { $status = "No reply" }
        }
        $pingresult | Add-Member noteproperty Status -value $status
        Write-Output $pingresult
      }
    }
}

Get-Content c:\computers.txt | ping-computer | Format-Table
```

You can see that the last line of our script is getting our list of computer names from C:\Computers. txt, piping them to the **Ping-Computer** function, and then piping the function's output to the **Format-Table** cmdlet. Here's how the function works:

We've enclosed the entire function's contents in a Process script block. That makes the function usable from the pipeline. Remember that PowerShell executes the Process script block once for each input object passed in from the pipeline. The **$_** variable will contain the current pipeline object.

First, we execute the Win32_PingStatus query, passing the **$_** variable as the address to ping. Note that this query executes *locally*; you are only contacting the remote computer via ping, not via WMI. We examine the results (usually only one result) that we get back by using a **ForEach** loop.

Within the loop, we create a new $pingresult object by using the **New-Object** cmdlet. We add several properties by using the **Add-Member** cmdlet and populate those properties with properties from the WMI instance: ResponseTime, StatusCode, ProtocolAddress, and Address. We then use a Switch construct to examine the StatusCode property and populate the **$status** variable with a text version of the status code. Notice that a Default condition in the Switch construct fills in the "no reply" status in the event that no reply was received. We used the **$status** variable to populate the last property that we added to the object. Finally, we output the finished $pingresult object to the pipeline using the **Write-Output** cmdlet. Here's our script's output:

```
ResponseTime   StatusCode    ProtocolAddress     Address      Status
------------   ----------    ---------------     -------      ------
                                                 DON-LAPTOP   No reply
0              0             ::1                 LOCALHOST    Success
0              0             fe80::e468:309...   DON-PC       Success
                                                 SERVER2      No reply
```

533

It's worth noting that on Windows Vista, the Win32_PingResult class will work with IPv6 and not just IPv4. You can see this in the ProtocolAddress property, where IPv6-style addresses are listed.

If we wanted to make this **Ping-Computer** function available in the global scope, we could dot source it. We'll delete the last line of the script, just leaving the function, and then dot source it:

```
PS C:\> . ./bigping
```

This defines the function in the global scope, rather than creating a new script scope for it. With the function defined in the global scope, we can use it at the command line, just like a cmdlet:

```
PS C:\> $results = get-content c:\computers.txt | ping-computer
PS C:\> $results


ResponseTime    :
StatusCode      :
ProtocolAddress :
Address         : DON-LAPTOP
Status          : No reply

ResponseTime    : 0
StatusCode      : 0
ProtocolAddress : ::1
Address         : LOCALHOST
Status          : Success

ResponseTime    : 0
StatusCode      : 0
ProtocolAddress : fe80::e468:3091:f2fc:8deb
Address         : DON-PC
Status          : Success

ResponseTime    :
StatusCode      :
ProtocolAddress :
Address         : SERVER2
Status          : No reply
```

Our **$results** variable contains the results of the pipeline we executed. Since it's a collection of our "PingResult" objects, we can treat **$results** like any other collection. For example, to examine the second object:

```
PS C:\> $results[1]


ResponseTime    : 0
StatusCode      : 0
ProtocolAddress : ::1
Address         : LOCALHOST
Status          : Success
```

Any time you need a function to return *rich* results—that is, more than just a simple value—a custom object is a good option. In this case, we've created a useful utility function that not only lets us know what computers were pingable, but provides other useful information as well. Because our function is returning a real object, we can pass those objects down the pipeline. For example, here's a command line that uses our function and only outputs the names of the computers that *were not* pingable. Further, we're only displaying the Address property of unresponsive computers:

```
PS C:\> get-content c:\computers.txt | ping-computer | where { $_.Status -eq "No reply" }'
>>| select Address

Address
-------
DON-LAPTOP
SERVER2
```

You can see how this sort of custom object lends itself well to filtering, sorting, and other functionality provided by PowerShell's other cmdlets.

A Practical Example

Note that the example we showed you earlier isn't *practical*, but we thought you'd like to see another. For this example, we're going to create a custom function called **Get-OSInfo**. It'll accept a computer name—either a single string or an array of strings—and for each one, it'll retrieve that computer's Win32_OperatingSystem class and output a custom object containing the computer's Windows build number, service pack version, and computer name.

Here's the script:

GetOSInfo.ps1

```
function Get-OSInfo {
    param([string[]]$addresses)

    function OutputInfo {
        param (
            [string]$computer,
            [string]$build,
            [string]$spver
        )
        $output = New-Object psobject
        $output | Add-Member NoteProperty ComputerName -value $computer
        $output | Add-Member NoteProperty BuildNumber -value $build
        $output | Add-Member NoteProperty SPVersion -value $spver
        $output
    }

    trap {
        OutputInfo $address,"Unknown","Unknown"
    }

    foreach ($address in $addresses) {
        $os = gwmi win32_operatingsystem -computer $address -ea continue
        OutputInfo $address $os.buildnumber $os.servicepackmajorversion
    }

}
```

Remember!
If you dot source this or add it to your profile, this function will be available from the command line and you can use it almost like a simple cmdlet.

To use this function:

```
Get-OSInfo @("don-pc","server2") | format-table
```

So, what's going on? We start by declaring a function that accepts a string array (which, remember, can consist of only one element, if we're only interested in one computer). We declare a function named **OutputInfo,** which actually outputs our custom object. It creates a new object, adds three NoteProperty members, and then outputs the custom object to the success pipeline (using an implicit **Write-Output** cmdlet).

We've defined an error handler in case WMI is unable to reach one of the computers we specified. If that happens, the trap handler calls the **OutputInfo** function, passing along "Unknown" values for the build number and service pack version number. The trap handler calls "continue," allowing the script to continue after the error.

Next is the main body of the script: A simple **ForEach** loop that contacts WMI and retrieves the Win32_OperatingSystem class. Notice the -**EA,** or -**errorAction,** parameter, which specifies that exceptions be raised (so we can trap them). If no errors occurred, then the script calls the **OutputInfo** function with the retrieved WMI information.

The beauty of building our own custom object is that we don't have to worry about formatting the output. Since our output values are in object properties, any of PowerShell's Format cmdlets can handle formatting for us:

```
Get-OSInfo @("don-pc","server2") | format-list
```

If we'd simply output string values, we would have needed to format them ourselves, which is much less efficient (anything that makes us do extra work is "inefficient" as far as we're concerned).

Chapter 41
Object Serialization

Occasionally, there's a need for objects to be represented in a more easily portable format, such as XML. Serialization is the process of taking an object and converting it into an XML representation. The reverse, *deserialization*, converts the XML back into an object—although the object is often less functional than it was prior to serialization, often including only property values and omitting methods since it is no longer "connected" to the real-world software that originally generated it. In other words, if you serialize a Windows service into an XML file, you can carry that to another computer and deserialize it back into an object. But that object won't be able to start and stop the original service; it'll simply be a way of examining the service's properties as they were at the time it was serialized. Serialized objects, then, are essentially a "snapshot" of an object at a specific point in time.

Windows PowerShell primarily uses the **Export-CliXML** cmdlet to serialize objects and save the resulting XML in a text file. For example, run this command:

```
PS C:\> gwmi win32_operatingsystem | export-clixml c:\test\win32os.xml
```

It results in the following XML representation (which we've truncated to save space):

```
<Objs Version="1.1" xmlns="http://schemas.microsoft.com/powershell/2004/04">
  <Obj RefId="RefId-0">
    <TN RefId="RefId-0">
      <T>
        System.Management.ManagementObject#root\cimv2\Win32_OperatingSystem
      </T>
      <T>
        System.Management.ManagementObject
      </T>
```

```
    <T>
        System.Management.ManagementBaseObject
    </T>
    <T>
        System.ComponentModel.Component
    </T>
    <T>
        System.MarshalByRefObject
    </T>
    <T>
        System.Object
    </T>
</TN>
<Props>
    <S N="RegisteredUser">
        Don Jones
    </S>
    <S N="SerialNumber">
        89580-378-1205931-71241
    </S>
    <U16 N="ServicePackMajorVersion">
        0
    </U16>
    <S N="SystemDirectory">
        C:\Windows\system32
    </S>
    <S N="SystemDrive">
        C:
    </S>
    <Nil N="TotalSwapSpaceSize"/>
    <U64 N="TotalVirtualMemorySize">
        5963004
    </U64>
    <U64 N="TotalVisibleMemorySize">
        2882304
    </U64>
    <S N="Version">
        6.0.6000
    </S>
    <S N="WindowsDirectory">
        C:\Windows
    </S>
</Props>
  </Obj>
</Objs>
```

The **Import-CliXML** cmdlet does the opposite, returning the XML to a static object inside the shell:

```
PS C:\> $os = import-clixml c:\test\win32os.xml
PS C:\> $os.servicepackmajorversion
0
PS C:\> $os.name
Microsoftr Windows VistaT Ultimate |C:\Windows|\Device\Harddisk0\Partition1
PS C:\>
```

PowerShell has a set of default rules used to serialize objects. However, you can customize the serialization by providing *serialization directives* in a type extension file (we first discussed these files in the "The PowerShell Extensible Type System" chapter).

Why Export Objects to XML?

Exporting, or serializing, objects to XML allows them to be persisted, or saved, as a static snapshot. One practical reason to do so is to share those objects with other PowerShell users. For example, you might want to export your command-line history to an XML file so that you can share it with another user—who could then import it to re-create your command-line history.

Another less obvious reason might be to get a snapshot of objects when you're not physically around. For example, suppose you have a long-running process that starts on one of your servers at 1:00 A.M. every morning. You know it should finish by 5:00 A.M. You could write a very short PowerShell script, like this:

```
Get-Process | Export-CliXML c:\1am.xml
```

And you could schedule it to run at 1:15 A.M., when the long-running process should be running. Later, at 5:30 A.M., you could run a second script:

```
Get-Process | Export-CliXML c:\5am.xml
```

When you arrive for work, you could grab both of these files and re-import them, effectively reconstructing the objects *as they were* when the XML file was created. This would let you examine the objects from that point in time, even though you weren't physically present then. For example, to compare the two sets of objects:

```
PS C:\> $1 = import-clixml c:\1am.xml
PS C:\> $5 = import-clixml c:\5am.xml
PS C:\> compare-object $1 $5
```

Using this example, the **$1** variable contains all of the objects that were running at 1 A.M. You can pipe **$1** to any other cmdlet capable of working with objects, allowing you to sort, group, filter, or format the process objects in any way. This ability to easily persist objects—a result of PowerShell's serialization capabilities—has myriad uses.

Creating Serialization Directives

You enter serialization directives into the type extension file within the <MemberSet> tag. In other words, you're starting with the following basic template for a type:

```
<Type>
    <Name>type name</Name>
    <Members>
        <MemberSet>
            <Name>PSStandardMembers</Name>
            <Members>
               ...serialization directives go here...
            </Members>
        </MemberSet>
    </Members>
</Type>
```

Review the "The PowerShell Extensible Type System" chapter if you need a refresher on type extensions. Remember, when you provide this PSStandardMembers member set, you're *overriding* PowerShell's default serialization rules. That means PowerShell will *only* use the method you specify to serialize the class type you've specified.

For the following examples, we'll be using the output of our **Ping-Computer** cmdlet. This is available in the SAPIEN Extensions for Windows PowerShell (PshX-SAPIEN) snap-in, which is available for download at www.PrimalScript.com/freetools. This cmdlet outputs objects of the type SapienPshX. PingResult. For each of our examples, we'll serialize using the following command:

```
ping-computer "localhost" | export-clixml c:\test\export.xml
```

For your reference, PowerShell's default serialization behavior results in the following:

```
<Objs Version="1.1" xmlns="http://schemas.microsoft.com/powershell/2004/04">
  <Obj RefId="RefId-0">
    <TN RefId="RefId-0">
      <T>
        sapienPshX.PingResult
      </T>
      <T>
        System.Object
      </T>
    </TN>
    <Props>
      <S N="ComputerName">
        localhost
      </S>
      <I32 N="StatusCode">
        0
      </I32>
      <I32 N="ResponseTime">
        0
      </I32>
      <S N="ProtocolAddress">
        ::1
      </S>
    </Props>
  </Obj>
</Objs>
```

As you can see, this default output displays the object's type (in <T> tags), the type it inherits from (the second <T> tag set), and then the object's properties (<S> is a string, <I32> is an integer, and so forth). Had we generated a collection of these objects, one <Obj> tag section would have been generated for each.

Serializing as a String

This technique allows you to serialize the object as a string:

```
<NoteProperty>
 <Name>SerializationMethod</Name>
 <Value>String</Value>
</NoteProperty>
```

Here's a complete example:

```
<Types>
  <Type>
```

```
        <Name>sapienPshX.PingResult</Name>
        <Members>
           <MemberSet>
               <Name>PSStandardMembers</Name>
               <Members>
                 <NoteProperty>
                     <Name>SerializationMethod</Name>
                     <Value>String</Value>
                 </NoteProperty>
               </Members>
           </MemberSet>
        </Members>
    </Type>
</Types>
```

And here's the result when we export **Ping-Computer localhost | Export-CliXML c:\test\export.xml**:

```
<Objs Version="1.1" xmlns="http://schemas.microsoft.com/powershell/2004/04">
  <S>
     sapienPshX.PingResult
  </S>
</Objs>
```

What this SerializationMethod property is doing is telling PowerShell to call the object's built-in **ToString()** method. In the .NET Framework, pretty much *all* classes inherit (eventually) from the System.Object class (although most classes have several ancestors between them and the top-level System.Object class). The System.Object class provides a simple **ToString()** method, which simply outputs the class's type name; many objects *override* this simple method and provide their own, more robust **ToString()** method. However, as you can see here, our sapienPshX.PingResult class simply utilizes the System.Object class's simpler method, so our export result simply contains the type name as a string.

Specifying the String Serialization technique is primarily useful when the type you're working with provides a useful and robust **ToString()** method of its own.

Specifying a String Source

Our next SerializationMethod property is similar to the previous one. We're still going to specify a String output, but this time we're going to add a source other than the object's **ToString()** method to get that string. Specifically, we're going to use a PowerShell script block, and its output will be used as the source for our final serialized XML. Here's a simple example:

```
<NoteProperty>
 <Name>SerializationMethod</Name>
 <Value>String</Value>
</NoteProperty>
<ScriptProperty>
 <Name>StringSerializationSource</Name>
 <GetScriptBlock>PowerShell Script Code Here</GetScriptBlock>
</ScriptProperty>
```

Here's a more complete example, where we're using a script to output only two of the object's four properties, along with a timestamp as a third property:

```
    <Type>
        <Name>sapienPshX.PingResult</Name>
        <Members>
```

```
            <MemberSet>
                <Name>PSStandardMembers</Name>
                <Members>
                  <NoteProperty>
                      <Name>SerializationMethod</Name>
                      <Value>String</Value>
                  </NoteProperty>
                  <ScriptProperty>
                      <Name>StringSerializationSource</Name>
                      <GetScriptBlock>
                        $newobj = new-object PSObject
                            $timestamp = Get-Date
                            $newobj | add-member NoteProperty Timestamp -value $timestamp
                            $newobj | add-member NoteProperty Computer -value $this.ComputerName
                            $newobj | add-member NoteProperty StatusCode -value $this.StatusCode
                            $newobj
                      </GetScriptBlock>
                  </ScriptProperty>
                </Members>
            </MemberSet>
        </Members>
    </Type>
</Types>
```

However, what we're doing is creating a new, blank object of the PSObject type, and storing it in **$newobj** variable (we covered the creation of custom objects in the "Creating Custom Objects" chapter). We're adding three properties—Timestamp, Computer, and StatusCode—and setting them to specific values. The special **$this** variable represents the original PingResult object, and we're accessing its ComputerName and StatusCode properties. Finally, we output **$newobj**, and that's what PowerShell uses to generate the string in our serialized XML:

```
<Objs Version="1.1" xmlns="http://schemas.microsoft.com/powershell/2004/04">
  <S>
    @{Timestamp=5/1/2007 10:15:12 AM; Computer=localhost; StatusCode=0}
  </S>
</Objs>
```

Remember, the three properties of our **$newobj** variable aren't broken down, because we've specified that the final serialization be a single string.

You can use property types other than a ScriptProperty type as the StringSerializationSource property. In this next example, we'll use a NoteProperty type, which is basically just a static text string:

```
<Types>
    <Type>
        <Name>sapienPshX.PingResult</Name>
        <Members>
            <MemberSet>
                <Name>PSStandardMembers</Name>
                <Members>
                  <NoteProperty>
                      <Name>SerializationMethod</Name>
                      <Value>String</Value>
                  </NoteProperty>
                  <NoteProperty>
                      <Name>StringSerializationSource</Name>
                      <Value>Static Text</Value>
                  </NoteProperty>
                </Members>
```

```
      </MemberSet>
    </Members>
  </Type>
</Types>
```

The result is the following:

```
<Objs Version="1.1" xmlns="http://schemas.microsoft.com/powershell/2004/04">
  <S>
    Static Text
  </S>
</Objs>
```

Not terribly useful, since every object of the specified type will always be serialized with this exact output, but it demonstrates that the StringSerializationSource property can be something other than a ScriptProperty type.

Controlling Serialization Depth

When you're working with hierarchical objects—such as file system folders, where one folder can contain additional folders, which can contain additional folders, and so forth—you may want to control the *depth* to which PowerShell serializes that hierarchy. If you don't, then serializing a top-level object, such as the root folder of a drive, will automatically serialize *the entire object hierarchy*—in other words, the entire drive, which can be time-consuming and produce unexpectedly large results.

Adding a depth-control serialization directive does *not* require you to specify any properties to be serialized; PowerShell will still follow its default rules, but it will do so only for the specified depth within the object's hierarchy. In other words, this serialization directive can stand alone. Here it is:

```
<NoteProperty>
  <Name>SerializationDepth</Name>
  <Value>2</Value>
</NoteProperty>
```

Serializing Only Specific Properties

Perhaps the most useful SerializationMethod technique is to export just specific properties of the object. Using this technique, you can ensure that you export only the *useful* properties of an object, meaning deserialized objects will contain only useful data. You may also wish to omit properties that won't have meaning later on, such as a constantly changing value like CPU utilization. The basic format is as follows:

```
<NoteProperty>
 <Name>SerializationMethod</Name>
 <Value>SpecificProperties</Value>
</NoteProperty>
<PropertySet>
 <Name>PropertySerializationSet</Name>
 <ReferencedProperties>
   <Name>property</Name>
 </ReferencedProperties>
</PropertySet>
```

You can include as many referenced properties as you want. Again, all of the properties you reference must already exist for the class you're working with; you'd use this technique mainly to "hide" properties of the class that you *don't* want to be serialized. Here's a full example:

```
<Types>
    <Type>
        <Name>sapienPshX.PingResult</Name>
        <Members>
            <MemberSet>
                <Name>PSStandardMembers</Name>
                <Members>
                  <NoteProperty>
                     <Name>SerializationMethod</Name>
                     <Value>SpecificProperties</Value>
                  </NoteProperty>
                  <PropertySet>
                    <Name>PropertySerializationSet</Name>
                    <ReferencedProperties>
                       <Name>ComputerName</Name>
                       <Name>StatusCode</Name>
                    </ReferencedProperties>
                  </PropertySet>
                </Members>
            </MemberSet>
        </Members>
    </Type>
</Types>
```

And here's the XML it creates:

```
<Objs Version="1.1" xmlns="http://schemas.microsoft.com/powershell/2004/04">
  <Obj RefId="RefId-0">
    <TN RefId="RefId-0">
      <T>
          sapienPshX.PingResult
      </T>
      <T>
          System.Object
      </T>
    </TN>
    <Props>
      <S N="ComputerName">
         localhost
      </S>
      <I32 N="StatusCode">
         0
      </I32>
    </Props>
  </Obj>
</Objs>
```

Notice that this output is identical to what PowerShell would create using its default rules, except that only two of our object's four properties are being serialized.

Controlling the Inheritance of Serialization Directives

We mentioned earlier in this chapter that nearly all classes inherit from the System.Object class, which is the top-level and most generic class available in the .NET Framework. Our serialized object XML, as in the example we just showed you, reflects this inheritance by listing not only our type, but the type from which it inherits:

```
<TN RefId="RefId-0">
  <T>
    sapienPshX.PingResult
  </T>
  <T>
    System.Object
  </T>
</TN>
```

More complex objects have a more complex hierarchy in their serialized XML. For example, here's a service, obtained by using the **Get-Service** cmdlet:

```
<TN RefId="RefId-0">
  <T>
    System.ServiceProcess.ServiceController
  </T>
  <T>
    System.ComponentModel.Component
  </T>
  <T>
    System.MarshalByRefObject
  </T>
  <T>
    System.Object
  </T>
</TN>
```

When defining a serialization directive, class inheritance comes into play. For example, in our prior example (selecting specific properties), we showed you the sapienPshX.PingResult class, and we selected two of its four properties. The properties we selected will normally be serialized for that class *and for any classes that derive from it.* Suppose we have a second class, named sapienPshX.BetterPingResult, which inherits from sapienPshX.PingResult. Without any serialization directives, only the ComputerName and StatusCode properties would be serialized for that inherited type, because it inherits from a type that *has* a specific serialization directive registered.

Create a type extension like this:

```
<Types>
   <Type>
      <Name>sapienPshX.PingResult</Name>
      <Members>
         <MemberSet>
            <Name>PSStandardMembers</Name>
            <Members>
              <NoteProperty>
                 <Name>SerializationMethod</Name>
                 <Value>SpecificProperties</Value>
              </NoteProperty>
              <PropertySet>
                <Name>PropertySerializationSet</Name>
                <ReferencedProperties>
                  <Name>ComputerName</Name>
                  <Name>StatusCode</Name>
                </ReferencedProperties>
              </PropertySet>
            </Members>
         </MemberSet>
      </Members>
   </Type>
```

```
<Type>
    <Name>sapienPshX.BetterPingResult</Name>
    <Members>
        <MemberSet>
            <Name>PSStandardMembers</Name>
            <Members>
              <NoteProperty>
                 <Name>SerializationMethod</Name>
                 <Value>SpecificProperties</Value>
              </NoteProperty>
              <PropertySet>
                <Name>PropertySerializationSet</Name>
                <ReferencedProperties>
                   <Name>ResponseTime</Name>
                </ReferencedProperties>
              </PropertySet>
            </Members>
        </MemberSet>
    </Members>
</Type>
</Types>
```

Now, our sapienPshX.BetterPingResult type will serialize with three properties: ComputerName and StatusCode (because its parent type, sapienPshX.PingResult, serializes with those properties), and ResponseTime, a property we've specifically selected for the type. You *can*, however, *block* this inheritance behavior in serialization directives. Here's the same example type extension file with a minor change, which we'll boldface:

```
<Types>
    <Type>
        <Name>sapienPshX.PingResult</Name>
        <Members>
            <MemberSet>
                <Name>PSStandardMembers</Name>
                <Members>
                  <NoteProperty>
                     <Name>SerializationMethod</Name>
                     <Value>SpecificProperties</Value>
                  </NoteProperty>
                  <PropertySet>
                    <Name>PropertySerializationSet</Name>
                    <ReferencedProperties>
                       <Name>ComputerName</Name>
                       <Name>StatusCode</Name>
                    </ReferencedProperties>
                  </PropertySet>
                </Members>
            </MemberSet>
        </Members>
    </Type>
    <Type>
        <Name>sapienPshX.BetterPingResult</Name>
        <Members>
            <MemberSet>
                <Name>PSStandardMembers</Name>
                <Members>
                  <NoteProperty>
                     <Name>SerializationMethod</Name>
                     <Value>SpecificProperties</Value>
                  </NoteProperty>
                  <NoteProperty>
```

```
            <Name>InheritPropertySerializationSet</Name>
            <Value>false</Value>
          </NoteProperty>
          <PropertySet>
            <Name>PropertySerializationSet</Name>
            <ReferencedProperties>
              <Name>ResponseTime</Name>
            </ReferencedProperties>
          </PropertySet>
        </Members>
      </MemberSet>
    </Members>
  </Type>
</Types>
```

Now, objects of the sapienPshX.BetterPingResult type will *only* serialize with a ReponseTime property, because we've turned off the serialization directive inheritance. Any types that happen to inherit from sapienPshX.BetterPingResult will still inherit its serialization directives, unless they also have the InheritPropertySerializationSet property set to FALSE.

Serialization: Now and Tomorrow

What's the purpose, then, of serialization, and why should you care about it? Today, serialization is a way of saving objects into a simplified, easily transportable format. For example, you might export a bunch of objects from one computer, move the XML file to another computer, and then import the objects from XML to work with them again. Saving objects is another good use of serialization: For example, by piping the **Get-History** cmdlet to the **Export-CliXML** cmdlet, you can save your command history in an XML file. You can then use the **Import-CliXML** cmdlet to import that file, pipe it to the **Add-History** cmdlet, and then "reload" your command history. This is useful when giving demonstrations, or when conducting various repetitive tasks.

In the future, serialization will play an important role in remote management. A future version of PowerShell will allow you to connect to remote copies of the shell and have them execute commands locally on the computer where they're installed. Those remote shells will then serialize the results of your commands, transmit the results—as a stream of XML text via an HTTP-like connection—back to you, where your shell will reconstruct the objects so that you can work with them. Being able to customize how objects are serialized will provide important capabilities at that time, in addition to the useful things you can do right now.

Chapter 42
Creating Custom Formats

Windows PowerShell uses XML-based files to define how various types of objects should be formatted. If you open the PowerShell installation folder, you'll see a number of files ending in ".format.ps1xml"; these files control the built-in formatting behavior that PowerShell ships with. You can create your own formats, as well.

Examining the Formatting Format

One of the easiest ways to see how these XML files work is to examine an existing type's formatting. For example, running **Get-EventLog System | Format-List** produces output like the following (which we've seriously truncated to save space):

```
PS C:\> get-eventlog system | format-list


Index              : 1888
EntryType          : Information
EventID            : 1103
Message            : Your computer was successfully assigned an address from the network,
                     and it can now connect to other computers.
Category           : (0)
CategoryNumber     : 0
ReplacementStrings : {}
Source             : Dhcp
TimeGenerated      : 4/18/2007 9:06:18 PM
TimeWritten        : 4/18/2007 9:06:18 PM
UserName           :
```

How does PowerShell know to select these particular properties and display them in this particular fashion? Well, if we pipe the **Get-EventLog** cmdlet to the **Get-Member** cmdlet, we'll see what type of data the cmdlet is returning:

```
PS C:\Users\Don> get-eventlog system | get-member

  TypeName: System.Diagnostics.EventLogEntry
```

We can then open the DotNetTypes.format.ps1xml file (located in PowerShell's installation folder, which is in the Windows system folder—System32 or System64) and locate the formatting for that type. It starts off with a <View> tag, which contains the entire definition for how we want to view, or see, items of this particular type. The <Name> tag of the view is what you'll use with the **-view** parameter of a formatting cmdlet to manually select the view. Notice that the <TypeName> tag is contained within a <ViewSelectedBy> tag: The <ViewSelectedBy> tag contains a list of things that will trigger PowerShell to use this view; any use of the System.Diagnostics.EventLogEntry type will trigger this view.

Next is the <ListControl> section, which actually defines the look of the view. Our list has one <ListEntry> tag, which consists of several <ListItems> tags. For each <ListItem> tag, the XML defines the property that will be shown: Index, EntryType, and so forth. These are the object properties that PowerShell selects when building the table we saw earlier. You'll notice that these properties are the columns that PowerShell displayed when we ran the **Get-EventLog** cmdlet. They weren't *all* displayed, though, because our PowerShell window wasn't wide enough. PowerShell displayed only as many columns as would fit, displaying columns in the exact order listed here in this XML:

```xml
<View>
        <Name>System.Diagnostics.EventLogEntry</Name>
        <ViewSelectedBy>
            <TypeName>System.Diagnostics.EventLogEntry</TypeName>
        </ViewSelectedBy>

        <ListControl>
            <ListEntries>
               <ListEntry>
                  <ListItems>
                    <ListItem>
                        <PropertyName>Index</PropertyName>
                    </ListItem>
                    <ListItem>
                        <PropertyName>EntryType</PropertyName>
                    </ListItem>
                    <ListItem>
                        <PropertyName>EventID</PropertyName>
                    </ListItem>
                    <ListItem>
                        <PropertyName>Message</PropertyName>
                    </ListItem>
                    <ListItem>
                        <PropertyName>Category</PropertyName>
                    </ListItem>
                    <ListItem>
                        <PropertyName>CategoryNumber</PropertyName>
                    </ListItem>
                    <ListItem>
                        <PropertyName>ReplacementStrings</PropertyName>
                    </ListItem>
                    <ListItem>
                        <PropertyName>Source</PropertyName>
```

```
                </ListItem>
                <ListItem>
                    <PropertyName>TimeGenerated</PropertyName>
                </ListItem>
                <ListItem>
                    <PropertyName>TimeWritten</PropertyName>
                </ListItem>
                <ListItem>
                    <PropertyName>UserName</PropertyName>
                </ListItem>

            </ListItems>
          </ListEntry>
        </ListEntries>
      </ListControl>
    </View>
```

This is a pretty simplistic example, but it does serve to illustrate the basics of how and why PowerShell's built-in formatting works. If you scroll to the top of the file, you'll notice that all the <View> tags are contained within a top-level <ViewDefinitions> tag, which is itself contained in the uppermost <Configuration> tag. That's more or less the whole of the formatting file.

Tip
These files are easier to work with in a dedicated XML editor rather than in Notepad. SAPIEN PrimalScript recognizes and color-codes XML files for easier editing, and the Enterprise edition of PrimalScript includes a Visual XML Editor, which can make XML editing and creation even easier.

By the Way...
If you just run Get-EventLog System without specifying the Format-List cmdlet, PowerShell displays the output in a table format. That's because the first view registered for the EventLogEntry type is a table-style format; when we specified a list format, PowerShell had to dig deeper to find a format for the EventLogEntry objects that used a ListControl type. Fortunately, there was one—otherwise, PowerShell would have constructed a list on its own, possibly using less relevant properties.

Constructing Your Own Format

A format file thus begins with a <Configuration> tag. Inside that is a <ViewDefinitions> tag, or *node*. Within that, you'll add a <View> node for each object you want to format. Within the <View> node, you'll define an arbitrary <Name> tag for your view, and you'll build a <ViewSelectedBy> node that tells PowerShell when to use your view. Optionally, the <View> node can also contain a <GroupBy> node, which specifies how PowerShell should group objects. For example, a folder listing is grouped by its parent. Thus far, then, a format file looks something like this:

```
<Configuration>
 <ViewDefinitions>
   <View>
     <Name>MyView</Name>
     <ViewSelectedBy><TypeName></TypeName></ViewSelectedBy>
```

```
        <GroupBy></GroupBy>
    </View>
  </ViewDefinitions>
</Configuration>
```

Actually, there's one meta tag that must appear as the first line in the actual file:

```
<?xml version="1.0" encoding="utf-8" ?>
```

This simply defines the file as XML. For the remainder of this chapter, we'll assume that any format files you're creating already have this line and just focus on the body of the file. Your file name must end in the .ps1xml extension. We recommend you give the file a meaningful name. You'll need to copy the file to any computer where you intend to use the custom formats. Later in the chapter, we'll show you how to load the files into PowerShell.

> **Tip**
> The <Name> of your view allows you to specify it when you use the Format-Custom cmdlet. This cmdlet has a -view parameter, which accepts the name of the view you want to use to format your output. This allows you to manually select a view, even if it doesn't match the data type of the objects you're trying to format.

Let's cover how that <GroupBy>node works. Typically, you'll populate it with two sub-nodes, <PropertyName> and <Label>:

```
<GroupBy>
 <PropertyName>Myproperty</PropertyName>
 <Label>My Prop</Label>
</GroupBy>
```

Now, when you select this view, PowerShell generates a new header with the label "My Prop" each time it encounters a new value for the MyProperty property. Grouping objects in this fashion isn't used a lot, though, so let's get back to our basic, in-progress format:

```
<Configuration>
 <ViewDefinitions>
   <View>
     <Name>MyView</Name>
     <ViewSelectedBy><TypeName></TypeName></ViewSelectedBy>
     <GroupBy></GroupBy>
   </View>
 </ViewDefinitions>
</Configuration>
```

From here, you have to decide if you want to make a list, wide, table, or custom view. We'll cover each of these views individually, in increasing order of complexity, but we'll start with the above basic template as our starting point for each. For all of our examples, we'll be using the System.Diagnostics.Process class, creating a custom view for objects of the Process type.

Wide Views

A wide view is probably the easiest to create, primarily because wide views use only a single object property—they're just not that complex. Here's a complete view:

```
<Configuration>
 <ViewDefinitions>
   <View>
     <Name>MyView</Name>
     <ViewSelectedBy><TypeName>System.Diagnostics.Process</TypeName></ViewSelectedBy>
     <WideControl>
        <WideEntries>
           <WideEntry>
              <WideItem>
                 <PropertyName>Name</PropertyName>
              </WideItem>
           </WideEntry>
        </WideEntries>
     </WideControl>
   </View>
 </ViewDefinitions>
</Configuration>
```

Notice that we've filled in the <ViewSelectedBy> section with a .NET Framework type name to which this view will apply. We've added a <WideControl> section, which includes a single <WideEntries> section. Within that, you're permitted one <WideEntry> section, which may contain a single <WideItem> tag. That tag includes the property name you want included in the view—just one property. This may seem like overkill to just display one property, but it's the same basic structure that the other types of views use, so a lot of the excess is just to maintain the structural consistency that XML requires.

You can manually select this view by running:

```
PS C:\> get-process | format-wide -view MyView
```

There's one alternative you can perform with a <WideItem> tag: Rather than containing a <PropertyName> tag, it can instead contain a <ScriptBlock> tag. For example, suppose we wanted all our process names displayed in uppercase:

```
<WideItem>
    <ScriptBlock>$_.Name.ToUpper()</ScriptBlock>
</WideItem>
```

We've used the special **$_** variable, which represents the current object, to access the Name property. Because the Name property is a string, it has a **ToUpper()** method. Thus, our wide view will display all process names in all uppercase characters.

List Views

List views are only slightly more complicated than wide views, because list views also display properties without a lot of extra formatting. Essentially, a list view is identical to a wide view, except that you can have multiple items—that is, properties or script blocks. Here's an example list view:

```
<Configuration>
 <ViewDefinitions>
   <View>
     <Name>MyView</Name>
     <ViewSelectedBy><TypeName>System.Diagnostics.Process</TypeName></ViewSelectedBy>
     <ListControl>
```

```
        <ListEntries>
            <ListEntry>
              <ListItems>
              <ListItem>
                  <Label>Name</Label>
                  <PropertyName>Name</PropertyName>
              </ListItem>
              <ListItem>
                  <Label>Process ID</Label>
                  <PropertyName>ID</PropertyName>
              </ListItem>
              <ListItem>
                  <Label>CPU Used</Label>
                  <PropertyName>CPU</PropertyName>
              </ListItem>
              </ListItems>
            </ListEntry>
        </ListEntries>
      </ListControl>
    </View>
 </ViewDefinitions>
</Configuration>
```

Also notice that each <ListItem> tag can have an additional <Label>tag. The <Label> tag is the text displayed next to the actual property value. The <PropertyName> tag, as in a wide view, is the property to display. As with a wide view, you can also substitute a <ScriptBlock> tag for a <PropertyName> tag; when you do so, you still provide a <Label> tag that PowerShell uses to label whatever the script block outputs.

You can manually select this view by running:

```
PS C:\> get-process | format-list -view MyView
```

....
Caution!
We're just using these views as examples; generally speaking, you wouldn't include two views with the same name in the same format file. It's actually not a problem to have two views with the same name, provided they're different layouts (e.g., wide and list), because PowerShell can distinguish them by the layout type. However, if you have two views that use the same layout and have the same name, you'll get unexpected results when trying to use that formatting file.

Table Views

Table views are incrementally more complex than a list view. Like a list view, you can define multiple properties to display (one per column). However, you must define the table's header—the first row, which displays labels for each column—in a separate section. Here's the first part of our example:

```
<Configuration>
 <ViewDefinitions>
   <View>
     <Name>MyView</Name>
     <ViewSelectedBy><TypeName>System.Diagnostics.Process</TypeName></ViewSelectedBy>
     <TableControl>
       <TableHeaders>
       <TableColumnHeader>
```

```
        <Label>Name</Label>
        <Width>20</Width>
        <Alignment>Left</Alignment>
      </TableColumnHeader>
      <TableColumnHeader>
        <Label>Process ID</Label>
        <Width>10</Width>
        <Alignment>Center</Alignment>
      </TableColumnHeader>
      <TableColumnHeader>
        <Label>CPU(s)</Label>
        <Width>4</Width>
        <Alignment>Right</Alignment>
      </TableColumnHeader>
    </TableHeaders>
  </TableControl>
 </View>
 </ViewDefinitions>
</Configuration>
```

As you can see, all we've done here is define the <TableControl> tag and add the <TableHeaders> section. Within it, we have three <TableColumnHeader> sections, one for each column defined. For each column, we define the text for the <Label> tag, the <Width> tag to define the desired width of the column, and the <Alignment> tag to define the column's alignment, which may be Left, Center, or Right. You need to keep track of the order in which you define the columns: If you define too many to fit on a user's screen, PowerShell will only display as many columns as it can in the order they're provided in this view. Also, your table *row* entries, which define the data shown in the table's rows, must occur in the same order as the table header, or the output won't make any sense.

We'll continue by adding the table row information:

```
<Configuration>
 <ViewDefinitions>
   <View>
     <Name>MyView</Name>
     <ViewSelectedBy><TypeName>System.Diagnostics.Process</TypeName></ViewSelectedBy>
     <TableControl>
       <TableHeaders>
        <TableColumnHeader>
          <Label>Name</Label>
          <Width>20</Width>
          <Alignment>Left</Alignment>
        </TableColumnHeader>
        <TableColumnHeader>
          <Label>Process ID</Label>
          <Width>10</Width>
          <Alignment>Center</Alignment>
        </TableColumnHeader>
        <TableColumnHeader>
          <Label>CPU(s)</Label>
          <Width>4</Width>
          <Alignment>Right</Alignment>
        </TableColumnHeader>
       </TableHeaders>
       <TableRowEntries>
        <TableRowEntry>
          <TableColumnItems>
           <TableColumnItem>
             <PropertyName>Name</PropertyName>
           </TableColumnItem>
           <TableColumnItem>
```

```
        <PropertyName>ID</PropertyName>
      </TableColumnItem>
      <TableColumnItem>
        <PropertyName>CPU</PropertyName>
      </TableColumnItem>
      </TableColumnItems>
    </TableRowEntry>
   </TableRowEntries>
  </TableControl>
 </View>
 </ViewDefinitions>
</Configuration>
```

We've added the <TableRowEntries> element, which includes a single <TableRowEntry> node. Within that is a single <TableColumnItems> element, containing one <TableColumnItem> tag for each column defined in the header. The <TableColumnItem> elements contain either a <PropertyName> tag or a <ScriptBlock> tag, which work exactly as they did in the wide and list views.

....

Remember!
Our example isn't including a <GroupBy> section, but it could—refer to our earlier discussion on the <GroupBy> element for information.

You can manually select this view by running:

```
PS C:\> get-process | format-table -view MyView
```

Custom Views

Custom views are a completely different beast, and they're much more complicated. They're made more complicated than necessary, really, by the fact that (as of this writing) the PowerShell SDK documentation doesn't address them, and PowerShell doesn't really ship with any examples. We'll do our best to de-mystify them for you here. They start off simply enough:

```
<Configuration>
 <ViewDefinitions>
   <View>
     <Name>MyView</Name>
     <ViewSelectedBy><TypeName>System.Diagnostics.Process</TypeName></ViewSelectedBy>
     <CustomControl>
       <CustomEntries>
       </CustomEntries>
     </CustomControl>
   </View>
 </ViewDefinitions>
</Configuration>
```

This is enough like the pattern of the other three view types that you can probably figure out what comes next: Within the <CustomEntries> section, we'll create <CustomEntry> elements that define our view. Within the <CustomEntry> nodes will be <CustomItem> elements that actually determine what gets displayed. You're right: That's what'll happen. It's what goes *inside* those <CustomItem> sections where it gets more complicated.

Here's a simple custom format. Really, this isn't any more complicated than a wide view, because this custom format is simply displaying the names of the Process objects. You'll notice that it takes more XML to get this result: For example, the <CustomItem> element has an <ExpressionBinding> sub-element that contains the familiar <PropertyName> tag. As with the other views we've covered, that <PropertyName> tag could also have been a <Scriptblock> tag:

```
<Configuration>
 <ViewDefinitions>
   <View>
     <Name>MyView</Name>
     <ViewSelectedBy>
        <TypeName>System.Diagnostics.Process</TypeName>
     </ViewSelectedBy>
     <CustomControl>
       <CustomEntries>
        <CustomEntry>
         <CustomItem>
           <ExpressionBinding>
             <PropertyName>Name</PropertyName>
           </ExpressionBinding>
         </CustomItem>
        </CustomEntry>
       </CustomEntries>
     </CustomControl>
   </View>
 </ViewDefinitions>
</Configuration>
```

Here's a slightly more complicated version: We've changed the <CustomItem> element to include a <Frame> tag, with the <LeftIndent> tag set to 4. This will "draw" an invisible "box" around our results, and indent the entire box by four characters. Within the <Frame> tag is another <CustomItem> element, this time with our <Scriptblock> tag and a <NewLine /> tag. The <NewLine /> tag places a blank space after each object that's output in our view. To save space, we're only including the <CustomControl> section of the XML—nothing else has changed:

```
    <CustomControl>
      <CustomEntries>
       <CustomEntry>
        <CustomItem>
          <Frame>
            <LeftIndent>4</LeftIndent>
            <CustomItem>
                <ExpressionBinding>
                  <Scriptblock>$_.Name.ToUpper()</Scriptblock>
                </ExpressionBinding>
                <NewLine />
            </CustomItem>
          </Frame>
        </CustomItem>
       </CustomEntry>
      </CustomEntries>
    </CustomControl>
```

Here's a further evolution. This time, we've added a <Text> tag to the custom item, creating a "Process:" label. We've also added an <ItemSelectionCondition> tag to the <ExpressionBinding> tag. Only processes with a Handles property greater than 50 will be selected to have their name displayed:

```
<CustomControl>
  <CustomEntries>
   <CustomEntry>
    <CustomItem>
      <Frame>
        <LeftIndent>4</LeftIndent>
         <CustomItem>
           <Text>Process: </Text>
            <ExpressionBinding>
              <ItemSelectionCondition>
                <Scriptblock>$_.Handles -gt 50</Scriptblock>
              </ItemSelectionCondition>
              <Scriptblock>$_.Name.ToUpper()</Scriptblock>
            </ExpressionBinding>
         </CustomItem>
      </Frame>
    </CustomItem>
   </CustomEntry>
  </CustomEntries>
</CustomControl>
```

Here's what a portion of the output looks like:

```
Process: ACPRFMGRSVC
Process: ACSVC
Process: ACTRAY
Process: ACWLICON
Process: AUDIODG
Process: AWAYSCH
Process: BTTRAY
Process: CSRSS
Process: CSRSS
Process: CSSAUTH
Process: DLLHOST
Process: DLLHOST
Process: DWM
Process: EXPLORER
Process: EZEJMNAP
Process: HKCMD
Process:
Process:
```

You'll notice that PowerShell does not display processes that don't meet the criteria, although the Process: label is still displayed, because that label is defined apart from the <ItemSelectionCondition> tag. So, PowerShell displays the label, regardless, using this view.

Our next step is to remove the <ItemSelectionCondition> tag, and to add some additional <Text> elements and a new <ExpressionBinding> tag. Now, we're displaying each process's ID in parentheses, next to the process name:

```
<CustomControl>
  <CustomEntries>
   <CustomEntry>
    <CustomItem>
      <Frame>
        <LeftIndent>4</LeftIndent>
         <CustomItem>
           <Text>Process: </Text>
           <ExpressionBinding>
             <Scriptblock>$_.Name.ToUpper()</Scriptblock>
```

```
      </ExpressionBinding>
      <Text> (ID: </Text>
      <ExpressionBinding>
        <PropertyName>ID</PropertyName>
      </ExpressionBinding>
      <Text>)</Text>
    </CustomItem>
  </Frame>
  </CustomItem>
  </CustomEntry>
  </CustomEntries>
  </CustomControl>
```

Here's a snippet of the output:

```
Process: ACPRFMGRSVC (ID: 1412)
Process: ACSVC (ID: 2436)
Process: ACTRAY (ID: 1488)
Process: ACWLICON (ID: 2696)
Process: AUDIODG (ID: 1236)
Process: AWAYSCH (ID: 4052)
Process: BTTRAY (ID: 680)
```

Combined with the <NewLine /> tag we used earlier, you can begin to see how fairly complicated formatting is possible. One last iteration:

```
<CustomControl>
  <CustomEntries>
   <CustomEntry>
    <CustomItem>
      <Frame>
        <LeftIndent>4</LeftIndent>
        <CustomItem>
          <Text>Process: </Text>
          <ExpressionBinding>
            <Scriptblock>$_.Name.ToUpper()</Scriptblock>
          </ExpressionBinding>
          <Text> (ID: </Text>
          <ExpressionBinding>
            <PropertyName>ID</PropertyName>
          </ExpressionBinding>
          <Text>)</Text>
        </CustomItem>
      </Frame>
      <Frame>
        <CustomItem>
        <NewLine />
        <ExpressionBinding>
          <Scriptblock>"Handles: " + $_.Handles '
            + " / CPU(s): " + $_.CPU</Scriptblock>
        </ExpressionBinding>
        <NewLine />
        </CustomItem>
      </Frame>
    </CustomItem>
   </CustomEntry>
  </CustomEntries>
</CustomControl>
```

This time, we've added an all-new <Frame> tag to contain new information. It starts with a <NewLine

/> tag, and then displays a text message including the number of handles and the CPU seconds measurement for the process. It concludes with another <NewLine /> tag. Examine this, and then examine a sample of its output:

```
Process: ACPRFMGRSVC (ID: 1412)
Handles: 135 / CPU(s): 0.1404009

Process: ACSVC (ID: 2436)
Handles: 257 / CPU(s): 0.624004

Process: ACTRAY (ID: 1488)
Handles: 85 / CPU(s): 0.1092007

Process: ACWLICON (ID: 2696)
Handles: 82 / CPU(s): 0.1404009
```

Custom views are certainly complex, and, trust us, we've barely scratched the surface of what they can do. However, this should get you started on creating your own custom formats. Why bother? One reason we can think of is to create output that's more suitable for management or auditing reports.

By the way, we generated all of this output after importing our format file by using the **Update-FormatData** cmdlet (of course), and then running:

```
PS C:\> get-process | format-custom -view myview
```

Where are custom views practically useful? We've mentioned elsewhere that PowerShell displays and formats all its built-in help using custom views; anytime you're dealing with especially complex data that needs to be laid out in a particular way—not necessarily a list or a table—then a custom view might make sense. Typically, however, administrators are usually working with several objects—such as processes, services, event logs, and so forth—and any time you've got a collection of objects, a list or a table is usually easier to make and presents the information in a way that's easier to use.

Importing Your Format

When you're ready with a working format, move the .ps1xml file to its permanent location. Personally, we like keeping these files in our personal documents folder ("My Documents" on Windows XP, or "Documents" on Windows Vista), so that our files "follow" us if we're using a roaming profile. We don't recommend storing your files in PowerShell's installation folder, since there's always a possibility that your files will be overwritten by some future update.

Before you can start using your new views, you have to import them into the shell. You'll first need to decide if you want your new formats to come *before* or *after* PowerShell's built-in formats. Remember, when PowerShell isn't given a specific view by name, it goes looking for one that matches the object type it's working with. The first matching view it comes across is the one it uses, so if your views are loaded first, then they'll become the defaults for your data types. If your views are loaded last, then they'll be available on demand, but they won't become the default views (unless PowerShell defines no other views for the object types you've selected).

- To load your files before PowerShell's, run **Update-FormatData -prependPath** *filepath*.

- To load your files after PowerShell's, run **Update-FormatData -appendPath** *filepath*.

Running the **Update-FormatData** cmdlet *registers* the view or views you've defined in the specified file and makes those views available to PowerShell's Format cmdlets.

....

Oops...

If you made a mistake in your format XML, PowerShell will display any errors when it tries to load the file. After fixing any problems, you'll need to close and re-open PowerShell before you can try to re-load your format file.

Unless you add these cmdlets to your profile, you'll need to run them each time you open a new PowerShell session; PowerShell does not persist this information in any other way. Also, keep in mind that you can digitally sign .format.ps1xml files just like .ps1 files; if your shell's Execution Policy requires a signature for scripts, then you'll need to sign your format files, also.

....

Warning

As you read this chapter, you might be tempted to simply modify the format files that shipped with PowerShell. Don't. These files are digitally signed by Microsoft. If you modify them you will break the signature, and unless you're Microsoft, you won't have any way to resign them. Also, when a new version of the file ships from Microsoft, your changes will be lost.

Formatting Rules

PowerShell's formatting rules are a bit complicated, so it's worth reviewing them. When PowerShell needs to format objects, it follows these rules and uses the *first rule that matches*. Also note that these decisions are all made by examining only the first object in the pipeline—all objects are formatted according to the decision applied to the first object:

- If you haven't specified a table, list, wide, or custom format (by using one of the Format cmdlets), then PowerShell will look to see if a view has been registered for the data type of the pipeline object. If at least one view has been registered, PowerShell will use the first one it finds—selecting table, list, wide, or custom based on whatever the view uses.

- If you used a Format cmdlet to specify a list, table, wide, or custom format, but didn't specify a particular view by name, PowerShell will grab the first registered view for the object's type that matches the layout you specified. If no registered view exists, PowerShell will "fake it" and do the best job it can to construct the appropriately formatted output for you, using the "default" properties defined for the object ("default" properties are defined in PowerShell's Types.ps1xml file).

- If you specified a list, table, wide, or custom format, *and* specified a particular view (by using the **-view** parameter of the Format cmdlet), PowerShell will look for that view. However, it'll only be able to use it if the view uses the same layout—list, table, wide, or custom. If the view you specify doesn't match the layout you specified, you'll receive an error.

- If there is no registered view for the type of object in the pipeline, and you didn't specify any formatting, PowerShell will use a table if the object has fewer than five properties. Otherwise, it'll use a list. PowerShell won't automatically select a wide or custom format under these circumstances. If PowerShell decides to use a list, it will—by default—only display properties that are marked as "default properties" for that object type in PowerShell's Types.ps1xml file. If that object type isn't defined in Types.ps1xml, or if no properties are marked as "defaults," then PowerShell will display *all* of the properties in a list.

Chapter 43
Windows Server 2008 R2 PowerShell Features

Windows Server 2008 R2 ships with Windows PowerShell v2.0. It also includes a number of new "solutions" for managing different Server 2008 R2 features or roles. A complete discussion is beyond the scope of this book, but we thought you'd be interested in a peek at what is possible. Consider this more of a tasting as opposed to a full entrée.

We've briefly covered the PowerShell Active Directory provider elsewhere in the book but here are some roles you are likely to use and how you might manage them with PowerShell.

Server Manager

While the graphical Server Manager tool is terrific, there may be times when you prefer to work from the command line. Windows Server 2008 R2 includes a command-line version of Server Manager called ServerManagerCMD.exe. However you can achieve the same functionality with PowerShell by loading the ServerManager module:

```
PS C:\> Import-Module ServerManager
PS C:\> gcm -mod Servermanager | select name

Name
----
Add-WindowsFeature
Get-WindowsFeature
Remove-WindowsFeature
```

As you can see there are only three cmdlets. None of the cmdlets have parameters that support remote computers, but if PowerShell v2.0 is installed and configured you can always use a remote session to run these cmdlets.

Get-WindowsFeature

The **Get-WindowsFeature** cmdlet will display all features and roles, regardless of their installation status:

```
PS C:\> Get-WindowsFeature

Display Name                                             Name
------------                                             ----
[ ] Active Directory Certificate Services               AD-Certificate
    [ ] Certification Authority                          ADCS-Cert-Authority
    [ ] Certification Authority Web Enrollment           ADCS-Web-Enrollment
    [ ] Online Responder                                 ADCS-Online-Cert
    [ ] Network Device Enrollment Service                ADCS-Device-Enrollment
    [ ] Certificate Enrollment Web Service               ADCS-Enroll-Web-Svc
    [ ] Certificate Enrollment Policy Web Service        ADCS-Enroll-Web-Pol
[X] Active Directory Domain Services                     AD-Domain-Services
    [X] Active Directory Domain Controller               ADDS-Domain-Controller
    [ ] Identity Management for UNIX                     ADDS-Identity-Mgmt
        [ ] Server for Network Information Services      ADDS-NIS
        [ ] Password Synchronization                     ADDS-Password-Sync
        [ ] Administration Tools                         ADDS-IDMU-Tools
[ ] Active Directory Federation Services                 AD-Federation-Services
    [ ] Federation Service                               ADFS-Federation
    [ ] Federation Service Proxy                         ADFS-Proxy
    [ ] AD FS Web Agents                                 ADFS-Web-Agents
        [ ] Claims-aware Agent                           ADFS-Claims
        [ ] Windows Token-based Agent                    ADFS-Windows-Token
[ ] Active Directory Lightweight Directory Services      ADLDS
[ ] Active Directory Rights Management Services          ADRMS
    [ ] Active Directory Rights Management Server        ADRMS-Server
    [ ] Identity Federation Support                      ADRMS-Identity
[ ] Application Server                                   Application-Server
    [ ] .NET Framework 3.5.1                             AS-NET-Framework
    [ ] Web Server (IIS) Support                         AS-Web-Support
    [ ] COM+ Network Access                              AS-Ent-Services
    [ ] TCP Port Sharing                                 AS-TCP-Port-Sharing
    [ ] Windows Process Activation Service Support       AS-WAS-Support
        [ ] HTTP Activation                              AS-HTTP-Activation
        [ ] Message Queuing Activation                   AS-MSMQ-Activation
        [ ] TCP Activation                               AS-TCP-Activation
        [ ] Named Pipes Activation                       AS-Named-Pipes
    [ ] Distributed Transactions                         AS-Dist-Transaction
        [ ] Incoming Remote Transactions                 AS-Incoming-Trans
        [ ] Outgoing Remote Transactions                 AS-Outgoing-Trans
        [ ] WS-Atomic Transactions                       AS-WS-Atomic
[ ] DHCP Server                                          DHCP
[X] DNS Server                                           DNS
...
```

This is a textual layout of what you see in the graphical Server Manager. But even though it is formatted text, PowerShell is writing objects to the pipeline, which means you can easily filter, sort, and select:

```
PS C:\> Get-WindowsFeature  | where {$_.installed} | Sort Displayname | Select DisplayName
```

```
DisplayName
-----------
.NET Framework 3.5.1
.NET Framework 3.5.1 Features
Active Directory Administrative Center
Active Directory Domain Controller
Active Directory Domain Services
Active Directory module for Windows PowerShell
...
Windows PowerShell Integrated Scripting Environment (ISE)
Windows Server Backup
Windows Server Backup Features
XPS Viewer
```

We've truncated the output but you get the idea. These are the features and roles currently installed on this Windows Server 2008 R2 system.

Add-WindowsFeature

Adding a feature is relatively straightforward, although the hardest part may be getting the proper feature name. The **Add-WindowsFeature** cmdlet supports the **-WhatIf** parameter so we can get a sanity check before committing:

```
PS C:\> add-WindowsFeature web-server -whatif
What if: Checking if running in 'WhatIf' Mode.
What if: Performing operation "Add-WindowsFeature" on Target "[Web Server (IIS)] Management Tools".
What if: Performing operation "Add-WindowsFeature" on Target "[Web Server (IIS)] Web Server".
What if: Performing operation "Add-WindowsFeature" on Target "[Web Server (IIS)] Security".
What if: Performing operation "Add-WindowsFeature" on Target "[Web Server (IIS)] Health and Diagnostics".
What if: Performing operation "Add-WindowsFeature" on Target "[Web Server (IIS)] IIS Management Console".
What if: Performing operation "Add-WindowsFeature" on Target "[Web Server (IIS)] Performance".
What if: Performing operation "Add-WindowsFeature" on Target "[Web Server (IIS)] Common HTTP Features".
What if: Performing operation "Add-WindowsFeature" on Target "[Web Server (IIS)] Static Content Compres...
What if: Performing operation "Add-WindowsFeature" on Target "[Web Server (IIS)] Default Document".
What if: Performing operation "Add-WindowsFeature" on Target "[Web Server (IIS)] HTTP Errors".
What if: Performing operation "Add-WindowsFeature" on Target "[Web Server (IIS)] Static Content".
What if: Performing operation "Add-WindowsFeature" on Target "[Web Server (IIS)] Request Monitor".
What if: Performing operation "Add-WindowsFeature" on Target "[Web Server (IIS)] HTTP Logging".
What if: Performing operation "Add-WindowsFeature" on Target "[Web Server (IIS)] Request Filtering".
What if: Performing operation "Add-WindowsFeature" on Target "[Web Server (IIS)] Directory Browsing".
What if: This server may need to be restarted after the installation completes.

Success Restart Needed Exit Code Feature Result
------- -------------- --------- --------------
True    Maybe          Success   {}
```

That all looks good so we'll go ahead and do it for real:

```
PS C:\> add-WindowsFeature web-server

Success Restart Needed Exit Code Feature Result
------- -------------- --------- --------------
True    No             Success   {IIS Management Console, Request Monitor, ...
```

You can either install high-level roles as we've done here, or you can use the **Add-WindowsFeature** cmdlet for more fine-grained feature installations.

Remove-WindowsFeature

Removing a role or feature couldn't be any easier with the **Remove-WindowsFeature** cmdlet:

```
PS C:\> Remove-WindowsFeature XPS-Viewer

Success Restart Needed Exit Code Feature Result
------- -------------- --------- --------------
True    No             Success   {XPS Viewer}
```

Be sure to look at Help and examples for all of these cmdlets.

Server Backup

Windows Server 2008 R2 includes a Windows Server Backup feature with an option for command-line tools. If you select this option, you'll have the opportunity to use PowerShell cmdlets. These cmdlets are stored in PSSnapin, which you need to load. We'll even use these cmdlets via a remote PSSession to a server named RESEARCHDC. We'll add the snap-in and take a look at what's inside:

```
[researchdc]: PS C:\> add-pssnapin windows.serverbackup
[researchdc]: PS C:\> get-command -pssnapin windows.serverbackup | Select name

Name
----
Add-WBBackupTarget
Add-WBBareMetalRecovery
Add-WBFileSpec
Add-WBSystemState
Add-WBVolume
Get-WBBackupSet
Get-WBBackupTarget
Get-WBBareMetalRecovery
Get-WBDisk
Get-WBFileSpec
Get-WBJob
Get-WBPolicy
Get-WBSchedule
Get-WBSummary
Get-WBSystemState
Get-WBVolume
Get-WBVssBackupOptions
New-WBBackupTarget
New-WBFileSpec
New-WBPolicy
Remove-WBBackupTarget
Remove-WBBareMetalRecovery
Remove-WBFileSpec
Remove-WBPolicy
Remove-WBSystemState
Remove-WBVolume
Set-WBPolicy
Set-WBSchedule
Set-WBVssBackupOptions
Start-WBBackup
```

We'll walk through a simple backup. The cmdlets are designed around a backup policy that specifies what you want to back up, where you want to back up to, and when. We first create an empty policy, and then define the files to back up:

```
[researchdc]: PS C:\> $policy = New-WBPolicy
[researchdc]: PS C:\> $files = New-WBFileSpec -FileSpec C:\scripts\*.*
```

We add the WBFileSpec object to the policy:

```
[researchdc]: PS C:\> Add-WBFileSpec -Policy $policy -FileSpec $files
```

Use the **New-WBBackupTarget** cmdlet to define a target location. We're going to specify a file share on another server in another domain:

```
[researchdc]: PS C \>$backupLocation = New-WBBackupTarget  -NetworkPath \\mycompany-dc01\files
```

Depending on your configuration you may need to specify alternate credentials. You also add this object to the policy by using the **Add-WBBackupTarget** cmdlet:

```
[researchdc]: PS C:\> Add-WBBackupTarget -Policy $policy -Target $backupLocation
WARNING: The backed up data cannot be securely protected at this destination. Backups stored on a
remote shared folder might be accessible by other people on the network. You should only save your
backups to a location where you trust the other users who have access to the location or on a net-
work that has additional security precautions in place.
```

```
Label                 :
WBDisk                :
WBVolume              :
Path                  : \\mycompany-dc01\files
TargetType            : Network
InheritAcl            : True
PreserveExistingBackup : False
```

There is a security warning because we specified a network share, but for our demonstration purposes this is fine.

We want to take advantage of the volume shadow copy service so we'll specify that as a backup option:

```
[researchdc]: PS C:\> Set-WBVssBackupOptions -Policy $policy -VssCopyBackup
```

Here's the **$policy** variable:

```
[researchdc]: PS z:\> $policy
```

```
Schedule            :
BackupTargets       : {\\mycompany-dc01\files}
VolumesToBackup     :
FilesSpecsToBackup  : {C:\scripts\*}
FilesSpecsToExclude : {}
BMR                 : False
SystemState         : False
VssBackupOptions    : VssCopyBackup
```

We are going to run this immediately by using the **Start-WBBackup** cmdlet:

```
[researchdc]: PS C:\> Start-WBBackup -Policy $policy
Initializing the list of items to be backed up...
```

```
Creating a shadow copy of the volumes in the backup...
Creating a shadow copy of the volumes in the backup...
Creating a shadow copy of the volumes in the backup...
Preparing to run a consistency check...
Scanning the file system...
Scanning the file system...
Scanning the file system...
Scanning the file system...
Scanning the file system...
Scanning the file system...
Scanning the file system...
Scanning the file system...
Volume 1 (100%) of 1 volume(s).
The backup operation completed.
```

The **Get-WBSummary** cmdlet provides the details:

```
[researchdc]: PS C:\> get-wbsummary


NextBackupTime                    : 1/1/0001 12:00:00 AM
NumberOfVersions                  : 1
LastSuccessfulBackupTime          : 9/21/2009 3:03:34 PM
LastSuccessfulBackupTargetPath    : \\mycompany-dc01\files
LastSuccessfulBackupTargetLabel   :
LastBackupTime                    : 9/21/2009 3:03:34 PM
LastBackupTarget                  : \\mycompany-dc01\files
DetailedMessage                   :
LastBackupResultHR                : 0
LastBackupResultDetailedHR        : 0
CurrentOperationStatus            : NoOperationInProgress
```

Now, the bad news: There are no PowerShell cmdlets for restoring data. You'll either need to use the WBADMIN.EXE command-line tool or the Windows Server Backup management console.

IIS

You can now manage most of IIS 7 on Windows Server 2008 R2 from a command prompt with PowerShell. As you can imagine, this is a very extensive topic that we can't cover in detail here. But we want you to know what to expect and hopefully pique your curiosity to discover more.

As with other new PowerShell features, after we've installed the Web Server role we need to import the WebAdministration module:

```
PS C:\> import-module WebAdministration
PS C:\> gcm -mod webAdministration | select Name

Name
----
Add-WebConfiguration
Add-WebConfigurationLock
Add-WebConfigurationProperty
Backup-WebConfiguration
Begin-WebCommitDelay
Clear-WebConfiguration
Clear-WebRequestTracingSettings
ConvertTo-WebApplication
Disable-WebGlobalModule
Disable-WebRequestTracing
```

```
Enable-WebGlobalModule
Enable-WebRequestTracing
...
Start-Website
Stop-WebAppPool
Stop-WebCommitDelay
Stop-WebItem
Stop-Website
```

As before, we've truncated the output, but there are cmdlets for just about anything you would need to accomplish.

Get-WebSite

Our Web server has just been installed which means it only has the default site which we can see using the **Get-WebSite** cmdlet:

```
PS C:\> get-website | select *


name                         : Default Web Site
id                           : 1
serverAutoStart              : True
state                        : Started
bindings                     : Microsoft.IIs.PowerShell.Framework.ConfigurationElement
limits                       : Microsoft.IIs.PowerShell.Framework.ConfigurationElement
logFile                      : Microsoft.IIs.PowerShell.Framework.ConfigurationElement
traceFailedRequestsLogging   : Microsoft.IIs.PowerShell.Framework.ConfigurationElement
applicationDefaults          : Microsoft.IIs.PowerShell.Framework.ConfigurationElement
virtualDirectoryDefaults     : Microsoft.IIs.PowerShell.Framework.ConfigurationElement
ftpServer                    : Microsoft.IIs.PowerShell.Framework.ConfigurationElement
Collection                   : {Microsoft.IIs.PowerShell.Framework.ConfigurationElement}
applicationPool              : DefaultAppPool
enabledProtocols             : http
physicalPath                 : %SystemDrive%\inetpub\wwwroot
userName                     :
password                     :
Attributes                   : {name, id, serverAutoStart, state}
ChildElements                : {bindings, limits, logFile, traceFailedRequestsLogging...}
ElementTagName               : site
Methods                      : {Start, Stop}
Schema                       : Microsoft.IIs.PowerShell.Framework.ConfigurationElementSchema
```

What else can you do with a Web site? We know that "website" is the cmdlet noun so we'll use **Get-Command** to find out:

```
[researchdc]: PS C:\> get-command -noun website | select name

Name
----
Get-Website
New-Website
Remove-Website
Start-Website
Stop-Website


PS C:\> stop-website   "default Web Site"
PS C:\> get-website
```

```
Name                ID   State   Physical Path               Bindings
----                --   -----   -------------               --------
Default Web Site 1       Stopped %SystemDrive%\inetpub\wwwroot http *:80:


PS C:\> start-website "default web site" -passthru

Name                ID   State   Physical Path               Bindings
----                --   -----   -------------               --------
Default Web Site 1       Started %SystemDrive%\inetpub\wwwroot http *:80:
```

We very easily stopped and re-started the default Web site. We used the **-passthru** variable on the last command to force the **Get-WebSite** cmdlet to write an object to the pipeline so we could verify that the site was back up and running.

New-WebSite

Adding a new Web site certainly seems faster in PowerShell. As long as the folder specified for the physical path exists, all you need is a simple command calling the **New-WebSite** cmdlet:

```
PS C:\> new-website -name "PowerShell TFM" -hostheader "PowerShellTFM" '
>> -PhysicalPath "$env:systemdrive\inetpub\wwwroot\pshtfm"
>>

Name                ID   State   Physical Path               Bindings
----                --   -----   -------------               --------
PowerShell TFM      2    Started C:\inetpub\wwwroot\pshtfm    http *:80:PowerShellTFM
```

How hard was that?

Managing Web Sites

Let's imagine we goofed when we created the PowerShellTFM site and it was supposed to be on port 8090. We can see the current Web bindings by using the **Get-WebBinding** cmdlet:

```
PS C:\> get-webbinding "PowerShell TFM"

protocol                                         bindingInformation
--------                                         ------------------
http                                             *:80:PowerShellTFM
```

By this point in the book you should be able to make a pretty good guess about what cmdlet to use to set a new binding:

```
PS C:\> set-webbinding -name "PowerShell TFM" -BindingInformation "*:80:*" -PropertyName Port
-Value 8090
PS C:\> get-webbinding -Name "PowerShell TFM" | select *


protocol             : http
bindingInformation   : *:8090:*
isDsMapperEnabled    : False
certificateHash      :
certificateStoreName :
ItemXPath            : /system.applicationHost/sites/site[@name='PowerShell TFM' and @id='2']
```

```
Attributes          : {protocol, bindingInformation, isDsMapperEnabled, certificateHash...}
ChildElements       : {}
ElementTagName      : binding
Methods             : {EnableDsMapper, DisableDsMapper, AddSslCertificate, RemoveSslCertificate}
Schema              : Microsoft.IIs.PowerShell.Framework.ConfigurationElementSchema
```

Did you correctly "guess" the **Set-WebBinding** cmdlet? We had to specify the binding to modify, a property and value.

IIS PSDrive

The WebAdministration module also installs a PSDrive called IIS. You can navigate your Web server as if it were a file system:

```
PS C:\> iis:
PS IIS:\> dir

Name
----
AppPools
Sites
SslBindings


PS IIS:\> cd sites
PS IIS:\sites> dir

Name               ID   State     Physical Path                 Bindings
----               --   -----     -------------                 --------
Default Web Site   1    Started   %SystemDrive%\inetpub\wwwroot http *:80:
PowerShell TFM     2    Started   C:\inetpub\wwwroot\pshtfm      http *:8090:*

PS IIS:\sites> cd '.\PowerShell TFM'
```

This isn't exactly like a file system. If you've used the registry PSDrive you'll see some similarities. For example, we need to use the **Get-Item** cmdlet:

```
PS IIS:\Sites\PowerShell TFM> get-item . | select *


PSPath                   : WebAdministration::\\RESEARCHDC\Sites\PowerShell TFM
PSParentPath             : WebAdministration::\\RESEARCHDC\Sites
PSChildName              : PowerShell TFM
PSDrive                  : IIS
PSProvider               : WebAdministration
PSIsContainer            : True
name                     : PowerShell TFM
id                       : 2
serverAutoStart          : True
state                    : Started
bindings                 : Microsoft.IIs.PowerShell.Framework.ConfigurationElement
limits                   : Microsoft.IIs.PowerShell.Framework.ConfigurationElement
logFile                  : Microsoft.IIs.PowerShell.Framework.ConfigurationElement
traceFailedRequestsLogging : Microsoft.IIs.PowerShell.Framework.ConfigurationElement
applicationDefaults      : Microsoft.IIs.PowerShell.Framework.ConfigurationElement
virtualDirectoryDefaults : Microsoft.IIs.PowerShell.Framework.ConfigurationElement
ftpServer                : Microsoft.IIs.PowerShell.Framework.ConfigurationElement
Collection               : {Microsoft.IIs.PowerShell.Framework.ConfigurationElement}
applicationPool          : DefaultAppPool
```

```
enabledProtocols            : http
physicalPath                : C:\inetpub\wwwroot\pshtfm
userName                    :
password                    :
ItemXPath                   : /system.applicationHost/sites/site[@name='PowerShell TFM' and @
id='2']
Attributes                  : {name, id, serverAutoStart, state}
ChildElements               : {bindings, limits, logFile, traceFailedRequestsLogging...}
ElementTagName              : site
Methods                     : {Start, Stop}
Schema                      : Microsoft.IIs.PowerShell.Framework.ConfigurationElementSchema
```

Or use the **Get-ItemProperty** cmdlet to retrieve a specific property:

```
PS IIS:\Sites\PowerShell TFM> (get-itemproperty -path . -name serverAutostart).value
False

PS IIS:\Sites\PowerShell TFM> (get-item .).limits


maxBandwidth      : 4294967295
maxConnections    : 4294967295
connectionTimeout : 00:02:00
Attributes        : {maxBandwidth, maxConnections, connectionTimeout}
ChildElements     : {}
ElementTagName    : limits
Methods           :
Schema            : Microsoft.IIs.PowerShell.Framework.ConfigurationElementSchema
```

To modify a Web site property, use the **Set-ItemProperty** cmdlet (which has an alias of sp) with the PSDrive provider. We can verify the change by calling **Get-ItemProperty**:

```
PS IIS:\Sites\PowerShell TFM> sp . -name limits.connectiontimeout -Value (new-timespan -min 1)
PS IIS:\Sites\PowerShell TFM> gp . limits.connectiontimeout.value


Days              : 0
Hours             : 0
Minutes           : 1
Seconds           : 0
Milliseconds      : 0
Ticks             : 600000000
TotalDays         : 0.000694444444444444
TotalHours        : 0.0166666666666667
TotalMinutes      : 1
TotalSeconds      : 60
TotalMilliseconds : 60000
```

We wanted to change the timeout value from 2 minutes to 1 minute. The value is stored as a TimeSpan object, which is why we used the **New-TimeSpan** cmdlet.

Virtual Directories

Use the **New-WebVirtualDirectory** cmdlet to create a new virtual directory. The specified physical path must already exist:

```
PS C:\> New-WebVirtualDirectory -site "PowerShell TFM" -name Files -PhysicalPath c:\scripts
```

```
Name                                             PhysicalPath
----                                             ------------
Files                                            c:\scripts
```

The **Get-WebVirtualDirectory** cmdlet naturally retrieves virtual directories:

```
PS C:\> Get-WebVirtualDirectory

Name            Physical Path
----            -------------
Files           c:\scripts
```

There's a lot of useful information here, which you can see by piping to the **Select-Object** cmdlet:

```
PS C:\> Get-WebVirtualDirectory | select *


path                   : /Files
physicalPath           : c:\scripts
userName               :
password               :
logonMethod            : ClearText
allowSubDirConfig      : True
PSPath                 : MACHINE/WEBROOT/APPHOST
Location               :
ConfigurationPathType  : Location
ItemXPath              : /system.applicationHost/sites/site[@name='PowerShell TFM' and
                         @id='2']/application[@path='/']/virtualDirectory[@path='/Files']
Attributes             : {path, physicalPath, userName, password...}
ChildElements          : {}
ElementTagName         : virtualDirectory
Methods                :
Schema                 : Microsoft.IIs.PowerShell.Framework.ConfigurationElementSchema
```

You can even see this virtual directory in the IIS PSDrive:

```
PS C:\> dir 'IIS:\Sites\PowerShell TFM'

Name                                             PhysicalPath
----                                             ------------
Files                                            c:\scripts
```

Remove-WebSite

Getting rid of a Web site is dangerously easy to do by using the **Remove-WebSite** cmdlet:

```
PS C:\> remove-website "PowerShell TFM"
```

We urge you to use the **–WhatIf** parameter first as a sanity check.

There's much, much more of IIS that you can manage with PowerShell and we expect to see future improvements and enhancements from the IIS team at Microsoft.

Remote Desktop Services

In Windows Server 2008 R2, Terminal Services has been rebranded as Remote Desktop Services or RDS for short. PowerShell support has been added and here's a quick peek at what you can look forward to.

The RDS PSDrive

The Remote Desktop Services team at Microsoft took a different approach when it came to offering PowerShell support. Instead of providing cmdlets, they leverage a PSDrive. Actually, there are only a few cmdlets:

```
PS C:\> import-module RemoteDesktopServices
PS C:\> get-command -module RemoteDesktopServices | Select Name

Name
----
Clear-PersonalVirtualDesktop
Get-VirtualDesktop
Set-PersonalVirtualDesktop

PS C:\> Get-VirtualDesktop -user research\rbiv

Name                          AssignedTo        Host
----                          ----------        ----
Vdi01.research.mycompany.local   RESEARCH\rbiv    r2-011.research.mycompany.local
```

However, to accomplish anything else requires use of the RDS PSDrive:

```
PS C:\> cd RDS:
PS RDS:\> dir


    Directory: RDS:


Name                  Type       CurrentValue  GP  PermissibleValues PermissibleOperations
----                  ----       ------------  --  ----------------- ---------------------
RDSConfiguration      Container                -                     Get-Item, Get-ChildItem
GatewayServer         Container                -                     Get-Item, Get-ChildItem
RDSFarms              Container                -                     Get-Item, Get-ChildItem
RemoteApp             Container                -                     Get-Item, Get-ChildItem
ConnectionBroker      Container                -                     Get-Item, Get-ChildItem
```

For example, to manage the configuration, set your location to the RDSConfiguration "folder":

```
PS RDS:\RDSConfiguration> dir


    Directory: RDS:\RDSConfiguration


Name                      Type       CurrentValue  GP  PermissibleValues PermissibleOperations
----                      ----       ------------  --  ----------------- ---------------------
Connections               Container                -                     Get-Item, Get-ChildItem, ...
LicensingSettings         Container                -                     Get-Item, Get-ChildItem
ConnectionBrokerSettings  Container                -                     Get-Item, Get-ChildItem
TempFolderSettings        Container                -                     Get-Item, Get-ChildItem
```

ProfileSettings	Container		-			Get-Item, Get-ChildItem
SessionSettings	Container		-			Get-Item, Get-ChildItem
VirtualIPSettings	Container		-			Get-Item, Get-ChildItem
UserLogonMode	Integer	0	-	0, 1, 2		Get-Item, Set-Item
RDSessionHostServerMode	Integer	1	-	0, 1		Get-Item
TimeZoneRedirection	Integer	0	No	0, 1		Get-Item, Set-Item

Let's change the maximum number of connections. First, here's the current setting:

```
PS RDS:\RDSConfiguration\connections\RDP-Tcp> dir .\MaximumConnections


    Directory: RDS:\RDSConfiguration\connections\RDP-Tcp


Name                Type       CurrentValue   GP   PermissibleValues  PermissibleOperations
----                ----       ------------   --   -----------------  ---------------------
MaximumConnections  Integer    4294967295     No                      Get-Item, Set-Item
```

The PermissibleOperations column provides a clue as to how we should proceed:

```
PS RDS:\RDSConfiguration\connections\RDP-Tcp> set-item .\MaximumConnections 1024
```

If we check again, we see the new value:

```
PS RDS:\RDSConfiguration\connections\RDP-Tcp> dir .\MaximumConnections


    Directory: RDS:\RDSConfiguration\connections\RDP-Tcp


Name                Type      CurrentValue   GP   PermissibleValues  PermissibleOperations
----                ----      ------------   --   -----------------  ---------------------
MaximumConnections  Integer   1024           No                      Get-Item, Set-Item
```

It is pretty easy to see all configuration values with a single PowerShell expression:

```
PS RDS:\RDSConfiguration> dir -rec | where {$_.type -notmatch "container"} | select
Name,CurrentValue

Name                                       CurrentValue
----                                       ------------
UserLogonMode                              0
RDSessionHostServerMode                    1
TimeZoneRedirection                        0
ConnectionStatus                           1
Type                                       Microsoft RDP 6.1
Transport                                  tcp
Comment
MaximumConnections                         1024
ClientWallPaper                            0
...
```

Or perhaps you'd like to see the currently installed published applications? Change to the RemoteApp "folder" and look at the RemoteAppPrograms "sub-folder":

```
PS RDS:\remoteapp> dir .\RemoteAppPrograms | Select Name

Name
----
calc
mspaint
powershell
powershell (1)
powershell (2)
PowerShell_ISE
PowerShell_ISE (1)
SnippingTool
wmplayer
wordpad
```

Each application has its own folder with its own configuration settings. Here are the values for the published application "PowerShell":

```
PS RDS:\remoteapp\remoteappprograms\powershell> dir | Select Name,CurrentValue |

Name                CurrentValue
----                ------------
DisplayName         Windows PowerShell
Path                %SYSTEMDRIVE%\WINDOWS\system32\WindowsPowerShell\v1.0\powershell.exe
PathExists          1
IconPath            %SystemRoot%\system32\WindowsPowerShell\v1.0\powershell.exe
IconIndex           0
IconContents        0,0,1,0,4,0,48,48,0,0,1,0,32,0,168,37,0,0,70,0,0,0,32,32,0,0,1,0,32,0,168,16,0,0,23...
CommandLineSetting  0
RequiredCommandLine
ShowInWebAccess     1
RDPFileContents     redirectclipboard:i:1...
UserAssignment
```

Perhaps you'd like to publish a new application. All we need to do is use the **New-Item** cmdlet to create a new entry in the RDS PSDrive:

```
 PS RDS:\> New-item .\RemoteApp\RemoteAppPrograms -Name "PrimalPad" '
>> -ApplicationPath "c:\windows\primalpad.exe" -ApplicationName "PrimalPad" -ShowInWebAccess 1
>>

PS RDS:\> dir remoteapp\remoteappprograms\primalpad | Select Name,CurrentValue

Name                                CurrentValue
----                                ------------
DisplayName                         PrimalPad
Path                                c:\windows\primalpad.exe
PathExists                          1
IconPath                            c:\windows\primalpad.exe
IconIndex                           0
IconContents                        0,0,1,0,9,0,128,128,0,0,1,0,32,0,40,...
CommandLineSetting                  0
RequiredCommandLine
ShowInWebAccess                     1
RDPFileContents                     redirectclipboard:i:1...
UserAssignment
```

We can now see the published application in our Web browser.

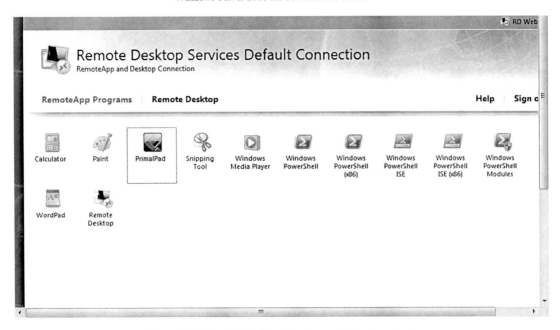

Figure 43-1: Remote Desktop Services published applications.

Finally, just because we have PowerShell doesn't mean you have to give up all of your terminal services command-line tools. They should still work within PowerShell. Here's a remote session to an RDS server where we've called query.exe to display all the current user sessions:

```
[r2-01]: PS C:\> query user
 USERNAME              SESSIONNAME        ID  STATE   IDLE TIME  LOGON TIME
 administrator         console             1  Active       none  9/21/2009  2:04 PM
 rbiv                  rdp-tcp#1           2  Active         51  9/21/2009  1:36 PM
 adeco                 rdp-tcp#3           3  Active         12  9/21/2009 12:37 PM
 administrator         rdp-tcp#0           4  Active          5  9/21/2009 12:41 PM
 bshakespeare          rdp-tcp#2           5  Active          6  9/21/2009  1:38 PM
```

In our opinion many of these PowerShell solutions in Windows Server R2 are clearly version 1 implementations and, as such, we expect to see improvements, bug fixes, and refinements over the next few years.

Chapter 44
The .NET Framework for Windows Administrators

With all this talk of the .NET Framework and Windows PowerShell, it's easy to think that you *need* to know about the Framework in order to use PowerShell effectively. Some of the more ambitious PowerShell users will blog at length about loading up .NET Framework assemblies and doing crazy stuff with them. Well, the news—good or bad, however you want to view it—is that you can be *very* effective in PowerShell *without* touching the .NET Framework directly. Sure, everything in PowerShell is .NET Framework under the hood, but PowerShell's primary purpose is to *adapt* the Framework into something more administrator-friendly. That said, the Framework has a lot of powerful capabilities lurking under the hood, and if you don't mind the complexity, PowerShell *will* let you access all that power. So, that's what this chapter is all about: understanding the Framework enough to be able to utilize it from within PowerShell.

What is the Framework?

The Microsoft .NET Framework is essentially a *huge* collection of prepackaged functionality provided to programmers by Microsoft, to make the programmers's work easier. For example, the .NET Framework knows how to send e-mail, how to resolve computer names to IP addresses, and how to ping a remote computer; if you're writing an application in the Framework, then you just instruct it to do those things, rather than writing them yourself. By building all this great functionality into the common Framework, Microsoft allows programmers to be more productive. All the programmers have to do (more or less) is piece together the various pieces of the Framework to accomplish whatever task they are trying to accomplish.

For example, if we sat you down with a copy of C++ and asked you to write a program that would stop a Windows service, would you know where to begin? We certainly wouldn't. Because that's such a commonly needed task, however, Microsoft built that functionality into the Framework in the form of the System.ServiceProcess.ServiceController class. See, the Framework consists almost entirely of these various *classes,* and they're organized into a fairly consistent naming convention—called a *namespace*—to help make them a bit easier to remember. For example, nearly anything having to do with the Windows system falls under the System namespace, including System.IO for input/output tasks (like writing files), System.XML for working with XML documents, System.Web for working with Web-related stuff, and so forth. A .NET Framework class serves pretty much the same purpose as a WMI class: The class describes how some piece of software functions. Think of a class as a *definition* for something; a definition for a service, for example, specifies that the service has a name, the ability to start, stop, and pause, and so forth. When you're actually talking about a *specific* service, then you're talking about an *instance* of that class. The instance has all the properties and methods that are defined in the class, and those properties and methods allow you to manipulate that instance—stopping it, starting it, reconfiguring it, and so forth.

So, at its heart, the Framework is an enormous collection of classes, which is referred to as a *class library*. And we do mean *enormous*: Visit the documentation at http://msdn2.microsoft.com/en-us/library/ms644560.aspx and you'll see exactly how enormous. But, by organizing classes into the various namespaces, the class library is somewhat easier to browse and learn about.

PowerShell's Framework Adaptation

Normally, PowerShell doesn't force you to work directly with the Framework's classes. Instead, PowerShell gives you task-oriented cmdlets, which simplify the underlying Framework classes and, in some cases, make them more consistent. For example, some Framework classes use a Length property to indicate their size, while others use a Count property; PowerShell "adapts" these so that they consistently appear to use the Count property when accessed from within PowerShell.

WMI is a really good example of the hard work PowerShell does to adapt Framework classes into something more administrator-friendly. For example, try running this:

```
PS C:\> gwmi win32_operatingsystem | gm


   TypeName: System.Management.ManagementObject#root\cimv2\Win32_OperatingSystem
```

We've retrieved a WMI instance and piped it to the **Get-Member** cmdlet (or the **Gm** alias). We see that the TypeName—that is, the Framework class name—is System.Management.ManagementObject. Okay, that means PowerShell asked the Framework to go get this particular WMI instance, and what came back was this object type. Let's look it up in the documentation (it's at http://msdn2.microsoft.com/en-us/library/system.management.managementobject.aspx). If we look at the *members*—that is, the properties, methods, and so forth—of this class, we see that there aren't that many properties and methods. There *certainly* aren't as many properties as PowerShell lists:

```
Name                   MemberType   Definition
----                   ----------   ----------
Reboot                 Method       System.Management.ManagementBas...
SetDateTime            Method       System.Management.ManagementBas...
Shutdown               Method       System.Management.ManagementBas...
Win32Shutdown          Method       System.Management.ManagementBas...
Win32ShutdownTracker   Method       System.Management.ManagementBas...
BootDevice             Property     System.String BootDevice {get;s...
BuildNumber            Property     System.String BuildNumber {get;...
BuildType              Property     System.String BuildType {get;set;}
```

```
Caption                                     Property     System.String Caption {get;set;}
CodeSet                                     Property     System.String CodeSet {get;set;}
CountryCode                                 Property     System.String CountryCode {get;...
CreationClassName                           Property     System.String CreationClassName...
CSCreationClassName                         Property     System.String CSCreationClassNa...
CSDVersion                                  Property     System.String CSDVersion {get;s...
CSName                                      Property     System.String CSName {get;set;}
CurrentTimeZone                             Property     System.Int16 CurrentTimeZone {g...
DataExecutionPrevention_32BitApplications   Property     System.Boolean DataExecutionPre...
DataExecutionPrevention_Available           Property     System.Boolean DataExecutionPre...
```

And that's just a partial list! No, the Framework object is much more generic. If we were actually using the Framework directly, we wouldn't have all of these properties; instead, we'd use the ManagementObject class's **Get()** method to retrieve the property we wanted. For example, object. Get("BuildNumber") would get the BuildNumber property. But in PowerShell, we don't have to do that, because PowerShell has *adapted* the object for us. The clue is in the TypeName shown by the **Get-Member** cmdlet:

```
TypeName: System.Management.ManagementObject#root\cimv2\Win32_OperatingSystem
```

PowerShell's Help tells us that it's adapted this object to directly represent the root\cimv2\Win32_OperatingSystem WMI class. What PowerShell has done is gone in and retrieved all of the WMI class properties, and constructed a customized object with all the properties that the WMI class has. That way, what we get in PowerShell "looks" like we think a Win32_OperatingSystem WMI class should look like. PowerShell also adapts the WMI class's methods, such as **Reboot()** and **Shutdown()**, so we can call them directly. The Framework would have us call the **InvokeMethod()** method, which is more cumbersome. By and large, then, PowerShell's adaptation makes it easier to work with Framework objects.

Adaptation Details

Sometimes, however, you need to work *directly* with the *actual* Framework object. Sometimes this is because PowerShell isn't adapting some function or feature that you want to use; often times, it's because—as in the case of WMI—PowerShell's adaptation is actually creating an entirely different object from the one the Framework returned. Therefore, PowerShell provides four different "views" of an object:

- The adapter view, which is called PSADAPTED.

- The actual, raw object, which is called PSBASE.

- Just the elements that PowerShell has added to the object, called PSEXTENDED.

- The adapter object itself, called PSOBJECT.

As we covered in the "Working with XML Documents" chapter, PowerShell does a ton of work adapting an XML document to look like an object hierarchy; XML looks nothing like that in the raw Framework world. For example, you can create and view a simple XML document object as follows:

```
PS C:\> $x = [xml]"<root><tag /></root>"
```

To see what PowerShell has done with that, just pipe the **$x** variable to the **Get-Member** cmdlet. PowerShell will claim you've got a System.Xml.XmlDocument type of object, which is true enough (the **Get-Member** cmdlet's output is lengthy, so we're not including it here—try it for yourself). However, if you look at the various other objects, you'll see something different. For example, try this:

```
PS C:\> $x.psbase


NodeType            : Document
ParentNode          :
DocumentType        :
Implementation      : System.Xml.XmlImplementation
Name                : #document
LocalName           : #document
DocumentElement     : root
OwnerDocument       :
Schemas             : System.Xml.Schema.XmlSchemaSet
XmlResolver         :
NameTable           : System.Xml.NameTable
PreserveWhitespace  : False
IsReadOnly          : False
InnerXml            : <root><tag /></root>
SchemaInfo          : System.Xml.Schema.XmlSchemaInfo
BaseURI             :
Value               :
ChildNodes          : {root}
PreviousSibling     :
NextSibling         :
Attributes          :
FirstChild          : root
LastChild           : root
HasChildNodes       : True
NamespaceURI        :
Prefix              :
InnerText           :
OuterXml            : <root><tag /></root>
```

Looking at $x.psadapted, however, reveals the *adapted* object, in which the XML document structure is converted into an object hierarchy:

```
PS C:\> $x.psadapted

root
----
root
```

The adapted object is what you work with normally, so just typing **$x** is the same as typing **$x.psadapted**. The point is that the PSBASE version—the raw object—provides very different properties and methods. So, what are the differences? Well, for example, the **$x** variable by itself won't allow us to access the native XML DocumentElement property:

```
PS C:\> $x.documentelement
PS C:\>
```

PowerShell simply returns nothing, because the *adapted* view of the **$x** variable doesn't have a DocumentElement property. However, we can access that by using the PSBASE view:

```
PS C:\> $x.psbase.documentelement

tag
---
```

```
PS C:\>
```

Thus, PSBASE is a means of accessing the raw, un-adapted Framework class. Most PowerShell objects are adapted to some degree or another; for example, let's look at the various views for a process object obtained by using the **Get-Process** cmdlet:

```
PS C:\> $p = get-process
PS C:\> $p.psbase

Length        : 70
LongLength    : 70
Rank          : 1
SyncRoot      : {acrotray, Ati2evxx, Ati2evxx, audiodg...}
IsReadOnly    : False
IsFixedSize   : True
IsSynchronized : False


PS C:\> $p.psextended

                                                                          Count
                                                                          -----
                                                                            70


PS C:\> $p.psobject

Members             : {Count, Length, LongLength, Rank...}
Properties          : {Count, Length, LongLength, Rank...}
Methods             : {Get, Set, Address, get_Length...}
ImmediateBaseObject : {acrotray, Ati2evxx, Ati2evxx, audiodg...}
BaseObject          : {acrotray, Ati2evxx, Ati2evxx, audiodg...}
TypeNames           : {System.Object[], System.Array, System.Object}

PS C:\> $p.psadapted

Length        : 70
LongLength    : 70
Rank          : 1
SyncRoot      : {acrotray, Ati2evxx, Ati2evxx, audiodg...}
IsReadOnly    : False
IsFixedSize   : True
IsSynchronized : False
```

You can see that the extensions—PSEXTENDED—is actually a count, since what the **Get-Process** cmdlet returns is a collection. Normally, the **$p** variable wouldn't have a Count property; the extensions—part of PowerShell's adaptation, in other words—provides this property. The PSBASE shows that the *normal* property name is Length. However, PowerShell adds the Count property to maintain consistency with other portions of the Framework, which use Count rather than the Length property. In other words, the PowerShell team decided to standardize on Count, and added it to those objects that were already using Length.

> **It's a Bypass!**
> If PSBASE still isn't making sense to you, then think about it this way: Normally, PowerShell tries to simplify Framework classes for you, and what you see in PowerShell is that "simplified" version. PSBASE allows you to bypass the simplification, when desired, and work directly with the "under the hood" Framework class.

Using Framework Objects Directly

Of course, you can use PSBASE to work directly with any Framework objects that PowerShell is retrieving for you. But what about *other* Framework objects, ones that PowerShell isn't already adapting and loading for you? PowerShell does have the ability to load Framework assemblies (DLLs) and utilize the classes they contain. Perhaps the best example we have of this is loading up the Framework's speech synthesizer (available in version 3.0 and later of the Framework).

Loading Assemblies into PowerShell

Framework classes are contained in assemblies, which are stored in files on your hard drive, primarily as DLL files in the %windir%\Microsoft.NET\Framework*version*\ folder. We want to work with the System.Speech.Sythesis.SpeechSythesizer class, which is conveniently documented at http://msdn2.microsoft.com/en-us/library/system.speech.synthesis.speechsynthesizer.aspx; even more conveniently, the documentation tells us right at the top of the page that this is in the System.Speech.dll file. Here's how to load the assembly:

```
PS C:\> [system.reflection.assembly]::LoadWithPartialName("System.Speech")
```

Simple enough. Now the classes within that assembly are available to us.

Using a Framework Class

When you load up a class for the first time, you're executing a special method of the class called its *constructor*. Sometimes, classes have multiple constructors that accept different input arguments; some classes will have a constructor that doesn't require any arguments at all. According to the SpeechSynthesizer class's documentation, the only available constructor for this class doesn't have any arguments at all. So, creating a new instance of the class is as easy as this:

```
PS C:\> $speech = new-object system.speech.synthesis.speechsynthesizer
```

We put the new instance into a **$speech** variable, which will give us access to its properties and methods:

```
PS C:\> $speech.speak("This PowerShell stuff rocks!")
```

Remember, piping the **$speech** variable to the **Get-Member** cmdlet will reveal its properties and methods; some of these may seem complicated because PowerShell isn't doing any adaptation for objects like this—you're getting the raw object from the Framework.

On our system, the default voice is a female voice. If we wanted to switch to a male voice, we'd—well, we'd look in the online documentation, is what we'd do. The page listing the members of the SpeechSynthesis class is at http://msdn2.microsoft.com/

en-us/library/system.speech.synthesis.speechsynthesizer_members.aspx, and we see a property named Voice. Clicking that property to learn more, we see that it's a read-only property. That means we can't change it, so it's not what we're looking for. Back to the members page.

There's a **SelectVoice()** method—that looks promising. The docs say that it takes one argument, which is the name of the voice to select. No clues on what might be valid values here, though, so it's off to our favorite search engine to try to find an example. We punch in **speechsynthesizer selectvoice method** and hope for the best; we're quickly sent to http://www.codeproject.com/useritems/ Vista_Speech_Recognition.asp?msg=1977267, which offers a full tutorial on the topic.

Why the Runaround?
Why are we sharing this exploration process with you? Because this book isn't going to be a complete reference—or even an incomplete reference—to the .NET Framework. Our goal is to show you how we find this information, so that you can duplicate our self-education techniques and learn to educate yourself about other useful Framework classes.

It turns out after reading the fairly lengthy tutorial that we could do this faster by using the **SelectVoiceByHints()** method, which allows us to pass a gender and age, and lets the Framework figure out what "voice" fits that. There's no clue as to how we specify a gender, so we decide to just guess. We run this in PowerShell:

```
PS C:\> $speech.selectvoicebyhints("male",35)
Cannot convert argument "1", with value: "35", for "SelectVoiceByHints" to type "System.S
peech.Synthesis.VoiceAge": "Cannot convert value "35" to type "System.Speech.Synthesis.Vo
iceAge" due to invalid enumeration values. Specify one of the following enumeration value
s and try again. The possible enumeration values are "NotSet, Child, Teen, Adult, Senior"
."
At line:1 char:27
+ $speech.selectvoicebyhints( <<<< "male",35)
```

Well, it bombed, but it gave us a great clue! Now we try this:

```
PS C:\> $speech.selectvoicebyhints("male","senior")
PS C:\> $speech.speak("How's this, young man?")
```

And it works great. So, you've seen how to actually find the assembly that a class lives in, load that assembly, create a new instance of a class, and then utilize the class—along with an Internet tour of how to find out *how to use a class*.

Fun (and Useful) Tricks With the .NET Framework

You can do a number of useful things with the Framework. In the next few chapters, for example, we'll show you how to use it to access databases, build your own graphical user interfaces from within PowerShell, utilize Web services, and much more. Right now, however, we offer a few short, incredibly useful techniques.

Sending E-mail

Sending e-mail from within PowerShell is easy, thanks to the Framework's built-in System.Net.Mail classes. And there's a bonus: Because these functions live in the base System.dll assembly, you don't need to load any additional assemblies into PowerShell! The starting point is the System.Net.Mail.

MailMessage class, which is a shortcut class used to create quick, ad-hoc e-mail messages. Once you create a new instance of the class, you simply set a few properties (such as the body of the message, who it's going to, and so forth), and you're done. Here's where you start:

```
PS C:\> $mail = new-object system.net.mail.mailmessage
```

Now, we need to create the sending and recipient e-mail addresses. Note that these are actually entirely new classes of the MailAddress type, so we'll create them and assign them to variables:

```
PS C:\> $from = new-object system.net.mail.mailaddress("don@sapien.com")
PS C:\> $to = new-object system.net.mail.mailaddress("jhicks@sapien.com")
```

Next, we'll assign the address in the **$from** variable to the From property of the message. Note that the To property of the message is actually a collection, because we can add multiple recipients. To add one, we'll use the collection's **Add()** method, passing in the address we want to add. We can do this as many times as needed to add all the recipients. Finally, we'll set the Subject and Body properties, which are simple text strings. Note that you *can* add attachments, set Bcc and Cc recipients, and so forth; look up the System.Net.Mail.MailMessage class in Microsoft's MSDN Library (http://msdn.microsoft.com/library) for details:

```
PS C:\> $mail.from = $from
PS C:\> $mail.to.add($to)
PS C:\> $mail.subject = "Test message"
PS C:\> $mail.body = "Hi, Jeffery!"
```

Last, we create one more new object, this time of the System.Net.Mail.SmtpClient class. Creating the class requires us to pass along the name of our SMTP mail server; we then use the SmptClient's **Send()** method, passing in our mail message object, to actually send the message:

```
PS C:\> $client = new-object system.net.mail.smtpclient("mailserver")
PS C:\> $client.send($mail)
```

And that's it. Of course, your mail server's security comes into play, as well: For example, if your SMTP server requires authentication, than this technique won't work as-is. Instead, you'll also have to set the Credentials property of the SmtpClient object. It can also use a custom SMTP port, be forced to use SSL, and so forth; consult its documentation in the MSDN Library for details on these options.

Resolving Names by Using DNS

Here's something fun to do with the System.Net.Dns class. This is an interesting class; if you look in the documentation at http://msdn.microsoft.com/library, this class is listed as *static*, with a comment that says, "The members of a static class are accessed directly without an instance of the class." That means you don't need to create an instance of the class by using the **New-Object** cmdlet; instead, you can use the class directly:

```
PS C:\> [system.net.dns]::gethostaddresses("msn.com")


IPAddressToString : 207.68.172.246
Address           : 4138484943
AddressFamily     : InterNetwork
ScopeId           :
```

```
IsIPv6Multicast    : False
IsIPv6LinkLocal    : False
IsIPv6SiteLocal    : False
```

This example illustrates the value of reading the documentation—without it, you could spend all day trying to run **New-Object System.Net.Dns** and just keep getting error messages. The documentation also reveals the other tasks this class can help accomplish, such as getting a host name by passing its IP address (reverse lookup), getting the DNS host name of the local computer, and so forth.

Accessing Remote Event Logs

The System.Diagnostics.EventLog class provides access to event logs, including those on remote computers:

```
PS C:\> $log = new-object System.Diagnostics.EventLog Application,Server2
```

The **$log** variable now represents the Application log of Server2. You can then use the log's **Clear()** method, for example, to clear it:

```
PS C:\> $log.Clear()
```

The log also provides **WriteEntry()** and **WriteEvent()** methods, which can be useful, as well as methods like **ModifyOverflowPolicy()**, which can reconfigure the log itself. From a practical perspective, the **Get-Eventlog** cmdlet is using this class and technique so you should rarely need to resort to using the raw class yourself.

Making a Notification Icon

The Framework has the ability to place a notification icon in the task bar notification area. Using it, you can display balloon tip-style notifications. You start by loading the System.Windows.Forms assembly into the shell:

```
PS C:\> [reflection.assembly]::loadwithpartialname("System.Windows.Forms")
```

Because we need an icon for this, we also need to load the System.Drawing assembly:

```
PS C:\> [reflection.assembly]::loadwithpartialname("System.Drawing")
```

Next, we create a new icon and load a standard Windows .ICO file:

```
PS C:\> $icon = new-object system.drawing.icon("c:\myscriptsicon.ico")
```

Now, we create a new NotifyIcon object and set its icon to be the icon we just created. We also set its Visible property to $True so that it displays:

```
PS C:\> $notify = new-object system.windows.forms.notifyicon
PS C:\> $notify.icon = $icon
PS C:\> $notify.visible = $true
```

Now we can display a balloon tip:

```
PS C:\> $notify.showballoontip(10,"Title","Message",[system.windows.forms.tooltipicon]::warning)
```

The last bit determines the icon shown in the balloon tip; you can select Error, Info, None, or Warning. The first number is the number of seconds that the balloon remains visible.

Chapter 45
Reading and Writing Information in Databases

Let's get one thing clear from the outset: This chapter isn't about managing database systems like Microsoft SQL Server or Oracle, and it isn't about designing and creating databases. Right now, none of those database management systems provide Windows PowerShell-specific capabilities for administration—that is, they don't provide cmdlets. Microsoft SQL Server does provide a set of .NET Framework classes called SQL Management Objects (SMO) to accomplish administrative tasks, but using them is more complicated than we can do justice to in a single chapter—it's a book of its own, and it's pretty difficult, compared to how easy it'll be once SQL Server provides a set of cmdlets for administration. Instead, our goal is to help you utilize existing databases—whether those are SQL Server, Microsoft Access, Excel spreadsheets, MySQL tables, or nearly any other type of database you may have—in your PowerShell scripts. We'll do so through the use of a few special .NET Framework classes.

Connecting to a Database

The first thing you'll need is a database *connection string*. The Framework treats SQL Server and other databases somewhat differently, so we'll start with a non-SQL Server connection. Go to www. ConnectionStrings.com and locate the type of database you want to connect to. We'll use an Access 2007 database; if multiple connection strings are shown, look for one that says "OLE DB" or "OLEDB." For example, the Access 2007 connection string is shown as follows:

```
Provider=Microsoft.ACE.OLEDB.12.0;Data Source=C:\myFolder\myAccess2007file.accdb;Persist Security
Info=False;
```

Of course, we need to modify that somewhat to meet our specific needs, primarily by specifying the correct path to the database file:

```
Provider=Microsoft.ACE.OLEDB.12.0;Data Source=C:\files\sample.accdb;Persist Security Info=False;
```

Finally, we'll paste that into PowerShell, assigning the string to a variable for easier use:

```
PS C:\> $connstr = "Provider=Microsoft.ACE.OLEDB.12.0;Data Source=C:\files\sample.accdb;Persist
Security Info=False;"
```

Next, we need to import the assembly that contains the Framework's database functionality: System. Data:

```
PS C:\> [system.reflection.assembly]::LoadWithPartialName("System.Data")
```

And we'll create a new OleDbConnection object. This is the object you use to connect to non-SQL Server databases (SQL Server uses a SqlConnection object—it has a different name, but you use it exactly as shown here). After creating the new object, we'll set its ConnectionString property to be our connection string, and then we'll open the connection:

```
PS C:\> $conn = new-object system.data.oledb.oledbconnection
PS C:\> $conn.ConnectionString = $connstr
PS C:\> $conn.open()
```

That's it! Our connection is open and the database is ready for use.

Building a Command

Next, we need to tell the database to do something. The instruction language used, no matter what type of database we're actually connected to, is the Structured Query Language, or SQL. This book isn't intended as a learning guide for SQL; suffice it to say that SQL has four main operations:

- **SELECT:** Use this operation to query rows from the database.
- **INSERT:** Use this operation to add rows to the database.
- **DELETE:** Use this operation to remove rows from the database.
- **UPDATE:** Use this operation to change existing rows in the database.

We're going to start with a SELECT query. We begin by putting the query itself into a variable:

```
PS C:\> $query = "SELECT * FROM Test ORDER BY ColumnA"
```

Next, we create a new Command object (specifically, an OleDbCommand; SQL Server uses a SqlCommand that works the same way). We'll set it to use our existing, open Connection, and give it our query text:

```
PS C:\> $cmd = new-object system.data.oledb.oledbcommand
PS C:\> $cmd.Connection = $conn
PS C:\> $cmd.CommandText = $query
```

Executing the Command and Working with the Results

Because our query is expected to return rows of data, we need to store those rows someplace. We'll use a variable; what comes back from the Command will be a DataReader object, containing the rows our query returned, and PowerShell will place that object into our variable:

```
PS C:\> $reader = $cmd.ExecuteReader()
```

As an aside, if our query *wasn't* expected to return any rows—if it were an INSERT, UPDATE, or DELETE query, for example—we'd use a slightly different method:

```
PS C:\> $cmd.ExecuteNonQuery()
```

Notice that we don't save the results into a variable this time, because there are no results expected back. However, in the first example above, we use the **$reader** variable, which contains our query results. The first thing we need to do is position the DataReader's internal "pointer" to the first row of data:

```
PS C:\> $reader.read()
True
```

The return value of TRUE, which could also have been saved in a variable, tells us that there's at least one row beyond this one when we're ready for it. Right now, we're on the first row of data and ready to access its columns. We have some choices in how we do this: If we know what order the columns are in the database, we can access the columns' values using their ordinal position:

```
PS C:\> $reader.GetValue(0)
Value1
PS C:\> $reader.GetValue(1)
Value2
```

If we only know the columns' names, and not their position, it's a bit trickier:

```
PS C:\> $reader.GetValue( $reader.GetOrdinal("ColumnA") )
Value1
```

Here, we've used the **GetOrdinal()** method to get the ordinal, and passed that to the **GetValue()** method, which only accepts ordinals. When we're done working with those rows and want to go on to the next one, we execute the **Read()** method again:

```
PS C:\> $reader.read()
True
PS C:\> $reader.read()
True
PS C:\> $reader.read()
False
```

When the **Read()** method finally returns FALSE, it means we've moved past the available data. Now, any attempt to access the columns will result in an error. Of course, in a script you'd be more likely to place this into a loop of some kind:

```
While ($reader.read()) {
    $reader.getvalue(0)
}
```

Remember: To change data, there's no **SetValue()** method; instead, you issue a *new* query using UPDATE. However, keep in mind that so long as a DataReader is open on a connection, you cannot use that connection for anything else—so you may have to create a second connection in order to make database changes. In order to free up the connection being used by the DataReader, close the DataReader:

```
PS C:\> $reader.close()
```

You should also close the overall database connection when you're finished using it:

```
PS C:\> $conn.close()
```

The SQL Server Difference

SQL Server works almost the same way, but has special Framework objects:

- For connections, use System.Data.Sql.SqlConnection.

- For commands, use System.Data.Sql.SqlCommand.

- Executing a command returns a System.Data.Sql.SqlDataReader.

Apart from these differences in object names, the objects work identically to their OleDb counterparts. The only other major difference is that the connection string expected by the SqlConnection object is somewhat different. The Connection Strings Web site (www.ConnectionStrings.com) lists the various SqlConnection strings available under the heading "SQL Native Client." For example:

```
Driver={SQL Native Client};Server=myServerAddress;Database=myDataBase;Uid=myUsername;Pwd=myPassword;
```

A number of variations exist depending on what kind of security connection SQL Server is configured to use, and so forth; the Connection Strings Web site lists them all and provides examples.

A Practical Example

Here's a real-world example: We'll populate a database with computer names and write a script that reads those names, retrieves the computers' service pack version numbers, and places those numbers into the database:

SPInventoryToAccess.ps1

```
# Assumes database is Inventory.accdb
# Assumes table name is SPInventory
# Assumes column names are ComputerName and SPVersion
# and that both columns are text (not numeric) values

function GetSP($computer) {
    $wmi = gwmi win32_operatingsystem -computer $computer
    foreach ($item in $wmi) {
        $item.servicepackmajorversion
    }
}

function SetSP($computer,$spack) {
```

```
$connstr = "Provider=Microsoft.ACE.OLEDB.12.0;" + '
  "Data Source=C:\users\user\documents\inventory.accdb" + '
  ";Persist Security Info=False;"

# Open Connection
$conn = new-object system.data.oledb.oledbconnection
$conn.ConnectionString = $connstr
$conn.open()

# Create query
$query = "UPDATE SPInventory SET SPVer = '$spack' " + '
  "WHERE ComputerName = '$computer'"

# Execute query
$cmd = New-Object system.Data.OleDb.OleDbCommand
$cmd.connection = $conn
$cmd.commandtext = $query
$cmd.executenonquery()

    $conn.close()

}

[system.reflection.assembly]::LoadWithPartialName("System.Data")

# Connection String
$connstr = "Provider=Microsoft.ACE.OLEDB.12.0;" + '
  "Data Source=C:\users\user\documents\inventory.accdb" + '
  ";Persist Security Info=False;"

# Open Connection
$conn = new-object system.data.oledb.oledbconnection
$conn.ConnectionString = $connstr
$conn.open()

# Create query
$query = "SELECT ComputerName, SPVersion FROM SPInventory"

# Get Records
$cmd = New-Object system.Data.OleDb.OleDbCommand
$cmd.connection = $conn
$cmd.commandtext = $query
$reader = $cmd.executereader()

# Read rows
While ($reader.read()) {
    $computer = $reader.getvalue(0)
    $spack = GetSP $computer
    SetSP $computer $spack
}

# Close everything
$reader.close()
$conn.close()
```

Note that our script makes some assumptions about the location and structure of the database, so we've documented those assumptions in the script's initial comments. We've created separate functions to retrieve the service pack version and to write the service pack to the database; this simply helps to encapsulate those particular tasks. Also notice that the SetSP function creates an all-new connection to the database. The following are some additional notes on what we did in the script:

- By using the same variable names as the main script, this function is creating *new* variables in its own private scope. See our discussion on scope in the chapter "Scripting Overview."

- The function can't use the main script's connection, because the DataReader is using that connection. So long as the DataReader is open, PowerShell locks that connection to the DataReader and you can't use the connection to issue other queries.

- Opening and closing a connection over and over again isn't necessarily resource-efficient, but it keeps the function self-contained. An alternative would have been to open a second connection in the main body of the script, and to pass that connection as a third input argument to the SetSP function. That way, the connection could stay open throughout the script and be re-used by the function. We'd just have to remember to close the second connection before the script finished.

Here's a complete walkthrough of the script, one section at a time. First up is our GetSP function, which simply uses WMI to query a specified computer. It outputs that computer's ServicePackMajorVersion property:

```
function GetSP($computer) {
    $wmi = gwmi win32_operatingsystem -computer $computer
    foreach ($item in $wmi) {
        $item.servicepackmajorversion
    }
}
```

Next is the SetSP function. We begin by defining our connection string:

```
function SetSP($computer,$spack) {
    $connstr = "Provider=Microsoft.ACE.OLEDB.12.0;" + '
     "Data Source=C:\users\user\documents\inventory.accdb" + '
     ";Persist Security Info=False;"
```

Then we open the connection:

```
    # Open Connection
    $conn = new-object system.data.oledb.oledbconnection
    $conn.ConnectionString = $connstr
    $conn.open()
```

And we create a new SQL UPDATE query. Notice our use of the input arguments, **$spack** and **$computer**, to provide values to the SQL query:

```
    # Create query
    $query = "UPDATE SPInventory SET SPVer = '$spack' " + '
     "WHERE ComputerName = '$computer'"
```

Finally, we create a new command, execute it, and then close the connection:

```
    # Execute query
    $cmd = New-Object system.Data.OleDb.OleDbCommand
    $cmd.connection = $conn
    $cmd.commandtext = $query
    $cmd.executenonquery()

    $conn.close()

}
```

Here's the first line of the script that executes—remember, the functions are just *defined* at this point; we haven't actually called them yet. The first line of the script loads the System.Data assembly:

```
[system.reflection.assembly]::LoadWithPartialName("System.Data")
```

Note that this won't create an error if the assembly is already loaded, so it's safe to execute even if the assembly might have already been loaded by something else. Next we define and open our connection to the database—the one that the main body of the script will use:

```
# Connection String
$connstr = "Provider=Microsoft.ACE.OLEDB.12.0;" + '
 "Data Source=C:\users\user\documents\inventory.accdb" + '
 ";Persist Security Info=False;"
# Open Connection
$conn = new-object system.data.oledb.oledbconnection
$conn.ConnectionString = $connstr
$conn.open()
```

We create a SQL SELECT query:

```
# Create query
$query = "SELECT ComputerName, SPVersion FROM SPInventory"
```

And then we execute that query, saving the resulting DataReader object into the **$reader** variable:

```
# Get Records
$cmd = New-Object system.Data.OleDb.OleDbCommand
$cmd.connection = $conn
$cmd.commandtext = $query
$reader = $cmd.executereader()
```

We use a loop to move through the returned rows one at a time, retrieving the first column as the computer name. The loop passes the computer name to the GetSP function to get the service pack version, and then passes both the computer name and service pack version to the SetSP function to update the information in the database:

```
# Read rows
While ($reader.read()) {
    $computer = $reader.getvalue(0)
    $spack = GetSP $computer
    SetSP $computer $spack
}
```

Finally, when we're all done, we close everything:

```
# Close everything
$reader.close()
$conn.close()
```

As you can see, working with databases is reasonably straightforward, and they provide a good deal of extra functionality for your scripts.

Note

If you have SQL Server 2008's management tools installed on your computer, you can run **Get-PSSnapin –registered** to see the name of the SQL Server 2008 cmdlet and provider snap-ins. Use the **Add-PSSnapin** cmdlet to add the cmdlet snapin, and you'll get a new cmdlet named **Invoke-SQLQuery**—this is an easier way to run a query against SQL Server without having to mess around with all the .NET Framework stuff.

Chapter 46
Working with Windows Forms

Windows Forms, or WinForms, are a segment of the .NET Framework that allows developers to create graphical applications. The idea is that all the common graphical user interface controls—buttons, check boxes, and so forth—are contained with the Framework itself, so that all you have to do is tell the Framework where to put them, what size to make them, and other details. The Framework actually takes care of drawing them and managing them on the screen. Because Windows PowerShell is built on the Framework, it can access all of WinForms, meaning you can use PowerShell to construct graphical user interfaces.

Caveats, Restrictions, and Can't-Dos

However, before we get carried away, you should know that building a GUI in PowerShell isn't necessarily easy. For one, there's no Visual Studio-like GUI that lets you drag UI elements around; instead, you'll be manually positioning these elements on a pixel-by-pixel basis. For another, PowerShell can't interact with *all* of the various controls that WinForms supports. That's because PowerShell has some restrictions on the type of events it can easily hook up to—which means now we need to discuss what events actually are.

Introducing Events

You've already learned that objects, generically speaking, have properties and methods. Properties describe what an object is and does, while methods tell an object to do something. Objects also support *events,* which are things that can happen *to* an object. For example, when you move your mouse around the screen in Windows, little "MouseMove" events are happening to everything you pass your mouse over. Most objects don't react to this particular event; others—like the window minimize and maximize controls in Windows 7—may react by highlighting themselves or some other action.

When an event occurs, we say that the event is *raised*. You can write code, called an *event handler*, which is executed when the event is raised. Event handlers are what allow you to *do* something when an event happens. For example, when a user clicks a button, the "Click" event is raised and your "Click" event handler executes (if you've written one). This is broadly referred to as *event-driven programming*, since your code only executes in response to events that are raised. This is a different model than the *procedural* programming normally done in PowerShell, where a script simply contains a set of instructions that are followed in sequential order—the script doesn't wait around for things to happen, it just executes one line at a time.

The number and type of events supported by a given control, such as a button or check box, is determined by Microsoft, and these are hardcoded into the Framework. So, if a particular control doesn't support a "MouseMove" event, then you won't be able to "detect" that event happening to the control, and you won't be able to write code that responds to that event.

When an event *does* occur to a control, the Framework sends your event handler some input arguments. These arguments allow your event handler to determine, for example, what control the event occurred to. Sometimes, the arguments might also contain *state* information, such as whether a Shift or Ctrl key was held down at the time the event occurred. The exact arguments passed into your delegate differ depending on the control and the event. For example, some simple controls, like buttons, pass a minimal number of arguments for their "Click" event; other, more complex controls might pass additional arguments for a "Click" event. The exact arguments passed by a particular control's event are collectively referred to as the event's *signature*. In a bit, we'll look at how you can access these arguments, but first let's start building a graphical user interface.

PowerShell and Events

PowerShell allows you to "connect" your code to an event, but *only if* the event uses a particular *signature*. We'll get into this in detail later in the chapter—it'll make more sense after we've shown you some of this working. The good news is that, as an administrator, you probably only want to create fairly simple graphical user interfaces, and PowerShell won't have any problems with those. So, let's get started.

But First…You Need to Read the Docs

Throughout this chapter, we're going to be referring to the .NET Framework documentation. You can find it online, for free, at http://msdn.microsoft.com/library. Because browsing through the documentation's table of contents is extremely time-consuming, we're primarily going to be relying on the search function within MSDN Library to look up specific classes by their type name. *We urge you to follow along.* We're not going to be republishing the information in the documentation, since what's online is already free and up-to-date, and if you're going to be working with WinForms, you're going to need to know how to use the documentation—so you might as well start getting used to it now!

Creating a Form

When you look at a window, or a dialog box, or pretty much anything similar in Windows, you're looking at a *Form*. A blank Form doesn't contain anything you can interact with directly, except perhaps minimize, maximize, and close buttons in the Form's title bar. Rather, a Form is a blank canvas on which other controls are placed. In fact, a Form is often referred to generically as a *container control*, meaning it is a control that can contain other controls.

To create a new Form, we first need to load the Framework assembly that contains the WinForms classes. Then, we'll instantiate a new Form, set some of its properties for size, appearance, and position, and then display the Form.

By the Way...

We'll be doing the majority of our work in a script, rather than from the command line. You can type everything we're showing you directly into the command line, but it's very time-consuming to keep retyping it over and over as you make tweaks. This is an instance where a PowerShell script is really the best way to do things.

```
# load WinForms
[Reflection.Assembly]::LoadWithPartialName("System.Windows.Forms") | Out-Null

# create form
$form = New-Object Windows.Forms.Form
$form.text = "PowerShell Menu"
$form.top = 10
$form.left = 10
$form.height = 250
$form.width = 200
$form.visible = $true
```

Of course, if you run this script, you'll see a window quickly appear and disappear. That's because PowerShell creates the **$form** variable within the scope of this script; when the script ends, the scope goes away—and so PowerShell discards **$form** and the window it represents disappears. Were you to dot-source this script, or simply type it into the command line directly, the window would stay visible. We can also make one minor change to the last line of our script:

```
$form.visible = $true
$form.showdialog()
```

This will remove our explicitly setting the Form's Visible property, and instead call the Form's **ShowDialog()** method, which makes the window *modal*. In other words, no other code will execute until the window is closed. Use the window's close button (in its title bar) to close it, and then PowerShell displays "Cancel," which is the value returned by **ShowDialog()** when you close a Form in this fashion. Here's the Form so far:

Figure 46-1: An empty Form.

Adding Controls

Okay, now we've got a window—what are we going to do with it? We could probably start by adding some controls. We're going to focus on the simpler controls provided by the Framework. Here are their Framework class names, along with the URL of the control's member list (listing its properties, methods, and events):

- **Label:** System.Windows.Forms.Label
  http://msdn2.microsoft.com/en-us/library/
  system.windows.forms.label_members.aspx

- **Button:** System.Windows.Forms.Button
  http://msdn2.microsoft.com/en-us/library/
  system.windows.forms.button_members.aspx

- **Check box:** System.Windows.Forms.CheckBox
  http://msdn2.microsoft.com/en-us/library/
  system.windows.forms.checkbox_members.aspx

- **Radio button (or option button):** System.Windows.Forms.RadioButton
  http://msdn2.microsoft.com/en-us/library/
  system.windows.forms.radiobutton_members.aspx

- **Text box:** System.Windows.Forms.TextBox
  http://msdn2.microsoft.com/en-us/library/
  system.windows.forms.textbox_members.aspx

- **Combo box (drop-down list box):** System.Windows.Forms.ComboBox
  http://msdn2.microsoft.com/en-us/library/
  system.windows.forms.combobox_members.aspx

- **List box:** System.Windows.Forms.ListBox
  http://msdn2.microsoft.com/en-us/library/
  system.windows.forms.listbox_members.aspx

To create a new control, all you need to know is its class name:

```
$button = new-object System.Windows.Forms.Button
```

To customize the control's appearance, simply modify one or more of its properties (which are listed on the respective members pages we referenced above). Note that each control will have a Top and Left property, which are measured from the *top-left corner* of the *parent control*. So, a Button control with a Top property of 10 and a Left property of 10 will appear 10 pixels down and 10 pixels to the right within whatever Form it is eventually placed in. To actually add the control to the Form, use the **Add()** method of the Form's Controls collection, as shown here:

```
# create button
$button = New-Object Windows.Forms.Button
$button.text = "Close"
$button.height = 20
$button.width = 150
$button.top = 2
$button.left = 25
$form.controls.add($button)
```

Make sure you move any call to the Form's **ShowDialog()** method to the *end* of this code! Right now, were you to run the Form, clicking the button wouldn't do anything. That's because we haven't created an event handler yet, nor have we "attached" the event handler to the button's Click event. Here's our Form with the button added:

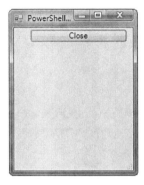

Figure 46-2: Adding a Button control.

You'll notice that we have some tweaking to do with that button's position, but hopefully you get the idea behind adding a simple control to a Form.

Creating Event Handlers

Event handlers are simply PowerShell script blocks, which execute in response to a given event. For simple events—that is, those using the simple signature we examined earlier—you can use a simple syntax to attach the script block to the desired event. As a general practice, we usually attach all of our event handlers *before* we add the control to the Form, so the following is a revised example of our script (to save space, we're omitting the code that builds the actual Form—we're assuming you still have that in there):

```
# create button
$button = New-Object Windows.Forms.Button
$button.text = "Close"
$button.height = 20
$button.width = 150
$button.top = 2
$button.left = 25

# create event handler for button
$event = {
    $form.close()
}

# attach event handler
$button.Add_Click($event)

# attach controls to form
$form.controls.add($button)

$form.showdialog()
```

The **$event** variable contains our script block—and notice that this is *not contained* within quotation marks! In the event handler code, we're simply calling the **Close()** method of our Form object. We attach our event handler to the Click event of the button by calling the **Add_Click()** "method." You can attach any event in this fashion: **Add_** followed by the event name, such as Click. We attach the button to the Form and show the Form as a dialog box.

So, the basic steps of working with WinForms are:

- Create the Form and set its properties.
- Create one or more controls and set their properties.
- Create event handlers and attach them to controls.
- Add the controls to the Form.
- Display the Form.

The tricky part, if there is one, is knowing what control properties and events are useful and tweaking property settings—like control positions and sizes—to achieve the appearance you're after.

Useful Control Events and Properties

Again, we're going to focus on a few basic controls, along with the Form itself. For each of these, we'll call out specific properties and events that we've found to be the most useful, but keep in mind that these are a very small subset of the controls' total capabilities; you'll need to review the Framework documentation (we gave you URLs earlier) for the complete details. Note that some properties, methods, and events might certainly qualify as "interesting," but are very complex to use with a Visual Studio-like graphical designer (and, even if you *have* Visual Studio, it won't do you any good in PowerShell). For example, creating a set of drop-down menus for a Form is pretty complex, and involves several different controls; creating this in PowerShell code is beyond the scope of what we're able to cover here.

Also, *all* controls have a Top, Left, Height, and Width property; we won't be adding those to any of the lists that follow, but you'll need to set them in order to achieve the appearance you're after. All controls also have a Name property, which you can set to create a name for the control; this isn't always terribly useful inside PowerShell, though, where you'll primarily refer to a control by the variable that "contains" the control. However, we'll show you some examples later where the Name property can be useful.

Forms

A Form represents a window, either one that's resizable, or a fixed-size dialog box. Interesting properties include:

- **ControlBox:** Either $True or $False; controls whether the Form has a "control box" in the upper-left corner of its title bar.
- **Controls:** A collection containing all the controls contained on the Form. Use this collection's **Add()** method to add new controls to the Form.
- **DialogResult:** You set this property before closing a Form that was displayed using the **ShowDialog()** method; this property determines the "result" returned by **ShowDialog()**—can be one of:
    - [System.Windows.Forms.DialogResult]::Abort
    - [System.Windows.Forms.DialogResult]::Cancel
    - [System.Windows.Forms.DialogResult]::Ignore
    - [System.Windows.Forms.DialogResult]::No
    - [System.Windows.Forms.DialogResult]::None

- o [System.Windows.Forms.DialogResult]::OK

- o [System.Windows.Forms.DialogResult]::Retry

- o [System.Windows.Forms.DialogResult]::Yes

- **FormBorderStyle:** Controls the border style of the Form. Set this to one of the following:

  - o [System.Windows.Forms.FormBorderStyle]::Fixed3D

  - o [System.Windows.Forms.FormBorderStyle]::FixedDialog

  - o [System.Windows.Forms.FormBorderStyle]::FixedSingle

  - o [System.Windows.Forms.FormBorderStyle]::FixedToolWindow

  - o [System.Windows.Forms.FormBorderStyle]::None

  - o [System.Windows.Forms.FormBorderStyle]::Sizable

  - o [System.Windows.Forms.FormBorderStyle]::SizableToolWindow

- **MaximizeBox, MinimizeBox:** Controls whether the Form has maximize or minimize buttons; set to $True or $False.

- **Text:** The text shown in the Form's title bar.

- **TopMost:** Set to $True or $False to control whether this Form appears "on top" of all other windows.

Interesting methods include:

- **Activate():** Gives the Form the *focus*, making it the active window.

- **BringToFront():** Brings the Form to the front of Windows' *z-order*, making it (at least temporarily) the topmost window, but not necessarily making it the *active* window.

- **Close():** Closes the Form.

- **Hide():** Hides the Form.

- **ShowDialog():** Shows the Form *modally*, meaning the remainder of the application (that is, your script) stops running until the Form is closed.

- **Show():** shows the Form *non-modally*, which means your application (your script) continues running.

Forms also have events that you can create event handlers for:

- **Click:** Raised when the Form is clicked.

- **Closing and Closed:** Raised when the Form is asked to close and when it finally closes.

- **Resize:** Raised when the Form is resized.

Labels

A label is simply a non-editable text area. You could use this to provide a label for a text box, for example. The only property you'll concern yourself with on a label is its Text property, which controls what the label contains. Labels don't have any frequently used methods or events.

Buttons

A Button is a clickable command button, which is placed on a Form or within another container. One interesting property is Text, which is the text that appears on the face of a button.

Buttons don't really have any methods that you'll frequently use. The main event you'll worry about is Click. The Click event is raised when the button is clicked.

Text Boxes

Text boxes provide a place for users to type textual input. Apart from their size and position controls, they have a few properties you might want to configure:

- **Enabled:** Set to $False to disable the text box (grey it out); the default, $True, allows the text box to function normally.

- **MaxLength:** The maximum number of characters that can be typed into the text box.

- **MultiLine:** Set this to $True to make the text box a multiline control with built-in word wrapping.

- **PasswordChar:** Set this to a single character, such as *, to force the text box to only display this character for whatever is typed.

- **ReadOnly:** Set this to $True to allow a text box to display text (e.g., you can change the Text property), but to prohibit editing of that text by the user.

- **Text:** Provides access to the text that has been typed inside the text box. You can set this property to pre-fill the text box, if desired.

We've never found ourselves using any of a text box's methods on a regular basis, although there are a couple of events you'll want to know about:

- **Click:** Raised when the text box is clicked.

- **Enter:** Raised when the cursor enters the text box.

- **Leave:** Raised when the cursor leaves the text box.

- **TextChanged:** Raised when the text inside the text box changes—even by so much as a single character. You have to be careful with this event; if your event handler changes the text, then *another* TextChanged event will be raised, which could easily create an endless loop.

Check Boxes

Check boxes are used to indicate "yes/no" choices. The primary properties you'll worry about are:

- **Checked:** $True or $False depending on whether the check box is checked.

- **Text:** The text that appears alongside the check box.

Check boxes don't really have any frequently used methods, but they do have a useful event:

- **CheckChanged:** Raised when the check box is checked or unchecked.

Radio Buttons

Radio buttons are used to present a short (usually three or fewer items) series of choices, from which the user selects a single choice. Important properties are:

- **Checked:** $True or $False depending on whether this radio button is selected.

- **Text:** The text that appears alongside the radio button.

Only a single radio button in a set can be selected at a single time. All radio buttons included on a Form are considered part of a set; if you want to have two sets of radio buttons, then at least one of those sets needs to be enclosed in another container-style control, such as a System.Windows.Forms.GroupBox control. Radio buttons don't have any especially important methods, but they do each have one important event:

- **CheckChanged:** Raised when the radio button is selected or cleared. Note that this event will usually raise twice: Once for the radio button that was just selected, and then once for the radio button which was subsequently cleared.

List Boxes

List boxes contain a list of text choices, from which the user may select one or more. Because multiselect list boxes are somewhat more complicated, we're mainly only covering a list box that's configured to allow a single item to be selected. Important properties are:

- **Items:** Retrieves a collection of the items within the list box.

- **SelectedIndex:** The zero-based index number of the currently selected list item; contains -1 if no item is selected.

- **SelectedIndices:** A collection of zero-based index numbers for selected items (if multiple-item selection is allowed).

- **SelectedItem:** The currently selected item.

- **SelectedItems:** A collection of selected items (if multiple-item selection is allowed).

- **SelectionMode:** The means by which items are selected; can be one of the following:

    o [System.Windows.Forms.SelectionMode]::MultiExtended—multiple items can be selected using Shift, Ctrl, and the arrow keys.

    o [System.Windows.Forms.SelectionMode]::MultiSimple—multiple items can be selected by holding down the Ctrl key.

    o [System.Windows.Forms.SelectionMode]::None—no items can be selected.

    o [System.Windows.Forms.SelectionMode]::One—one item can be selected (this is the default).

- **Text:** The text of the currently selected item.

There is a useful method you should know about:

- **FindString():** Finds the first item in the list that matches the specified string (useful for finding the index number of an item when all you know is the item text).

And, of course, an event or two:

- **SelectedIndexChanged:** Raised when the selection changes.

- **TextChanged:** Raised when the Text property is changed.

The tricky part with a list box is, of course, getting items into it: You have to use the Items collection, which has an **Add()** method:

```
$listbox.items.add("New Item")
```

Each time you add an index, it is added to the *end* of the list. However, the method also outputs the new index number. If you don't simply want that number displayed as script output, either capture it in a variable or pipe it to the **Out-Null** cmdlet:

```
$listbox.items.add("New Item") | Out-Null
```

Combo Boxes

A combo box can take one of two main Forms. A true *combo box* allows you to select items from a drop-down list, and to type your own value, which isn't on the list. A more limited Form, the *drop-down list*, only permits you to select an item from the list. Useful properties are:

- **DropDownStyle:** Determines the style of the combo box, and can be:
    - o [System.Windows.Forms.ComboBoxStyle]::DropDown—for a true combo box.
    - o [System.Windows.Forms.ComboBoxStyle]::DropDownList—for a drop-down list.
    - o [System.Windows.Forms.ComboBoxStyle]::Simple—for a combo box where the drop-down portion is always visible.
- **Items:** The items in the list—this works the same as the Items property for a combo box, which we've already discussed.
- **SelectedIndex, SelectedItem:** Both refer to the selected list item, either by index or by the item text.
- **Text:** The text in the combo box.

There aren't any major methods to call to your attention, but there are some events:

- **SelectedIndexChanged:** Raised when the selected list item is changed.
- **TextChanged:** Raised when the text is changed (see our comments about this event in the Text box for some cautions).

You add items to the drop-down list in the same way that you add them to a regular list box.

Displaying Forms

You have to use the **ShowDialog()** method so that everything stays on one thread—this means your Form will "block" the shell. **ShowDialog()** populates the Form's DialogResult property; code WITHIN the Form can set this property to return a result to the shell or calling script or whatever. If you just use the **Show()** method, then the Form spins on a new thread, and PowerShell can't stay "connected" to the Form's events—so it's effectively useless.

A Practical Example

We wanted to build a quick little graphical utility that would allow a technician to quickly retrieve key operating system information from a remote computer. The trick is, we didn't want the technician to have to know the computer names: Instead, we'd read those in from a text file (we're hardcoding the file name, since we don't want technicians to have to provide it, but you could prompt for that, if desired), allowing us to give each technician just the computer names they need to work with. So, here's our first go-round—we'll show you the entire script first, and then break down each piece:

WinForms1.ps1

```
function CheckOS {
    Param([string]$computer=$env:computername)

    $wmi = gwmi win32_operatingsystem -computer $computer

    # create output form
    $form = New-Object System.Windows.Forms.Form
    $form.text = "OS Info for $computer"
    $form.top = 10
    $form.left = 10
    $form.height = 200
    $form.width = 250
    $form.formborderstyle = [system.Windows.Forms.FormBorderStyle]::FixedDialog

    # create text box
    $textbox = New-Object system.Windows.Forms.RichTextBox
    $textbox.top = 2
    $textbox.left = 2
    $textbox.width = 246
    $textbox.height = 196
    $textbox.readonly = $true
    $textbox.text = "OS: {0} `nBuild: {1} `nServicePack: {2}" -f `
    $wmi.caption,$wmi.buildnumber,$wmi.servicepackmajorversion
    # add control to form
    $form.controls.add($textbox)

    # show form
    $form.showdialog() | Out-Null
}

# load WinForms
[Reflection.Assembly]::LoadWithPartialName("System.Windows.Forms") | Out-Null

# create form
$form = New-Object System.Windows.Forms.Form
$form.text = "Check OS Info"
$form.top = 10
$form.left = 10
$form.height = 280
$form.width = 200
$form.formborderstyle = [system.Windows.Forms.FormBorderStyle]::FixedDialog

# create label
$label = New-Object system.Windows.Forms.Label
$label.text = "Select computer to query:"
$label.top = 2
$label.left = 10
$label.width = 180

# create button
$button = New-Object Windows.Forms.Button
$button.text = "Select"
$button.height = 20
$button.width = 180
$button.top = 230
$button.left = 10

# create event handler for button
```

```
$event = {
    $form.dialogresult = [system.Windows.Forms.DialogResult]::OK
    $form.close()
}

# attach event handler
$button.Add_Click($event)

# create list box
$listbox = New-Object Windows.Forms.ListBox
$listbox.height = 200
$listbox.width = 180
$listbox.top = 20
$listbox.left = 10

# populate list box
$names = get-content c:\computers.txt
foreach ($name in $names) {
    $listbox.items.add($name) | out-null
}

# attach controls to form
$form.controls.add($button)
$form.controls.add($listbox)
$form.controls.add($label)

# show form
if ($form.showdialog() -ne "Cancel") {
    if ($listbox.selectedindex -ne -1) {
    CheckOS $listbox.selecteditem
    }
}
```

The first thing our code does is define a function—that's not actually executing until later, though, so we'll skip it. The first *executable* code in our script is loading up the Windows.Forms assembly:

```
# load WinForms
[Reflection.Assembly]::LoadWithPartialName("System.Windows.Forms") | Out-Null
```

Next, we create a new Form. We apply several attributes to it, including a dialog box-style border:

```
# create form
$form = New-Object System.Windows.Forms.Form
$form.text = "Check OS Info"
$form.top = 10
$form.left = 10
$form.height = 280
$form.width = 200
$form.formborderstyle = [system.Windows.Forms.FormBorderStyle]::FixedDialog
```

Then we create a label, so that the user has some idea of what this little utility is going to do:

```
# create label
$label = New-Object system.Windows.Forms.Label
$label.text = "Select computer to query:"
$label.top = 2
$label.left = 10
$label.width = 180
```

Next up is a button:

```
# create button
$button = New-Object Windows.Forms.Button
$button.text = "Select"
$button.height = 20
$button.width = 180
$button.top = 230
$button.left = 10
```

Next is the button's event handler. Notice that all this is doing is setting a DialogResult for the Form, and then closing the Form:

```
# create event handler for button
$event = {
    $form.dialogresult = [system.Windows.Forms.DialogResult]::OK
    $form.close()
}
```

Now we add the event handler to the button's Click event:

```
# attach event handler
$button.Add_Click($event)
```

Next, we create a list box and populate it by reading computer names from a text file:

```
# create list box
$listbox = New-Object Windows.Forms.ListBox
$listbox.height = 200
$listbox.width = 180
$listbox.top = 20
$listbox.left = 10

# populate list box
$names = get-content c:\computers.txt
foreach ($name in $names) {
    $listbox.items.add($name) | out-null
}
```

Now we're ready to add our three controls to the Form:

```
# attach controls to form
$form.controls.add($button)
$form.controls.add($listbox)
$form.controls.add($label)
```

And now we show the Form. Notice that we're calling the **ShowDialog()** method as part of an If block. We're checking to see if the **ShowDialog()** result is "Cancel" or not; if it isn't, we check to see if an item is selected in the list box. If one is, we'll call the function we defined at the beginning of the script, passing the selected list box item as the function's input argument:

```
# show form
if ($form.showdialog() -ne "Cancel") {
    if ($listbox.selectedindex -ne -1) {
    CheckOS $listbox.selecteditem
```

```
    }
}
```

Here's what the Form looks like:

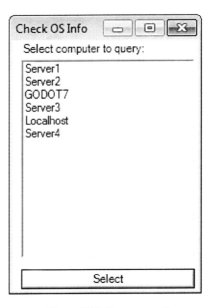

Figure 46-3: Form example.

The function retrieves information from WMI—specifically, the Win32_OperatingSystem class. It then creates a *new* Form, adds a rich text box, and fills that box with the information we've selected. Finally, it shows the Form as a dialog box:

```
function CheckOS {
    Param([string]$computer=$env:computername)
    $wmi = gwmi win32_operatingsystem -computer $computer

    # create output form
    $form = New-Object System.Windows.Forms.Form
    $form.text = "OS Info for $computer"
    $form.top = 10
    $form.left = 10
    $form.height = 200
    $form.width = 250
    $form.formborderstyle = [system.Windows.Forms.FormBorderStyle]::FixedDialog

    # create richtext box
    $textbox = New-Object system.Windows.Forms.RichTextBox
    $textbox.top = 2
    $textbox.left = 2
    $textbox.width = 246
    $textbox.height = 196
    $textbox.readonly = $true
    $textbox.text = "OS: {0} 'nBuild: {1} 'nServicePack: {2}" -f '
    $wmi.caption,$wmi.buildnumber,$wmi.servicepackmajorversion

    # add control to form
    $form.controls.add($textbox)
```

```
    # show form
    $form.showdialog() | Out-Null
}
```

Here's the dialog box displayed by the function:

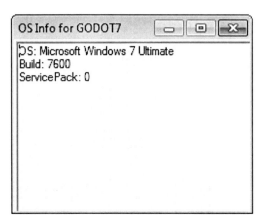

Figure 46-4: OS info Form.

The only thing we don't like about this utility is that it has to be run *each time* you want to query a computer. Instead, we'd like it to re-display the first Form, so that another computer can be selected. It should continue doing that until we close the Form by clicking its "Close" button (in the title bar).

The way we're choosing to do that is to move the CheckOS function *inside the button's Click event handler*. Here's the revised script, where you'll notice the relocated CheckOS function. Also within the Click event handler is the call to CheckOS, which checks to make sure a computer name was selected before continuing:

WinForms2.ps1

```
# load WinForms
[Reflection.Assembly]::LoadWithPartialName("System.Windows.Forms") | Out-Null

# create form
$form = New-Object System.Windows.Forms.Form
$form.text = "Check OS Info"
$form.top = 10
$form.left = 10
$form.height = 280
$form.width = 200
$form.formborderstyle = [system.Windows.Forms.FormBorderStyle]::FixedDialog

# create label
$label = New-Object system.Windows.Forms.Label
$label.text = "Select computer to query:"
$label.top = 2
$label.left = 10
$label.width = 180

# create button
$button = New-Object Windows.Forms.Button
$button.text = "Select"
$button.height = 20
$button.width = 180
```

```
$button.top = 230
$button.left = 10

# create event handler for button
$event = {
  function CheckOS {
    Param([string]$computer=$env:computername)

    $wmi = gwmi win32_operatingsystem -computer $computer

    # create output form
    $form = New-Object System.Windows.Forms.Form
    $form.text = "OS Info for $computer"
    $form.top = 10
    $form.left = 10
    $form.height = 200
    $form.width = 250
    $form.formborderstyle = [system.Windows.Forms.FormBorderStyle]::FixedDialog

    # create richtext box
    $textbox = New-Object system.Windows.Forms.RichTextBox
    $textbox.top = 2
    $textbox.left = 2
    $textbox.width = 246
    $textbox.height = 196
    $textbox.readonly = $true
    $textbox.text = "OS: {0} 'nBuild: {1} 'nServicePack: {2}" -f '
    $wmi.caption,$wmi.buildnumber,$wmi.servicepackmajorversion

    # add control to form
    $form.controls.add($textbox)

    # show form
    $form.showdialog() | Out-Null
} #end CheckOS function

    if ($listbox.selectedindex -ne -1) {
        CheckOS $listbox.selecteditem
    }
} #end $event scriptblock

# attach event handler
$button.Add_Click($event)

# create list box
$listbox = New-Object Windows.Forms.ListBox
$listbox.height = 200
$listbox.width = 180
$listbox.top = 20
$listbox.left = 10

# populate list box
$names = Get-Content c:\computers.txt
foreach ($name in $names) {
    $listbox.items.add($name) | out-null
}

# attach controls to form
$form.controls.add($button)
$form.controls.add($listbox)
$form.controls.add($label)

# show form
$form.showdialog() | Out-Null
```

At the end, we've piped the output of the **ShowDialog()** method to the **Out-Null** cmdlet, because at that point, we don't care what the dialog box's result is—the only way the dialog box can be closed is to click its "Close" button, which means our script is finished.

Working with Event Arguments

In our examples thus far, we've ignored the fact that data is passed into each event handler. For the most part, we haven't *needed* any data; we just needed to know that the event occurred. That's probably the case for *most* events, actually, but the Framework does sometimes provide additional information that you can work with inside your event handlers. In an event handler, you have two special variables that you can work with: The **$this** variable represents the control that the event occurred to. For example, if a button was clicked, **$this** would *be* that button. This allows you to assign the same event handler to multiple controls' events, since you can always use **$this** to figure out which control actually received the event, and to work with that control directly.

The **$_** variable represents the *event arguments* that were passed into the event. Sometimes, as with a button's MouseClick event, the arguments are of a specific type—MouseEventArgs, for example. Those types may have particular properties. For example, a MouseEventArgs argument has a Buttons property, which allows you to determine *which mouse button* was used to click the control. Here's an example:

```
Switch ($_.Button) {
    System.Windows.Forms.MouseButtons.Right { "Right button"; Break }
    System.Windows.Forms.MouseButtons.Left { "Left button"; Break }
}
```

A complete discussion of every type of possible event handler signature, and every possible event argument construction, is beyond the scope of this book—that's what the Framework documentation is for, actually. For example, if we search for the System.Widows.Forms.Button class, and then click on its MouseClick event, we see that the *event handler* is listed as a MouseEventHandler. Clicking on that event handler reveals that it passes in the *sender* argument (which becomes the **$this** variable in PowerShell), and *e* (which becomes the **$_** variable in PowerShell), which is a MouseEventArgs argument. Clicking on MouseEventArgs displays information about it; scrolling to the bottom provides a link to the MouseEventArgs Members, which displays all the properties and so forth that **$_** would contain in PowerShell.

Hold on to Your Hat...

One reason that PowerShell can work with all these varied event signatures is due to a feature called contra variance in the Framework. Essentially, PowerShell can handle any event that passes a sender argument (which becomes the **$this** variable), and a second argument that is either of the type EventArgs, or of a type that inherits from EventArgs.

For example, look up the System.Windows.Forms.TreeView control in the Framework documentation, and click on the TreeNodeMouseClick event. That takes you to the documentation for that particular event, where you'll see that it wants a TreeNodeMouseClickEventHandler; click that, and you'll see that the second argument is a TreeNodeMouseClickEventArgs (we know, these crazy names kill us). Click that second argument and, finally, you'll see that it inherits from MouseEventArgs. Click that and you'll see that it inherits from EventArgs. Whew!

So, because the second argument in the event is a descendent (albeit second-generation) of EventArgs, PowerShell can "hook" an event handler to that event. Some events, however, may have additional parameters, or may have a second parameter that does not inherit from EventArgs. In those cases, PowerShell might not be able to "hook" your event handler to the event quite as easily. It is possible to create an event handler capable of dealing with a different event signature, but it's outside the scope of what we can cover here. And, if you're sticking with the basic WinForms controls and their common events, you won't need to know how to do that.

Using the **$_** and **$this** variables provides additional flexibility in your event handlers. Keep in mind that the overall design philosophy of event-driven programming, which WinForms uses, is as follows:

- Write enough code to get your interface looking like you want.

- Write event handlers that respond to user actions.

In other words, all of your "juicy" code will be in your event handlers, as shown in our WinForms2.ps1 example. This can make your scripts a bit tough to read—and, frankly, a real pain to debug, sometimes—but it's the way things need to be done to properly leverage WinForms.

Now that you've gone through the chapter you may think you'll never want to create a Windows Forms PowerShell script. Fortunately there is an easier way. SAPIEN Technologies has a free tool for generating WinForms PowerShell code. Go to http://www.primaltools.com/downloads/communitytools/ and download PrimalForms Community Edition. This application lets you create a Form in a WYSIWYG editor. Drag and drop controls on the Form, define properties and events, and customize as you need. You can then export the Form to a file, which creates a PowerShell script to generate the Form. All you have to do is add in your PowerShell code to tie everything together. Here's an example.

We have a PowerShell function to return the boot time for a given computer:

Get-BootTime.ps1

```
Function Get-Uptime {
 Param([string]$computername=$env:computername)
$os=Get-WmiObject win32_operatingsystem -computername $computername -ea SilentlyContinue
 if ($os.lastbootuptime) {
   Write-Host ("Last boot: {0}" -f $os.ConvertToDateTime($os.lastbootuptime))
   Write-Host ("Uptime   : {0}" -f ((get-date) - $os.ConvertToDateTime($os.lastbootuptime)).
tostring())
```

```
  }
  else {
    Write-Warning "Failed to find or connect to $computername"
  }
}
```

We would like to turn this into a graphical tool. We load up PrimalForms Community edition and begin dragging, dropping, and configuring the graphical elements on our Form.

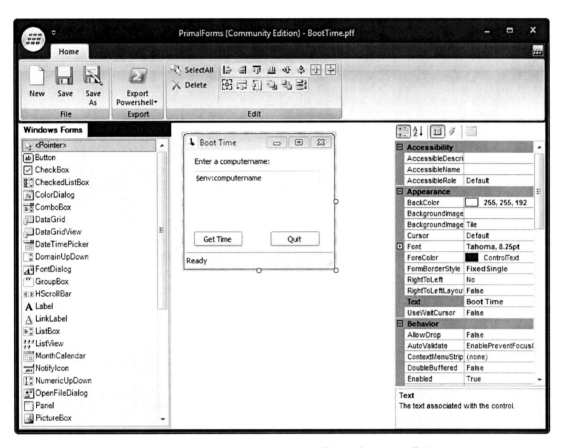

Figure 46-5: Creating a Form with PrimalForms Community Edition.

We can drag Form controls from the left panel to the Form and configure them in the right panel. The Form won't do anything until the "Get Time" button is clicked. We need to tie an event handler to this control. We select the button, and then click the lightning bolt icon on the Properties panel. This changes the view to show events.

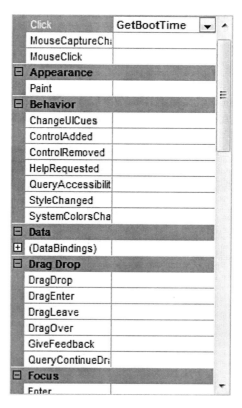

Figure 46-6: Defining an event.

In the appropriate event, in this case Click, we enter the name to use for the associated PowerShell code. This will create a script block in the final script with that name and all we have to do is write the code. PrimalForms handles generating code for all of the WinForms elements, which is usually the most tedious part of the process. We'll use the same code block for the Form's Shown event.

PrimalForms Community Edition doesn't have a script editor. So you need to export the Form to a file or if you have PrimalScript you can export to a file and continue editing. If you need to modify the Form, you have to return to the Forms editor and repeat the process, copying and pasting code from earlier versions.

When we load the exported Form in PrimalScript, we see the empty script blocks waiting for us:

```
#------------------------------------------------
#Generated Event Script Blocks
#------------------------------------------------
#Provide Custom Code for events specified in PrimalForms.
$GetBootTime=
{
#TODO: Place custom script here

}


$btnQuit_OnClick=
{
#TODO: Place custom script here

}
```

We can also see where these events have been added to the controls:

```
$btnGo.BackColor = [System.Drawing.Color]::FromArgb(255,240,240,240)
$btnGo.Name = 'btnGo'
$System_Drawing_Size = New-Object System.Drawing.Size
$System_Drawing_Size.Width = 75
$System_Drawing_Size.Height = 23
$btnGo.Size = $System_Drawing_Size
$btnGo.UseVisualStyleBackColor = $False

$btnGo.Text = 'Get Time'

$System_Drawing_Point = New-Object System.Drawing.Point
$System_Drawing_Point.X = 12
$System_Drawing_Point.Y = 117
$btnGo.Location = $System_Drawing_Point
$btnGo.DataBindings.DefaultDataSourceUpdateMode = 0
$btnGo.add_Click($GetBootTime)

$form1.Controls.Add($btnGo)
```

We already know our PowerShell function works, so all we have to do is integrate the output to the Form:

```
$GetBootTime=
{

    $errorActionPreference="SilentlyContinue"
    $rtbResults.Clear()

    $computername=$txtComputername.Text
    $statusBar1.text="Connecting to {0}" -f $computername.toUpper()

    $form1.Refresh()

    $os=Get-WmiObject win32_operatingsystem -computername $computername -ea SilentlyContinue

    if ($os.lastbootuptime) {

        $line1="Last boot: {0}" -f $os.ConvertToDateTime($os.lastbootuptime)
        $line2=$rtbResults.text="Uptime    : {0}" -f ((get-date) '
            - $os.ConvertToDateTime($os.lastbootuptime)).tostring()
        $rtbResults.Text=$line1+ "'n" + $line2
    }
    else {

        $rtbResults.Text=("Failed to connect to {0}" -f $computername.toUpper())
    }

    #clear variables
    Clear-Variable line1
    Clear-Variable line2
    Clear-Variable os

    $statusBar1.text="Ready"

}
```

The computername parameter from the function comes from the Form's computername text box:

```
$computername=$txtComputername.Text
```

We've added some PowerShell commands to manipulate Form elements like the status bar to provide information to the user:

```
$statusBar1.text="Connecting to {0}" -f $computername.toUpper()
```

As you can see our original code is basically unchanged. All we've done is use some variables to make it easier to display the information in the final Form:

```
$os=Get-WmiObject win32_operatingsystem -computername $computername -ea SilentlyContinue

if ($os.lastbootuptime) {

    $line1="Last boot: {0}" -f $os.ConvertToDateTime($os.lastbootuptime)
    $line2=$rtbResults.text="Uptime    : {0}" -f ((get-date) '
        - $os.ConvertToDateTime($os.lastbootuptime)).tostring()
    $rtbResults.Text=$line1+ "'n" + $line2
}
```

Here's the final graphical result.

Figure 46-7: A PrimalForm in action.

PrimalForms includes several sample Forms, scripts, and a Getting Started Guide, which we encourage you to review. You'll also find other examples on the SAPIEN blog (blog.sapien.com).

PowerShell Forms for Professionals
If you liked the free PrimalForms Community Edition, then you will definitely want to check out the commercial version of the product, PrimalsForms 2009, which includes an integrated script editor, a script packager, object browsers, Form preview, and much, much more. Details and a trial download can be found at http://www.primaltools.com/products/info.asp?p=PrimalForms.

Chapter 47
Working with the Web

One of Windows PowerShell's cooler features is its ability to tap into the .NET Framework's strong Web connectivity. We were originally going to call this chapter, "Working with Web Services," because "Web Services" is such a buzzword these days—but we realized that "Web Services" means a very specific thing and involves protocols like the Simple Object Access Protocol (SOAP). While that's all well and good, it's also pretty darn complicated, and it's not really all PowerShell can do. PowerShell can pull information from the Web in a lot of different ways, and we wanted to be able to touch on some of the other ways that aren't specifically "Web Services." But first, let's make sure we're on the same page with what happens when we use PowerShell to pull information from a Web server.

Retrieving Data from the Web

Basically, the entire point of the HTTP protocol that makes the Web work is that a client sends a request for a given Web page to a server, and the server (we hope) responds by sending the text of that Web page back to the client. Now, sometimes servers go through a lot of effort to produce that page. For example, servers running a server-side language like ASP.NET, or PHP, or ASP often have to process a lot of programming instructions, access databases, and so forth in order to dynamically "construct" the page requested by a client. In the end, though, what's transmitted to the client is just pure, simple text.

The type of text transmitted back is important, too. For example, most Web pages use a language called HTML, which you've no doubt seen. When this text is received by a Web browser, it *renders* the HTML, meaning it uses the HTML instructions to create the final page that you're accustomed to seeing. Sometimes, though, a Web server will send something other than HTML. A blog, for example, is in an XML format called RSS. Even a Web service uses HTTP, although the text it sends is in an XML format called SOAP (usually; other formats exist for Web services, too).

When you work with data from the Web in PowerShell, though, you're going to be working with that raw, under-the-hood text transmitted by a Web server. PowerShell doesn't render HTML into a pretty page, and it doesn't format an RSS feed the way Internet Explorer or another Web browser might. Instead, you'll be working directly with the text exactly as it was transmitted by the Web server. Sometimes, you might just save that information to a file, so that it can be opened by a "smarter" application, like Internet Explorer; other times, especially when the text is in an XML format, you might use PowerShell's own capabilities to extract bits of data from what the Web server sent you.

A Simple Request

You use the .NET Framework's System.Net.WebRequest class to make a Web request to a specific URL. It looks like this:

```
$Request = [System.Net.WebRequest]::Create("http://www.sapien.com")
```

The request doesn't *do* anything; it just sort of sits there on your computer. To transmit it, you ask the Framework to retrieve the response to that request:

```
$response = $request.GetResponse()
```

And that's it: The **$response** variable will contain your HTTP response. As a simple thing, you can check the response's StatusCode property to see if it's "OK:"

```
$response.StatusCode
```

In fact, these three lines of code can combine to make a pretty useful little utility, which we'll write as a function:

```
Function Ping-WebServer {
 Param([string]$url)
 $request = [System.Net.WebRequest]::Create($url)
 $response = $request.GetResponse()
 If ($response.StatusCode -eq "OK") {
 $True
 } else {
 $False
 }
}
```

Pass this function the URL of an intranet (or Internet, for that matter) Web server and the function will output $True if that server is reachable via HTTP, and if the server responds correctly. This is a nice little utility that you could incorporate into a larger script that checks the status of various resources on your network for you. The trick with it is that we didn't care *what* the response was; we just cared that there *was a response*.

Working with XML Data from the Web

But what if you *do* want to work with the information that the Web server sent back? In that case, we might opt to work with a more full-featured object: The System.Net.WebClient. For example, Microsoft publishes an RSS feed at http://www.microsoft.com/technet/security/bulletin/secrss.aspx, which lists the latest Microsoft security bulletins. RSS is simply an XML format, and we know from our chapter,

"Working with XML Documents" that PowerShell knows how to work with XML. So, we'll use the WebClient to retrieve that RSS feed, and then use PowerShell's XML capabilities to create some formatted output from the feed's contents.

We have to start by loading the Framework assembly that contains the WebClient class, and then we'll ask it to download the entire RSS feed into an XML variable:

```
[System.Reflection.Assembly]::LoadWithPartialName("System.Web") | Out-Null
$webclient = new-object System.Net.WebClient
$url="http://www.microsoft.com/technet/security/bulletin/secrss.aspx"
[xml]$data = $webclient.downloadstring($url)
```

Now we need to examine the data. First, we'll check to make sure we *got* some data, by checking to see if the **$data** variable is null or not:

```
if ( $data -ne $Null) {
```

Now we'll start creating our output, starting with the RSS channel title and the date it was last updated:

```
Write-Host $data.rss.channel.Title -backgroundcolor Yellow -foregroundcolor blue

Write-Host "Last Updated" $data.rss.channel.LastBuildDate 'n
```

Next, we'll write the title of the first item. Notice that we're setting a variable, **$i**, equal to zero, and using it to access the first rss.channel.item element:

```
$i=0
do {
write-Host $data.rss.channel.item[$i].Title -foregroundcolor White
```

Depending on the severity of the current item, we'll set its description color to be red, yellow, or green:

```
#color code description based on severity
if ($data.rss.channel.item[$i].Description -Like "*Rating:Critical*") {
    $color="Red"
}

elseif ($data.rss.channel.item[$i].Description  -Like "*Rating:Important*") {
    $color="Yellow"
}
else {
    $color="Green"
}
```

Last, we'll actually write the description, using the color we selected:

```
Write-Host $data.rss.channel.item[$i].Description 'n -foregroundcolor $color
```

Now we increment the **$i** variable by one and continue looping until we've reached the end of the RSS items:

```
$i++
} until ($i -gt ($data.rss.channel.item).count)
```

}

Finally, here's what happens if our original **$data** request was null:

```
else {
 Write-Warning "Could not get  $url"
}
```

Here's the entire script, with some additional comments to help you follow the flow:

Get SecurityRSS.ps1

```
#Get-SecurityRSS.ps1
#Query Microsoft's Basic Security Feed for latest bulletins
#Critical bulletins will be displayed in Red
#Important bulletins will be displayed in Yellow
#Everything else will be displayed in Green

[void] [System.Reflection.Assembly]::LoadWithPartialName("System.Web")
$webclient = new-object System.Net.WebClient
$url="http://www.microsoft.com/technet/security/bulletin/secrss.aspx"
## Get the Web page into a single string
$data =[xml]$webclient.downloadstring($url)

if ( $data -ne $Null) {
 Write-Host  $data.rss.channel.Title -backgroundcolor Yellow -foregroundcolor blue
 Write-Host "Last Updated" $data.rss.channel.LastBuildDate 'n
 $i=0
 do {
 write-Host $data.rss.channel.item[$i].Title -foregroundcolor White
 #color code description based on severity
 if ($data.rss.channel.item[$i].Description -Like "*Rating:Critical*") {
     $color="Red"
 }
 elseif ($data.rss.channel.item[$i].Description  -Like "*Rating:Important*"){
     $color="Yellow"
 }
 else {
     $color="Green"
 }
 Write-Host $data.rss.channel.item[$i].Description 'n -foregroundcolor $color
 $i++
 }
 until ($i -gt ($data.rss.channel.item).count)
 }
else {
    Write-warning "Could not get $url"
}
```

This example showed you how to retrieve a Web page into a string. In our example, we converted that to XML by declaring the **$data** variable as an [XML] type, but you could use [string] instead if you were retrieving a normal HTML page. Once you've got that HTML page, you can work with the contents however you want to.

Using a Proxy Server for Web Connections

The examples we've shown thus far assume that you have an unimpeded connection to the Internet—that is, you either don't have a Web proxy server to deal with or the proxy server is capable of working "invisibly." If that's not the case, then you'll need to take a few additional steps. Note that these can be tricky and you'll probably have to do some experimentation to find the exact combination that works for you. Just be prepared for things to not work properly the first time, since every proxy configuration is different!

In *many* cases, the System.Net.WebClient or System.Net.WebRequest class will be able to read and use the proxy settings configured in the Internet Options control panel application. Try ensuring that those settings are properly configured first: Open the Control Panel, double-click Internet Options, select the Connections tab, and then click LAN Settings (this may differ slightly on various versions of Windows). If set to "automatic proxy configuration," Windows relies primarily on the WPAD host identified by your DHCP server.

Alternately, you can create a new System.Net.WebProxy class:

```
PS C:\> $proxy = new-object System.Net.WebProxy
```

Once you've done that, you can set the proxy server address:

```
PS C:\> $proxy.Address = "http://myproxy.mycompany.com"
```

You can specify that Windows pass along your logon credentials to the proxy:

```
PS C:\> $proxy.UseDefaultCredentials = $true
```

It is possible to provide alternate credentials to the proxy server as well. However, the technique is a bit complicated due to the way the Framework classes are designed. For more information, go to http://msdn.microsoft.com/library, search for "System.Net.WebProxy," and then read the information provided for the Credentials property. You'll need to create a new instance of the ICredentials interface, and then use its **GetCredentials()** method. Credentials can be supplied on a per-URI basis, so this is something you really have to think through carefully. Whenever possible, we find that configuring a proxy through the Internet Options Control Panel application is far easier.

Once you've gotten your proxy configured the way you want it, you have to assign it to the WebClient or WebRequest:

```
PS C:\> $webrequest.proxy = $proxy
```

Then you can successfully issue your request, which should now be directed to your proxy server. However, we don't want to understate the complexity of using the WebProxy class in environments with unusual older proxy servers; we've been in some situations where we've simply never been able to get the WebProxy to connect properly. If you run into difficulty, please drop by the forums on www.ScriptingAnswers.com and ask for help; in a book like this we can't deal with every individual situation that may come up, but in the discussion forums, we definitely can.

Working with "Real" Web Services

PowerShell can natively work with "real" Web services—that is, those which communicate using a Web services protocol like SOAP—but it needs some help from you to do so. The .NET Framework requires a *Web services description language* (WSDL) *proxy* in order to handle communications between the Framework and the remote Web service; unfortunately, PowerShell can't build such a proxy itself. Microsoft Visual Studio comes with a command-line utility called Wsdl.exe, which can build such a proxy, but for the purposes of this book, we're not assuming you have access to a licensed copy of Visual Studio.

In his blog, PowerShell MVP Keith Hill shows how you'd build a proxy, assuming you *did* have access to Visual Studio's Wsdl.exe utility. The full post is at http://keithhill.spaces.live.com/blog/cns!5A8D2641E0963A97!512.entry. The proxy looks like this, with the first line using Wsdl.exe to compile a WSDL proxy from a weather-forecasting Web service:

```
PS C:\> wsdl.exe http://www.webservicex.net/WeatherForecast.asmx?WSDL
```

Next, he uses the C# compiler to compile the proxy:

```
PS C:\> csc /t:library WeatherForecast.cs
```

Then he loads the compiled proxy assembly into PowerShell:

```
PS C:\> [Reflection.Assembly]::LoadFrom("$pwd\WeatherForecast.dll")
```

With the assembly loaded, he creates a new instance of the object representing the Web service:

```
PS C:\> $weatherService = new-object WeatherForecast
```

And finally calls the Web service's **GetWeatherByZipCode()** method, storing the results in the **$forecast** variable:

```
PS C:\> $forecast = $weatherService.GetWeatherByZipCode(80526)
```

Last, he displays the contents of the **$forecast** variable:

```
PS C:\> $forecast
```

A further discussion—since it requires Visual Studio—is beyond the scope of this book, but we wanted you to see that it's *possible* and give you an idea of where to go if you want more information.

A Practical Example

This'll be fun: Bing (formerly known as Windows Live Search) is capable of returning search results in RSS format, which we learned how to read earlier in this chapter. Combining that with some of the knowledge from the chapter "Creating Custom Objects," we've written a function that will accept a query term, and then return a set of custom objects representing the search results. We added the Get-SearchResults function to our profile so that it is always available. Here's the function:

BingSearch.ps1

```
Function Get-SearchResults {
    param([string] $searchstring=$(throw "Please specify a search string."))

    $client = New-Object System.Net.WebClient

    $url="http://www.bing.com/search?q={0}`&format=rss" -f $searchstring
```

```
[xml]$results = $client.DownloadString($url)
$channel = $results.rss.channel

foreach ($item in $channel.item) {
    $result = New-Object PSObject
    $result | Add-Member NoteProperty Title -value $item.title
    $result | Add-Member NoteProperty Link -value $item.link
    $result | Add-Member NoteProperty Description -value $item.description
    $result | Add-Member NoteProperty PubDate -value $item.pubdate
    $sb = {
        $ie = New-Object -com internetexplorer.application
        $ie.navigate($this.link)
        $ie.visible = $true
    }
    $result | Add-Member ScriptMethod Open -value $sb
    $result
  }
}
```

This is using the System.Net.WebClient class to retrieve a Bing results page. Notice that we're passing the RSS format request in the URL itself; this is a feature of Bing that we're simply capitalizing on. We go through each search result and create a new custom object. That object has properties for the Title, Link, Description, and PubDate, and a ScriptMethod named **Open()**. This ScriptMethod is just a PowerShell script block, which we defined in the **$sb** variable: It creates a new instance of Internet Explorer, navigates to the page represented by the current search result (accessing the URL via $this. link), and makes the browser visible. Finally, the function outputs the search result.

Here's how to use it:

```
PS C:\> $hits = get-searchresults "PrimalScript"
PS C:\> $hits


Title                     Link                      Description               PubDate
-----                     ----                      -----------               -------
SAPIEN Technologies, Inc. ... http://www.sapien.com/     PrimalScript a scripting I... Thu, 20 Aug 2009
PrimalScript: The ONLY Uni... http://www.primaltools.com... More than just an admin sc... Wed, 26 Aug 2009
SAPIEN Technologies, Inc. ... http://www.primalscript.co... SAPIEN Technologies: Scrip... Fri, 28 Aug 2009
PrimalScript free download... http://www.freedownloadsce... PrimalScript free download... Tue, 11 Aug 2009
PrimalScript 2009 released... http://blog.sapien.com/ind... The SAPIEN Technologies Bl... Tue, 21 Jul 2009
Primalscript is a scriptin... http://www.hallogram.com/p... Primalscript is the leadin... Sat, 16 May 2009
PrimalScript Software Info... http://primalscript.softwa... Review This review applies... Mon, 10 Aug 2009
Primalscript                http://www.sapien.com/down...                           Thu, 27 Aug 2009
FACT: PrimalScript Sucks    http://primalscriptsucks.com What do thousands of scrip... Thu, 20 Aug 2009
Free primalscript Download... http://wareseeker.com/free... Free primalscript Download... Sat, 29 Aug 2009

PS C:\> $hits[0].title
SAPIEN Technologies, Inc. - VBScript Editor, PowerShell Editor, ASP ...

PS C:\> $hits[0].link
http://www.sapien.com/
PS C:\> $hits[0].open()
```

As you can see, we're able to access individual search results, such as $hits[0] to access properties like Title and Link, or the method we created—**Open()**—to open the search result in a new Internet Explorer window.

Chapter 48
Creating PowerShell Advanced Functions and Scripts

Windows PowerShell v2.0 introduced the ability to create cmdlets not only in a .NET Framework language (which we cover in the next chapter), but also in PowerShell's simpler scripting language. In fact, a cmdlet isn't all that different from a filtering function (which we cover in the chapter, "Script Blocks, Functions, Filters, Snap-ins, and Modules"): The cmdlet has a name, has input arguments—which, as a cmdlet, are referred to as *parameters*—and has three unique stages: BEGIN, PROCESS, and END. OK, we need to be honest. You really aren't going to create a true cmdlet with a script. In PowerShell v2.0 you can create an *advanced function* that behaves almost like a compiled cmdlet.

Design Guidelines

Each advanced function that you write should perform only *one* task, and that task should align directly to an administrative task that you might normally accomplish manually, such as creating a user or restarting a computer. Function naming should follow standardized PowerShell naming guidelines, including the use of a verb, a dash, and then a singular noun. Verbs should come from the standardized list of PowerShell verbs (which we covered in the chapter, "Best Practices for Scripting").

Whenever it makes sense, an advanced function should accept pipeline input. For example, if a function is designed to accept a user name as input, then it should be able to have a collection of user names piped in from the pipeline also. Advanced functions should *always* produce objects as their output; this enables the objects to be used by other cmdlets, such as Sort, Group, Where, Select, and so forth; we explain how to create output objects in the chapter, "Creating Custom Objects."

Functions vs. Scripts

There really isn't much difference between an advanced function and an advanced script. All of the techniques we will be discussing in regards to functions apply equally to a script. One benefit of using a function is that you can use a simple verb-noun name.

```
Dir | get-fileDetail | export-csv report.csv
```

You could also use a script file, but then you would need to specify the full path and your script execution policy would also apply.

```
Dir | c:\scripts\get-filedetail.ps1 | export-csv report.csv
```

The approach you choose is up to you.

Advanced Function Lifecycle

When you execute an advanced function, PowerShell follows a very specific set of steps:

1. PowerShell maps input parameters, something we'll discuss later in this chapter.
2. PowerShell executes the BEGIN script block, if one exists.
3. For each object piped in from the pipeline, PowerShell executes the PROCESS script block, if one exists. So, if four objects are piped in, the PROCESS script block will execute four times.
4. PowerShell executes the END script block, if one exists.

Each of the three script blocks—BEGIN, PROCESS, and END—can write objects to the pipeline by using the **Write-Output** cmdlet. PowerShell collects these objects together and sends them to the next cmdlet in the pipeline. Cmdlets can (and should) use the **Write-Debug, Write-Verbose, Write-Error**, and **Write-Warning** cmdlets to write debug information, verbose status information, errors, and warnings.

Creating an Advanced Function

It's easier to create a fully functional advanced function if you follow a simple set of steps.

Step 1: Start with the Basic Function Structure

The basic structure of an advanced function begins with the keyword **Function**, followed by the contents of the function itself. Here's a bare-bones example:

```
Function Get-Something {
  [CmdletBinding()]
  Param()
  BEGIN {}
  PROCESS {}
  END {}
}
```

The **Param** area is where you define the cmdlet's parameters, and this is an important step that sets cmdlets apart from normal functions. The BEGIN, PROCESS, and END script blocks are where you place the cmdlet's function code. No code should exist outside these three script blocks. If you don't need one of the script blocks, you can omit it.

Step 2: Define Attributes

You can define four different attributes for an advanced function, which helps PowerShell understand certain aspects of the function's operation. These are defined as part of the [CmdletBinding] attribute. Within this attribute we can define these values:

- **SupportsShouldProcess:** Indicates that the function can reconfigure the system, and is designed to work with the **-whatIf** and **-confirm** parameters. You do not need to define -**whatIf** and -**confirm** yourself, but you do have to code your function to handle PowerShell's ShouldProcess functionality (which we'll cover later).

- **DefaultParameterSet=***set_name*: If the function defines multiple parameter sets (which we'll cover shortly), this is the set that is used by default. If a user wishes to use a different set, PowerShell will be able to tell by the parameters they specify.

- **ConfirmImpact=***level*: Specifies the lowest level at which confirmation should be requested. PowerShell defines a built-in function called ShouldProcess, which queries the user and asks whether an operation should be performed. Your function is responsible for calling ShouldProcess before performing any potentially damaging actions; ShouldProcess will be called only then the setting of ConfirmImpact (which defaults to "medium") is equal to or greater than the value of the built-in **$ConfirmPreference** variable. ConfirmImpact, then, is a way of roughly defining how severe your advanced function's actions might be; PowerShell users can set **$ConfirmPreference** so that they're only prompted for actions of the severity level they choose. By default, **$ConfirmPreference** is "High," meaning that any advanced function with a ConfirmImpact of "Low" or "Medium" won't normally prompt for confirmation.

....

How Confirmation Works

Any advanced function with a ConfirmImpact equal to or higher than the contents of $ConfirmPreference will automatically prompt the user for confirmation when the function is run. These functions also support the use of the -confirm parameter; when this parameter is specified by the user, the function will also prompt for confirmation, regardless of the contents of $ConfirmPreference. A user can also specify -confirm:$false, which will suppress the normal automatic confirmation prompts.

- **-snapin** *name*: You can specify this attribute multiple times, and it simply documents the PSSnapIns that this cmdlet depends upon.

Attributes are defined as follows:

```
Function  Get-Something
    [CmdletBinding(
    SupportsShouldProcess=$False,
    ConfirmImpact="None",
    DefaultParameterSetName="")]
  Param()
 BEGIN {}
}
```

Step 3: Define Parameters

Within the parameter block, you'll define the function's parameters. Keep in mind that parameter names should be clear, and whenever possible should be consistent with the parameter names used by "real" PowerShell cmdlets. For example, if your cmdlet needs to accept a computer name, the accepted parameter name is -**computerName**, not -**comp**, or -**remote**, or -**machine**, or anything else. Review other PowerShell cmdlets to find a consistent parameter name whenever you can.

Once you've decided on a parameter name, you need to decide what attributes the parameter will have. Some options are:

- **Mandatory:** Indicates that the cmdlet cannot run unless this parameter is specified.

- **ValueFromPipeline:** Indicates that this parameter can accept incoming pipeline objects that are of the same data type as the parameter.

- **ValueFromPipelineByPropertyName:** Indicates that this parameter can accept incoming pipeline objects, and will search those objects for a property name that corresponds to the parameter name.

- **Position:** If the parameter name doesn't need to be specified, then the parameter is positional, and you need to decide which position it will occupy.

- **Alias:** An alias that you can use instead of the full parameter name, such as -**CN** for -**computerName**.

- **ParameterSetName:** Specifies which *parameter set* this parameter belongs to. A cmdlet can have multiple parameter sets, and each set must have at least one parameter that is unique to that set, and that is not used in any other set.

- **ValueFromRemainingArguments:** Indicates that this parameter accepts all remaining arguments which haven't been matched to another parameter. This parameter, then, is a "catch all" parameter for anything else the cmdlet user specifies when running the cmdlet.

- **HelpMessage:** A short description of the parameter and its purpose.

- **Switch:** Indicates that the parameter doesn't accept a value; if it's specified, then the parameter is considered True; if the cmdlet is run without the parameter, then the parameter is False.

A few options allow you to specify whether a parameter accepts null or empty values as input:

- **AllowNull:** This parameter is allowed to be null ($null).

- **AllowEmptyString:** This parameter is allowed to contain an empty string ("").

- **AllowEmptyCollection:** This parameter accepts a collection, but the collection may be empty, containing no objects.

Finally, several options allow you to specify input validation. PowerShell will reject parameter values that do not meet whatever validation rules you specify:

- **ValidationCount(min,max):** The minimum and maximum number of arguments that this parameter can accept.

- **ValidatePattern(regex):** A regular expression that will be used to validate input; only input values matching the regular expression are accepted.

- **ValidateRange(min,max):** The minimum and maximum numeric values that the parameter can accept.

- **ValidateScript(script block):** A script block is used to validate the input for this parameter; if the script block returns $True, then the input is considered valid.

- **ValidateSet(string[]):** An array of string values that are acceptable choices for this parameter.

- **ValidateNotNull():** Specifies that the parameter value cannot be null ($null).

- **ValidateNotNullorEmpty():** Specifies that the parameter value cannot be null ($null) or an empty string ("").

You also need to select an appropriate data type for the parameter, such as [string] or [int]. You should also decide if the parameter can accept a collection of items, such as [string[]] or [int[]]; any parameter that accepts pipeline input is, by definition, going to need to accept a collection and its data type should reflect that by including [] after the data type name: [Boolean[]], [regex[]], [string[]], and so forth.

An example parameter might look like this:

```
param(
[Parameter(Position=0, Mandatory=$False, ValueFromPipeline=$True)]
[string]$computername=$env:computername)
```

Let's break that down a bit: Inside the main Param() block, each parameter starts with a [Parameter()] declaration, which includes the parameter's attributes. In this particular parameter it is defined as the first parameter, is not required, and can accept a pipelined value. After that, you include the parameter's variable name, which is **$computerName** in this case. We've cast it as a string and provided a default value.

If you have more than one parameter for your cmdlet, and you often will, simply separate them by commas:

```
Param(
 [Parameter(
 Position=0,
 ValueFromPipeline=$True)]
 [string]$computerName,

 [switch]$recurse
)
```

Positional Parameters

A positional parameter is one with the Position() attribute specified. For these parameters, users of the cmdlet can specify a value in the proper position and do not need to type the parameter's name. For example, consider this parameter definition:

```
Function Get-Something {
 Param(
        [Parameter(Position=0)][string] $parm1,
        [Parameter(Position=1)][int] $parm2,
        [int]$parm3
        )
}
```

This cmdlet could be called in *any* of the following ways:

```
Get-Something -parm1 "Hello" -parm2 5 -parm3 100
Get-Something "Hello" 5 -parm3 100
```

The value in the first position (position 0) will be mapped to the **$parm1** variable, while the value in the second position (1) will be mapped to the **$parm2** variable; the **$parm3** variable is not set up as positional, so if you use it, you must specify the parameter name.

Specifying Default Values

You can specify default values, which will be used whenever a cmdlet is run and a given parameter is not specified. For example:

```
Function Get-Something {
 Param(
       [Parameter(Position=0)][string] $parm1="Hello",
       [Parameter(Position=1)][int] $parm2,
       [int]$parm3
       )
}
```

If you run this cmdlet without specifying the **$parm1** variable, then **$parm1** will contain "Hello," its default value. You should always provide a default for any parameter that may be used but that is not marked [Mandatory].

Parameter Sets

Parameter sets allow different cmdlets to be called in different ways. For example, if you run **Help Receive-Job**, you'll see that the cmdlet has six distinct parameter sets. Used one way, the cmdlet needs a job identifier and can accept a runspace object. Used another way, the cmdlet needs a job identifier and a computer name. PowerShell can tell the difference between these two sets because they each contain at least one unique parameter name: -**Session** and -**computerName** respectively.

In an advanced function, this would be defined by using something like this:

```
Function Receive-PSJob {
 Param(
       [Parameter(mandatory=$True,Position=0)][psjob]$job,
       [Parameter(parametersetname="One")][remoterunspaceinfo]$session,
       [Parameter(parametersetname="Two")][string[]]$computerName
       )
}
```

Pipeline Parameters

PowerShell provides two ways of matching incoming pipeline objects to the parameters of your cmdlet. There are some limitations to how this works: Each parameter set can have no more than one parameter of a given object type set to **ValueFromPipeline**. This, then, is legal:

```
Param([Parameter(ValueFromPipeline=$True)][string]$parm1,
      [Parameter(ValueFromPipeline=$True)][int]$parm2)
```

Because the **$parm1** and **$parm2** variables are different types of objects—string and integer. If you pipe integer objects into this cmdlet, PowerShell will place them into **$parm2**; if you pipe in string objects, PowerShell will place them into **$parm1**. However, this example is illegal:

```
Param([Parameter(ValueFromPipeline=$True)][string]$parm1,
      [Parameter(ValueFromPipeline=$true][string]$parm2)
```

Here, we've specified two [string] objects for pipeline input. If you pipe strings into the cmdlet, PowerShell won't be able to tell if it should use the **$parm1** or **$parm2** variables, and it won't try to pass the pipeline objects into both parameters.

Keep in mind, though, that the following *is* legal:

```
Param(
 [Parameter(ValueFromPipeline=$True,ParameterSetName="One")][string]$parm1,
 [Parameter(ValueFromPipeline=$True,ParameterSetName="Two")][string]$parm2,
 [Parameter(Mandatory=$True,ParameterSetName="One")][string]$computername,
 [Parameter(Mandatory=$True,ParameterSetName="Two")][string]$username
)
```

If you run this cmdlet with the mandatory parameter -**computerName**, PowerShell will know you're using the parameter set named "One," and will bind incoming string objects from the pipeline to the **$parm1** variable, which is in the same parameter set. On the other hand, if you specify the -**userName** parameter, then PowerShell knows you're using parameter set "Two," and incoming strings from the pipeline will be placed into the **$parm2** variable, which is part of the same parameter set.

PowerShell has a second way of binding pipeline input, which is **ValueFromPipelineByPropertyname**. Consider this example:

```
Param([Parameter(ValueFromPipelineByPropertyName=$True)][string]$index)
```

When you pipe an object into this cmdlet, PowerShell will look to see if the object has an Index property—which matches the parameter name, -**index**. If the object has an Index property, then its value—but not the entire object—will be placed into the **$index** variable.

Parameter Best Practices

- Don't use multiple parameter sets unless you have to—they definitely complicate things.

- Always specify an object type, such as [string], for each parameter that isn't a [switch] type.

- Add input validation, using the Validate attributes, whenever you can. Doing so helps PowerShell filter out inappropriate input, so that you don't have to write code which does so.

Step 4: Select Methods

Script cmdlets can have the basic "methods" we've already mentioned: BEGIN, PROCESS, and END. You simply provide code for the ones that are appropriate for your cmdlet. The BEGIN script block executes first, and then your PROCESS script block executes once for each piped-in object; any parameters that are bound to pipeline objects will only contain one object at a time. Essentially, PowerShell is performing a **ForEach** loop for you, so that your PROCESS script block only has to deal with each single object once. Finally, after all pipeline objects have been processed, the END script block runs.

If your cmdlet doesn't accept pipeline input, then you'll usually just provide a BEGIN script block. You don't need to provide any script blocks that you don't use; for example, if you *do* accept pipeline input, but don't need to perform any kind of "set up" (opening a database connection or other initial work), then you might not have a BEGIN script block.

If your cmdlet does accept pipeline input, then you *must* provide a PROCESS script block. Any parameters that you've defined as accepting pipeline input will only contain objects when your PROCESS script block is running; they may be empty within the BEGIN or END script blocks.

Step 5: Add Calls to ShouldProcess

If your cmdlet is defined with SupportsShouldProcess and ConfirmImpact (which we described earlier in this chapter), then you'll make calls to the **ShouldProcess()** method only from within your PROCESS script block. Calling **ShouldProcess()** is easy: Just use the built-in **$pscmdlet** variable, which is available from within any advanced function:

....

Note

You can't call ShouldProcess from the BEGIN or END script blocks; you'll only use ShouldProcess from within the PROCESS script block.

```
$result = $pscmdlet.shouldprocess("Target information")
```

This will result in a message something like the following when you use the -**confirm** parameter:

```
Confirm
Are you sure you want to perform this action?
Performing operation "test-test" on Target "Target information".
[Y] Yes  [A] Yes to All  [N] No  [L] No to All  [S] Suspend  [?] Help (default is "Y"): y
```

The string you pass to the **ShouldProcess()** method should describe whatever your cmdlet is about to modify—that is, the *target* of the cmdlet's activity at that moment. The result of **ShouldProcess()**—which we stored in the **$result** variable in our example—will either be $True or $False, depending on whether the user selected "Y" or "N." If the user selects "A" or "L," **ShouldProcess()** returns $True or $False, as appropriate, and then *continues to return that same value* on any subsequent calls within the same PROCESS script block. If the user selects "S" for "Suspend," PowerShell takes over and provides a nested prompt; you don't need to do anything about that. Another way to code **ShouldProcess()** looks like this:

```
If ($pscmdlet.ShouldProcess("Object name") {
  # take action - user said Yes
} else {
  # user said No
}
```

Step 6: Add Your Code

At this point, your function structure is done; you're ready to add whatever code you need to the BEGIN, PROCESS, and/or END script blocks. Add your code, test the function, and you're done!

Remember: Your function must appear in your script *before* you can use it. That is, the advanced function's definition and structure must be above any lines of script which call the function. Functions obey all of PowerShell's rules for scope, which we discussed in our chapter entitled, "Scope in Windows PowerShell."

Common Parameters

A very nice feature with advanced functions, which we've alluded to, is that your function can take advantage of the common parameters that all cmdlets access such as **-WhatIf**, **-Confirm**, **-Verbose**, and **-Debug**. Let's take a moment to make sure you understand how to take advantage of these features.

WhatIf and Confirm

In order to use the **-WhatIf** or **-Confirm** parameters, your function must use CmdletBinding and set SupportsShouldProcess to True:

```
[CmdletBinding(SupportsShouldProcess=$True)]
```

Once enabled, you can run your script or function like this:

```
PS C:\test> gc servers.txt | Get-OS -whatif
What if: Performing operation "Get-OS" on Target "chaos".
What if: Performing operation "Get-OS" on Target "xp01".
What if: Performing operation "Get-OS" on Target "testdesk01".
```

Or this:

```
PS C:\test> gc servers.txt | Get-OS -confirm

Confirm
Are you sure you want to perform this action?
Performing operation "Get-OS" on Target "chaos".
[Y] Yes  [A] Yes to All  [N] No  [L] No to All  [S] Suspend  [?] Help (default is "Y"):
```

Verbose

The **-Verbose** parameter can be a helpful feature for anyone running your script or even for debugging purposes. You do not need [CmdletBinding()]. By default, using **-Verbose** doesn't do much more than this:

```
PS C:\test> "chaos" | get-os -verbose
VERBOSE: Performing operation "Get-OS" on Target "chaos".
```

However, throughout your script or function you should insert commands by using the **Write-Verbose** cmdlet where you want to provide verbose feedback:

```
Write-Verbose "Connecting to $computername"
```

When you use the **-Verbose** parameter, then these lines will be written to the Verbose pipeline and made visible.

Debug

In a similar fashion you can use the **-Debug** parameter and include the **Write-Debug** cmdlet lines in your advanced function or script:

```
Write-Debug "$(get-date) Processing $computername"
```

You won't see anything until you use the **-Debug** parameter with your function or script:

```
PS C:\> "chaos" | get-os -debug
DEBUG: 04/22/2009 16:10:51 BEGIN

Confirm
Continue with this operation?
[Y] Yes  [A] Yes to All  [H] Halt Command  [S] Suspend  [?] Help (default is "Y"): A
DEBUG: 04/22/2009 16:10:59 Processing chaos

Confirm
Continue with this operation?
[Y] Yes  [A] Yes to All  [H] Halt Command  [S] Suspend  [?] Help (default is "Y"): A

Confirm
Are you sure you want to perform this action?
Performing operation "Get-OS" on Target "chaos".
[Y] Yes  [A] Yes to All  [N] No  [L] No to All  [S] Suspend  [?] Help (default is "Y"):
DEBUG: 04/22/2009 16:11:05 computername = chaos

Confirm
Continue with this operation?
[Y] Yes  [A] Yes to All  [H] Halt Command  [S] Suspend  [?] Help (default is "Y"):


SystemDirectory : C:\Windows\system32
Organization    : SAPIEN Technologies
BuildNumber     : 6001
RegisteredUser  : Jeffery Hicks
SerialNumber    : 89587-448-2973025-71837
Version         : 6.0.6001

DEBUG: 04/22/2009 16:11:06 END

Confirm
Continue with this operation?
[Y] Yes  [A] Yes to All  [H] Halt Command  [S] Suspend  [?] Help (default is "Y"):
```

As you can see, this also prompts you to step through each line.

Adding Help

Perhaps the greatest feature with advanced functions and scripts is Help. All you need to do is define your Help elements in a special comment block at the beginning of your script or function. Here's an example:

```
<#
.Synopsis
    Get computer operating system information.
.Description
    This function will connect to a computer using WMI and return
    Operating System information.

.Parameter Computername
    What is the name of the computer to query? The default is the local computer.
.Parameter Logname
    What is the name of the event log to backup? The backup will fail if the
```

```
    file already exists.
.Parameter Filepath
    What is the path for the backup file? This path is relative to the remote
    computer and must be a local drive.
.Parameter Clear
    Clear the event log if it successfully backed up
.Example
    PS C:\> get-os

    Return OS information for the local host.
.Example
    PS C:\> "serverA","serverB","ServerC" | get-os | Select CSName,Caption,CSDVersion,OSArchitect
ure

.ReturnValue
    None
.Link
    Get-WMIObject


.Notes
 NAME:      Get-OS
 VERSION:   1.0
 AUTHOR:    Jeffery Hicks
 LASTEDIT:  4/16/2009 5:00:00 PM

#requires -version 2.0
#>
```

The layout should be pretty self-explanatory. Once added, you can use PowerShell's Help feature with your function like any other cmdlet:

```
PS C:\> help get-os

NAME
    Get-OS

SYNOPSIS
    Get computer operating system information.


SYNTAX
    Get-OS [[-computername] [<String>]] [-Verbose] [-Debug] [-ErrorAction [<ActionPreference>]]
    [-WarningAction [<ActionPreference>]] [-ErrorVariable [<String>]] [-WarningVariable [<String>]]
    [-OutVariable [<String>]] [-OutBuffer [<Int32>]] [<CommonParameters>]


DETAILED DESCRIPTION
    This function will connect to a computer using WMI and return
    Operating System information.


RELATED LINKS
    Get-WMIObject

REMARKS
    To see the examples, type: "get-help Get-OS -examples".
    For more information, type: "get-help Get-OS -detailed".
    For technical information, type: "get-help Get-OS -full".
```

As with a traditional cmdlet, you can also provide examples for Help:

```
PS C:\> help get-os -examples

NAME
    Get-OS

SYNOPSIS
    Get computer operating system information.

    ------------------------ EXAMPLE 1 ------------------------



    PS C:\> get-os

    Return OS information for the local host.
    ------------------------ EXAMPLE 2 ------------------------



    PS C:\> "serverA","serverB","ServerC" | get-os | Select CSName,Caption,CSDVersion,OSArchitect
ure
```

How terrific is that!

A Practical Example

Let's walk through the entire advanced function process, from the beginning, step by step. We'll create a practical advanced function that might prove useful in your own administrative scripts, and we'll
make an effort to use as many features and options as possible, so that you can see several of them in
action. Our example function will restart, shut down, log off, or power down remote computers. It'll
accept computer names from the pipeline, and will output objects that indicate which operations were
successful:

Reset-Computer.ps1

```
Function Reset-Computer {
<#
.Synopsis
    Remotely restart or shutdown a computer.
.Description
    The function will Restart, Shutdown, PowerDown, or Logoff
    a remote computer.
.Parameter Computername
    What is the name of the computer to remotely control. This
    parameter has an alias of CN.
.Parameter Force
    If specified, force all applications to close on the remote machine.
.Parameter Operation
    What do you want to do with the remote computer. Valid choices are
    Restart, Shutdown, PowerDown, or Logoff.
    The default is Restart. This parameter has an alias of OP.
.Example
    PS C:\> reset-computer server01 -force

    This will restart computer server01, forcing any open applications to close.
.Example
    PS C:\> get-content fileservers.txt | reset-computer -op Logoff
```

```
    In this example, all the computers listed in fileservers.txt will be
    piped to Restart-Computer. Each computer will be logged off.
.Example
    PS C:\> "lab01","lab02","lab03" | reset-computer -op shutdown -force -verbose

    Shutdown computers lab01, lab02 and lab03 forcing applications close and
    displaying verbose information about what the function is doing.

.ReturnValue
    [BOOLEAN]

.Link
   Get-WMIObject

.Notes
 NAME:      Reset-Computer
 VERSION:   1.1
 AUTHOR:    Don Jones/Jeffery Hicks
 LASTEDIT:  4/22/2009 5:00:00 PM

#requires -version 2.0
#>

 [CmdletBinding(
  SupportsShouldProcess=$True,
  ConfirmImpact="high"
  )]

param (
    [Parameter(
     ValueFromPipeline=$True,
     Position=0,
     Mandatory=$True,
     HelpMessage="Computer name(s) to target")]
    [Alias("CN")]
    [String[]]$computerName,

    [Parameter(
     Mandatory=$false,
     Position=1,
     HelpMessage="Restart,Shutdown,PowerDown, or Logoff")]
    [Alias("OP")]
    [ValidateSet("Restart","Shutdown","PowerDown","Logoff")]
    [String]$operation="Restart",

    [Parameter(
     HelpMessage="Forces applications to close")]
    [Switch]$force
    )

BEGIN {
    Write-Debug "In the BEGIN script block."
    Write-Debug "passing value of operation $Operation to switch"
    switch ($operation) {
        "Logoff"    { $opcode = 0 }
        "Restart"   { $opcode = 2 }
        "Shutdown"  { $opcode = 1 }
        "PowerDown" { $opcode = 8 }
    }
    if ($force) {
       Write-Verbose "Using Force option"
       Write-Debug "Adding 4 to opcode ($opcode)"
        $opcode += 4
```

```
    }
    Write-Debug "Win32Shutdown opcode is $opcode"
}
PROCESS {
    trap {
        Write-Debug "trap called"
        Set-Variable -Name connected -Scope 1 -Value $false
        Write-Verbose "Connection to $computername failed"
        continue
    }
    Write-Verbose "Attempting connection to $computername"
    $connected = $True
    $wmi = Get-WmiObject win32_operatingsystem -computername $computerName -enableAllPrivileges
-ea "Stop"

    Write-Debug "Creating custom PSObject"
    $obj = New-Object PSObject
    $obj | Add-Member NoteProperty ComputerName $($computerName)
    $obj | Add-Member NoteProperty Success $false

    if ($connected) {
        Write-Debug "Connected is True"
        foreach    ($os in $wmi) {
            Write-Verbose "Attempting operation $opcode on $computername"
            if ($pscmdlet.shouldprocess($computername)) {
                Write-Debug "Calling the Win32Shutdown() method"
                $return = $os.win32shutdown($opcode)
                Write-Debug "return is $($return.returnvalue)"
                if ($return.returnvalue -eq 0) {
                    $obj.Success = $true
                }
                else {
                    Write-Debug "Action failed. Return is $return.returnvalue"
                }
            }
        }
    }
    Write-Debug "writing custom object to the pipeline"
    Write-Output $obj
}
END {
 Write-Debug "In the End script block"
 }
} #end function
```

Once loaded, here's how you might use it:

```
gc c:\files\computers.txt | reset-computer -op "Shutdown" | ft –auto
```

We'll walk through this example—it's reasonably complicated, so we'll break it down into the smallest chunks possible. We'll skip the Help definition section as that is self explanatory. The main body of the function begins with the [CmdletBinding()] type, which indicates that our function supports the ShouldProcess technique, meaning you can call it by using the -**WhatIf** and -**confirm** parameters, even though we don't have to specifically define those parameters:

```
[CmdletBinding(
  SupportsShouldProcess=$True,
  ConfirmImpact="high"
 )]
```

Next is our first parameter definition, **$computerName**. We've indicated that it is an array of strings, and that it can accept a collection of strings from the pipeline. It's mandatory, and positional, meaning that if it's used, its parameter name doesn't need to be specified—just its value. We've given it a **CN** alias:

```
param (
    [Parameter(
     ValueFromPipeline=$True,
     Position=0,
     Mandatory=$True,
     HelpMessage="Computer name(s) to target")]
    [Alias("CN")]
    [String[]]$computerName,
```

Next up, we define our **$operation** parameter. It has an **OP** alias and is not mandatory. We've provided a default value of "Restart". This parameter can accept only one of four possible values: Restart, Shutdown, PowerDown, or Logoff (which are not case-sensitive). PowerShell will automatically reject any other values for us, so we don't have to check these ourselves:

```
    [Parameter(
     Mandatory=$false,
     Position=1,
     HelpMessage="Restart,Shutdown,PowerDown, or Logoff")]
    [Alias("OP")]
    [ValidateSet("Restart","Shutdown","PowerDown","Logoff")]
    [String]$operation="Restart",
```

Finally we have the **$force** parameter, which is a switch—that means it doesn't need a value specified:

```
    [Parameter(
     HelpMessage="Forces applications to close")]
    [Switch]$force
```

In our function's BEGIN script block, we're going to translate the desired operation, and whether it should be forced, into the necessary numeric code. We looked these up on the Internet by using a search engine to find the Win32_OperatingSystem class, and then examined its Win32Shutdown method. Forcing the operation simply requires us to add 4 to the normal operation code, so we do that.

....

Plan Ahead
We've added numerous Write-Verbose expressions throughout the function to display informational messages. These messages will only be seen when using the common -Verbose parameter. We've also sprinkled some Write-Debug expressions as well to present more technical information if the -Debug parameter is used. We recommend you use either or both of these commands throughout your script or function. There's no performance penalty, and when the time comes to debug your script, you've already built in debug functionality.

Note that the BEGIN script block is not its own scope: The **$opcode** variable will be "seen" by the PROCESS and END script blocks:

```
BEGIN {
    Write-Debug "In the BEGIN script block."
    Write-Debug "passing value of operation $Operation to switch"
```

```
    switch ($operation) {
        "Logoff"    { $opcode = 0 }
        "Restart"   { $opcode = 2 }
        "Shutdown"  { $opcode = 1 }
        "PowerDown" { $opcode = 8 }
    }
    if ($force) {
        Write-Verbose "Using Force option"
        Write-Debug "Adding 4 to opcode ($opcode)"
        $opcode += 4
    }
    Write-Debug "Win32Shutdown opcode is $opcode"
}
```

Our PROCESS script block begins with an error trap:

```
PROCESS {
    trap {
        Write-Debug "trap called"
        Set-Variable -Name connected -Scope 1 -Value $false
        Write-Verbose "Connection to $computername failed"
        continue
    }
```

The only error we expect is a failure of WMI to connect to the specified computer, so if that happens we're writing out a verbose message. We exit the trap handler with the **continue** keyword, meaning PowerShell will go back and pick up at the line following the one that caused the error. The most important thing to notice here is that trap handlers are their own scope; any variables we create or change will be changed only within this scope. Our desire, however, is to change a variable named **$connected**, which exists in the function's scope—one level up from the trap handler.

Scope Hierarchy

The trap handler is its own scope, which is a parent of whatever scope contains the trap. Since the trap is contained within a cmdlet, the cmdlet is the parent of the trap. Therefore, the function's scope is the parent scope of the trap scope.

In order to change that parent scope variable, we use the **Set-Variable** cmdlet. We give it the variable name, the desired value, and a **-scope** parameter, which refers to the parent scope. A **-scope** value of 0 refers to the current scope, 1 refers to the parent, 2 refers to the parent's parent ("grandparent"), and so forth.

Next, the real PROCESS code begins. We'll write out a verbose message indicating which computer we're connecting to, we'll set our **$connected** variable to $true (we're optimists), and tell the **Get-WmiObject** cmdlet to retrieve the Win32_OperatingSystem class from the first computer. We've set its **-ErrorAction** (EA) parameter to "Stop" so that any errors result in an exception, which activates our trap handler:

```
    Write-Verbose "Attempting connection to $computername"
    $connected = $True
    $wmi = Get-WmiObject win32_operatingsystem -computername $computerName -enableAllPrivileges
-ea "Stop"
```

At this point, our **$connected** variable will be $true if the trap handler never ran—meaning we connected successfully. If a connection error occurred, our trap handler set the **$continue** variable to $false, and will resume execution at the following line. The following three lines simply create a new, custom object and add two properties: ComputerName and Success. We default the Success property to $false (we've stopped being optimists at this point):

```
$obj = New-Object PSObject
$obj | Add-Member NoteProperty ComputerName $($computerName)
$obj | Add-Member NoteProperty Success $false
```

We only want to perform the next bit if we're actually connected, so we check the value of the **$connected** variable. If it's $true, we'll run through the WMI objects that we got back (we're only expecting one, but this is how you have to work with WMI), and we write a verbose message indicating what we're about to do:

```
if ($connected) {
    Write-Debug "Connected is True"
    foreach    ($os in $wmi) {
        Write-Verbose "Attempting operation $opcode on $computername"
```

Before we continue, we call the **ShouldProcess()** method, passing along the computer name we're currently targeting. This gives the user the chance to review the operation and decide whether to continue—if they've specified the -**confirm** parameter, or if their system **$ConfirmPreference** is set to "High" or lower. We configured our cmdlet to have a "high" impact in the first line of the cmdlet definition, because we think restarting a computer is a pretty severe impact:

```
        if ($pscmdlet.shouldprocess($computername)) {
```

If ShouldProcess returns $true, then we'll attempt to execute the specified operation—shut down, power off, and so forth. The WMI method returns a value, and zero indicates success. So if we get a zero, we'll change our custom object's Success property to $true; otherwise, we leave it at $false:

```
            Write-Debug "Calling the Win32Shutdown() method"
            $return = $os.win32shutdown($opcode)
            Write-Debug "return is $($return.returnvalue)"
            if ($return.returnvalue -eq 0) {
                $obj.Success = $true
            }
            else {
                Write-Debug "Action failed. Return is $return.returnvalue"
            }
        }
    }
}
```

Next, we write the custom object to the pipeline:

```
Write-Output $obj
```

And finally, we wrap up our cmdlet. We're not using the END script block, but we left it in, with no code except for a **Write-Debug** cmdlet, as a placeholder:

```
END {
 Write-Debug "In the End script block"
 }
```

Finally, it's time to call our script. We create a text file containing several computer names, one computer name per line, and pipe them to our new cmdlet. We pipe the results to the **Format-Table** cmdlet and let it run:

```
gc c:\test\computers.txt | reset-computer -op "Shutdown" | ft –auto
```

We'll use one more test, this time without piping input:

```
Reset-computer "localhost" –op "Logoff" -confirm
```

You'll notice that most of the complexities of this task didn't have anything to do with an advanced function per se; they'd be complex if this was a normal function or script. The advanced function itself doesn't add much complexity to the task at hand, but it does make this functionality easier to reuse, and to use right within the pipeline.

Proxy Script Cmdlets

PowerShell v2.0 gives you the ability to retrieve the metadata of a normal cmdlet into a variable. *Metadata* is essentially a description of a cmdlet—its syntax, parameters, and so forth. For example, we'll start by retrieving the **Write-Host** cmdlet using the **Get-Command** cmdlet:

```
PS C:\> $wh = gcm write-host
```

Next, we'll create a new .NET Framework object from the System.Management.Automation. CommandMetaData class. This is part of Windows PowerShell's engine, so you don't have to do anything fancy to get this part of the Framework up and running—it's already there:

```
PS C:\> $metadata = new-object system.management.automation.commandmetadata $wh.implementingtype
```

This retrieves the metadata for the **Write-Host** cmdlet, which we can view simply by typing $metadata and pressing Enter:

```
PS C:\> $metadata

Name                    : Write-Host
CommandType             : Microsoft.PowerShell.Commands.WriteHostCommand
DefaultParameterSetName :
SupportsShouldProcess   : False
SupportsTransactions    : False
ConfirmImpact           : Medium
Parameters              : {[Object, System.Management.Automation.ParameterMetadata],
                          [NoNewline, System.Management.Automation.ParameterMetadata],
                          [Separator, System.Management.Automation.ParameterMetadata],
                          [ForegroundColor, System.Management.Automation.ParameterMetadata]...}
```

What's more interesting, though, is what another PowerShell class can do. The System.Management. Automation.ProxyCommand class has a static method called **Create().** Pass it the metadata for a cmdlet, and it'll produce an advanced function that "wraps" around the real cmdlet:

```
PS C:\test> [system.management.automation.proxycommand]::create($metadata)
[CmdletBinding()]
param(
```

```
    [Parameter(Position=0, ValueFromPipeline=$true, ValueFromRemainingArguments=$true)]
    [System.Object]
    ${Object},

    [Switch]
    ${NoNewline},

    [System.Object]
    ${Separator},

    [System.ConsoleColor]
    ${ForegroundColor},

    [System.ConsoleColor]
    ${BackgroundColor})
begin
{
    try {
        $outBuffer = $null
        if ($PSBoundParameters.TryGetValue('OutBuffer', [ref]$outBuffer))
        {
            $PSBoundParameters['OutBuffer'] = 1
        }
        $wrappedCmd = $ExecutionContext.InvokeCommand.GetCommand('Write-Host', [System.Management.
Automation.CommandTypes]::Cmdlet)
        $scriptCmd = {& $wrappedCmd @PSBoundParameters }
        $steppablePipeline = $scriptCmd.GetSteppablePipeline($myInvocation.CommandOrigin)
        $steppablePipeline.Begin($PSCmdlet)
    } catch {
        throw
    }
}

process
{
    try {
        $steppablePipeline.Process($_)
    } catch {
        throw
    }
}

end
{
    try {
        $steppablePipeline.End()
    } catch {
        throw
    }
}
<#

.ForwardHelpTargetName Write-Host
.ForwardHelpCategory Cmdlet

#>
```

You can rename this script cmdlet to something other than **Write-Host** if you want to, but it'll essentially work the same as the "real" **Write-Host** cmdlet. But wait, there's more.

Once you've got that cmdlet metadata (we stored it in the **$metadata** variable), you can manipulate it. For example, we'll change the name of our new cmdlet to **Write-OtherHost**:

```
PS C:\> $metadata.name = "Write-OtherHost"
```

We can also remove parameters, such as the **-BackgroundColor** parameter:

```
PS C:\> $metadata.parameters.remove("BackgroundColor")
```

Now, we can produce a modified advanced function:

```
PS C:\test> $code=[system.management.automation.proxycommand]::create($metadata)
PS C:\test> write "Function Write-OtherHost { $code }" | out-file write-Otherhost.ps1
PS C:\test: get-content write-Otherhost.ps1

Function Write-OtherHost { [CmdletBinding()]
param(
    [Parameter(Position=0, ValueFromPipeline=$true, ValueFromRemainingArguments=$true)]
    [System.Object]
    ${Object},

    [Switch]
    ${NoNewline},

    [System.Object]
    ${Separator},

    [System.ConsoleColor]
    ${ForegroundColor})

begin
{
    try {
        $outBuffer = $null
        if ($PSBoundParameters.TryGetValue('OutBuffer', [ref]$outBuffer))
        {
            $PSBoundParameters['OutBuffer'] = 1
        }
        $wrappedCmd = $ExecutionContext.InvokeCommand.GetCommand('Write-Host', [System.Management.
Automation.CommandTypes]::Cmdlet)
        $scriptCmd = {& $wrappedCmd @PSBoundParameters }
        $steppablePipeline = $scriptCmd.GetSteppablePipeline($myInvocation.CommandOrigin)
        $steppablePipeline.Begin($PSCmdlet)
    } catch {
        throw
    }
}

process
{
    try {
        $steppablePipeline.Process($_)
    } catch {
        throw
    }
}

end
{
    try {
        $steppablePipeline.End()
    } catch {
        throw
    }
```

```
}
<#

.ForwardHelpTargetName Write-Host
.ForwardHelpCategory Cmdlet

#>
 }
```

Now our new **Write-OtherHost** advanced function has all the features of the **Write-Host** cmdlet, but without the **-BackgroundColor** parameter.

The practical upshot of all this is that you can modify built-in cmdlets by wrapping them in an advanced function, and modifying their parameters. For example, if you don't want to allow people to change the background color of output, then you'd give them a replacement Write-Host—in the form of an advanced function that lacked the **-backgroundColor** parameter.

Chapter 49
Creating PowerShell Cmdlets and Snap-Ins in the .NET Framework

This is *definitely* an advanced topic. Before you proceed, you should know that cmdlets can only be written in .NET Framework languages, such as Visual Basic .NET (VB) or C# (pronounced "C Sharp"). We're not here to teach you those things, and, in fact, we're assuming that if you're reading this chapter, you're already familiar with programming in those languages. Cmdlet development is also *definitely* beyond the scope of "systems programming" or "administrative scripting," which is what the rest of this book is about. However, at the time we're writing this, nobody else has really documented cmdlet development, so we figured we'd give it a shot. Honestly, if you're already pretty familiar with VB or C#, then writing a cmdlet isn't really that difficult.

We also need to point out that this short chapter is obviously not a complete work on cmdlet development. We could (and others have) write a complete *book* about this subject; our goal here is just to give you an overview of what cmdlet development looks like and give you a jumping-off point for further exploration, if you find that this topic interests you.

Incidentally, the previous chapter on advanced functions introduces a lot of techniques and concepts which *do* carry over directly into .NET Framework-based cmdlets. So, if you've read the previous chapter, then you're halfway there, and this chapter will probably give you enough additional information to create some pretty powerful cmdlets.

Much of the sample code in this chapter is taken from SAPIEN Technologies' extensions for PowerShell, a free snap-in you can download from www.primaltools/community. That isn't an open-source project, so we won't be sharing the source code for all of the cmdlets in that snap-in. However, if you visit www.CodePlex.com, and search for "PowerShell," you'll find a number of other projects that *are* open source, and you can check out their source code. Don wrote a game that runs as PowerShell cmdlets, and you'll find it on CodePlex at www.codeplex.com/powerquest.

Some Terminology and the Basic Process

Remember that cmdlets live in snap-ins, which are basically .NET Framework DLL files. A snap-in can contain more than one cmdlet, but you have to add the entire snap-in and all its cmdlets to PowerShell at the same time; you can't pick and choose. So, creating a new cmdlet involves first creating a snap-in for the cmdlet to live in; from there, you can start adding cmdlets to the snap-in.

When you're finished programming a snap-in (and its cmdlets), you must *compile* it into a finished DLL. That DLL must exist on any system that needs to use the snap-in and the cmdlets it contains. The DLL must initially be *registered* so that PowerShell can detect its existence, and then you can add it to the shell by using the **Add-PSSnapin** cmdlet. If you later recompile a snap-in, you can just drop the new DLL on top of the old one; there's no need to re-register it. But you will need to restart PowerShell.

Getting Started: You Need an Environment

Don't think for a moment that you're going to get away with using Notepad to create cmdlets. Yes, it's physically possible, but only a madman would try. Instead, you'll need a copy of Visual Studio 2005 or later (or one of the free "Express" editions of Visual Studio, at least). Or, if you happen to have SAPIEN PrimalScript 2009, you'll find that it does a bang-up job for cmdlet development as well as PowerShell scripting. Because we *do* happen to have PrimalScript 2009, we'll be using it and giving you directions to follow along (you can get a free trial of the software from www.primalscript.com/downloadtrial).

You're also going to need the System.Management.Automation DLL, and you will not believe how far out of their way Microsoft has gone to make this thing difficult to find. Start by going to www. microsoft.com/download, and in the download search box (not the "all Microsoft.com" search box), type "framework sdk", and then click Go. You're looking for the .NET Framework 3.0 SDK for your platform (x86 or x64); Microsoft seems to move this thing constantly and it can be quite infuriating to locate. Worse, when you finally get it, you're going to have to install pretty much all of it in order for the "Reference Assemblies" to be installed. We haven't figured out which little component of the SDK does this, so we typically just install the whole SDK on a virtual machine, grab the Reference Assemblies from the Program Files folder, and then copy them over to the computer we're actually working on. Fun, huh? Next time you talk to someone at Microsoft, ask them why the heck they can't ship this one little DLL with PowerShell itself.

....

Don't Get Excited
By the way, don't get excited if you find System.Management.Automation.ni.dll. That won't help you; that's a pre-compiled version that's actually used by PowerShell, but you can't use it to make new cmdlets. Sorry.

Once you get this thing onto your system, it should be in \Program Files\Reference Assemblies\Microsoft\WindowsPowerShell\v1.0. There are actually five total DLLs that you'll need:

- Microsoft.PowerShell.Commands.Management.dll

- Microsoft.PowerShell.Commands.Utility.dll

- Microsoft.PowerShell.ConsoleHost.dll

- Microsoft.PowerShell.Security.dll

- System.Management.Automation.dll

Creating a New Snap-In

To get started, go to PrimalScript's File menu and select New > Project. Then, select either Visual Basic Projects or C Sharp Projects, depending on which .NET Framework language you plan to work in. In the Templates window, select Windows PowerShell Snapin. Give your snap-in a name (we're using "TestToys"), specify a location for it on your hard disk, and then click OK.

When PrimalScript displays the workspace browser (usually on the right of the screen), double-click PSSnapin.vb. This is the file that defines your snap-in. Really, all you need to do is modify the strings returned by the various functions, such as the name, vendor name, description, and so forth. You can use the AssemblyInfo.vb files to set the information that is displayed when someone right-clicks the DLL file in Windows Explorer and selects Properties. This information includes the version number, title, description, copyright information, and so forth.

That's it—you've made a snap-in! Of course, without a cmdlet in there, it won't do much good.

This would be a good time, however, to add a reference to the System.Management.Automation.dll. In PrimalScript, expand the References node in the Workspace browser, and you'll probably see the reference already in there; right-click and remove it. We're going to re-add it, just to make sure it has the correct path for *your* system. Right-click References and select Add Reference; on the .NET tab, click the Browse button, find System.Management.Automation.dll, and then double-click it. Now you should have the proper reference in your project—why not save it at this time?

Creating a New Cmdlet

To begin adding a new cmdlet, right-click the project name ("TestToys," in our case), and select Add > Add New Item. From the list of categories, select Windows PowerShell Cmdlet, and then select Windows PowerShell Cmdlet from the Templates window. Create a name for your cmdlet—we're going with PingComputerCmdlet—and click OK. To begin working with your new cmdlet, just double-click its .VB file to open that file in the editor window.

Our goal is to create a cmdlet that accepts one or more String objects, which we expect to either be computer names or IP addresses. We'll define a **-name** parameter to accept this input, but we also want to accept input from the pipeline. We want our cmdlet to attempt to ping each specified address, and, if it's successful, to output that same address. Essentially, we're building a filter: Computer names go in, but only the ones that we could successfully ping will come out. We can then pipe those successful names to some other cmdlet, which attempts to connect to those computers.

Naming Your Cmdlet

The first thing you need to do is pick a name for your new cmdlet. You'll notice that the cmdlet code starts with something like this:

```
<Cmdlet(VerbsCommon.Get, "PingComputerCmdlet", SupportsShouldProcess:=True)> _
```

That's definitely not correct. Rather than VerbsCommon.Get, we want to specify another verb: Ping. The PowerShell SDK lists the allowable verbs. The documentation starts at http://msdn2.microsoft.com/en-us/library/ms714674.aspx, but we're specifically interested in those verbs that are at http://msdn2.microsoft.com/en-us/library/ms714428.aspx. We see that the Ping verb is listed as a Diagnostic Verb, meaning it'll be VerbsDiagnostic.Ping. We'll change the noun portion of our cmdlet name to Computer, resulting in the following:

```
<Cmdlet(VerbsDiagnostic.Ping, "Computer", SupportsShouldProcess:=True)> _
```

Because our cmdlet doesn't do anything potentially dangerous, we're not going to support the **-Confirm** or **-WhatIf** parameters. Therefore, we're going to set the SupportsShouldProcess metavariable to FALSE:

```
<Cmdlet(VerbsDiagnostic.Ping, "Computer", SupportsShouldProcess:=False)> _
```

That leaves us with this as our entire cmdlet code:

```
<Cmdlet(VerbsDiagnostic.Ping, "Computer", SupportsShouldProcess:=False)> _
Public Class PingComputerCmdlet
    Inherits Cmdlet

    '<Parameter(Position:=0, Mandatory:=False)> _
    'Public Property Name() As String
    '   Get
    '       Return ""
    '   End Get
    '   Set(ByVal value As String)
    '   End Set
    'End Property

    Protected Overrides Sub ProcessRecord()
        Try
            Throw New NotImplementedException()
        Catch ex As Exception

        End Try
    End Sub

End Class
```

By the Way...
You may have noticed that we're programming our cmdlet in VB. You're welcome to use C#, if you prefer; the online documentation we've referenced provides examples in C# (which is one reason we decided to go with VB—just to be different).

Now we're ready to start creating input parameters for our cmdlet.

Creating Cmdlet Parameters

The cmdlet template provided in PrimalScript has a block of comments that show how to declare a PowerShell cmdlet parameter. We're just going to uncomment that block and use it as-is. Because our cmdlet can't operate without some input, we're setting our parameter to Mandatory and we'll leave it named "**-Name**".

```
<Parameter(Position:=0, Mandatory:=True)> _
```

We're also going to declare a variable, which will hold whatever data is passed in through this parameter. The variable declaration occurs *outside* the parameter's Property block:

```
Dim Address As string
```

Notice that we've defined this as a single string, not an array. Keep that in mind.

Also notice that the Get block simply returns the current property value. We're storing the current value in Address, so when the Get block is called, we simply want to return whatever's in Address:

```
Get
     Return Address
End Get
```

Similarly, when new data is passed into the parameter via the Set block, we want to put that data into our Address variable so that we can work with it. Therefore, we'll modify the Set block. The variable "value" is provided for us as the variable that receives incoming data; we'll just transfer that into our Address variable for long-term storage.

```
Set(ByVal value As String)
     Address = value
End Set
```

So, our entire parameter declaration looks like this:

```
Dim Address As String
<Parameter(Position:=0, Mandatory:=True)> _
Public Property Name() As String
    Get
        Return Address
    End Get
    Set(ByVal value As String)
        Address = value
    End Set
End Property
```

Since this is the only parameter we need, we're *almost* done with this part. If we did create additional parameters, they'd all need a unique Property name, and they'd need a unique Position value. The Mandatory value could be modified for each one as appropriate. Typically, parameters aren't any more complicated than this.

Input Validation in Parameters

You could, if you wanted to, perform some input validation in the Set block to make sure that any incoming data is what you expect. For example, let's say we created a parameter that was accepting date input. To check and make sure we got a date, we could do something like this:

```
<Parameter(Position:=0, Mandatory:=True)> _
Public Property Today() As String
    Get
        Return TodayDate
    End Get
    Set(ByVal value As String)
     If isdate(value) Then
            TodayDate = value
        Else
            Throw New Exception("Bad input")
        End If
    End Set
End Property
```

Here, we've used an If/Then block to determine if the incoming data is a valid date or not. If it is, we go ahead and put it into our storage variable, TodayDate. Otherwise, we have VB throw an exception, which would be passed up to Windows PowerShell.

Pipeline Parameters

We did say that we wanted our **-name** parameter to accept input from the pipeline, so we need to modify it slightly by adding an additional attribute to its declaration:

```
Dim Address As string

<Parameter(Position:=0, Mandatory:=True, ValueFromPipeline:=True)> _
Public Property Name() As String
    Get
        Return Address
    End Get
    Set(ByVal value As String)
        Address = value
    End Set
End Property
```

By adding the ValueFromPipeline attribute, we're telling PowerShell that complete input objects can be fed to this parameter from the pipeline. That's an important distinction: We want the *complete* input object, which we're expecting to be a String collection. Another option is to only have the parameter accept a single *property* from the pipeline objects. To do that, you'd specify the ValueFromPipelineByName attribute instead. If we did that, then the input objects would have to have a Name property, which would match the name of our parameter. PowerShell would *just* feed the Name properties of input objects to our parameter.

Overriding an Input Processing Method

Finally, we have to "override" one of the cmdlet's default input processing methods. All cmdlets are built from a template that's essentially built into PowerShell; whenever PowerShell executes a cmdlet, it automatically executes three distinct phases. Remember, these all happen for *each* cmdlet that is run. They are:

- **BeginProcessing:** This is called when the cmdlet is initially executed.

- **ProcessRecord:** This is called once for each input object that is passed to the cmdlet.

- **EndProcessing:** This is called after all input objects have been sent to the cmdlet for processing.

The template that cmdlets are built on defines three methods that correspond to these "execution phases." The trick is that the template's methods *don't do anything*. So, if we do nothing else with our cmdlet, all three methods will execute without error, but nothing will happen. In order to have our cmdlet do useful work, we have to *override* at least one of these methods, substituting our own code for the template's empty methods.

If your cmdlet doesn't accept pipeline input, then it should override the EndProcessing method. Our cmdlet *does* accept pipeline input, so we must at least override the ProcessRecord method:

```
Protected Overrides Sub ProcessRecord()
    Try
        Throw New NotImplementedException()
    Catch ex As Exception
```

```
        End Try
    End Sub
```

Here's how this works: If 10 objects are pipelined into our cmdlet, then the cmdlet's **ProcessRecord()** method will be executed *10 times*. Each time, PowerShell will set our input parameter **-name** to a new pipeline input object. In that fashion, we'll be processing all 10 input objects, although our cmdlet only has to worry about processing one of them at a time.

The default code PrimalScript gives us simply throws an exception indicating that the **ProcessRecord()** method hasn't yet been implemented. We'll remove that default code and substitute our own.

Coding the Cmdlet

One of the reasons we like working in VB rather than C# is because VB has a neat object called My, which contains a lot of cool functionality. For example, **My.Computer.Ping()** is a method that pings a computer by name or IP address, and returns a TRUE or FALSE value if the computer was reachable or not. Since we already know that our Address variable will contain the address we want to ping, it's pretty easy to build the functional code of our cmdlet:

```
    If My.Computer.Network.Ping(Address) Then

    End If
```

Now all we need to do is create some output. That is, if the ping was successful, we want to output the same address we received as input. PowerShell provides a built-in **WriteObject()** method that will do the trick:

```
    If My.Computer.Network.Ping(Address) Then
        WriteObject(Address)
    End If
```

That's a pretty straightforward, yet useful, cmdlet.

Your finished .VB file should look something like this:

```
Imports System.Management.Automation

<Cmdlet(VerbsDiagnostic.Ping, "Computer", SupportsShouldProcess:=False)> _
Public Class PingComputerCmdlet
    Inherits Cmdlet

    Dim Address As String

    <Parameter(Position:=0, Mandatory:=True, ValueFromPipeline:=True)> _
    Public Property Name() As String
        Get
            Return Address
        End Get
        Set(ByVal value As String)
            Address=value
        End Set
    End Property

    Protected Overrides Sub ProcessRecord()
        If My.Computer.Network.Ping(Address) Then
        WriteObject(Address)
```

```
     End If

  End Sub

End Class
```

Compiling the Snap-In

Now we're ready to compile the cmdlet into a DLL. From PrimalScript, this is pretty easy: From the Build menu, select Build Workspace. Note that PrimalScript requires you to have installed the .NET Framework SDK in order for compilation to work; that's because PrimalScript is simply calling on the compilers provided with the Framework SDK. If you installed the Framework SDK in order to obtain PowerShell's reference assemblies, then you should be ready to go.

Registering the Snap-In

The .NET Framework (just the Framework runtime, not the whole SDK) includes an **InstallUtil.exe** utility that registers assemblies like your new snap-in. To use it, open a new PowerShell window and type this:

```
PS C:\> set-alias installutil $env:windir\Microsoft.NET\Framework\v2.0.50727\installutil
```

Note that this is a reference to the .NET Framework 2.0 folder; this is okay even if you're using v3.0 of the Framework, because v3.0 is really just a set of add-ons to 2.0. PowerShell itself is written and compiled in v2.0.

Next, run this:

```
PS C:\> installutil "path\file.dll"
```

You'll provide the complete path and file to your snap-in DLL. Make sure your snap-in DLL is someplace permanent; once you register it this way, PowerShell will always look for it in that location.

Adding the Snap-In

You can add registered snap-ins by using the **Add-PSSnapIn** cmdlet. If your cmdlet is named TestToys, just run this:

```
PS C:\> add-pssnapin testtoys
```

That's it—you should be able to run the **Get-PSSnapIn** cmdlet and see your new snap-in. To see the cmdlets included in your snap-in run:

```
PS C:\> get-command -pssnapin testtoys

CommandType     Name                  Definition
-----------     ----                  ----------
Cmdlet          Ping-Computer         Ping-Computer [-Name] <String> [-Verbose] [-Debu..
```

If you want your snap-in to be available every time you start PowerShell, don't forget to add it in your profile.

Removing the Snap-In

If for some reason you need or want to remove the snap-in after it has been registered, the easy approach is to use the **installutil** alias:

```
PS C:\> installutil /u "filepath\testtoys.dll"
```

If that fails, you might need to delete the registry entry under HKLM:\SOFTWARE\Microsoft\ PowerShell\1\PowerShellSnapIns, and then restart PowerShell.

Using the New Cmdlet

We're going to read a list of computer names from a text file and pipe them to the **Ping-Computer** cmdlet. The contents of the text file are as follows:

```
DON-LAPTOP
LOCALHOST
DON-PC
SERVER2
```

Of these, only the second and third names are actually reachable on our network. Here's the cmdlet in action:

```
PS C:\> get-content c:\computers.txt | ping-computer
Ping-Computer : An exception occurred during a Ping request.
At line:1 char:44
+ get-content c:\computers.txt | ping-computer <<<<
```

Oops! Well, not everything goes perfectly the first time. Unfortunately, there's no super-easy way to debug cmdlets. You basically have to try and analyze what happened, modify the cmdlet, re-compile it (which will require you to shut down PowerShell so that the snap-in DLL can be overwritten), and then try again.

Debugging Cmdlets

After a bit of fussing, we got things working properly:

```
PS C:\> get-content c:\computers.txt | ping-computer
LOCALHOST
DON-PC
```

The problem, it turns out, is that the **My.Computer.Ping()** method will generate an exception if it's unable to resolve a name to an IP address. On our test network, which doesn't use DNS, it wasn't able to resolve the first name to an IP address, so it wasn't able to even try pinging it. We solved the problem by simply adding some VB error trapping to our cmdlet, so that any exceptions wouldn't cause it to quit:

```
Protected Overrides Sub ProcessRecord()
    Try
        If My.Computer.Network.Ping(Address) Then
            WriteObject(Address)
        End If
    Catch ex As Exception
    End Try
```

```
    End Sub
```

This isn't a great practice, programming-wise; we *should* be checking to see what error occurred and handling it, if possible. But we know that about the only thing that can go wrong is for the name-to-IP address resolution to fail, and there's nothing we can do about that if it happens—so we haven't put any "error handling" code in the Catch block.

Here's the revised .VB file:

```
Imports System.Management.Automation

<Cmdlet(VerbsDiagnostic.Ping, "Computer", SupportsShouldProcess:=False)> _
Public Class PingComputerCmdlet
    Inherits Cmdlet

    Dim Address As String

    <Parameter(Position:=0, Mandatory:=True, ValueFromPipeline:=True)> _
    Public Property Name() As String
        Get
            Return Address
        End Get
        Set(ByVal value As String)
            Address=value
        End Set
    End Property

    Protected Overrides Sub ProcessRecord()
        Try
            If My.Computer.Network.Ping(Address) Then
             WriteObject(Address)
            End If
        Catch ex As Exception

        End Try

    End Sub

End Class
```

Making Help

By default, when someone uses the **Get-Help** cmdlet (or the **Help** function) to ask for help on your cmdlets, PowerShell looks for an XML-formatted Help file located in the same folder as your snap-in DLL. This XML format is *complicated*, and it's absolutely not worth your time to cobble one together manually. Fortunately, a member of the Windows PowerShell team took the time to build a graphical tool capable of creating PowerShell-compatible Help files. Download it from http://www.wassimfayed. com/PowerShell/CmdletHelpEditor.zip, run it (be sure to read its documentation), and then you're ready to go. Your snap-in has to be pretty much finished before you can begin authoring the Help file; the utility looks at your snap-in and sets up appropriate sections for each cmdlet, each parameter, and so forth.

It's All in the Framework

While we certainly haven't shown you every possible permutation of cmdlet development, we've definitely given you a kick-start. Hopefully, if you're already experienced in VB or C#, you'll have enough to begin creating your own cmdlets and snap-ins and extending the capabilities of Windows PowerShell.

However, as you've seen here, the actual process of creating a cmdlet or snap-in is pretty straightforward. It's the *functionality* of your cmdlets—the code that makes them do whatever it is you want them to do—that's complex. For that, we can't provide a lot of help: You'll need to dig into Microsoft .NET Framework development much deeper than we can do in this administrator-focused book. We do know that many administrators have some programming experience in their background, and that you may already have some Framework familiarity. For those administrators, diving in and creating cmdlets should be pretty simple now that you've seen how it's done.

A Practical Example

Although the example we showed you is definitely practical, we want to do something a bit more complicated to wrap up this chapter. Our goal is to redo our **Ping-Computer** cmdlet so that it outputs a custom object type for each computer name provided to it. Each of those objects will expose a number of properties, including the computer name that we attempted to ping, whether it was successful, and other statistics. Such a custom object is more flexible because we'll be outputting an object even if a ping fails; this allows a subsequent pipeline cmdlet, such as the **Where-Object** cmdlet, to filter the results for whatever you have in mind at the time.

> **This is Rocket Science**
> Well, it's not exactly rocket science, but this is a much more complicated and .NET Framework-centric example. We won't be explaining all of the underlying Framework concepts in exhaustive detail, so if this is a bit over your head, that's okay; you're not missing anything that's actually important to the day-to-day operation of PowerShell. If you're diving this far into cmdlet authoring, we're assuming that you have a good Framework grounding in the first place.

We'll start by defining a new class named PingResult. In .NET Framework, a class is basically the description of what a given object will look like. In this case, we've simply defined four basic properties. Notice that we declare an "internal" variable, whose names we start with an underscore (that's our convention, not something you *have* to do). These variables hold the actual property values; the four Property routines provide a means of changing and retrieving those values.

Next up is our actual cmdlet class. You'll notice that we've abandoned the special **My** object and switched to using WMI to perform the ping; that's because the WMI Win32_PingStatus class provides more detailed information, rather than just a "success" or "failure" rating. Our cmdlet's **ProcessRecord()** subroutine is called once for each pipeline object passed into the cmdlet; for each one, it attempts to ping the computer name provided. It constructs a new object of our PingResult type and populates the object's properties from values provided by the Win32_PingStatus class. Each PingResult object is written to the output pipeline.

First up, the PingResult class:

PingResult.vb

```
Public Class PingResult

'the following is one line
 Private _ComputerName As String, _StatusCode As Integer, _ResponseTime As Integer, _
ProtocolAddress As String

  Public Property ComputerName() As String
```

```
        Get
            Return _ComputerName
        End Get
        Set(ByVal value As String)
            _ComputerName = value
        End Set
    End Property

    Public Property StatusCode() As Integer
        Get
            Return _StatusCode
        End Get
        Set(ByVal value As Integer)
            _StatusCode = value
        End Set
    End Property

    Public Property ResponseTime() As Integer
        Get
            Return _ResponseTime
        End Get
        Set(ByVal value As Integer)
            _ResponseTime = value
        End Set
    End Property

    Public Property ProtocolAddress() As String
        Get
            Return _ProtocolAddress
        End Get
        Set(ByVal value As String)
            _ProtocolAddress = value
        End Set
    End Property

End Class
```

To add a class in PrimalScript, right-click on your workspace name, Select Add > Add New Item, and then pick Class from the Code section. Here's the revised cmdlet file:

PingComputerCmdlet.vb

```
Imports System.Management.Automation
Imports System.Management

<Cmdlet(VerbsDiagnostic.Ping, "Computer", SupportsShouldProcess:=True)> _
Public Class PingComputerCmd
    Inherits Cmdlet

    '<Parameter(Position:=0, Mandatory:=False)> _
    'Public Property Name() As String
    '    Get
    '        Return ""
    '    End Get
    '    Set(ByVal value As String)
    '    End Set
    'End Property

    Private _Name As String
    <Parameter(Position:=0, Mandatory:=False, ValueFromPipeline:=True, _
     HelpMessage:="The name or IP address to ping")> _
    Public Property Name() As String
```

```
        Get
            Return _Name
        End Get
        Set(ByVal value As String)
            _Name = value
        End Set
    End Property


    Protected Overrides Sub ProcessRecord()
        Dim Result As New PingResult

        'define query
        Dim Searcher As New System.Management.ManagementObjectSearcher( _
        "SELECT * FROM Win32_PingStatus WHERE Address = '" & _Name & "'")

        'execute query
        Dim PResults As System.Management.ManagementObjectCollection
        PResults = Searcher.Get()

        'run through results
        Dim PResult As System.Management.ManagementObject
        For Each PResult In PResults
            Result.ComputerName = _Name
            Result.StatusCode = PResult.GetPropertyValue("StatusCode")
            Result.ProtocolAddress = PResult.GetPropertyValue("ProtocolAddress")
            Result.ResponseTime = PResult.GetPropertyValue("ResponseTime")
            WriteObject(Result)
        Next

    End Sub

End Class
```

Before you compile this, you'll likely need to set Option Strict to Off.

When you use this new version, you can pipe in the contents of a file, or, as in this example, create a new array of strings and pipe that into the cmdlet:

```
PS C:\> @("localhost","don-pc","mediaserver","testbed") | ping-computer

ComputerName                StatusCode      ResponseTime ProtocolAddress
------------                ----------      ------------ ---------------
localhost                   0                          0 ::1
don-pc                      0                          0 fe80::e468:3091:f2...
mediaserver                 0                          0 192.168.4.103
testbed                     0                          0
```

You'll notice that the ProtocolAddress property contains the actual address that responded—in most cases, those are IPv6 addresses, since those computers are newer versions of Windows (running Windows Vista) that automatically configure themselves to use IPv6.

Also notice the value of outputting objects from the cmdlet, rather than just simple strings. Now, PowerShell's formatting cmdlets can take over and create lists and tables automatically by using the objects' properties. Even the **Get-Member** cmdlet can help, as shown here, by displaying the properties. Notice the TypeName: It consists of our snap-in's name (PrimalToys), and the class name we created in VB:

```
PS C:\> $results = @("localhost","don-pc","mediaserver","testbed") | ping-computer
PS C:\> $results | gm


   TypeName: PrimalToys.PingResult

Name                 MemberType     Definition
----                 ----------     ----------
Equals               Method         System.Boolean Equals(Object obj)
GetHashCode          Method         System.Int32 GetHashCode()
GetType              Method         System.Type GetType()
get_ComputerName     Method         System.String get_ComputerName()
get_ProtocolAddress  Method         System.String get_ProtocolAddress()
get_ResponseTime     Method         System.Int32 get_ResponseTime()
get_StatusCode       Method         System.Int32 get_StatusCode()
set_ComputerName     Method         System.Void set_ComputerName(String value)
set_ProtocolAddress  Method         System.Void set_ProtocolAddress(String value)
set_ResponseTime     Method         System.Void set_ResponseTime(Int32 value)
set_StatusCode       Method         System.Void set_StatusCode(Int32 value)
ToString             Method         System.String ToString()
ComputerName         Property       System.String ComputerName {get;set;}
ProtocolAddress      Property       System.String ProtocolAddress {get;set;}
ResponseTime         Property       System.Int32 ResponseTime {get;set;}
StatusCode           Property       System.Int32 StatusCode {get;set;}
```

While we won't pretend that creating cmdlets is *easy*, it is at least straightforward. Any complexity comes entirely from the complexity of the Framework itself, and not from the very small amount of overhead required to actually create a cmdlet or a snap-in.

Chapter 50
Transactional Operations

Windows PowerShell leverages the transactional file and registry systems present in Windows Server 2008, Windows Vista, and later versions of Windows.

Version-specific Information Follows
The information in this chapter does not apply to Windows XP, Windows Server 2003, or any prior version of Windows.

A *transaction* consists of a set of steps that are normally individual, independent operations, but which are "packaged" into a single operation. For example, when you delete a file under normal conditions, the file is deleted and stays that way. With a transaction, you might bundle several file deletions into a single *transaction*. At any time, you can *roll back* the transaction to undo all of the deletions made to that point; you can also *commit* the transaction to make all of the deletions permanent.

The purpose of transactions is to take several independent, yet related steps and make them into a single, *atomic* operation, meaning that either *all* of the operations succeed as a unit, or that none of them occur at all. Suppose, for example, that you have a home directory related to a user who has left the company. You also have several other directories which contain shortcuts into that user's home directory. You want to delete all of the shortcuts and the home directory; however, if any single delete operations fail, you don't want *any* of the deletions to become permanent: It's either all, or nothing. That's exactly what a transaction enables.

Beginning a Transaction

PowerShell needs to be told that you want to begin using its transactional capabilities. To do so, simply use the **Start-Transaction** cmdlet:

```
PS C:\> Start-Transaction
```

Note that you can only have a single transaction in effect at one time. It's not possible to have two transactions running in parallel so that you can choose which transaction a particular operation becomes a part of.

Wait... Only One Transaction?

It can *look like* PowerShell supports nested transactions. For example:

```
PS C:\> Start-Transaction
PS C:\> Start-Transaction
```

This might make it appear as if you've created a second, nested transaction within the first. But you haven't; the second **Start-Transaction** cmdlet simply re-uses the transaction created by the first. However, PowerShell *does* remember how many times you've run the **Start-Transaction** cmdlet; that'll become important when you're done with the transaction.

Multiple Transactions

Um, okay, it turns out you *can* have multiple transactions. Normally, when you're using the **Start-Transaction** cmdlet without any parameters, only a single transaction exists. It's scope-independent, which means scripts and other child scopes don't have their "own" transactions; they all share a single, common, global transaction.

You *can* create an independent transaction, using the **-Independent** parameter of the **Start-Transaction** cmdlet. The independent transaction isn't considered a "child" of the global transaction, but once you begin an independent transaction, all transactional operations will use it until it's completed or rolled back. We'll look at some examples of this behavior at the end of this chapter.

Transactional Operations

Transactional operations are conducted by using PowerShell's various ***-Item** cmdlets, such as **Get-ChildItem**, **Remove-Item**, **New-Item**, and so forth. Currently only the Registry PSProvider supports transactions:

```
PS C:\> get-psprovider | where {$_.Capabilities -like "*transactions*"}

Name                Capabilities                           Drives
----                ------------                           ------
Registry            ShouldProcess, Transactions            {HKLM, HKCU}
```

We'll use this for our demonstrations. The trick with transactions is that operations performed using these cmdlets *are not normally part of a transaction,* even if a transaction is in effect. In other words, assuming we've started a transaction by running the **Start-Transaction** cmdlet, the following command will occur immediately and will not be part of the transaction:

```
PS HKCU:\> new-item MyCompany
```

In order to have an operation become a part of an active transaction, you have to add the -**UseTransaction** parameter to the cmdlet:

```
PS HKCU:\> new-item MyCompany -usetransaction
```

Supported Transactional Operations

Currently, only the Registry PSDrive provider support transactions. Other PSDrive providers may gain transactional capabilities in the future, and third-party PSDrive providers also have the option of adding transactional capabilities.

Rolling Back or Committing a Transaction

Once you've started a transaction, you have two ways to complete it. Your first option is to run the **Complete-Transaction** cmdlet to commit the transaction, making any changes made "inside" the transaction permanent. Your second option is to run the **Undo-Transaction** cmdlet to abandon the transaction, "undoing" all of the changes made "inside" the transaction.

Using our previous example to illustrate these options:

1. You run the **Start-Transaction** cmdlet.

2. You run **new-item "MyCompany" –useTransaction**.

3. You run **new-itemproperty MyCompany -name "Location" -value "Las Vegas" –useTransaction** to add a registry value.

4. You run **Get-Item MyCompany** but you'll get an error about missing keys.

5. You run the **Complete-Transaction** cmdlet.

6. You run **Get-Item MyCompany**. This time, you get a result since the changes have been committed.

Multiple Calls to Start-Transaction

Earlier, we told you that you can run the **Start-Transaction** cmdlet multiple times, and PowerShell will simply re-use the transaction from the first time you run **Start-Transaction**. We also said that PowerShell keeps track of each **Start-Transaction** call; in order to complete a transaction, you have to run the **Complete-Transaction** cmdlet *the same number of times* as you've run **Start-Transaction**. In other words:

1. Run the **Start-Transaction** cmdlet.

2. Run the **Start-Transaction** cmdlet.

3. Run one or more transacted operations.

4. Run the **Complete-Transaction** cmdlet. At this point, *the transaction is still open*.

5. Run the **Complete-Transaction** cmdlet again—now, the transaction is actually complete.

This paired behavior does not apply to the **Undo-Transaction** cmdlet; when you run **Undo-Transaction**, the current transaction is cancelled and rolled back, no matter how many times you've run the **Start-Transaction** cmdlet at that point.

Independent Transactions

We promised to provide an example of how independent transactions work, and so here we go. You might find it helpful to have REGEDIT.EXE open so you can track progress:

1. Run the **Start-Transaction** cmdlet. This starts a new, global transaction.

2. Run a transacted operation, such as our steps to add the MyCompany registry value. This operation belongs to the global transaction.

3. Run **Start-Transaction –independent** to begin a new, independent transaction.

4. Run another transacted operation, such as creating a second registry key and values. Remember to use the **-UseTransaction** parameter. This operation belongs to the independent transaction.

5. Complete the independent transaction by running the **Complete-Transaction** cmdlet. At this point you should have the second registry item you created.

6. Run a third transacted operation by creating yet another registry item. Again, don't forget to use **-UseTransaction**. This operation belongs to the first transaction you started—the global one.

7. Roll back the global transaction by running the **Undo-Transaction** cmdlet. At this point you should have the second registry key because that occurred inside the independent transaction, which was committed and not rolled back.

Although the sequence of commands may make it seem as if the independent transaction is nested within the global one, "nested" isn't really an accurate term. The independent transaction is committed or rolled back independently, and isn't dependent upon the global transaction.

Practical Example

We'll conclude this chapter with a slightly more practical example modifying the registry. Let's imagine a situation where you want to add some keys and values to HKLM. Naturally if there is an error anywhere in the process you will want to rollback and undo any changes:

Demo-Transaction.ps1

```
#requires -version 2.0

Trap {
  Write-Warning $($_.Exception.Message)
  Undo-Transaction -verbose
  return
}

$path="HKLM:\System"

#Turn of the error pipeline
$errorActionPreference="SilentlyContinue"

#default rollbackPreference is on errors
Start-Transaction -RollbackPreference "Never"

New-Item -Path $path -name "MyCompany" -ea Stop -UseTransaction | Out-Null
New-Item -Path (Join-Path $path "MyCompany") -name "Config" -ea Stop -useTransaction | Out-Null

$Config=Join-Path $path "MyCompany\Config"

New-ItemProperty $Config -name "Server" -value "FX123" -ea Stop -useTransaction | Out-Null
```

```
New-ItemProperty $Config -name "LastUpdate" -value (Get-Date) -ea Stop -UseTransaction | Out-Null
New-ItemProperty $Config -name "UpdatePath" -Value "\\FS876\Updates" -ea stop -UseTransaction | Out-Null
New-ItemProperty $Config -name "version" -type "DWORD" -value 1 -ea Stop -useTransaction | Out-Null

Complete-Transaction
Write-Host "Registry update successful" -foregroundcolor Green
```

The script starts by defining a Trap which will display any error messages, rollback, and transactions using the **Undo-Transaction** cmdlet. After setting some variables we start the transaction process:

```
Start-Transaction -RollbackPreference "Never"
```

By default PowerShell will automatically roll back transactions on any error, but for the sake of illustration we are going to configure PowerShell to never automatically rollback. The main part of the script creates some registry keys using the **New-Item** cmdlet. Notice the -**UseTransaction** parameter:

```
New-Item -Path $path -name "MyCompany" -ea Stop -UseTransaction | Out-Null
New-Item -Path (Join-Path $path "MyCompany") -name "Config" -ea Stop -useTransaction | Out-Null
```

The script then creates some registry values using the **New-ItemProperty** cmdlet. Again, notice the use of the -**UseTransaction** parameter:

```
New-ItemProperty $Config -name "Server" -value "FX123" -ea Stop -useTransaction | Out-Null
New-ItemProperty $Config -name "LastUpdate" -value (Get-Date) -ea Stop -UseTransaction | Out-Null
New-ItemProperty $Config -name "UpdatePath" -Value "\\FS876\Updates" -ea stop -UseTransaction | Out-Null
New-ItemProperty $Config -name "version" -type "DWORD" -value 1 -ea Stop -useTransaction | Out-Null
```

Assuming no errors occurred, the transaction is committed by using the **Complete-Transaction** cmdlet and the script ends:

```
Complete-Transaction
Write-Host "Registry update successful" -foregroundcolor Green
```

But let's see what happens when something goes wrong. We'll introduce an error into the script:

```
New-ItemProperty $Config -name "UpdatePath" -type "FOOBAR" -Value "\\FS876\Updates" -ea stop
-UseTransaction | Out-Null
```

Here's what happens when we try to run the script:

```
PS C:\> C:\scripts\demo-transaction.ps1
WARNING: Could not bind parameter 'Type'. Could not convert "FOOBAR" to "Microsoft.Win32.
RegistryValueKind". The possible enumeration values are "String, ExpandString, Binary, DWord,
MultiString, QWord, Unknown".
VERBOSE: Performing operation "Rollback" on Target "Current transaction".
PS C:\>
```

The warning message comes from the Trap, and you can also see that the **Undo-Transaction** cmdlet is called because we used the -**Verbose** parameter.

Writing PowerShell commands to leverage transactions takes a little practice and a lot of testing. Unfortunately, until more PSProviders support transactions, you won't have many opportunities.

Chapter 51
Working with Events

Many classes in the .NET Framework expose *events*, which are special notifications that occur in Windows, generally on a timed basis or in reaction to something that happens in the operating system. For example, one of the classes in the .NET Framework is a *timer*; creating an instance of this class and piping that instance to the **Get-Member** cmdlet reveals a couple of events:

```
PS C:\> $timer = new-object System.Timers.Timer
PS C:\> $timer | gm


   TypeName: System.Timers.Timer

Name                       MemberType   Definition
----                       ----------   ----------
Disposed                   Event        System.EventHandler Disposed(System.Obj...
Elapsed                    Event        System.Timers.ElapsedEventHandler Elaps...
BeginInit                  Method       System.Void BeginInit()
Close                      Method       System.Void Close()
CreateObjRef               Method       System.Runtime.Remoting.ObjRef CreateOb...
Dispose                    Method       System.Void Dispose()
EndInit                    Method       System.Void EndInit()
Equals                     Method       System.Boolean Equals(Object obj)
GetHashCode                Method       System.Int32 GetHashCode()
GetLifetimeService         Method       System.Object GetLifetimeService()
GetType                    Method       System.Type GetType()
InitializeLifetimeService  Method       System.Object InitializeLifetimeService()
Start                      Method       System.Void Start()
Stop                       Method       System.Void Stop()
ToString                   Method       System.String ToString()
```

AutoReset	Property	System.Boolean AutoReset {get;set;}
Container	Property	System.ComponentModel.IContainer Contai...
Enabled	Property	System.Boolean Enabled {get;set;}
Interval	Property	System.Double Interval {get;set;}
Site	Property	System.ComponentModel.ISite Site {get;s...
SynchronizingObject	Property	System.ComponentModel.ISynchronizeInvok...

Responding to .NET Framework Object Events

The big event we'll be looking at is **Elapsed**, which occurs—or is *fired*, in programmer-speak—every time the timer "ticks." You determine how often that occurs by setting the timer's Interval property to a specific number of milliseconds, and then setting the timer's Enabled property to $True. Here's how:

```
PS C:\> $timer.interval = 1000
PS C:\> $timer.enabled = $true
```

If you're following along in the shell, then you'll have an **Elapsed** event firing off every second—the problem is, right now, Windows PowerShell basically ignores the event; it hasn't *registered* to actually do something when the event occurs.

> **Where Do We Get This Stuff?**
> Honestly, once we start talking about .NET Framework objects, we're leaving the realm of
> PowerShell scripting and moving firmly into the world of Framework development, just like a C# or
> Visual Basic developer. We can't possibly provide a reference on all the objects and events that are
> available—there are literally tens of thousands. What we can do—and will do, in this chapter—is
> show you how to work with object events that you've already discovered, perhaps through a good
> book on Framework development, or by browsing the online MSDN documentation at http://msdn.
> microsoft.com/library.

So let's decide what we want to *happen* when the timer "ticks." How about making the console beep?

```
PS C:\> $action = { [Console]::Beep(440, 300) }
```

We've just created a script block that makes the console beep. Now let's tell PowerShell to execute that script block when our timer's **Elapsed** event fires:

```
PS C:\> Register-ObjectEvent $timer "Elapsed" -SourceIdentifier "BeepALot" -Action $action
```

We've created an *event subscriber,* or what some folks would call an *event sink.* We named our subscriber "BeepALot," and in just a few seconds we will become very annoyed at all the beeping. When we want PowerShell to *stop* paying attention to the **Elapsed** event, we simply unregister our subscriber:

```
PS C:\> Unregister-Event BeepALot
```

One thing we learned while experimenting with this capability is not to use the **Write-Host** cmdlet as an event action, at least not for an event that's firing every second. What happens is that **Write-Host** fires so fast and frequently that you don't get a chance to type in the **Unregister-Event** cmdlet! We wound up just having to close the shell to shut it up. Live and learn!

More Event Capabilities

PowerShell has several cmdlets designed to deal with events. We'll look at some of these in more detail in a moment, but for now let's just see what they all are:

- **Register-ObjectEvent:** As we demonstrated, this subscribes PowerShell to a .NET Framework object event.

- **Unregister-Event:** Again, we demonstrated how this removes an event subscription.

- **Get-EventSubscriber:** This cmdlet lists all of the current event subscriptions that are registered with the shell.

- **New-Event:** This cmdlet actually creates and fires a new event *within the shell*. This is a bit different from an event fired by a .NET Framework object; think of it as a custom event.

- **Register-EngineEvent:** Unlike **Register-ObjectEvent**, which subscribes to a .NET Framework object event, this cmdlet subscribes to a custom event that you fire by using **New-Event**.

....

Built-in PSEvents

The various –Event cmdlets can also work with—specifically, let you register for—events fired by the PowerShell engine. PowerShell.Exiting is one such event, and it is fired when the shell begins to exit.

- **Remove-Event:** This cmdlet removes an event from the shell's event history.

- **Get-Event:** This cmdlet retrieves a list of events that have occurred within the shell—think of it as the event history log, in a way.

- **Wait-Event:** This cmdlet causes the shell to pause, or *block*, until the specified PSEvent occurs (is "fired"). When the shell is blocking, you can't do anything else—it's basically waiting for the event and won't do anything but that.

Responding to Custom Events and Shell Engine Events

Let's start by registering for a shell engine event—we'll have the message "Bye!" display just before the shell exits:

```
PS C:\> Register-EngineEvent "PowerShell.Exiting" -action { Write-Host "Bye!!" -foregroundcolor green}
```

This registers a subscriber for the PowerShell.Exiting event; when the event is fired, we'll see "Bye!!" on the command line. Test this by simply running **Exit** in the shell. However, before testing it, try getting a list of event subscribers, to prove that we've registered for the event:

```
PS C:\> Get-EventSubscriber


SubscriptionId    : 1
SourceObject      :
EventName         :
SourceIdentifier  : PowerShell.Exiting
Action            : System.Management.Automation.PSEventJob
HandlerDelegate   :
SupportEvent      : False
ForwardEvent      : False
```

```
PS C:\>
```

We could, of course, unregister the subscriber at this point:

```
PS C:\> unregister-event powershell.exiting
```

It *is* possible to have more than one subscription for the same event; when the event fires, each subscriber's action will be executed. To unregister one of these subscribers, you'll have to not only specify the event—such as PowerShell.Exiting (which is called the SourceIdentifier)—you'll also have to specify the SubscriptionId (shown in the output of the **Get-EventSubscriber** cmdlet) by using the **-SubscriberID** parameter of the **Unregister-Event** cmdlet.

Let's look at a related example: responding to a custom event. We have to start by making up an event name, called a SourceIdentifier. We'll use "My.Custom" for this example, and respond to the event by writing a message to the console:

```
PS C:\> register-Engineevent "My.Custom" -action { Write-Host "Fired!" –foregroundcolor Magenta }
```

Now, we can fire the event by using the **New-Event** cmdlet:

```
PS C:\> new-event "My.Custom"


ComputerName     :
RunspaceId       : 55837796-4401-41fb-9240-df9b4e28ebf0
EventIdentifier  : 1
Sender           :
SourceEventArgs  :
SourceArgs       : {}
SourceIdentifier : my.custom
TimeGenerated    : 8/31/2009 10:43:03 AM
MessageData      :


Fired!
PS C:\>
```

You can see our "Fired!" output, but you also see the object—an *event* object—which was returned by the **New-Event** cmdlet. Piping that to the **Out-Null** cmdlet will suppress that output and create a cleaner event reaction:

```
PS C:\> new-event "My.Custom" | out-null
Fired!
```

A Practical Example

Why use custom events: anytime you need a fixed reaction to occur, and you want to be able to trigger that action from anywhere in the shell. Think of an event subscriber as a sort of "universal function" that can be easily executed whenever you like. For example, you might want to create an event that writes information to a log file. In this case, you'll not only need to trigger the event, you'll also need to pass along some information to be written into the log file. That information will be passed as an *event argument*.

We'll start by registering our custom event subscriber, including the action:

```
Register-EngineEvent "Custom.Log" -Action {$args | Out-File $env:temp\log.txt -Append}
```

The magic bit in this subscriber registration is accessing the event argument that we'll pass in later. Within the event's action, the **$args** variable represents the event arguments that we pipe to the **Out-File** cmdlet. We can trigger this event as follows:

```
New-Event "Custom.Log" -EventArguments "$(get-date) Log this!" | Out-Null
```

Our first argument, "$(get-date) Log this!" goes into **$args** and our event subscriber appends this information to a fixed log file. When we're done, we need to make sure we unregister the event subscriber:

```
Unregister-Event "Custom.Log"
```

While custom events like this one certainly aren't something you'll probably use every single day, they definitely have some interesting uses in a production environment.

Appendix A
Automatic Variables in PowerShell

PowerShell defines a number of automatic variables that you can use. Note that some of these are context-dependent, meaning they're only available in certain situations. Also, while the majority of these are defined by PowerShell (meaning they're available under any hosting application), some of these are defined by PowerShell.exe and are only available to scripts running under that host, or under a host that is fully emulating PowerShell.exe.

Variable	Purpose
$$	The last token of the last line received by the shell
$?	$True is the last operation succeeded; otherwise, $False
$^	The first token of the last line received by the shell
$_	The current pipeline object (used in script blocks, filters, the **ForEach-Object** cmdlet, and the **Where-Object** cmdlet)
$Args	An array of the parameters passed to a function
$commandLineParameters	Accumulates command-line and pipeline paramaters
$culture	Contains culture (locale) information
$DebugPreference	The action to take when information is written to the debug pipeline ("Continue" means to display it; "SilentlyContinue" suppresses it)

Variable	Purpose
$Error	A collection of objects for which an error occurred
$ErrorActionPreference	The action to take when information is written to the error pipeline ("Continue" means to display it; "SilentlyContinue" suppresses it)
$False	Boolean value FALSE
$foreach	Refers to the enumerator in a foreach loop
$Home	Specifies the user's home directory; same as %homedrive%%homepath%
$Input	Contains the collection of pipeline objects sent to a script block
$LastExitCode	The exit code of the last external executable that was run
$MaximumAliasCount	The maximum number of aliases available
$MaximumDriveCount	The maximum number of drives available
$MaximumFunctionCount	The maximum number of functions available
$MaximumHistoryCount	The maximum number of entries saved in the command history
$MaximumVariableCount	The maximum number of variables available
$PsHome	The folder where Windows PowerShell is installed
$PSVersionTable	Contains PowerShell version information
$Host	Provides an interface to the hosting application
$OFS	Output Field Separator: Use when converting an array to a string; by default, is a space character
$ReportErrorShowExceptionClass	When $True, shows the class name of displayed exceptions
$ReportErrorShowInnerException	When $True, shows the chain of inner exceptions for displayed exceptions
$ReportErrorShowSource	When $True, shows the assembly name of displayed exceptions
$ReportErrorShowStackTrace	When $True, shows the stack traces for displayed exceptions
$ShouldProcessPreference	Specifies the action to take when a cmdlet is used with -confirm
$ShouldProcessReturnPreference	Value returned by ShouldPolicy
$StackTrace	Contains detailed stack trace information about the last error
$True	The Boolean value TRUE
$UICulture	Contains UI culture (locale) information

Variable	Purpose
$VerbosePreference	The action to take when information is written to the verbose pipeline ("Continue" means to display it; "SilentlyContinue" suppresses it)
$WarningPreference	The action to take when information is written to the warning pipeline ("Continue" means to display it; "SilentlyContinue" suppresses it)

Appendix B
Common .NET Framework Data Types

As we discussed throughout this book, PowerShell relies on the underlying .NET Framework types to handle data manipulation. This is a benefit for you, because those underlying Framework types pack in a lot of useful functionality. Our goal in this Appendix is to provide a quick reference to those types' *most useful* methods and properties—not a comprehensive reference, but rather a listing—with examples of those properties and methods that an administrator will get the most use from.

In the reference tables that follow, method names are always followed by (), but property names are not. That's how you can tell the difference between a property and a method.

[Boolean] [Bool] • System.Boolean
Contains TRUE/FALSE values

Name	Purpose	Example
ToString()	Returns a string representation of the object; e.g., the word "TRUE" or "FALSE."	$var.ToString()

[Byte] • System.Byte
Contains byte values

Name	Purpose	Example
ToString()	Returns a string representation of the byte.	$var.ToString()

[Char] • System.Char
Contains individual characters

Name	Purpose	Example
ToString()	Returns a string representation of the object; e.g., the character itself	$var.ToString()

[DateTime] • System.DateTime
Contains date and time values—note that the methods and properties produce output based upon your system's regional settings. For the below example, assume that $d or $t contain a date, time, or date/time value.

Name	Purpose	Example
Add()	*This method requires you to create instances of the Framework's TimeSpan class; instead, use one of the AddX() method below.*	
AddDays()	Adds the specified number of days	$d = $d.AddDays(2)
AddHours()	Adds the specified number of hours	$t = $t.AddHours(24)
AddMilliseconds()	Adds the specified number of milliseconds	$t = $t.AddMilliseconds(1000)
AddMinutes()	Adds the specified number of minutes	$t = $t.AddMinutes(-30) *Adding a negative number results in subtraction*
AddMonths()	Adds the specified number of months	$d = $d.AddMonths(6)
AddSeconds()	Adds the specified number of seconds	$t = $t.AddSeconds(60)
AddTicks()	Adds the specified number of ticks (a *tick* is a 100-nanosecond unit)	$t = $t.AddTicks(100)
AddYears()	Adds the specified number of years	$d = $d.AddYears(100)
Date	Extracts the date from the value	$d.Date
DateTime	Extracts the date and time from the value	$d.DateTime
Day	Extracts the day of the month from the value	$d.Day
DayOfWeek	Extracts the day of the week from the value	$d.DayOfWeek

Name	Purpose	Example
DayOfYear	Extracts the day of the year (Julian date) from the value	$d.DayOfYear
GetDateTimeFormats()	Returns an array with all possible string representations of the date	$d.GetDateTimeFormats()
Hour	Extracts the hour from the value	$d.Hour
IsDaylightSavingTime()	Returns $True or $False if Daylight Saving Time is active	$d.IsDaylightSavingTime()
Kind	Indicates whether the time is based on local time, Coordinated Universal Time (UTC), or neither	$d.Kind
Millisecond	Extracts the milliseconds from the value	$d.Millisecond
Minute	Extracts the minutes from the value	$d.Minute
Month	Extracts the month from the value	$d.Month
Second	Extracts the seconds from the value	$d.Second
Ticks	Extracts the ticks from the value. A tick is 100 nanoseconds.	$d.Ticks
TimeOfDay	Extracts the time of day from the value	$d.TimeOfDay
ToBinary()	Returns a 64-bit integer value representing the date	$d.ToBinary()
ToFileTime()	Returns a Windows file time	$d.ToFileTime()
ToFileTimeUtc()	Returns a Windows file name translated to Coordinated Universal Time (UTC)	$d.ToFileTimeUtc()
ToLocalTime()	Converts the time to local time	$d.ToLocalTime()
ToLongDateString()	Converts the value to a long date string	$d.ToLongDateString()
ToLongTimeString()	Converts the value to a long time string	$d.ToLongTimeString()
ToOADate()	Converts the value to an OLE Automation date	$d.ToOADate()
ToShortTimeString()	Converts the value to a short time string	$d.ToShortTimeString()
ToString()	Returns a generic string representation of the date.	
ToUniversalTime()	Converts the value to Coordinated Universal Time (UTC)	$d.ToUniversalTime()
Year	Extracts the year from the value	$d.Year

[Decimal] • System.Decimal

Contains decimal values

Name	Purpose	Example
ToString()	Returns a string representation of the decimal	$var.ToString()

[Double] • System.Double

Contains double-precision floating-point numeric values

Name	Purpose	Example
ToString()	Returns a string representation of the number	$var.ToString()

[Float] [Single] • System.Single

Contains single-precision floating-point numeric values

Name	Purpose	Example
ToString()	Returns a string representation of the number	$var.ToString()

[Hashtable] • System.Collections.Hashtable

Contains associative arrays (also called dictionaries or hashtables; see page 186)

Name	Purpose	Example
Add()	Adds an element with the specified key and value	$ht.Add("Key","Value")
Clear()	Clears the hashtable of all elements	$ht.Clear()
Contains()	Returns $True if the hashtable contains the specified key	$ht.Contains("MyKey")
ContainsKey()	Returns $True if the hashtable contains the specified key	$ht.ContainsKey("MyKey")
ContainsValue()	Returns $True if the hashtable contains the specified value	$ht.ContainsValue(5)
Count	The number of key/value pairs in the hashtable	$ht.Count
IsFixedSize	$True if the hashtable is a fixed size	$ht.IsFixedSize
IsReadOnly	$True if the hashtable is read-only	$ht.IsReadOnly
Item	Gets or sets the value associated with the specified key	$ht.Item("MyKey") = "MyValue" Write-Host $ht.Item("MyOtherKey")
Keys	Gets an array of the hashtable's keys	$a = $ht.Keys

Name	Purpose	Example
Remove()	Removes the element having the specified key	$ht.Remove("MyKey")
ToString()	Returns a string representation of the entire hashtable	$ht.ToString()
Values	Gets an array of the hashtable's values	$a = $ht.Values

[Int] • System.Int32
Contains 32-bit (regular) integer values

Name	Purpose	Example
ToString()	Returns a string representation of the number	$var.ToString()

[Long] • System.Int64
Contains 64-bit (long) integer values

Name	Purpose	Example
ToString()	Returns a string representation of the number	$var.ToString()

[Regex] • System.Text.RegularExpressions.Regex
Contains regular expression strings; below examples assume $r contains a valid regex

Name	Purpose	Example
GetGroupNames()	Returns an array of capturing group names for the regex	$r.GetGroupNames()
GetGroupNumbers()	Returns an array of capturing group numbers that correspond to the group names in an array	$r.GetGroupNumbers()
GroupNameFromNumber()	Gets the group name that matches the specified number	$r.GetGroupNameFromNumber(1)
GroupNumberFromName()	Gets the group number that matches the specified name	$r.GetGroupNumberFromName(0)
IsMatch() *Returns $True is a single match is found*	1. Returns $True if the specified string matches the regex 2. Start the regex comparison at a specified character position 3. Returns $True if the specified string matches the specified regex	1. $r.IsMatch("Test") 2. $r.IsMatch("Test",2) 3. $r.IsMatch("Test","\w+")

Name	Purpose		Example	
Match() *Returns the first match found*	1.	Returns a match where the specified string matches the regex	1.	$r.Match("Test")
	2.	Start the regex comparison at a specified character position	2.	$r.Match("Test",2)
	3.	Returns a match where the specified string matches the specified regex	3.	$r.Match("Test","\w+")
Matches() *Returns an array of all matches found*	1.	Returns a collection of matches where the specified string matches the regex	1.	$r.Matches("Test")
	2.	Start the regex comparison at a specified character position	2.	$r.Matches("Test",2)
	3.	Returns a collection of matches where the specified string matches the specified regex	3.	$r.Matches("Test","\w+")
Replace()	Within the specified input string, replace all strings that match the regex with the specified replacement string		$r.Replace("Input","Replace")	
Split()				
ToString()	Returns the regex expression as a string		$r.ToString()	
Options	Returns the options that the regex uses to operate		$r.Options	
RightToLeft	Returns $True if the regex searches from right to left		$r.RightToLeft	

[Scriptblock] • System.Management.Automation.ScriptBlock

Contains strings which are used as script blocks

Name	Purpose	Example
Invoke()		
InvokeReturnAsIs()		
ToString()	Returns a string representation of the script block	$var.ToString()
IsFilter		

[String] • System.String

Contains True/False values. Examples below assume that $s contains "SAPIEN Press"

Name	Purpose	Example
Chars	Converts the string into an array of [char] objects	$c = $s.Chars
EndsWith()	Returns $True if the string ends with the specified character(s)	$s.EndsWith("Press") $True
IndexOf()	Returns the character position of the specified string	$s.IndexOf("SAP") 0
IndexOfAny()	Returns the index of the first occurrence of any character in the specified array	$a = @("A","P") $s.IndexOfAny($a) 1
Insert()	Inserts the specified string at the specified index position	$s = $s.Insert(5," Insert") $s SAPIEN Insert Press
IsNormalized()	Returns $True if the string is in the "C" Unicode normalized form	$s.IsNormalized()
LastIndexOf()	Returns the last index position of the specified string	$s.LastIndexOf("s") 11
LastIndexOfAny()	Returns the last index position of any character in the specified array	$a = @("r","e") $s.LastIndexOfAny($a) 9
Length	Returns the length of the string	$s.Length 12
Normalize()	Returns a version of the string which is in the normalized Unicode form "C"	$s = $s.Normalize()
PadLeft()	Adds the specified number of spaces to the left of the string	$s.PadLeft(5)
PadRight()	Adds the specified number of spaces to the right of the string	$s.PadRight(5)
Remove()	Deletes the specified number of characters beginning at the specified position	$s.Remove(0,7) $s Press
Split()	Returns an array of strings, using the specified character to split the existing string into individual elements	$t = "One,Two,Three,Four" $t.Split(",")
Substring()	Retrieve the specified number of characters starting at the specified position	$s.Substring(2,7) PIEN Pr
StartsWith()	Returns $True if the string starts with the specified character(s)	$s.StartsWith("Press") False
ToCharArray()	Converts the string into an array of [char] objects	$c = $s.ToCharArray()
ToLower()	Returns a lowercase version of the string	$s.ToLower() sapien press
ToUpper()	Returns an uppercase version of the string	$s.ToUpper() SAPIEN PRESS
Trim()	Removes whitespace from the beginning and end of the string	$s = $s.Trim()

Name	Purpose	Example
TrimEnd()	Removes whitespace from the end of the string	$s = $s.TrimEnd()
TrimStart()	Removes whitespace from the beginning of the string	$s = $s.TrimStart()

We have omitted some of PowerShell's types, such as [XML] and [WMI], because PowerShell provides a better adaptation for these types of objects that you get just working with the Framework type. Refer to the appropriate chapter on these technologies for more information. We've omitted the [ADSI] type adapter here because it's discussed more thoroughly in the chapters dealing with ADSI and directory services.

Appendix C
Regular Expression Syntax

PowerShell uses a fairly standard implementation of regular expression syntax; Web sites like www.regegbuddy.com, www.regular-expressions.info, and www.regexlib.com provide tools, tutorials, and examples that can be used in PowerShell without any major adjustments. This Appendix is not intended as a tutorial; rather, it's intended as a quick reference to the major syntax elements supported by PowerShell. Our "Regular Expressions" chapter covers using regular expressions and provides several real-world examples.

Standard Regular Expressions Format	Logic	Example
value	Match the exact character specified	"book" -match "oo" (matches "oo")
.	Match any single character	"copy" -match "c..y" (matches "copy")
[*value*]	Match at least one of the characters in the brackets	"big" -match "b[iou]g" (matches "big")
[*range*]	Match at least one of the characters within the range; use – to specify a contiguous range	"deal" -match "d[a-e]l" matches ("deal")
[^]	Match any character except those in the brackets	"hand" -match "h[^brt]nd" matches ("hand")

Standard Regular Expressions Format	Logic	Example
^	Anchor match to the beginning of the string	"book" -match "^bo" (matches "bo")
$	Anchor match to the end of the string	"book" -match "ok$" (matches "ok")
*	Match zero or more instances of the preceding character	"shaggy" -match "g*" (matches "gg")
?	Match zero or one instance of the preceding character	"hairy" -match "r?" (matches "r")
\	Match the character that follows as a literal character (escaped)	"$5.00" -match "\$5" (matches "$5")
\w	Match a word – any character except whitespace	"SAPIEN" -match "\w" (matches "S")
+	Match one or more instances of the preceding directive or character	"SAPIEN" -match "\w+" (matches "SAPIEN")
\W	Match any non-word character (space, tab, etc)	"One Two" -match "\W" (matches the space)
\s	Matches any whitespace character	"One Two" -match "\s" (matches the space)
\S	Matches non-whitespace character	"abcde" -match "\S+" (matches "abcde")
\d	Matches any digit	"abc123" -match "\d" (matches "1")
\D	Matches any non-digit	"abc123" -match "\D" (matches "a")
{n}	Specify exactly n matches	"abc" -match "\w{2}" (matches "ab")
{n,}	Specify at least n matches	"abc" -match "\w{2,} " (matches "abc")
{n,m}	Specify at least n matches, but no more than m matches	"abc" -match "\w{2,3}" (matches "abc")

Appendix D
Reading PowerShell's Help

By now you know how easy it is to ask PowerShell for help and how a well-written cmdlet is self-documenting. But deciphering a help screen can be a little confusing to first-time PowerShell users. We want to show you how easy it is to read a help screen.

Here's what you might get when asking for help on the **Get-Service** cmdlet:

```
PS C:\ > help get-service

NAME
    Get-Service

SYNOPSIS
    Gets the services on a local or remote computer.


SYNTAX
    Get-Service [[-Name] <string[]>] [-ComputerName <string[]>] [-DependentServices] [-Exclude
<string[]>]
    [-Include <string[]>] [-RequiredServices] [<CommonParameters>]

    Get-Service -DisplayName <string[]> [-ComputerName <string[]>] [-DependentServices] [-Exclude
    <string[]>] [-Include <string[]>] [-RequiredServices] [<CommonParameters>]

    Get-Service [-InputObject <ServiceController[]>] [-ComputerName <string[]>]
[-DependentServices] [-
    Exclude <string[]>] [-Include <string[]>] [-RequiredServices] [<CommonParameters>]
```

The Synopsis should be self-explanatory. But what about the Syntax section? The first thing to notice is that there are three different ways you can use **Get-Service**. Each version has its own syntax, although with this cmdlet, they are very similar.

Anything you see in square brackets is optional. You don't have to specify it as a parameter. If it is a required item—more on that in a bit—PowerShell will prompt you for a value like this:

```
PS C:\ > get-eventlog

cmdlet Get-EventLog at command pipeline position 1
Supply values for the following parameters:
LogName:
```

When you see something like <string[]>, this is informing you of the expected type for that particular parameter. Thus, the displayName parameter for **Get-Service** is expecting a string value:

```
-displayName <string[]>
```

The [] characters after the 'string' indicates that the parameter can accept an array of strings and most likely accepts pipelined input.

```
PS C:\> "Print Spooler","Windows Update","Credential Manager" | get-service

Status   Name         DisplayName
------   ----         -----------
Running  Spooler      Print Spooler
Running  wuauserv     Windows Update
Stopped  VaultSvc     Credential Manager
```

Some PowerShell parameters are positional. That is, you don't have to specify the parameter name. PowerShell will determine the parameter property based on the position. Ever wonder why you can run an expression like this without having to specify any parameters?

```
PS C:\ > get-service spooler
```

If you look again at the syntax for the first variation, notice that **-name** is in square brackets:

```
Get-Service [[-Name] <string[]>]
```

This indicates that the parameter name is not required and is a positional parameter. The **Get-Service** cmdlet only has one such parameter.

If you need a bit more clarification, look at the full help for a cmdlet:

```
PS C:\ > help get-service -full
```

In addition to the summary we've already looked at, you get full information about each parameter. Here's an excerpt for **Get-Service**:

```
PARAMETERS
    -ComputerName <string[]>
        Gets the services running on the specified computers. The default is the local computer.

        Type the NetBIOS name, an IP address, or a fully qualified domain name of a remote computer.
```

To
        specify the local computer, type the computer name, a dot (.), or "localhost".

        This parameter does not rely on Windows PowerShell remoting. You can use the ComputerName
parameter
        of Get-Service even if your computer is not configured to run remote commands.

```
        Required?                       false
        Position?                       named
        Default value                   Localhost
        Accept pipeline input?          true (ByPropertyName)
        Accept wildcard characters?     false

    -DependentServices [<SwitchParameter>]
        Gets only the services that depend upon the specified service.

        By default, Get-Service gets all services.

        Required?                       false
        Position?                       named
        Default value                   False
        Accept pipeline input?          false
        Accept wildcard characters?     false
...
```

Notice that these parameters are not required, which we already knew because they were enclosed in square brackets.

The Name parameter has a position value of 1, which means the first string after the cmdlet name will be treated as a service name. Again, this confirms what we already knew, because -**name** was shown in square brackets in the help summary. The
-**Include** parameter is not positional:

```
        Position?                       named
```

The help syntax informs you that you must specify the parameter name.

Look at the default value for the -**name** parameter. Help tells you that it is the * wildcard. Finally, you can also see that the parameter can accept pipelined input. Since all the parameter is expecting is a string, you can run an expression like this:

```
PS C:\ > @("spooler","alerter","browser") | get-service

Status     Name             DisplayName
------     ----             -----------
Running    Spooler          Print Spooler
Stopped    Alerter          Alerter
Running    Browser          Computer Browser
```

Each array value is piped to **Get-Service**, which assumes the value passed is the name of a service.

The last piece of important information in PowerShell help is to look at what types of objects the cmdlet can accept as input and what type of objects, if any, the cmdlet produces:

```
INPUTS
    System.ServiceProcess.ServiceController, System.String
        You can pipe a service object or a service name to Get-Service.
```

```
OUTPUTS
    System.ServiceProcess.ServiceController
        Get-Service returns objects that represent the services on the computer.
```

This snippet from the **Get-Service** help shows that the cmdlet can accept either a service object or a string and that it returns a ServiceController object. You can confirm that by running an expression like this:

```
PS C:\ > (get-service spooler).GetType()

IsPublic   IsSerial  Name                              BaseType
--------   --------  ----                              --------
True       False     ServiceController                 System.ComponentModel.Component
```

With a little practice, you'll be able to decipher the mysterious PowerShell help screens, which will make you a more efficient PowerShell user.

Note that, in PowerShell v2, the **Get-Help** cmdlet (which lies underneath the more-familiar **Help** function) supports a new parameter: -**online**. Using this parameter forces PowerShell to open a Web browser and display cmdlet help from Microsoft's Web site; this online help us typically more recently-updated than what shipped with PowerShell and may contain additional examples. For example, running **Help Get-Service –online** will retrieve the online help for the **Get-Service** cmdlet. When possible, we advise always checking the online help if you're having trouble with a cmdlet or need to see the most recent examples.

Index

X–Y–Z

PrimalScript® 2009
THE MOST ADVANCED SCRIPTING IDE AVAILABLE

ChangeVue™ 2009

INTUITIVE | POWERFUL | SCALABLE
VERSION CONTROL

Using source control is an indispensable safety net for any professional developer, regardless of programming language or file size. Not only does source control provide an inherent backup mechanism by storing versions of any file you add to a repository, it also provides an effective means of coordinating who works on what in a team.

Source control is not limited to developers. System and network administrators should use source control to manage their library of production scripts. From the single administrator who needs a backup and versioning solution to a team that wants change control so that there's no confusion about who has the latest version, ChangeVue is an easy to use solution.

ChangeVue 2009 provides a lightning fast, set-up in minutes way of adding source code control to your environment. No matter whether you work alone, or in a small team, ChangeVue 2009 can adapt to your needs.

Download a fully functional 45 day trial from:

www.primaltools.com

SAPIEN

PrimalMerge™ 2009
COMPARE | CONTRAST | COMBINE

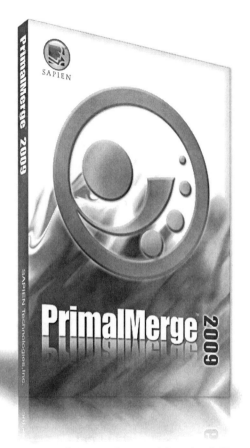

Comparing the contents of two, almost identical files by hand, can be a tedious and error prone operation. PrimalMerge streamlines the process using its Visual Differencing Engine. In a clear, color- coded visual environment, you can select the differences you want to individually keep or reject, or simply review all of the differences and accept them as a set. You are in complete control from start to finish.

Download a fully functional 45 day trial from:

www.primaltools.com

SAPIEN

PrimalXML™ 2009

CREATE, EDIT, AND MANIPULATE XML FILES

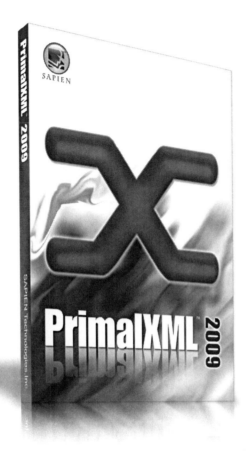

Working with XML as text can be tricky, tedious and difficult. Why not use a tool that is specifically designed to edit, manipulate, and create XML files? PrimalXML is just that tool. It provides you with the core set of functionality that you need to get your job done.

PrimalXML 2009 is chock full of the features that you need like book-marking, find and replace, and copy, clone and paste of attributes. And the Windows 7/Vista ribbon interface helps keep it simple to use.

Download a fully functional 45 day trial from:

www.primaltools.com

SAPIEN

LaVergne, TN USA
14 October 2010

200648LV00003B/3/P